# The French Revolution in Europe

## Volume 8 of 9: Coalition to Treaty of 1815

by

Albert Sorel

Translated by Frank H. Wallis, PhD

Waterbury, CT

*The French Revolution in Europe. Volume 8 of 9: Coalition to Treaty of 1815.*

Translation Copyright © 2023 by Frank H. Wallis (1957-). All rights reserved. Permission is granted to make and reproduce direct quotes, but not more than a total of five hundred words, with complete scholarly attribution. Excerpts and direct quotes longer than this must receive permission from the publisher. Paraphrasing of this work is encouraged, but must be acknowledged in a footnote, end note, or parenthetical reference, with name of author, title of work, date of publication, and page number(s).

Published in the United States of America.
ISBN: 979-8371321015

frank.h.wallis@gmail.com

Other Frank H. Wallis, PhD, translations include:

*Blanche of Castile, Queen and Regent of France, 1188-1252.* From Élie Berger, *Histoire de Blanche de Castille, Reine de France* (1895)

*History of the Roman Emperors.* 6 vols. From Louis-Sébastien Le Nain de Tillemont, *Histoire des empereurs et des autres princes* ...(1690-1732)

*Charles VII.* 6 vols. Gaston du Fresne de Beaucourt. (1881-91)

Cover photo courtesy of the Metroplitan Museum of Art, New York. Title: "Napoléon I" (1812), by Jean-Baptiste Isabey. Oval miniature, 2-1/4 x 1-3/8 in. (56 x 36 mm). Gift of Helen O. Brice, 1942. Accession Number: 42.53.5.

# Contents

*Translator's Preface* p. *xii*

# Section One

## The Coalition

**Chapter I.    Defection of Prussia and Austria, 1812 - 1813.** p. 1

I. Catastrophe of the *Grande Armée*. – The XXIXth newsletter. – Maret in Vilnius. – Napoléon in Warsaw, December 1812.

II. Views of Alexander. – Triumph of Russia. – Return of Alexander to his plans for the kingdom of Poland; opposition in Russia; difficulties with Austria and the Russians. – Views on Germany, national unity, the Empire, the German Committee of Stein. – France, the return to the old boundary of the Rhine on the East; the Scheldt to the North. – Action inside, Bernadotte and Moreau. – Overtures to Prussia; York, November and December 1812.

III. Convention of Tauroggen. – Embarrassment, crisis and duplicity in Berlin. – Prussia turns towards Austria; Mission of Knesebeck in Vienna, December 1812. – Defection of York, Convention of Tauroggen, December 30th. – How it is taken in Berlin. – Mission of Hatzfeld in Paris.

IV. Grand Design of Metternich. – The Austrian auxiliary corps, *de facto* neutrality. – Metternich's plan to break away from the alliance, and go to mediation. – Intermediate nuances, overtures to France, 9 December 1812. – Views on peace, destruction of the Grand Empire; procedure with Napoléon, ulterior motives of a regency of Marie-Louise.

– Napoléon claims 30,000 men; refusal, proposal for mediation, Bubna's mission to Paris, 20 December 1812.

V. NAPOLÉON IN PARIS. – Blame and disaffrtion; abandonment of the Grand Empire; illusions on the conservation of natural limits. – Interview of Napoléon with Bubna, 31 December 1812. – Illusions of Napoléon on Franz II and Austria, the family alliance; views of regency of Maria-Louisa and coronation of the King of Rome. – To what extent he accepted the mediation of Austria, January 1812.

VI. ARMISTICE OF ZEYCS. – How Metternich interprets and turns this conditional acceptance into breach of the alliance. – He receives overtures from Russia; armistice between the Austrian corps and Russia, 30 January 1813. – Armaments; implicit denunciation of the French alliance; mediation insinuation in France; how it will lead to rupture. – Overtures to Russia and Prussia; how mediation will lead to coalition.– The Confederates of the Rhine committed to defection, February 1813.

VII. TREATY OF KALISCH. – Proclamation of Koutousof; Germany called to emancipation, January 1813. – Friedrich-Wilhelm III leaves for Breslau; his perplexities. – He decides for a Russian alliance; negotiation of Knesebeck at the Russian headquarters; differences over the reconstruction of Prussia; Alexander reserves Poland. – Russian counter-proposal; treaty of alliance of 28 February 1813.

VIII. THE ALLIES MANIFESTO. – Negotiation between Alexander and Austria; offer of Italy, March 1813. – Appeal to the peoples; threats to the German princes, manifesto of Koutousof, 29 March 1813. – Fundamental equivocation on the limits of France, the legitimate limits. – Saxony reunited with Prussia; invasion of this kingdom. – Italy offered to Austria; concert between Austria and Russia, 29 March 1813. – Despite the differences, the node of the coalition.

IX. REGENCY OF MARIA-LOUISA. – The peace party in Paris. – Napoléon sees clearly the intentions of the allies and prepares an all-out war. – The regency of Maria-Louisa; attempt at rapprochement with Pius VII; new Concordat. – How Napoléon conceives peace; declaration to Schwarzenberg, maintenance of the Grand Empire. – He renounces Spain. – Last review, April 1813.

## Chapter II.  Austrian Mediation, 1813. p. 69

I. BREAK IN THE ALLIANCE. – Armaments of Austria; mediation; promise to the allies to go over to their side if Napoléon rejects the conditions of Austria as mediator, and resolution to impose on Napoléon conditions which, in advance, they know he will not accept. – Narbonne replaces Otto in Vienna, March 1813; hostility he finds. – Conditions of peace indicated by Metternich, 7 April 1813. – Exchange of notes, audience of Franz II and Narhonne; rupture of alliance declared, 23-26 April 1813.

II. ENGLAND AND PRUSSIA. – Why England hesitates to enter into the coalition; success of his policy; the Mediterranean as English Lake; general hostility to peace. – Refusal to accept the mediation of Austria, March 1813. – Mechanics of treaties; how England will be mistress of war and peace. – Views of the Low Countries, the new kingdom of Austrasia, from the Elbe to the Scheldt. – Sending of negotiators to the continent.

III. BERNADOTTE AND MURAT. – Enlisting of French kings: alliance of England with Bernadotte, March 1813. – Practices around Murat; return of Murat in Naples; his ambitions for the kingdom of Italy. – The English proconsul in Palermo, exile of Maria-Carolina. – Murat is moving towards defection, negotiations with Austria, sudden return to Napoléon, April 1813.

IV. ARMISTICE OF PLEISWITZ. – Victory of Napoléon at Lutzen; Napoléon at Dresden, 8 May 1813. – Austria's armed neutrality; passage to hostility: true conditions inn the peace of Austria, 7 May 1813. – Minimum indicated to Napoléon. – More extended conditions settled between Austria and Russia; concerted joint action, 16 May 1813. – Napoléon thinks of turning towards Russia.– Declaration at Bubna, 16 May. – Caulaincourt mission to Tsar Alexander; Bautzen, 20 May 1813. – How Napoléon decided on an armistice. – The negotiation; confidences of Caulaincourt. – The Convention of 4 June.

V. THE TREATY OF REICHENBACH. – Franz II approaches the allies, military conferences, 134. – Treaty between England and Prussia, 14 June; between England and Russia, 15 June. – Conferences between Austrians, Russians and Prussians on the conditions of peace; preliminary bases of 18 June. – Extension of these bases; Russian note of 19 June; the greatest extent, the old limits. – Possible agreements between Austria, Russia, and Prussia against France, settled on 24 June, signed on 27 June. – Napoléon invites Metternich to come and see him at Dresden.

VI. THE DRESDEN INTERVIEW. – Meeting of 26 June between Napoléon and Metternich. – Extension of the armistice to 10 August, mediation by Austria accepted. – Battle of Vittoria, evacuation of Spain. – Bernadotte among the allies; Conference of Trachenberg. – Moreau.

VII. CONGRESS OF PRAGUE. – The derisory congress. – Metternich and Franz II. – New insinuations to Murat. – Instructions from Napoléon to Narbonne and Caulaincourt. – England adopts the program of 2 June. – Caulaincourt in Prague; statements by Metternich. – The reality of the facts. – Exchange of notes at Prague. – Napoléon's secret instructions to Caulaincourt. – Austrian ultimatum; the secret of peace in 60 hours, 8 August. – Concessions of Napoléon, 10 August. – They arrive too late; breakup of Congress, August 10$^{th}$. – Austrian declaration of war. – Permanent conditions of war, the coalition of 1709 and that of 1813.

## Chapter III. Fall of the Grand Empire, 1813 - 1814. p. 151

I. TREATY OF TOEPLITZ. – Arrival of Moreau, Battle of Dresden. – Crisis of the coalition; superior role of Alexander. – The treaty of 9 September. – Defection of Bavaria. – Bernadotte aims for the crown of France. – Battle of Leipzig; Napoléon's interview with Merveldt, 17 October; new concessions. – He treats through insurgent Germany. – Murat surrenders to Austria. – Napoléon recrosses the Rhine.

II. VIEWS OF ALLIES ON PEACE. – Metternich, opposition to Alexander's views on Poland. – Germany confederated and neutralized by itself. – Metternich approaches England; Aberdeen. – Austria's desire to treat with Napoléon weakened; the regency. – Stratagem to detach the French from Napoléon; natural limits. – With what reservations Alexander agrees. – First overtures to Nicolas-Auguste Saint-Aignan, 26 October.

III. THE FRANKFURT OVERTURES. – The allies at Frankfurt. – Overtures to Saint-Aignan; feints of Metternich; the note of 9 November. – Ambiguity on natural limits. – Disavowal of Hardenberg, Aberdeen, Castlereagh. – Plan of operations drawn up.

IV. RESPONSE OF NAPOLÉON. – Public opinion in Paris, how they misunderstand the intentions of the allies. – Talleyrand. – The royalists; Bernadotte's party. – Return of Napoléon, 10 November: he renounces Spain. – Arrival of Saint-Aignan; the reply of 16 November. – Desire for peace. – Caulaincourt in foreign affairs. – Metternich's dilatory answer; the manifesto of the allies, 1 December.

V. DEFECTION OF MURAT. – Treaty of Valençay, 11 December. – The session of the Legislative Body; opposition; the bases of Frankfurt. – The brother kings. – Caroline negotiates with Austria. – Return of Murat. – Duplicity of Metternich; England and Russia. – Neipperg at Naples. – The Treaty of 11 January 1814. – Napoléon's last days in Paris, he foresees the Bourbons.

## Chapter IV. Congress of Châtillon, Jan. - March, 1808. p. 201

I. DIVERGENCE AMONG ALLIES. – The allies after crossing the Rhine; Alexander, the all-out war; distrust of Metternich; Alsace and Poland; Bernadotte; Metternich's desire to negotiate with Napoléon. – Arrival of Castlereagh at Freiburg, his instructions. – Agreement with Metternich.

II. PROTOCOL OF LANGRES. – The allies at Langres, deliberations on politics and the war, memoir of Metternich. – Observations of the allies. – Resolution of 29 January 1814.

III. FIRST TALKS. – Plenipotentiaries at Châtillon. – Conference of February 5th. – Napoléon gives *carte blanche* to Caulaincourt. – Conference of February 7th. – Suspension, 9 February.

IV. NAPOLÉON AT NOGENT. – The night of 7 to 8 February. February news on the morning of the 9th; Napoléon regains hope.

V. BASES OF TROYES. – Difference among the allies on the reconstruction of Europe. – News from Paris, royalist emissaries. – Alexander and the liberals; England and the Bourbons. – Deliberations on peace 12-14 February; ultimatum of the 15th.

VI. THE ALLIANCE OF CHAUMONT. – Napoléon's victories; he returns to the "natural limits". – The allies at Chaumont. – English proposal for a general alliance; treaty of 1 March.

VII. ULTIMATUM OF THE ALLIES. – Conference of 10 March at Châtillon; Conferences of the 12th and 13th; disavowal of the Frankfurt overtures.

VIII. THE ROYALISTS. – The royalists in Paris; Vitrolles mission. – Vitrolles in Troyes, 16 March; the allies and the Bourbons. – Emissary of the Comte d'Artois, 20 March.

IX. BREAKUP OF THE CONGRESS. – Last talks, 15-19 March. – Collapse of the Empire in Paris. – Napoléon's conversation with Wessenberg, 28 March; the abdication offered to Austria. – The allies before Paris; capitulation, 31 March.

## Chapter V. The Peace of 1814. p. 257

I. TALLEYRAND. – Parties in Paris; perplexity of Talleyrand; the regency. – The Bourbons and the old limits. – Entry of the allies. – Declaration of 31 March. – The provisional government; Alexander and the Bourbons. – The forfeiture. – Plots against Napoléon. – How Alexander prepared the abdication.

II. ABDICATION. – Napoléon at Fontainebleau. – The Day of the Marshals. – Caulaincourt and the Marshals at Alexander's. – Defection of Marmont. – Chateaubriand. – The constitutional articles of the Senate. – Treaty of 11 April with Napoléon. – Departure for the island of Elba.

III. TREATY OF PARIS. – Character of the Restoration. – Triumph of Alexander. – Armistice Agreement, 23 April. – Arrival of Louis XVIII; Tallryrand and Alexander at Compiègne. – Entry of the King into Paris. – The Charter. – The conditions of peace. – Articles reserved; the Congress, 30 May. – Departure of the allies.

# Section Two

## Treaty of 1815

### Chapter I. Congress of Vienna, June 1814 – March 1810. p. 295

I. THE RESTORATION. – Louis XVIII is unaware of France, but he knows Europe. – Infirmity of his government.

II. CONFLICTS AMONG THE ALLIES. – Adjournment of the congress; Alexander in England. – Confirmation of the Treaty of Chaumont. – Causes of conflict; the question of Saxony and Poland. – The reconstruction of Prussia. – Opposition in Russia to the restoration of Poland. – Views of Austria on question of Italy. – Murat, Austria, and the Bourbons. – The Germans.

III. INSTRUCTIONS OF LOUIS XVIII. – Talleyrand informed of the conflicts of the allies. – How France drew peace from them. – How it made a policy with the obligations imposed on it by the allies. – Disinterestedness, legitimacy, balance, secondary States. – Applications in Italy and Germany. – Superiority of this policy. – But antagonism with Russia.

IV. PRELIMINARY QUESTIONS. – Arrival of the plenipotentiaries in Vienna; efforts of the four to exclude France from the congress. – Arrival of Talleyrand; how he foiled these combinations. – Conference of 30 September. – Interview with Alexander. – Embarrassment of Castlereagh. – Metternich and the question of Naples. – Conference of 8 October. – Progress of Talleyrand.

V. QUESTION OF SAXONY AND POLAND. – Parties in Vienna. – What delayed the congress; how questions arose between Alexander and Castlereagh. – Castlereagh and Metternich brought together, approach Talleyrand. – Interview between Alexander and Talleyrand, 22 October. – Metternich and Hardenberg against Russia; intervention of the King of Prussia; perfect union with Alexander. – General anxiety in Vienna. – The Committees. – Agreement between Louis XVIII and Wellington. – The *Mémoire rationné sur la Saxe*, 2 November.

VI. TREATY OF 3 JANUARY 1815. – Taking possession of Saxony by the Prussians, 10 November. – Alexander's insinuations to Talleyrand on the subject of Naples. Was there any question of an alliance and of the left bank of the Rhine? – Agitation in Vienna. – How one was led to a transaction. – The Statistical Commission. – Intervention of England; the triple alliance between England, Austria, and France. – Rolling of the questions of Saxony and Poland; the Prussians on the Rhine.

VII. THE FALL OF MURAT. – Murat and France. – He approaches Napoléon and breaks with Austria.

## Chapter II. Final Act in Vienna, 1815. p. 343

I. RETURN OF NAPOLÉON. – What decided Napoléon to return to France. – Departure of Louis XVIII. – Napoléon tries to negotiate with the allies.

II. NAPOLÉON OUTLAWED. – The news in Vienna, declaration of 13 March. – The new announcement of the alliance of Chaumont. – Consequences for France; Talleyrand loses all his advantages. – Views of the English. – Of the Austrians. – Of Alexander.

III. FOUCHÉ. – The party of Orléans in France; Fouché: his ambitions, his intrigues in Paris and Vienna. – His maneuvers in Ghent. – Alexander and the English in Vienna. – Fall of Murat.

IV. TREATY OF 9 JUNE. – The final act; Italian affairs. – German affairs; disappointment of the patriots. – The Germanic Confederation. – The Low Countries, Switzerland. – Eastern affairs.

## Chapter III. Waterloo. March – June, 1815. p. 367

I. THE LAST BATTLE. – Conditions in which it engaged; the arbitration of Louis XVIII. – Napoléon. – Wellington. – Blücher. – Catastrophe.

II. THE SECOND ABDICATION. – Napoléon in Paris. – Desire for revolution. – Why he renounced it.

III. WELLINGTON. – The provisional government and Fouché. – Commissioners sent to Haguenau; misunderstanding of allied dispositions. – Wellington and Pozzo working for the Bourbons. – Commissioners sent to Wellington; he dispels the ambiguity.

IV. THE SECOND RESTORATION. – Capitulation of Paris, 3 July; Article XII. – Return of Louis XVIII; Fouché and Talleyrand to the ministry. – The Prussians in Paris; return of Louis XVIII.

V. THE EXILE OF NAPOLÉON. – First question to settle, the fate of Napoléon. – He surrenders to the English; Saint Helena.

## Chapter IV. Treaty of 20 November 1815. p. 389

I. THE QUESTION OF ART. – Solitude and impotence of Louis XVIII. – How he will truly become King. – Museums.

II. PROJECTS OF PARTITION. – Deliberations of the allies; the conference. – Threats and revenge from the Germans. – Superiority of Alexander. – How the English ambassadors worked for the same ends as he, for other motives. – Their remonstrances in London. – Metternich. – The Prussians. – Summary of requirements. – The question of Alsace and Lorraine. – The ultimatum of the four.

III. THE DUKE OF RICHELIEU. – Disgrace of Talleyrand. – Letter from Louis XVIII; Alexander. – Richelieu in government. – Last concessions of the allies.

IV. THE SIGNATURE. – End of Murat; execution of Ney. – The peace treaty. – Renewal of the alliance of Chaumont; the system of congresses; the Holy Alliance. – Liberation of territory in 1818.

## Chapter V. Europe and the French Revolution. p. 411

I. THE WAR. – Conclusion of this book; permanent character of this history; the war of limits. – Permanence of the motives of the coalitions. – Constant effort of France to leave its limits and of Europe to make it return there.

II. TREATY OF 1815. – Character of the treaties of Vienna. – Causes of weakness of these treaties; ignorance of the characters, traditions, interests of the peoples. – How the treaties of 1815 were destroyed in the Low Countries, Italy, and Germany. – Fault committed with regard to France; how it was led to destroy the order established in 1815.

III. THE REVOLUTION. – That the war of limits was only the form of deeper struggles. – Permanent character of the national genius of the peoples of Europe. – Particular character of the motives which move them at different times. – How the Revolution of 1789 was nationalized in France. – In the other nations of Europe. – Democracy and nationality in the 19th century. – The right of people to dispose of their fate; French principle. – How Napoléon drew the destinies of the new Europe. – Grandeur of the French people in this history.

**Index** p. 427

# Translator's Preface

Albert Sorel (1842-1906) published *L'Europe et la Révolution française: la Coalition, les Traités de 1815.* (Paris, 1904), as the eighth of eight prose volumes, not including the General Index, volume nine. The series was a monumental history of state relations as they were stimulated by the Revolution of 1789 and its effects in Europe. What took place in France would not be contain-ed in that nation state, as new ideas gained a foothold, and as the *status quo* powers tried in their own way to deal with radical change.

Sorel was born in Honfleur, Normandy, the son of a wealthy manufacturer. Destined for business, he instead followed a strong literary interest but compromised a bit by attending law school and entering the Foreign Ministry in 1866. After the Franco-German War of 1870 Sorel entered the *Ecole libre des sciences politiques* (now known as *Sciences Po*) and gained distinction as a lecturer in diplomatic history. Some of his lectures were modified into book format, e.g., *Histoire diplomatique de la guerre franco-allemande* (1875). In that same year he became general secretary of the newly created office of the Présidence du sénat. For 30 years he worked on *L'Europe et la Révolution*, and also managed to publish documents and ancillary monographs to his great life work. Sorel was nominated nine times for the Nobel Prize in literature, between 1903 and 1906.[1]

This eight volume work met my criteria for selection as a candidate for translation: 1.) the highest level of scholarship, marked by thorough command of all the primary sources; 2.) the ability to

---

1 Nomination Archive. NobelPrize.org. Nobel Prize Outreach AB 2021. Fri. 17 Dec 2021. <https://www.nobelprize.org/nomination/archive/show_people.php?id=8665>

analyze and explicate questions which arise from exploration of a thesis. It is also a sort of tribute to happy memories of many discussions on the European state system I was privileged to have had with Paul W. Schroeder (1927-2020), at the University of Illinois.

Note: the only author preface in the entire nine volume work appeared in volume one. It helps to read it to understand his thesis of national character informing political choices in State systems and relations. In the 19th century, especially after the 1870 War, it was unlikely any historian in France would be untouched by nationalism.

Full proper names are given at their first appearance, and sometimes with dates of birth and death, and brief biography. Subsequent volumes will follow Sorel and give only the last name or common aristocratic title. These can be found in each volume's index, and the General Index, which is to be volume IX of this series. I also follow Sorel in citing sources which already appeared in previous volumes in an abbreviated form.

I use end notes for the citations instead of the original footnotes for a much cleaner page appearance. Footnotes with (*, †, etc.) are mine, as is information within brackets [ ]. To comport with current norms of genderless English, I have dropped the French sexing of nouns. France is not "she," but "it"; nations are not "she," but "it". I have expanded and updated many biographical details of people for whom Sorel often identified with only a surname or title.

Frank H. Wallis
Waterbury, CT

Page left intentionally blank.

# Section One

## The Coalition

## Chapter I: Defection of Austria and Prussia

### 1812 - 1813

**I. Catastrophe of the *Grand Armée***

The mainspring of the Grand Army was distorted.[1] Winter had not yet announced that, disbanded, it was already scattered. Greed, from top to bottom, destroyed discipline. One thought only of keeping loot and provisions. Suddenly, on 4 November the snow fell, then, on the 6th, the cold set in, sudden and intense. Napoléon was that day not far from Smolensk, at Dorogobuje. There he received the first notice of the conspiracy of Mallet du Pan. The emotion he felt was profound. Paris had not yet known the great failure; there was no suspicion in France that the retreat was turning into a disaster; and yet, at the mere sound of the Emperor's death, the whole scaffolding of the Empire so skillfully bound together had threatened to crumble. From then on, the resolution to hasten his return grew apace; hence also the concern to show that he was alive, alert, and the importance given in the bulletins on his health. However, he deferred, to retain what remained of the army; he even exposed himself, without military necessity, and only to raise morale. But everything was sinking. Inhumanity rose with misery and despair; selfishness became fierce. It was the struggle for life in all its horror. Ney commanded the rear guard, fighting, rifle in hand, as in the winter of 1793. The soldiers obeyed him not because he was a marshal and a duke without horses, without escort, without councils of war, the muddy boots, the head decked out in a scarf under the deformed hat. He was obeyed because he revealed himself to be the leader, by virtue of his valor. He was the conscience and the honor dominating this oblivious and stupefied crowd which crawled on the snow.

On the banks of the Beresina, around 22 November there was a thaw and breakup, the abyss of mud, the poisoning of the swamp, even worse than the cold. The bridges remained free for a long time. The herds of men, harassed, lay down, refusing to go any further; then, at the approach of the Russians, they wanted to pass all at once, jostled each other, threw themselves into the water which was carrying it, and broke the bridges.

Napoléon, until then, in his letters, had concealed things: a few words only, brief and imprecise. Faced with this hideous rout, he confessed.

> The army is numerous, but horribly disbanded. It takes fifteen days to hand it over to the flags; and a fortnight, where could we get them? Perhaps this army will only be able to rally behind the Niemen. It is possible that I believe my presence in Paris necessary. I would very much like there to be no foreign agent in Vilnius. The army is not beautiful to show. It's been a fortnight since I've received a courier and I'm in the absence of everything.[2]

Eighteen couriers were missing. He found them, for the most part, on 2 December. They brought him the details of the Mallet affair and the news from Spain, always at worst. He wrote in haste and everywhere, sent General Montesquiou to Paris, without bridling. Incidentally, this officer had the "victory of the Beresina, 8 flags, 6,000 prisoners, 12 pieces of cannon" published in all the gazettes of Prussia and the Confederation, then he gave Paris, the Empress, "details on the good health of the emperor and on the state of the army."[3] The XXIXth *Bulletin*, 3 December, ends with these words: "His Majesty's health has never been better." To Maret: "We are starving!"

The letters from Paris left him no longer in doubt: he had to return, precede the sinister revelation, prepare minds for it by gradation, suppress all reflections by his presence, shake the whole Empire with his energy. On 5 December, he left the army in the greatest secrecy and left by sleigh for Vilnius. Thus, thirteen years before, he abandoned his army in Egypt; but then he ran to France to repair disasters incurred by others; he arrived there like hope. This time disaster struck him in his own work; he left behind him despair, he sowed anxiety under his feet, he brought stupor, discouragement.

However, in Vilnius, Maret, strove to put on a good face, official in the midst of diplomats in search of news, agents of bad talk, spies of all kinds, and the most dangerous, because they were inevitable, the officers in observation of the allied staffs of Austria and Prussia. The couriers from Warsaw denounced the suspicious attitude of the Austrians: Schwarzenberg, who commanded the auxiliary corps, spared the Russians, and spared his own troops even more. It was the game of 1809 which was beginning again, reversed. From the Prussian frontier, word was sent that the Prussians and Russians, instead of fighting, should approach each other and exchange emissaries.

Maret learned on 28 October of the evacuation of Moscow. For lack of victory news, he gave parties. There was prodigious dancing throughout the Empire: in invaded Prussia, in conquered Austria, in Spain on fire, in Warsaw, even in Vilnius. They were dancing at Bignon's, imperial commissioner, on 28 November; Maret, alarmed as he was, made an act of presence. Suddenly, at a word spoken to him, he disappeared. A Pole, Count Abranowics, with whom Bignon was staying, returned, telling the truth about the crossing of the Beresina. The party stopped, the dancing ceased; colloquies in low voices, cries of women; each escaped, trembling for his family, for his country.

On 10 December, Napoléon arrived in Warsaw, where the news of the misfortune had preceded him. He found the government in disarray, the Poles in despair. On the 11th, from Kutno, he wrote to Maret, whom he was leaving to cover his political retreat, to notify the diplomats of his departure and to invite them to return to Paris. One line indicates that he was thinking of negotiating with Vienna: "Austria must have a capable minister in Paris." On the 14th, he asked, from Dresden, the Emperor his father-in-law to increase the Austrian auxiliary corps to 60,000 men, and the King of Prussia to raise his to 30,000 men. He sent him Narbonne, on a mission of containment and also of insinuation: a marriage between the prince royal and a Bonaparte princess.

What remained of the army was draining away, calamitous. They saw arriving, like a dying wave, in Vilnius, "a kind of crowd like a legion of reprobates." An officer named Roche, who remained in the town, was seized with such horror that he died. Many had gone mad. The masses were sustained only by exaltation, and an obstinate stubbornness to live. They found straw, linen, fire, provisions; they were finally able to feed themselves; many died. Then the drift continued towards Germany, an uncertain river, wandering along all the slopes, and tracing its course only by the fringe of bloody foam, the horrible alluvium of corpses. Prussia could raise its head: the Grand Army was no more than a sham, and the immense bogeyman of the month of June only an object of derision for the Prussians.

## II. Views of Alexander

The pride of the Russians rose in proportion. They glorified themselves. They revealed themselves to themselves, they made themselves known to the universe: "What a great nation we are, above all the others!" Souvaroff, in 1799, worked only for "foreign powers," and he could not succeed in "delivering them from the yoke of the French." Koutousof saved the fatherland. Let no one speak of the Spanish: apart from a few bands, they were neither brave nor active; the gentlemen served the usurper, the soldiers fled, their generals allowed themselves to be beaten! Above all, let's no longer talk about the "infamous" Corsican: "This beggar took us for Germans!" Nothing remained of his stolen reputation but a fugitive, "a coward filled with vanity and presumption, spoiled by the fortune and cowardice of his enemies and who loses his head, the cowardest of men as soon as he finds that we resist him and defeat him."[4] Tchigagof had "the beautiful dream of catching him in a net, crowning the countryside with a prodigious bear hunt!"[5]

Alexander advanced to the West in triumph over the monster, restorer of the kings, liberator of the people. He marched in his dream of 1804: Napoléon overwhelmed, France in rout, the Revolution repressed. Supremacy passed to the grandson of Catherine the Great, to the heir of Peter the Great. Continental peace was now a Russian affair. But the enchantment in which Alexander found himself did not make him lose sight of reality; this hero looked at his feet. He saw Poland there. Czartoryski reappeared with the circumstances of his policy; the story goes back to the conditions of the autumn of 1805, when Russian armies pressed the Prussian border and it was wondered in Russia whether Warsaw would be taken as collateral, paying for the alliance, even before have concluded it.[6] Czartoryski wrote to the Tsar, 9 October, 6 December, 27 December: "If Your Imperial Majesty, at the moment when the Polish nation expects the vengeance of a conqueror, stretches out your hand and offers willingly what for them was the object of the fight, the effect will be magical."[7] Let Alexander carry out what Napoléon had hoped for without accomplishing it, let him resurrect Poland, let him return it to the Poles and make himself king of it! What an entry into the campaign and what a gift of joyful accession of the new Caesar to the nations of Europe!

The hero of the crusade glorified himself; politics advised and moderated him. No doubt there were Poles fascinated by Napoléon to the point of self-annihilation, but we have to take into account the character of this nobility, always at a gallop, plumed, prancing, running to extremes: "a patriotism, a disinterestedness without limits, an ambition, an unbridled vanity."[8] One had to reckon even more with Russia. The Poles took part in the war; their horsemen entered the city of Moscow, sacked Smolensk, and the devastation of Russia awakened the ancient hatred. Old Russians were all about revenge, and after revenge, contempt. Pure and simple annexation and subjugation, that, according to them, was all that Poland deserved and all that the interests of Russia required.[9] The rest would be dangerous, "a disastrous combination." Woronzof wrote to Rostopchine:

> I hope by God's goodness that all these advertisements are false. I have known for a long time that the Poles desire it to be, their vanity cannot bear to no longer be a nation. But if we don't want to form the Kingdom of Poland only from the Duchy of Warsaw, that is ridiculous and that will not satisfy the Poles, for they want to recreate their kingdom in its ancient integrity, and encompass all that Austria and Prussia possess and have possessed.

Nesselrode wrote to the Emperor: "The measure would be eminently anti-national" in Russia; and to win over the Poles, it would be necessary to sacrifice "for the sole pleasure of satisfying the whims of this light and restless nation" the territories attributed to Russia by the three partitions from 1772 to 1795. It "cannot enter into the head of a reasonable man and sincerely devoted to the interests of Russia." How could one believe "that in the heart of a Pole there can ever enter the desire for a Russian Poland?" They will want it Polish; to give them a national constitution is to invite them to independence. How would the Tsar reconcile this double and contradictory character, of autocrat on this side of the Polish frontier, of constitutional king beyond? The constitution of Poland would be by example a continuous provocation to revolution. Finally, to rebuild the whole of Poland, it would be necessary to compensate Austria and Prussia for what would not be given back and what one should ask of them. This would be to raise, at the moment of renewing the coalition, that question of Poland which broke it in its beginnings. This would break it again, and the first effect would perhaps be to throw Austria and Prussia into the arms of France instead of detaching them, which remained the first condition of success.

They were *raisons d'État*. Alexander knew its value. He did not give up his favorite dream; but he understood that to hasten things would be to compromise them, and, placed in the position in which Napoléon found himself in 1807, he used the same expedients. He let Czartoryski's emissaries stir up the Poles and adjourn Polish affairs. This country remained the stake in the game, whether it was the revolutionary Convention that played the game, the Emperor Napoléon, or the Tsar of Russia, restorer of law!

With Poland thus maintained outside the law, the question arose of the appeal to other peoples, of the use that would be made of them and of the way in which their deliverance would be regulated. In Austria, everyone understood it in the same way as the old Russians with regard to Poland: to exploit national revolutions, since the great error of the times wanted that to be the only way of recruiting armies and training soldiers; but, the ground swept, immediately use these same forces to force the peoples to rest, after having restored them to peace. The Russians were about to enter Germany. Stein accompanied Alexander; he sent note after note. The poet and publicist Arndt, a refugee in Russia, helped him with all his ardor and all his eloquence. Stein expected from Alexander what Johann von Müller and many Germans had hoped from Napoléon: the regeneration of Germany. Like them, he thought that the impetus could only come from outside. It required "unity and speed." These qualities were not to be found in the courts of Germany, among "the cabinets, ministers, generals, mistresses and *valets de chambre*" who formed their entire government.[10] The great object, according to Stein, was to return Germany to the Germans, to check "the seditious spirit, the felony of the German princes," to sweep from Germany those masters "who have unworthily betrayed her," those "cowards who have sold the blood of their peoples to prolong their shameful existence"; to abolish forever "the monstrous constitution" of the Treaty of Westphalia, and to "form an empire which would contain all the moral and physical elements of force, liberty and light, and which could resist the restless ambition of France." What would Emperor Franz and Metternich, King Friedrich-Wilhelm III and Hardenberg think of it? what would the Bavarian and the Badois think, and all those confederates of the Rhine whom it would be a question of detaching from France and enlisting in the coalition? Threatening them with a return to the suzerainty of the Empire was not the way to turn them away from Napoléon; there was a risk of making the Corsican the preserver of the independence of the kings. Alexander postponed this great problem again, but giving Stein more freedom than he gave Czartoryski; he had no fear then of dissatisfying his ministers, generals, monks, and boyars; he allowed the German Committee of Stein to agitate Germany to extinction and to promise, in its name, greatness and liberty to this delivered nation, provided that it contributed to its own deliverance.

In this Europe torn from French supremacy, how far would the repression of France be pushed? It was meditated on in the Russian chancellery, at the same time as the reconstitution of Germany. On this great problem, solved in advance in his mind, Alexander consulted Roumiantsof and Nesselrode, the chancellor in title and the young secretary of state who insinuated himself more and more into the confidence of the Tsar. Roumiantsof opined that Russia had received from on high the "heavenly mission" to deliver and pacify Europe, to "plow with danger the whole field of the European commune," but the other powers would seek to deprive him of all part in the harvest: it was therefore important that Russia should operate alone and pay itself as it pleased. Nesselrode issued a noticeably different opinion, and his opinion prevailed. Russia, according to Nesselrode, could not accomplish its task alone, or if it found itself forced to do so, it would have no resource but to treat with Napoléon, if necessary on the principle of the *status quo*, contented with having thrown the colossus down and broken the yoke of the blockade. But Russia did not win this huge victory to stop there.[11]

> The strings are stretched as much as possible. It is therefore a stable and solid state of peace which the well-understood interests of Russia demanded, after success against the French armies guaranteed its preservation and independence.... The most complete way in which this object could be achieved would be, no doubt, that France should be driven back within its natural limits; that all that is not situated between the Rhine and the Scheldt, the Pyrenees and the Alps should cease to be either an integral part of the French empire, or even dependent on it.

Let us dwell on this text, it is important for what follows. We must not isolate the words *natural limits* from the context, we must not above all forget that it is a Russian minister who is speaking to the Emperor of Russia, and that these words do not have, for them, the value that they had taken hold in France since 1792. In the eyes of Nesselrode and his master, the Rhine was a natural limit, from Basel to the Lauter, as from the Lauter to Cologne; the Meuse and the Moselle were equally natural limits, and so too the Scheldt. However, in this plan of 1812, it was a question of the Rhine, an old limit, still natural, from Basel to Lauter, and of the Scheldt.[12] This was how the Russians understood it in 1804, in the instructions given to Novossiltssof, and it is in this sense that it must be understood in Nesselrode's memo.[13]

Nesselrode concluded: "This is certainly the maximum of all the wishes that we can form." But, he added,

> they could not be realized without the cooperation of Austria and Prussia. The external development of our plan is therefore subordinated to the dispositions that these two powers will make appear; it will only be able to unfold as these decide, therefore, the results to which we must aim will also be more or less limited. They consist ... in wresting from the domination of France as many countries as possible.[14]

However, to not revolt the French and not induce them to make common cause with Napoléon, this idea will be concealed behind the head until the moment when it becomes realizable.

It was first a question of pushing the war. Bernadotte will be the igniter of the defection of the German princes, the teaser of the defection of the dignitaries and beneficiaries of the Empire in France, and, at the same time, the trainer of the constitutional republicans or monarchists. It was the time of his lofty coquetry with Mme de Staël; the time also, when, by the back door, he received Alexis de Noailles, unofficial emissary of Louis XVIII.

Bernadotte had this advantage, that he entered into all combinations; he was at the same time the suitor of Benjamin Constant, the sword that the Jacobins needed, the king that the Constitutionalists needed, the protector of the Republic for some, the restorer of the monarchy for others: Cromwell, Monk, Lafayette. The Bourbons were looking for him as they had been looking for Pichegru. Bernadotte dreamed of working only for himself. He also considered himself fit to stand in for the Republic, the Empire and royalty, Napoléon, Louis XVIII, Louis-Philippe, and even his brother-in-law, Joseph Bonaparte. He prided himself on deceiving them all, preventing them from each other and, necessary to all, to make him their arbiter and the supreme expedient to which all should rally.

His hand, very expert, was found in another intrigue which reveals the subtle depth of Russian combinations and the singular knowledge that Alexander and his agents had of the illusions of the French. The design was not new. It had been thought of in 1805; Strogonof advised him in 1807; it had been discussed at Abo between Bernadotte and the Tsar: it was a question of winning Moreau over to the coalition. It was not to oppose to Napoléon a captain, his rival at the time when they fought under the same standard, and who passed for his master in the minds of the rebels of Paris, since Bonaparte had banished him. The Russians didn't think they needed him; they considered themselves capable of unmasking the false great man; Moreau only seemed useful to them to unite in France and reassure the former Republicans, the liberals, disaffected with Napoléon but still attached to the glory of France and intractable on the article of limits. How could one believe that the allies were thinking of dismembering, of swallowing up the Republic, when one would see at the head of their armies the hero of Hohenlinden, the victim of the trial of Pichegru, the exile of 1804?[15]

With Austria, necessity was pressing. Undoubtedly the very secret arrangement concluded in Vienna in July had served, as we say today, as counter-assurance to Russia and paralyzed the effects of the treaty of 14 March with Napoléon. Austria had shown itself loyal to Russia in this disloyalty; but it was important to extend the same arrangements to the new countryside, to prevent Austria from furnishing succors to France, and finally to attract it to the coalition. There remained in Vienna, even after the official break, a Russian agent, Otto, who, secretly, maintained the threads.[16] On 5 November a M. de Boutiaguine arrived there: he was received with great mystery by Metternich and developed the proposals which the Tsar had had Lieven set out in his letter of 2 October. Rasoumovsky, who had remained in Vienna as a private individual, renewed the same appeals to Metternich a fortnight later: "Is Austria not disposed to seize the favorable moment to break with France and bind itself to Russia?" Metternich slipped away. Alexander rightly judged that it would first be necessary to force his hand, and then fulfill it. Knowing the views of the general-in-chief, Schwarzenberg, on this article, he wasted no precious time in prematurely negotiating an alliance, and he went straight to the first chapter: to establish in law the neutrality which had in fact existed since the beginning of the war between the Russians and the auxiliary corps which was methodically retreating before them. He dispatched, in the last days of December, Anstett to the headquarters of Schwarzenberg, with the mission of offering and the power to conclude an armistice. Then he turned to Prussia, believing that he could use it more deliberately with this Court and that, Prussia won over, it would involve Austria.

Personal relations had never been severed between the two sovereigns; although officially at war, they stuck to this word of Friedrich-Wilhelm III in March 1812: "We will always remember that we are united, that we must always become allies again."

Prussia was the power which had suffered the most from Napoléon, and whose territory was the first to meet before the Russian army. It was in this passage that it was necessary to ring the first strokes of the bell and give the first stroke of the helm: the call to kings and the call to peoples. On the other hand, if the design on Poland were to be realized, Prussia would be the first of the interested powers which it would be advisable to disinterest; it was a question of obtaining from them a renunciation, in favor of Russia, on the recovery of their Polish provinces, Posen and Warsaw, and that they seek conveniences elsewhere. Lieven had written it to Hardenberg on 2 October. Colonel Boyen had reported these words from the Tsar:

> If the king accedes to it – to the alliance – I not only guarantee him all his present possessions, but I undertake not to lay down arms until the king has returned to possession of all the provinces he has lost in Germany or will have been compensated in another way, namely by Saxony, which seems to me suitable for this.

The provinces Alexander already largely occupied, and he advanced there every day; it remained to engage the Prussian government and compromise it with Napoléon in such a way that it found itself at the discretion of Russia and could only be saved by the Russian alliance.

The Russians had gained access to General York, who was serving in the auxiliary corps. Following an illness of the general-in-chief, Grawert, York had taken command of this corps. On November 1st, the Russian general Essen wrote to him from Riga, announcing Napoléon's retreat: "It depends on you to break the chains of Prussia: lock up Macdonald at Mittau, march to the Prussian frontier; your example will exalt your fellow citizens, you can be the liberator of your fatherland and of the whole of Germany!" York sent this missive to the King. In the meantime, a very shrewd Italian, the Marquis Paulucci, replaced Essen in the government of Riga. He wrote to York on 14 November, urging him to follow the example of the Spanish officer La Romana.[17]

A contemporary reported, "York is a man of great character and heroic fearlessness in fire; but his is a hard, intractable character; he is violent, hateful and rude, and it is difficult to have him as a comrade and as a subordinate."[18] More difficult still to hang him for dupe. A man playing his head to break Napoléon's yoke, he had no intention of handing himself over to Alexander. He answered finely, on 20 November: "The case of La Romana is not mine. La Romana knew what he could expect, for his country, from the allies to whom he gave himself." York sent one of his *aides-de-camp* to the King for instructions, and another to Vilnius to ascertain the state of affairs there. This officer was back on 8 December. He spoke of survivors, ghosts, and army spectres. York reassured himself. Alexander then informed him through Paulucci that he pledged not to lay down his arms until he had succeeded in obtaining for Prussia a territorial aggrandizement considerable enough to make it resume among the powers of Europe the the place it occupied before the War of 1806. That very day, 18 December, Macdonald began his retreat from

Mittau to Tilsit.

Macdonald, without realizing all the danger, formed suspicions and informed Berthier. He wrote on 2 December: "General York absolutely performs only the strictest duty and conducts himself only to save appearances and the honor of the Prussian arms." A few days later on 10 December 1812 he formally demanded the recall of York and several of his officers.

### III. Convention of Tauroggen

In Berlin, Hardenberg and his master put more form into it, and Napoléon's minister, Saint-Marsan, brought infinitely less clairvoyance to it. Hardenberg corresponded with Metternich. He did not yet dare abandon himself to the hope of a return of fortune. He could not believe the extent of Napoléon's defeat, he dreaded his terrible responses. On 30 November, Captain de Schack arrived, *aide-de-camp* of York. Neither the King nor his minister consented to give an order which might compromise them.

The Chancellor redoubled his protests to Saint-Marsan, who redoubled his credulity:

> I still find him (the Chancellor) as confident and as sincere as in the past, and he is of such a character that he would hardly hide plans for a change of political system... Some public marks of benevolence and interest for this country on the part of His Majesty the Emperor, some demonstration which would give confidence, satisfaction for the conduct held during the campaign, would, I believe, have a very great effect and would absolutely nullify the intrigues of some plotters.[19]

On 14 December, Napoléon's visit to Dresden was known in Berlin. The next day, a letter from Serra, Minister of France in Dresden, announced the imminent arrival of Narbonne in Berlin, with a mission for the King, and the order to Saint-Marsan to deliver a letter from the Emperor to Friedrich-Wilhelm III.[20] The letter, dated Dresden, on 14 December, requested that the Prussian Auxiliary Corps be increased to 30,000 men. Saint-Marsan immediately went to Hardenberg to obtain an ordinance from the King. He found the Chancellor "in the best spirit," "honest, loyal," as usual. He showed Prussia so imbued with its fidelity that it was already demanding its reward. Hardenberg, he wrote, thought and insinuated that upon peace "skillful and solid," the Emperor, to "form himself a constant ally of France and a barrier for the north," might propose "not to reunite Poland to Prussia, but to make the King of Prussia King of Poland."

Friedrich-Wilhelm III received Saint-Marsan at Potsdam on the 16th. "I have found," said this imperturbable optimist, "the king in the best disposition, abandoning himself to all the loyalty and frankness of his character, judging things soundly, and calculating the genius and strength of your Majesty."[21] The King read the letter from Dresden, "protesting his attachment to the system he adopted, which he would never change." He understood no doubt, from the system he had been following since November 1805, and Saint-Marsan from the system of fidelity to the forced alliance of 1812; then, after asking for time to reflect, he "slipped" that the limitation of his forces to 42,000 men made it very difficult for him to comply with the Emperor's wishes and that, on the other hand, if Napoléon were to evacuate the Prussian positions, he would dispose of the occupying troops: the Prussians would replace them in the garrisons, with every advantage. He was skillfully taking advantage of Napoléon's first admission of embarrassment to get rid of his shackles. Moreover, redoubled politeness. Informed of Maret's forthcoming visit, the King offered to furnish him with lodging, put his carriages and his livery at his disposal, eager to show the public, "at this moment, the value he makes of a minister of His Majesty." Through this unctuous verbiage infiltrated the first insinuation of this intermediary of Austria who will become the key of European policy. Saint-Marsan wrote:

> I have no reason to suspect that the court of Russia has hitherto made any proposition to the latter; but the Baron de Hardenberg told me that he thought he was certain that some had been done to that of Austria to seek to detach her from your Majesty's alliance; that it was answered that Austria would not change her system, but that she would undertake to transmit to Your Imperial and Royal Majesty proposals for peace if Russia so desired.[22]

However, events were rushing forward. York was in danger of being driven into some dreadful extremity. It could not be left unanswered indefinitely; this was addressed to him on 21 December: Beware of pranks, do not stretch the rope too tightly, do not forget that Napoléon was a man of genius, inexhaustible in resources; to behave, moreover, according to the circumstances. Nothing was prescribed, nothing was forbidden; they left it to York; they reserved the right to approve or disavow it, which made it possible, while waiting for "circumstances," to protest the firm intention in which they were to persevere in the alliance.

Maret arrived on 23 December, saw the King and Hardenberg, and allowed himself to be persuaded by the loyalty of the gesture, the loyalty of the King's countenance, Hardenberg's skill in insinuating that loyalty is the finest of calculations. "The work for the increase in the quota is not yet signed," said this minister, "but the king's approval is certain."

The Prussians had long had neutrality at heart; duplicity, since 1807, had taken its place. Despite the disaster of the Grand Army, Macdonald remained intact and fell back on Prussia; Augereau was still occupying Berlin with 12,000 men, and as long as he was there, a Prussian Fructidor always seemed to be feared: this *sans-culottes* duke remained a man, from the first alert, to treat the King of Prussia, his ministers and all his Court as he had in Paris, in 1797, treated the agents of the sovereign people. Add that this double game, which was a necessity for them, also entered into their tastes and their calculations. Hardenberg once wrote in his diary, "Why not crush the French in the retreat?" "We must strike and annihilate," the King ordered his minister.[23] But if it was really on their mind, they confided it only in the ear, behind closed doors. They flattered themselves that they would find in Austria a double guarantee, both against the Russians, allies tomorrow, than against Napoléon, yesterday's ally, the Russians demanding passage and Napoléon demanding soldiers to bar their way. Hardenberg, Ancillon, Knesebeck held council on 25 December. The hour awaited with so much angst for six years, the hour of virile resolutions had sounded. They recognized this, but concluded that if the moment to act had come, the circumstances demanded they act with circumspection. This was the King's opinion. It was therefore agreed to enter into negotiations with Vienna, to send Knesebeck thither, and they busied themselves in drawing up their instructions in consequence.

He had to ascertain the intentions of Austria; if Austria was decided to turn against France, Knesebeck would declare that such was also the intention of the King, but that Prussia could not currently take the initiative. It armed, but as long as the alliance between

Vienna and Berlin had not been concluded and the armaments completed, "it will be absolutely necessary to maintain, as before, the appearance of perfect harmony with France." The King would like for Prussia the complete restitution of the territories which it possessed before 1805, for Europe the state of peace of the treaties of Lunéville and Amiens, for Germany the dissolution of the confederation of the Rhine and the partition of supremacy between the North, to Prussia, and the South, to Austria, the Main marking the separation. But, the instructions added,

> until everything is ripe for the execution of the plan, the interests of the two powers demand that they continue to play, with as much circumspection as skill, the role of France's faithful ally and to keep her in perfect security, not to expressly decline new demands on its part and to nourish it with vain hopes.

Under this mantle, Prussia would be able to press on with its preparations: the auxiliary troops to be supplied to France would serve as a pretext for this. Hardenberg wrote to Gneisenau in London: "Napoléon demands the raising of the auxiliary corps to 30,000 men. It requires a drawstring on the upper Oder. We take advantage of this to increase our army and concentrate our forces, as we had done and planned in the spring of last year.[24]

But it was necessary to keep up appearances, Friedrich-Wilhelm III concealing his intentions so well that his people were not far from imputing his treasonable conduct to him. Everyone, at the sight of the wrecks of the Grand Army, measured the extent of the shipwreck and realized that there was an opportunity for salvation, then for revenge. It may be said that all Prussia was convinced of this; they asked to run to arms, and could explain neither the state of genuflexion in which their King remained before the Emperor, nor these levies of men destined to fight against their own country; people were astonished, they were scandalized by the intimacy displayed with Saint-Marsan, by so many dinners offered at gala events and very ostensibly to French people staying or passing through, to Maret, to Augereau, finally to Narbonne, who had preceded Maret, who remained after him and who pushed his little matrimonial mediation.

Hardenberg did not uncover without temper, in the agitations of the public, in the intrigues of the secret societies, the hand of the man whom he considered a dangerous revolutionary, Stein. "Nothing more urgent, without a doubt, than to repress these effervescences in principle," he wrote. Then Ancillon said,

> It is very sad that since 1809 there have spread in the minds maxims subversive of every social order. Many people have convinced themselves that the nation can take the initiative, and that this nation is them. They must be repressed, it is the best way to give confidence to the French.

The people did not understand these double and triple bottom policies. They must honor what they love and believe in the beauty of the cause to which they sacrificed themselves. The diplomats set down illustrious traps: they had never, by the play of their machinations, aroused enthusiasm. Prussia expected not advice of prudence, orders to be silent and to keep quiet, but the battle cry, the sounding of trumpets. York made the gesture and gave the eagerly awaited signal.

Invested with the most formidable responsibility towards his country, York was inspired only by political feeling: he was a people and he acted as a poor soldier would have done, placed in the outposts as a lost sentinel, as the last of the peasants of old Prussia acted in seeing the liberators arrive. The King had left him the option between military servitude and civic duty, between discipline and national conscience: this soldier obeyed the voice that came from the highest and commanded the most imperiously. But this soldier with a Prussian soul was at the same time a shrewd Prussian. He performed an act which decided the destinies of his country; he did it both instinctively and with advice: he was rash, and was so with policy. On 2 January 1813, the King and Hardenberg were still struggling to swim between two waters, hardly daring to come to the surface to breathe for a moment, when they learned that the defection they were working to spin with such insidious industry, a corps of the Prussian army had spontaneously consumed it. The flag was engaged, the King's honor compromised and the nation called to arms by a formidable clarion call: the war of independence was announced as a revolution.

Macdonald retreated to Tilsit, leaving York and his Prussians in the rear. York was withdrawing very slowly; the Russians worried him little; however, it happened that on 24 December the Russian General Diebitsch cut him off from Macdonald. That same evening, York and Diebitsch met at the outposts. Diebitsch declared that he had orders not to treat the Prussians as enemies, and that the Russian generals possessed powers to conclude a convention of neutrality. York said nothing, took no sides, but he let the Russians put themselves in a position to bar his way. On the 26th he received a message from Paulucci, with Alexander's letter of the 18th, which offered the alliance and promised the reconstitution of Prussia. It was food for thought. Lacking orders from Berlin, York temporized again and saw Diebitsch again. They agreed that hostilities would in fact cease, and that they would both maneuver so as to appear, Diebitsch to cut the road, and York to escape before superior forces.[25] By this verbal arrangement, he thought he had avoided all difficulties. On the 27th, he sent Count Henckel de Donnersmarck to Berlin to instruct the King. On the 29th, he stopped at Tauroggen, very close to the Prussian frontier: it was there that Seydlitz found him, one of his envoys, who was returning from Berlin, with the remarkable instruction not to commit "mischief," to act according to the circumstances, and for all light the opinion that the King remained attached to the French treaty. On the same day he received a note from Macdonald inviting him to join him at Tilsit.

The Russians were measuring all the consequences of the defection of a Prussian corps, at the first encounter, on the threshold of Germany. Clausewitz, who accompanied the Russian army, augured ill of York's hesitations. He proceeded to Tauroggen, where he arrived on the evening of the 29th; he carried a letter from the Russian general staff, declaring that Wittgenstein's army would be on the 31st on the left bank of the Niemen, cutting the road from Tilsit to Koenigsberg. York didn't give him time to deliver the envelope. As soon as he saw it, he apostrophized him:

> Back! don't come near me! I don't want to deal with you anymore. Your damned Cossacks let a message pass from Macdonald ordering me to march on Piktupôhnen, and effect my junction with him there. There is no more hesitation: your troops are not arriving, you are too weak; I have to march; I forbid you all these negotiations which would end up costing me my head.

Clausewitz begged York to read the letter he brought him before going any further. When he realized the danger in which the progress of Wittgenstein placed him, and learned that, failing to decide before the 31st, he would be treated as an enemy, York changed his language. He said, "Clausewitz you are a Prussian. Do you believe in the sincerity of this letter? Can you give me your word of honor that Wittgenstein will really be, on the 31st, at the points indicated there?" Clausewitz vouched for the sincerity of the statement; as for the execution, he reserved himself: "Your Excellency knows that in war, with the best will in the world, one is often forced to remain within the lines one has prescribed for oneself." York had called his chief of staff. He remained pensive for a few moments, then, taking Clausewitz's hand: "You have me. Tell General Diebitsch that we will talk tomorrow morning at the Poscherun mill and that I am already resolved to separate myself from the French and their affairs." He added: "I won't do things by halves; I will also procure Massenbach for you."

Massenbach commanded the part of the auxiliary corps which had followed Macdonald. York had on hand a cavalry officer of this troop; he asked him: "What do they say in the regiments?" And as the officer could find no words to express the joy of his comrades at the thought of breaking with the French: "You may say so, you young people; me, old man, I feel my head shaking on my shoulders." He called his officers together and said to them:

> Gentlemen, the French army is annihilated by the avenging hand of God. The time has come when we can regain our independence by uniting with the Russian army. Let those who are determined like me to sacrifice their lives for the country and for liberty follow me; let the others withdraw. If things turn out well, perhaps the king will forgive me; otherwise I'll lose my mind. In this case, I recommend to my friends my wife and my children.

A unanimous cry answered him: "We are with you!"

The next morning, 30 December, Diebitsch, accompanied by Clausewitz and Count Dohna, met at the mill of Poscherun. York, who had brought with him Colonel de Roeder and Major de Seydlitz: six persons, five of whom were Prussians by birth. Clausewitz and Dohna were already in Russian service; the others gave themselves up to Russia. On the spot, the agreement was signed. It was an entirely military arrangement, without the slightest political addition. The Prussians marked out the territory they would occupy between Memel and Tilsit; this territory and their army corps would be in some way neutralized and would remain so until they had received orders from the king. In any case, they would have free passage and would engage not to serve against Russia for three months. The thing done, York sent two letters he had prepared, one for Macdonald and the other for the King, very brief.[26]

Massenbach and his detachment received an order to leave Macdonald. On 31 December, in the morning, they had disappeared. Macdonald learned the news at the same time as he received the missive from York.[27] He immediately decided to evacuate Tilsit. York replaced him on 1 January 1813. On 3 January, this general addressed a second letter to the King, this one developed, and in which he explained the reasons for his action.

> I did it without Your Majesty's order. Circumstances and serious considerations will justify it to contemporaries and posterity. It is reserved for Your Majesty, as in 1805, to be the liberator and protector of your peoples and of the peoples of Germany. It is too obvious that the hand of Providence has driven everything. But the opportunity wants to be seized quickly. Now or never, it's time to conquer liberty, independence, greatness. The pusillanimous needed an example; Austria will follow your Majesty's. I do not ask him for any consideration for my own person. However I die, I will die for Her. [?]

The first ring of the great cosmopolitan army was broken; the first blow of the national revolution of Europe was struck, Napoléon's system of alliances was shattered. The example was going to be contagious in Germany, it was like a tocsin that was to resound throughout the Confederacy. Scant, no doubt, next to a catastrophe like that of the Grand Army, than the march to the right or to the left of ten thousand Prussians; but a great deal more than the defection of the most enchained, the most fearful, the most humbled of Napoléon's vanquished, who had become his allies by force.

The Tauroggen agreement was immensely far-reaching, and it is no exaggeration to compare, for the extent, these talks of December 1812, in the plains of Poland, to those other conferences, equally confused, uneasy, obscure, which had led, in 1792, Brunswick to beat a retreat on the plains of Champagne. Like the act of Brunswick, that of York can only be explained by the general appearance, the atmosphere, the passing wind, the weather, in a word, what is called fatality, because the direction escaped to individual will and that everything took place with the help of all. At the end, just as at the beginning of the Great War, Prussia marked time and gave the signal for one of those evolutions of things which made Goethe say on the evening of Valmy: "A new era is beginning." It was one, indeed, and the reverse of the other defection from Prussia to Europe of the allied kings against the French Revolution, in 1792; defection to France, fighting against the Europe of insurgent nations, in 1812.

These were the actions which the King of Prussia could not conceive. His royal vanity disapproved of them when he did not command them, and it was not in his character as a king ever to command them. York, by his loud call of trumpets, disconcerted the pedantic and gloomy fugue of the official Prussian music. A general had allowed himself to act on his own, without orders, which amounted to disobedience and almost treason! The prince, as commander of the army, was offended; his policy was upset in all his machinations, and seeing them suddenly jerk and become entangled in their straps, he felt dizzy; but the core of the man was brave, the heart of the King was patriotic, and this prince, eternal victim of his indecision, felt a heartbeat on seeing that one of his subjects had dared to accomplish what he dared not even think, and the public will said to him: *vox populi, vox Dei*. However, it was not necessary to let it appear, or even admit it, to become aware of it. The first movement, the natural one, was joy; the second, mood and anxiety; the third, dissimulation.

On 2 January, Prince Wilhelm (the future Emperor of Germany) recounted:

> ...it was three o'clock, the king was about to go out for his daily walk (in Potsdam) with the prince royal, prince Frederick and myself, when Count Henckel appeared in the orangery of the new garden, where we had dined... the king went away with him... After half an hour, full of anxiety for us, he returned. His countenance breathed an air of satisfaction that we had not seen in him for a long time: it delighted us all the more because it contrasted more with the words he addressed to us: – Count Henckel has brought me unfortunate news: York capitulated with his corps; they are prisoners of the Russians; the days of 1806 seem to begin again. – We stood petrified.

Hardenberg showed himself, in these encounters, to be a man of fine dress, and never to lose his head. He went to the most urgent and immediately thought of the change that this *coup de partie* brought to the great game of indemnities and compensations. The reiterated offers of Alexander, by Lieven, by Boyen, by Paulucci, assumed an entirely different character after the act of York; it was becoming evident that affairs would end, after more or less detours, in this arrangement. Hardenberg changed faces. The instruction drawn up for Knesebeck, at Vienna, subordinated the whole action of Prussia to an understanding with Austria. Hardenberg added to it, that same day, 2 January, this postscript that: "in the event that the Russians cross the Vistula and present themselves on the Oder, the king does not want to conclude anything with them without the consent of Austria; but he wishes this assent and, according to him, it is in the interest of Austria to give it." It was not an easy task to manage: it was necessary to face on all sides and to trick everyone; with Saint-Marsan, Narbonne, and Augereau to hold them in illusion, to persuade them that he remained faithful, to declare it to the Prussian people, by all the official speeches, all the ostensible gestures, that is to say to show defection to the national cause to veil the defection from the enemy; to trick York so that he could neither say nor even believe himself approved; try to untangle Alexander's game, if he was sincere in his offers and how he intended the reconstitution of Prussia and Germany; not to surrender to him, while securing his alliance; secure Austria, if need be, against the Russians, if they tried supremacy in the manner of Napoléon, and yet not bind themselves with Austria to the point of not being able to treat with Alexander if it was in their interest; finally to appear sorry when, deep down, they were exulting.

In the evening there was a ball to which the princes were invited. They refused to go there. "And why?" asked the king to them. "This is not what can turn you away from it." The next day, January 3, Krusemarck left to resume his post in Paris: his instructions required him to march with Austria. On the 4th, Knesebeck set out for Vienna, to deliberate on this common march.

Saint-Marsan knew nothing yet; prudence dictated that he should be allowed, to the end, to sleep off his confidence. On January 4th he attended a grand dinner at Augereau's, with Narbonne, Hardenberg, and Hatzfeld. During dinner, he was given a letter from Macdonald, sent by Berthier, relating the event. The letter was read at table. "The Baron de Hardenberg seemed appalled." Augereau, Saint-Marsan, and Narbonne "exhausted the material."[28]

> The Baron de Hardenberg agreed with us, as did the Prince de Hatzfeld. He went immediately to the king, who has just returned to town. He proposes to dismiss York, to have him arrested if possible, to give command to General Kleist, to recall the troops, and to send Prince Hatzfeld to Paris.

Narbonne and Saint-Marsan went to the King, who lavished assurances of loyalty, testimonies of indignation. They were told that Friedrich-Wilhelm III's first words had been: "There is enough to have a stroke. What should be done?" Saint-Marsan opined that all the troops of the Prussian contingent should be placed under command of Murat, general-in-chief since the Emperor's departure. The King said: "Not only is the opinion of the Comte de Saint-Marsan good to follow, but it is a matter of law." So it was decided, and Saint-Marsan was informed of it, on 5 January.

This diplomat had to admit to himself, however, that something was suspicious about the whole affair. He received communication of a letter which Major de Natzmer, private *aide-de-camp* to the King, was instructed to take to Murat, at Elbing. The King said: "This measure aroused my indignation as much as my surprise. Major von Natzmer bears my orders to dismiss General York and have him arrested. I need not say that I do not ratify the convention." Natzmer left Berlin on the evening of 5 January; but instead of going to Elbing, to Murat, he made a detour to Alexander's headquarters: he carried a verbal communication to the Tsar: the King approved the convention of Tauroggen, but he could not ratify it publicly; when the Russian army had reached the Oder, he would be ready to sign an offensive and defensive alliance with Alexander.[29]

Narbonne, however, whether he conceived the suspicions which were later credited to his perspicacity, or whether he felt himself at the end of his mission, decided to uncover its real object.[30] On 7 January he went to take leave of Hardenberg; and insinuated to him that nothing would be more apt to strengthen the alliance with France than a marriage between the Crown Prince and a princess of the imperial family, a Beauharnais or a daughter of Murat. Of course, Hardenberg, apologized for not answering before referring to the King, and the effect of this reference was a note he wrote in his diary: "We will apologize on the parleys begun for a princess of Austria. Hatzfeld is not to make any advances. Above all, his mission is only a mask."

This mission, announced on 4 January, was taking place in full light, under the eyes of Saint-Marsan. Hardenberg kept him informed of the smallest details; he had him read the instructions "in the original." They expressed "the king's indignation."[31] He confided to him, moreover, that this prince had, on the request of Narbonne, "certainly manifested whether he rejected it entirely or whether he would adopt it in certain cases." He did not disguise the possible advantages; but he was a father; he reserved his son's feelings; however, "if the advantages were considerable, such as to place the monarchy in a higher rank than that in which it is now," in short, if the marriage were to be concluded, it would never be without a dowry, and the Prussians already indicated that they would like to receive, the Duchy of Warsaw, for example. Saint-Marsan half-heard him. He mandated, "All this is consistent with his upright and loyal character. Experience has matured this prince." Saint-Marsan reported, in support, this speech he had from authorized confidants:

> It is true that most of my subjects are indisposed against the French, and that is quite natural; but unless they are impelled to it by unbearable demands of sacrifice, they will not stir. I believe I have certain data that Austria will hold firm in her alliance with France. If it weren't, my position is very different from that of this power. I am France's natural ally. Tell the Emperor that for precuniary sacrifices I can make no more; but that if he gives me money, I can still raise and arm 50 to 60,000 men in his service.

It would have been a masterpiece not only to have Napoléon thus annul the interdict placed on the Prussian army, but also to have him pay for the troops destined to fight him. France's natural ally! This was the proposal that the governments of Paris had so often launched from the Provisional Executive Council and the Committee of Public Safety towards Berlin. It had remained there without an echo. However, the sentence smelled of 1792. The brave Augereau found himself quite comforted by it. "I have the greatest confidence in the King of Prussia's devotion to His Majesty the Emperor; but we should also have a little more confidence in him. This country is maintained only by the calm of its sovereign."[32] Hardenberg wrote in his diary on January 5: "Saint-Marsan and Hatzfeld dined at my house. Need to hide the real system from the first, as we did to Goltz and everyone else." Thus weighed down, Hatzfeld left for Paris on 11 January 1813.

## VI. Grand Design of Metternich

An Austrian envoy, charged with a somewhat analogous mission, had preceded him there. With slightly different maps and a longer range combination, the same game was being played in Vienna as in Berlin. Prussia, still occupied by a French corps, crafted more cynically; Austria, removed from the theater of war, could bring more elegance and refinement to it. Metternich had been preparing for this crisis for a long time. Metternich had said, "In a war between France and Russia, Austria will have a flank position which will allow her to be heard before and after the fight." Before, no, and neutrality had, under Napoléon's hand, been transformed into an alliance; but, in the hands of Metternich, the alliance turned into *de facto* neutrality, and the famous flank position was revealed.[33] It was a question of occupying it. On one crucial point his calculations deceived him. He believed in wintering in Russia, in a second campaign in 1813: the retreat from Moscow surprised him, the disaster disconcerted him. He refused to believe it was so deep, especially irreparable. The fear of an offensive return from Napoléon never ceased to haunt him. "The destruction of the army of Russia would not prevent France from setting up another one," he said at the beginning of November. He calculated the interested help of the German Confederates. "As for the idea of being able, in the present war, to free Germany, he still saw no likelihood of it. It would be necessary," wrote a diplomat of his friends, "to want to carry out such a project, to be prepared in advance for a war of several more years, which Austria certainly is not."[34]

However, by the indistinct gleams that came from Russia, his mind worked, and, without yet seeing the goal within reach of his hands, without yet discerning the directions to take, he speculated, he plotted; he foresaw a mediation which would make Austria arbiter of the peace; but he immediately perceived the danger, and this danger was twofold: in the first place, a victory for France; in the second place, a victory of the enemies of France, and then the pretensions of Prussia to dominate Germany, the pretensions of Russia to govern Europe, to extend into Poland, to push into the East, in short one in the Confederation of the Rhine, the other in emancipated Europe, resuming, for their own benefit, the role of Napoléon. Austria could not admit it at any price: what was the use of overthrowing Napoléon, already shaky, to rebuild an edifice much more formidable to the

Austrian monarchy than the Grand Empire would henceforth be? These were, moreover, only proposals for the future; at the present, Austria found itself doubly bound, both by the treaty of 1809, which limited its army to 150,000 men, and by the treaty of 1812, which placed 30,000 men in the service of Napoléon. These 30,000 men, the auxiliary corps commanded by Schwarzenberg, remained intact; the first point was to regain free disposal, to evade Napoléon's pressing demands for an increase in strength, but not to reject them, however, for that was the only way to obtain him the license to arm and to put himself back, without inspiring him with distrust, in condition to fight him. The second point was to remain with Russia on the footing of neutrality, to stop the Russians at the frontiers of Gallicia, to hold them in suspense, leaving them to hope for an early alliance. Finally, it was necessary to encourage Prussia to revolt, and for the example it would set, and for the perilous situation in which it would place itself, which would allow Austria either to take advantage of its rout, or to await events, to solicit them skillfully, to reserve every chance. Preparing Europe for Austrian arbitration; to ensure that, after having successively reassured and disturbed everyone, Austria, in the event of Napoléon's final victory, would find clients everywhere; in case of defeat of the French, everywhere of the allies, and that it consummated, to its advantage, the ruin of the Grand Empire or the ruin of Europe; in short, when the time comes, disposing of 300,000 men, a decisive support in the struggle, put the Austrian alliance in the auction of Europe; to give oneself to whoever would pay the best, whoever would procure the most land and who would offer the most guarantees, except to prefer, basically, that it was not France and that interests agreed with grudges; above all to avoid being crushed by the enemy masses before having been able to intervene, such was the very complicated plan formed by Metternich. To execute it, it was necessary, first of all, to reconstitute the military state of Austria, then more than insufficient. This work required time and money. Time would be obtained from Napoléon; silver, from England.[35] "The simple roads were impassable," reported a confidant of Metternich in this crisis, Friedrich von Gentz. "We had to establish our system on intermediate nuances, which dispensed us both from ranking ourselves in pure loss among the number of enemies of France and from falling out irrevocably with the powers leagued against her."[36]

The first of these shades of passage, and not the least uncertain, was that which separated the alliance with France against Russia from the mediation between Russia and France, which would lead, by subtle gradations of color, to the alliance with Russia against France. In fact Austria was neutral with regard to Russia. In law it remained Napoléon's auxiliary; the art consisted in reducing the fact and the right to a single term, mediation. Metternich insinuated it as an evolution of the alliance; if Napoléon lent himself to it, neutrality with regard to the two belligerents would be the consequence.

On 9 December, Metternich sent a letter, which was really an instruction, to Floret, accredited to Vilnius, with the Duke of Bassano. Nothing, he said, could at this moment induce the Emperor Alexander to a separate peace; a general peace was only possible, by admitting that the Emperor Napoléon wills it; and Austria is the only power that can procure it. "Austria alone contains at this moment, by the calm and by the imperturbable firmness of its attitude, 50 million men ready to rise for a cause which would depend on a single word from the sovereign of Austria to make it look general." Austria only breathed peace and proposed to undertake the work. "Austrian steps in England and Russia must be entirely left to us as to form." Austria would not confine itself to speaking with words, but speak on its own behalf. "It must be Austria speaking the language of peace to all, France that of an ally, and the other powers that of the most complete independence."

The bottom of the mechanics, if one can say, was double, and with double meaning the declaration. A confidential letter which accompanied the ostensible dispatch already betrayed it sufficiently: "Austria has long since seen herself reduced to the rank of powers of the second order by France and by Russia." It "finds itself in a situation which would allow it to take, without prior negotiations with any power, the initiative of the steps which it wishes to concert with France." While waiting for it to impose itself, Austria emphasized the extent of the service it offered: it was necessary

> all the ascendancy that she never ceased to keep on public opinion in England so that she even managed to make herself heard there. They are convinced that winter will be enough to expel the French from Spain. We would reject there, without even discussing them, all proposals for peace that would come there on the part of France. The cry of uprising against the current preponderance of France is universal.

As for Prussia and Germany, even Austria, if Napoléon "does not come to the aid of the governments by measures very opposed to those which, until now, have served as a basis for his policy, the latter will end up being unable to repress the impulse which the peoples receive from current events." Metternich now raised the revolutionary bogeyman against France and threatened to unleash the monster! Nothing better demonstrates the immensity of the change accomplished in Europe.

Hardenberg, who was residing in Vienna for the regency of Hanover, wrote to the Count of Münster, King George's minister for that former electorate, on 22 December: "The Vienna cabinet takes such a high tone *vis-à-vis* Napoléon, which can only be explained by the conviction that Austria could talk to him with impunity." This diplomat whose report was composed to be read to the English ministers, continued:

> Metternich has conceived a grand plan for Europe, which however he still only calls a political dream. Its main features are that France should be confined within its natural limits between the Rhine, the Alps and the Pyrenees, that Germany should be divided into several large independent States, the independence of which would be guaranteed by Austria and by Prussia, which should be restored to the rank of a great power; it would be necessary, in his opinion, to divide Italy into two great kingdoms, reserving, on that side, for Austria, which, moreover, would return to its lost possessions, the frontier of the Mincio; that the Porte should at last be restored to the frontiers which it had in Europe before the Peace of Bucharest, and Russia should be restricted to the limits which it had before that of Tilsit.

Metternich foresaw, correctly, that Napoléon would never consent to it and that he would recommence the struggle as long as he had an army to risk. Peace as Metternich conceived it, peace with repressed and weakened France, could only be understood with a regency of Maria-Louisa, a tutelage of the Emperor Franz, and that would have been a masterstroke.[37] Metternich was already thinking about it, he thought about it for a long time. This combination presupposed the death or forfeiture of Napoléon; the hazards of war might bring death; the consequences of war, decay. But Metternich did not lose himself in speculating about prospects; if he had a piercing gaze, his gait remained measured. He was still on the news from Smolensk, and for the moment he was contenting himself with concerting some accommodation which, "while diminishing the preponderance of France, would nevertheless consolidate her new dynasty and not increase the power of Russia."

However, the "political dream" seemed one day on the point of coming true. On 12 December, rumor spread of the catastrophe of the Grand Army, of Napoléon's flight, of his very disappearance.[38] Count Hardenberg said:

> The impression which this news and the idea of the possibility that he had been taken or had perished momentarily produced here is difficult to describe; the majority of the public did not hide their joy, and Count Metternich would, at that moment, have desired better than to come to an understanding as soon as possible with the powers at war with France, especially with England.

The news of the pretended victory over Beresina, especially the announcement of Napoléon's passage through Vilnius and Warsaw, cooled him and brought him back to measures of temporization. For a moment he thought his system doomed in advance and all his grand political designs annihilated in the bud. It was only on the 15th that he had any positive information.

Victor de Broglie, sent by courier from Warsaw, arrived bearing the *XXIX Bulletin*. He had found on the road the rumor of the disaster "confusedly but universally diffused"; "the uprising of minds against France broke out on all sides." The French ambassador, Otto, immediately went to Metternich.[39]

> The Count's embarrassment was so visible that I can only attribute it to the interest he takes in our successes. He seemed to fear for the alliance, and he forgot himself several times so far as to tell me that if Austria took another course, she would soon see more than fifty million of men on his side. According to him, all of Germany, all Italy would declare for her. We make the biggest efforts to win Austria, Italy is offered, the Illyrian provinces, the supremacy of Germany, finally the restoration of ancient splendor and the imperial crown.

At all events, and on the eve of the auction, Metternich insinuated the price that Napoléon would have to pay for Austria's loyal attitude, if

Austria decided on the side of "loyalty."

Shortly afterwards came Napoléon's letter to the Emperor Franz, from Dresden, on 14 December, requesting the elevation of the auxiliary corps from 30,000 to 60,000 men. It was an opportunity to resume the maneuver begun on the 9th, but the instructions sent to Floret, in Vilnius, had become useless. Paris was the place to go, and it was decided to send General Bubna there, who had given proof of expertise. Bubna received an instruction from the Emperor, dated 20 December 20.[40] He was charged with seeing, listening, but not negotiating. He could only express wishes in favor of a negotiation through Austria. On an article, it would be formal: "He will take care not to leave any doubt to Napoléon that any more active cooperation on our part would be illusory"; nothing beyond the auxiliary corps, and of this corps itself the best employment henceforth would be "to place it, so to speak, in line with the rest of the Austrian army"; in reality, to extricate it imperceptibly from the French army to merge it with the rest of the troops of the Emperor Franz II. Bubna would not hide from Napoléon that a "general peace, on broad bases, could alone repair the disasters of the present campaign." He will express apprehensions on the peril with which Russia threatened the allied States of Napoléon, the Duchy of Warsaw, Prussia; he must show how important it would be if Austria "presented to Russia an imposing mass of resistance." All of these insinuations tended to uncover by what gratification Napoléon would reward the alliance if he wanted it, or on what conditions he would accept the intervention. Bubna must not fail to point out the interest for Austria "to be as soon as possible in the knowledge of the overtures of the Emperor of the French."

Metternich, moreover, like Hardenberg in Berlin, declared himself on all occasions the first partisan of the French alliance; he complained of being the butt of denunciations, calumnies, attacks of every kind from the Russian and English faction, from the faction which urged defection with regard to France and alliance with Russia. It was, in his mind, a means of preparing Napoléon for the offers of intervention, which would have the implicit consequence of abrogating the treaties of 1809 and 1812, on the limitation of the Austrian forces and the auxiliary corps. He mixed insinuations of good offices with protestations of fidelity. Otto wrote,

The government has been firm enough to maintain the alliance system, and it may be said that the latest setbacks have only served to confirm its provisions. The restoration of peace is currently Austria's dearest wish. Tell us frankly, the Minister repeated to me just now, what you want to do and put us in the position of acting towards you as a good ally, and towards others as an independent power. – May he (Napoléon) have complete confidence in us.[41]

It remained to be seen how Napoléon, accustomed to all the tricks and machinations of politics, was going to judge these contests of feints in Berlin and Vienna.

## V. Napoléon in Paris

On 16 December 1812, the *Moniteur* published the *XXIV Bulletin*. On the 18th, Napoléon arrived. He found Paris in consternation, all souls in anguish: after other wars, they were looking for the dead; this time they were looking for the survivors. Around him silence, less prompt obedience; no advice or criticism; but no energy; brains seemed empty. Everything fell on him alone, the responsibility for the disaster, the measures of reparation and revenge, and he felt that faith had disappeared. Everyone blamed him, criticized him; one denounced faults, one invented them if need be, as formerly the strokes of genius. The murmur of some, yesterday, became the talk of all: it was not for France that he undertook this war and that he claimed to support, against all politics, all reason, all common sense; it was for him alone, for his insatiable ambition; France defended herself on the Rhine, not on the Niemen and the Vistula! The Rhine barrier only seemed more precious. This Republican limit took on some sacred character. France would never give it up. Europe would not cross it. Informed people repeated what they were already whispering: that since Lunéville and Amiens, Europe which had recognized, without ulterior motive, the limit of the Rhine to France, asked only to respect it; the highest pretensions of enemies had never reached that far. So the Emperor, who had compromised everything, now threatened to lose everything.

As soon as he ceased to appear to be the instrument of public safety and of the fortune of all, Napoléon became the peril of everyone. The wise had long thought that this could not last; everyone now had the instinct, and soon with new sacrifices will come the desire that it not last. They did not see the end: since the adventure of Malet, the veil was torn asunder, and behind the veil of the temple they uncovered, as in the time of the ancient gods, inert marble and an empty sanctuary. The end appeared as necessary as it was simple: the end of Caesar or that of Paul I: a helping hand, a struggle: reliance on the clever to engineer the affair, on the violent to execute it: this kind of man had never been lacking since the Revolution. A woman of wit, on a retreat from gallantry, taking refuge in intrigue, under one or the other figure friend and client of Talleyrand, wrote in her notebook this remark of the Prince Vice-Grand Elector: "It is necessary to destroy by any means. This man is no longer worth anything for the kind of good he could do. We need liberty to remain, we need laws."[42] They are talking again about Sieyès, who, it seems, still excited.

The common people alone persisted in trust: they believed in the conspiracy of the elements, as in the conspiracy of kings. They felt the tide rising. As the war approached the frontier, they will have the instinct that the Revolution is at stake, that the fatherland is threatened, and under the influence of the necessities which caused the *levée en masse* in 1793, they will push further or let grow in the great army, closing ranks. Likewise also the officers of the young army, of career and vocation, who remained in France or in Germany, who still believed in the genius of the Emperor, who had not seen the retreat and imagine that nothing was simpler than a new Austerlitz and another Jena. It is here, in the people who provided soldiers, in this warrior youth who provided officers, that the mainspring remained. Napoléon tended it to break it. The Senate voted, the ministers signed an order, and the machine moved again, until the sources that fed it were exhausted. But this same Senate will vote a need for the deposition of the Emperor same as the early raising of conscripts, ripe for an Imperial Thermidor. Napoléon harangued the senators, discoursing before the councilors of state: this man of action drowned in words; he was in the tribune pleading his destiny, seeking arguments; he covered himself with words. He, whose great skill was to express the force of things in action, finding it hostile, strove to turn it around, with the blows of decrees. He forgot that if his orders carried so far, it was because he decreed general opinion. Whatever he ordered and whatever he still obtained, he no longer led. He directed, in France, with effort. In Europe, he no longer commanded: he negotiated; he disputed over the text of treaties; he invoked the letter; no longer a dictator, but a solicitor of alliances and auxiliaries.

 On 31 December, in the evening, he received Bubna.[43] The audience lasted two and a half hours, during which Napoléon talked a great deal. He was in substance disposed to peace with honor. He relied on the Emperor of Austria: he was his brother, his ally: the alliance was established for eternity! "But Austria's role will change. She is going to become a main party in the war; but if she wants us to listen to her, she has to arm herself." However, if he urged Austria to support diplomacy by deploying forces, he meant forces intended, in the event of failure of the negotiation, to support France. He asked if Metternich had set his sights on peace. He indicated Portugal restored to the Braganzas; Naples remaining with Murat, Spain with Joseph, but evacuated of French troops; England, by reciprocity, would evacuate Sicily; not a village in the Duchy of Warsaw! As the price of peace with England, he would give Illyria to Austria. Under these conditions, he was not opposed to Austrian mediation. An illusion, and this was a capital fact here, had taken hold of his thoughts, which will never come out of them and, in many encounters, will cloud his judgment. In his passionate tenderness for his son, on whom all his ambitions were henceforth concentrated, he could not imagine that concern for the fate of this child did not govern Austrian policy as it absorbed French policy. He was the father; Franz II was grandfather: the child bound them irrevocably. If he kept his clairvoyance in the face of Metternich's Machiavellianism, he didn't doubt, he didn't want to doubt Franz's final loyalty. He pushed the superstition of State pardon to the point of imagining that it must operate this miracle of animating, by introducing into it a heart, what he so aptly called in 1805 "this skeleton of Franz II." He forgot that if Franz had found the entrails of State to hand over his daughter, he would also find enough to take her back; that he would erase his signature with the same hand that signed the marriage contract; that in his eyes the King of Rome counted no more than any Archduke, even an Archduchess. Finally he did not suspect that the interest of Austria could be to overthrow him from his throne, to dismember his Empire and to despoil his son to keep him in guardianship in a France annexed and dependent on the House of Austria, as Naples and Spain were still part of the French Empire.

 We see him in these days of perplexity constantly preoccupied with attaching the King of Rome and the Empress to the Empire, and by this attachment, with tightening the Austrian alliance. He had the precedents of the coronation of the crown princes searched.[44] On 2 January 1814, he held a council, as at the time of the marriage: Talleyrand, Cambacérès, Maret, Caulaincourt, Champagny, all the former, present or future Ministers of Foreign Affairs, and the two State Councilors in external relations: La Besnardière and Hauterive. Was it appropriate to await the overtures of peace or to take the initiative, was it appropriate to apply directly to Russia, or to accept the intervention of Austria? Talleyrand, Caulaincourt, Cambacérès the four others opined for direct negotiation, for Austrian mediation.

On the 5th, a private council deliberated the question of the coronation and that of the regency. A new search for precedents on the regency of queens, the association of the kings of the Romans with the Empire.[45] The Pope remained hostage, available. Napoléon will use him. He flattered himself that these measures would interest the Austrians, appease the cabals of the Court, and convince the Emperor. Maret wrote to Otto on 7 January:

> A draft regulation is under deliberation at the Council of State for the coronation of the Empress and King of Rome. Our constitutional laws prohibit the regency of women. A draft *senatus-consultum* was drawn up to make modifications to it and would leave to His Majesty the option which he might soon be in the position of using, of entrusting the regency to Marie-Louise. The coronation will take place next February. The coronation will probably be done by the hand of the pope and Paris will bring together an affluence similar to that which M. de Metternich witnessed at the coronation of the emperor.

This was followed by the insinuation of a letter from Franz II to his daughter, authorizing her, "to give her word that nothing can harm the friendship and the alliance which so happily exist."

This was the answer that Napoléon wanted to the letter he sent the same day to his father-in-law, and to understand its significance, it was necessary to know this affair of the coronation, the coronation and the regency, the main support of his arguments. He resumed, this time, specifying the terms, the points touched upon in his interview with Bubna. First the apology: "I never met the Russian army that I did not beat it. The Russians didn't take a cannon from me; they didn't take a single eagle from me. My guard never yielded."[46] Then the phantasmagoria of resources: "Men, horses, money, they (France) offer me everything. I have a billion one hundred million in cash." He was sure of Spain. He was thinking of retracing his steps in Russia. "I will not make any move for peace; however, I will not refuse those which Your Majesty wishes to do."

Thus, he accepted the intervention of Austria; but he did not admit the break or even the suspension of the alliance of 1812 and he insisted on the doubling of the auxiliary corps. If Russia rejected peace, wrote Maret to Metternich, by the same letter, "His Majesty would declare the independence of the empire threatened; he would call 500,000 men to arms, you would be obliged to do the same on your side. You would then become the main party in the great controversy." In the directions given to Otto for his talks with Metternich, he clearly indicated in what spirit, under what reservations, the Emperor could be inclined to accept the intermediary:[47]

> His Majesty will not refuse the step which Austria wishes to take. He will even see it with pleasure, in the hope that Austria is firmly resolved to act, if the dispositions of Russia render this step unnecessary, with due vigor, and to increase his auxiliary corps to 60,000 men.

As for the terms of peace:

> None of the territories united by *senatus-consultum* can be separated from the empire. Such a separation would be considered a dissolution of the empire itself. To obtain it, 500,000 men would have to surround the capital and be encamped on the heights of Montmartre.[48]

Illyria, Dalmatia, Corfu, part of Spain, not united constitutionally, Illyria could therefore be considered "as an object of compensation for concessions made by the English government." If Russia claimed to grow at the expense of Prussia, Austria, the Duchy of Warsaw, of Turkey, Austria would be the first interested in seeing that this did not happen; it will convince itself that the only way to bring about peace is to continue the war. "Explain yourself so that the case occurring, it is a stable and irrevocable thing agreed, and that we can count with certainty on the cooperation of thirty thousand more men." Napoléon placed as much insistence on binding Austria through him as Metternich brought persistence on detaching himself by the same procedure. He did not want to admit the very idea of this detachment.

> When Minister Metternich gave you to understand that a change of system would in a short time place more than fifty million men on the side of Austria, because all of Germany and all of Italy would be ready to declare themselves, he spoke to you in a language which cannot be his own, but that of the enemies of the alliance. (Then) His Majesty should immediately and without hesitation declare to his people that the imperial consideration of France and its preponderance over Italy are threatened, put a war contribution of 25 *centimes* per *franc*, which would produce 200 million, call the second ban on the national guard and make a war armament of 600,000 men, and it would be impossible to stop events.[49]

Thus, on the one hand, a terrible war, on the other the succession of Austrian blood in France, consecrated by law and religion. Napoléon did not seem to doubt the choice of Franz, he still seemed to believe, if not in the devotion, at least in the political clairvoyance of Metternich.

> We are not unaware of the bad dispositions of the whole household of the Empress of Austria, and all our confidence resting on the Emperor and his minister; the speeches made to you by M. de Metternich necessarily had in your eyes, as in ours, a very great importance. The Emperor has a right to be suspicious, having been deceived so often.[50]

## VI. Armistice of Zeycs

It will be so again, and more insidiously than it had ever been. Metternich, while waiting for Bubna's courier, speculated with Count Hardenberg, unofficial from England, with Humboldt, Prussian envoy, and gradually accentuated, extended his "intermediate nuances." Always preoccupied with an invasion by the Russians, an occupation of Gallicia, a reconstitution of Poland; always frightened of an offensive of Napoléon which would begin like 1805 and 1809; always governed by this master idea of entrenching himself in neutrality until he was in a position to speak and act, but, until then, to fully arm and remove Austria from the theater of the war, he endeavored to turn it towards the North; at the same time he got rid of Napoléon and the Russians. York's defection facilitated his maneuvers: he saw his interest in throwing the Prussians into the arms of Russia. Napoléon would become more accommodating if he let Austria defect at ease and gain time to dictate peace. One reads in a letter from Hardenberg:[51]

> Count Stadion is convinced that Count Metternich wants the same end as us, with the exception, however, of the annihilation of the dynasty of Bonaparte, of which neither he nor the Emperor wants to be the instrument; but that he wishes to arrive at this goal, in his own way, by temporizing and still preserving the work of his creation, the alliance with France. However attached the Emperor may be to the Archduchess his daughter, and although religiously bound by the faith of his engagements, he will sacrifice one and the other of these ties step by step to circumstances influencing the happiness of his States.

On 11 January, Metternich received Bubna's report of the 31 December interview. He brushed aside, as useless verbiage, Napoléon's restrictions on his consent. From the whole context, he isolated and detached this text: the acceptance of mediation, the authorization, the very advice to arm. He immediately embarked on a diplomatic campaign and the armaments began. Meanwhile, Knesebeck arrived. Metternich saw him on 12 and 14 February. With his German partners he willingly affected some Machiavellian pedantry and refined on the "elegances" of procedure. The alliance of Prussia with France, he told him, had such a character of manifest constraint, that it permitted a sudden leap into the opposite camp.[52] Since the marriage of the Archduchess, the same had not been true of the link between France and Austria. Austria could not escape it by a violent disengagement. The dignity of the monarch would be compromised. The principal work of the cabinet must therefore be to recover all its liberty in a dignified and juridical manner, and to be freed from the treaty by Napoléon himself. The first article was to recover "mobility"; Austria now possessed it entirely. It could turn freely to one side or the other. The second article was to offer at the same time mediation to England and Russia: Austria did it. This second step taken, next was to find the basis of a lasting peace; Austria hoped to persuade Napoléon to propose it. As for the fourth step, namely whether Austria undertook to support these peace proposals with all its might and to go over to the side of whoever would accept them, it was not explained yet.

On the 15th, a courier brought the letters from Paris of 7 February, namely, Napoléon for Franz II, and Maret for Metternich. It is here that we must touch on the point of the ambiguity created and exploited by Metternich. Napoléon accepted mediation only to draw Austria into his camp and enchain them; Austria offered it only to make itself free to pass into the enemy camp. Napoléon flattered himself that negotiation must end with the engagement of the whole Austrian army, and that to begin with, Austria will increase auxiliary corps to 60,000 men. Metternich saw in his procedure the means not only of refusing the supplement of 30,000 men requested by Napoléon, but of recalling the 30,000 others, those of the treaty of 1812. Napoléon urged Austria to arm, with a view to strengthening the alliance; Metternich requested this authorization with a view, if need be, to turning the forces thus increased against Napoléon. Metternich took Napoléon at his word, but he took the word in a quite different sense from that which Napoléon gave it. From conditional mediation accepted by Napoléon, he concluded with mediation without conditions. He wrote to Count Zichy, minister in Berlin, correcting the nuances, but basically confirming the remarks made to Knesebeck.[53] "We have achieved the first goal we set out to achieve." He advised the King of Prussia to go to the only part of his states of which he was master, Silesia, the rest being occupied as much by the French as by the Russians. He would assemble 50,000 men there under the pretext of defending the line of the Oder, of distancing his army from old Prussia, and of removing it from the contagion of the example of York. He would thus detach this army from that which Napoléon was assembling in Berlin and would find himself, under the pretext of arresting the Russians, in a position to give them his hand.

    The Prussians thus encouraged, exhorted and driven to defection, led, so to speak, to Russia, Metternich turned to Otto. He insinuated that the Prussians deserved some reward, which would at the same time be high politics: "It is very unfortunate that the duchy, Warsaw, cannot be reunited with Prussia, which would be then strong enough to form together with us a barrier against Russia." As for the 30,000 men, he hid the intentions of the Emperor his master.[54] To distract Otto, he entrusted him with all the official details of his mediation with the English and the Russians. It was a means of involving Napoléon in this negotiation, and once he had implicitly accepted it, of declaring to him that, by virtue of this very mediation, Austria can no longer supply one from the belligerents an auxiliary corps; he must withdraw from the alliance, with Napoléon's consent, under the eyes of his ambassador!

He wrote a long letter to Maret and another to Bubna: "It is reserved for the Emperor of the French to make us regard the present war as Austrian; the first step is taken; he accepted our intervention – a word which you will carefully use on all occasions, instead of that of mediation."[55] The mediator, in fact, undertook to support his proposals. Now, Metternich intended to become a mediator only to bind himself to Russia, Prussia, and England. The effect of his procedure was to be, not to bind Austria to Napoléon, but to draw Napoléon into the net whose threads Austria would tighten and from which he would no longer emerge. Franz enhanced his minister's communications with a beautiful letter "to his good brother and son-in-law."[56]

There upon came a report from Schwarzenberg, commandant of the auxiliary corps dated 8 January and related the overtures made by Anstett, Alexander's envoy: the great desire of the Tsar and the entire Russian army to take advantage of the opportunity presenting itself to renew relations; "that everything was prepared to bring Austria back into possession of her ceded provinces"; that Russia only aimed to restore balance in Europe; "that the restoration of Poland could never enter into his sights, just as little as the change of ruling dynasty in France; that these solemn assurances should infinitely facilitate the means of reaching agreement"; and, to conclude, Anstett proposed an armistice of three months, having, he said, Marshal Koutousof the powers to sign it. Schwarzenberg was very favorable to it, the armistice kept his army intact and, moreover, halted the progress of the Russians in the Duchy of Warsaw at the former limits of Austria in 1809.

This was anticipating the wishes of the Emperor Franz. He replied to Schwarzenberg on 24 January: "If you were to come to the conclusion of a suspension of hostilities, you should not lose sight of the importance of covering as much of the territory of the Duchy of Warsaw as possible." The less the Russians occupied, the less they would be entitled to lay claim to, and because the Russians were talking of restoring Austria to its lost provinces, the policy demanded that the Russians be taken at their word and secure, already, territories to claim.

The armistice was signed on 30 January at Zeycs: "Given the severity of the season and other equally pressing circumstances." It was unlimited; a concerted movement plan was appended to it.[57] From then on Schwarzenberg methodically withdrew before the Russians.

Austria had recovered the disposition of its auxiliary corps at the same time as the mobility of its policy. Zeycs presented the counterpart and complement of Tauroggen a month later.

Count Stackelberg, Russian Minister at Vienna before the rupture, resided at Gratz and kept in communication with Metternich; this minister asked him for an interview and began the intervention procedure. In order that Otto should not entertain any suspicions, he hastened to confide in him and announced to him that M. de Lebzeltern had been sent to Alexander.[58] He attributed the initiative of the Stackelberg parleys: this Russian had arrived quite elated with victory; Metternich had him brought down to earth: "Here, my dear Stackelberg, you look like a man who is seeing the light of day for the first time, he dazzles you. We see more clearly." He said to Otto, "This is a big step, this first move from Russia. Count on us, we won't let go of anything, absolutely nothing. The emperor ordered the mobilization of 100,000 men, including the auxiliary corps."[59] There was an insinuation intended to reassure Napoléon about this armament and, at the same time, to remove his consent to the fusion of the auxiliary corps into the main body of the Austrian army. He added, to prepare Napoléon for a more considerable armament and to come to the abrogation of the restrictive treaty of 1809: "Up to now the war is not Austrian. If it becomes so in the sequel, it is not with 30,000 men, but with all the forces of the monarchy that we will attack the Russians." And, the better to lull Napoléon's suspicions, he revealed a whole web of betrayals between agents of Alexander and the Poles, "that nation which breathes nothing but scheming and intrigue, which has only been Polish since it ceased to be, which apparently cajoles France, which promises at the approach of danger loyalty and love to Russia." It was an invitation to Napoléon to dissolve the Duchy of Warsaw, to restore the Austrian parts of it to Austria, the rest to Prussia, without scruple for the Poles, and to make a bulwark of it against Russia.[60]

Thereupon he despatched the go-betweens with instructions. In Berlin, Zichy reassured the Prussians on the defection which he would advise them. The conditions were not the same for the two sovereigns, he would say, "but their interest is the same. This interest is permanent; it appears to the Emperor so pronounced that a change of political attitude cannot destroy it or even harm it." Franz wrote it in his own hand to Friedrich-Wilhelm III.[61] Lebzeltern went to meet Alexander with a letter from the Emperor of Austria, and Wessenberg set out for London.[62]

These two instructions cast an oblique but penetrating light on Metternich's designs. He refined on the nuances: the intermediary and the mediation. "As a mediating power, we would have to dictate the terms of peace." They were only at mediation, but "it is up to the belligerent powers themselves to feel all the interest they have in leading us to extend the attitude of simply intervening power and to change it into that of mediating power." He went further:

> As soon as Napoléon begins to fear that we will change our current attitude from intervening power to armed mediator, it is in the natural interest of the opposing party to accept our intervention to make us pass to the role of mediator, to which the Emperor will be far from refusing in the sequel.

As for the bases of peace,

> it is now less a question of the detailed bases of future peace than of the first and general ones on which a negotiation could be based. It will then be a meeting place. Prague would seem to us the most suitable.

That is to say, following the tactic of 1805, one would first produce general propositions, still rather vague, the minimum of what one would require later; they would serve as a primer for negotiation, and, once this negotiation had begun on this provisional and fallacious basis, it would be taken up again in underpinnings, extended, and developed according to the circumstances of war and the fortune of arms. Never, even in this first period, even in these first talks, was there any question of fixing immutable conditions of peace, to be accepted or refused by yes or by no, to be signed in 24 hours; on the contrary, and it is in this way that it will henceforth be appropriate to interpret the proposals of the allies, if one wants to penetrate politics, unravel their artifice and know their true significance.

Metternich himself commented on these instructions in his conversations with Hardenberg, the Hanoverian. He told him, and repeated it to Humboldt, that "when the game was well underway," Russia with 200,000 men on the Oder, if Prussia declared itself, if Sweden landed 30,000 men, if Denmark remained neutral, Austria would declare neutrality; it would form, in the meantime, an army of 100,000 effective combatants, 150,000 with the depots, on the destination of which France, in spite of the protests of Austria, would always retain doubts, while, from that moment, he would give the most positive assurances to Russia and Prussia that these forces would never act against them; finally, that having meanwhile come to an agreement on the basis of peace with the powers at war with France, Austria would declare itself against anyone who refused peace; a threat which, assuming an understanding had been reached with England, Russia and Prussia, could only be directed against France.[63]

Concerned to remove the theater of war and to prevent "the Confederates of the Rhine" from falling on the rich countries of the Austrian States; foreseeing at the same time that these states, when the time came, would willingly change their confederation, Metternich urged the principal among them to temporize, to draw their armaments at length, in short to slip away their defection. He drew the King of Saxony, honest and limited, into the net of the intervention.[64] He wrote to Binder, in Stuttgart, "If the king hastens to bring his forces to an available state, he increases both the chances of sacrifices for his own states and those of the continuation of war." Passing through Munich, the Austrian ambassador to France spoke similarly. He opened up about it with Mercy-Argenteau, Napoléon's envoy, a family minister, a mixed diplomat who, in Vienna, one might think was just as Austrian as French: "Is France not strong enough in its limits of the Rhine, to need other titles to its influence in Germany?" He spoke of the evacuation of the Hanseatic towns, of Illyria. "The current state of affairs can no longer stand, it requires sacrifices on the part of the Emperor Napoléon."[65] The defection of Austria, consummated in fact, was no more than a diplomatic secret; that of Prussia was about to declare itself publicly.

### VII. Treaty of Kalisch

The Russians had entered East Prussia. Kutousof issued a proclamation dictated by the Tsar:

> Providence has blessed the efforts of the Emperor my master. Independence and peace will be the results. His Majesty offers his assistance to all the peoples who, drawn today against him, will abandon the cause of Napoléon to follow only that of their true interests. It is especially to Prussia that this invitation is addressed. It will be glorious for His Majesty the Emperor to put an end to the evils he is experiencing, to help restore Frederick's

monarchy to its brilliance and extent, and to be able to give the King of Prussia proof of the friendship he never ceased to keep.

This imperial counterpart to the famous manifesto of the convention of November 1792 was in East Prussia the signal for a veritable revolution.[66] People cheered the Russians, run to arms. York, although publicly disavowed and under prosecution, remained general-in-chief and put himself at the head of the movement. Stein arrived on January 23rd, installing himself with the full powers of commissioner of Alexander, and acted as dictator of public safety. He convened the States of the province, which would provoke a general uprising. Stein's appeals, his signals, his examples were addressed to all of Germany. He lifted the blockade, stamped contributions, contracted a loan, gave Russian paper currency. Despite the resistance of the intimidated administrators and counter-orders from Berlin, he put the whole country in a fever. In a fortnight he did more for the reform of the State, for the regeneration of the Prussian nation, than his year of ministry. All the armament of the people, all the organization of the *landwehr* and the *landsturm*, which the Government took over, proceeded from his dictatorship. The King decreed, a few weeks later, only accomplished facts.

Friedrich-Wilhelm III inclined to the part suggested to him by Metternich, to retire to Breslau, in faithful Silesia, to assemble there all the troops he could levy, and to show there at least a phantom of government. Hardenberg arranged the departure in the greatest secrecy, as an escape. On the night of 19/20 January, Natzmer returned from Russian headquarters: he had seen Alexander on the 12th; he brought back the strongest entreaties to ally himself with Russia, the confirmation of the promises already made by Lieven, reiterated by Boyen, to reconstitute Prussia, but above all, the advice to withdraw from the perils of Berlin, to recover the independence of the Crown. The same message arrived from Vienna on the 21st, with Knesebeck's report: Austria promised nothing, but it approved of the defection and the Russian alliance. However, Friedrich-Wilhelm III still hesitated. Hardenberg persuaded him, kidnapped him, so to speak, only by assuring him that Augereau was going to invest Potsdam and arrest him. He left on the morning of the 22nd. "Little dinner at my house," Hardenberg wrote in his diary. "Marshals Augereau, Ney, Desaix, Sébastiani, Saint-Marsan. I announced the King's departure, which took place in the morning, with the troops, without touching Berlin.

Pretext for departure: the formation of a new army as a contingent." Friedrich-Wilhelm III arrived at Breslau on 25 January. Soon the troops flowed there, then the government rallied there, Hardenberg and, a little later, Scharnhorst. On the 28th the King received a courier from Krusemarck, relating the audience which this envoy had had with Napoléon on the 15th January. The Emperor affected confidence in the loyalty of the King, he insinuated that he might abolish certain clauses of Tilsit which were too harsh for Prussia; he even hinted at advantages, and tried to sow jealousy, to stir up the anxiety he knew reigned in Prussia with regard to Russia: "As for the Duchy of Warsaw, it may be indifferent to me that it retains the present form, whether it passes to Austria or Prussia; but to Russia, never!"

The same day two letters from Alexander arrived, one dated the 6th, the other the 21st of January.[67] They were outpourings of magnanimity.

> By my religion, by my principles, I like to repay evil with good, and I will not be satisfied until Prussia has resumed all her splendor and her power. To achieve this, I offer Your Majesty not to lay down arms until this great goal has been achieved. But your Majesty, on your side, must frankly join me. Never has a decision been more important than the one you are about to make. It can save Europe or destroy it forever.

Very adroitly, Alexander endorsed York's act: "I hope that General York has acted in accordance with Your Majesty's intentions. I cannot express enough the pleasure I feel in thinking that our troops have not longer to fight yours." In attenuating the character of Stein's dictatorship the Russian commissariat was transformed into an anticipated delegation of the King:

> I have invested with my full power a Russian dignitary, but one of your Majesty's most faithful subjects, the Baron de Stein. I hope by this I have given proof to Your Majesty how much the preservation of your States to their legitimate sovereign is close to my heart.

Napoléon, the bitter enemy, demanded acts which would be a real betrayal of the King towards his own cause, his subjects, his crown, and for all advantage he indicated, very vaguely, some part of the Duchy of Warsaw, from which it would be necessary to first dislodge the Russians. Alexander, the friend of the heart, always regretted and always desired, asked only a defection to the forced alliance, the divorce of the marriage void in its substance and in its cause; he formally promised to raise Prussia in splendor and dignity, and with Alexander spoke the whole Prussian nation. Friedrich-Wilhelm III felt carried away in spite of himself. It was as if backwards that he entered his own history. Memories of 1805, 1806, and 1807 obsessed him: he doubted his ally, his people, himself. Russia was luring him into the abyss! the enthusiasm of his people prevailed in revolution! Before acting, even speaking, he would like to be sure of assembling his troops with enough mystery and rapidity so that the corps of Augereau and Ney, so that the terrible Davout, would not surprise him in some formation, and not annihilate his monarchy before Alexander had time to save it. By taste, by habit, by necessity, he had to continue to pretend, and in this extremity he found himself again with the perplexities, the duplicities, the troubled and slow combinations of 1805 and 1806. He calculated that the great Russian army, 100,000 men, would not be concentrated at the mouths of the Vistula until the end of February, and that it would need to recover. Prussia would not be ready until March. Until then, it was necessary to trick Napoléon, to arm themselves under the guise of stopping the Russians; then to claim the fortresses of Silesia, and if Napoléon refused to evacuate them to make some pretext to break, when able; finally, if Napoléon perceived this plan, to obtain Russian aid in haste and in mass.[68]

But the slope was rapid, the impulse irresistible, and we will see Friedrich-Wilhelm III driven to reconquer his kingdom as he was in 1806 to lose it. It was a Louis XVI who marched, without knowing it, to a Valmy, to a Jemappes who would make themselves for royalty. His people were advancing, they were following. Measures followed one another timidly, uncertain at first then more and more significant, chained by a mysterious force which imposed decrees on the King, the dispatches, the treaties which he signed with a hesitant hand. On 28 January he created an Army Committee, made up of Hardenberg, Hake, and Scharnhorst, whose re-entry was an event. On the 29th, he announced to Alexander, by the Count of Brandenburg, that he was ready to respond to his appeal and was going to send an envoy, Knesebeck, hastily recalled from Vienna. He arrived in Berlin on 3 February, and the same day the King signed an ordinance for the creation of a corps of volunteers, in reality the nation's call to arms. However, Hardenberg wrote on the 4th in his diary: "The king does not yet know well what he wants." Friedrich-Wilhelm III was bewildered, disconcerted, like all his diplomats, like all his gentlemen, by the rising tide, the outburst of the people; the demand for political liberty was very close to the demand for national independence.[69]

Finally he meditated, with perplexity, on the promises of Alexander. The reconstitution of Prussia! but where, how? To be immediate, by returning Warsaw and Posen to him, or else in the future contingents of the war, to the detriment of the German brothers and in the wastelands of the conquests?[70] To despoil a king, by virtue of the laws of war, was an act with which a King of Prussia had never troubled himself; did the King of Saxony hesitate to enrich himself with the spoils of Prussia? But if he had no scruples about the act, Friedrich-Wilhelm III had doubts about the success. The King of Saxony remained on his throne. Napoléon protected him. If this kingdom was good to take, it was hard to conquer. On the contrary, Warsaw and Posen were available, close at hand.

On 8 February, Friedrich-Wilhelm III made up his mind and Knesebeck's instructions were sent, along with an autograph letter to the Tsar. The letter, flabby and cold, from the chancellery, minuted by Hardenberg, did not come from an exalted heart which gives itself; it betrayed a businessman negotiating a contract, getting ready to haggle over the price, to argue over the term. At the moment of taking the plunge, the King of Prussia began by retreating. He would only give himself the compensations in his pocket, his campaign plan in hand, and 100,000 Russians around him. By these marks alone, he would recognize the hand of divine Providence signing the treaty; then, he would let his heart speak, abandon himself to gratitude, and open his arms to his friend, his eyes wet with tears! The draft treaty delivered to Knesebeck bore this:

> The independence of Prussia can only be assured by restoring to her the strength she had before the war of 1806, and by increasing it if possible by acquisitions in the north of Germany. His Majesty the Emperor of all the Russias undertakes not to lay down arms without the consent of His Majesty the King of Prussia, unless he has restored to his said Majesty all the countries and states which he possessed before the War of 1806, or their equivalent, those of the House of Hanover excepted. This restitution must extend particularly to the part of the Duchy of Warsaw which belonged to Prussia.

Prussia would line up 80,000 men, Russia 150,000, whom it would undertake to muster on the Oder and bring to the Elbe before 15 April. To these pretensions, which thwarted Alexander's desires and imposed a battlefield on him militarily, were added the difficulties arising from the very character of the negotiator, one of the Prussians, said Stein to Alexander, "whose march is more hidden, but no less treacherous," than that of the declared adversaries of Russia in Berlin; "false, systemic mind," and open deceit.

It was part of the King's "plan" not to speak out further until he had the Russians' answer; but his people exceeded him: voluntary enlistments, monetary donations, everything poured in, with beautiful pathetic scenes of farewells and benedictions, songs inspired by patriotism. Out of national momentum universal compulsory service entered into the laws of the Prussian monarchy. At the same time York was publicly absolved, 12 February 1813, and restored to his command, which, in fact, he had never left.

Of so many rowdy oaths to expel and exterminate the French, Saint-Marsan who arrived at Breslau on 29 January, remembered only this oath from the chancellor: "Baron de Hardenberg has sworn to me twenty times today that the system has not changed, that no direct overtures have taken place for Russia ... that the king's conduct proves his loyalty."[71]

Accordingly, Hardenberg proposed to procure a truce between France and Russia, on condition that the French would withdraw behind the Elbe; he demanded the custody of the Silesian fortresses occupied by France, plus Danzig, and lastly a remission of 45 million on the arrears of the war contribution. Napoléon would thus have assured Prussia the freedom of its armaments, paid subsidies, and finally opened the roads to the Elbe, where we have seen that King Friedrich-Wilhelm III intended to attack and annihilate the French by 15 April. An instruction to this effect was sent to Hatzfeld, and Saint-Marsan received the confidence. He persisted in his confidence, attributing the movements of Prussia to the alarm caused him by Napoléon's refusal to recognize his neutrality and "to the mistrust which we showed him."[72]

However, Knesebeck arrived at the Russian headquarters at Klodova, and there he found dispositions very different from those he had expected. Indoctrinated by Stein on the "half-wills" of the King and the bad will of his advisers, Alexander returned to the views suggested to him in 1805 by Czartoryski: to force the hand of the King of

Prussia by invading his estates and by the uprising of its peoples; then reserve the faculty, according to the circumstances and according to its own conveniences, to restore this king in his power and splendor. "Friendship, trust, perseverance and courage, Providence will do the rest!"[73] But Russia would promise nothing, and less than anything in the world the Duchy of Warsaw. He found himself all the more at ease that the Prussian people instinctively worked for him, understanding nothing of the King's hesitations, of Hardenberg's subtleties.

Alexander received Knesebeck on 15 February and took in very bad part Friedrich-Wilhelm III's precautions, his slowness in separating from Napoléon, sparing the man who had sacrificed him, haggling with his savior. He said: "There is no need for treaties. Prussia must break immediately."[74] Prussia must be reconstituted, he wished it to be, and its accomplishment would be the work of war. He put on the table the annexation of Saxony in compensation for the Duchy of Warsaw. "Prussia must necessarily be enlarged," he continued. Knesebeck observed, "But this way of doing feels a bit French, the conquering." Alexander replied: "The conduct of Saxony does not permit of treating her otherwise than as a conquered country." He added: "We would compensate the King of Saxony somewhere, in Germany, in Italy..."

Knesebeck exhibited his draft treaty. One Russian wrote, "We could have believed that it was Prussia which had delivered Russia from the yoke of the French!" Nesselrode replied, on the 21st, with a counter-proposal which put things in perspective:

> The entire safety and independence of Prussia can only be firmly established by restoring to her the real strength she had before the war of 1806. His Majesty the Emperor of all the Russias undertakes not to lay down arms as long as Prussia will not be reconstituted in its statistical, geographical and financial proportions conforming to what it was before the aforementioned period. It will be preserved between the various provinces which must return under the Prussian domination the unit and the district necessary to constitute an independent body of State.

In particular, a territory would be joined to old Prussia which, in all respects, would bind this province to Silesia. Russia expressly excluded from this reconstitution of Prussia the possessions of the House of Hanover. For the rest, they neither promised nor forbade anything: the Duchy of Warsaw remained her conquest; to Prussia to help herself and to contribute with all the force of her arms to her own recovery. However, after the express stipulation of a piece of the Duchy of Warsaw to join old Prussia in Silesia, it became clear that Russia reserved most of it for itself.

Knesebeck refused to sign, whereupon an impatient Alexander "planted him there."[75] He sent Anstett to Breslau to rush the negotiation and wrote in his own hand, on 24 February, to Friedrich-Wilhelm:

> It is impossible for me to conceal from Your Majesty the painful impression produced on me by the communication M. de Knesebeck gave me of the instructions last given to General von Krusemarck in Paris. As soon as the enemy was annihilated, forgetting all the past, I flew before you, because the thought of the reintegration, of the very enlargement of Prussia, was always nurtured in the intimacy of my feelings. The time has come when we can achieve. You have to enter it.

He entrusted this letter to Stein, whom he recalled from Kœnigsberg:

> He is certainly one of the most faithful subjects your Majesty possesses. During almost a year that he stayed with me, I got to know and respect him even better. He is acquainted with all my intentions and my desires regarding Germany, and will be able to give you an exact account of them.

Willy-nilly, the Prussian army must pass from the role of auxiliary of Napoléon against Russia to that of auxiliary of the Russian army against Napoléon; that Prussia submit to the conditions of its liberator as it submitted to those of its conqueror; that Friedrich-Wilhelm III understood the role that Alexander reserved for him, that of lieutenant general of Russia in Germany, and with his *ukase* Alexander sent him a minister of his choice and of his confidence, this Stein once dismissed, abandoned without regrets to the revenges of Napoléon, Stein who had just revolutionized old Prussia, who would claim to rule the King and whose sight would awaken the most burning of all the old wounds, that of self-love, susceptibility. "It is clear, the king ordered Hardenberg on the 21st, that they want to entrain us, at all costs, and compromise us."

However, he could no longer mislead the French nor push his

armaments further without being sure of Russia. Napoléon put appearances against him and provided, by persisting in occupying Prussia and its fortresses, sufficient grounds for a manifesto of rupture.[76] The resolution taken, or rather suffered, thus the impatience succeeded the calculated slowness. Hardenberg sent a courier to Knesebeck on the 23rd, urging him to conclude; he added: "The treaties with England and Sweden, modeled on that of Russia, are ready." But the days went by without news, in the most cruel anxiety. On the 25th, only a note from Anstett announced his arrival in Breslau. He requested an interview with Hardenberg to communicate to him his full powers, the counter-draft treaty, and a letter from the Tsar to the King. Stein, ill, had to give up delivering it in person.

The treaty was not what the Prussians would have wanted, but circumstances pressed, the movement of public opinion dictated; they decided to conclude without further discussion. The Russian text, signed at Breslau on the 27th, was taken to Kalisch, where Russian headquarters were, by Anstett on the 28th, accompanied by Scharnhorst as a military adjutant. Said the Tsar to Knesebeck, "The king had more confidence in me, he signed without changing a word." Emotion cut him off for a moment, then he exclaimed: "Providence sends me help. But the king can be sure that I would rather die than abandon him."

The official instrument was dated Kalisch, 28 February 1813, and bears the signatures of Hardenberg and Koutousof:[77]

> The total destruction of the enemy forces which had penetrated into the heart of Russia paved the way for the great epoch of independence for all the States which will want to seize it to free themselves from the yoke that France has imposed on them for so many years. In leading his victorious troops beyond his frontiers, the first feeling of His Majesty the Emperor of all the Russias was that of rallying to the fine cause which Providence so visibly protected his former and dearest allies, in order to accomplish with them destinies which hold both the rest and the happiness of peoples exhausted by so many commotions and so many sacrifices. The time will come when treaties will no longer be truces, when they can once again be observed with that religious faith, that sacred inviolability on which the consideration, the strength and the preservation of empires depend.

This preamble constituted the declaration of the rights of Europe according to Russia and the manifesto of the policy that Alexander was to make prevail in Europe for several years. It proclaimed the lofty motives which the Tsar proposed; it set the tone for the new language of the chancelleries and solemnly affirmed this paradox destined to make a fortune in history, that religious faith, the inviolability of treaties, will consecrate the return to the sacred principles of an ancient law. However, these principles had never prevailed in the past; this right was known only through the declamations of publicists and the violations of rulers that they had never experienced, but whose imaginary memory lent a body to all the illusions of hope.

There followed articles no less important for the realities of affairs than the declarations of doctrine. They form the starting point, or rather the resumption of an alliance which, contracted in 1764, renewed in 1813, lasted until 1878, governed the 19th century, organized Germany in the Prussian way after having reconstructed in the Russian: an offensive and defensive alliance whose primary ostensible object was to "reconstruct Prussia" and to deprive France of "any influence whatsoever in northern Germany" (Article 1); immediate cooperation of the two armies; no peace or truce except by mutual agreement (Article 6); invitation to Austria to enter the alliance as soon as possible (Article 7). Then secret articles relating to the reconstruction of Prussia, and which reproduced verbatim the Russian counter-project.

Alexander achieved his goal. Without tying his hands, he secured the support not only of the Royal Prussian army, but of the Prussian national insurrection, and under this impulse from all of Germany, he became the proven leader of the grand coalition of the peoples, the leader of the independence crusade. He placed the King of Prussia on his left, and he would take care of placing the Emperor of Austria on his right, for the solemn entries he intended to make in the freed capitals.

## VIII. Manifesto of the Allies

Lebzeltern, who arrived at Russian headquarters on 5 March, was received by the Tsar on the evening of the 8th. His instructions directed him, under the guise of intervention, to test the Russians on the alliance and find out what they would offer. Alexander did not let Lebzeltern struggle with insinuations. He got straight to the point and said:[78]

> Is it possible that, always enclosed in vagueness, you want either to be divined, or that we throw ourselves into your arms without you deigning to tell us a single thought of yours? You want the good of the European cause? That is; me, above all, I desire that Austria regains its old attitude and all its possessions; that Prussia emerge from this struggle independently and with a degree of consistency; May Germany be freed from the French yoke and free, or rather subject as before to the domination of your sovereign. – Do you wish, Sire (said Lebzeltern), that I transmit this base as yours? – Tell me as secretly as possible if it suits you," replied Alexander; give me this one or another, I give you my word to produce it like mine, and you will make use of it as you please.

Then he added:

> You can fear nothing, all my army and that of the king will act with vigor; enter into possession of the Tyrol, from Italy to Mantua, at your convenience. Declare that you only want to take possession of what belongs to you, that you do not want to make war on France, that you will place yourself between the powers which will want to attack it we will assist you in everything. Then talk about a general congress, and finally then you will negotiate in the forms you want. If England brought exaggerated pretensions to it, well, we would understand each other, the interests of the Continent above all.

It was, as with Prussia, very skillful magnanimity. If Austria entered into these views, it would find herself, in fact, at war with Napoléon, and, in fact, allied with Russia and Prussia, for it would present to the two parties, Napoléon on one side, Alexander and Friedrich-Wilhelm III, as his own terms of peace, the terms agreed with Russia and Prussia against Napoléon; there would then be nothing left but to declare the alliance. Lebzeltern discerned it very well; the proposals appeared advantageous, and he hastened to transmit them to Vienna.

Alexander went to Breslau on 15 March. On the 16th, Prussia declared war on France. Alexander remained close to the King until the 19th. This was the occasion for ovations, accolades, reviews, with a great display of oaths and enthusiasm. However, the staffs arranged their movements. Gneisenau had arrived from London, quite elated by the new sight which, on his way, his country had given him. Stein took part in the deliberations: he intervened as the spokesman for Germany before Prussia and Russia; he signed with Nesselrode, on 19 March, a convention in which the two sovereigns regulated the conduct of their troops in the territories they would occupy, the Confederation of the Rhine and the countries united to the French Empire. They would announce that their object was the deliverance of Germany; they would invite princes and peoples there. "Any German prince who does not respond to this appeal within a fixed time will be threatened with the loss of his States." The crusade of kings proceeded like the revolutionary crusade 20 years earlier, and it held the rights of princes just as much as the Convention on the Rights of Peoples. "It will be necessary," said Cambon when proposing the decree of 15 December 1792, "to tell the peoples who would like to keep their privileged castes: 'You are our enemies,' and then treat them as such, because they will want neither liberty nor equality. " It was not then permitted for peoples to be free except in the Jacobin way; states were only permitted to be independent in the Russian and Prussian fashion. A committee composed of delegates from Prussia and Russia, to which would be added delegates from the other allied states, would administer the occupied countries, would carry out requisitions there, would organize an army of the line, a militia, a *levée en masse*. There would be formed five large sections of these countries: 1) Saxony, 2) Westphalia, 3) the duchies of Berg, 4) the departments of Lippe, 5) the departments of Bouches-de-l'Elbe and Mecklenburg.[79]

One recognizes in these measures the thought of Stein. Tsar Alexander pronounced the excommunication of the princes who would not unite. They would be guilty of national *lèse-majesté*, expropriated, ostracized from Europe. As for Saxony, which offered itself the first blows, it would not even have the option. The King of Saxony, Duke of Warsaw, had been one of the provocateurs of the war; he would be its first victim. Prussia henceforth had only to treat this prince as an enemy and his kingdom as a conquered country.[80]

On 20 March, the Treaty of Kalisch was published in its ostensible part, and, on the 25th, the appeal to the German nation, inspired by Stein and which was only the fiery commentary on the preamble to the alliance. It bore, ironically, the signature of Koutousof, who had come to Germany by passing over the belly of Poland, and speaking in the name of the copartners of three partitions:

LL. MM. the Emperor of Russia and the King of Prussia only came to help the princes and peoples of Germany to recover those hereditary lands of the peoples, which were taken from them, but which are imprescriptible in their liberty and their independence. Honor and country! let every German still worthy of the name join us with promptness and vigor! that each, prince, noble or placed in the ranks of the men of the people, second of his property and his rank, of his body and his life, of heart and mind, the liberating projects of Russia and Prussia!

The confederation of the Rhine, that deceitful chain by means of which the spirit of usurpation again tied up dislocated Germany, can no longer be endured. His Majesty the Emperor of Russia thereby announces the relations which he wishes to have with regenerated Germany and its constitution. The more the bases and the principles of this work are modeled after the ancient spirit of the German people, the more Germany, rejuvenated, vigorous, united, will be able to reappear with advantage among the nations of Europe.

Never had such language been held by kings. Never had such words been hurled at the peoples before the French Revolution, and since that revolution, never had an appeal for independence had such a resounding in the souls of the people. France, in 1792, had preached war and cosmopolitan revolution; Russia, in 1813, unleashed the war of nationality. The proclamation of Koutousof was to produce in Germany and in Italy, where it had its echo, effected infinitely more powerful than the decree of 19 November 1792 had been able to produce. The disappointment which followed after 1815, the sacrifices of the peoples and the triumph of the kings, was neither less profound nor less painful than that of the peoples invaded and insurgent after the first exit of the Republic in 1792, and the installation of the republic in "liberated" countries.

Moreover, the manifesto spoke neither of Poland, which had ceased to exist by the very act of the liberators; nor of Holland, out of consideration for the English who intended a king for it; nor of Italy, to spare the proprieties of Austria. It ended with this declaration intended to seduce the French, at least to disarm them, inciting them to separate their cause from that of Napoléon:

May France, beautiful and strong by herself, occupy herself in the future with her internal prosperity. No foreign power will disturb it, no hostile enterprise will be directed against its legitimate limits. Let France know that the other powers will lay down their arms only when the bases of the independence of all the peoples of Europe are established and assured.

The text does not say *natural limits*, which, despite the ambiguity about the course of the Rhine and the Scheldt, would have been too precise and compromising before anything had been agreed. But *legitimate limits* reserved all combinations and ulterior motives, above all that of the 1792 limits, legitimate as far as limits could be, because they were those of the *legitimate monarchy*, prior to this revolution whose effects it was claimed to annihilate and the memory to be abolished. Were these legitimate limits, in the eyes of the allies, those of 1795, declared constitutional by the Convention, or those of 1801, declared constitutional by the Emperor in 1804? Did they attribute to the Treaty of Lunéville a unique character of imprescriptibility, when so many other treaties concluded before or after that one, and declared equally eternal, fell, repudiated, torn, abrogated by them? It is up to the French to flatter themselves with it, if they wished, and according to the vanity of their illusions. The point was to persuade them that implacable war pursued only Napoléon; that the Grand Empire and its supremacy were alone at stake and that France, provided that it allowed the edifice to be razed and the justice of the allies to pass, must find itself at home, happy and pacified. One might be surprised that such deep and remote calculations should be discovered in a proclamation which seems improvised with enthusiasm, to the fanfares of the trumpets, and signed on a drum, by an army general who did not refine words. One would be strangely mistaken. All the words were pierced, hollowed out, so to speak, hollowed out like counterfeit money. This device was designed in 1805 and elaborately fleshed out since then. Nothing better connected than the articles of April 1805 and Koutousof's manifesto. Nothing is more significant than comparing together the only two official and public texts that we possess on the intentions of the allies in 1813, the initial text, that of 26 March in Kalisch, and the final text, that of 1 December in Frankfurt, the one which preceded the Congress of Prague, and the other which preceded the Congress of Châtillon.

Kutusof's proclamation said:

> France beautiful and strong by itself. No hostile business will be directed against its legitimate boundaries.

The Frankfurt statement:

> The allied sovereigns want France to be big, strong and prosperous. The powers confirm to the French empire an expanse of territory that France has never known under a king.

Nothing of *natural limits*: they will insinuate themselves into words, but will never be defined and even less will they be written in manifestos. The secret of the negotiations of 1813 lies entirely in this ambiguity.

Hardly had war been declared when the new liberators of Europe showed the world how they treated kings when kings kept their word and that word had been given to France. The King of Saxony was held up as an example to the general defection of the Confederates. Blücher, renewing Frederick's methods and rediscovering the paths of the Seven Years' War, entered Saxony on 26 March; he immediately called the people to insurrection: "Get up! unite with us; your sovereign is in the hands of the foreigner, he no longer has his liberty of action." On 9 April, Stein installed himself as chairman of the central administration committee. The peculiarity of the affair is that, at this very moment, Friedrich Augustus was escaping from the French alliance and negotiating, secretly, a defection disguised under the label of neutrality and the cloak of Austrian intervention.

Meanwhile Alexander pressed the Austrians.[81] Otherwise, he said to Lebzeltern, "the allies reserving to act on the north of Germany, abandon to Austria all the courts of the south." "The Emperor gives *carte blanche* to the Emperor of Austria," wrote Lebzeltern. Nothing better done to reassure Metternich. But he reserved for himself, by more complicated means, a more important role. If Alexander claimed to set himself up as a dictator of peace, Metternich flattered himself that he would at least become its chancellor. He aspired for his master the supreme arbitration which Russia had arrogated to itself in advance. He therefore continued, imperturbably, on his way. On 23 March, he wrote to Lebzeltern, proposing an arrangement which would make it possible to get rid of the Polish army of Poniatowski, who had taken refuge in Cracow, and which was very embarrassing for Austria and, despite its weakness, also hindered the Russians. "The march of recent events puts us in the painful position of having to allow the Poles to place themselves within our armistice radius," wrote Metternich.[82] But, "desiring to give the courts of Prussia and Russia proofs of his entire confidence," the Emperor resolved to take a decisive part "in favor of the removal of the Poles." And here was the insidious way he was going to get them out of the armistice radius. The secret convention of 30 January covered them; it would be agreed, by a secret and temporary convention, to suspend the armistice. The Russians would denounce it by the impossibility where the allies find themselves of leaving in their flank and behind their back a hotbed of movements and insurrection such as the Polish army offers. The armistice denounced,

> we will declare to the Polish authorities, civil and military, that we can no longer cover them with our line, that, consequently, they have the choice of disbanding if they want to remain in the duchy, or else of crossing the Austrian States to go win such a point from Germany that they want to choose.

It was up to the Russians, if they knew how to do it, to poach or hire these Poles. The round played, the armistice restored, everyone will return to their positions, Austria drawing its auxiliary corps from the French alliance and the Russians establishing themselves quietly in the Duchy of Warsaw. Metternich said: "You can confide under the seal of secrecy to Their Imperial Majesties that we will immediately send off the army corps which leaves the left bank of the Vistula in Bohemia, where it will join the army which is forming in this kingdom." The convention was signed at Kalisch, on 29 March, by Lebzeltern and Nesselrode. Austria, although under the mask, had acted as a coalition. It was coming closer by crawling, but was really coming closer, both in combined movements and in its announced intentions.

    Thus the foundations of the coalition were laid, the cornerstones in place. The fundamental alliance, that of Prussia and Russia, was nearly stopped by the same obstacles which from 1792 to 1795 delayed, prevented and finally broke the first coalition, the rival covetousness of the allies over Poland. But it was nothing. Kalisch's alliance withstood all attacks, and the most formidable, those of the diplomats of Russia and Prussia, always suspicious, always jealous of each other. It was not only the friendship of the sovereigns which brought about this change. The sovereigns loved each other, but this attachment had not prevented Alexander, in 1805, from meditating on the dismemberment of Prussia, and Friedrich-Wilhelm III, in 1805, in 1806, and in 1812, from allying himself with Napoléon against Alexander. So something more happened, which forced the hand of princes and diplomats, made the friendship of the princes unalterable and the alliance indissoluble. This new agent was the one who, from then on, and for two years, will take hold of history, the great unknown, the mysterious god, destiny on the move, European nations, the Russian nation the first, then the German nation, which pushed and moved everything. It was by throwing himself into this current, and letting himself be carried by it, that Alexander arrived at Koenigsberg, at Breslau with such a force of impetus that it overthrew all the dykes; it was the current which in turn carried Friedrich-Wilhelm III. The heartfelt affection of sovereigns was tempered by the ordeal and came out of it sealed by the popular hand. The exaltation of the peoples for independence ensured the loyalty of the kings. In 1792, it was a question, between the allied kings, only of bargains of men and lands, and they ended as they had begun, by haggling, competition, and estrangement. In 1813, the question posed was that of the independence of peoples; the princes must proclaim it, they must act as if they wanted it, for the peoples believed in it, and this faith of the peoples alone commanded sacrifices, furnished the offerings without which the gods do not grant victory in human blood and cannon fodder. Now, this faith was all the real strength and all the nerve of the coalition.

## IX. Regency of Maria-Louisa, 1813

Going back 20 years, everything seemed out of place: Paris gave the aspect of Vienna, Berlin, or Mainz in 1792: heavy and unpopular militarism, violent conscription, arbitrary levies, innumerable auxiliaries, cosmopolitan armies, wars of calculations, politics, supremacy; in the midst of the preparations for a colossal struggle, the scope of which the country had not yet grasped and in which it would lose interest were it not for the terrible harvest of men, official balls, command parties: said a contemporary who had been in the Russian war and foresaw the German war, "gloomy balls, where I thought I was dancing on tombs."⁸³ This separation of the cause of France and that of the Emperor, of the interests of the country and those of the sovereign, which the allies had always considered a necessary condition for the success of their enterprise, which, from 1805, they sought to provoke, which they endeavored to provoke by the ambiguous declarations of their emissaries, the ambiguity of their declarations and the work of their friends in France, operated of itself and without it costing them anything, by the mere selfishness of men and their extraordinary ability to turn things to their liking by imagination.

In the world of opponents, interested parties, and clever men, the Grand Empire was spoken of as a gigantic encumbrance in the history of France. Who still cared about Poland? The Confederation of the Rhine would dissolve: France would be all the more free of its movements. Was Holland indispensable and did French Belgium need this "barrier" turned against Europe? We forgot the time when it was a matter of honor to reign over Italy, to "free" it. Westphalia, Naples, Spain finally, parasites of the Empire, which gnawed at its extremities! In the departments, in modest families, only the empty homes, the call-ups and re-calls of conscripts, the interminable list of the dead and that of the designated victims of the war were considered. They cursed this war which never ended and of which only the suffering was measured since the reverses had started again. They reproved it, they repudiated it with violence. We found ourselves saturated with glory, to the point of nausea. Thus travelers embarked for the opulent islands and the countries of gold discover the danger with the shaking of the storm and curse their mad confidence, the temerity of their chief, the ship, the pilot, the sea and the gods whose oracles have deceived! Everything seemed good to throw overboard, which would make it possible to regain ground. It was hard to understand why Napoléon refused to disembark this excess load which threatened to sink the ship and even so many useless passengers. We called for rest with all the more impatience as we felt more convinced that it would be enough for France to want its own security, its own tranquility, and to obtain them from the Emperor, to live henceforth great, prosperous, intact in its natural limits, in Europe delivered and peaceful. Universal peace by the renunciation of France, a concept as chimerical in 1813, as universal fraternity by French conquest in 1792. Said a general, and one of the harshest among the censors, "Napoléon, like a mastiff, only let go what was torn from him by breaking it."⁸⁴ It was because Napoléon did not judge of them like the vulgar, who, to see conquests threatened, immediately declared them useless. He knew by what stages France had marched from Paris to Moscow, by what evolution it had carried the conquest, then the defense, from the Rhine to the Vistula, from the Alps to Calabria, from the North Sea to the Adriatic, from Cadiz to Hamburg. Between the coalition and him, there was still all the thickness of central Europe, an enormous rampart if he won, the void if he was defeated. He foresaw that the retreat would take place by the same paths as the conquest, and that once begun, if once driven back, it would stop neither at the Elbe nor at the Rhine itself; that if it were reduced to recrossing that river, Europe would recross it in his tracks; in short, that in defeat it would always be necessary to retreat, as in victory it had been necessary always to advance: Wagram overturning on Friedland, Jena, Austerlitz, Hohenlinden, Marengo, Lodi, Fleurus, Jemmapes, Valmy. He pictured to himself the fatal symmetry of war, the tipping of the Grand Empire, the European invasion flowing back into the invasion of Europe by France, and the Grand Empire going away in pieces, eaten away, undermined by this deluge, as it had formed in layers, alluvium from the rising tide.

  He therefore over-armed. He must win again and, as always, since the first outing in 1792, play all for all. He pretended to regard the campaign of 1812 as an accident: nothing but an army to rebuild and revenge to take! He knew how to contain himself in the face of defection itself. On 10 January he experienced the capitulation of York; either that, on the basis of the erroneous notions of his agents, he did not discover at first the importance of them, or that it suited him, to keep Prussia as long as possible at his discretion, to appear to believe in the good faith of Friedrich-Wilhelm III and, to spare public opinion, not to publicize this disruption of his alliances, he took note of this fact to motivate his new requests for conscripts. "What was enough yesterday is not enough today. The insolence of the victors of Louis XIV and the shame of the treaties of Louis XV seem to still threaten us," he had Regnault say to the Senate. "It is the return of these ignominious times that it is a question of preserving France." He exclaimed "I will even arm the women!"[85] The *senatus-consultum* of 11 January placed 350,000 men at its disposal, cohorts, freed from the preceding classes, levied on the class of 1814. Thanks to the pusillanimity of Prussia, to the embrace with which it still suffocated it, thanks to the slowness and complicated calculations of Metternich, he still hoped to arrive in time, and, as in 1805, as in 1806, to break the coalition into its members. He said of the Prussians, "It is not a nation. They do not have any national pride; they are the Gascons of Germany. The Prussians are stale. We have always despised them." As for the Germans, don't be stunned by their effervescence: "The German is not murderous enough to make a revolution!"[86]

He was soon informed about Austria, and his first sounding did not deceive him. On 2 February he gave audience to Bubna. This general tried to insinuate to him, by the most watered-down combinations of his diplomatic pharmacy, the retreat of the auxiliary corps and the *de facto* armistice with Russia. Napoléon felt bitterness and venom:

> Sir, it's a bad play, it's contrary to the treaty, it's a first step towards defection. You have changed the system. We are going to turn the world upside down. The hope for peace is lost. I accepted your intervention for peace, but an armed mediator does not suit me. It will happen that the viceroy of Italy will be obliged to evacuate Warsaw, to leave the Vistula, to go behind the Oder; it will cause a bad sensation in my army and in France.

He then spread out in threatening, incoherent remarks: "It was not anger, it was a man struck by a completely unexpected idea, of which he knows how to appreciate all the importance, and which is deeply concerned," said Bubna. All of Metternich's "intermediate nuances" unfolded before his eyes, and he pierced to the bottom: an armed mediation! However, he relented, always flattering himself that, victorious over the Russians, he would contain the Austrians and that the family spirit, joined to a natural prudence, would retain or delay Franz II the time necessary to reduce him to composition.

The police bulletins were becoming alarming. There was some revolutionary agitation in Provence; royalist machinations were spoken of in the West; in Belgium, a real resistance to conscription; in Holland, troubles, panics of bad omen. Gendarmes were exhausted in pursuit of conscripts; it almost took an army to recruit another. As in those times of Louis XIV whose memory Napoléon evoked, as in 1710, during the disasters of the War of Succession, the woods were filled with refractories. This was not the time to cry treason and call out barren alliances. Napoléon therefore continued to affect confidence in his confederates: "I am satisfied with the conduct of my allies; I will not abandon any; I will uphold the integrity of their states."[87]

As much to bind the Austrians as to compromise them before Europe and turn the alliance into a show, for lack of being able to translate it into military acts, he announced in the newspapers and prepared the *senatus-consultum* regulating the regency of the empress, and coronation of the King of Rome. But this legal guarantee was not enough for him. He saw near the disaster, his death, in Russia, and from afar, in Paris, the conspiracy, the revolution. He wanted supreme protection for his son, above the force of arms, above even treaties, laws, *senatus consulta*, and as he does not have it, he asks for it from the powers that are beyond this world, thus through the Church that he wanted his pragmatics to be sealed.[88] The *raison d'État* which, in 1804, led him to be consecrated by the Pope led him to desire that the Pope consecrate his son, and reasons of the heart were added *raison d'État*. This affair was intimately involved in the negotiations for a new Concordat with Pius VII.

This Pope was still interned at Fontainebleau. Napoléon had offered him an interview: "Perhaps we will achieve the much-desired goal of bringing down all the difficulties which divide the State and the Church."[89] The pacification of the West, the submission of Belgium, the appeasement of Catholics throughout France would, he thought, be the consequence; but the consecration of the King of Rome seemed to have been the main thought, as in 1802, during the Concordat, the establishment of Consular power.

On 19 January, Napoléon surprised Pius VII at Fontainebleau, garlanded him, dazzled him, caressed him, threatened him, and finally wrested from him the promise of an agreement which was signed on 25 January.[90] It was in principle, but in terms so obscure that they committed nothing, the transfer of the Holy See to Avignon and, implicitly, the renunciation of temporal power. On 7 February the *senatus-consultum* relative to the regency was promulgated; the new Concordat was on the 13th. The Pope almost immediately disavowed, if not his signature, at least the consequences that Napoléon claimed to draw from it. Napoléon ignored him. For the moment, the Concordat gave the appearance of religious peace, and Napoléon wanted no more. When he left Paris, he would leave behind the spectacle of a united, submissive France, in a beautiful government setting.

On 30 March appeared letters patent which conferred the regency on Maria-Louisa. Otto, whom Napoléon considered too lacking in perspicacity, had been replaced by Narbonne, a man of the Court, a man of war, better to observe, to show more countenance, and better to fulfill the character of a family ambassador.[91] He would also know how to insinuate better, and with more authority. Because Austria wanted peace, wrote Maret on 29 March, "let her go to Russia and ask her to open negotiations immediately. We would agree to an armistice. The armistice once admitted, the language and the forces of Austria would promptly bring about the conclusion of peace." Prussia would pay the price, instead of gaining the Duchy of Warsaw, as Metternich proposed. The Emperor, continued Maret, believed he had found in Prussia the intermediate state which Europe needed in the northeast. "It was a mistake. A power whose treaties are only conditional cannot be a useful intermediary. It does not guarantee anything. It is only a subject of discussion and is not a barrier." In the event of a common victory, they would share it. It had five million inhabitants. "We would form three states. A million would remain with Prussia on the right bank of the Vistula; two million would go to Austria, and two million to Saxony and Westphalia. The best lot would go to Austria, Silesia." This beginning posed, as if by digression, Maret returned to the continuous theme of Napoléon: let Austria intervene; that they arm well. But intervention and armament would only be done in agreement with France, by virtue of the alliance and with a view to consolidating it. As soon as the French army was on the Elbe, Austria would make its declaration to Alexander and, while acting with France, would exercise its mediation with a view to a general armistice which would precede the negotiation of peace. As for Prussia, it would be restrained by terror, while waiting for the hour to annihilate them.[92]

With Schwarzenberg, who returned as ambassador on 7 April, and had his audience on the 9th, the Emperor took up the same remarks:[93] the armistice, a congress in Prague, for example, then Austria passing over to the side of France. He said he wanted peace, but a peace that would not affect his prestige.

> The English believe that France is crushed, they will ask me for Belgium. My position is difficult: if I made a dishonorable peace, I would lose myself. I am new, I have more consideration to keep for public opinion, because I need it. By publishing a peace of this nature, one would hear, in truth, at the first moment, only cries of joy; but soon the government would be highly blamed, I would lose the esteem and at the same time the confidence of my people, because the Frenchman has a lively imagination, he loves glory, exaltation, he is

"fibrous." Do you know where must we look for the first cause of the fall of the Bourbons?

Delicately with Napoléon, more vigorously with Maret, Schwarzenberg painted the weariness of Europe, the revolt of the peoples, the general despair which united them: "No one will move where your armies are; as long as they are not there, the fire that you thought was extinguished will throw up a new flame." Then he spoke of the conditions of peace, presented them under the cover of England: the mouths of the great rivers of Germany, Holland, independent Italy, Venice, the Cape, Malta, and he added: "I believe that Russia would never make peace without agreeing with the British cabinet."[94] He carried away this impression that "to justify himself and save his glory *vis-à-vis* France, the Emperor will want to assert maritime and commercial advantages." Now, he added, this was the article on which England will be the most recalcitrant.

Besides, of the indemnities from Austria, not a word. It is because to give Austria what Austria coveted, Napoléon would have had to strip himself of his most brilliant conquests: Milan, Venice, which he had been so reproached for having surrendered in 1797 and 1801, in order to obtain the natural frontiers, and which he had only been able to resume after Austerlitz. Italy, the first prestige, the splendor of the Republic, the luxury of French glory! He could only give to the princes whose alliance he desired the territories which he had taken from them, and he had taken them precisely to reduce these princes to peace. By restoring them to their former power, he would restore to them the means of combating it; he would recover and restore them themselves to the state in which they were before 1805, before 1807, before 1809, and the causes of these wars would reappear of themselves as soon as he had suppressed their effects. Finally, he furnished them, by restoring a part to them, the means of recovering the rest; he interested them in his downfall.

From Spain, he seemed to expect nothing more. He emptied it, little by little, of the remnants of the army which he had gradually engulfed there. He sent orders to Joseph, in cipher, and in quadruplicate! "that lost time is irremediable; that affairs will turn out badly if he promptly puts no more activity and movement in the direction of affairs"; and he commanded him "to be always ready to take the offensive, to threaten to move on Lisbon and to conquer Portugal, if the English should weaken their army of Spain."[95] Paradoxical order, an order of sinister irony to a distraught king, who had lost two-thirds of his kingdom, who returned to his capital and left it, like the bad sailor who, under the headwind, brings his crippled ship to the coast, disembarks and re-embarks.[96] In the public, at Court, and Napoléon knew it, only one wish was expressed: the recall of Joseph to France, the return of Fernando to Spain. Napoléon inclined to it; Spain was a gangrenous member, he would amputate it. "If I need to, I will withdraw my army from Spain, I will arrange with the junta, I will send them their Fernando, and all will be said," he told Schwarzenberg. But he had little time left, if he wanted to be proud of it, for on 23 March Joseph left Madrid, this time never to return. The evacuation from Spain had begun and was only a matter of stages.

Napoléon left on 15 April. On Sunday the 11th, he reviewed the guard for the last time, at the Carrousel.

> For the French Empire, it was a question of being or not being. These soldiers, France's hope, these soldiers her last drop of blood, also played a large part in the restless curiosity of the spectators. On the day of danger, Napoléon was all of France.[97]

Thus still thought the man of the people and the soldier who cried: "Long live the Emperor!" But apart from them, wrote Schwarzenberg, "everyone without exception is war-weary. It must be admitted that tempers are well raised, and that Paris has changed a great deal over the past eleven months; finally everything depends on one man: he is the emperor." And this man, at the moment of engaging this supreme part, repeated again, as at the time of his triumphal ascent: "I am the work of circumstances, I have always marched with them."[98] Circumstances were what had changed most in Europe, and they worked against him.

1. For this volume: *Archives des Affaires étrangères*; *Correspondance de Napoléon*; supplement by Lecestre; *Traités de la Russie*; Publications of the Société d'histoire de Russie; *Hansard*; Correspondence published by Ducasse, Bailleu, Archives of Woronzof, and Stern; *Mémoires* and correspondence of Talleyrand, Metternich, Pasquier, Castlereagh, Nesselrode; histories of Fain, Bignon, Thiers, Ernouf, Lefebvre, Martens, Ranke, Duncker, Oncken, Pertz, Cavaignac, Fournier, Arneth, Bernhardi.
2. To Maret, 29 novembre 1812.
3. Molodetchna, 2 décembre 1812. Montesquiou left on the 3rd, at daybreak.
4. Letters of Woronzof, December 1812, April 1813. Compare Tolstoy, *War and Peace*.
5. Tchigagof's letter to the Emperor, *Société d'histoire de Russie*, VI.
6. See vol. VI.
7. Letter of 27 December 1812, *Mémoires de Czartoryski*.
8. Words of the Countess Potocka, *Mémoires*.
9. Alexander to Czartoryski, 25 January 1813; Martens, III; *Mémoires de Nesselrode*, January 1813; letter of Woronzof, 27 January 1813; summary of transactions of the Russian cabinet, *Société d'histoire de Russie*, XXXI.
10. Memos of September and November 1812.
11. *Société d'histoire de Russie*, XXXI; *Mémoires de Nesselrode*, December 1812; Martens, III, p. 94 et suiv., VII, p. 63 et suiv.
12. This is how Martens understands it in his commentary: "To drive France back to its ancient limits between the Rhine, the Alps, the Pyrenees and the Scheldt," III; "bring France back to its old historical borders." VII. See Congress of Châtillon.
13. Compare the articles of the treaty of 11 April 1805.
14. Cf. instructions of 1804 and Treaty of 1805.
15. Pingaud, *Bernadotte*, ch. VI; "Les dernières années de Moreau," *Revue de Paris* (15 décembre 1899); Hyde de Neuville, *Mémoires*, I, ch. XII.
16. Martens, III, p. 87 et suiv; Oncken, *O. und P.*, I. p. 23 et suiv.
17. La Romana left Denmark in August 1808, agreed with the English, and brought his auxiliary corps back to Spain.
18. *Mémoires de Langeron*. Campaign of 1813.
19. Reports of 1 and 9 décembre 1812.
20. Reports of Saint-Marsan, 11, 12, 15 décembre; Serra to Saint-Marsan, 14 décembre 1812.
21. To Napoléon, 17 décembre 1812.
22. Report to the Emperor, 19 décembre 1812.
23. 28 December 1813. Oncken, *O. und P.*
24. Hardenberg to Gneisenau, 29 December; Instruction to Krusemarck, 31 December 1812; Instruction to Knesebeck, 2 January 1813. (Oncken.)
25. Compare, in 1794, the maneuvers of Moellendorf preparing the defection of Austria and initiating the negotiations in Basel.
26. Martens, VII, p. 60.
27. Macdonald, *Souvenirs*, p. 184 et suiv.; letter of 31 décembre 1812.
28. Report of Saint-Marsan, 4 janvier 1813; Fain, *Manuscrit* of 1813; Villemain, *Souvenirs*.
29. Cf. in Oncken, II, p. 555, Hardenberg's statement to Ompteda on 6 January, and the letter to Gneisenau on 9 January.

30 Villemain, I, p. 240.
31 Reports of Saint-Marsan, 11, 12 janvier 1813.
32 Augereau to Berthier, 12 janvier 1813.
33 Oncken, *O. und P.*, I, pièces. Letter of Metternich to Hardenberg in Berlin, 5 October 1813; II,extracts from the reports of Count Hardenberg, Minister of Hanover to Vienna; *Mémoires de Metternich*, I, p. 124 et suiv.
34 Hardenberg, from Vienna to Munster and London, 9 November 1812.
35 Oncken, II, liv. VIII, ch. III. See in particular the notes et memos of Radetsky. Fournier, *Napoléon*, III, ch. IV.
36 *Dépêches aux hospodars de Valachie*, I; Metternich, to Wessenberg; mission to London, 8 February 1813.
37 Oncken, *O. und P.*, II, p. 101-102.
38 Report of Hardenberg, 24 December 1812.
39 *Souvenirs du duc de Broglie*, I, p. 198; Otto to Maret, 16 décembre 1812.
40 20 December 1812. (Oncken.)
41 Reports of Otto, 28 December 1812, 8 January 1813.
42 Lamy, *Mémoires de Mme de Coigny*.
43 Report of Bubna, 2 January 1813. (Oncken, *O. und Pr.*)
44 22 December 1812. The brief, by Regnaud, was submitted on the 29th; Masson, *Napoléon et son fils*.
45 Memo of 10 janvier, by Barbier. (Masson.)
46 Oncken, *O. und Pr.*, I, p. 393, text following the Archives of Vienna.
47 Maret to Otto, 7 janvier 1813.
48 Parma, Isle of Elba, Piedmont, Tuscany, Piacenza, Roman States, Holland, Hanseatic Cities, Oldenburg, Lauenburg.
49 Report of Otto, 16 décembre 1812.
50 On these cabals and on this Empress, Maria-Ludovica d'Este, Franz's fourth wife, cf. Masson, *Marie-Louise*.
51 At Münster, 13 January 1813. (Oncken.)
52 Report of Knesebeck, in Onken, *0. und P.*, I.
53 To Zichy, 16 January 1813. (Oncken.)
54 Report of Otto, 18 January 1813.
55 To Maret, 23 January; to Bubna 25 January 1813. See above, instructions to Wessenberg, 13 February 1813.
56 23 and 24 Janaury 1813.
57 Text in Martens, III, p. 89.
58 Reports of Stackelberg, 26 January; of Otto, 26 January 1813.
59 Report of Otto, 13 February 1813.
60 Metternich to Bubna, 6 February 1813; Ernouf, *Maret*, ch. VIII; Bignon, XI, p. 503; *Souvenirs d'un diplomate*. See Otto's report above, 18 January 1813, p. 48.
61 Metternich to Zichy, 30 January; Emperor to the King of Prussia, 28 January 1813.
62 Instructions for Lebzeltern; Franz II to Alexander, 8 février 1813. Instructions for Wessenberg, 8 February 1813. (Arneth, *Wessenberg*.)
63 Hardenberg to Münster, to London, 7 February 1813, in French.
64 André Bonnefons, *Un allié de Napoléon*.
65 Metternich to Binder, 18 February 1813; Bignon, XI, p. 433.
66 This whole part has been remarkably studied and exposed by Cavaignac, II, ch.

VIII: the origins of the uprising in East Prussia; Stein's Russian full powers; ch. IX, the Estates General of Koenigsberg; ch. X, the landwehr of the eastern provinces; ch. XII, comparison between the Prussian organization in 1813, the volunteers and the *levée en masse* of the French Revolution.
67 Bailleu, 240-242.
68 King to Hardenberg, 26 February 1813. (Duncker.)
69 Reports of Zichy; Oncken, II, p. 578-84, *O. und P.*, II, p. 240; Cavaignac, II, p. 354-55.
70 Views of Prussia on Saxony, in v. VII.
71 Report of 15 February 1813.
72 To Prince Eugène, 18 February 1813.
73 Letter Alexander to the King, 24 February 1813.
74 Report of Knesebeck, 18 February 1813. (Oncken, *O. und P.*, I)
75 Alexander to Roumiantsof. (Martens, VII, p. 73.)
76 Hatzfeld's report on talks with Napoléon, 5-14 Feb. 1813. (Oncken.)
77 Martens, VIII.
78 Report of Lebzeltern, 8 March 1813. (Oncken.)
79 Conventions, 4 April 1813. (Martens, VII.)
80 Alexander to Nesselrode, 23 March 1813.
81 Reports of Lebzeltern, 22-29 March 1812. (Oncken.)
82 Oncken, *O. und P.*, II, 201-04.
83 Fezenzac, *Campagne de Saxe*, I.
84 Thébault, V, p. 8.
85 To Bubna, 1 mars 1813.
86 Conversation with Bubna; Bubna reports. (Oncken.) Napoléon judges them like Stendhal: "The true German is a tall blond man, of indolent appearance." Sagan, June 1813: in full insurrection of Silesia.
87 Speech to the Legislative Body, 14 February 1813.
88 Conversation related by Barante, I, p. 270.
89 To Pius VII, 29 décembre 1812.
90 Pasquier, II, ch. II; D'Haussonville, V, ch. LV, LVI; De Clercq, II, p. 377.
91 Narbonne, named on 5 mars 1813.
92 "At the slightest insult from a city, from a Prussian village, burn it down, even Berlin." To Eugène, 5 mars 1813.
93 Report of Schwarzenberg, 14 avril 1813. (Oncken.)
94 Conferences of 8, 9, 10 April 1813.
95 To Clarke, 9 février 1813.
96 *Mémoires militaires de Jourdan*, ch. XXIII; *Mémoires du roi Joseph*, IX, liv. XII.
97 See the admirable tableau of Balzac, "La dernière revue de l'empereur," in his *Femme de trente ans*.
98 Barante, conversation at the Tuileries, I, p. 171.

Page left intentionally blank.

# Chapter II: Austrian Mediation

## 1813

### I. Rupture of the Alliance

Intervention was, for Austria, only a way out of the French alliance and a way into the coalition. Metternich would have preferred, first of all, to stop in between, to entrench himself in the passage, to make it a place of safety, as the great diplomatic warehouse of Europe, of which he would be the arch-broker. He soon recognized that he should, and would, opt for the coalition; he judged that the most expedient would be to allow himself to drift imperceptibly there by breaking, in formal terms, the ties with France. He pressed the armaments, and as the treasury was very dry, he persuaded the Emperor to issue *assignats*. It was not without difficulty. The Emperor was afraid of everything: of this paper money, of this army which risked bringing war on him before he was ready, of his terrible son-in-law, not of his anger, but of his bursts of genius and his surprises; finally and especially of the German people who came out of the borders, threatening to propagate the revolution as far as Austria. Koutousof's proclamation seemed to him imbued with the worst Jacobinism; he was terrified of it beyond what could be said. On this article, Metternich, who shared his alarms and added to them the disgust of a "principled" gentleman, was not in a position to reassure him. "This appeal to the peoples made all the rulers of Germany shudder," wrote Stackelberg on 11 April.[1] It was one of the fundamental articles of Metternich's plan to release these princes from their French confederation and to attract them to the future coalition. While Koutousof enlisted the peoples, he occupied himself with embattling kings. It was important, he instructed Lebzeltern, to declare that the powers of the second and third rank must lose none of their present strength, but that they desired to see them enjoy all the rights of sovereignty with the greatest independence. This language will succeed completely in the courts of the South and will have more effect than all possible negotiations.[2] The Bavarians were just waiting to be convinced.[3]

The Russians were urging: "Let Austria join us, let her listen to the voice of her true friends, let her listen to that of her peoples and of almost all of Germany."[4] Metternich decided to move from one nuance to another more marked. On 2 April he announced to Stackelberg that if Napoléon rejected mediation,

> Austria will employ the forces which Providence has placed in her hands, to co-operate in the most perfect agreement with the allied powers, in the establishment of an arrangement based on the principles which His Imperial Majesty believes necessary for the existence of his Empire and the well-being of Europe.

Now he knew perfectly well that these principles Napoléon, even defeated, would not subscribe to. Mediation would therefore be rejected by him, he himself would throw Austria into the camp of the allies; defection would be elegant and legal, the public and posterity would let themselves be lured into the merry-go-round and would pay homage to the perfect correctness and the classic "purity" of the procedures and "principles" of the House of Austria!

With regard to the Prussians, he entered into more open confidence in proportion as his policy obliged him to reckon more with them. He took pride in refusing the Silesia offered by Napoléon, and this proof of disinterestedness given, he developed his system to Humboldt, who wrote of it: "The fundamental point of this system is the close and unalterable union of Prussia and Austria."[5] Hardenberg immediately responded in the same effusive tone and added:

> There are above all two subjects on which it is absolutely important to consult together without the slightest loss of time: the affairs of Germany and those of Poland. We also feel it at the Russian court. You know, dear Excellency, that especially the affairs of Germany, according to our wish, should only be regulated by common agreement with you.

He proposed a secret conference between Nesselrode, Metternich, and himself. Metternich declined the invitation, which he considered premature, and announced that he was dispatching Stadion on a special mission to Russian headquarters.[6]

The interview would perhaps have compromised him and, in any case, singularly embarrassed him with Narbonne. This gallant man had remained a very gallant man. He put some "swagger" into it during the retreat from Moscow; he indulged in some ridicule in his embassy.[7] "He has a mania for wanting to succeed through women," said Napoléon. He had been received with open arms by the Emperor and his minister.

> He kept a large house, he was eagerly invited to all the meetings; high society followed the example of the masters; but the devil lost nothing by it. Narbonne disentangled very well what was hidden in hatred and hope under these demonstrations of command.

He knew German and could discern, from the gazettes, the agitation propagated among the people. He did not conceal the gravity of this fermentation which threatened, he wrote, with the most violent, the most general explosion in Germany. They seem to have prepared, wherever the Russians, "every means of converting every German into a bitter enemy of the French. I say each German because we affect above all not to recognize any state division," that we "kindle the common hatred that must be felt by all who live from the Rhine to the Niemen." One

> seems to transform the councils of Russia, Prussia and Sweden into a committee of public safety.... Everything here seems to present the same picture that Prussia offered before the battle of Jena.[8] He noted the clamors of society which, as a whole, pushes for war with the most delirious passion.... The Austrian corps which is in front therefore does not want to fight! I see all the cafes and all the meeting places breathing nothing but hatred of the French name, and attributing only to it the desperate state of finances, the annihilation of trade and the appalling high cost of everything that is not a commodity of the first and strictest necessity. If I look at the army, there is not an officer who does not tremble at the idea of waging war for us

and who, believing that he no longer has to deal with the same Frenchmen who have so often humiliated them, does not think or say that the time has come when it will be so easy to reconquer with wear and tear the honor and Austrian territory. (In summary) We have for us, as you told me with so much reason, only the Emperor, M. de Metternich and M. de Schwarzenberg.[9]

Could they even count on Metternich? From their first meeting, Narbonne suspected the intentions of this minister.[10] He claimed, he said, to put himself in a position to be able to say, when the time came:

> I wanted, above all, to try to bring true peace, but I did not neglect to ensure all the means of making war; France does not want to accede to reasonable proposals accepted by all the powers; it is I who now propose that you put us at the head of these powers, and take in Europe the attitude and the rank that suits us.[11]

Did Narbonne pierce this very subtle game on his own, or was he informed by some interested confidant? Still, when he received the instruction from Paris on 29 March, he did not hesitate to push hard. On 7 April he went to see Metternich and had a long and important interview with him. "While chatting, I said that I thought I had the very natural certainty that the Emperor could not and did not want to see in the Emperor of Austria an arbiter who would declare himself and fight against any of these parties who would call for his judgment. any." This was precisely, reported Narbonne, Metternich's hidden plan; he made no reply to this observation, and he asked in his turn:

> If this is a *sine qua non* condition of the other powers, will not the Emperor Napoléon withdraw from what he has put forward, and, in order to give a lasting peace, and impossible without it, will he not renounce reunions made so new, which become infinitely less useful to him since there is no longer any question of the continental system? We do not pronounce, in any way, the name of Spain, nor that of Holland, of which there is reason to believe that England would like to speak: that concerns France directly and solely.

Already there had been talk of Holland, and Narbonne had remained convinced that England would never consent to leave it to France.[12] Metternich again insisted on the eastern barrier, and the utility of forming for Prussia a kingdom of Poland, with the Duchy of Warsaw. Narbonne saw where he was leading him, but he was not finished. As he spoke, according to his instructions, of dismembering Prussia, instead of constituting a kingdom in Poland, and of growing Saxony or Westphalia from its debris, Metternich said: "What we need is that the Confederation of the Rhine does not go as far as the Niemen." He continued: "Austria cannot fight to retain for France the protectorate of the Confederation of the Rhine." And here is the suppression of the Confederation of the Rhine which was added to the other conditions. "All of these explanations always happen in the smoothest and seemingly most trusting way," Narbonne said. He took up the subject of the partition of Prussia and spoke of "entering Silesia." Metternich replied, "That could only be in the case of war, and then convenience would decide. "In all this, then, you want nothing for yourself?" – Impossible, answered the Austrian, that the Illyrian provinces should not return to Austria; the Emperor had, more or less, made the commitment, and it would not present difficulties. On that Narbonne said:

> Am I not to conclude that your project is, leaning towards France, to fight against her, if she does not accept what you consider acceptable? – This comes naturally from the situation of things, from our position; of course all the favor is for France. And is that why you send M. de Stadion to the headquarters of the Emperor of Russia? – This is not yet definitively decided, but it is almost certain. – Are you waiting, continued Narbonne, for the first victory to make up your mind?

And Metternich: "You are wrong; believe that the day after this victory, we would speak to you in a more pronounced tone than today." "Faith, I think you would be very foolish," retorted Narbonne, who saw in Metternich's remarks only a boast, and did not guess in it the avowal of an understanding already far advanced with the allies. There remained the positive proposals: the immediate opening of negotiations with Russia; the armistice; the auxiliary corps increased to 50,000 men; the concentration of 40 to 50,000 men in Bohemia; the entry of Austria into the war, as the main party, with 100,000 men. Metternich listened to them *ad referendum*, and Narbonne left him a note which was only a reproduction of the dispatch of 29 March.[13]

Insinuations, digressions, direct or implicit declarations, the talks could be summed up in these terms: Austria considered the continental system as abrogated, and at the same time its engagements on the blockade; it went from intervention to mediation proper and indicated that it would decide against whoever rejected its conditions; as for such conditions, it was Illyria to Austria, the Duchy of Warsaw to Prussia, renunciation of the protectorate of the Confederation of the Rhine, and implicitly of the Hanseatic cities, not to mention Holland and Spain, which would be the requirements of England. Metternich's reply to Narbonne's note arrived on 12 April, in the form of an extract from the instructions given that day to Schwarzenberg. It confirmed all the apprehensions that the interview on the 7th might have given rise to:

> It emerges from the nature of things, and we are very glad to see that the Emperor Napoléon shares our conviction, that the course of events, the bringing together of the theater of war, no longer require the Emperor to take part as a power simply auxiliary to the war, if, against our dearest wishes, it should continue.

This supposed concession of Napoléon was drawn from the fact that he had first demanded 30,000 men in Poland, then a concentration of 40 to 50,000 men in Bohemia, then an armament of 100,000 men with a view to a common action against the allies. Metternich concluded from this that, by the very fact, Napoléon detached Austria from the treaty of 1812, because he proposed to substitute for it a more extensive alliance. On this sophistry of rare impertinence, he declared:

> We can therefore only share the opinion of the Emperor of the French, that the stipulations of limited help in our treaty of alliance, are not applicable to the circumstances of the moment. The Emperor will not limit his steps in favor of the cause he believes he must plead – that of peace – to mere words, and if possible exaggerations in the views of the Allied cabinets should prevail over the reason and moderation that will not cease to profess His Imperial Majesty, he will without hesitation put an important force in the balance of the power which we regard, even disregarding the immense complications of the present moment, as our most natural ally.

Here is by this text, viscous and colorless, the smooth and consummated defection, the treaty of 14 March 1812 erased: a new alliance to be tied, if indeed Austria agreed to it. This is what Count Metternich called the second step in his oblique march, and he congratulated himself on it as an effect of the "extreme skill" that he deployed, "of an eminently favorable situation, which escaped the eyes of superficial observers."[14] As for the regency of Maria-Louisa, it counted for nothing. "She is looked upon by enlightened men as a symptom of the last weakness," Gentz wrote.[15] "Several people imagine that this step was taken by Napoléon only to flatter the court of Vienna. If that had been his goal, we can say that he completely missed it." It was more readily attributed to his discords with his brothers, and it was one more crack that was discovered in the facade of the building.

Narbonne insisted. He declared that Napoléon considered the auxiliary corps as part of his army, and he assigned him his post of war. Metternich ducked into the undergrowth. "We only want peace; but on what basis to establish it? Do you know yourself what France wants? The Emperor claims to yield on nothing. The Hanseatic cities, for example, he persists in holding." However, the auxilliary corps withdrew. Narbonne asked for explanations. Metternich answered: The corps numbered more than 30,000 men, he could only withdraw! To this extraordinary argument of an ally who defected on the pretext that he had put in the alliance more troops than the treaty had, and that this body being indivisible, the surplus must carry the mass, Narbonne was indignant:

> The first step you take is to violate the treaty that still stands. I can no longer delay explaining myself to you. The Emperor, my master, desired and still desires good understanding between France and Austria. To this end he closed his eyes to several steps and particularly to the armistice concluded without his consent by a body under his orders.

The next day, he sent a formal note to Metternich, inviting him to instruct the commander of the auxiliary corps to keep "the positions assigned to him by the armistice, and to await there the orders that His Majesty will please the Emperor of the French to give it to him."[16]

Metternich did not answer. Very worried, very irritated also, offended in his sense of the honor of arms, Narbonne ventured a step which was not prescribed to him and which turned out to go far beyond Napoléon's intentions. After having, by his note of the 31st to Metternich, noted the disagreement, which, in procedure, led to accepting the debate, he brought it before Emperor Franz. He obtained an audience and went there on 23 April.[17]

Franz was shorter-witted than his minister and less smooth-talking. He did not understand the "intermediate nuances," and, when Narbonne invoked the treaty of March 1812, he said to him: "But it was your very master who canceled it by proposing and urging me to take the mediation army. It is my conviction that I cannot be at war and a mediator at the same time." Narbonne would have had a fair game of recalling that the offer had come from Austria, an offer of intermediary, and not of mediation; that Napoléon had lent himself to it only with a view to consolidating and extending the alliance, and that he had in no way accepted armed mediation; that, moreover, the effect of this mediation should be, according to him, to throw Austria with all of its forces on the side of Napoléon; that Austria had let it be understood; that it was only to come to this that Napoléon urged them to arm. Franz II said: "Finally, it is my conviction; I want all my troops to be united to act in agreement with the Emperor." Narbonne asked, "So they will all be destined to fight for him?" – "Yes, if he hears, as I hope, reasonable proposals." He stammered a few confused words about the Rhine, and Italy, then "Take care, Ambassador, I have reason to believe that we will not be happy with your last note." Narbonne begged him not to abandon his son-in-law. The loyal Austrian, forced into his last entrenchments, invoked the ultimate reason of politicians in need of avowable reasons to justify their conduct: "No, I can't change my resolution; it is my conviction, and my conscience commands me to do so. Otherwise I would be responsible before God!"

Narbonne came away very moved from this audience where he had led, rather inconsiderately, Franz to transform a hypocritical and underhanded defection into an accomplished and avowed defection. Meanwhile, he heard that the King of Saxony was turning to the same defection as Austria.[18] He wrote to Napoléon, "The conversation I had this morning with the Emperor is far from having diminished this mistrust." – distrust of the final course that Austria would take –

and I find there words which seem to me to leave few doubts about the kind of subterranean connection which exists between this cabinet and all sovereigns now at war with Your Majesty. It is therefore quite simple that Humboldt and Stackelberg repeat everywhere that the Austrian government is too advanced to dare to retreat, and what I thought might be a subtlety takes on the full character of the truth.

Then, alluding to rumors about the King of Saxony:

All this calls for more than suspicion, without however giving certainties. They flatter themselves that they will have 180,000 men in line on the 1st of July, and then, Sire, what are called here reasonable conditions will be discovered, which are very far from those which Your Majesty has given me a glimpse of.

These 180,000 men would support the decrees which Austria intended to dictate if, between now and then, the Emperor had not imposed any by one of those prodigies to which he had accustomed people. "Twice this was told to me." However, he did not despair of bringing them to neutrality or of compelling them to do so.[19] Three days later, on April 26th, Metternich, in a dry note, declined all claims, referring to his earlier explanations.[20]

These remarks smelled of war. On 21April, Count Hardenberg, always well informed, wrote to Münster in London:

He (Metternich) is too attached to the State, and he has too much ambition not to want to restore it to its former luster, and he is at the same time too enlightened to hope to achieve this goal through France, if even she offered him as a reward for her assistance in the present struggle aggrandizements for Austria.

## II. England and Prussia

These notices were addressed to the Prince Regent of England. So far, England had not appeared; step by step they advanced on the stage and there resumed a decisive role which befit its employment as general treasurer of the coalitions. However, it still reserved itself. England doubted the resolutions and armaments of Austria, and especially those of Prussia.

The English ministers regarded catastrophe as inevitable

henceforth; they only wanted to intervene in Germany to strike the decisive blow and remove their main guarantee, the Low Countries. The Duchy of Warsaw, the Confederation of the Rhine, and the reconstruction of Prussia and Austria mattered little to them and counted only as means, in the background. The Mediterranean remained on the first floor, and in that direction everything was successful for them: the royalty of Joseph was crumbling in Spain under their blows; that of Murat would fall like rotten fruit on its stalk: all they had to do was shake the tree. They occupied Portugal, under the pretext of protecting its independence; Sicily, under the pretext of protecting the monarchy there. Their agent, Bentinck, held the Bourbons there in handcuffs, under the pretext of snatching them from the claws of Napoléon. Portugal, Spain, Sicily, Naples, and, beyond, all Italy to defend, that is to say, to win the commercial supremacy of England; as many commercial treaties as restorations; as many outlets and warehouses to open as there were peoples to deliver. The English ministers saw it clearly, in 1813, as much as Catherine II had 20 years before, and they fought Napoléonic despotism on the coasts and on the seas just as this great Empress crushed the French Revolution in Warsaw and planned to exterminate the French Revolution in Constantinople. The Bank of London quantified the profits of the operation, and British commerce pointed to the new markets of the globe, the islands and colonies of France and Holland, Spanish America in insurrection. England was enriched by the general distress, by the unemployment of the manufactures of the Continent, by the ruin of all the distraught navies. No more competitors, no more neutrals, those parasites of maritime warfare! It is explained that the cabinet waited, in order to provide subsidies to the allies, to be sure that they would work for England and that the definitive peace would become the English peace, those of 1763. They did not yet see the time come to impose it.

Wessenberg, who arrived on 29 March, found little haste in London.[21] No doubt Russia gained all the prestige lost by France and they returned to the fine arrangements of 1804, but only towards Russia. Wessenberg wrote,

> The selfishness of the British Government has never been more pronounced than it is today, and the result is a blindness from which it will, I fear, only be cured by great misfortunes. Believing itself sure of Russia, it imagines it can do without the rest of the continent and above all can do

without peace with France. It is clear that its policy will always be a system of war so long as it is exclusively concerned with maritime commerce. The English speak of a war in Germany as one would speak of a war in India.[22]

The prince regent, inflated by Münster, very Hanoverian and very little Austrian, showed himself cold; Castlereagh, less than pleasant: he didn't want to hear of peace; he even feared that the rumor of a negotiation would spread among the public, so badly would it be received and would compromise the Cabinet. In short, he declined the intermediary, and *a fortiori* the mediation of Austria.[23]

The former Prussian agent Jacobi, who had been on the lookout since 1807, arrived in London shortly after Wessenberg. He was better received there. It is that instead of mediation he spoke of an alliance, and that Prussia found itself in the money relationship at the discretion of the English. Finally, it was realized in London that, without Prussia, Russia would not take the offensive. Hardenberg had commissioned Jacobi to communicate to the English ministers the Treaty of Kalisch, with the secret articles, and he proposed to take these stipulations as bases of the agreements to be concluded between Prussia and England. In the Treaty of Kalisch, we read Article 6, that seemed likely to give the English confidence and satisfaction: it was the one where the allies undertook "not to negotiate in particular with the enemy, not to sign either peace, nor truce, nor any convention other than by mutual agreement." If Prussia took an identical engagement with England, Russia, being already bound with Prussia, will be bound at the same time with England. Neither Prussia, nor consequently Russia, could "negotiate in particular with the enemy, sign peace or truce" except by mutual agreement with England. No coalition, for lack of money, was possible without it. No peace, the coalition made, would be possible without its consent. England, which, by its subsidies, would hold the war, would hold, by these clauses, the wires of all the negotiations; it would sit in all the conferences and in all the congresses; one could begin without it appearing, nothing to be finished without it: it would appear, it would lay down conditions, and neither Prussia nor Russia would sign except on these conditions, or at least on accepted conditions. All overtures made to Napoléon by Austria without the consent of England would therefore be only pretenses or preliminaries which would not bind the coalition definitively. This combination, imagined in 1805 and inserted in the April treaty, intended to serve as a charter for the coalition of the time, took on capital importance here. This was the permanent undertone of all overtures to peace, the end of things that must be clearly discerned from the beginning, otherwise one would run the risk of taking for serious – if not sincere – proposals that never were, for the reason that England refused to adhere to them.

It is understandable that this clause immediately disposed the English to listen to the Prussian envoy. There was another, intended to seduce the prince regent: it was the creation "of a considerable new kingdom, from the Elbe to the Scheldt perhaps, which would contain the old Hanoverian possessions and would be assigned to an English prince." Chancellor Hardenberg wrote,

> An enlargement of the house of Hanover, which would place an intermediate state between Prussia and France, and would form a natural alliance between Prussia and England, would in no way be contrary to our interests; but (he added), Prussia would have to be enlarged in proportion.

A new kingdom of Austrasia which would make England mistress of eastern Germany, maritime Germany, Holland and the Netherlands, which would give her the coasts from the Weser to the Scheldt, was not to displease London; but one did not see in it with so favorable an eye the condition placed there by Hardenberg, the proportional aggrandizement of Prussia. The dull rivalry of Guelph and Hohenzollern; one suspected behind this affair a rather obscure machination which neither facilitated nor hastened things.[24] However the Prussians declared their pressing need for money and arms. "The fear of a separate peace between Russia and France haunts the English government like a specter," wrote Lieven. They decided to help Russia and to supply arms to Prussia.[25] Did Castlereagh then re-read Pitt's old notes and did something of the soul of this implacable enemy of French greatness seep into the souls of his successors? The only hope of hastening the fall of the colossus, the fear of missing the opportunity to strike the last blow, the fear of discouraging Europe by delaying revenge and the slaughter, triumphed over their bad humor against Austria and their little confidence in Prussia. Lord Cathcart, accredited to Alexander, followed Russian headquarters. Lieutenant General Charles Stewart, brother of Castlereagh, was accredited to the Prussian Government. They were going to resume the negotiations at the point where Novossiltsof had left them, back to the conditions of the eve of Austerlitz, that is to say, the repression of France within its old limits and, consequently, the overthrow of Napoléon.

## II. Bernadotte and Murat

It was in the same spirit that the English negotiated with Bernadotte, but here they had, if not complete confidence in the man, at least the persuasion that they operated without failure. Their correspondence from Paris showed the expediency of one of those internal diversions, one of those subterranean stirrings of opinion which England had made use of, with so much success, at all times, and with more efficiency than ever since the Revolution. Nothing seemed to them more apt to stir up the zeal and to nourish the gratuitous or interested illusions of the friends of England, than an intervention of Bernadotte in the war. It would give a party which had not yet dared to declare itself a leader, a figurehead, a pretext for intrigues, plots, mines, and artifices.

Surrounded, in his staff, by French *émigrés* in relation with Constitutionalists and even Republicans, Bernadotte was the right man to bring together those who flattered themselves to fight the Emperor while loving France, and to serve the cause of liberty by working to overthrow the Empire. The work that Talleyrand and Fouché were pursuing in Paris, in the councils of boudoirs, he would undertake in broad daylight. He would be a very active dissolver of public opinion in France, the most active even, until the day when Moreau decided to return.[26] He offered the English another advantage, that he would find his interest in the great design of the Guelph kingdom: this plan involved the expropriation of Denmark, dismembered or indemnified, and the attribution of Norway to Bernadotte. He had been promised by Alexander; he had the promise confirmed, albeit in rather vague terms, by the English. For a million sterling, he undertook, by a treaty signed at Stockholm, 3 March 1813, to cross into Germany with 30,000 men, and to support the operations of the Russian army. The English cabinet added to the promise of Norway that of Guadeloupe, which completely compromised Bernadotte with regard to France. But this clause remained secret. As for the French public, the language of the unofficial, the letters of the dazzled, like Mme de Staël, finally the *gasconades* of Bernadotte in person, would strengthen it in the belief that this former Minister of War of the

Directory, the man of confidence of the Republican Party in 1799, this sworn Fructidorian, this notorious anti-Brumairian, could only work to guarantee natural limits. In fact, Bernadotte associated himself with a policy whose first article was the destruction of these limits and the favorite combination an Anglo-Hanoverian kingdom extended to the Scheldt. This alliance was a masterstroke. The English expected a contagious example. They were preparing another, the scandal of which would have a still wider repercussion, and would cause a deeper shock.

Murat had abruptly left the Grand Army.[27] From when he entered Prussia he wanted to leave, and on 17 December 1812, he had a lively scene at Gumbinen with Davout, who came to ask him for his orders. Davout found him leaving the table, with Berthier. "Without reason and without any preamble," Murat told him "that no one in Europe trusted his (Napoléon) thought, that he could have made his peace with the English." He said it in such a way as to make it understood that he regretted not having done it. He praised the royal prince of Sweden, Bernadotte, which was hardly less significant. Davout represented to him "that he was king only by the grace of the emperor and the blood of the French; that he was also a French prince and that his duty required him not to make peace with the enemies of the emperor without his approval." To which Murat replied "that he was King of Naples as the Emperor of Austria was Emperor of Austria, and that he could do whatever he wanted."[28] Because for two years already, he thought he was threatened with the fate of Louis. Jealous of his wife Carolina, less as husband than as king, he suspected her of conspiring with Napoléon to dethrone him, and, on his part, he neglected nothing to make his wife's regency unpopular. On 4 February he was in Naples; he found an enthusiastic reception there. Durant, the Minister of France, wrote that the Queen was doing her best to bring Murat back to himself.

> Although she clings no less to the power and brilliance of the throne, her heart and her reason agree in making her feel that for the King, for her, for her family, there is no other guarantee than the very power of the Emperor, and that it is solely in his hands that they must place their destinies.[29]

One of Murat's first acts, however, was to rush to Vienna, with secret and entirely personal instructions, without the knowledge of his

French ministers and of his foreign minister, Gallo (Prince Cariati). This prince had to say and said to Metternich,

> that the king desired only the preservation of the throne of Naples, that he would renounce his pretensions to Sicily; sure, however, that his existence would sooner or later be threatened by France, and knowing the liberal views of (the Emperor of Austria), he desired to have a guarantee which would assure him of his future existence; that this guarantee could be given to him only by Austria, and that he was ready, on the other hand, to support our march (that of Austria) if necessary, by all his military forces.[30]

He found in Napoléon's attitude a pretext for the suspicions which it suited him to justify his conduct. A "most disturbing" letter, and then silence.[31] Napoléon had written two letters to the Queen, but so lively that she had concealed them from her husband.[32] It is difficult to believe that Murat had not had some echo of the very harsh words spoken about him by Napoléon, and of which this letter to Eugene gives an idea: "I find the conduct of the king very extravagant and such that I needn't have him arrested for an example. He is a brave man on the battlefield, but he lacks combination and moral courage."[33] He had read this note inserted in the 27 January 1813 number of the *Moniteur*:

> The King of Naples, being indisposed, had to leave command of the army, which he handed over to Viceroy Eugène. The latter is more accustomed to a large administration; he has the complete confidence of the Emperor.

Murat considered himself more than ever under the influence of forfeiture and confiscation. While he already felt Napoléon's hand resting on his crown, the Italians came to him, begging him to reign. Clinging to the throne of Naples out of self-love, he glimpsed the glory of becoming the liberator of Italy, of consecrating by national suffrage his granted royalty, and from intruder king to king brother-in-law, becoming direct king by grace of the Revolution. This phantom of high politics would hide from his eyes the defection in which he was smoldering.

Italy was not shaken by the same earthquakes as Germany. There was, however, agitation there, and with the prospect of the fall of Napoléon, one saw reborn the troubles, the plots which had accompanied, in 1799, the collapse of the republics of the Directory. The purely revolutionary party, the *carbonari* now mixed with men from the middle classes, these "enlightened men" who had hoped for the advent of liberty, from French domination, who were no longer satisfied with civil liberty, who dreamed of political liberty, and even more, national independence, Italy for the Italians; for the *carbonari*, in the form of a republic; the others, in the form of a monarchy, but in both cases united and national. Add to this the agents of the ancient dynasties, the papalines, the counter-revolutionaries, to whom, as to the French *émigrés*, any alliance seemed good to annihilate the work of the Revolution; they would burn Italy, the Austrians would extinguish the fire and suppress the incendiaries. It took a man of prestige to put all these elements into combustion. Murat seemed to some, the patriots, loyal enough and glorious enough to take on the task; to others, advantageous enough and stupid enough to be their dupe, while waiting for him to become their victim. Both sides circumvented him, intoxicated him with flattery. He responded with bluster, "promising mountains and wonders, saying that it was finally necessary to restore Italy's liberty, that he was the man to give it to her and that he would give it to him."[34] In short, jumping on his own bait, and posing as a paladin of the independence and unity of Italy.

    The Englishman Bentinck, proconsul of Sicily, well informed by his spies, closely followed these movements, excited people's minds, and, by his agents, kept the thread of all intrigues. This protector of legitimacy used it with the Bourbons of Sicily as formerly, in Holland, the ministers of the Directory with the Batavian republicans. He proceeded by riots, threats, police, military investment of the palace. He was, with his proteges, in open combat. Maria-Carolina denounced him in London, stirred up the people against him, and tried to lead the Sicilian troops. The imbecile Fernando, torn, as always, between fear of his wife, fear of the English, fear of being killed, at least imprisoned, fear of being disturbed in his hunts and his entertainments, abdicated, in turn, in favor of his son and regained power. Bentinck, fearing to be accused in parliament of playing the role that Napoléon had played in Spain in 1808, decided to keep Fernando on the throne, but by monopolizing the government, which he did on 9 February. Then he busied himself, by bad means, intimidation, in getting rid of the Queen. He succeeded. Maria-Carolina embarked on 2 April, trying to reach Austria. The King of Sicily found himself in a private charter, and the Queen, sister of Marie-Antoinette, wandering the seas, pushed back from shore to shore, at a time when the allies were busy dethroning the King of Saxony. Thus was the work of restoration prepared.

Master of Sicily, Bentinck undertook to become master of Naples, and thereby the rest of Italy. He multiplied emissaries and secret intrigues. He entered into occult and shady negotiations with Murat. While he presented himself to patriots and legitimists as the champion of liberty for some, of the rights of others, while he showed Great Britain ready to support the enterprise of each, he exhorted Murat

> to declare himself the champion of Italian freedom, praised his valor, his military skill, affirmed that his reunion with the allies would decide the success of the enterprise, that the disturber of the world would be crushed; that Joachim would be hailed King of Naples by the allies.

Such were Bentinck's insinuations, and this Englishman flattered himself that they were listened to, so much so that he sent a scout to London to bring back confirmation of his promises.

But in this first sentence of his defection, Murat had to, as he did until the catastrophe of his life, confuse both himself, his advisers, his instigators, and his accomplices. This unfortunate man was obsessed with the reign: if he believed his Crown was threatened by Napoléon, he offered himself to the allies; if he began to hope again for the Emperor's pardon, he would return to France. As soon as he sat down again, he regained his common sense, he understood that the allies would never accept him in good faith; that Napoléon, no doubt, after having enthroned him, could with the reverse of his pen cast him from the throne; but he felt that the only serious chance of remaining king consisted in remaining the ally of the emperor who had made him a king. Finally, a soldier at heart, he retained a French heart, warm, naive; child of the streets of France, reformed soldier of the *ancien régime*, enthusiastic volunteer of the Revolution, despite the braiding of his costumes and his favorite embroidery. He said to Durant,[35]

> How can the Emperor fail to recognize by what advantage I would be to him in Italy? I already have 30,000 men under arms; I will soon have 40,000. The army of Naples today provides security for Italy. If the Emperor will not believe in the sincerity of my assertion, let him at least believe in the instigations of my own interest. What guarantee could their promises have in my eyes? Don't I know that my destiny is an emanation from that of the Emperor? It is from him that I hold my crown. I want to keep it no doubt, but above all I want to keep my honor; let the Emperor say a word, and I will take care of the defense of Italy. I will defend it for him, for his system, without mixing any calculation that is personal to me. That if the Emperor, in his future plans, still believes my presence useful to the grand army, he tells me, and I go there; but, may his heart not be closed to me; may he give me back the consideration I need to serve him well, and may by devoting my life to him, I may at least know that he is doing me justice!

It was thus that in that spring of 1813, rotten with betrayal, Murat, learning that France was running to arms, that the German confederates were showing themselves faithful, and that the great march forward was about to begin again, wrote to the Emperor on 12 April, the letter of a captain surprised in marauding, to a. colonel of whom he was the spoiled child:

> My soul was shattered when you showed me distrust, when you seemed to want to humiliate me in the face of Europe. How, Sire, could you have doubted one who, since the beginning of his military career, has given you only proofs of devotion and fidelity, whose only object was his thoughts than glory, His Majesty's service, the greatness of France?

But Bentinck was watching him and Metternich was setting his net. This minister wrote to Count Mier on 20 April: "We are ready to listen to the king; the emperor only wants to see the king govern peoples who have devoted all their attachment to him." Then he spoke of mediation: "The mediating power no longer has a choice; she could succeed only so long as she was actually prepared to back up her words with war. Accordingly His Majesty musters great military forces."

## IV. Armistice of Pleiswitz

Meanwhile the Tsar and the King of Prussia had repaired to Dresden on 24 April. They saw Cathcart and Charles Stewart arrive there, both furnished with powers to treat. England declined the mediation, but in doing so pushed Austria into the coalition, for Austria could not otherwise prove the sincerity of its intentions or otherwise obtain the subsidies indispensable to act effectively. They found themselves inclined to hasten, more than Metternich would have liked, her secret agreements with Prussia and with Russia, when Napoléon's appearance on the scene rendered the intervention, if not a seriousness which it never had, at least an apparent consistency and some *raison d'être*, in form and expediency.

Napoléon had rebuilt an army with 200,000 men at his disposal. The French regiments trained and formed *en route*. They still lacked stamina, but they showed spirit. The presence of the Emperor electrified them. "Never had recruiting produced such a strong and fine breed of soldiers," said one officer. Blended with the remnants of the Grand Army, this youth recalled to mind, without the disastrous disposition to panic, the troops which Dumouriez and Kellermann hardened and trained in 1792. But the artillery was badly harnessed, and the cavalry insufficient. Finally, these Frenchmen found themselves mixed up with too many Germans.[36] The Confederation of the Rhine counted for a third of the 170,000 men that Napoléon carried into Saxony. France already saw itself as invaded in its own army.

Arrived at Erfurt on 28 April, Napoléon defeated on 2 May, at Lutzen, in Saxony, the Prussians and the Russians. Lacking cavalry, he could not pursue and destroy them. However, it was a brilliant entry into the campaign, calculated to excite the troops, to show that he was still the formidable leader of war that he had been; but it was only a success, it was not a great victory, the clap of thunder that would have been needed, the crushing blow of Jena. Napoléon made of the battle all the brilliance he could in Vienna and among his confederates.[37] He judged that Lutzen should bring Austria back to him. "The proposal to have an armed mediation accepted is too ridiculous for the Emperor of Austria not to understand it; it must be said bluntly, it is to want to put the interests of France at the mercy of the Empress and of M. de Stadion," wrote Caulaincourt in Narbonne on 4 May. Caulaincourt, who accompanied the Emperor, a sort of minister for foreign affairs in succession, between the general staff and the campaign chancellery, held the pen, but we recognize the style of 1809, after Wagram.

However, Napoléon treated them strangely. He blamed Narbonne for having pushed things too far and defined things too clearly.[38] He still hoped to take them back:

> The Emperor loves his father-in-law, he wishes to spare him inevitable misfortunes, if he lets himself go with the advice of inspiration and of the English clique. It was with a view to sparing its weakness and not putting the ministry in the position of going back on a false determination that we wanted to gain time. It was evident that if events were against us, the opinion of his people would lead the Emperor of Austria, and range him against us, while the French army, victorious as it was, it was in the interest of Austria to stay with France. Your Excellency's hasty explanation has the advantage of releasing us from all ties with this power, but the Emperor would have preferred your reserve to have spared him this false step.

He went to Dresden on the 8th; he wished to give an example to the Confederates of the Rhine, and to the peoples a warning. He had just learned, by a letter from Friedrich Augustus and by reports from Narbonne, that Saxony had adhered to Austrian mediation and that the movements of its troops were strangely turning to defection.[39] Add the hateful demonstrations of the people, agitated by Stein and the German patriots. Napoléon addressed to the King of Saxony a veritable ultimatum; he put him on notice to join his troops to the Grand Army, to declare that he was still part of the Confederation of the Rhine, that he had no treaty to the contrary to this confederation, otherwise "I declare him a felon, out of my protection, and consequently he has ceased to reign."[40] A municipal deputation, according to the rites, awaited him at the entrance to the town. He said,

> You deserve that I treat you like a conquered country. I know what insults you lavished on France, what hostile transports you indulged in, when the Emperor Alexander and the King of Prussia entered your walls. Your houses present to us the remains of your garlands, and we still see on the pavement the dunghill of the flowers which your young daughters have sown in the footsteps of monarchs. However, I want to forgive

everything. Bless your king, for he is your savior.

The King of Saxony arrived on the 12th, submissive, reconquered, and perfectly loyal in his resipiscence. Napoléon made a point of publicly manifesting their understanding; but the people remained hostile, and the army, forced to serve, were dissatisfied and smoldering with defection. Friedrich Augustus brought back from his wanderings in Germany and Bohemia some very disquieting information about the attitude of Austria. Intercepted letters succeeded in unmasking all that was suspicious in its mediation, scheming with the allies, attempts to hire Napoléon's confederates, and intention finally to go to war, if its peace conditions were not accepted, as soon as it felt able. Senfft, Minister of Foreign Affairs to Friedrich Augustus, had seen Metternich. Speaking of himself, he reported,

> It was easy for him to disentangle that the court of Vienna had no serious hopes for peace, nor any fixed plan for the terms to be offered, and were basically decided on war against France; one therefore sought, according to the expression of Metternich himself, only to ensure success and to gain time to complete the preparations which one announced should be finished so as to be able to enter in the campaign at the end of May.[41]

"The information we find in Dresden should no longer leave any doubt," Fain said correctly. And nowadays, a German historian said: "Napoléon would have been the only one to be mistaken." We will see that he was not mistaken.

Lutzen's battlefield served Metternich's calculations; it made mediation possible; it procured for Austria the delay it needed, the means of luring Napoléon, of dragging him along, of keeping him in suspense, and of putting itself in the spotlight. What Metternich learned from the recriminations of the allies, Prussians against Russians, Russians against Prussians, was not to annoy him. Austria would take the direction of politics and war as soon as it entered the scene. If Napoléon had crushed the allies, he would once again have become master of the world; if he had been routed, the supremacy would have passed to Alexander; Austria would have been no more than a chancellery in succession, and an auxiliary corps of the coalition. He was "in the ebb and flow of agitations, news, apprehensions, conjectures," a singularly perilous and difficult pass for Metternich: his master, both wavering and stubborn, the public carried away in turn turned and bewildered, not understanding, condemning the delays in declaring war.[42] Metternich showed himself superior by self-control, following, dexterity, flexibility in parades.[43] This man of the world, this political dandy, with a white and nervous hand, displayed the composure, the eye, and the energy of an old pilot.

The allies solicited him; Napoléon, incompletely victorious, would be forced to enter the "forms." Metternich wrote, "It was a question of preventing him from following his usual tactic, that is to say of turning towards Bohemia, in order to strike against us a great blow, the consequences of which would have been incalculable for Austria." He said to Count Hardenberg, "Towards the end of the month the Bohemian army should be ready to act: in the meantime he expected to agree with the other powers on the question of mediation, and until this time he still wanted to temper with Napoléon." It provided that "war between Austria and France must break out by the refusal that Bonaparte will undoubtedly give to the proposals that Russia, Prussia and Austria will jointly make to him."[44]

The end of the matter therefore consisted in proposing to him conditions which one would be sure to see him reject, and the choice was not difficult, knowing his views, the necessities of his policy, and the quite recent declarations that he had made to Schwarzenberg. Napoléon could not retreat without losing his prestige, admitting defeat, exposing himself to new demands from the allies, Metternich knew that the leaders of opinion in Paris would make a weapon against him by refusing to meet preliminary conditions which, in the state of mind in France, one would consider not only acceptable, but excellent. In this way, Napoléon would be engaged in a negotiation, the least effect of which would be to deepen the separation between him and the French. He would have lost the offensive advantage, the superiority of numbers, the confidence of the generals, the enthusiasm for war.

"The transition from neutrality to war will only be possible through armed mediation," Metternich had told Franz II. He was about to take that step. On 7 May he drew up instructions for Stadion which he despatched to Alexander: he developed his ideas on armed mediation and laid down the "views of peace" to be proposed to Napoléon; they were: 1) The suppression of the Duchy of Warsaw and the return, as far as Austria is concerned, to the state prior to 1809; 2) the restitution to Prussia of her former possessions in northern Germany; 3) the abandonment by France of all it possessed in Germany beyond the Rhine; 4) independent Holland; 5) the restitution of all the French provinces in Italy; 6) the restoration of the Pope; 7) for Austria, the frontier before Lunéville, the Mincio or the Oglio, plus the Tyrol and the country of the Inn, Illyria, Dalmatia, and the restitution of all that the treaty had taken away from it from 1809; 8) cessation of Napoléon's supremacy in Germany; 9) the Kingdom of Italy out of the hands of the Emperor of the French.[45] These, according to Metternich, were the conditions for a good continental peace, but he recognized that one must distinguish between a maximum and a minimum, according to the chances of war. On the war itself, he expressed himself clearly: "The Count of Stadion will prove that we aspire above all to bring the term closer together, or by a prompt agreement with the powers, or by operations which allow us to bring our forces beyond our frontiers." In support, Stadion would produce

> military estimates which will leave the Emperor Alexander nothing to be desired on the details of the movements of our army ... He will neglect nothing to bring about an instantaneous negotiation, and to agree on the bases of an active military co-operation on our part in the case of the failure of our care in favor of peace.

The same day, Franz wrote to the Tsar. He wished for a peaceful arrangement, but immediately added:[46] "Our united forces, directed from a fixed point of view, and in the most perfect harmony, will make us, there can be no doubt, assuming the contrary, arrive at the noblest goal that the powers can propose." On 8 May, Stadion set out: he was in a position to bring to an end "the instantaneous negotiation" and to establish between Austria and the allies "the most perfect accord," which was the primary aim of his assignment.[47]

It remained to bind Napoléon the time it would take to establish the agreements. Metternich saw Narbonne on 7 May.[48] He was careful not to declare to him the maximum of his conditions and what he considered to be the bases of a good peace would be discovered successively, at the congress. He contented himself with insinuating that in the Russian proposals he rejected two-thirds, he accepted one. But on these two-thirds, any more than on the propositions themselves, he did not express himself clearly. He was careful not to articulate the main article of the instructions to Stadion, the essentials of a good peace: according to Austria, namely the reconstitution of the Austrian monarchy as it was in 1805. He did not explain. Narbonne pressed him: "What should, without doubt, give the greatest hope of seeing peace concluded, is the knowledge of the conditions which you are ready to have accepted and to support; you promised to give it to me, and I claim it." Metternich rambled on, spreading himself in circumlocutions. Narbonne, who remembered their interview of April 7th, questioned him: "Doesn't all this mean that you want the Emperor to accept the Rhine as the frontier, including Holland?" – "Yes, without doubt, and it is more for his interest than for ours." – "So, successively," continued Narbonne, in his report,

> I made particular reference to M. de Metternich the cession of the Illyrian provinces, the dissolution of the Confederation of the Rhine, the abandonment of the new united departments, the destruction of the Duchy of Warsaw and the enlargement of Prussia operated according to this which would be agreed between the great powers, which would remain guarantors of the state of things and true protectors of the princes of the Confederation.

Metternich added that to dissuade Russia from talking about Italy and Spain, it had to adopt a threatening attitude. As for Holland, the Count appeared, in his own name, to abandon it to France, but Narbonne knew that these departments formed the portion reserved for England, and he could not flatter himself that England would find it convenient to leave it to France. Thus, in addition to these five Austrian points: 1) the suppression of the Duchy of Warsaw; 2) the Hanseatic towns and the 32nd military division;[49] 3) Illyria; 4), the aggrandizement of Prussia; 5) the dissolution of the Confederation of the Rhine, one must understand that the allies would require others, e.g., Holland on the part of the English, the evacuation of Italy wanted by the Russians, not to mention the reconstitution of Austria on the footing of 1805, claimed by Austria from Russia. Is it permissible to believe that if Napoléon accepted the five Austrian points, Austria would make war on the English and Russia to keep Holland, Spain, and Italy for Napoléon, where they claimed to establish itself and take its conveniences?

On the 11th Metternich drew up instructions for Bubna, which he sent to Napoléon. "This fat, cunning man" knew how to make the emperor speak and report what he heard. His mission was to initiate mediation, to engage Napoléon in it through moderate proposals. The nine points laid down in the Stadion instruction, and the five points indicated to Narbonne, dwindled to three, that is to say the minimum of the Austrian claims: 1) dissolution of the Duchy of Warsaw; 2) renunciation of annexed departments in Germany, the 32nd military division; 3) Illyria to Austria, "with a good border on the side of Italy"; plus (Bubna will only touch upon it if it sees fit) "another boundary arrangement between us and Bavaria," which would mean the Tyrol and the Inn district. There would be no question of the reconstitution of Prussia; as for the dissolution of the Confederation of the Rhine, Bubna would only possibly present it as a probable claim "of the powers." He would propose, if Napoléon deemed it appropriate, to negotiate an armistice. He indicated Prague as the place of the meeting of a congress. If Napoléon accepted this, then he would be entitled to believe that Austria "will defend the cause she pleads, by force of arms," for it is in these very terms that Bubna will make it known to Napoléon that, if he refused, Austria would declare war on him.[50]

While Bubna was on his way to Dresden, Stadion met Nesselrode at Goerlitz. On 13 May they had talks, at the end of which Nesselrode summarized the conditions of Austria in these terms: 1) restoration of Austria to the state of power and extent in which it was in 1805, with, in Italy, the border of the Po and the Mincio; 2) reconstitution of Prussia under the conditions fixed by the Treaty of Kalisch; 3) dissolution of the Confederation of the Rhine and restitution of the countries annexed in 1810; 4) annihilation of the Duchy of Warsaw. Nesselrode added,

> Such are the conditions which the Cabinet of Vienna regards as immediately Austrian, and which it is determined to uphold *vis-à-vis* France. If Napoléon has not accepted them before 1 June, the Austrian armies act. Although sure that the conditions put forward above would never be accepted by France, Austria wishes that, in order to facilitate the means for her to persevere to the end in the line of conduct she has drawn up, we adopt the forms through which it believes it must pass in order to bring about the transition from mediation to cooperation.

"It would therefore like" that in articulating these conditions, Russia would include "even bases such as independence of Spain, Holland, and arrangements for Italy, necessary for the restoration of a stable peace." Stadion was authorized "to agree on the general principles of a plan of operation"; he only asked for a commitment, that "whatever the setbacks," to push the war "with perseverance and with all of the means."

Stadion joined the allies at Wurschen, and there Nesselrode, by a note of 16 May, declared that Russia add to the Austrian conditions: 5) separation from Holland; 6) the restoration of the Bourbons in Spain; 7) Italy free in all its extent from the government and influence of France. Hardenberg adhered to this note of 16 May on behalf of Prussia, with this addition: "It (this peace) should be accepted in a completely positive manner and without delay, and the retreat of the French armies must immediately follow adherence from the Emperor Napoléon to these conditions." Nesselrode concluded: "Such are the principal bases which His Majesty regards as invariable conditions." These principal and invariable bases would still be only the bases of a preliminary peace, England not being included in them. The intervention of England, inevitable during the conferences, would call everything into question.

The same day, 16 May, Stadion attended a council of war at Alexander's where Wolkonski, Toll, and Knesebeck drew up a plan of operations which he immediately transmitted to Vienna. There was established, says a Russian document, "a complete understanding between Austria and us on the proposals to be addressed to France, as well as on the procedure to be followed in common, if our overtures, as everything led us to believe, were rejected by Napoléon."[51]

And, however, Bubna would "put forward" to Napoléon, as bases "of a possible continental peace": 1) the dissolution of the Duchy of Warsaw; 2) France's renunciation of the departments across the Rhine in Germany, that is, the countries annexed in December 1810; 3) the return of the Illyrian provinces to Austria, with a good border on the side of Italy. He would insinuate as probably having to be postponed by the powers the renunciation of the protectorate over Germany, that is to say the dissolution of the Confederation of the Rhine. He would also insinuate a border arrangement between Austria and Bavaria. He would add that Austria had little hope of the adhesion of England, which "can only be forced into peace by a continental peace which would leave her entirely isolated and abandoned to the efforts of France."

Thus everything was calculated to lure Napoléon into the trap: watered down and limited proposals from Austria to induce him to mediation and congress; growing demands, to the congress, to throw it out of itself and to induce it to retract this acceptance. If, extraordinarily, he did not pierce the plot, the insolent pretension of Prussia, which recalled the ultimatum of 1806, would provoke his anger and lead him to destroy everything. Then the game would be played. France, which would only be made aware of the ostensible and restricted proposals of Bubna, the first three points, the minimum of the Austrian claims, would know that Napoléon refused this moderate, conciliatory peace, which left France its natural frontiers with Italy, Holland, perhaps the Confederation of the Rhine, in short the essence of the Grand Empire, and that he broke the Austrian alliance for having persisted in the Duchy of Warsaw, in the Hanseatic cities, in Illyria; that he disregarded the "admirable advice sincerely given" by Metternich.[52]

Now, warned by Narbonne, Napoléon had no illusions about the character of the Austrian proposals, about the gradations that would follow, and he knew that everything depended on the war. But he found himself at an impasse. If he refused to negotiate on the bases of Metternich, he assumed before Europe, before his allies, before the French, whom he felt was slipping away from him, the responsibility for the war and gave Austria a pretext to come out against him. If he accepted, he ran the risk of losing the fruits of his victory in dangerous, useless negotiations, and he would become entangled in the network hatched by Metternich, allow Austria to complete armaments, would leave, at the shadow of diplomacy, to organize a formidable coalition which would embrace it, the day when it believed itself strong enough to reveal its true intentions. His whole work was at stake. It was not a question, as Metternich insinuated, of pacifying Europe. It was a question of renouncing to dominate it, of seeing it unite again against France. It was necessary, as in 1795, as in 1798, as in 1800, as in 1805, 1806, 1809, to choose between a struggle to the death and the pure and simple return of France to its old limits. It was from the Grand Empire that they claimed to expropriate it first, then from the Empire itself and from the conquests of the Republic. Napoléon clearly discerned it; however, he still flattered himself that he could turn the positions of his adversaries, cut them off, divide them, and disconcert them in turn.

On 14 May, Caulaincourt wrote to Narbonne:

> Newly intercepted letters from M. de Stahrenberg to M. de Nesselrode and from M. de Humboldt to the King of Prussia leave no doubt as to the duplicity of M. de Metternich. The King of Saxony handed over to His Majesty all his notes with Austria. If circumstances became serious, which the Emperor did not think, it can't escape you that he would make arrangements with Emperor Alexander. For these two sovereigns to get along, it takes very little. What matters to Russia? The Continental System and Poland. We renounced the continental system for Russia; Italy, Germany and Spain are much more important to the Emperor than Poland. You know better than anyone that the Emperor has no madness in mind, that he has always looked at Poland as a means, but not as a main affair. He can therefore only escape Austria by satisfying Russia on this point, we have a means of humiliating Austria, and even of reducing her to nothing, for what concessions would not the Emperor Alexander make if, to get him out of trouble, Poland was ceded to him? A mission to headquarters would split the world.

Such were Napoléon's ulterior motives, his secret conjectures, his illusory speculations, when he received Bubna on the 16th of May.[53] Bubna gave him a letter from Franz II dated 11 May. Napoléon let him develop his "forms" and lay his "bases"; then, with that incoherence of thought and expression which gave his words a powerful and savage eloquence:

> I don't want your armed mediation. You're just confusing the question. You say you can't do anything for me; you are therefore only strong against me. It is a subtlety that I do not admit, to say that all this does not alter your system of alliance with me; it's a discourse that can be given to the women you want to seduce. You don't get anything by beating a Frenchman. I will not cede anything, not a village of all that is constitutionally united to France. A man who, from a private individual, has reached the throne, who has spent twenty years under grapeshot, does not fear bullets, does not fear threats. I do not value my life, as little as that of others I do not esteem it more than that of a hundred thousand men; I will sacrifice a million if necessary. You will force me only by multiplied victories I will perhaps perish, and my dynasty with me. I don't care about all that. You want to snatch Italy and Germany from me, you want to dishonor me, sir! Honor above all! then the

woman, then the child, then the dynasty. We are going to upset the world and the established order of things. The existence of monarchies will become a problem. The best of women will be its victim; she will be unhappy. France will be handed over to the Jacobins. The child in whose veins Austrian blood flows, what will become of him? What is closest to my heart is the fate of the King of Rome; I don't want to make Austrian blood odious to France!

Weigh this word, which rises to the lips like the height of the heart of a beleaguered genius; it reveals the secret of the Grand Empire, and this intimate weakness which will, if not offend the judgment, at least slow down the blows of the Emperor, clinging to the end to this hope, that by dint of beating the Prussians and the Russians, he will oblige Austria to remain his ally, to appear, at least, to have helped him. Then, abruptly returning to business:

> I bought Illyria with the loss of a million men; you won't get it by force without sacrificing as much. You want to fish in murky water. You don't win provinces with rose water; these are means that can be used to seduce women. You begin by asking me for Illyria, then you will ask me for the country of Venice, then the Milanese, Tuscany, and you will force me to fight against you; better start there. Yes, if you want to have provinces, blood must flow. Pushed back to Frankfurt, I would have told you the same thing; I have only one idea about it; my policy is frank and open.

He would have read the note that, the same day, Nesselrode was drafting and which became the preliminary charter of the new coalition, that he would not have used any other language. However, he changed his mind. Caulaincourt had a discussion with Bubna on the 17th, and said to him:

> The Emperor seems disposed to grant some advantages to Austria, if they can serve to re-establish peace; but he does not want the circle of Popilius drawn for him. As to the substance, he rejects mediation, but he consents to the meeting of a congress in an intermediate town, with or without England. He notifies this in a letter to the Emperor Franz, and he adds, in another letter, I am determined to die, if necessary, at the head of what France has of generous men, rather than become the

laughingstock of the English and to make my enemies triumph.

Bubna took away these letters for Franz II, dated 17 May.[54] The next day Caulaincourt wrote to Narbonne:

> The emperor read his father-in-law's letter. His Majesty found him full of protest, assurances and a very cajoling tone. He instructs me to tell you that, of course, he cannot recognize any armed mediation. Austria must explain what she wants, because from Brabant to Tuscany, from Lorraine to Venice, one can suppose her sights of interest. No doubt we could get along better.

Napoléon had passed through such formidable crises in 1805, in 1806, in 1809; but he saw clearly, his combinations formed like an electric spark, immediate, luminous, striking a blow from a distance. In 1805, he threw himself between the allies, disconcerted them, made a corner, separated them. From now on, it is they who, approaching, pushed him back, tossed between their camps. He groped in the fog, fidgeted, struggled.

He did not deny Austria a tip, but nothing more, or "the good hand" of the middleman. It was repugnant to him to abandon the arbitration of peace to Metternich. He found himself in the situation he foresaw before his interview with Bubna, and he turned to Alexander. He sent him Caulaincourt:

> My intention is to build him a golden bridge to deliver him from the intrigues of Metternich ... If I have sacrifices to make, I prefer that it be for the benefit of the Emperor Alexander, who makes me a good war, and of the King of Prussia, in whom Russia is interested, only for the benefit of Austria, who has betrayed the alliance, and who, under the title of mediator, wishes to arrogate to herself the right to dispose of all, after doing the part that suits her. All the honor of this peace would therefore go to the Emperor Alexander alone.

Caulaincourt would indicate: the Confederation of the Rhine limited to the Oder, a line from Glogau to Bohemia: Prussia would lose there 1,500,000 souls, who would go to Westphalia; in compensation, it would receive the Duchy of Warsaw, with Danzig, the whole of the Vistula, or four to five million inhabitants. France and Russia would be separated.⁵⁵ This project would destroy Poland forever. The famous ultimatum of 1810, "the Kingdom of Poland will never be restored," would become a reality. Napoléon, moreover, did not stick strictly to these proposals:

> Without stopping at this or that part of the instructions, you must seek to enter into a direct negotiation on this basis (which the Emperor of Russia alone would have the honors of the peace). Once we come to talk to each other, we will always end up agreeing.

At the same time, Napoléon pressed measures and especially Eugène's demonstrations. He said,

> It is important for Austria to see your encamped divisions and the armed places as soon as possible... Make it known in the gazettes of Turin and Milan and everywhere that you will soon have 150,000 men. Engage the King of Bavaria to fortify in the Tyrol some gorges ... and some forts, to be master of the passes and to contain the inhabitants.

In short, "to gain the upper hand over Austria; let me be the one threatening..."⁵⁶

On 18 May, Macdonald informed the general-in-chief of the Russian army that Caulaincourt requested an audience with the Tsar. The answer was delayed until the next day, and when it returned, copied from a minute of Alexander, saying that this emperor was on the run, that the general-in-chief did not know when he could take his orders. The leave was dry. Nesselrode toned it down slightly: "However pleased His Majesty would have had in expressing to you the feelings he keeps for you personally, he regrets that circumstances object to him admitting you to his headquarters." And he invited him to transmit his communications through Austria.⁵⁷ The step however did not remain without effect: the Russians informed Metternich of it, who did not fail to be moved by it and found in it more powerful motives to get closer to the allies.

But Napoléon also gave it to him not to hasten his movements. On 20 May the allies were defeated at Bautzen. It was not a complete victory, and with this victory, Napoléon would know no more. His army was tired. "I was hoping to settle with Austria," he said later.⁵⁸ Like the ship which, in heavy weather and contrary wind, takes reefs, steers badly, runs tacks to exhaustion, it returned once again to the Austrian side, which it must necessarily reach, because the others were intractable.

He did not know the exact situation of the allies and their perplexities. Forced to evacuate Breslau, to partially abandon Silesia, they saw, in their rear, Berlin threatened, Hamburg recaptured. The Russian general Michael Barclay de Tolly declared that the state of his troops obliged him to withdraw towards Poland: he asked for six weeks to recover and begin again in Silesia. Austria demanded as much to effect its junction. Separated from the Russians, without the support of the Austrians, Friedrich-Wilhelm III thought himself lost. Louis-Alexandre Andrault, Comte de Langeron [1763-1831] wrote:

> Napoléon then had 130,000 men and we did not have 80,000. We had no more ammunition. We couldn't risk a fight. He could not experience failure. If he had continued the war, he would have forced us to retire behind the Oder. It was on this aspect that we decided. We could hardly have stayed there. He could have thrown us back to the Vistula, then he would have had very advantageous chances of concluding peace; Austria would have been unable to declare against him; the Prince Royal of Sweden could not or dared not join us.

An armistice alone could save them, and the appearance of Caulaincourt at the outposts gave some hope of opening a negotiation. On the night following the battle, Alexander had Franz II write, via Stadion: "Nothing can shake me in my perseverance, I count more than ever on the prompt cooperation of Austria." On the 22nd, Stadion wrote to Berthier: "Their Majesties have found in the account given by M. de Bubna of the conversation with the Emperor Napoléon, the opinion that he thinks that an armistice might prepare the way," to a negotiation; they are ready to send officers with powers to the outposts.

Napoléon was expecting reinforcements, horses, equipages. He awaited the effects of the measures that Eugène was about to take in Italy. A few days later he wrote:

> I decided for two reasons: my lack of cavalry, which prevents me from striking strong blows, and the hostile position of Austria. This court, under the most amiable, the most tender colors, I would even say the most sentimental, wants nothing less than to force me, by the fear of its army assembled in

> Prague, to restore to it Dalmatia, and Istria, and even beyond the Isonzo. She also wants the left bank of the Inn and the land of Salzburg.... War with her is to be expected. What leads me to stop during my victories are the armaments of Austria and the desire to gain time so that your army (Eugène's) can be encamped at Laybach, and have two armies. Austria's insolence has no end. If we gave her what she wants now, she would want Italy and Germany afterwards; certainly she will have nothing from me.[59]

But one thing was not to give in to Austria, not to humble oneself before them and even inflict a lesson on them, another thing to let them carry out their plan, start the struggle again and, as he said to Bubna: "To make odious Austrian blood to France!" He hoped to reconcile everything, political calculations, military necessities, by gaining time, by regaining the ascendancy.

Add the news from Paris. Maret, so courteous, so cautious, wrote to him, after having noted the joy of victory:[60]

> If, during the campaigns which preceded the last, one sought in a success only the presage and the guarantee of a new glory, today that the confidence is shaken, that such serious questions must be solved on the field of battle, we only want to see in it a pledge given by fortune for rest and peace. Nations don't die; they tire of the necessity of always conquering. You have conquered the moderation which is in your resolutions, but which might have appeared without dignity in reverses, will henceforth do no harm to your glory, and this peace, the only wish, the pressing need of France, will always be a glorious peace.

Maret, who arrived on 22 May, could only verbally support these respectful but significant remonstrances. Add again the murmurs of the generals, the lack of initiative of the lieutenants, their consideration, their discouragement too; the butchery of Bautzen, the relentlessness of the enemy disturbed them deeply. "My friend, towards the end of the battle, the Emperor is insatiable in combat; we will all stay there, that is our destiny!" said Duroc to Marmont.[61] A few moments later a bullet killed him.

Finally, and above all, the thought which henceforth never left him, which interposed itself between his genius, all of direct action, and the reality of business; her purest thought no doubt, but which, like the most transparent water, diverted her gaze and distorted objects, her son's thought.[62] The concern for another himself, more precious, more tender, exposed to more hazards, for which he feared what he had never feared for himself, the catastrophe, this continual game battles. This preoccupation with the future, with the morrow which belongs to no one, made him circumspect, introduced feeling into his policy, which had known only *raison d'État* and necessity. Defeat was the abyss: formerly he did not stop his gaze there, and he passed over it and pierced beyond it; now he plunged into it: he saw the image of a child in distress, and the vision horrified him. He tried to trick, to compromise with destiny.

It would have taken an Austerlitz; Napoléon found neither the army, nor the enthusiasm, nor the plan; he asked fortune for a delay, and he resorted, to await the stroke of genius and the opportunity, to political combinations. They tempted him because they veiled the military inertia to which he saw himself constrained, because he did not despair of holding Austria back, of softening Franz II, of disconcerting Metternich: the congress would offer the means. He could only arrive at this congress by entering "into the Austrian forms". But if he sacrificed it to Franz II, he thought it a good idea to hand the honors to Alexander.

On 25 May, Caulaincourt wrote to Nesselrode: "I am flattered that there is no longer any objection to H.M. the Emperor Alexander granting me the honor of paying court to him." On the 26th, Napoléon dictated instructions for an armistice which would prepare for a congress. This armistice was to last three months, or at least the whole time of the negotiations, each one remaining in the position he occupied. Napoléon was keen to mention the congress in the armistice agreement itself, believing that it was thus thwarting a calculation by the allies. "They don't want a congress, and they want to continue the war in the hope of dragging Austria into pronouncing a sentence, an unseemly and absurd thing," Maret wrote to Caulaincourt.[63]

However, Napoléon declared war on Sweden, as Swedish troops had entered Hamburg. It was an aggression that he could not tolerate in the face of the confederates of the Rhine and the Germans in insurrection. But in all his letters from that time these words recur: "There is nothing to do but to gain time.... Save time, without upsetting Austria"; work to eventually renew the covenant; "beat the campaign. Does she want to keep the Ottoman Empire? You can embroider two months on this canvas and give rise to twenty letters."[64]

The commissioners met near Liegnitz on 30 May. On the side of the allies were generals Schouvalof and Kleist, and on the French side Caulaincourt.

From Erfurt, the Duke of Vicence passed among the allies to come under the influence of Talleyrand and serve his plans.[65] He had entered into a relationship of trust with Nesselrode, then adviser to the Russian Embassy in Paris, who was sending secret correspondence to the Tsar through Speransky. He said:

> It was my conversations with M. de Talleyrand and a few other people opposed to Napoléon's growing ambition that paid the price. M. de Caulaincourt, then French Ambassador to Russia, rallied to this opposition. In secret conversations he had made the Emperor Alexander aware of the dangers with which his master's ambition threatened Russia. In the spring of the year 1810, the Emperor Napoléon, dissatisfied with his correspondence, had called him back. The Emperor Alexander, not wishing to lose such a valuable source of information, advised him to make use of my intermediary on his return to send it to him. All these men did not believe they were betraying their master, but preserving him from the fiery passions by preventing him from pursuing these endless wars which depopulated France, impoverished it, and could end in terrible disasters.[66]

One could not, however, confuse Caulaincourt in the troop of partisans of the Empire without the Emperor, nor doubt the "loyalism" of his personal devotion to Napoléon so often and so warmly declared.[67]

Convinced that a conversation between the Emperor of Russia and himself could put everything in order and settle everything in a few hours;[68] fascinated by Talleyrand, garlanded by Alexander, indoctrinated by Metternich; believing in the magnanimity of the Tsar, in the virtues of the King of Prussia, in the principles of the Emperor of Austria, Caulaincourt seems to have imagined that Europe, sympathizing with France, desired, like the French, only peace within the limits of Lunéville, the natural limits. These limits seemed to him impassable to armies, immutable in treaties. He imagined himself working for the good of Europe, for the good of France, for the good of the Emperor by facilitating the execution of their generous intentions for the allies, by forcing Napoléon's hand as far as possible and by leading him, if necessary in spite of himself, to enter into designs which he persisted in disregarding, forcing him to sign a peace that would consolidate his dynasty. These illusions alone explain the very singular steps which he took in this meeting and which denote, on his part, the most blind confidence in the intentions of Russia.

On the 30th, after the delimitations had been debated, from which the Russians claimed to exclude Hamburg, and the duration, which they claimed to reduce to one month, taking advantage of a moment when the Prussian Kleist had left the chamber, Caulaincourt took apart from Schouvalof, assured, he declared that his confidences would only be reported to Alexander.[69]

> Let's try to arrange things. The Emperor Napoléon has, I believe, consented to the mediation of Austria. Let's take advantage of the moment, it's good; we are in a moment of weakness, our troops are dispersed. General Bertrand is on the side of Striegau. The other columns present the flank to you while marching; when we are successful, we can no longer be made to listen to reason. You let us do it, so our troops are tired; this is our moment of weakness. But don't forget what I'm telling you, we're going to have considerable reinforcements. If we set foot in the Duchy of Warsaw, the war will last for years.

Schouvalof did not fail to report to the Tsar, the same day, these surprising insinuations: "And really, there are some which would cost him his head, if we knew it." Could it be a ruse of war, a means of assuring himself of the weakness of the allies, of their powerlessness to attack when Napoléon believed himself in a position to crush them? Schouvalof suspected it. However, he added, "it sounds like he wants a great failure for the French army to conclude peace as soon as possible." The next day, 1 June, talks resumed. Reinforcements did not arrive, said Caulaincourt; if the Russians did not act, then they could not; the Cossacks acting in the rear of the army could intercept all communication.[70] And in the evening, in his report to Napoléon: "An *aide-de-camp* to the Duke of Ragusa was caught yesterday in a cavalry affair. I am in the middle of a swarm of Cossacks." He added:

> M. de Schouvalof told me, in front of his colleague, that he could assure me that the Emperor Alexander was without passion in this matter, that he sincerely wanted peace, that everything would prove it and that if we also wanted it sincerely that he would accept the armistice as they propose it.

On 2 June the commissioners drafted a text. Caulaincourt referred it to Napoléon. Then, taking Schouvalof aside, he said to him: "In two months the French army will be doubled. If you are sure that Austria is acting with you, you do well not to dream of making peace with us; but if you are not sure, you have no time to waste." Napoléon wanted to make peace, "without foreign influence." Then, after pointing out the dispersion and disarray of the French army:

> Why didn't you back up your claims with strong attacks? Do you know that the armistice is all to our advantage? The Emperor Napoléon was in such a hurry to know if it was concluded that not only did he send me three couriers yesterday to find out if I had finished, but he himself came to meet mine.

Is it, Schouvalof concluded, "conviction or frankness, or desire that we act before the Austrian army begins its operations?"

The draft armistice was sent to Napoléon. However the allies obtained from Austria the decisive move, of which Caulaincourt said: "If you are sure that Austria is acting with you, you do well not to think of making peace with us." Metternich received, on 29 May, the news of Bautzen, the almost desperate appeal of the allies. It seemed to him that the hour had struck. "My decision was taken. It was a question of stopping Napoléon in his forward march and fixing the Emperor Alexander and King Friedrich-Wilhelm on the resolution that the Emperor my master would take."[71] This armistice that Napoléon then wanted to gain the ascendancy over Austria, Austria wanted it to gain from Napoléon; each in order to arm and negotiate against the other. But what was most urgent for Metternich was to hold the allies in confidence and Napoléon in suspense for as long as necessary. He despatched a courier to Bubna, instructing him to insist on mediation with Napoléon, and he persuaded the Emperor Franz to approach the Russian headquarters.

Emperor Franz II left with his minister on 1 June. On the way they met Nesselrode, who was going to find Metternich in Vienna with a copy of the armistice plan.[72] Franz and Metternich provided the answers to the questions that Nesselrode had a mandate to ask them: "Will Austria draw the sword? What is the time when Austria will begin hostilities?" Nesselrode accompanied them to Gitschin, to the castle of the Count of Trautmansdorf, where they arrived on 3 June. Metternich wrote:

> According to the short conversation I had with the Count de Nesselrode, it seems to me beyond doubt that he will leave us satisfied and convinced that in no case will we abandon the cause. Our soldiers are happy with the military direction taken by the allies. What would seem to us to serve our interests better than anything else would be the conclusion of the armistice.[73]

Napoléon waited with a strange impatience; a fever entered it, the fever of uncertainty, the need to end, in whatever way it might be, an affair in which he reproached himself for having gotten into it. On 2 June he told Caulaincourt to cut the dispute in two: if the allies granted him 20 July, he would yield on Hamburg, but on Breslau, which he occupied and which the allies wanted him to evacuate, it was impossible. Berthier wrote, "His Majesty asks me to write to you that the question of Breslau is a question of honor to which one cannot yield." And the Emperor himself: "This armistice... is not honorable for me..." Doubts besieged him. He had Caulaincourt write: "How are you ignorant, you who know the relations of Austria, if the armistice is not a disastrous thing for us, since at the moment of denouncing it, Austria will intervene and resume color?" And on the other hand, the same day: "I am tired of this negotiation which lasts so long. Try to end it today." On the night of the 3rd to the 4th, he ordered the marshals to be ready to march in the morning, and Caulaincourt to finish it one way or the other, convinced that the enemy only wanted to gain time. But the allies accept his conditions, and on the 4th the armistice was signed, at Pleiswitz, "on the bases fixed by the Emperor."

It was to last until 20 July,[74] the date then fixed by Schwarzenberg for the completion of the preparations in Austria.[75] It was a purely military act: not a word was said either of the mediation or of the peace congress. A notice written before Alexander's eyes said:

> It is enough to take a look at it to be convinced how much it differs from all the armistices which Napoléon has concluded up to now. Among the advantages which result from it, we must certainly place in the first line that it saves us the time to fix in an irrevocable manner our relations with Austria. We have the certainty of continuing the war with the cooperation of Austria, unless the perfect harmony which reigns between her and us imposes on Napoléon to the point of making him subscribe to

an honorable peace for Russia, advantageous for its allies and beneficial for Europe. An accession to the alliance which remains between Russia and Prussia is already negotiated with Count Stadion for the case of war, and General Foll (Phull) leaves today for Prague, in order to agree with Prince Schwarzenberg of a plan of operations.[76]

No sooner had Napoléon ratified it than he regretted it. "Fatal knot, where all the chances and destinies of the campaign are tied," he said later. He tried to justify himself by an error, the least admissible for a head of empire and a man such as himself. He said to Gourgaud: "Yes, I know very well that I did wrong. We must do this justice to Soult, he approved of my idea of not signing the armistice; but Berthier and Caulaincourt pressed me."[77]

## V. Treaties of Reichenbach

The armistice was a curtain. Behind, in the intermission, the capital scenes of the drama took place. Emperor Franz II remained at Gitschin, where he was surrounded by a small court, chiefly of soldiers, who under the cloak prepared the joint operations. By a note of 7 May. Metternich invited the allies to conclude a possible treaty for the case of war and to determine the bases of peace to propose Napoléon, which would form the pivot of the turning movement of Austria. On 13 June, Schwarzenberg presented the Emperor with a plan of operations which was adopted on the 15th in a council attended by Metternich.

The English had been at Reichenbach, in Silesia, not far from the Bohemian border, since the last days of May.[78] It was with the Prussians that they first met. They refused to pay a pound sterling before the Prussians had consented to the abandonment of the territories intended for the enlargement of the future kingdom of Hanover, namely the bishopric of Hildesheim, the parts of the former electorate of Hanover and Ost-Friesland united either with the kingdom of Westphalia or with the French empire in 1810, departments of Ems-Oriental and Ems-Supérieur, which had to be conquered. The Prussians struggled in extreme necessity: no money, no arms, no ammunition. They went where the English wanted. The English, by reciprocity, brought them a considerable guarantee, that of the Treaty of Kalisch: the reconstruction of Prussia into a State equivalent to that of

1806. They also guaranteed, for half, "a federative paper" that the allies would put ongoing up to £5 million. Prussia guaranteed, for its part, the restoration of the ducal houses of Brunswick and Hanover. It undertakes to put 80,000 men into the field, for £666,666. This treaty was signed on 14 June 1813.

The next day, 15 June, also at Reichenbach, the English signed with Russia. England paid £1,000,000, plus £500,000 intended for the maintenance of the Russian fleet which had taken refuge in English ports and which was placed at the disposal of the British Admiralty. It guaranteed the "federal paper" Russia undertook to procure the increase of the House of Hanover. Finally, the essential article, identical in the two treaties, which joined them together, bound them with the Treaty of Kalisch and made it the foundation of the coalition:

> Article VII. The two high contracting parties (England and Prussia, England and Russia) will act in the most perfect concert as regards military operations, and will communicate to each other frankly what concerns their policy. Above all, they undertake reciprocally not to negotiate separately with their common enemies, sign no peace, no truce, no convention whatsoever other than by mutual accord.

But Kalisch's treaty said:

> Article VI. H. M. the King of Prussia and H. M. the Emperor of Russia reciprocally undertake not to negotiate in private with the enemy, to sign either peace, or truce, or any convention whatsoever, other than by mutual agreement.

Thus Prussia could not negotiate or treat for peace without Russia, Prussia and Russia could not negotiate or treat without England. It follows that the three powers were entirely bound for negotiation as for peace. These arrangements canceled in advance, as definitive, the proposals that Metternich might make to Napoléon, as long as England would not have accepted them. There you have thus dissipated the ambiguity of this mediation and of this congress about which so much has been disputed, because one started, gratuitously, on the sole words of Metternich, from this postulate that Metternich's proposals were sincere and definitive, that the allies adopted them with this character and that if Napoléon, taking Metternich at his word, had accepted them purely and simply, the war was ended on the continent, by this very advantageous peace for France.[79]

However, three commissioners: Nesselrode, Hardenberg, and Stadion had drawn up, on 12 June, not without effort and tension, a plan for the bases of peace.[80] Austria would notify Napoléon of these bases which he must accept before 20 July and which it considered as "conditions *sina qua non* of peace": 1) The dissolution of the Duchy of Warsaw, 2) The enlargement of Prussia following this dissolution and by the cession of the city and territory of Danzig, 3) The restitution of the Illyrian provinces to Austria, 4) The re-establishment of the Hanseatic cities, at least of Hamburg and Lübeck, as independent cities, and an arrangement on the surrender of the other parts of the 32nd military division. To these four bases which would form the Austrian ultimatum, were added, 5) dissolution of the Confederation of the Rhine. Austria would push its insistence to the point of breaking off negotiations; 6) reconstruction of Prussia, approaching as closely as possible its extent before 1805. Austria would support this question with the same warmth as the preceding one.

The Prussians had raised very strong objections to the reduction of the Austrian ultimatum to the first four points. When challenged by Hardenberg, Stadion had to reassure him, and he did so in positive terms:

> In stating the four points which H. M. the Emperor of Austria would make his own cause, he had declared at the same time that he would still support the following two with all the weight of his mediation, that there could therefore never be any question of helping the Emperor Napoléon by force of arms, but that the two courts could count on the military efforts of Austria only for the first four.

The peace they were going to negotiate, said Hardenberg, must be something other than a bad armistice. England would never be satisfied with the first four points, and they would be deprived of English subsidies, which were so necessary. Nesselrode supported these observations. Metternich had foreseen them; in a telegram addressed to Stadion on 14 June, he informed him that the negotiations which were opening, leave to England the faculty of intervening there. The allies, while dealing in the first line with objects which agree with the views of England, separate themselves from them neither in form nor in substance. Thus the relations and engagements of Russia and Prussia towards England and Sweden remain intact.

Finally Kalisch's two allies declared "to accept negotiation only in the form of treating of preliminary points which would prepare the general peace in the event that England should wish to take part in it." Consequently it was stipulated:

> The two courts regard the negotiation opened at this moment only as preliminaries; any conditions beyond those proposed by Austria would still remain to be dealt with when England would take part in the negotiation and would have to negotiate on completely new bases, those of the compensations of maritime peace, joined to continental peace.

It was further resolved to invite England and Sweden to the negotiation. Finally "the definitive transaction to be concluded with Napoléon was to be preceded by the execution of the preliminary articles," and was to include, in addition to the four points, the evacuation of the Prussian fortresses of the Oder and of Danzig. All these precautions, and in particular the last, had only one reason: the fear that Napoléon would accept the first four conditions and in this case, the means of pushing him to break, by an unexpected demand, that he would consider dishonorable.

Metternich received a very vivid impression of this fear when, on 17 June he presented himself to Alexander at Reichenbach. The Emperor said, "But what will become of our cause if Napoléon accepts mediation?" Metternich replied:

> If he declines it, the armistice will cease as of right, and you will find us among the ranks of your allies. If he accepts it, the negotiation will show, beyond doubt, that he does not want to be wise, nor fair, and the result will be the same. In any case, we will thus have gained the time necessary to be able to establish our army in positions from where we can take the offensive.

There would always be time, according to him, to discover the other conditions, the reserve conditions, which would decide Napoléon to break if the first had induced him to negotiate. They would find there this advantage of having attracted him to negotiations, of having made the hope of peace shine before his armies, of having shaken his marshals who were weary, of seducing his ministers who breathed only treaties, finally of having him a compromise before the party of peace, which grew every day, which would make him solely responsible for the continuation of the war and would never forgive him for having refused so favorable a treaty. They would thus thwart his calculation which was to denounce to France the demands of the allies and to prove "by the sacrifices which are asked of her, the essential necessity of continuing the war."[81] It would be separated from France, which would amount to turning it militarily and taking it from the rear. The art would consist in presenting to the French the first four points as the only conditions of the treaty, not to speak to them about preliminaries to persuade the army and the public in France that it was a question of total and definitive peace. With one word, "yes," it was concluded and Austria took the side of France! Metternich excelled at these games of phantasmagoria.

But, at the same time, he became more and more involved with the allies, certain that Napoléon would refuse. On 18 June, the bases, with their gradations, were fixed. Metternich proposed to the Tsar that he send one of his trusted officers to the staff of Schwarzenberg, Napoléon's former auxiliary corps, which, detached from the French alliance, "would no longer be but one with that of the Emperor Franz II." Whereupon he returned to Gitschin. No sooner had he turned his head than mistrust resumed and the bases, even aggravated by points 5 and 6, seemed insufficient to the Russians.

Nesselrode sent him an urgent note on 19 June. Tsar Alexander declared to the Emperor Franz II that "it was impossible for him to conclude peace with France on the conditions which form the *sine qua non* of Austria ... All peace would only be a truce ... if, as the final result of so much effort and sacrifice, powerful barriers were not raised against France." What he meant by that were the barriers of the April 1805 treaty with England, those which Nesselrode himself set up in December 1812, that is to say the return of France to its former limits.

Metternich received this note on his return to Gitschin on the 21st. He also found there a letter from Maret inviting him to go to Napoléon in Dresden. Napoléon had heard of his interview with

Alexander. He wanted to maintain it in turn. Before facing this meeting which could decide the war, Metternich made a point of clearing everything with the allies, and to arrive at Napoléon with the coalition in his pocket. The arrival of Nesselrode made things easier for him. He arrived on the 23rd with a draft convention between Austria, Russia, and Prussia, prepared in a conference held on the 21st, "with the return of France, Austria and Prussia to their ancient limits."[82] But to declare it in advance would have been to arouse public opinion in France, to make the war popular, to unite Napoléon and the French people and to break the most insidious and most effective of the combinations of his diplomacy. He indoctrinated Nesselrode. He read to the Emperor Franz II a report which removed the sovereign's last hesitations. As a result, he pressed Bernadotte's accession and movements: "I admit that I am counting prodigiously on the effect of his cooperation," the military effect first, and political effect above all. Then, convinced, if not of abusing, at least of confusing Napoléon, he obtained from Franz II this declaration: "Once the war has begun, the three allied courts will set as the goal of their common efforts the articles set out by the Russian and Prussian cabinets in their 16 May notes, giving them the greatest extent."[83]

This note added to the four points of the Austrian ultimatum and to points 5 and 6 which Austria pledged to support: Austria as it was in 1805; the complete emancipation of Germany from French influence, which involved the abandonment of Westphalia and Berg; free Italy, in all its parts, from the government and influence of France, that is to say, the abandonment not only of Venetia, but of Lombardy, Piedmont, Tuscany, Rome, Parma, and Naples; the separation of Holland and France; the restoration of the Bourbons in Spain. These were, according to Metternich, the conditions for a good peace. It would remain, France expelled from Germany and Italy, to make peace excellent, by giving to these conditions "the greatest extent," which meant the left bank of the Rhine and the Netherlands, at least as far as the Scheldt.

The agreement which was established, on this principle, between Metternich and Nesselrode received the approval of Franz II, and thus were drawn up the articles of the Treaty of Reichenbach, between Austria, Russia, and Prussia, with a view to the event that Napoléon should reject the mediation of Austria. The first article was:

His Majesty the Emperor of Austria having invited the courts of Russia and Prussia to enter under his mediation into negotiations with France for a preliminary peace which could serve as a basis for a general peace, and His Majesty having fixed the conditions that he believes it necessary to restore a state of balance and lasting tranquility in Europe, he undertakes to declare war on France and to join his arms to those of Russia and Prussia if, until the 20 July of this year, France did not accept these conditions.

These conditions, listed in Article 2, were the first four points. But it was well stipulated that if Napoléon accepted them, they will only be used for a preliminary peace, being able to be used as a basis for a general peace. The text did not say that Russia and Prussia will not raise other demands in the negotiation, and, to mark their intentions, they added that the fate of the Duchy of Warsaw will be settled without France, by the three co-partnering powers. Article 6 made it very clear what the Allies' claims will be in the negotiations, indicating the conditions Austria promised to uphold if Napoléon rejected the four points. These were the articles stated by the Russian and Prussian cabinets in their note of 16 May, "giving them the widest scope." Within this scope one must understand the powerful barriers of the Russian note of 19 June, and the demands of England, without which Prussia and Russia pledged not to negotiate or sign peace.[84] Austria in turn undertook Article 7 "not to enter into any arrangement or negotiation except by common accord with Prussia and Russia," that is to say, with England. Austria will employ in the war "all the forces at her disposal," at least 150,000 men, who will join at least 150,000 Russians, and 80,000 Prussians.

These agreements were settled when, on 24 June, Metternich left for Dresden; but they were not signed until the 27th of June at Reichenbach, after Metternich's interview with Napoléon. This artifice of chancery would enable Metternich to speak to the Emperor with the authority of a coalition member and to attest, if need be, to his honor as a German count, that Austria was still free from all engagement.

Furnished with this talisman which made him invulnerable and, if need be, invisible, Metternich believed himself in a position to approach Napoléon, to disturb him, to force him to betray his hidden views and to draw him into the impasse; above all, to discover his conditions of peace and to appreciate by that how many points it would be necessary to unmask, four, five, or six, to be sure that he would refuse.

Bubna came and went from the allies to Napoléon, carrying notes and sayings.[85] He announced that Russia and Prussia had joined the mediation, but that England had refused. He left this impression, which Napoléon translated in a letter to the King of Württemberg:[86]

> England has declined the overtures which Russia and Prussia have offered her and seems resolved to make peace on principles which these powers, which no one will suspect of being favorable to me, have found so absurd and so inadmissible that they didn't even want to hear them. In the moment of their intoxication, the powers proposed to me as a basis of peace the treaty of Lunéville; England indignantly rejected it as too favorable to France.[87]

While waiting for things to take shape, Napoléon struck terrible examples in Germany, at Hamburg, where Davout had entered.[88] He tried to shake up and bring back public opinion in France, which was too inclined towards peace. He wrote to Savary:

> The tone of your correspondence does not please me; you always annoy me with the need for peace. I know better than you the situation of my empire. I want peace. I am more interested in it than anyone; but I will not make a peace which would be dishonoring and which would bring us back to a fiercer war in a month.

He wrote to Cambacérès:

> I have seen more than twenty letters from foreign ministers who write at home that we want peace at all costs in Paris, that my ministers send it to me every day. All the chatter of ministers about peace do my affairs the greatest harm. People in Paris have very false ideas if they believe that peace depends on me. The claims of the enemies are excessive and I know very well that a peace which would not be in conformity with the opinion that we have in France of the strength of the empire would be very frowned upon by everyone.[89]

He ordered Rémusat, in charge of the entertainment department, to get the actors to leave, and with some display, as if the whole Comédie-

Française, including tragedy, were to get under way. This caravan would make Paris, London, Spain think "we're having fun in Dresden."

They weren't having fun. They were morose, murmuring against war, longing for peace; the mere word armistice brought back a little good humor. Napoléon told them, "I see that you no longer want to go to war. Berthier would like to hunt in Grosbois, Rapp to live in his beautiful hôtel in Paris."[90] All had only one fear, and they expressed it, that "Napoléon does not decide quickly enough to subscribe to the enemy's conditions." In the midst of these harassments of his family, Napoléon found himself alone to judge affairs, to provide for them, and for the first time perhaps this isolation weighed on him.[91] He found himself hesitating between Maret, persuaded of Austrian avarice, who urged Napoléon to satisfy it, and Caulaincourt, infatuated with Russian disinterestedness, who urged Napoléon to throw himself into Alexander's arms.

Add what he learned from Bernadotte, the formidable effect of the intervention of this ex-marshal, the intrigues which must ensue, the reawakening of the old plots of 1800, 1804, 1808, 1809, further aggravated by the new prestige of the character. Add Murat's intrigues with Bentinck, denounced to him and which confirmed his presentiments only too well. Add the bad letters from Spain, where everything was going from bad to worse, where the French army was retreating, where the English were still advancing. A battle lost, and Spain would have to be evacuated.[92] Finally, the rumor that transpired in the reports of spies, of the comings and goings of soldiers, diplomats to Gitschin, Reichenbach, the arrival of the English, the mysterious movements of Metternich. It is understandable that Napoléon wanted to confer with this minister, to try to pierce up to date his views on peace, his views on the day after the congress, and above all the secrets of the allies as to what they were able to conclude, if Austria entered into their agreements, and to what extent.

### IV. Interview in Dresden

Napoléon was staying at the Marcolini Palace. On entering it on 26 June, Metternich was struck "by the expression of painful anxiety which could be read on the faces of the courtiers, the generals bedecked in gold" who thronged his way.[93] Berthier said to him in a low voice: "Don't forget that Europe needs peace, especially France, which only wants peace." Napoléon received him in a gallery, standing as he walked, sword at his side, hat under his arm. He came to meet him, asked for news of the Emperor, then his features darkened:

> If you want peace, why come so late? It seems that it no longer suits you to guarantee the integrity of the French Empire; why didn't you deny that you didn't say it earlier? I win two battles; you come to talk to me about armistice and mediation. Without your disastrous intervention, peace between the allies and me would be made today. Admit it, since Austria took the title of mediator, she is no longer on my side; she is no longer impartial, she is an enemy.

Metternich replied that it depended only on the Emperor to give peace to the world. Napoléon replied that he was ready to make peace, but rather than sign a dishonorable one, he would perish. "I wrote it to the emperor, my honor above all, and then peace!" He reproduced arguments familiar to him, which he gave to Schwarzenberg: "Your sovereigns born on the throne can allow themselves to be beaten twenty times and always return to their capital; I cannot, because I am an upstart soldier. My domination will not survive the day when I cease to be strong, and therefore to be feared." Then correcting himself: "Well, let's see, let's deal, I consent to it, what do you want?" Then Metternich, without specifying, spoke of respect for rights, of peace guaranteed under the aegis of an association of independent states. Napoléon said:

> Let's speak more clearly. I offered you Illyria to remain neutral. Does it suit you? My army is quite sufficient to bring the Russians and Prussians to their senses, and your neutrality is all I ask. – Oh! Sire...why shouldn't Your Majesty double your forces! It is up to you to fully dispose of ours. Yes, things have reached the point where we can no longer remain neutral; we must be with you or against you.[94]

Then Napoléon endeavored to ascertain the true state of the Austrian forces. He took Metternich to his study, where there were pointed cards. He affected to know everything, better than Metternich himself, and he argued about it, or rather he talked about it for more than an hour, Metternich giving him, here and there, a few replies, but avoiding giving him any information. Then they returned to the gallery and resumed their choppy dialogue, with the march interrupted by stops. These were the commitments of the allies, those of Austria, if there were any, that he wished to learn. He took a guess: "I know what happened between Prussia and Russia. There is talk of a treaty with a third power." But this "recognition" remained in vain. Metternich remained silent. Also silent on the conditions of peace that Austria would propose to the congress, that they would accept, that they would finally impose by armed mediation.

> Well what do you mean by peace? Do you want to strip me? Do you want Italy, Brabant, Lorraine? I won't give up an inch of ground. I make peace on the status quo ante bellum... I will even give part of the Duchy of Warsaw to Russia; I won't give you anything, because you didn't beat me; I will give nothing to Prussia, because she has betrayed me; if you wanted Western Gallicia, if Prussia wants a part of its former possessions, it can be done, but against compensation. Then you will have to compensate my allies. Illyria cost me 200,000 men to conquer; if you want to have it, you must spend an equal number of men.

This Illyria offered by allusion, taken up by threat, Napoléon no doubt thought to move Metternich by it and, thereby, to provoke him to some imprudence. Metternich was still silent. Then Napoléon showed that he had seen the plans of his enemies:

> By the way, you want Italy, Russia wants Poland, Prussia Saxony, and England wants Holland and Belgium. You all aspire only to the dismemberment of the French Empire. And I would have to evacuate Europe, half of which I still occupy, bring back my legions with their butts in the air behind the Rhine, the Alps and the Pyrenees to rely for a doubtful future on the generosity of those for whom I am today the victor! In what attitude do they want to put me in front of the French people? The Emperor is strangely mistaken if he believes that a mutilated throne can be a refuge in France for his daughter and his grandson. Ah! Metternich, how much did England give you to decide to play this role against me?

As he was gesticulating, his hat fell on the floor. Metternich hinted that fortune could betray France: Napoléon had only an army of children. Napoléon, then, would got carried away as to say: "You are not a soldier. You don't know what goes on in the soul of a soldier. I grew up on battlefields and a man like me cares little for the lives of a million men."[95] He added that in Russia only 30,000 French had died. The rest were Polish, German. So Metternich, very well informed of what was being said in Paris and even in the Emperor's entourage: "Why make such a statement to me within four walls? Let's open the doors, and may your words resound from one end of France to the other! It is not the cause that I represent that will lose out." They walked with long strides, and the hat, on the floor, came and went, kicked by Napoléon. There was a silence. Metternich watched this disastrous hat; smiling, very upright, very fat, like a man who is no longer playing the courtier and picking up objects from the ground. Napoléon sensed the ridicule, stooped, took the hat, and the incident created a diversion.[96] Night came, Napoléon uttered a few more threats, recriminated against the marriage: it was a fault, "It may cost me my throne, but I will bury the world in ruins." This bluster appeased him; he politely dismissed Metternich, escorted him to the door: "We will see each other again, I hope!" And putting his hand on his shoulder: "Do you know what will happen? You will not make war on me." Metternich had not uncovered Austria's peace terms, those which would hand it over to the allies if Napoléon refused them. He had contented himself with saying that his master, in the event of this refusal, would recover his liberty of action; as for Napoléon, he had neither accepted nor declined mediation, and he had only formally refused a cession of territory.

Metternich had therefore not, in procedure at least, accomplished his mission. He resumed and continued the talks on forms with Maret. He had a serious reason for dragging the discussion out. As far as he was concerned, there was no doubt that it would be war, because Austria was committed to it in the event of Napoléon's refusal of the conditions which would be proposed, and these conditions would certainly be rejected by Napoléon. But, if he had paid off in his conversation with the Emperor, the figures that Napoléon had detailed to him, left him with doubts. "I was wondering if it wouldn't be desirable to gain a few weeks to complete our order of battle." He sent a courier to Schwarzenberg: "Would the extension of the armistice be useful to us? What would be the last possible term?"

While awaiting the answer, he slipped notes with Maret, and resumed the debate on the continuation or total or partial suspension of the alliance of 1812,[97] which gave Schwarzenberg's courier time to arrive; he asked for 20 days: "I shall consider myself lucky to obtain this delay, but a single day more would put me in embarrassment." It was the extension of the armistice to 10 August. It was difficult to obtain it from Napoléon, more difficult still to obtain it from the allies. Metternich wrote to his father, "I succeeded by the boldest stroke, by prolonging the armistice for twenty days, which I took it upon myself to stipulate, in the name of the powers, without saying a word to them, because from their knowledge, the thing became impossible."[98]

These dilatory remarks had led him to 29 July. Napoléon had formally renounced the alliance; but on the congress there was no agreement. They were discussing the accession of England. Metternich had listened a lot. Marshals, generals, diplomats "expressed their ever-increasing concerns." On the evening of the 29th, he announced his departure for the following morning; in the night, Napoléon had changed his mind. What reflections, what calculations decided him? A letter from Maret to Narbonne allows us to surmise: the hope of inducing Austria to prolong the negotiation, and, when the term came, if the allies denounced the armistice, the obstinate hope that Austria would remain calm, that he would continue to negotiate while fighting, and finally the belief that Austria remaining neutral, he would then be in a position to crush the Russians and the Prussians.[99] On the 30th, just as Metternich was about to get into the carriage, Napoléon sent for him, and the convention was signed there and then. Mediation of Austria for general or continental peace was accepted; a congress of French, Russians, and Prussians would meet, under this mediation, before 5 July, in Prague, and, verbally, Napoléon gave up to denounce the armistice before 10 August; Austria reserved the right to have the same commitment accepted in Russia and Prussia.[100]

Schwarzenberg gave a date of 10 August. Metternich had the courage to propose it to Napoléon, and the skill to obtain it. However, if Napoléon consented to it with so much ease, it was because he considered this extension to be profitable for him. "After 10 August, the armistice is against us," wrote Maret, some time later.[101]

On the evening of the 30th, Napoléon received a courier from Spain.[102] This country was lost. Joseph, with his treasures, his many pictures, his confidants, his government, his house, his court, fell back heavily on France.[103] It was not really a flight like in Prussia in 1806, but rather a move with coaches and escort, like that of the Bourbons of Naples or that of the Braganzas when Napoléon decreed that they had ceased to reign. Wellington's victory at Vittoria on 21 June turned it into a rout. This victory uncovered the French frontier, and Napoléon, who had planned to take England from the rear by the Indies, found himself taken from the rear by the English on the Pyrenees.

The convention of 30 June had fixed 5 July for the meeting of the envoys. This day passed without any news of the adhesion of the allies; now, without prolongation of the armistice, Napoléon would not consent to open the congress. He deferred the appointment of his plenipotentiaries, and he contented himself with giving, on 9 July, at Narbonne, the order to go to Prague, in his capacity as ambassador to the Court of Vienna, telling him to inquire about the extension of the armistice, on the projects of the powers, and in particular, to observe the armaments, preparations and military positions of Austria. Narbonne set out the same day. On the 11th he wrote from Prague that he had seen Metternich in passing. This minister agreed that peace was in the hands of Austria "in the sense that if she united with France, the allies would not even think of trying to fight."[104]

Metternich went to his master. The ratification of the 30 June convention was singularly dragging on. He succeeded in removing the resistance of the Russians and Prussians only by the promise he made to them and the guarantees he gave them of very effective assistance from Austria after 10 August. Nesselrode said,

> Prince Metternich offered us a conference. I went there with Prince Hardenberg and the Baron de Humboldt. This conference was one of the stormiest I have ever attended, but the importance of rallying Austria was so great that it had to pass through all the conditions it stipulated. The sovereigns fled no less irritated than their representatives at Ratjiborszye at the idea of a congress and the delay it brought to the resumption of hostilities.[105]

Thus the delay which Napoléon consented in part by condescending towards Austria and with a view to obtaining its alliance, or at least ensuring its neutrality, but Austria employed it, in agreement with the allies, to prepare the formidable aggression of the three armies united against Napoléon, and at the same time diversions which might prove fatal to him, against his lieutenants dispersed in northern Germany, as much to restrain the peoples as to supply the troops. These considerations led the allies to deal with Bernadotte.

This ingenious Gascon, who with a thrust would, he said, annihilate the Corsican, and with a slash of the marshals, his former comrades-in-arms, was very slow in translating his boasting into exploits.[106] Alexander feared that, his pin drawn from the game, Bernadotte would re-embark for his adopted kingdom, or at least would content himself with a war of containment, sparing his army, to impose himself on everyone, during the peace. He summoned him. The fact is that Bernadotte, warned that Napoléon was making common cause with Denmark, had no more resources of ambition except on the side of the allies.[107]

He found Alexander and Friedrich-Wilhelm III at Trachenberg Castle in Silesia on 9 July. The soldiers who on 16 May had drawn up the first war plan at Wurschen, then prepared its extension. They called Bernadotte to their conferences, both to secure his support and to receive from his mouth advice on the art of beating the French. The Austrians did not sign the protocol which was adopted on 12 July, but this protocol nevertheless regulated their role as if already there was no doubt about their participation in the war. Stadion, who was at Trachenberg, was not officially informed, but it is impossible that without the admission of Austria, Russians, Prussians and Swedes thus disposed of his future contingent in the coalition. The plan decided upon at Trachenberg proceeded from the Napoléonic system, to act in masses, to attack, to push to the limit:[108]

> It has been agreed to adopt as a general principle that all the forces of the allies should always go to the side where the greatest forces of the enemy will be found...; 1) The combined armies must, before the expiration of the armistice, be returned, part of the allied army in Silesia, 90 to 100,000 strong..., to Jung-Bunzlau and Brandeis, to join in the most short notice to the Austrians, in order to form with it in Bohemia a total of 200 to 220,000 combatants...; 2) The army of the Royal Prince of Sweden will assemble with a force of about 70,000 men, to move towards the Elbe, heading immediately for Leipzig...; 3) The Austrian army, united with the allied army, will deploy, according to the circumstances either by Eger and Ihof, or in Saxony, or in Silesia, or on the side of the Danube; 4) All the united armies will take the offensive and the enemy's camp will be their rendezvous.

In his conversations with his new friends, Bernadotte bewildered them, bewildering himself with his blandishments; here and there his thought escaped him. Austria was to be, he told Stadion, "the tomb of Napoléon's greatness."[109] He strove for this, but he prided himself on bringing neither hatred nor anger to it. "Relation by marriage to the family of the Emperor of the French, long cherished by him, I cannot be his personal enemy. I am willing to reduce him to the old bounds of France, but not to contribute to overthrowing him, and his family, from the throne." He did not intend to be "the wandering knight of the liberty of Europe... It is to have Norway that I join the great cause." However, if it happened that "by an internal revolution, Napoléon lost the throne of France," he implied that he could be called there in his place. He said a little earlier to a French *émigré*,[110]

> They no longer want Bonaparte in France, but they ask me not to act against my native country, not to lose thereby the popularity I enjoy. If Napoléon is overthrown, I can to play the greatest role possible, to dispose of the regency.

At Stralsund, where he returned on 17 July, he found brilliant encouragement. It was a letter from his stormy friend Mme de Staël, dated from London. She had seen the Prince Regent, Castlereagh, Canning. "Society England came to my house. I miss Sweden as a homeland, because your fiery gaze is my homeland. God grant that the war in which you will triumph is renewed!"[111]

At the same time she informed him of the probable arrival of their friend Moreau. The conqueror of Hohenlinden was not a candidate for the imperial throne; at most he would be in the consulate of a republic restored by the magnanimity of Alexander. "Besides," he wrote to Bernadotte, "if the nation desires the Bourbons, I would see them take over the government with pleasure, under conditions which ensure freedom." But blinded as he was by hatred of Napoléon, Moreau was not yet so blinded as to forget the horror inspired in his compatriots by the allied emigrants abroad. "I am ready to enter France at the head of the French troops, but I do not conceal from you my repugnance to march there at the head of the foreign troops," he said.[112] In short, a civil war, auxiliary to the invasion, here is that turning movement he thought of serving his country!

Alexander did not reserve him for this equivocal role. By calling him to his staff, he called there a great name, capable of disturbing minds in the French camp, a contagious example and perhaps a secret of victory. He had no idea of making him a [General] Monk of the Bourbons or the [President] Washington of a republic. When his thoughts began to float towards France, what he cherished in his dreams was a constitutional monarchy, *à la* Staël, *à la* Benjamin-Constant, indebted, disarmed, garlanded, of which he would be the protector and the idol, and whose king, created by him, drawn by him from the ranks, would reign at his discretion and would take, in his escort, on his left, his rank beside Friedrich-Wilhelm III. These daydreams brought him singularly closer to Bernadotte, and Bernadotte, whose political flair was singularly keen, did not fail to lend himself to this game wherever he suspected some malcontent to cling to. "If we fell from a cloud, Moreau, you and I, in the middle of the Place Vendôme," he wrote to Lafayette, "we would at first be a little embarrassed by our persons, but who knows if it would not result in a revolution?" And here was a new intrigue which matured in the shadow of the armistice, becoming entangled in Metternich's plot, already so complicated.

### VI. Congress of Prague

The Prague Congress was only a solemn sham.[113] Everything flowed in formalities, everything happened in merry-go-rounds, false entries, false exits, staging games. On 12 July the Russian envoy, Anstett, and the Prussian Humboldt arrived. They were the first; they were keen to occupy the place, for their role in the comedy was to prevent everything:[114] the object of the congress, Anstett's instructions said, was to specify the real conditions of peace and to convince Austria of the impossibility of living in peace with Napoléon, that is, of declaring war on him. The congress, if it led to anything, was to result only in an agreement on preliminary conditions: if Austria seemed to want to moderate those which had been decided upon at Reichenbach, Anstett would oppose it and would immediately demand something more rigorous. If Napoléon accepted them, Anstett would say he had no powers to treat, even *sub spe rati*; he could only take note *ad referendum* of Napoléon's consent. Finally, the allies should not lose sight of the fact that no definitive peace could be concluded without the consent of England. Anstett, personally an enemy of Napoléon, had only to consult his hatred to fully penetrate his instructions.[115] Humboldt received similar ones.

Metternich, before going to Prague, went to take his emperor's orders at the castle of Brandeis, and tried to obtain his final consent to war, for he had had to negotiate, steal with his master as much as with Napoléon and with the Russians. Franz II, short and sly, was still worried, he did not dare, without demonstrable necessity, to face this scandal: the break with his son-in-law, and face this peril: a fourth war with Napoléon, on the Austrian border. He had to be brought there step by step; "Napoléon had to utter the word and force him to break off." Metternich worked to familiarize him with the idea of the impossibility of avoiding war if Napoléon refused a peace based on "a fair balance."[116] This prince, whose scruples were, in reality, only precautions, was sometimes frightened by the dangerous games of his minister. He considered him too reckless and also too shrewd; but, deep down, he felt on board with him, and wanted him to succeed. He saw in Metternich, and not without some concern for jealousy, another self, more intelligent, who offended him; however, he followed him, but on tiptoe, constantly turning to make sure that retreat remained an option. He let him engage in such a way as to profit from war if it became inevitable or presented itself to his advantage; at the same time he reserved his consent, so as to be able to give, without sin, all the words of honor that Napoléon would need, in case Napoléon should decide for peace, especially in case he should prevail in war, which would allow him to assert his good faith and obtain some relief.

To persuade him, Metternich sent him, on 12 July, a long apologetic memorandum in which his whole maneuver was summed up. The Emperor read it; but did not surrender yet. The next day, on arriving in Prague, Metternich saw Humboldt. This Minister wrote, "In clearly giving me to understand that he believed war to be inevitable, he was saying that the impossibility of a solid peace, down to the last evidence, must be shown by the present negotiations, to the Emperor Franz."[117]

This solid peace was nearer than one would have dared to hope, which news from Spain revealed. Vittoria looked decidedly like a disaster wrote Bubna, on 5 July, from Dresden where he was collecting impressions, "The disorder must be like that of the retreat from Moscow; the French generals lost all their artillery, all the baggage, including that of the king; they must find themselves cut off from communication with Bayonne." Bernadotte being bound, Metternich took care of Murat.[118] Mier wrote to him from Naples: "The king refuses the 20,000 men that Napoléon asks of him. If the French gazettes continue to insult him, he will dismiss the minister from

France." All the Emperor's methods persuaded him more and more that the Emperor Napoléon nourished against him hostile projects... "that it only takes a *senatus-consultum* to deprive him of his kingdom." Napoléon spared him only because of the war: victorious, he would crack down. "Their Majesties are impatiently awaiting the response to Cariati's proposals as to what action to take in the event of war between Austria and France. The king is still determined to support our interests. Please give me your instructions." These instructions were specific:

> Will the king, until events have developed, observe neutrality? In that case, he must not interfere with our operations, and he should come to a secret arrangement in this sense. Does he want to take an active part in the war? In this case it is necessary to come to a formal treaty with Austria and join the coalition.

Metternich promised absolute secrecy, and he added this insinuation:

> We share the conviction that the King can only ensure his existence definitively by linking it to that of Austria. How to effectively hide that he has done too much not to have attracted all the animadversion of the Emperor of the French?[119]

However, the French plenipotentiaries did not hasten to appear. It was because the hesitation of the allies to prolong the armistice, the delays in the conferences opened on this subject at Neumarck the claim of Austria to ensure the direction of the congress, to become the broker and the privileged agent in exchange for peace and to collect in kind its fees; its armaments, the unambiguous movement of its troops, the comings and goings of diplomats and soldiers at the Russian headquarters, the secret advice Napoléon received on the Trachenberg conferences, confirmed his secret suspicions.[120] Was Austria marching to war? Until the last moment he hesitated to believe it. On 16 July alone he designated Narbonne and Caulaincourt as plenipotentiaries; he did not sign the decree until the 18th.

The Emperor wanted peace, said Maret to Narbonne on 17 July 1813, but if it was not to take place, it must be ensured that he did not have to declare himself before 10 August and that hostilities not resume until 1 September. "The events in Spain – the evacuation of Madrid, the battle of Vittoria – give important reasons for seeking to gain time." The Emperor wanted to know the true situation of things in this country. He wanted to wait for the harvest: "His Majesty needs by opening the countryside to find the barns full" and to measure "the immensity of the forces" that he concentrated in Franconia, Bavaria, and Italy. Finally he hoped that passions would calm down and that the game of diplomacy would use the delay, at least as much as the activity of the intendants. Napoléon realized Austria's interest in extending the armistice: Metternich "hopes for peace," he needed time for negotiations; it rearmed, and it would be stronger on 10 September than on 10 August; therefore he must lend himself to the prolongation of the armistice, and Napoléon flattered himself with profiting from it in spite of himself, against him if need be.

If the hope of involving Austria obliged the enemies to prolong the negotiations until September, that is what the Emperor wanted, as Muret said.[121] Or, if the allies denounced the armistice, Austria would remain quiet and the negotiations continued; that is what the Emperor prefers. He was strong enough to leave 100,000 men in an observation corps at Dresden, and go and crush the Russians and Prussians. These three chances, calculated at Dresden, during the convention of 30 June, were all favorable.

As for thinking that Austria itself would denounce the armistice and turn against France, he refused to do so, despite all the clues he had: "If Austria were to come out against us without hearing us, there would be nothing to do. But we can't stop at this proposition..." They were not ready; it will take 40 days.

The instructions drawn up on 22 July for Narbonne and Caulaincourt, prescribed them to

> allow nothing that does not breathe the desire for peace, and an honorable peace. They must not rush the progress of the negotiations. They will let everything be said and will respond by taking *ad referendum*. They will send a courier while awaiting the reply.... His Majesty does not reject the possibility that new circumstances, new combinations may lead him to enter into a system with Austria, but in the present situation of things, such is not his thought. Austria, being mediator, has nothing to ask and nothing to obtain.

An assignment would encourage him to want a new one. It was in the interest of France that it wins nothing. As for the bases, indicate only one *uti possidetis ante bellum*. "There can only be talks in the negotiations of States whose fate has changed since 1812 and not before." This was followed by meticulous prescriptions on precedents, the communication of powers, ceremonial, written negotiations, all preliminaries and all procedural deadlines. In transmitting these instructions to Narbonne, Maret commented on them: "You will not lend yourselves until further notice to any official communication; you will limit yourself to relations of etiquette and politeness."

Napoléon did not yet despair, thanks to these complications of form and under the cloak, of insinuating himself between the allies and dividing them.[122] We read in the common instruction of the 22nd: "The intention of the Emperor is to negotiate with Russia a peace which will be glorious for this power and which will make Austria pay, by the loss of its influence in Europe, the price of her bad faith and the fault she committed in violating the alliance of 1812 and thus bringing France and Russia together." The next day, 23, Maret wrote to Narbonne: "You couldn't be too well with M. de Metternich. The reluctance of the Russians to negotiate is a reason to see if we can come to an agreement with Austria. Its neutrality would win us out." Maret concluded: "You will receive with this letter more powers; until the convention is signed in Neumarck, you must have your hands tied." Informed that he would be immediately, Napoléon set out on the 24th for Mainz, where he had summoned Maria-Louisa. He wanted to prepare this Empress for the official break with Austria, and at the same time to maintain family relations between her and her father which would make it possible, when the time came, to reconnect with Franz II and his Government. He wanted to demonstrate before all of Europe his conjugal faith, his paternal love, and to show that his attachments of heart were not at the mercy of politics.[123] He was thinking of death, especially since he had seen Bessières and Duroc fall very close to him; perhaps he had even sought it, perhaps he would find himself forced to seek it in disaster: the Empress's regency then appeared to him as the safety of the Empire and the guarantee of the King of Rome.[124] He wanted to give Maria-Louisa his last instructions. Finally, he was concerned with ensuring retirement in the event of an unfortunate war.

When Caulaincourt learned of his instructions, he deplored them. His conviction of the necessity of peace was hurt, his zeal hampered, his policy disconcerted. He wrote it to the Emperor: "Whatever my repugnance for such illusory negotiations, I understand above all my duties and I obey. Tomorrow I will be on my way." He begged the Emperor not to make the break with Austria inevitable:

> Austria is already too compromised to retreat, if the peace of the Continent does not reassure her. Your Majesty knows very well that it is not the cause of this power that I pleaded with her. Certainly it's not even his 150,000 bayonets that I want to remove from the battlefield, although this consideration deserves some attention, but it is the uprising of Germany which the old ascendancy of this power may bring about, which I beg Your Majesty to avoid at all costs.[125]

It was too late. Envoys from Russia and Prussia asked Metternich what Austria would do if Napoléon broke the armistice before 10 August. Metternich answered, on 23 July, that his master would consider this act as an offense to the mediator, and that the allies could, by this very fact, enter Austria. He only negotiated to reach the term fixed by Schwarzenberg.

On 25 July a conference was held between this general, Metternich, and Radetzky.[*] Informed of the commitments made by Bernadotte at Trachenberg, the Austrians decided, at the request of Tsar Alexander, that the Russian corps intended to go to Bohemia to link its operations to those of the Austrian army could enter as early as 10 August if, on the 9th, the preliminary peace was not signed. Only then did the allies agree to ratify the extension of the armistice verbally agreed on 30 June between Napoléon and Metternich. Franz II thus eventually opened his border to the Russians.[126]

Russia and Prussia were both tied to England. England then said its word, which henceforth, in all the affairs of the coalition, remained the last. The English general Nugent was at Prague, in communication with Metternich, in communication with Lord Cathcart, who had remained close to the allies. He communicated to him instructions which he had received from Castlereagh, dated 5 July. Nugent conferred on the 27th, with Metternich.[127] England appropriated the Russian and Prussian program of 16 May, the same as in the Treaty of Reichenbach of 27 June, Austria had eventually adopted and to which the allies reserved giving "the greatest extent," was already the reconstruction of Austria on the scale of 1805, the Confederation of the Rhine dissolved, Holland evacuated, and the abandonment of Italy. Thus, Austria had not yet communicated to

---

[*] Johann Josef, Graf Radetzky von Radetz (1766-1858), Czech general.

Napoléon its four preliminary points, and it was agreed in advance that of the four allies, three would not conclude peace on these conditions, and Austria agreed with them. It was enough for Napoléon to refuse the minimum for this strange mediator to join the allies and demand the maximum. It is very likely that the same courier brought conclusive words on the article of subsidies, and guarantees, at least verbal, on that of the indemnities of Italy, this essential chapter of the Austrian peace, from Leoben to the treaty of 1805, in passing through Lunéville.[128] In any case the four-way cartel was, in fact, knotted against France, and the adhesion of England carried away the English peace concerted already by Alexander, that is to say the conditions of the treaty of April 1805, the return to the old limits. During this decisive interview, as Nugent expressed some fears that the arrival of Caulaincourt would delay or prevent the war. Metternich replied to him, "It will make no difference, for the conditions proposed are such that they will be very difficult to accept, and moreover, they may be made worse." Franz in turn gave his approval on 2 August. Metternich said, "Never had a monarch had the entrails of the state like him."[129] And from then on, the tone rose. Count Hardenberg wrote to Munster on 28 July:

> It is difficult for me to express to Your Excellency the change which has taken place in the last few days in the Emperor's dispositions and in the tone taken by Count Metternich and all those who until recently spoke only of peace. Today we only talk about war and its necessity. Count Metternich repeats on every occasion that he no longer burdens himself with correspondence and notes, nor with four or six conditions of peace; that war is needed. (He adds) It is to Napoléon himself that this result is due.

It was only a question of winning on 10 August, that is to say, of moving towards rupture by putting formalities into it and by throwing the responsibility on Napoléon. These forms were the whole object of the exchange of notes which took the disappointing name of the Congress of Prague. Of all these forms, the simplest and most effective was to reveal and notify Napoléon of the famous bases only at the last hour and when there was barely time to reply by return post.

Narbonne was already in Prague; Caulaincourt joined him there on 28 July. "From what M. de Narbonne told me," he wrote to Maret on arriving on 28 July, "we are here on a volcano and the moments are counted; our delays had a bad effect. Everything I hear makes me doubly regret that the Emperor has tied your hands to you, as to me, more than he had promised." He untied them himself. Sorry to find himself in Prague "without the means to do good" as he understood it, he took them on, with his private authority.[130]

He went the same day to see Metternich who paid him back on the spot, as usual, his official visit. Caulaincourt was alone. "Stripping off his diplomatic character," he asked Metternich if he was surprised to see him in Prague.[131] Metternich replied that he viewed his appointment "as a happy achievement." Caulaincourt resumed,

> Certainly, if you start from the point of view of intentions. I speak to you today as an old friend and the man who knows the individuals and the issues as well as I do. We will talk tomorrow as envoys. Well, how about peace? – It depends on one man. – Everything depends on a preliminary question: have you decided not to accept a neutrality for which you will be offered advantages, and to go to war with us, or not? The Emperor believes you want peace, or failing that, well-paid neutrality. – Well! write to Napoléon that if he wants to get lost, he has only to follow these ideas; that we will go to war, that nothing can prevent the declaration of war on the 11th, only the signing of peace on the 10th. In any case, resumed Caulaincourt, do not expect a negotiation before the return of the Emperor, which will not take place until the 5th. I'm here with no instructions other than to delay. We will come to you with all the quibble questions. (Then) What will the Emperor do the day when he is certain that all his positions on the Elbe are turned, that you and the allies are stronger than him? I don't know... Ask for anything that is fair and especially anything that presents the idea of a real basis for pacification, you will get it more easily than a little, because Napoléon will say of it: Austria is decided on war rather than a truce; if you ask little of him, he will make no sacrifice for peace and he will believe that he is coming to terms with you at the expense of the belligerent powers...

He would have added as Metternich told Anstett: "Just tell me if you have enough troops to make us reasonable for once?"[132] On both questions, politics and the military, Metternich replied to the duke "that he would be served as he wished." Whereupon, as he was taking his leave, Caulaincourt made to him this declaration of more consequence than all the chancellery notes and all the written haggling:[133]

> You do not see in me the representative of the Emperor's whims, but of his true interest and that of France. I am just as European in present matters as you can be. Bring us back to France by peace or by war, and you will be blessed by 30 million French people and by all the enlightened servants and friends of the Emperor.[134]

These remarks were too significant and Metternich found in them the last encouragement for the scabrous operation which remained for him to carry out, that is to say, to break the ambiguity which he had so artfully maintained and to declare formally, what would be, after the 10 August, in the role of Austria. He explained it to Caulaincourt, who wrote on 30 July to the Minister,

> From the various conversations I have had with him, and in which I thought I had to confine myself to listening, it seems to me that things are much more mature than people think in Dresden. The result of all he told me is that Austria will do everything for peace, but that she is seriously prepared for war and is even determined to do so, in case peace does not come. According to him, Austria is in a situation which does not allow it to be neutral.

Metternich said it, with this mental restriction that his engagements had been taken, but that in taking them he had reserved the right not to reveal them until 10 August; he was concerned to spin the defection until that date and to prepare Napoléon to receive official notice of it: when he sent it, he would have saved form and would be in a position to respond to the French: the Emperor wanted it! Caulaincourt understood it with an ulterior idea, that peace was possible, that by giving oneself to Austria one would procure this honorable and salutary peace and that those who would be its instruments would have deserved the country well. The same day, 30 July, he collected, in the company of Narbonne, this declaration by Metternich:[135]

> It will probably only be on the 10th day that we will know the Emperor's thoughts, and this day can be peace or war. But be sure that, after this day of the 10th, nothing can prolong the armistice. I give you my word here that we will arrive at this time without Austria having the shadow of an engagement with any other power, and that only now will it be decided with whom we will fight. We very much want it not to be against you, but we have great difficulty in hoping for it. What is impossible is for us to remain neutral.[136]

But the same day, Metternich wrote to Stadion, at the headquarters of the allies:[137]

> M. de Caulaincourt, who is animated by the best spirit, confirmed to me that from my trip to Dresden the Emperor Napoléon is under the most complete illusion as to the true position of things. Disconcerted for a long time in all his calculations, always clinging in preference to the idea that flatters his views, he also seems completely convinced, at the present time, that Austria will never take sides against him, that he harbored the conviction in Moscow that the Emperor Alexander would lend himself to peace.

And further:

> M. de Wacquant goes to the Allied headquarters to remain there as military commissioner. He is furnished by Prince Schwarzenberg with a letter of credence for the general-in-chief of the Russian and Prussian armies. His orders are to follow in all respects the directions Your Excellency may wish to give him.[138]

However, there remained a concern: if Napoléon accepted the conditions that would be put to him? And an unknown:

> It's hard to imagine how it would even be physically possible to come to a conclusion in five days time. The fact, however, is not impossible with the particular character of man on which peace ultimately depends.

Gentz wrote, August 4:[139]

> For a fortnight the appearance of our cabinet has been absolutely changed. The Emperor and some of his special confidants who would consent to war only because they no longer knew how to combat the reasonings of M. de Metternich or thwart the skillful measures by which he dragged them on in spite of themselves, are now declared themselves and no longer see any other chance or other choice. This change has been brought about in part by the progress which armaments have made and by the courage which an enormous mass of men and united means inspires in the most fearful; but largely also by the unheard-of and inexplicable conduct of Napoléon. The only key to this conduct is found in the supposition that he never seriously believed that Austria would take part in the war; and this supposition has been confirmed to us again by Caulaincourt, who knows him as well as anyone.

Squabbling began: there was endless debate whether the role of the mediator would be to carry letters, to carry words, or to settle verbal controversies; whether Metternich would act as broker or arbitrator; whether one would govern according to the precedents of Ryswick, those of Teschen, or those of Rastadt, the procedure of this congress condemned in advance never to open.[140]

Napoléon returned to Dresden, considering the resumption of hostilities as henceforth inevitable, at the end of his patience with his two families, the natural and the ally, his brothers and his father-in-law.[141] Let the King of Westphalia know, he instructed Berthier, in Mainz, that "if he does not submit to obeying all the marshals," he will never have a command in the French army. "What has just happened in Spain is making people increasingly aware of the importance of holding on to these principles... that war is a profession, that you have to learn it. The King of Spain, to whom I once made similar observations, is in tears at not having understood them well."

His ambassadors did not give him more satisfaction, as he considered them insufficient, entangled in the plots of Metternich. However, what did this minister mean when he declared to the French: "It will only be at this moment – 10 August – that it will be decided who we will fight with." What were, definitively, those conditions of peace which he affirmed that if accepted they would retain Austria; if they were repulsed, they would throw it into the camp of the allies? Metternich did not yet explain it in official form.

Could it be those which Bubna had insinuated on 16 May, those which Metternich had indicated on the 7th at Narbonne and which were more extensive?

On 5 August, Napoléon dictated to Maret a confidential instruction for Caulaincourt to find out, under the seal of secrecy,

> in what manner Austria understands that peace can be made, and whether, the Emperor Napoléon adhering to his proposals, Austria would make common cause with us, or whether she would remain neutral; as soon as the Emperor is certain of Austria's word, he will give instructions accordingly to his plenipotentiaries. (To make known) that one wishes in twenty-four hours to write its conditions under its dictation (of Metternich); that in three days your answer will be given; that His Majesty wishes M. de Metternich to be very sure of the Emperor of Austria's approval.

Caulaincourt received this letter on 6 August and immediately went to Metternich; but this minister had gone out. Time was lost. Finally, Caulaincourt met him in the evening and communicated to him in complete confidence.[142] To be foreseen, it did not seem any less em-barrassing. Metternich once thought it highly doubtful that it was "even physically possible to come to a conclusion in five days time." There were only four left. Napoléon's expressed desire that Metter-nich "be very sure of the Emperor of Austria's approval" provided him with the means to gain two days out of these four. He went to fetch this assurance at Brandeis, where the Emperor was. He also esti-mated Napoléon's next step dictated by his anxiety about the arma-ments of Austria. "The more he seems to be afraid of us, the firmer you have to talk to him; the more he seeks to separate us from our allies, the closer we must bond with them."

Caulaincourt had urged Metternich to force the note. Metter-nich, who knew Napoléon very well, could not flatter himself that he would intimidate him by raising the bar. Quite the contrary. But, desiring "to give the allied courts a new proof of our firmness and of a loyalty which must bind them more intimately to us"; judging that Napoléon, having promised secrecy, could not publish these condit-ions and use them "to justify in the eyes of France and her allies the renewal of the war"; persuaded that even rigorous conditions would be approved in France and that in any case Napoléon would be reproached there for having rejected them, he did not hesitate to advise his master to increase the points from four to six, a sure way, according to him,[143] to decide the refusal. If Napoléon, whom he considered "almost certain," pushed them back, Austria will have shown its firmness and loyalty to the allies. If Napoléon accepted them, this reply had the advantage of shortening the transactions and making their conclusion possible. He was so convinced of the refusal, that he had commissioned Gentz to write the manifesto of rupture.[144] But Metternich considered this case "very unlikely." The Emperor, decidedly won over to war, "no longer seeing the possibility of arriving at peace as a result of the negotiat-ions established at Prague," considered himself "entitled to present his ultimatum."

Metternich returned to Prague on the evening of the 7th, communicated his reply to Humboldt and Anstett, and saw Caulaincourt. After asking him for the secret,[145] "what he is about to say must never be quoted," he continued: "Austria is still not linked either with Russia or with Prussia." It would be "for the cause of Europe if peace is not made on the 10th."

> The current gait is a gait of strength or finesse. His Majesty (the Emperor of Austria) could have stopped at the natural idea that the Emperor Napoléon only wants to know the views of the powers, in order to draw from them some means to justify the war and to continue it. But, in this very hypothesis, which His Majesty rejects, he believes his views so just and so much in the interest of France and his son-in-law, that he would still find a reason to explain himself. If it is a step of force, which is the opinion to which the emperor attaches himself, it is necessary to explain oneself, to speak clearly and frankly. It is what I am going to do.

He then read the Emperor's instructions:

> Knowing by preliminary confidential explanations the conditions which the courts of Russia and Prussia *seem to set for peaceful arrangements*, and uniting myself to their points of view, because I regard these conditions as necessary for the well-being of my States and of the other powers, and as the only ones which can really lead to general peace, I do not hesitate to state the articles which contain *my ultimatum*. I expect a yes or a no on the 10th. I have decided to declare on the 11th that I join my forces with those of the allies...

The conditions followed. "I wrote them based on what he told me," Caulaincourt reported.[146]

> Dissolution of the Duchy of Warsaw and its distribution between Austria, Russia and Prussia; hence Danzig to Prussia.
>
> Restoration of Hamburg and Lubeck as Hanseatic free cities and eventual arrangement and bound to general peace on the other parts of the 32nd military division, and on the *renunciation of the protectorate of the Confederation of the Rhine*, so that the independence of all sovereigns of Germany is placed under the guarantee of all the powers.
>
> *Reconstruction of Prussia with a tenable border on the Elbe.* Cession of the Illyrian provinces to Austria.
>
> *Reciprocal guarantee* that the state of possession of the great or small powers, such as it will be fixed by peace, cannot be changed or harmed by any of them.

Metternich added, "by order of the Emperor," that failing acceptance on 10 August,

> we will declare war on France on the morning of the 11th such overtures that one might want to make to us beyond the 10th will be linked as little to the Prague negotiations as the conditions put forward at this moment would have the least value beyond the same term. Our alliance with the powers now at war with France taking its beginning on the 11th, we will receive, beyond this term, no more communication which would be addressed to us separately.[147]

So he uttered the words "alliance with the powers at war with France"; he said under what conditions Napoléon's refusal would lead Austria to join the coalition; but he did not say that he would engage to obtain immediate peace from the allies on these conditions, if Napoléon accepted them, nor that Austria would make war to impose them on the allies. He did not explain himself on the capital question, namely, whether the allies and Austria would not claim to give peace a greater extent; whether the points of the ultimatum constituted preliminaries or a definitive treaty; if, in a word, Napoléon, who by saying no would certainly have war, would be sure, by saying yes, of obtaining peace on the terms of the ultimatum.

These words: conditions which the courts of Russia and Prussia s*eem to set for peaceful arrangements* – the ultimatum did not say a definitive peace; these other words conditioned the only ones which could really lead to general peace; the reservations made previously about Holland, an English affair, and Italy, a Russian affair, and that the ultimatum did not either confirm or withdrew, all these nuances and restrictions were such as to lead one to believe that this Austrian *ultimatum* constituted only the *minimum* of the Allies' conditions. The deadline fixed by Austria proved that its alliance with Russia was made, if not signed, a conditional and term alliance, but was already agreed upon, even in the detail of execution, since on the 11$^{th}$, and war would be declared.

Caulaincourt, however, did not hesitate to believe that peace was possible, even to consider peace as made by the sole *yes* of Napoléon, and he urged the Emperor to pronounce it.[148]

> No doubt Your Majesty will see in this ultimatum some sacrifices of self-esteem, but France will not make any real. Please, Sire, put in the balance of peace all the chances of war. See the irritation of people's minds, the state of Germany as soon as Austria declares herself, the weariness of France, her noble devotion, her sacrifices after the disasters of Russia. The hours are now counted.

And, the next day, to Maret: "I pity you with us. This whole thing was so badly handled. Never wanting to give anything up in time, we spoil everything and lose everything."[149]

Metternich kept the allies informed; as Humboldt showed some concern:

> I was told that on the 11th war would still be declared whatever Napoléon's replies; that the Emperor of Austria wanted neither an alliance with France nor neutrality, that he embraced entirely the cause of Prussia and Russia.[150]

Caulaincourt's report did not reach Dresden until the 9th, at three o'clock in the afternoon. For Napoléon's reply to be delivered in Prague on the 10th, it would have had to leave Dresden on the evening of the 9th.

Napoléon found himself taken aback: thus he used it once after his victories, at the time of Lunéville and Pressburg. Convinced that if they negotiated, the demands would get worse as they went along, he had only to compare the six points of the ultimatum to the three points of Bubna on 16 May to make sure. But he did not want to incur the responsibility for the break. Encouraged by Caulaincourt and Maret, impressed, no doubt, more than he cared to say, by the state of mind in his army, he consented to a compromise. He dictated two notes for Caulaincourt, one very restricted, the other more extensive, to be revealed only in case the first was not accepted. This second note, the only one to consider, said: 1) dissolution of the Duchy of Warsaw; 2) Danzig free city; 3) indemnity to the King of Saxony by a cession of 500,000 souls taken largely in Austrian Silesia and Prussia; 4) cession to Austria of the Illyrian provinces, with the exception of Istria, Trieste, Goritz, and Villach. Napoléon considered Istria necessary for the defense of Venice, and Villach for that of the Tyrol; 5) integrity of Denmark.[151] It was repugnant to him to capitulate so quickly, in front of the hourglass which passed, as well as in public. He imagined that if the armistice were really denounced on the 10th by Austria, hostilities, according to the terms of the convention, not being able to recommence until the 17th, the negotiations could be continued until that day. Finally, it had become a habit with him, a sort of state maxim, not to send dispatches with the ink still wet and the paper lukewarm from improvisation. "He wanted to let the night pass over such important resolutions," said Maret.[152] He took a middle ground. Bubna had returned to Dresden to watch and listen. He received him and spoke to him for two hours, emphasizing the scope of his concessions, the impossibility of pushing them further. Could he return Hamburg and Lubeck? How would he pursue the war against the English? If maritime peace joined continental peace, that would change the question.

> You see I want to do a lot for peace: my allies are losing, I am abandoning a whole nation that has done a lot for me; but do not treat me as if I were already beaten, do not take the certain for the uncertain; you would not demand more if I had lost four battles.

Bubna carried away the impression that Napoléon had made up his mind, that he judged his situation for the truth, but that he intended not to deal with the knife at his throat: "Don't rush me like that," he said, "I want peace, but all the negotiations in the world have taken time!" He would have liked Bubna to go to Prague and report the interview in person to Metternich. Bubna evaded the request: his foot hurt and he had great difficulty in standing up during the audience. He contented himself with despatching a courier, and Napoléon flattered himself that, informed in this way, Metternich would await communication from Caulaincourt.[153]

When he received Bubna's letter, Metternich no doubt felt he had great reason to make the ultimatum worse. If he had sincerely wanted to negotiate, he would have allowed discussion on the articles discarded or amended by Napoléon: the whole of Illyria and the Hanseatic towns. But he did not understand it that way, and, to tell the truth, he was no longer its master. The day of the 10th passed without the courier from Caulaincourt being reported; Anstett and Humboldt were on the lookout, watch in hand. As midnight struck, they notified Metternich that their powers had expired.[154] Metternich declared the congress dissolved, and an hour later Humboldt wrote to Hardenberg: "Our wishes are fulfilled, my dear baron; what we have negotiated since 4 January is achieved."[155] War was declared by Austria on France, and Narbonne received his passports. "I had the signals lighted, which were kept ready from Prague to the Silesian border, to announce that the negotiations were broken off and that the Allied armies could cross the Bohemian border," Metternich recounts.

On 11 August, Caulaincourt presented himself in the morning at Metternich's with Napoléon's counter-proposals. He received, as an official answer, the notification, in the name of Prussia and Russia, of the dissolution of the congress and of the rupture. Metternich added that mediation was over; but that Franz "would none the less support with the greatest zeal the cause of a peace, but a real peace, with his new allies."[156]

Caulaincourt still believed it was possible to treat. Metternich, out of politeness and a sort of diplomatic modesty, if only to put off the scandal for a few hours, consented to talk with the Duke of Vicenza academically, that is to say in the language of chancelleries, in all superfluity and insignificance of purpose. He took the opportunity, however, to ask at any chance for the whole of Illyria with Trieste. But before waiting for an answer, he notified, on the 12th, Austria's declaration of war. Napoléon's reply arrived on the 13th, in the form of a dispatch from Maret to Caulaincourt. Napoléon yielded both on the article of the reconstitution of Prussia and on the dissolution of the Confederation of the Rhine; he abandoned Illyria, except Istria and Trieste, "because for us it is Venice"; finally the 32nd military district, the departments of North Germany, except Hamburg and Lubeck. "In short, it all depends on Austria," concluded Maret. Austria declared that it could no longer do anything without Russia: Russia arrived on the 15th, in the person of Alexander, accompanied by the King of Prussia. Alexander, from the first word spoken to him, refused to hear anything. On the 16th, Metternich informed Caulaincourt of this, who immediately left town. Thus, concluded a Russian historian, the goal which the Russian government had since the month of December 1812. The armistice had produced the most favorable effects for the coalition: the Russian reserves had arrived, Prussia had completed its *levée en masse*, Bernadotte brought up his contingent, Austria finally threw all its forces in the balance. Metternich made the decisive contribution: he believed himself master of affairs, having played Napoléon, and capable of ousting Alexander from the supremacy of Europe. On a single point, his calculations were disappointed, and they were by an element which did not enter into it, with which he did not count, the revolt of a soldier's soul at the moment of going over to the enemy, and the beating of a man's heart under the cast-off of a king of adventure.[157]

Metternich urged Murat to sign a secret alliance convention that would "definitely ensure his existence." By one of the abrupt movements with which he was familiar, under the impact of one of those impulses which formed his whole military genius, like a horse which swerves and rears at the moment of charging at the terrified and rushing in the trap, Murat escaped from the impasse into which the Austrians had engaged him, resumed the high road, and ran to the guns. On a letter from the Emperor, he set out for Dresden on 2 August, and arrived there just in time for the resumption of hostilities.[158]

The war therefore began again, the endless war, which had lasted since 1792, and for the same reasons which had made it last 20 years and had extended it to the extremities of Europe. In reality, for anyone familiar with the treaties of April 1805, those of June 1813, the declarations of Alexander, Hardenberg, Metternich, the English, even Bernadotte, there is no room for doubt. What the allies wanted was the destruction of the Grand Empire, the ruin of French supremacy, the repression of France within its old limits, and as a final consecration, the downfall of Napoléon, if the war did not kill him. In reality, what Napoléon defended on the Elbe, what he must inevitably lose if he was repulsed, these were the bridgeheads and outposts, that the Committee of Public Safety of the Year III and the Directory had successively drawn on the map, conditions of the conquest and conservation of natural boundaries. Mazarin and Louis XIV, to push themselves to the Rhine, by Alsace, had consented to secularizations in Protestant Germany and organized the Line of the Rhine; to secure Flanders and the County, France had to invade Germany and the Low Countries: it was in Holland that it had conquered these countries, it was in Holland that it almost lost them, the day when Holland escaped its domination. In the same way, and on a larger scale, the Republic and the Empire, to assure France of the whole of the Rhine, from Huningue to Holland, consummated, in Germany, the work of secularization, created the Confederation of the Rhine, subjugated Holland, then annexed it. To submit Austria to it, it was necessary to expel it from Italy, and to keep Italy, to possess the passes and put Switzerland in guardianship. Colbert and Louis XIV had dreamed of dominating the Mediterranean; the Republic had planned, and Napoléon undertook to make it a French lake. As England did not consent to it, and no more admitted France mistress of Genoa, sovereign of Naples, or as guardian of the Adriatic than regent of Antwerp, Sieyès imagined and Napoléon accomplished, to reduce to the continental system, that is, the coalition of the continent against England.

Now this system was faltering and we will see it undermined and crumble, wall after wall, tower after tower, as it was built. In this destruction of the Revolution and the Empire, the blockade, in the hands of England, turned against France and the coalition reversed. The allies will take the Grand Empire from the rear, reverse history, successively dislodge France from all its entrenchments: namely, the Duchy of Warsaw, Danzig and the Hanseatic cities, the coasts of the Baltic and those of the North Sea, the Confederation of the Rhine, Holland, Switzerland, Belgium, Italy; to cross the rivers, the Elbe, the Rhine, to annihilate the dykes and barricades erected by it, and, from barrier to barrier, to drive it back by all the roads by which it had passed. They must renew and regain lost battles, unroll and tear up treaties, annihilate the Moskva: this is done in December 1812; annihilate Friedland and Tilsit: done at Kalisch, at Reichenbach, from February to June 1813; annihilate Wagram and Vienna. This was what Metternich claimed to be doing in Prague, and that had been done, except for Pressburg, Amiens, and Lunéville. Brought back to where they were in 1798, the allies claimed to accomplish what they planned then and what they did in part: drive the French out of Italy, return Naples to the Bourbons, Milan to Austria, to seize Holland and Belgium, to exchange them, finally to reconquer the left bank of the Rhine, to bring back France to the old limits and to even trim them if possible. They had conceived only two motives for undergoing these conquests: the strength of France and the indemnities it distributed: the force defeated, the indemnities would remain and the spoils would increase them tenfold. What *raison d'État* will advise them to tolerate, when France was defeated, an extension of French power which they had, on so many occasions and with so much determination, fought against! Moderation? They had never known it, and who would have taught it to them since 1792? Justice? They only practiced the old law of Israel, the law of retaliation, and in fact of public law, reprisals. Such is the symmetry of this history the same motives which led France to conquer the continent and to upset it led the continent to conquer and dismember France.

The coalition being victorious, it was according to the aborted designs of the defeated coalitions of 1793, 1799, 1805, 1807, 1809 that we must judge the designs of 1813. Then, we discover the sequence, and considering by what links they hold with the past, one will include and understand the persistence of it, one will realize that there existed in the mind of the allies an idea behind the forehead, extremely old, extremely inveterate, which gives the key of all the agreements, reveals some secrecy, which in a word, runs the whole affair.[159]

The story continued in its alternatives. The allies wanted to reduce Napoléon to the minimum possible power, but they revealed their intentions only by degrees, as soon as the war allowed them to realize them. That is why they negotiated by fighting. Napoléon will only cede what he deems irretrievably lost; thus in Prague: the Duchy of Warsaw, Illyria, then at the last moment, the Confederation of the Rhine, part of the 32nd military division. On the Elbe, the allies demanded Germany, Holland, Italy; on the Rhine they will demand: the German left bank and Belgium, the old limits. As Napoléon said, "that it would be necessary, to obtain it, that 500,000 men were encamped on the heights of Montmartre," the allies will push to Montmartre and will treat in Paris. To imagine, in this march, another possible interruption than that of a French victory, is to create an obstacle which does not exist anywhere either in the minds of men or in the nature of things, which did not stop France when it left its old limits in 1792, which will not stop the allies in 1813, when they are masters of bringing it back there. It is therefore the war which, until the end, will decide everything.

1. Martens, III, Notice on the treaty of Reichenbach
2. Dispatch of 23 March 1813 to Lebzeltern.
3. Martens, VII, p 113.
4. Nesselrode to Stackelberg, 11 March 1813.
5. Report of Humboldt, 31 March 1813.
6. Hardenberg to Metternich, 11 April 1813.
7. Arrived in Vienna on 17 March; *Journal de Castellane*; Conversation of Napoléon with Schwarzenberg, 8 April 1810; *Souvenirs du duc de Broglie*; Villemain; Lefebvre, V; Fain, *Manuscrit de 1813*, I.
8. Report of 6 April 1813.
9. Reports of 1 and 7 April 1813.
10. Report of 24 March 1813.
11. Reports of 24 March and 1 April 1813.
12. Report of 25 March 1813.
13. Report of 7 April; verbal note from Narbonne to Metternich after their morning conference, 7 April 1813.
14. Gentz, letter of 14 April 1813.
15. *Ibid.*
16. Report of 20 avril 1813. – Note of 21 April, Fain.
17. "Précis del'audience donnée par S.-M. l'empereur d'Autriche à l'ambassadeur de France," 23 avril 1813.
18. The King of Saxony left Regensburg on the 19th to go to Linz and meet there with Franz II. He took with him his confessor and the princes of his house. Serra to Narbonne, 22 April 1813.
19. Report to Napoléon, 23 avril 1813.
20. Text in Fain.
21. Arneth, *Wessenberg*, I, ch. XII: mission to England; Letters of Woronzof; Martens, XI, notice on the treaty of Reichenbach; Ranke, V, liv. IV, ch. XXIII and XXIV.
22. Report of 10 May 1813.
23. Report of Wessenberg, 9 April 1813.
24. Instructions Jacobi, Breslau, 26 March 1813. (Oncken, *O. und P.*, II, ch. IX.)
25. Martens, XI: Notice on the Convention of Reichenbach.
26. Christian Schefer, *Bernadotte roi*, ch. II; Léonce Pingaud, *Bernadotte, Napoléon et les Bourbons*, ch. X, XII; *Souvenirs de Saint-Chamans*.
27. Helfert, *Joachim Murat*; *Köningin Carolina von Neapel*; *Maria-Carolina von Oesterreich*; Botta, trad. Fr., V, liv. XXVI; Gervinus, trad. Minsen, III, ch. III; Cresceri, *Memorie*; *Mémoires de Desvernois*; *Lettres inédites de Murat* (*Revue de Paris*); Weil, *Le prince Eugène et Murat*: Sources, V, p. 201; Duforcq, *Murat et la question de l'unité italienne en 1815*; Bianchi, *Storia documentata della diplomazia europea in Italia*.
28. Davout to Duroc, 3 février 1813; Helfert, *Murat*, reports of Count Mier, minister of Austria to Naples; Weil.
29. Report of Durant, 10 mars 1813.
30. Metternich to Mier, 20 April 1813: "Prince Cariati has acquitted himself *vis-à-vis* me of the commission with which he is charged. He told me." (Helfert, Weil.)
31. "I learned for the first time that he had received, at this time, a letter from the

Emperor which made a deep impression and which, being still the last remaining communication between the two monarchs, had left the king's heart open to the most disturbing thoughts." Report of Durant, 31 mars 1813.
32. They have not been found. See in the Correspondence the note placed under n° 14502, and Helfert, *Maria Carolina*, p. 508, footnote.
33. Napoléon to Eugène, 20 janvier 1813.
34. Botta, V, p. 365.
35. Report of Durant, 31 mars 1813.
36. On 10 May, when the Elbe was crossed, out of four corps and 60,000 to 70,000 men, 109 battalions, 28 squadrons, 18 batteries, there were 3 regiments of cavalry and 5 of German infantry; 9 Italian, Illyrian, Swiss, Spanish infantry regiments. (Hausser, IV, p. 138.)
37. To Franz II, to the King of Württemberg, to Jérôme, 3-4 mai 1813.
38. See above the note of 21 April and the interview of 23 April.
39. 20 avril 1813. Oncken, II, p. 637; Bonnefons, *Un allié de Napoléon*, p. 376, 413, 416 et suiv. Thiers, XV, p. 208 209, 402, 412.
40. To Caulaincourt, 8 mai 1813. (Bonnefons, p. 420 et suiv.)
41. *Mémoires du comte de Senfft*; Sainte-Beuve, *Nouveaux lundis*, IX, article on Bignon; Bonnefons, p. 311, 418 et suiv; Oncken, *O. und P.*, II, p. 282 et suiv; Zeitalter, II, p. 637; Fain, I, p. 387-89.
42. Cf. *Souvenirs du duc de Broglie*, I, p. 222.
43. "He does not waver in the execution of his plan." Report of Count Hardenberg, 12 May 1813. (Oncken.)
44. *Mémoires de Metternich*; Report of Count Hardenberg, 9 May 1813.
45. The treaty of 11 April 1805 reserved it for one of Bonaparte's brothers, probably Joseph.
46. Oncken, *O. und P.*, II, Annexes.
47. Franz to Friedrich-Wilhelm, 17 May 1813. (Ranke, IV.)
48. Report of Narbonne, 7 mai 1813
49. These terms embarrassed the departments formed in 1810: Ems-Oriental, Ems-Superior, the Lippe, the Weser, with Bremen, the Elbe, with Hamburg.
50. Instructions to Bubna; Franz II to Napoléon, 11 May 1813. (Oncken.)
51. Overview of Russian Transactions, XXXI, p. 314.
52. Thiers, XV, p. 345.
53. Report of Bubna, 16 May 1814. (Oncken.)
54. The boundaries of Austria in 1805; Italy entirely withdrawn from France. Notes from Nesselrode, 13 and 16 May, in agreement with Stadion.
55. Instructions for Caulaincourt, 17 May 1813. Notes for Caulaincourt. (Lefebvre.) Full powers for Caulaincourt in view of an armistice, 18 May 1813.
56. Eugène, 18 mai; cf. *id.* 12 mai 1813.
57. Miloradovitch to the Marshal, 19 May; Nesselrode to Caulaincourt, 20 mai 1813.
58. Gourgaud, II, p. 71.
59. To Clarke, 2 juin; to Eugène, 1 and 2 juin 1813.
60. Maret to the Emperor, 8 mai 1813. (Ernouf.)
61. Marmont, V, liv. XVII.
62. On the obsession of this thought, see Masson, *Napoléon et son fils*.
63. Instructions for Caulaincourt, 26 mai; Maret to Caulaincourt, 29 mai 1813.

64 To Maret, 12 juin 1813. (Lecestre; Fain, I, 2nd part, ch. IX.)
65 *Mémoires de Talleyrand*, I, p. 320, 401, 413-14, 438; Masson, *Joséphine répudiée*, p. 51.
66 *Lettres et papiers du chancelier comte de Nesselrode*, II.
67 "My sword and my emperor made me what I am. The current generation does not know the Bourbons and consequently does not deal with them; the old people have forgotten them, and the Vendéens, if they remember their courageous efforts for these princes, have not lost the memory of their long abandonment and of their stay on the Ile Dieu. I also know and think all this." (To Napoléon, 3 mars 1814.)
68 "A mission to headquarters would divide the world," to Narbonne, 14 May 1813.
69 This conversation, according to the reports of Schouvalof, of 31 May and 2 June 1813, communicated to the Congrès des sciences diplomatiques à la Haye, by Baillen, *Annales internationales d'histoire*, congrès de la Haye, n° 3. Compare, below, the analogous remarks made by Caulaincourt to Metternich, the day of his arrival in Prague, 25 July 1813. In his letter to the Emperor of 1 June, Caulaincourt reported on the details of the technical negotiation, and he added: "As for at the peace negotiation, I have not yet been able to talk in particular with Count Schouvalof."
70 It seems that Napoléon remained under this impression. He gave to Las Cases (*Mémorial*) among the reasons that determined him to the armistice: "The rear was exposed and covered by the enemy." Langeron commented: "There could only be behind inconvenient partisans to the truth, but not dangerous." (*Mémoires*, Campagne de 1813.)
71 *Mémoires*, I, p. 134 et suiv.
72 Martens, III, p. 102 et suiv. – Russia, XXXI: Nesselrode mission to Vienna, Gitschin agreement.
73 Metternich to Stadion, 3 June 1813. See June 6, the same eagerness to know if the armistice has been concluded. (Oncken.)
74 De Clercq, II, p. 332. (Oncken, II, p. 660.)
75 Stadion to Metternich, 3 juin 1813. (Oncken.)
76 Russie, XXXI. *Aperçu des transactions*, p. 311; Stadion to Metternich, 3 June 1813: Propositions relative to the plan of campaign. (Oncken.)
77 Ségur, V, p. 119: criticism of the armistice from the French point of view; Oncken, II, p. 629: criticism of the armistice from the point of view of the allies.
78 Russie, XXXI, p. 316; text, Martens, XI, p. 169; III, Notice on the treaty of Reichenbach; Metternich to Stadion, 6, 8, 11, 14 June 1813; Oncken, *O. und P.*, II, ch. VI.
79 Thiers, XV, p. 343.
80 Report of Stadion and pieces in Oncken. (*O. und P.*, II, p. 336.)
81 Hardenberg to Münster, 21 June 1813. (Oncken.)
82 *Mémoires*, I, p. 160.
83 Report to the Emperor, 24 June; letter to Stadion, 23 June 1813. (Oncken.)
84 Cf. note of 16 May; bases of 12 June; Russian note of 19 June; Austrian conditions of a good peace.
85 Fain: notes from Maret and Metternich 15-22 June 1813; Ernouf, ch. XLI; Oncken, *O. und Pr.*, I, p. 383.
86 Dresde, 13 June 1813. Cf. Fain, II, p. 17.

87 Mistake. Compare above, Nesselrode's note of 19 June 1813, and Reichenbach's clauses.
88 Cf. to Davout, 7, 18, 24 juin (Lecestre); letters of Davout, 11 and 13 juin (*Corr.* IV); *Mémoires de Puymaigre*, p. 152: of Thiébaut, V, p. 49 et suiv; 101 et suiv; 142 et suiv; 160.
89 To Savary, 13 juin; to Cambacérès, 18, 30 juin 1813. (Lecestre); *Mémoires de Pasquier.*
90 Fain, I, p. 430, II, p. 74.
91 Ernouf, after the notes of Maret. *Mémorial*, VI, p. 57; Fain, II, p. 75, note.
92 Giving up even then, and Wellington won on 21 June 1813, at Vittoria.
93 On this interview: account of Fain, II, ch. IV, which Fain takes from Maret (Ernouf, *Maret*, p. 562) and which Maret must have written after a conversation with Napoléon, but from a distance, because he alludes there to peace conditions which were not notified to him then; Metternich's stories, the first summary and immediate, of 26 July 1813 (Oncken, *O. und P.*, pieces, II, p. 678), the other detailed, taken up, arranged in dialogue, in the *Mémoires: Sur l'histoire des alliances*, I, p. 147, II, p. 461. Critique of these texts, Oncken, *O. und P.*, II, p. 385.
94 Fain, p. 40. In Metternich there is no mention of Illyria.
95 A cruder expression, said Metternich, in a footnote.
96 Compare his conversation with the Queen of Prussia at Tilsit, VII, p. 183.
97 Fain, II: Notes of Maret and Metternich, 27, 28, 29 June; Bignon, XII, ch. IV.
98 Letter of September 1813. (*Mémoires*, I, p. 258.)
99 23 juillet 1813. Retrospective.
100 Simple mediation and not armed mediation, as it is said in the *Memoirs* of Metternich, I, p. 385.
101 To Narbonne, 23 juillet 1813. – See Fournier, III, p. 145, note; Ernouf, p. 563-66.
102 Notes of Maret. (Ernouf, p. 506-67.)
103 On this retreat rich in picturesque incidents, see the *Mémoires d'Espinchat*, II, ch. XX-XXI; Jourdan, *Mémoires*, ch. XXI-XXV: "On 12 July, the king went to Bagneres, and Marshal Jourdan returned to his home." Cf. *Mémoires de Miot*, *Mémoires du roi Joseph.*
104 Report of Narbonne, 11 juillet 1813.
105 Nesselrode, *Autobiographie.*
106 Pingaud, *Bernadotte*, ch. XIII, Stralsund to Trachenberg, May-August 1813. – *Mémoires de Suremain.*
107 The treaty, which had been negotiated for several weeks, was signed on 10 July in Copenhagen. (Du Clercq, II, p. 386; Fain, II, p. 15.)
108 Russie, XXXI, p. 330.
109 Report of Stadion, 14 juillet 1813. (Oncken.)
110 Surmain, p. 287. Cf. Langeron, p. 455.
111 Blennerhasset, *Mme de Staël*, III; Gautier, ch. XXII.
112 6 mai 1814. Pingaud, ch. XIII, XIV.
113 "No Congress was more derisory" (Nesselrode, *Autobiographie*.)
114 Martens, III, note on the Treaty of Toeplitz of 9 September 1813.
115 Anstett, of French origin, was involved since 1805 in a number of Anglo-Russian intrigues against Napoléon. See the report of Narbonne, 10 juillet 1813;

Fain, II, p. 72; Ernouf, p. 569-70.
116 Reports of Hardenberg, 2 May 1813.
117 To Hardenberg, 13 July 1813.
118 It was even more so by a treaty of 22 July, with Russia. (Trietschke, I, p. 468.)
119 Mier to Metternich, 29 June 1813; Metternich to Mier, 16 July and 3 August 1813; Helfert, *Murât*; *Marie-Caroline*; Correspondence of Bentinck (Weil, I, p. 53-172.)
120 On this negotiation and the multiple incidents to which it gave rise, and the conferences of Neumarck, see Fain, II, ch. VII, and exhibits; Russia, XXXI, p. 318; Martens, III, p. 110; Oncken, II, p. 653.
121 To Narbonne, 23 juillet 1813.
122 Bignon, XII, ch. IV and V; Fain, II, ch. VII; Ernouf, ch. LXIII, notes of Maret; Lefebvre, *Le congrès de Prague*.
123 "When this trip was known in Prague, to say that His Majesty, going to Wurzburg, could not resist the desire of the Empress and her desire to spend thirty-six or forty-eight hours with this princess." (Maret to Narbonne, 24 juillet 1813.)
124 Masson, *Marie-Louise*, p. 496-500" correspondence of Maria-Louisa and Franz II; *Napoléon et son fils*, ch. IV.
125 Bignon; Thiers.
126 Convention of Neumarck, 26 July 1813. (Fain, II, p. 162.)
127 Nugent to Cathcart, Prague, 27 July; Cathcart to Castlereagh, 6 August; Castlereagh to Cathcart, 5 July 1813. Oncken, annexes; Castlereagh, *Letters and dispatches*. (Martens, XI report of Lieven, 16 July 1813; Ranke.)
128 Were closer relations between England and Austria established that very day? Metternich obtained from England the supremacy of Italy. We have said it. Nicomede Bianchi published, *Storia della diplomazia europea in Italia*, I, annexes p. 333, a protest which would have been addressed to Paris, on 26 May 1814, by Metternich to Castlereagh. This note refers to the negotiations which have already been initiated with regard to the execution of the secret treaty signed in Prague on 27 July 1813 and ratified in London on 23 August, and summarizes its content with precision: this treaty, by its articles 4, 9, 10, "absolutely decisive" reserved to Austria "the supreme direction and the definitive organization of Italy, with the exception of the former States of the King of Sardinia, in concert with England." The kingdom of Italy passed to Austria. No trace of the treaty has been found either in the archives of the record office, or in Vienna or Berlin. As for Metternich's protest, of which no trace has been found either, it was sent to Turin, in copy, during the Congress of Vienna, by Saint-Marsan, then entered the service of Sardinia. Saint-Marsan's journal does not mention it. (Rinieri, *Correspondenza dei cardinali Consalvie Pacca, 1814-1815, preceduta da un diario inedito del Mse di San Marzano*.)
129 Martens, III, p. 115.
130 To Maret, 28 juillet 1814.
131 Report of Metternich to Franz II, 28 July 1813. (Oncken.)
132 Report of Anstett, 28 July 1813. (Martens, III, p. 114.)
133 Compare Talleyrand at Erfurt.
134 No mention of these confidences in Caulaincourt's report to the Emperor of July 30, nor in the letters to Maret of the same day; simply these words: "I saw M. de

Metternich at four o'clock the very day of my arrival. Immediately afterwards, he visited me and I dined at his house with M. de Narbonne and our whole legation ... I held myself in the absolute reserve prescribed for me."

135 Caulaincourt and Narbonne to Maret, 30 juillet. Caulaincourt's report to Napoléon, of the same day: "He repeated to me several times what he had, he told me, already announced to M. le Duc de Bassano and to M. de Narbonne, and what he considered a duty of honor to convey to Your Majesty that, on 10 August, if the bases of peace were not signed, a declaration would necessarily accompany the denunciation of the armistice. Until that time, he says, Austria will not enter into any engagement; but there are two points on which he cannot leave us in any doubt; it is that it will not be neutral, and that it will wage war."

136 They would arrive without Austria having the shadow of an engagement. See the Treaty of Reichenbach, 27 June, the declaration to the English, 27 July, above. Version of Thiers (XVI, p. 152) Metternich would have added: "So let no one come after the event to tell us that we have deceived you. Until 10 August at midnight, everything is possible, even at the last hour; last 10 August, not a day, not a moment of respite from war, war with everyone, even with you!" – "Calm, sad and grand language," said Thiers, and p. 189: "M. de Metternich repeated those things which he had already said to M. de Narbonne, in such a calm, firm tone, with expressions of such affection for M. de Caulaincourt, and such manifest sincerity, for one must not, like the vulgar, imagine that a diplomat necessarily lies, that M. de Caulaincourt, could not resist so much evidence. So, with his usual veracity, he wrote immediately to M. de Bassano..."

137 30 July 1813. (Oncken, *O. und P.*, II, p. 440.)

138 "...(Napoléon's) ministers were completely deceived by the Austrian cabinet." (Langeron, p. 202, note.)

139 To Sir George Jackson, who accompanied Sir Charles Stewart as a diplomat. (Oncken, *O. and P.*, II, p. 440.)

140 Exhibits in Fain.

141 Letter and orders to Eugène, and to Berthier, 28, 31 juillet 1813. (Lecestre.)

142 Report of Caulaincourt, 6 août 1813.

143 To Stadion, 6 August 1813. (Oncken.)

144 Gentz, *Tagebücher*.

145 Report of Caulaincourt, 8 août 1813.

146 Text from Caulaincourt. Cf. Oncken, *O. und P.*, II, p. 450, note 684; Thiers, XVI, p. 217. Italics indicate conditions added to Reichenbach's four points.

147 Metternich to Stadion, 8 August 1813.

148 Caulaincourt to Napoléon. 8 août 1813.

149 To Maret, 9 août 1813.

150 Ranke, IV, p. 419.

151 Maret to Caulaincourt, 10 août 1813.

152 "The affairs of foreign relations are affairs which must be treated at length; you must always keep my letters three or four days under your bedside before sending them off." (to Champagny, 1 avril 1811.)

153 Report of Bubna, 9 August 1813. (Oncken.)

154 Notes of Anstett and Humboldt, 10 Augsut 1813. (Fain.) Caulaincourt to Maret, 10 août 1813.

155 Allusion to the instructions given in January to Knesebeck with a view to an

alliance with Austria. (Ranke, IV, p. 421.)

156 Caulaincourt to Maret, 11 août 1813; Note of Metternich, 11 August. (Fain.)

157 Metternich to Mier, 16 July 1813.

158 On the continuation of the negotiations of Metternich and Bentinck with Murat, see the correspondence of Naples, Vienna, London, Palermo. (Weil, I, pp. 57-172.)

159 Compare the state of things in 1709, at the time of the Hague preliminary. "I was convinced," said Saint-Simon, "that no one wanted peace, from rage against the king's person and from jealousy against France, all had seized on a plausible pretext to set him aside." It was then a question of forcing France to give up Spain and to begin its borders. "Their design only tended to a general destruction of France." Look at the 40 articles of the Hague preliminaries, not to mention what the Empire, the King of Prussia, and the Duke of Savoy claimed during the general negotiation for the definitive peace! It was then that Louis XIV appealed to the nation: "The more ease and desire I have shown in dissipating the suspicions that my enemies affect to retain from my power and my designs, the more they have multiplied their pretensions, so that by degrees adding new demands to the first, they also made me see that their intention was only to increase at the expense of my crown the neighboring States of France and to open easy ways to penetrate into the interior of my kingdom, whenever it would be convenient to their interests to start a new war. The one that I support and that I wanted to finish would not even have ceased when I had consented to the proposals they made to me." *Saint-Simon*, ed. Boislisle; Masson, *Journal de Torcy*.

# Chapter III: Fall of the Grand Empire

## 1813

### I. Treaties of Toeplitz

Moreau, who left the United States on 21 June, arrived in Sweden on 26 July, re-embarked there on 6 August, for Pomerania, and met Bernadotte at Stralsund.[1] Pichegru died in prison, Bernadotte stood on the steps of a throne, so Moreau could measure the contrast; with Pichegru he only went to conspiracy and civil war, with Bernadotte he marched to a foreign alliance.[2] He made his way to Berlin, where the people cheered him, obsessed with Italian or German deserters who marched to his orders. Alexander received him as a friend, paid him the first visit in the company of the King of Prussia; but he did not award him the supreme command with which Moreau had flattered himself. Schwarzenberg was in possession of the title of generalissimo; Austria had demanded it. Alexander gave him the rank of field-marshal: "You will be my adviser, my best friend"; and he placed him in his train, in the section of defectors and foreign auxiliaries, which brought together a great man, Stein, who was working for his country; the Swiss Jomini with his genius, which was of the second order, and his information, which was of the first; a number of French *émigrés*, such as Rochechouart and the Corsican Pozzo di Borgo, who continued his vendetta against the Buonapartes. There had been D'Antraigues, assassinated in July 1812, figured in the front ranks, charged with the portfolio of the friends of Paris, whose policy was to triumph with the coalition and whose wishes were to be fulfilled. "They made me give in to a wasp," wrote Moreau to his wife. He felt, from the start, out of place and downgraded.

He nevertheless put himself in character, which was to lead the French astray and to agitate public opinion. He did more, and it was precisely what the allies expected of him: he gave the advice of a man who knew his comrades in arms, advice too enlightened and which was only too effectively followed:

> Expect defeat wherever the Emperor shows in person. Avoid coming to blows with him as much as possible. Attack and fight the lieutenants wherever they can be reached. Finally, the beaten and weakened lieutenants ... unite with the existing forces all those that can be joined, march on him, wrest victory from him, by some losses that will have to be paid for, and give him no more respite.

This was the whole spirit of the second campaign of 1813, as penetrating and as formidable in scope against Napoléon as Carnot's famous plan was against the Allies in 1794.[3]

Moreau's advice was only too sound, and Napoléon, unfortunately, lent himself to it only too well. It came precisely to this war of lieutenants that Moreau declared so dangerous for him, so favorable to the allies. Instead of forming a mass and pressing forward as in the days of Austerlitz, Friedland, and Wagram, he was scattered, wanting to keep everything, and reduced to defending himself everywhere. He resolved to remain in Saxony to maintain the war in the center of Germany and to retain the German princes in the Confederation. He instructed Vandamme and Gouvion to oppose the march of the Austrians on Dresden through Bohemia. He instructed Oudinot to march on Berlin, to oppose the junction of the Prussian army in the north with the army of Silesia, to worry the Prussians, to dissolve the *landwehrs*, to bring back the Poles: operations of high concept, but too extensive, and too divergent. On the other hand, the allies had learned at his school. All their plans only tended to envelop him, and in such a superiority of numbers, with such clubbing blows, that all his genius would be turned, so to speak, and as if reduced to nothing. They marched on Dresden. On 26 and 27 August, Napoléon fought there and won: it was the last of his great battles, but one without a future. The battle was still his, but the consequences eluded him.

During the second day, around noon, at the hour when the

movement of retreat of the allies was pronounced, Moreau rode on horseback near Alexander, behind a Prussian battery, between two Englishmen, Cathcart and Wilson. A bullet shattered his left leg. He fainted and expired a few days later. The event justified his forecasts. On the 28th and 29th, Vandamme, powerless to stop the Austrians in their retreat, was himself beaten and routed on 30 August: 82 guns and 7,000 men lost or taken prisoner: it was the Battle of Kulm. On the 29th, Macdonald was beaten by Blücher, another rout: 100 guns, 10,000 men lost, the rest in disarray; it was the Battle of Katzbach. On 30 August, Oudinot, beaten on the 23rd at Grossbeeren, arrived exhausted at Wittenberg; he lost 12,000 men. In five days Napoléon found himself deprived of 100,000 men, of his convoys, of his artillery; he lost the offensive; his army, all in training, disbanding.

The quarrels which had been smoldering for weeks then broke out between the Emperor and his generals, and which suddenly revealed the wound becoming poisonous; violent scenes where all the soldierly rudeness of these illustrious upstarts was unleashed, preface and presage of the noisy defections of 1814. Letters from Bernadotte to Oudinot, Ney, Murat, Berthier, urging peace, were revealed to Napoléon by Oudinot. The others, who would have preferred to keep the secret, then decided to go to the Emperor. Ney alone, it is said, entered first. The discussion became resounding; the marshals appeared. "Traitor!" cried Napoléon to his brother-in-law, and as Berthier took up this apostrophe: "And you too! old fool, what are you getting into? Shut up!" A few days later it was Macdonald's turn:

> What have you done with the army I entrusted to you? – Sire, you no longer have an army; there are only poor people dying of hunger; go to traverse these mountains, you will find there your soldiers per hundreds, died of misery; you have lost everything; you have only to think of peace.

Napoléon concentrated what remained to him. The fate he had conjured at Dresden was to be fulfilled at Leipzig.

These three days, from August 27 to 30, which transformed Napoléon's victory into an irreparable defeat, had been days of cruel perplexity for the allies. From the start, the coalition passed through the formidable ordeal in which all the preceding coalitions had sunk: military recriminations, political recriminations, Austrians against Russians, Russians against Germans and Austrians, Prussians shouted at by everyone, but facing up, barking, biting everything in the world; the English disconcerted and already ready to tie up the subsidy bags. Metternich, very troubled, weighed the responsibilities that his master and his compatriots were already throwing on him. The three sovereigns met at Dun Castle, near Toeplitz. Nothing shows the reversal of affairs better. Stifling rivalries, pride and suspicions, to think only of providing together for the common peril, they held on: the rout of Vandamme, on 30 August, gave them courage and showed them that they had been right. That day the coalition was sealed: then came the news of the other successes, Katzbach, Grossbeeren; the final success no longer seemed doubtful.

However, the causes of disagreement were not lacking. In Germany, the defection of the Confederates was announced: at Grossbeeren, the Saxons of Macdonald's army had passed to Bernadotte. The fall of the Confederation of the Rhine therefore seemed only a matter of weeks. All the allies agreed in wanting to dissolve it; but what to do with Germany? What would be done with the Duchy of Warsaw, with Italy, in short, of which the Austrians were always thinking. Formerly the left bank of the Rhine had been conquered by the French in Italy; this time it seemed that Italy would be conquered on the Rhine by Austria.

Alexander played a superior character here. It was then that he really showed himself to be the regulator, or as they began to say in the classic jargon of the time, the king of kings, the Agamemnon of the new Iliad. He never for a moment lost sight of the plan of reign conceived in his youth, the reality of his mature age: to reconstitute Europe and take the place in the supremacy of the continent usurped by Napoléon; neither the revenge of his arms, nor the revenge of his own injuries. As much as he had shown himself to be undulating and fugitive during the Tilsit alliance – because, deep down, he did not want to, he laughed did not like his own policy, that of mask and passage, as much from Moscow one saw him resolute, followed, wanting his actions, marching towards his goal, which was the destruction of the Grand Empire, of the Western Empire and the downfall of Napoléon: him or me! to the accessible extremities, to the end, that is to say, to Paris. His persistent thought was to push the struggle "to the last result," to "pursue the war to the bitter end; not to compromise with a treacherous enemy; to destroy his armies, to overthrow his power";[4] he considered that time could only offer the allies better chances and decide, in their own eyes, their superiority. He would plant the two-pointed cross in the metropolis of the West, the sacred city of the Revolution, the city of the regicides, of the Convention, of the imperial coronation; he would dominate France, that Poland of the Latins. He would give institutions to the country of Montesquieu and a king to the Revolution. The destinies hatched by him from Tilsit were about to be accomplished; the time had come to reveal his genius, the time when the unknown politician hidden under the chimerical, the undecided and the dreamer, whose secret he had only discovered, one day, the secret of his mother, was going to come out of his cloud and reveal himself to the world. From a distance, he knew how to charm and win over the French, repeating and causing them to be repeated constantly that he separated from the cause of Napoléon the cause of their liberties and that of their borders: simple and profound political remarks, which were to have and had for first effect of making them consider as the approach of the liberator the invasion of the allies towards the French border, which unlike all invasions, this one would have the object of respecting and guaranteeing. He knew how to decide the adventure in crises by going to the vanguard, where the Prussian Blücher, tireless and insatiable, advanced always ready to sound the charge. Finally and above all he dictated the very political treaties drawn up on the model which had prevailed at Kalisch, and which all tended to this object: to reserve the disputes by reserving the claims of each one on the common conquests. Let's take first, then everyone will recognize their catches!

On 9 September, two treaties identical in substance, and almost identical in form, were signed at Toeplitz, between Russia and Austria, Russia and Prussia.[5] They confirmed the treaties already concluded either by Russia or by Prussia: "They do not intend to infringe in the least the previous and particular engagements, also defensive, which they have contracted with their respective allies," that is to say, Russia with Sweden in 1812, with Prussia, at Kalisch, with England at Reichenbach, Prussia with England, also at Reichenbach. The treaties of Toeplitz renewed and further clarified the formula of not entering into "negotiations for peace except by common accord." The allies promised each other in the most solemn manner not to listen to any insinuation or proposal addressed to them, directly or indirectly, by the French Cabinet, without communicating it to each other.[6] They determined, as the object of their common efforts, in separate and secret articles, in the first line, the following four points: 1) the reconstruction of the Austrian and Prussian monarchies on the scale nearest to that on which they were in 1805; 2) the dissolution of the Confederation of the Rhine and the complete and absolute independence of the intermediate States between the borders of the Austrian and Prussian monarchies, reconstructed according to the scale mentioned above, and the Rhine and the Alps on the other; (3) The restitution to the House of Brunswick-Lüneburg of Hanover and its other possessions in Germany; 4) an amicable settlement between the three courts of Russia, Austria, and Prussia on the future fate of the Duchy of Warsaw.

To give these provisions "all the desired precision," these additional articles: 1) the restitution of the countries which were united to France under the name of the 32nd military division; 2) that of the provinces and countries of Germany possessed by French princes.

These were the conditions of the notes of 16 May, those of Reichenbach, the real conditions of Prague. It remained to give "the greatest extent" and to add to it, according to the Russian note of June 19th, "powerful barriers against France." They prepared the means. A separate and secret Article II read: "The high contracting parties in no way intend to prejudice by the preceding article (the four points) any engagements which they may have contracted with other powers in the sense of the aim which they offer themselves."

There were some with Sweden, some could be discovered with England, which would precisely define this greater extent of the peace treaty, and it was a means of bringing Holland, the left bank of the Rhine, the limit of the Scheldt, Belgium, Italy, of which there would be no question in the preliminary bases.

Metternich did not fail to draw some procedural vanity from the insidious elegance of these forms. He wrote to Josef von Hudelist, back in Vienna, where he was acting for foreign affairs: "...to a greater extent, we appear moderate, and that I have caused the only articles which directly concern France to be placed in a secret convention, which is known only to the three courts."[7]

England found its proprieties in the article relating to Hanover. and signed, on 20 September, in London, with Russia and Prussia, a convention relating to the issue of paper money and subsidies.[8] These arrangements were completed by a preliminary treaty of alliance concluded at Toeplitz on 9 October between England and Austria: it contained the exclusive clause of negotiations, conventions and treaties otherwise than by common accord.[9]

At the same time, on 8 October, Metternich, carried out an accommodation almost as important in his eyes as the defection of Bavaria:[10] "Bavaria disengages itself from the bonds of the Confederation of the Rhine, and it will immediately join its armies with those of the allied powers." Austria guaranteed it: "the free and peaceful enjoyment as well as the full and entire sovereignty of all its States," except for rectifications of frontiers with indemnities. The treaty assigned as the objective of war: "the dissolution of the Confederation of the Rhine and the complete and absolute independence of Bavaria, so that, freed from all ties and placed outside all foreign influence, she enjoys the fullness of its sovereignty."[11] This treaty was to procure the defection of the other Confederates. The bait was the guarantee of their possessions acquired from the hands of Napoléon as the price of their defection from the Holy Roman Empire; it was the guarantee of their full and entire sovereignty, which ruined, in its germ, any project of reconstitution of the Holy Roman Empire and of reducing "thirty little despots, to the role of governors of provinces." Metternich attributed to this article a capital importance. Already the words *entire and absolute independence* of the States, inserted in the secret articles of Toeplitz, without Hardenberg having taken sufficient notice of them, prejudged the question. The arrangement of 8 October made it henceforth an Austrian question.

Alexander spurred on Bernadotte, who was decidedly sparing himself too much and operating too far from the coalition. The bullet of his friend Moreau did not tempt him, and it was another end which he proposed to himself with the French.

He entered the war, wrote Münster a few weeks later, in the hope that his old comrades, the French generals, would abandon the Corsican to join him. The idea of making himself king of France possessed him. Not succeeding in overthrowing his personal enemy, he nevertheless would like not to fight the French, to maintain his supposed popularity among them. He managed the Swedes to keep an honorable retirement and seemed to care little about the fate of others.

Pozzo di Borgo, whom Alexander had sent to him, wrote on 7 September: "The prince's idea of showing himself to the French as their future liberator takes more sway over his imagination every day. All his speeches, all his steps visibly tend to this end." On the battlefield of Grossbeeren, covered with French corpses, he said to Pozzo: "France is most worthy!" Whereupon, the Corsican, ironically: "So she's mine!" And, a short time later, to Rochechouart, charged with carrying him the cordon of Saint-Georges and encouraging him on the offensive: "Do you hear, my friend, who would have said, twenty years ago to poor Sergeant Bernadotte: You will be treated as Monsieur my brother and friend by the Emperor of Russia, the Emperor of Austria and the King of Prussia?" He took the cord of Saint-Georges: "It honors me infinitely; I am to life and death with the Emperor Alexander." But, as Rochechouart urged him to march:

> Get along well, my friend; a lot of caution is needed in my situation; it is so delicate. Besides the very natural repugnance I have to shed French blood, I have my reputation to uphold. I'm not mistaken: my fate is not due to a battle; if I lose it, I will ask Europe for a six-franc crown, no one will lend it to me. If I could blame only Napoléon, it would soon be over. Bonaparte is a rascal, he must be killed; as long as he lives he will be the scourge of the world; no more emperor is needed, this title is not French; France needs a king, but a soldier king; the race of the Bourbons is a worn-out race which will never get back on the water. Who is the man who suits the French better than me?

He reserved himself. However, he had to do it well; Napoléon declared war on him on 14 October. Bernadotte operated his junction with the army of Silesia.

Napoléon enveloped by the allies, gave battle on 16 and 17 October at Leipzig, which the Germans called the Battle of the Nations. On the 18th, this battle was lost, the Bavarians had defected on the 14th; the Saxons passed to the allies on the 18th, in the very midst of the action. Whereupon this cry of anger and despair resounded in the French ranks: "It's Bernadotte's cannon!" Bernadotte consummated the rout. For it was "the hideous rout": the army of conscripts, crippled, exhausted, ruined, no longer held together; exaltation had fallen, morale lost.

On the 17th, Napoléon said to Austrian General Merveldt, a prisoner, whom he dismissed on parole:[12] "Will this war last forever!" It would be time to finish it once. "Sire, it is the general wish and peace is in your Majesty's hands. It would have depended on him to conclude it at the Congress of Prague. – We were not in good faith, we ended up." Then pushing right to the fact that he suspected under those "tricksters." – Resumed Napoléon, "Why don't we accept the proposal to negotiate! You can see that England does not want peace!" Merveldt assured the contrary. Napoléon said,

> Well! let England give me back my islands, and I will give her back Hanover. I will restore the united departments and the Hanseatic towns. – I believe, Sire, that they will insist on the independence of Holland. – Well, we would have to agree on this independence, but that will not be easy with the maritime principles of England. – It would be a generous resolution and a great step towards peace. I remember that Your Majesty told me long ago that it was necessary for the peace of Europe that France should be separated, by a belt of small independent States, from the other powers. Let Your Majesty return to these principles which you had conceived in moments of calm and reflection, and you will ensure the happiness of Europe.

Napoléon did not dispute. There was a moment of silence, which Napoléon broke with this observation:

> But all this will not bring us to peace. How to negotiate with England, who wants to impose on me not to build more than thirty ships in my ports! – The English, Sire, think this conduct so inadmissible that they have not dared to articulate it until now.

And the ingenious Austrian took up the theme to insinuate an article which had not yet been mentioned to Napoléon and which was, in 1813, as in 1797 and in 1801, the essential article for Austria, Italy.

> England can hide only with the extent of the coast which Your Majesty possesses from the Adriatic to the North Sea, he (Your Majesty) would have, within a few years, a navy double or triple his own. How can this impending superiority be obviated if not by fixing the number of vessels which could be built in the ports of France, unless Your Majesty returns to the stipulations which you yourself established by placing yourself at the head of the government of Italy, namely to want to restore independence to this country to continental and general peace?

It was not precisely the text, it was even less the spirit of the commitment. Napoléon had written, "In no case do I have the project or the intention of joining the crown of France to that of Italy"; he intended it "for one of his legitimate children,[13] male, either natural or adopted"; but he would keep it "until the Mediterranean has returned to its natural state." This is how he understood, and he could not understand otherwise, Merveldt's insinuation, and it was in this sense that he added, agreeing that this condition would be more admissible than the limitation of the number of vessels: "In any case, I will not hear the restoration of the old order of things in Italy. Countries united under one sovereign would be suitable for a general system of politics in Europe." He meant: a French prince, by his hand. But the Austrian, who perhaps knew the articles of Toeplitz, and who in any case was not unaware that Italy would form the lot and the reward of Franz II, gave to the proposition a far wider meaning, that is to say Napoléon's pure and simple renunciation of Italy and the attribution of the entire kingdom and of the French departments, in part, at least, to Austria. They moved on to the Duchy of Warsaw: "Your Majesty has given it up, I suppose? – Yes, I offered it, and we didn't see fit to accept it. – Spain could still be a bone of contention. – I was forced to leave Spain; this question is thus decided by that." He spoke of an armistice; he would place himself behind the Saale. Merveldt did not hide from him that the allies hoped "to see him cross the Rhine again this autumn. "For that, I must lose a battle." He had also said: "I will make sacrifices, even great sacrifices, but there are things on which my honor depends and which above all, in my position, I could not part with, for example, the protectorate of Germany. "

Germany, after having abandoned Napoléon, rose against him. In 1799 Macdonald had evacuated Italy amid a "torrent of insurrections"; and here, a deluge rising on all sides, around the rutted causeways the French army, in the mud and the rain, flowed towards the Rhine, harassed by its enemies, reprobated by populations, which, more afraid, became hostile; all the cowardice of the great, all the servility of the humble who, since 1795, had smoothed the paths of conquest, turned into betrayals, insults and low revenge on the vanquished. The soldiers, in despair, cried out with hunger, misery, fever, as at Leipzig, at Macdonald: "Marshal, save your children!"[14] The marshals, rebellious since the beginning of the war, recriminated brutally. As the Duke of Taranto asked the Duke of Castiglione for an explanation of an order from the Emperor: "Does the b... know what he is doing!" replied the Duke of Castiglione. "Haven't you noticed he's lost his mind! The coward, he abandoned us, sacrificing us all, and do you think me good enough or stupid enough to have me killed or hanged, for a suburb of Leipzig? You had to do like me, go away!"

On 23 October, they arrived in Erfurt, trying to gather the fugitives, to comfort them. There had been formed stores there; they plundered them. A marshal was going to the castle to take Napoléon's orders to occupy a position that would cover the city. He met Murat.

> F. said to him this king, find the bad one; otherwise he will end up losing himself with us. – What do you want me to do about it? said the Emperor to the same marshal; I give orders and no one listens. I wanted to bring together all the crews, no one came.

Murat had given himself up. On October 16, after the first day at Leipzig, an emissary from Metternich brought him these proposals: England, in agreement with Austria, would engage to make him obtain King Ferdinand's renunciation of the kingdom of Naples; it would guarantee him this kingdom and its independence, it would even procure for him, in addition, certain advantages, provided that he left the French army and sent no troops to the assistance of the viceroy of Italy. "I decided on the spot," said Murat, "to ask the Emperor to return to Naples."[15] However, a soldier at heart, he fought at Leipzig, valiantly as usual, and helped to cover the retreat.

It was in Erfurt, where five years before he held his imperial assizes and his court of kings, gave a spectacle to the world of Alexander's embrace and the "benefit of the gods," invited to his banquet these allies today relentless in his quarry; in this same Erfurt, now the cemetery of his army, the tomb of his prestige, that Napoléon saw his brother-in-law for the last time. This king returned to Naples as he had come from it; the impossibility for him "to remain in any uncertainty." He saw his crown (his prize money) hanging by a thread held by Metternich. Now it belonged to this man. "I showed Napoléon ... such a firm decision for this part (to return to Naples), that I wrested his consent, and lost no time in running away, lest he revoke it. Our farewells were not too cordial."[16] He was quite determined to behave like a king, to think only of himself, and to leave the adventure, in the German style, like the Bavarian, with the guarantee of his kingdom and his sovereignty.

Jérôme, however, evacuated Cassel. Even before the battle had decided his fate, he was thinking of leaving. On 12 October 12, he said to Reinhard quite deliberately: "My intention is to stay." Reinhard pointed out to him that if the [German] princes remained, "it was in the hope that they would embrace what they call the common cause, and this, he said, is what your Majesty cannot and will not do." Jérôme remained pensive, but ordered horses for any event, every night. On the 26th, he heard the cannon: at six o'clock he left on horseback, surrounded by an escort which he called his guard, and made his way to Cologne. Thus ended the Kingdom of Westphalia.[17]

Napoléon resumed his calamitous retreat. On the 29th, at Hanau, the Bavarians tried to bar his way. The army faced. As the guard did not arrive: "We are f.....!" cried Macdonald, "if he does not come quickly." – "I can do nothing about it," answered Napoléon. He was impassive, indifferent, witnessing his own catastrophe as before in Russia, as later at Waterloo. On 31 October he reached Frankfurt, on 2 November, Mainz. The French had abandoned the right bank of the Rhine and retreated to the left bank: they returned to the positions of 1799.

## II. Views of the Allies on Peace

Metternich was made prince and Blücher at the same time became marshal: the one who had struck the fairest, and the one who had struck the hardest. These high rewards called for, by contrast, example and punishment. The King of Saxony saw himself treated by his "brothers" as the Pope had been by the "usurper": he was taken captive to Berlin and his States were put under sequestration. The allies, who claimed to suppress the work of the French Revolution, went back, naturally, to the time of the partitions of Poland, to the time when Stanislas Poniatowski was transported to Russia with his throne: the ex-king placed in the invalids and the ex-throne in the cabinet of curiosities.

Metternich had long suspected and now clearly discerned Alexander's designs: he would make himself King of Poland; Saxony would compensate the Prussians Posen and Warsaw for not being returned to them. The reconstitution of a Poland in the hands of Alexander involved Austria's renunciation of the part of Gallicia ceded in 1809 and perhaps the forced exchange of the rest. What compensation would be awarded to him? Gallicia was a good conquest, well attached to the monarchy, and which provided good recruits. But this exchange seemed insignificant compared with the danger of a Russia overflowing at the gates of Germany, weighing, without counterweight, on the East. What would be the use of having shaken the supremacy of Napoléon, if one substituted for it that of Alexander, with Prussia at Dresden, in the heart of Germany, threatening Vienna, pretending to the Empire?

The revolutionary movement of the Germans terrified Metternich, after having offended him from the start. He reckoned that the sovereigns would be in a position to stifle it, after having animated and exploited its flame. Victorious over France, Germany would fall back on itself and crush itself under its own weight, as was the tradition. The Germans, for a moment united against the "hereditary enemy," were already quarreling among themselves over the allocation they would make of their own homeland, delivered by their peoples. Stein, advocated a great empire, with an elected diet and a powerful emperor, the secondary princes reduced to the role of provincial governors.[18] Hardenberg thought of a division of supremacy between Austria and Prussia. Metternich was repelled by one or the other combination: no empire; Austria not admitting a Hohenzollern German emperor and judging the crown henceforth too heavy for the Habsburgs. Nor did he consent to the dualism suggested by Prussia: that would have been permanent rivalry. What suited Austria was quite simply a Confederation of the Rhine demarcated under the name of Germanic Confederation, into which Prussia would enter for its bare minimum, into which Austria would exercise the hegemony that Napoléon had granted himself in 1806. The confederate princes, kept in their possessions, happy to have drawn from so many trials the object of their traditional ambitions of districts and autonomy, would be grateful to Austria, which guaranteed them these possessions. They would establish a clientele for it and would assure it of an interested support, both against the encroachments of Prussia and against the revolutionary demands of the peoples. Hence the importance that Metternich attributed to his treaty with Bavaria, the foundation stone of the future edifice, and to the treaties he arranged, on the same conditions, with the other Germans.[19]

He found in a number of Russians favorable dispositions. Most of them, great scoffers of Prussia and its king, thought it appropriate to lower the boastfulness and curb the Prussian gluttony. Wrote a Russian diplomat, "The interest of Russia seems to demand that Germany become a mass heavy enough not to be imbued with the ambition of conquest, while preserving however an attitude imposing enough to repel attacks from without."[20] It was enough to unite them, on the outside, against France, and it was fitting that, on the inside, they remained divided. Alexander was not unaware of the advantage of this, and now that at the call of Koutousof and under the spur of Stein, Germany had regimented itself, that he had drawn from it all that he expected, he was inclined, for the rest, to let dreams vanish into promises and fine words. He adhered to the treaty which guaranteed sovereignty to Bavaria.[21]

It was more difficult to contain Prussian greed, turned on Saxony. In this affair, Metternich could expect nothing from Russia, any more than from the article on Poland. He sought support from the side of the English, who were no more interested than Austria in establishing Russian supremacy over Europe. Austria's conduct at Prague had lifted the prejudices of the English. Metternich endeavored to obtain confidence and to establish an understanding as soon as the new ambassador to Franz II arrived. Lord Aberdeen, barely 30 years of age, was a young lord of high birth, great fortune, and fine dress; in the absence of diplomatic experience, which he completely lacked, he possessed calm, reserve, even disconcerting coldness. "A badly groomed young bear," Metternich said at first. He quickly recovered from this impression; but the interviews were quite difficult: Aberdeen did not know German, Metternich spoke French perfectly, but Aberdeen, who did not understand him very well, spoke it with difficulty; Metternich understood English and spoke it little: they were forced to converse in two languages, Aberdeen using his and Metternich speaking French. He judged Aberdeen to be loyal, well intentioned towards Austria, with a certain chivalric background of admiration for Napoléon, of sympathy for the French army, very rare in this profession, especially in England. Metternich could take advantage of this against the enraged ardor of the Prussians and the glorious stubbornness of Alexander. Stadion, who frequented Aberdeen soon after at the Châtillon congress, lightly complained of "his diplomatic innocence." It was undoubtedly a quality in the eyes of Metternich, and he did not allow, as soon as he noticed it, to take advantage of it.

He undertook it at Prague, at Toeplitz, and more than once during the route which they followed together towards the Rhine.[22] He found him in the disposition he desired. They must, he told him, restrict the power of France, but why refuse any negotiation? It would be good to negotiate, were it only to throw on Napoléon the odiousness of the prolongation of the war. Basically, a good peace had to be the goal of this war.

When Merveldt reported the conversation Napoléon had had

with him on 17 October, Metternich saw it as bait. If the fundamental object of the war could be attained by this process, it would be a mistake not to stop there, for the vain pleasure of dethroning Napoléon and reorganizing the government of France. In England, the rulers, since 1804, especially since the treaty of April 1805, had not changed their minds on this article: the dethronement of Napoléon alone would guarantee them the peace they wanted, peace within the old limits. But this downfall and above all the establishment of the restored monarchy, they could not ostensibly give as an object of war. The Parliament, although very bitter against Napoléon, would not have allowed the war to be prolonged for an intervention in the internal affairs of France, when the essential object of the frontiers would be reached. It was therefore necessary to maneuver in secret against the Empire and the Emperor, and the ministers made no mistake of it, but they could not openly refuse to enter into negotiations, at least in pure form.

Now, neither Metternich nor his master dreamed then of dethroning Napoléon. It was here that, with Franz II, the "entrails of the State" were reconciled with the heart. The Bourbons, in mourning for Marie-Antoinette, did not smile on Maria-Louisa's father. A defeated Napoléon, humiliated, driven back within the old limits, reduced to impotence, cornered, very likely to some constitution that would curb his power, a Napoléon "husband and son-in-law," and this time, in truth, successor and nephew of Louis XVI, that was what suited the house of Austria. Let us add that of all the combinations, that of Bernadotte, Viceroy or Lieutenant-General of Russia, was the one which least suited him. If France needed a tutelage, Austria, mother-in-law and grandmother, seemed quite appropriate. Napoléon was neither invulnerable nor above all immortal: war offered hazards; a regency, under the high hand of Metternich, would bring together all the advantages: law, "principles" and politics, therefore, negotiating peace with Napoléon, while continuing to press him through war; force him to make the last sacrifices: peace at the discretion of the allies, abdication in favor of his son, which would cut short the aims of Alexander, and stop his triumphal march on Paris. The French in front of peace with Maria-Louisa and Napoléon II, the regency would profit from it, when the time came, and here, suddenly, Austria carried to this hegemony of Europe which Alexander aspired. The object of this combination consisted in associating the French with it, in exciting a movement of opinion in France, and in forcing, through the

French themselves, the hand of Napoléon.

Metternich had known him for a long time, he had followed very closely and maintained the provisions of the friends of peace and the "friends of Austria" in Paris. More than ever, he believed he could count on Talleyrand. He flattered himself that he found in him the collaborator needed to install the regency and then lead it in the Austrian way. He was informed of Talleyrand's views on peace, and these were precisely the ones he wanted to prevail. It would be more difficult to win over the French. He would achieve this through skillfully graduated games of perspective. He said:

> Knowing thoroughly the public mind in France, I was convinced that in order not to embitter it, in order to present it rather with a bait which would be seized, one would do well to flatter the national self-esteem and to speak, in the proclamation, of the Rhine, of the Alps and Pyrenees, as being the natural frontiers of France... With the aim of isolating Napoléon still further, and at the same time acting on the spirit of the army, I proposed, in addition, to attach to the idea of natural borders the offer of immediate negotiations.[23]

Moreover, and at the same time, he would propose "to take the war to the other side of the Rhine, to the heart of France." They would see the effect that the invasion would produce on the minds of the people, they would be well off and remain masters of giving the proposals, in the event of a congress, and according to the occurrences of the war, more or less scope, because they would negotiate on the march: in no case would an armistice be granted. If Napoléon accepted the bases presented to him and if war turned to the advantage of the allies, they would, at their discretion, push back the border, by the very game of the negotiation engaged with more or less equivocation on the limits of the Pyrenees, the Alps and the Rhine. The base would move with the terrain of the negotiation and the very person of the negotiators. If Napoléon, who would certainly not be caught in the deception, were to refuse, he was lost in public opinion. His refusal denounced to the public, the public would not forgive him. The process was classic, the allies had already experienced it; it would succeed against Napoléon, as formerly against Louis XIV, and more certainly, as Napoléon possessed only personal prestige without the dynastic tradition.[24]

Franz II approved of this plan, which "reserved the largest part for events." The hardest part was getting Alexander there. Metternich represented to him that there would be no formal "opening," that the bases would only be presented in an unofficial way and as an unofficial indication with a view to a preliminary negotiation; that, however, the war would continue and that they would remain free to raise the demands. But, objected Alexander, as well as formerly to the four points: "If Napoléon, confident in the chances of the future, took a prompt and energetic resolution and accepted this proposal in order to thus settle the situation?" Metternich replied, and it was his belief, that "Napoléon would never voluntarily take that course."

Alexander knew, moreover, that they were not committing themselves to anything, as negotiations could only be opened and definitive peace concluded with the consent of England. It was, basically, to return to the spirit and the gradations of the treaty of April 1805, that *vade mecum* of the Tsar. He surrendered, but not without expressing his reservations, the main one being the assurance that Napoléon would not accept: "Reluctant to agitate before the time a question all the more delicate – the downfall of Napoléon – because he was not indifferent to the personal feelings of one of his most intimate allies," Franz II, fearing that if he opposed any negotiation, Austria and perhaps Prussia would give up the march forward; "holding in his heart the secret of peace," and subordinating all dealings with his allies to his real object, which was to "drag them with him to the left bank of the Rhine," he planned

> that as events decided in favor of the allied courts, they would be easily disposed to raise their pretensions; that, according to this, the conditions of peace becoming more burdensome for the Cabinet of the Tuileries, the latter would be so much the less accessible to the counsels of prudence; finally, that the fate of arms alone could give rise to combinations decisive enough to bring about the downfall of Napoléon.[25]

Then, assured that he was not binding his hands nor turning aside from the paths he had prescribed, he gave license to Metternich.

This minister found under his hand the man he needed to fulfill the role of "messenger" in the tragicomedy of high intrigue which he was preparing. It was the Baron de Saint-Aignan, Minister of France at Weimar, brother-in-law of Caulaincourt, who was said to be subject, like him, to the influence of Talleyrand; man of the world and career diplomat, possessing precisely the dose of "seriousness" and self-conceit needed to be duped by some, and, unwittingly, to dupe others. He was captured at Weimar, 24 October, and taken prisoner, following the coalition chancellery. Metternich, who knew him, began it on 26 October, in vague and general remarks on peace and on the harm Napoléon had done himself by refusing to understand and follow his advice.[26] He said:

> The Emperor has been under the illusion for two years. He thought he was making peace in Moscow; then he persuaded himself that he would make it in Dresden and that we could not make war on him. Now who can calculate the consequences of this campaign? We sincerely wanted peace; we still want it and we will do it; it is only a question of approaching the question frankly and without detour. The Duke of Vicenza knows that there is between us, under the seal of secrecy, a writing which could bring peace to a conclusion in sixty hours. The Emperor Napoléon accepted it except for two articles. War had to be declared. In a nine-hour conversation with the Emperor, I had told him about it five times, but nothing could make him believe it.

Metternich expressed the fear that the character of the Emperor Napoléon was an obstacle to peace; that then it would be a disastrous war; that Germany would, by itself and by a spontaneous movement, have 300,000 more men on his frontiers "that the Germans were a gentle people, honest and removed from all violence; that this people was in revolution only because the Emperor Napoléon had offended it, had done nothing for it and had exasperated the sovereigns." He added, "England was much more moderate than was thought," but he was careful to insinuate the independence of Holland. He was careful not to confide to Saint-Aignan the secret of peace in 60 hours: the proposals then communicated to Caulaincourt were too far removed from those which Metternich intended to make henceforth. It would be enough to have launched the sentence which would make its way. To speak of such a secret was to encourage everyone to guess it, and everyone would guess it according to their wishes, would propagate it as they pleased, and the mystery would give it a kind of authenticity. In short, by legend, he was preparing Saint-Aignan for the stratagem. All this conversation, intended for confidences and indiscretions, had no other object than to deceive the gallery, to nourish the illusions of the abused, like Caulaincourt, and to furnish arguments to the clever, like Talleyrand.

On the evening of the 29th, judging Saint-Aignan in good standing, Metternich wrote to Schwarzenberg: "I have arranged this matter with the Emperor Alexander, and we are going to send Saint-Aignan to the Emperor Napoléon with a reply to the overtures he has made to Merveldt." However, he postponed the expedition, a few points remaining to be fixed. They were on the evening of the 29th, at Meiningen, through which passed the august procession. Friedrich-Wilhelm III was absent. Hardenberg, when he learned of the project, disapproved of it. As for Aberdeen, Metternich pretended with him to believe that Napoléon would accept the conditions. Aberdeen, tended in person to be gentle, would be seduced by it; but he would not fail to warn his Government, and nothing would be agreed upon, even on the preliminary bases, so long as the English ministers had not agreed.

In any case, it was, from the start, well established, and subsequently the English negotiators took note of it more than once, that Metternich's proposals, his eventual overtures to the French, his proclamations, and in general his whole procedure, were only of an unofficial character, so that the English could, if need be, "dismiss the parts ... as being officially unknown to them." Metternich was charged with drafting the proclamation which would insinuate the ambiguity, the soul of the whole machination.

### III. Overtures at Frankfurt

The allies had decided to stop in Frankfurt. Metternich arrived there on 4 November as coalition prime minister.[27] The city filled with diplomats, generals, solicitors, intriguers, a whole headquarters, a whole traveling congress: Hardenberg, Humboldt, and Knesebeck for Prussia; soon after it was Stein, appointed administrator of the conquered countries.[28] Stadion, *ad latus* of Metternich; Nesselrode, who was becoming more and more important in Russian affairs; Pozzo, Anstett; Cathcart, Aberdeen, and Charles Stewart; finally the two emperors. The King of Prussia alone was still missing. The old city celebrated, pulling from the attics the German flags and lanterns that had been extinguished since the famous celebrations of the coronation of Franz II in 1792, banquets and balls, which the Revolution had so violently disconcerted, resumed after 21 years, and this time nothing seemed more likely to stop it than moderation alone or the magnanimity of the allies. Everything breathed war. On 7 November, a conference took place between Schwarzenberg, the Austrian Radetzky and the Prussian Gneisenau. The chiefs of staff each developed their plan. Radetzky proposed to remake, to reconstitute in Frankfurt and not to resume active hostilities until 20 November; Gneisenau opined for the immediate passage of the Rhine between Mainz and Strasbourg by the great army, that of Schwarzenberg, while Blücher would invade Belgium and deliver Holland. Then they adjourned.[29]

Metternich took advantage of this respite to initiate his negotiation, and he did so as a consummate director, by an act of high comedy, in which he played, in the grand style, the character of Scapin of Court and State. Saint-Aignan had been driven to Frankfurt. On 8 November, Metternich summoned him and resumed his remarks, specifying them:

> No one resented the Emperor Napoléon's dynasty. We were ready to get along. Conditions to be established were naturally to set limits to the power of England and France. England, moreover, had much lower pretensions than was claimed. She was ready to give back to independent Holland what she would not give back as a French province.

These words contained the stuff of two misunderstandings, to put it politely. *No one was angry with the Emperor's dynasty*, in the sense that if the Emperor Alexander wanted to dethrone Napoléon, if he planned to replace him with Bernadotte, his plan, although very concerted, had not been recorded in any protocol. Metternich could therefore say nobody, that is to say, no juridical person, either official or formal. As for Holland, it was less a question of restoring islands and colonies than of increasing its extent by means of Belgium, in whole or in part, as far as the Scheldt, perhaps, but with Antwerp, at least.[30]

The next day, deliberation on war plans was resumed in the presence of Hardenberg at Metternich's, without anything definitive being decided, except the decision to resume the offensive as soon as they found themselves in a position. That same day, 9 November, Saint-Aignan was again summoned to Metternich's at nine o'clock in the evening. Metternich was alone; he was leaving, he said, for the Emperor Alexander, and it was in concert with this sovereign that he was going to entrust to Saint-Aignan with "words that this diplomat should take to the Emperor." Whereupon Nesselrode arrived and said that "one could regard M. de Hardenberg as present and approving everything that was going to be said," an affirmation, as we shall see, exactly contrary to reality. Metternich then developed his insinuations but he did not submit any notes. Saint-Aignan asked permission to summarize Metternich's words in writing and retired to an adjoining room for this purpose. The note he wrote recognized the "indissoluble bonds" of the allies, England's adherence to the coalition; consequently the uselessness, henceforth "to think either of an armistice or of a negotiation which did not have a general peace as its first principle"; "that the allied sovereigns were *unanimously agreed on the power and the preponderance that France must preserve in its integrity, and by confining itself within its natural limits, which are the Rhine, the Alps and the Pyrenees.*" Independence of Germany was a *sine qua non* of peace; likewise the independence of Holland and that of Italy; the frontier of Austria, on this side, still to be determined; finally the restoration of the Bourbons in Spain. "England was ready to make the greatest sacrifices for peace founded on these bases and to recognize the liberty of commerce and navigation, to which France is entitled." A congress could open on the spot, "without however the negotiations suspending the course of the military operations."

Metternich came to find Saint-Aignan in the room where he was writing and asked him "if he had any reluctance to see the English ambassador, who had just arrived." Saint-Aignan had no difficulty there, quite the contrary. He returned to the living room, greeted each other, and Metternich would have added, in the introduction: "Here is Lord Aberdeen, Ambassador of England, our intentions are common, so we can continue to explain ourselves to him." Saint-Aignan read out his note. Aberdeen followed the text with some difficulty; could he really grasp the nuances? However, coming to the article "of England's greatest sacrifices," he says "that she possessed much, which she would give back with both hands," but there he made the reservation "that she would never consent to anything that might infringe its maritime rights." He added that, besides, he very much wanted to know France and Paris, and spoke of the esteem which the English nation had for the French.

The allies, to complete the bait, did not fail to designate, at least for public opinion, the man who seemed to them the most likely to enter into their views. It was precisely the one whose name Talleyrand and his friends would not fail to put forward, and whose credit Saint-Aignan would hasten to publish everywhere. Already, on 26 October, Metternich had shown him "the esteem that the Emperor of

Austria had conceived for the Duke of Vicenza." He renewed this assurance.

> He instructed me to tell the Duke of Vicenza that he was preserved the feelings of esteem that his noble character has always inspired and that they would willingly hand over to him the interests of Austria and those of everyone else, if possible, to decide according to the principles of fairness that we know of.

Schwarzenberg, who came up, associated himself with these words. Nesselrode, who had been absent, returned and added this compliment that Alexander "would never change his opinion of his loyalty and his character, and that things would soon be settled if he were entrusted with negotiation."

On this subject they separated. Convinced that it was enough to pronounce the words *natural limits* for Parisians, fascinated by these words alone, to take them literally. Convinced that they would not ask for any other explanation and would consider this indication as a basis for a definitive peace, Metternich took care, in order to save his retreat, in the unlikely event that Napoléon took him at his word, to remove from his communication any official character and concerted. He wrote to Caulaincourt on 10 November:

> Monsieur your brother-in-law returning to France, it would have been impossible for me not to charge him with a word for Your Excellency. The Emperor ordered me to talk with M. de Saint-Aignan. He will render an account to His Majesty the Emperor of my words and those of M. de Nesselrode; chance brought the English ambassador to my house when we were together. I did not hesitate to let him take part in our interview. M. de Saint-Aignan will have fulfilled his task perfectly by faithfully reporting our words; we have taken great care to exempt him from any objection or remark.

This letter put things in perspective of a conversation ordered by the Emperor of Austria, between a passer-by, Saint-Aignan, and two of the ministers of the coalition, Metternich, who joined, we do not say in what capacity, visitor or negotiator, Nesselrode; the chance arrival of Aberdeen; nothing official, words to report and which did not commit anyone, because Metternich could not propose anything in the name of Austria alone, nor propose anything in the name of the allies without their formal consent. This was not the way to present new "overtures" of peace or to "lay the foundations" to be accepted by yes or by no. Saint-Aignan himself, transmitting his report to Maret, wrote:

> I told M. de Metternich that the note I was taking was for me alone and that I would not put it before the Emperor. This writing is not official. The expressions are vague. I had no reason to ask for a clearer explanation.

Metternich wanted to take a copy of it; Saint-Aignan did not think he had to refuse: "it would have been to give it more importance than it should have."[31]

The note indeed remained singularly ambiguous on the essential point, that of the limits. When Saint-Aignan, "subscribing to his own words" from Metternich, writes: "the natural limits, which are the Rhine, the Alps and the Pyrenees," he meant it, and all the French should have heard it as him, quite simply from the limits of Lunéville. We already know, and we will soon see even more precisely, what different meaning the allies gave to it. For them and for Metternich, these words *natural limits* and *limits of the Rhine* could lend themselves to the most variable of interpretations.[32] There was interest in letting the illusion spread in France, and skill in this new series of "nuances" consisted, as in the days of Dresden, in not defining anything. Napoléon would understand and say no; public opinion would be mistaken and would condemn the Emperor.

Metternich immediately wrote to Hudelist: "I do not believe that Napoléon is giving the affair any real follow-up. But we had to, in every respect, take a step, to clarify and at the same time obtain weapons within the nation." Hardenberg had stayed at home. When, in the evening, he learned of the interview, he noted in his diary: "Peace proposals without my participation, by Saint-Aignan Rhine, Alps, Pyrenees, absurdity, great stuff this." Stewart, as soon as he was informed, was offended; he only calmed down when Hardenberg assured him that "the document drawn up by M. de Saint-Aignan is and remains an unofficial document without any authenticity."[33] On reflection, Aberdeen, who possessed neither instructions nor powers, felt very embarrassed. He referred it to his minister, Castlereagh, and two weeks later notified his express reservations in the form of a note to Metternich:[34]

The undersigned, having arrived at Prince Metternich's, found there a document drawn up by M. de Saint-Aignan, in the form of an unofficial minute of a confidential conversation. After reading this document, the undersigned, in the presence of H.H. Prince Metternich and Count Nesselrode, with whom the interview had taken place, protested against the turn of the paragraph where England is mentioned. The language used by the undersigned on this occasion expresses the sincere wish of England for a peace which, based on equitable conditions, would assure the independence and tranquility of the Continent and the real happiness of France itself. His remarks on the content of the document drawn up by M. de Saint-Aignan were limited to the passage where England was mentioned, and if he did not push them further, it was not because he thought that the piece was complete on its own, but because he viewed the communication as private and unofficial, and one in which he probably had no part.

It was with these comments, added to the prior reservations and formalities of Alexander, that it is necessary to interpret these terms of the note of Saint-Aignan "that the allied sovereigns were unanimously in agreement." The intentions of the English showed themselves very clearly. We read in a memorandum which is among the Castlereagh papers, that France, brought back to its old limits, would soon find itself in a position to attack Germany again.[35] It therefore had to be contained, and the idea of the 1713 barrier reappeared with the same conditions of European peace: "An intermediate state between France and the Bas-Rhin," made up of Belgium with the territories between Meuse, Moselle and Rhine, joined to Holland. These views were connected with the Guelph kingdom, Germany's market and England's foothold on the Continent. The English ministry inclined to it. Castlereagh wrote on 13 November to Aberdeen, that is to say a day before Saint-Aignan informed Napoléon of the feigned offer of "natural limits" unanimously presented by the allies, including England:[36]

> Lord Aberdeen will not be surprised to learn that after such a flood of success, the English nation would probably look with defiance on a peace which did not strictly confine France within its ancient bounds; even on this condition, peace with Napoléon would never be popular, because one would never believe that he could wish to maintain it. The cabinet is determined to use all its influence to prevent the allies from rushing an arrangement that would not present solid guarantees. Consider that to take Antwerp from France is above all other objects most essential to British interests.

Always concerned to see the continental allies collect the subsidies and suspend the war as soon as their own conveniences were satisfied, the ministers instructed Cathcart to propose "a treaty of general alliance" against France, among all the powers of Europe.[37] Alexander did not care; it would have been to chain him too closely and impose a "capitulation" on his dictatorship. Besides, was not the object attained by separate treaties? It would be completely so if England, consenting to sacrifices, restored its colonies to France in compensation for the restitutions claimed from France on the Continent. Pozzo di Borgo received the mission to develop these views in London.[38]

On 19 November a new council of war had been held at Frankfurt, and this plan was decided upon: to occupy Holland and Switzerland, these two bastions henceforth turned against France; the march of the main army, Schwarzenberg on Langres, and Blücher operating on the left bank of the Rhine. On the taking of military possession of Switzerland, difficulties arose between Austria, determined to ignore it, and Alexander, who suddenly made himself the champion of Swiss neutrality, which, together with the still defective state of Blücher's army, delayed the crossing of the Rhine. Add the timidity and uncertainty of the King of Prussia, who arrived on 13 November. "He would like to remain with folded arms in Frankfurt," wrote Hardenberg, and the King wrote to him some time later: "This unfortunate invasion that is planned in France makes me shudder; we risk spoiling everything and losing the finest fruits of our efforts." 3 Metternich, on the contrary, considered that all was well: "We are firmly and surely going to work," he told Hudelist on 18 November. All in all, Schwarzenberg's political plans and military plans prevailed. They did not stop, but did not plunge into France blindly and they made arrangements to make peace there, with Napoléon himself, on the most extensive conditions that war would allow.

## IV. Response of Napoléon

The English were in Bayonne, Holland was invested, Belgium rose, the great army of the allies was on the Rhine, all the bastions, all the advanced forts had succumbed, or if they stood, they were like Hamburg, so many islets in the flood, useless, like the stranded and scattered vessels of a squadron in distress. France invested was under the blow of the invasion. In Paris, everything was intrigue and conspiracy, preparation for the next day, evolutions and defections. Talleyrand and his associates; Louis, who served the Unholy Mass in 1790; Dalberg, whom Napoléon made duke and who corresponded with Petersburg as "friend of Russia"; Antoine-Anasthase Roux-Laborie, master in cabals; always in the intrigues; then "the army of women," among whom there were conspiracies, who received advice, surprise half-confessions, informing, transmitting, possessing affiliations everywhere in Russia, Italy, Austria, sometimes reviving, sometimes unraveling in plots the old loves: the Duchess of Courlande, niece and favorite of Talleyrand, his delight, his confidante, and his adviser; the Duchess of Dalberg, who figured in the Empress's household, and warned the allies that they were expected in Paris with open arms; Mme de Vaudémont, correspondent of Fouché, halfway between Benevento and Otranto, and whose name recalled the illustrious betrayals of the time of Louis XIV,[39] as spirit of the League, temperament of the Fronde, but domesticated, who did not ask revolutions, said a woman "than to pass by her room, without finding out where they are going next"; and on the *entresol*,* Madames de Coigny and de Chastenay.[40] It was no longer the death of the Emperor that was feared, it was the fall of the Empire that was speculated upon. It will fall, but which way? Who will take over affairs? It was here that Talleyrand insinuated himself into the foreground. By other means, he arrived at the same combinations as Metternich: peace and regency. The peace of which he must be the great broker, perhaps the arbiter; the regency of which he would become the tutor of another Congress of Westphalia, another Anne of Austria, another Mazarin. Fouché was missing: Napoléon has sent him to Illyria to cover the retreat, less for the good that he might do there than for the harm that, meanwhile, he would not do in Paris.[41] In the world of the new rich and the new nobles, there was an increasing inclination towards the faction of the

---
\* A sort of mezzanine.

friends of Antraigues and the "friends of England"; it was thought that if Napoléon survived, there would be general ruin; but a salvation of fortunes could only come from peace, and peace only from allies.

This peace, which France desired, which Europe desired, Napoléon alone, out of the vanity of an upstart and conqueror, out of selfishness, out of madness perhaps, refused it at Prague!

> Hence there is a sort of satisfaction at the reverses experienced by the Emperor, because they were a punishment for his ambition. Disaffected minds separated France from its chief, and the humiliation of the Emperor seemed to console the ills of the country. The public effects were down to 50.[42]

The skillful, who had their funds in England, speculated on the decline. One did not yet say our friend the enemy! but one thought: bad news, good news, battle lost, security won! It would be over soon!

Talleyrand alone, perhaps, who knew Europe, who, from the beginning of the war, considered that peace would only be possible and lasting by returning to the old boundaries, foreseeing the demands of the allies and resigning himself to them in advance. He wrote,[43] "The powers soon after cannot take too much security if they don't want to be forced to start over again at fresh expense next year."[44] But he kept his plausible conjectures to himself; the illusions of others served his calculations too well. Metternich entertained them, Talleyrand did not dissipate them. These others were everyone, from those who claimed to be the best informed of Austria's secrets, like Caulaincourt, to the lowest of the short-story writers. No one doubted – the "friends of England" had been repeating this for 12 years – that the resolution of the allies was to spare France and give it peace on the conditions it wanted. This illusory concept then became like a fundamental maxim of Parisian politicians. Peace within the limits of Lunéville and Amiens! France, respected by the princes who would have had the honor of conquering it, admired by nations delivered, like them, from the tyrant, would prosper within these limits prescribed by nature, and would gain more liberty there.

A few royalists were beginning to murmur the name of the Bourbons. Some avoided listening. Some, like Talleyrand, because they feared disgrace or proscription; mostly because they did not know these princes. One cannot imagine to what extent they were forgotten, ignored even in families attached to the old monarchy. The rout of the Spanish royalty had deprived Joseph of the little philosophical prestige with which his friends flattered him. Eyes turned to Bernadotte's panache; the "Prince of Sweden" had the female politicians on his side, Mme de Stael, Mme de Chastenay.

> Bernadotte was then the true object of general confidence. Could this man of war, having become sovereign and whose glory was French, enter his country by force of arms, to carve up the provinces and deliver them up to foreigners? He was brave, he was from Béarnais. It was before him that Paris was to open up, and he would be its protector.[45]

A second-hand Henri IV. Thus reasoned, in 1792, the unfortunate royalists, when they saw the army of Condé forming the rear guard of the invasion: thus speculated the enlightened revolutionaries on the Duke of Brunswick, this *philosophe* prince," of whom one had expected at one moment, the regeneration of France. Benjamin Constant turned these nonsense intellectuals into a system and he deduced a sensational brochure: *De l'esprit de conquête et d'usurpation dans ses rapports avec la civilisation européenne.* [On the spirit of conquest and usurpation in its relations with European civilization.][46] Bernadotte, who added to the trophies of victory the suffrages of reason, would raise the republican assemblies from their ashes, oppose to a servile senate a patriotic tribunal, treat with Europe, restore to the nation its imprescriptible rights. He would constitute France, decree the downfall of Napoléon, restore the monarchy if necessary, but with liberty. "The hero has only to stamp his foot, and anarchy disappears, the French people resurrect." What the liberals of 1817 will say of the Prince of Orange, another "favorite" of public opinion: "A Protestant sovereign is what France needs." Protestant, Bernadotte was just enough to satisfy the legislators of the former Civil Constitution and the Institute atheists; he attended the Lutheran sermon, in Swedish, which he did not understand; he asked only to hear, at Saint-Denis, the Latin mass of Henri IV, the text of which he would not have understood either. Benjamin Constant assumed the role of draft Montesquieu of the imperial debacle. Chateaubriand was destined to be a precursor of the Restoration: he was preparing, in the shadows, his pamphlet *De Buonaparte et des Bourbons*, getting ready to reveal the Bourbons to France, and if the Bourbons still had royal blood and political sense, to reveal France to the Bourbons.

Napoléon returned to Saint-Cloud on 10 November, full of bitterness against his servants, especially against his brothers: "It is in my destiny to see myself constantly betrayed by the dreadful ingratitude of the men whom I have most filled with benefits."[47] He presided over the Council of State on 11 November, and asked for financial means. They discussed; each, nodding, thought of peace. Napoléon realized this, and crudely showed things as they were.

> We must dissolve the triumvirate which once divided Poland and which has just reformed with the audacious project of making us experience the same fate. You talk too much about peace, gentlemen. I see it well, we are not Romans. Do you want to descend from the rank in which I placed France, do you want to become a simple monarchy again, and no longer be an empire? This is what will happen to you if you lose Holland. You need the mouths of the rivers and this barrier to the north. Rather than return it, I will cut the dikes and return it to the sea.[48]

The advisers didn't believe it. Since 1795, all the governments had held the same speech, and these combinations which had led the French to Moscow, had not prevented the allies from arriving at the Rhine. Besides, they would put things right and deliver France from this nightmare of 20 years. Who bothered about the Grand Empire? This empire was suffocating France! As for the fate of Poland, no one feared it, sure as one felt of the magnanimity of Alexander, of the greatness of soul, of the generosity of the English, and of their peace of Amiens. Nothing was capable of shaking this relentless illusion. The more Napoléon insisted on the necessity of dominating Holland and Germany in order to keep the limits, the more he persuaded people of his senseless stubbornness, of his culpable blindness.

The same day he received Roederer, inquired about Jérôme, who was on the run; of Louis, wandering; of Joseph, at Mortefontaine, but all three still kings at heart, carrying their crowns in their suitcases, their kingdoms on the soles of their boots and clinging to their parchments.

> Did he still want the throne of Spain? – Sire, he thinks, I presume, that it would still be possible for him to negotiate. – Chimera! They don't want him. They regard him as incapable. They don't want a king who always lives with the women, playing games. The king depends on women, his houses, his furniture. Me, I care neither for Saint-Cloud nor for the Tuileries. We would burn that, that I would be indifferent to it. I count my houses for nothing, the women for nothing, my son a little. It is one of my faults to have believed my brothers necessary to assure my dynasty, my dynasty is assured without them.[49]

He spoke of Eugène, whom he was thinking of for the Italian crown, if he had to abdicate it: "He has honor, the king has none. There are only two motives that turn men away from evil deeds: religion and honor. Of religion the king has none. My father-in-law has no honor, but he has religion."[50] He returned to Joseph, who at least claimed his primogeniture.

> He would be my eldest Elder! He for our father's vineyard, no doubt! – In the case of the opening of the regency, Sire? – Oh! in that case he would cause trouble, I expect that. See the story. Everything has been quiet this year. M. de Talleyrand was quiet. I haven't had any intrigues like Fouché did with Talleyrand three years ago. If I had the king here – Joseph – and his great friends, the Clément de Ris and others, they would turn everything upside down.

This conversation, carried away in form, but perfectly considered as to substance, announced serious resolutions on the subject of Spain. Napoléon had been brooding over them for several months. He sent Laforest to Valençay, very secretly, with credentials, and this letter for Fernando, Prince of Asturias:[51]

> My cousin, the present circumstances of the policy of my empire lead me to desire an end to the affairs of Spain. I wish to remove all pretext for English influence, and re-establish the bonds of friendship and good neighborliness which have existed for so long between the two nations.

It was to bring things back to April 1808, the day Fernando arrived in Bayonne, to bring them back there to start them upside down and decree oblivion over five years of atrocious war and so many French people needlessly sacrificed.

In the meantime, on 14 November, Saint-Aignan arrived with his report. Napoléon received it on the 15th. He wrote that same day to Fouché, "You will do all you can to prevent people in this country (Italy) from being misled by the fallacious promises of Austria and by the fallacious language of Metternich." Such was his impression, very direct and very lively, on the first acquaintance he took of these "overtures" of Frankfurt. He pierced the pretense of it, and it was the whole spirit of the reply which he sent to Metternich, by Maret, on 16 November. Under the impact of the experience of Prague, which justified his forecasts only too well, he opined that the allies would have a fair chance to disavow the verbal insinuations reported by a Frenchman without powers and without mission; that it would therefore be important to obtain confirmation of it in writing, which the allies would easily grant, if they were sincere. He did not think (and he was right) that the words reported by Saint-Aignan constituted an ultimatum to be accepted or rejected by yes or by no; he saw in it an unofficial suggestion with a view to negotiations to be resumed, to be reopened, and the indication of a preliminary basis to be extended or restricted; now, in this respect war could serve him as well as the allies. He therefore confined himself to simply announcing the dispatch of an envoy. According to the wishes of the allies, he designated Caulaincourt; which indicated a desire for conciliation.[52] He reserved the right to explain himself later on the bases, according to the response that the allies would make and according to the turn that military events would take. He reasoned cautiously; but he reckoned without the cunning of Metternich and the echoes which this minister had arranged for himself in Paris. Napoléon negotiated only in view of the allies and the realities of war; Metternich operated only in view of the public and of opinion in Paris, and he had hit the nail on the head.

Saint-Aignan was widespread in Paris; his brother-in-law Caulaincourt even more so. They met at Mme de Coigny's, at Mme de Vaudémont's, who gave a dinner every week; where they met every evening, with Mme de Laval, Pasquier, Molé, Dalberg, Lavalette, Vitrolles, who knew how to listen and hear, a number of friends, confidants or associates of Talleyrand, finally "a count of S., former envoy from Persia to the court of France, Piedmontese by his mother, c... German by his wife, English by his alliances, Russian by a cousin, French by conquest and spy by taste, status and habit."[53] Pasquier recounted, "There were voluntary, calculated indiscretions, and the proposals of which M. de Saint-Aignan had been the bearer were soon known in Paris." Metternich had told Saint-Aignan: "The Duke of Vicenza knows that there is between us, under the seal of secrecy, a writing that could conclude peace in sixty hours." All of Paris was soon in on this secret and knew that "a few hours have caused everything to be lost in Prague,"[54] and what peace: not only the limits, but Westphalia, Berg, Holland, Italy, in short everything that was not specified in the 8 August ultimatum! Now, after so many disasters, Saint-Aignan still brought the much-desired peace, the "peace of the limits," that which Napoléon was not able to content himself with, and which France still missed. No one doubted either the sincerity of the allies or the authenticity of the proposals; Saint-Aignan had been "formally charged with it by M. de Metternich and M. de Nesselrode"; England "declared that it was willing to make the greatest sacrifices to conclude a peace which would be founded on these bases" (!) "She has a lot, but she would give back with both hands!"[55]

*Bases! The bases of Frankfurt!* These words were now on everyone's lips. These bases were certain, because they were reasonable, because the limits were imprescriptible, and all the governments had declared it since 1795, so everyone believed it blindly. Everyone spoke as if he had seen the marvelous parchment on which it was enough to affix a signature to put an end to all the evils of France and Europe and to repair with a stroke of the pen the double fault that it had become, a classic to reproach Napoléon: having broken the peace of Amiens not having stopped after Austerlitz. Pasquier reported,

> The desire to see him accept them (these bases) was universal, and a sort of league was formed in the palace, in the city, in the council, to push Napoléon along this path of safety. M. le Duc de Vicence was its soul and M. de Talleyrand was no stranger to it.

The Minister of the Treasury, Mollien; that of the police, Savary "were most pronounced for a prompt and frank acceptance." Berthier and "almost all the *aides-de-camp* thought the same." Valletta was working on it in the dark cabinet, and Pasquier informed the Emperor of this through the bulletins of "what was being said in Paris."

There was a general outcry against Maret, who was accused of being the author of the unfortunate reply of 16 November. Caulaincourt, enlightened by the Prague conferences on the real dispositions of the allies, and very exactly informed by his brother-in-law, M. de Saint-Aignan, did not hesitate to regard the latest proposals as an ultimatum on which it was essential to explain frankly, if the negotiation was not to be broken off.[56]

And all Paris repeated it after him, Napoléon ended by worrying about such general disapproval; he sacrificed Maret and replaced him in Foreign Affairs by Caulaincourt. At the same time Pierre-Antoine Daru left as Secretary of State to take over the war administration.

Maret's letter, which Metternich received on 25 November, provided him with the opportunity to perpetuate the ambiguity and to check Napoléon in the face of public opinion, without committing himself to anything. He replied to Maret that before accepting a congress, the allies wanted to have "the certainty that Napoléon accepted the general and summary bases that I indicated in my interview with the baron de Saint-Aignan." He avoided, moreover, specifying them, precisely what Napoléon wanted to obtain from him; the words "general and summary bases" betrayed the intention of discovering other, more specific and detailed requirements in the negotiation; the terms "indicated in my interview with the Baron de Saint-Aignan" brought the feigned overtures back to their true character, added no official guarantee, even less any collective guarantee.

This letter was delivered to Caulaincourt. He answered it on 2 December. It was, in principle, adherence to a peace based on the balance of Europe and – Napoléon insisted on what Metternich left ambiguous – "on the recognition of the integrity of all nations within their natural limits," and in particular, "to the general and summary bases which were communicated to M. de Saint-Aignan."

Metternich now thought himself sure of public opinion in Paris. He had on his side the credulity, perhaps the confidence, of Napoléon's new minister. He caused the approval on 4 December of a declaration intended by the sovereigns to make known to the French people the views of the allies at the moment when they were preparing to cross the Rhine, which they pretended to wish to assign as a limit to France. It was a work that he rightly considered to be one of his masterpieces. In this play, the only one involving the allies, he was careful not to reproduce – Alexander moreover would not have allowed it, nor Aberdeen – the sentence of Saint-Aignan: "That the allied sovereigns were unanimously in agreement on the power and the preponderance that France must preserve in its integrity and by confining itself within its natural limits, which are the Rhine, the Alps and the Pyrenees."

The natural limits, the Rhine, the Alps, the Pyrenees vanished. There remained only ambiguous and vague expressions: 1) The allied powers do not make war on France, but on this preponderance which, for the misfortune of Europe and France, the Emperor Napoléon too long exercised outside the limits of his empire. 2) Sovereigns want France to be big, strong and happy. 3) The powers confirm to the French empire an expanse of territory that France has never known under its kings.

Metternich wrote: "Our moral purpose is obvious as we are working to act on the interior of France." Aberdeen said: "We thought it appropriate, given the happy turn of events, to abandon the determination of the borders Rhine, Alps, Pyrenees."[57] Said an official Russian document,

> By this solemn manifestation of their intentions and wishes, the Allied cabinets had as their principal object the separation of the cause of Napoléon from that of the French people, and thus of removing the obstacles which a national resistance might have opposed to the armies of the coalition.

This resolution and the welcome given to Caulaincourt's letter when it arrived in Frankfurt on 5 December clearly reveal the illusion in which the politicians of Paris were. They imagined that a very simple yes, addressed on 16 November to the proposals of Saint-Aignan, would have forced the hand of the allies. They saw on 5 December what one would have seen on 25 November at the news of the acceptance of "the general and summary bases." Metternich brooded over his reply for five days, and wrote on 10 December to Caulaincourt. Noting "with satisfaction that the Emperor had accepted the essential bases" of peace, the sovereigns were going to bring this declaration, without delay, "to the knowledge of their allies," that is to say that they were going to consult the English, not with a view to the opening of a congress, but with a view to "preliminary conferences, so as to establish the bases and the mode of a definitive pacification."[58] It was so untrue that a yes would have sufficed to accommodate everything, that a whole month passed without there being any question of negotiating and that the preliminary conferences did not open until 5 February 1814, two months later.

Twenty thousand copies of the declaration were thrown beyond the Rhine and distributed throughout France "by all means in the power of the allies." It was dated 1 December. When it arrived in Paris, the public and politicians agreed to join the game: they read the text as Metternich had desired; and they saw, in imagination, the fascinating words the *limit of the Rhine* spring up from the sympathetic ink, "between the lines";[59] the sacred line of Basel to Holland was drawn on the map in luminous relief. They learned that Napoléon refused it, and it was henceforth the most ineradicable of legends.

## V. Defection of Murat

Napoléon himself began the liquidation of the Grand Empire. He got rid of Spain and the Spaniards. The treaty was signed at Valençay on 11 December. It returned to Spain the Bourbon kings with its continental and colonial territories as they existed at the time of the Treaty of Utrecht. Napoléon thought at the same time of freeing the Pope, and he sent to him, at Fontainebleau, the Bishop of Piacenza to negotiate his departure and his return to Rome. Pius VII replied that he would treat only at Rome itself, and Napoléon had henceforth no other resource but to send him back there.[60]

On 9 December he had opened the session of the chambers:[61] sessions on levies of men and levies of taxes. His speech was only the last echo of those that France had heard for 22 years, each time the Government demanded a new effort and proclaimed the need to restart the war: "France itself would be in danger, without the energy and the union of the French. It is up to you to set an example of an energy that commends our generation to future generations." Let them not say of us: "They sacrificed the first interests of the country! they recognized the laws which England sought in vain for four centuries to impose on France."[62] Speaking of peace negotiations: "I have ordered that you be given all the original documents. You will learn about it through a commission."

Caulaincourt would even have liked a publication. It would have, he wrote to the Emperor on 23 December, "the double advantage of giving France a pledge of your moderation and of proclaiming the public and reciprocal commitment for the allies not to demand more and for Your Majesty not to grant less." Caulaincourt no doubt imagined that reading these pieces would convey to the minds of the

French people the conviction with which he was animated. Napoléon did not consent to this. Saint-Aignan's report was singularly amended. The essential remained, the sentence on the limits; but, in the document thus accommodated, it took on more importance, I don't know if more official; in short, the proposals took on infinitely more pronounced base figures, and there followed an effect very different from that expected by the Emperor. Caulaincourt received commissioners of the Senate at the archchancellor's, who listened to him in silence. Then D'Hauterive was charged with indoctrinating those of the Legislative Body, among whom were François-Marie Raynouard and Joachim-Joseph Lainé. They showed themselves to be more inquisitive, less easygoing, visibly inclined to blind belief in the allies, to undisguised distrust of Napoléon. They thought it was enough to take note of the overtures; but they thought it useful to bind Napoléon. They asked him for a promise to France, to Europe, in positive and formal terms, to accede to these overtures. Raynouard, one of the commissioners, said "that the downcast, enervated public spirit could not otherwise rise again." He continued,

> The Legislative Body should declare to the Emperor that when he was raised to the throne by the will of the nation, he had promised to defend the borders and to preserve the integrity of the territory of the empire that today today he was summoned to keep his promise; that there would be no sacrifices that were not made to contribute with him to the acquisition of this oath, but that the wishes of the French stopped there, and that all that extended beyond this interest could be sacrificed for peace.[63]

The Senate voted an address of platitude. It would be without interest if the rapporteur, Fontanes, had not confirmed, accentuated, and officially specified the overtures of Frankfurt and the refusal of peace by Napoléon:

> M. le Prince de Metternich and the Russian Minister, M. le Comte de Nesselrode, both, named of their courts, laid before him (M. de Saint-Aignan), in a confidential interview, the preliminary bases for a general pacification. The English ambassador, Lord Aberdeen, was present at this conference. Notice that last point, senators, it is important.

The Legislative Body, through the mouth of Lainé,[64] one of the next architects of the restoration of the Bourbons, replied with remonstrances, regretting the illusion of peace, the Emperor's refusal, demanding control, the tribune. Napoléon answered in a few words: "Béarn, Alsace, Franche-Comté, Brabant are under attack. I call on the French to help the French. The foreigner will flee or sign the bases that he himself has proposed. There is no longer any question of recovering the conquests that we had made."[65] Then, on 31 December he declared the assignment closed.

Laine's remonstrances had the same effect on the public as the manifesto of the allies: they began to speak of liberty as they spoke of peace; people believed in the efficacy of the speeches of this Legislative Body, silent since Brumaire, as well as in the sincerity of the sovereigns of Europe, united for twenty-two years. In short, public opinion gave reasons for detaching itself from Napoléon.

Napoléon, in this disarray of his empire and faced with the resistance of his servants, had recourse to the expedients of the Revolution: he took up the language, the measures, and, as he said some time later, he put on his boots of 1793. Thus the decree of December 26th which revived the commissioners of the executive power of 1792 and the representatives on mission of 1793. The brother kings, the Bonapartes found themselves once again brought together around Paris; they too operated their retreat on history and went back to the starving and uncertain times, to 1795.[66] Napoléon wrote to Louis:

> You are no longer King of Holland. The territory of the empire is invaded, I have all Europe armed against me. Do you want to come as a French prince? I will receive you ... you will be my subject. If, on the contrary, you persist in your ideas of king and Holland, move away forty leagues from Paris. (And to Joseph) France is invaded, Europe all in arms against France, but above all against me. You are no longer King of Spain; do you wish, as a French prince, to line up with the throne? You will have my friendship, your prerogative, and will be my subject. Is this not possible for you? You must withdraw to forty leagues from Paris. You will live there in peace, if I live. You will be killed or arrested there if I die.[67]

Louis and Jérôme agreed to move away to forty leagues: that was still, in their opinion, to look like kings. Joseph, always political and who kept his thoughts behind his head, contented himself with the title; he became King Joseph, king of what? king of nothing, king like a prefect baron, a senator count. He opted for the confidence of the Emperor, the prerogative in the Empire, and the place closest to the throne, that of lieutenant general in the regency. "Friends of order and wise ideas, wrote a diplomat in 1805, would believe they had found the complement of the benefits of Providence, if the death of Napoléon could put Prince Joseph in his place."[68] Joseph put himself in the first rank of these wise men. He had wasted two years at Naples, lost his genius in Spain; were the predicted times approaching?

Murat judged them come and jumped the ditch. Alone of the Napoléonic kings, this lateral king still survived. He only used this remnant of life to betray his master, and his royal prerogative only to pact against his country. Napoléon discerned his movements.[69] To stop him, if it was still possible, he sent Fouché to him, who was returning from Illyria, retiring before the Austrians. If Fouché did not keep Murat, Murat at least would keep Fouché away from Paris. Murat, to motivate the defection he was preparing, had asked the Emperor to proclaim the independence of the Italians and "to unite Italy into a single nation."[70] On the 27th, Caulaincourt, in a composite report with Durant's correspondence, concluded: "The object of the king is to make Italy independent." He added: "Your Majesty has made it a nation. Most Italians want to have a political existence. The King of Naples noticed it. He will make every effort to make this opinion burst on all sides, and to unite, if he can, all the members of Italy." But was it appropriate to form only one monarchy? Caulaincourt, imbued with the traditions of Talleyrand, as if he had had before his eyes that minister's reports to the Directory, opined in favor of division: Murat in Naples, a neutral state in the center. However, he advised tacking, letting Murat sleep off his illusions: in peace, everyone would go home, the Duke of Tuscany, the Pope and Murat himself. In the meantime, occupied with such glorious designs, "this prince will seek less to obtain from allies what he will hope to obtain from Your Majesty ... he will not openly detach himself from Your Majesty's cause."

But it was too late and Murat had turned to the side of the allies. Metternich had seized the moment with Murat, just as he had conducted the intrigue against Napoléon, from Dresden to Frankfurt, all the easier in promises as he knew the allies resolved to ratify nothing, and that he was engaged to do nothing without them. His calculation consisted in separating Murat from Napoléon, in discrediting him in France and in Europe, in wearing him out in Italy, in pledging himself there and in expelling him from it, if he did not fall through his own failure. As for the motives which led Murat to listen to him, Fouché deduced them with the sagacity of a defecting master, who, in all likelihood, was already meditating on his own.[71] The King, he wrote, showed himself offended at not having received from Napoléon the superior command of Italy, pressed by his subjects, jealous of the dignity of their king as much as of their own independence, pressed by the patriots of Italy: "The word independence has acquired a magical virtue!" Finally, pressed by his friends in Paris who wrote to him: "The Emperor can do nothing more, even for France; how would he guarantee your states! Think of yourself, count only on yourself. He would sacrifice you to a shack."

And, very ironically, the former emissary of Terror said in his report to Napoléon:

> Your enemies oppose to the picture of the situation of France that of the immense advantages which his accession to the coalition presents to the king: this prince consolidates his throne, enlarges his States, instead of making to the emperor the useless sacrifice of his glory and his crown; he is going to shed on both the most stunning brilliance by proclaiming himself the defender of Italy, the guarantor of her independence. If he declares himself for Your Majesty, his army abandons him, his people rise up. If he separates his cause from that of France, all Italy hastens to his flag.

Before he returned to Naples, Caroline was won over to Austria. Metternich had deceived her by the same artifice he had used to induce Murat to leave the army and with which he deceived the French at Frankfurt. He showed him the recognition of his crown by England, this English peace which Napoléon had promised since 1800 and which he seemed more than ever unable to provide. He sent him a Neapolitan, Schinina, who painted for him the rout of Napoléon, presented to him as a model the defection of Bavaria, an old house, steeped in the traditions of monarchical honor, and allies of the imperial family! Caroline could not fail to be moved by this royal example. The agent spoke with so much force about the events to be foreseen, that the Queen resolved to summon Count Mier, the Austrian envoy, to the palace. She told him "how touched she had been by the friendly and generous proceedings of her Emperor," that she "was determined to enter into negotiations with Austria," and invited him to bring her a memorandum on the state of affairs.[72] Mier immediately set to work. There was, he said, no salvation for the kingdom except in the protection of the allies. He urged the Queen to act, in her capacity as regent, to save the crown, the state, her husband, her dynasty, concluding with this sentence, probably whispered by Metternich, who knew the woman in this improvised queen so well:

> This is the moment, and perhaps the only one that will ever come, when the queen can display the great qualities that heaven has so richly bestowed on her and unveil to the eyes of the universe the virtues indispensable for a sovereign, that she possesses in such an eminent degree.

On 28 October, Mier was again called to the palace. That day, to remove the last hesitations, he launched the argument without reply. He declared himself authorized to make known that

> Aberdeen, English Ambassador to the Court of Vienna, is authorized to sign, conjointly with Austria, a treaty with the King of Naples, on the supposition that His Majesty should declare himself for the cause of Europe and that Austria declare itself in favor of such an arrangement.[73]

Now, Austria not only promised, but urged the Queen to sign. She repeated, "She had made up her mind to enter into negotiations with Austria," and already she "promised not to take a man of her army out of the kingdom."

On 4 November, Murat unexpectedly returned to Naples. "To spare his self-esteem and not offend his character, jealous of royal power," the Queen begged Mier to keep their arrangements secret. "She wanted all her ideas and determinations to seem to come from him; besides, she promised to make the king do whatever Austria wanted." On the 8th, Murat received Mier. He said to him,

> The first step is done; I left the French army in accordance with the wishes of Austria and England; I have decided not to provide the troops that are (Napoléon) asked of me: my decision is taken; I want to unite with the allies, defend their cause, contribute to driving the French out of Italy, and I hope that I will be made to share in the advantages which will result from it.

By this he meant the remains of the Pope, for whom "the city of Rome with a nice borough, a good and sure income and plenty of incense should suffice." Mier left for Germany to report to Metternich and take orders from the allies.[74]

Murat would very much have liked Bentinck to give the precious pledge of an armistice to future accommodation: "On the sea side, I can join the Austrian army with my troops." But Bentinck refused any suspension of arms. Said this provident Englishman,

> There are no funds to be made on Murat. The treaty not only creates a rival for us, it can make Murat master of Italy. When the viceroy Eugène has been thrown back on the Alps, the Italians will certainly gravitate towards his side (Murat), while, if the protection and assistance of England extended over them, this great force would have undoubtedly turned on our side.[75]

These views tended to expel every French element from Italy, to substitute British hegemony for Austrian hegemony; they did not stop being political, and perfectly English. But, in the crisis they were passing through, it was important, above all, to remove Murat from the coalition and strike that resounding blow: the defection of the Emperor's brother-in-law. This is what Metternich was very actively working on in Frankfurt.

Metternich had caused the allies to decide that an Austrian negotiator, provided with formal credentials, would go to Naples. He charged Count Neipperg with this mission, predestined to intrusion into the private affairs of the Bonapartes. Neipperg was adroit, amiable, skillful in leading women; he hated Napoléon and the French.[76] "Count Neipperg will make the king understand that his fate is in the hands of Austria, which alone can bring the powers, which have authorized it, to accede to the treaty which it will make with Naples." England and Russia had authorized the negotiation; they had not engaged to accede to the treaty, and by their authorization to negotiate, they were bound only towards Austria; they were by no means so towards Murat. Aberdeen, moreover, had taken care to declare that: "the British government will never agree to intervene in an act which, guaranteeing the kingdom of Naples to Murat, would not bear the formal mention of the merits of the legitimate claims of the royal family of the Two Sicilies and would not consent to give him a fair compensation."[77]

Fouché, however, had been in Naples since 30 November. He stayed there until 18 December. His influence seems above all to have been employed in throwing on Murat's defection an ugly veneer of hypocrisy, in grafting duplicity on treason.[78] Was Murat a possible instrument, in France and in Europe? Did he play on it as in Paris several skillful, in their own way, speculated on Bernadotte? If the defection succeeded, did he want to be part of it, to open up access to the allies? If Napoléon won again, did he manage to prove that he had done everything to keep Murat for France? Did he flatter himself of an arbitration between Napoléon and his brother-in-law, perhaps even of the arbitration of Italy? Napoléon kept him away from Paris and affairs; his object was to return there, to make himself necessary there, to be there when things were decided, and to play a hand in all intrigues. His letters permit all conjecture and his acts contradict them all. The impression that remains is that he neither decided nor prevented anything, that he paraded on the stage his clean-shaven face, his equivocal gesture, all his disturbing garb of a dark and complicated Machiavellian, high policeman of all police, who did not allow a revolution to take place without his leading the machinery, nor a betrayal whose plots he did not weave: in short, the perfect agitator he knew he was, the great unrecognized draft that he showed each time that he claimed to touch foreign affairs and rub shoulders with Europe, in 1798 in the Cisalpine, in 1810 during the negotiation with England, which brought about his disgrace; such will appear until the end of his career, in 1815, and after the most extraordinary of his prestidigitations, his entry into the cabinet of Louis XVIII. "It is a humiliating thing for the human species that the contrast and the confusion of his ideas."[79] He wrote it of the King of Naples, and the historian cannot read it without thinking it about the Duke of Otranto.

Neipperg, soon joined by Mier, arrived on 31 December 1813. At his request, Bentinck sent his private secretary, Graham, to him to confer on affairs of war and those of Sicily. Neipperg had infinitely more difficulty in drawing this Englishman into his "forms" than in captivating Murat. He displayed, moreover, the qualities of cunning and seduction which had recommended him to Metternich's choice, garlanding the Queen, indoctrinating the King. Blinded to the point of believing Austria sincere when he guaranteed his an establishment in Italy and promised good offices with the allies, fascinated by his own glory, imagining himself to be the idol of the Neapolitans, the liberator of Italy, the savior of Europe, the very benefactor of France, as he would help to bring peace, this unfortunate drank his shame and, like a soldier of fortune who ended up as a defector, he signed his judgment and his condemnation.[80] But it was the soul of a barbarian conqueror, swollen and floating, stormy and childish, susceptible to those flashes of conscience which suddenly reveal to the fornicator the horror of his sin, the vengeance of the betrayed god, and the worst hellish torture, the very deprivation of this god. He wept bitterly.[81] He wept over the brave soldier Murat who, leaving for war in 1792, wrote to his father: "The greatest sacrifice I can make with my life is undoubtedly to die with my brothers in defense of the republic. Tell them that it is their interest that I defend, that it is our common cause that I serve." That Murat had just died of malarial fever from having wandered in his dreams along the marshes of old Europe. A few days later, King Murat, reassured by the cheers of these same *lazzaroni* who had killed the soldiers of Championnet and applauded in 1799 the tortures of the Republicans,[82] exalted by the flatteries of his courtiers (there were then *carbonari*, and were not the least enthusiastic and the least shrewd), saw deputies from Rome arriving for him who begged him to take possession of "their city." The populace was preparing to pillage the rich and expel the French. He said to Mier:[83]

> I did everything that Austria wanted; I blindly signed the alliance which the Count of Neipperg submitted to me. I place my interests entirely in the hands of the Emperor Franz II, and place myself with confidence under the aegis of the loyalty of the Austrian government; I am convinced that I will never repent of it. But I repeat to you again that you must enlarge me, make me stronger so that I am no longer a burden to you. You will derive no benefit from all these little states which you wish to establish in Italy. Put me in a position to always be able to maintain an army of 60,000 men, and the peace of Italy, your influence will be assured there. I act like the King of Naples and silence all other secondary considerations. The Neapolitans must be grateful to me for the proof of devotion I give them. My conduct will prove to sovereigns that I am worthy of occupying a place among them.

Durant said shortly after, "The king deceives the emperor, deceives his allies and deceives himself... He does not have 25,000 men. The soldiers in this army will desert. The rest only undertook to march because we made a promise to these soldiers that we would not fight.

If the king refuses to keep his promise, they will keep it for him."[84]

The treaty, signed on 11 January 1814, contained two parts: an ostensible one, the alliance, the guarantee of the crown of Naples to Murat, the promise of the good offices of Austria to make accede to it the allies; a secret one, the promise of Austria to intervene to obtain, in return for an indemnity, the formal renunciation of Ferdinand, to employ his good offices to hasten peace between Murat and England; finally the promise of 400,000 souls to be taken from the Roman State.[85] The price of betrayal would be paid by apostolic Austria at the expense of the Church and the papal domain.

Bentinck consented to sign on 3 February an armistice agreement; but he formally refused any accession to the treaty of peace, on the pretext that the advice received by him from Aberdeen on the subject of the negotiation between Austria and Naples did not sufficiently clearly imply the power to treat of peace and recognize Murat. 1 He was not mistaken, and the fact is that after having received from Metternich the communication of the draft treaty, Castlereagh wrote to him:

> The undersigned has the honor of acknowledging receipt to the Prince de Metternich of the draft treaty between His Majesty the Emperor of Austria and the person who currently exercises the government of Naples. However painful the impression felt by the Prince Regent when he had to note that it had been believed, in the general interest, necessary to conclude an arrangement which will constitute an obstacle to the restitution of His Sicilian Majesty in his hereditary States at the time of the signing of the general peace, the undersigned did not hesitate to send to the Minister of His Royal Highness accredited to the Court of Palermo the instruction, a copy of which is attached, enjoining him to cease hostilities immediately.

An armistice, and nothing more! As to peace, Castlereagh asked to confer with the Court of Palermo, as to his future indemnity, before "there can be any question of terminating the state of war now existing between H. M. Briton and the Government of Naples." The affectation of not naming Murat, of not writing the words *King of Naples* showed how far England was then from recognizing him, and, in reality, they never recognized him. Austria alone could have reminded them of their quasi-engagement at Frankfurt, when Neipperg was sent, and they took no notice, being interested in invalidating their own treaty themselves, and in getting rid of Murat as soon as Murat would have helped them get rid of Napoléon in Italy.

On 14 January the French envoy received notice of the break with Napoléon; on the 16th he left Naples. The betrayal was accomplished, the bell ringing, and Metternich had achieved his ends. This deception completes shedding light on the history of the character of the Frankfurt "overtures." It was the same game, played by the same skillful man, with the same accomplices: Nesselrode silent character, Hardenberg absent. As for Aberdeen, he got off with showing himself to the resistance of his colleague in Palermo, and incurring the same disavowal of his Government as in the Saint-Aignan affair: disavowal, but not blame nor regret, because everything was arranged, in both cases, according to the interests of English policy. It was part of the British Ministry's plans to remove Murat from Napoléon, but not to keep him in Naples, and it suited this calculation that Murat should be recognized by only one of the allies, which would not entail, with regard to him, any warranties from others. By the treaty of 11 January Franz II gave only one more word; it would only be a word to repeat. He had found means, by successive scratchings and surcharges, of transforming his alliance with Napoléon, his son-in-law, into an alliance against France; his "state entrails" and his imperial conscience would suffer no more from dethroning Murat to put his aunt and mother-in-law Maria-Carolina in her place, than from dethroning Napoléon, his own daughter and grandson. As for Metternich, he had conducted this negotiation with Caroline Bonaparte as a *roué* might conduct a pact of love with a giddy, greedy, gallant woman. Neipperg gave the word for the whole comedy when he once said to Graham: "Let's start by driving the French out of Italy, then we can always beat Murat."[86] Murat's fate would be decided in France. Murat, in reality, would lose his throne as he had won it. In vain he pretended to untie himself from France, and whatever he did, he would not detach himself from it.

Napoléon was preparing to leave Paris. On the 21st he wrote to Savary: "Depart this night from the 21st to the 22nd and before five o'clock in the morning, the pope to go to Savona."[87] After Valençay, Fontainebleau; the prisons were empty. After the evacuation of Spain, Poland, Germany, Illyria, there was the abandonment of Italy which announced itself and the Restoration which prepared. Napoléon did not conceal that his defeat would result in the return of the Bourbons. "All the powers and even England have recognized these limits" – the natural limits – he told La Besnardière, first clerk of foreign affairs:

> All states have grown; to want to bring France back to its ancient state would be to degrade and ruin it. The system of bringing France back to her old limits is inseparable from the re-establishment of the Bourbons, because they alone could offer a guarantee of the maintenance of this system, and England feels this well. Neither the empire nor the republic, if upheavals caused it to be reborn, would ever subscribe to such a condition. (Continued La Besnardière) As for Her Majesty, her resolution is immutable. She would not leave France less great than she received her. If, therefore, the allies wanted to change the accepted bases and propose the old limits, she saw only three parties either to fight and conquer, or to fight and die gloriously, or finally, if the nation did not support her, to abdicate.[88]

Napoléon inquired about the Bourbons, about their characters: "Believe me," he said to La Valette, who repeated it to Molé, "if I should be killed, my succession will not now devolve to the King of Rome. At the point where things have come, there is only a Bourbon who can succeed me?"[89] Caulaincourt left on 4 January. He left a cipher with Talleyrand, to let him know of the signing of the peace.[90] He said sadly to Rayneval who was accompanying him,"We are going, to fulfill a very difficult task, above all very useless, because, believe me, whatever we do, the era of the Napoléons is coming to an end, and that of the Bourbons is beginning again."[91]

By one of those inconsistencies of which he had given so many marks in his relations with his brother Joseph, by a last trait of that superstitious weakness which he could not shake before his "elder," Napoléon left him the government of France, the custody of of his wife, the tutelage of his son, even though he considered him incapable of commanding a regiment, of making a decision, of giving an order, that he suspected him of all ambitions, attributed to him all perfidy, and to tell the truth that he took away, with regard to this depository of his power, "emperor of anxieties, and husband of jealousies." On 24 January, he signed the letters patent conferring the regency on Maria-Louisa, with two advisers, Cambacérès for the civilian, Joseph for the military, and on the 25th, "at three o'clock in the morning, after having burned his most secret papers, he went."[92]

1. Pingaud, *Les dernières années de Moreau*; Rochechouart, *Souvenirs*.
2. Dumouriez, in London, offering himself to everyone, rejected everywhere, was reduced to the role of parasitic adviser. He drew up plans: one among others, dated 12 June 1813, which he described as sublime: to throw the Swedish army on the coasts of Flanders and Normandy! For Moreau, said Langeron, "he only wanted to overthrow Napoléon to put himself in his place, not as emperor, but as head of a republic he dreamed of until his death." (Langeron, *Campagne de 1813*.)
3. Thiébault, V, p. 81.
4. Russie, XXXI. *Aperçu*, p. 360, 395, 400-01.
5. Russia, XXXI. *Aperçu*. Resumption of hostilities, p. 334. Martens, III. Notice on the treaty with Austria, and text of articles; VII, notice on the treaty with Prussia, Toeplitz, 9 September 1813.
6. Article IV of the secret articles of the two treaties, identical.
7. Fournier, *Der Congress von Chatillon*, p. 7, note.
8. Martens, XI, p. 189.
9. Article IV, Angeberg, *Le Congres de Vienne et les traités de 1815*.
10. Martens, VII, p. 115.
11. Oncken, II, p. 698; *id*. liv. IX, ch. VII.
12. Report of Merveldt, 17 October 1813.
13. Decree and speech in the Senate, 18 March; to the Emperor of Austria, 17 March 1805.
14. *Souvenirs*, p. 222 et suiv. It is the most pathetic picture of this disaster, by a man who had seen those of 1799. (Ségur, VI. Thiébault, V.)
15. Declaration of Murat to the Austrian envoy in Naples. Mier's report, 16 December 1813. (Weil.)
16. Report of Mier, 16 December 1813. (Weil.)
17. Report of Reinhard; Ducasse, *Les rois frères*; Lang; Klein-Schmidt; Goecke.
18. Pertz, *Stein's Leben*; Treitschke, I, liv. I, ch. 3; Oncken, II, liv. IX, ch. VI; Martens, VII, note on Tœplitz; Ranke, IV, liv. IV. Conclusion.
19. Treaties with Württemberg, 2 November; with Baden, 20 November; with Hesse-Darmstadt, 23 November; Nassau, Saxe-Coburg, 23, 24, November 1813.
20. Memo of Alopeus, October 1813. (Martens, III.)
21. 16 November 1813. (Martens.)
22. Martens, XI. Notice on a note of Nesselrode, 5 février 1814. Cf. *Europe et Révolution*, VI, p. 371, 418-19.
23. *Mémoires*, I, p. 172, 262.
24. It is necessary to refer again, in this meeting, to the negotiations of 1709, so luminous by reflection. The Duke of Maine wrote on 3 June 1709 to Madame de Maintenon: "Under the shadow of talking about peace, they only thought of better dealing the mortal blow that they had been preparing for us for a long time."

"It is the heart of the French for their master that the king must bring back. This heart and bowels of the people... he possessed them as long as he was known by himself, and he was the greatest king in the world, his conquests having been bounded only by his own will... Now..., these people thought they had been sacrificed to the immoderate desire of their king to extend the borders. They (the

French) seem to have embraced the speeches of our enemies, who publish, to make our amiable master odious to the nations, that he aspires to universal monarchy." (Boislile, *Saint-Simon*, XVII, appendice X.

25 Russie, XXXI: "Déclaration des cabinets alliés, événements qui accompagnèrent l'entrée des alliée à Paris." Martens, IV, p. 150.
26 Report de Saint-Aignan, 10 novembre 1813. Compare with the truncated text printed in the *Moniteur*, deleted 20 janvier 1814, and reproduced by Angeberg, full text in Bichon, XIII, p. 23. See Thiers, XVII, p. 163; D'Haussonville, *Mélanges le congrès de Châtillon*.
27 He called himself a coalition minister. Letter to Caulaincourt, 15 February 1814. (Fain, *Manuscript of 1814*, p. 313; Fournier, *Châtillon*.)
28 Convention of 21 October 1813. (Martens, IX, p. 138.)
29 Oncken, II, p. 715-18; Fournier, p. 15-16.
30 Hardenberg to Münster, 12 October 1813.
31 To Maret, 15 novembre 1813.
32 Martens, III, p. 150-53; VII, p. 63.
33 Fourmer, *Châtillon*, p. 34, note; p. 248: letter to Hudelist, 9 November, and p. 359, Hardenberg.
34 Aberdeen to Metternich, 27 November 1813.
35 Memo of German origin, most likely.
36 *Corr.* I, p. 73. See, p. 89, the letter of 7 December on Saint-Aignan's note: "I cannot hide from you the government's uneasiness on reading the minute of Saint-Aignan, and, very certainly, such a document, if it is published by the enemy, without a counter-document from us, will excite painful impressions in this country." – See: *Congrès de Châtillon*, p. 246, 264, 297.
37 Martens, XI: notice on the note of Nesselrode of 5 février 1814.
38 Nesselrode to Lieven, 20 novembre; instruction of Pozzo, 16 December 1813.
39 On the Prince of Vaudémont and his two nieces, Mlle de Lislebonne and Mme d'Espinoy, *Saint-Simon*, year 1707.
40 *Mémoires* of Pasquier, Miot, Vitrolles, Mme de Chastenay, duc de Broglie, Castellane, Rœderer, Norvins, Thiébault, Barante, notes of the Comte Mole, fragments published by Gustave Bord, *Revue de la révolution* (1888). Etienne Lamy, *André de Coigny et ses mémoires*; Masson, *Marie-Louise*, ch. XI.
41 Madelin, *Fouché*, ch. XXI. Appointed governor of Ilyria on 17 July 1813, he arrived in Laybach on the 29th.
42 Miot, III, p. 344.
43 To the Duchess of Courlande, 20 janvier 1814; Lettenhove, *Revue d'histoire diplomatique*, II.
44 "The sole purpose of obliging France to observe for a long time the peace treaty which will be agreed upon is to put her, by the peace itself, in no condition to contravene it, by peace or by force, all that she occupies in the Low Countries, without exception; otherwise, the slightest place that will be left to her, will be a means of returning to it some day." Extraordinary of the *Gazette d'Amsterdam*, 18 juin 1709. (Boislisle, *Saint-Simon*, XVII, appendice.)
45 Chastenay, II, p. 268.
46 31 décembre 1813, 1 janvier 1814. Pingaud, *Bernadotte*; Memo to Bernadotte; On Mme de Staël and the sovereign protestant, *id.*, p. 170.
47 To Cambacérès, 6 novembre 1813. (Lecestre.)

48 Notes of Molé.
49 "Order that, if ever the English arrive at the castle of Marracq (near Bayonne) we burn the castle and all the houses which belong to me, so that they do not sleep in my bed." To Caulaincourt, 15 novembre 1813.
50 "State religion," like the entrails; it did not prevent him from "placing with his daughter as a consoler this rascal Neipperg." (Gourgaud, VIII, p. 330.)
51 12 novembre 1813. (Lecestre.)
52 Ernouf, ch. LXV. Notes of Maret.
53 Lamy, *Mémoires de Mme de Coigny*.
54 Caulaincourt to Hauterive, 8 mars 1814.
55 *Mémoires de Pasquier*, II, p. 104; Thiers, XVII, p. 43 et suiv; D'Hausonville, *Mélanges*, p. 125.
56 *Pasquier*, II, p. 108.
57 To Castlereagh, 4 December 1813; Russie, XXXI, survey, IV part. Déclaration de Francfort; Metternich, I; Metternich to Hudelist, 6 December 1813. (Fournier.)
58 Metternich to Wessenberg, 6 December 1813.
59 Metternich, I, 252. Compare with opinion in 1805, vol. V.
60 D'Haussonville, V, ch. LVII; Pasquier, II.
61 Thiers, VII, p. 163-78.
62 Compare Danton, 31 janvier 1793; Barère, 1 août 1793; Cambacérèe, 3 mars 1795; Committee of Public Safety, 27 avril 1795; Directory, 28 octobre, 7 novembre 1795; Proclamations of 21 octobre, 1 décembre 1805, 23 octobre 1806; Messages of 19 and 27 novembre 1806; Tilsit, juillet 1807; Message of 10 décembre 1810, and 9 juin 1811.
63 Notes by d'Hauterive, session of the Legislative Commission, 24 December 1813.
64 Fontanes, 27 décembre; adresse 29 décembre 1813.
65 30 décembre 1813.
66 Méneval, III, p, 176; Miot, III, p. 351; Ducasse, Lecestre; Masson, *Marie-Louise*.
67 To Louis, 4 or 5 janvier; to Joseph, 7 janvier 1814.
68 Lucchesini, 25 September 1805.
69 Lumbroso, *Muratiana*. Correspondence of Fouché. – Norvins, III. – Madelin, *Fouché*, ch. XXI-XXII. – Weil, I-III. – Reports of Durant, Caulaincourt, and the correspondence of Bentinck, Mier.
70 To Napoléon, 10 novembre 1813.
71 To Napoléon, 27 décembre 1814. (Lumbroso.)
72 Memo from Mier to the Queen. (Weil.)
73 Wenz, secretary of the Austrian legation, to Bentinck, 14 December 1813. (Weil)
74 Report of Mier, 16 December 1813.
75 Bentinck to Castlereagh, January 1814. (Weil.)
76 Frankfurt, 10 December 1813. (Weil.) Oncken, II, p. 715.
77 Aberdeen to Bentinck, 12 December; to Metternich, 11 December 1813. Metternich agreed on 12 December. (Weil.)
78 For example, Murat's letters to Napoléon, 21 and 25 December 1813. Fouché was then in Rome; he continued to advise Murat.
79 To Caulaincourt, 12 janvier 1814. (Weil, IX, p. 403.)

80 To Napoléon, 25 décembre 1813. See Bianchi, I, ch. I; Pasquier, II, ch. VII; *Mémoires de Desvernois*; Helfert, *Murat*.
81 "So I'm a traitor, what can I do? it's too late!" To Mme Récamier, *Souvenirs de Mme Récamier*, I, p. 249.
82 The English entered the port. "Vesuvius had just burst and was throwing flames. Murat was on horseback at the head of his guards; the crowd surrounded him shouting *Long live King Joachim!* He had forgotten everything, he seemed drunk with joy. The the next day, a big show at the Saint-Charles theatre. We also applauded the envoy of Franz II." (Chateaubriand, *Mémoires d'outre-tombe*.)
83 Report of Mier, 16 February 1814. (Helfert.)
84 D'Hauterive to Caulaincourt, 28 February 1814. Conversation with Durant.
85 Angeberg, p. 39 et suiv. On the secret articles see, Weil, III, p. 641.
86 Weil, III, p. 355.
87 Lecestre.
88 La Besnardière to Caulaincourt, 19 janvier 1814. [Sorel has misspelled Besnardière as Besnadière, or *vice versa*.]
89 Pasquier, II, p. 115, 139.
90 *Souvenirs* of Mme de Coigny. Conversation Talleyrand.
91 Viel-Castel, *Restauration*, I, p. 127; D'Haussonvule, *Mélanges*, p. 172.
92 Masson, *Marie-Louise*.

# Chapter IV: Congress of Châtillon

## 1814

### I. Divergence Among Allies

The war resumed. Blücher and his Prussians crossed the Rhine at Mainz, marching towards the Ardennes. On the 20th, Schwarzenberg's army passed through Basel. This operation was not accomplished without a draw with Alexander: the Tsar wanted to "put the whole of Europe against France," but he spared the Swiss.[1] On the 29th, the Diet of Zurich declared that the act of mediation had been abrogated and broke with France, which, from the point of view of the allies, put everything back in order. The headquarters moved to Freiburg.

Metternich had news from Paris. Someone asked Talleyrand what he thought of the state of affairs: "I believe," he replied, "that this is the beginning of the end." The Senate began to stir. The Empress wrote his father a lamentable letter. Napoléon was never tied up like this. On the Italian side, "we no longer have any worries." He had an hour of fulfillment and posed before posterity in the pose of a gallery painting: "We can rightly estimate that our headquarters is now the world."[2]

However, he still had concerns, and very serious ones. With success, the views of the ardent, the enraged, as Metternich called them, were given full scope. What had once been whispered was now being declared aloud: pushing the war of extermination, striking down the criminal, dethroning him, changing the dynasty. Russians urged: "The real glory, the real theater of war, was to fight within France, to force her to desist from the tyranny she has exercised and will exercise again over Europe, if we do not disable her once and for all from molesting others."[3]

Add the almost avowed designs of Alexander on Bernadotte and the candidacy openly put forward by this former Marshal of France as he and his Swedes approached the frontiers of his former country. Gentz wrote,

> The project of this court (Austria) could never have been to exchange one danger for another, and to destroy the preponderance of France in order to prepare and favor that of Russia. The sincere wish of the Cabinet of Vienna was to make peace with Napoléon, to limit his power, to guarantee the sovereigns against the projects of his restless ambition, but to keep him and his family on the throne.

These were, on the part of Napoléon's father-in-law and the minister who had made the marriage of 1810, identically the same views as in 1791, in the days of Varennes and Pilnitz, those of Louis XVI's brother-in-law, Léopold, and of the minister who had made the marriage of 1770, Kaunitz.[4]

These calculations led Metternich to spare Prussia. The fear in which he was to see the Russians masters of Gallicia and all-powerful in France led him, to ward off the worst evil, to consent to the least: he listened to Hardenberg, who made with him, the good German, the anti-Russian, and persuaded him that if an arrangement were made between them about Saxony, the King of Prussia would ratify it, separate from Alexander, and help Austria to oppose the Tsars views on Poland. This misunderstanding, which lasted a long time and which was, at the Congress of Vienna, the cause of long and obscure disputes, arose in the first days of January, 1814. Hardenberg, who was working to secure Saxony on both sides and who was sure of Alexander's guarantee, wrote in his diary, 8 January 1814: "Conference with Metternich. He accedes to the plan affecting Saxony." That same day, Metternich received a letter from Caulaincourt dated Lunéville, 6 January, and it betrayed concern, a desire to negotiate.

This letter contained perfectly founded observations which show that Napoléon had clearly discerned Metternich's play. Caulaincourt was surprised at the delays Metternich had taken in responding to "full and complete adherence to the bases that Your Excellency has proposed by common agreement with the ministers of Russia and England, and with the admission of Prussia." It was difficult to admit

> that Aberdeen had powers to propose bases without having any to negotiate; His Majesty does not insult the allies by believing that they were uncertain and that they are still deliberating; they know only too well that any conditional offer becomes an absolute commitment for the person who made it as soon as the condition he has placed there is fulfilled. In any case, we should expect to have on 6 January the answer that Your Excellency announced to us on 10 December.[5]

Caulaincourt had powers and he waited at the outposts for the necessary passports to go to Metternich. He attached to his official message a special letter: he congratulated Metternich on his elevation to the rank of prince and he added, alluding to very significant confidences that Metternich had surely not forgotten:[6] "My stay at Prague has made me appreciate these relations (with the Prince) too much for me not to always put them among the things I must most desire. We want peace; I hope that Your Excellency will believe in the sincerity of this wish when I express it to you."

Metternich desired peace no less; but how? With Napoléon or without Napoléon? The peace concluded at Basel, at Lunéville, in a congress, or dictated at Paris, after a triumphal entry, passing over the body of Napoléon and the remains of the Grand Army? While waiting for agreement to be reached on this article between the allies, Prince Metternich took care to hold Caulaincourt under illusions. He wrote to him, on 8 January, refining on the equivocation of Frankfurt and preparing his retraction by the means he had always reserved for himself: "The suppositions that Your Excellency admits that it was Lord Aberdeen who proposed the bases and that he was provided with powers to that effect, are in no way founded." Here, then, is England out of the debate, and the so-called pact of Frankfurt broken. He added on the 14th that Castlereagh was about to arrive; he invited Caulaincourt to come closer, and he indicated to him Châtillon-sur-Seine as the most suitable place for negotiations.

On the 16th, he sent a letter from Basel to Schwarzenberg, then marching to Langres, in which his concerns and his secret desires were betrayed:[7]

We are approaching a grave hour; our enterprise for the salvation of Europe will be crowned if the ground does not slip under our feet. Lord Castlereagh will arrive here tomorrow at the latest. Salvation depends on the first conversation I have with him. If he lets go like the others, new measures will have to be taken. In this case, it is of the utmost importance that you do not stretch out any further. It does not enter our mind to sacrifice a single man to put Bernadotte on the throne of France. You think I'm going crazy. Yet it is the question on the agenda.[8]

The English Cabinet had decided to send a plenipotentiary to the future peace congress, and as the allied sovereigns dealt directly with affairs, as they were assisted by their chancellors and foreign ministers, England could not do less than to accredit its Minister for Foreign Affairs to them.[9] Among the views which Castlereagh was called upon to develop, one of the chief ones was to draw together and bind up in one instrument the various treaties of the coalition, so as to insure the vigorous pursuit of the war and to secure the order of things that would establish peace; in the front line the constitution of the barrier state, Holland augmented by Belgium, seen, at all times, as fundamental in the eyes of the English. As for the proposals presented to Saint-Aignan, the English ministers considered: "that they went back to the deluge";[10] they held them to be devoid of any official character, and moreover they were quite ready, if one were forced to take them as bases, to quibble very legally on these terms of the note: "The power and the preponderance that France must preserve in its integrity, and by confining itself within its natural limits which are the Rhine, the Alps and the Pyrenees."

These terms, opined these subtle lawyers of the Crown, did not signify that the territory of France must extend to these limits; it was only about its power and its preponderance. Although it may exercise some influence over small States on this side of the Rhine, this influence must be so limited that it cannot extend, and its preponderance, beyond the Rhine.[11] There was another point which the English ministers had no less at heart, and that was the future government of France. They thought, as Pitt once did, that peace would be lasting only if France were driven back to its old limits; but they also thought that the old kings, the Bourbons, alone could accept this peace with dignity and observe it sincerely. Castlereagh wrote Aberdeen, on 10 December 1813, "If the Bourbons were restored, hostilities would immediately cease"; and no sooner had he left London than Cooke, the Under-Secretary of State for Foreign Affairs, wrote to him on 5 January: "Be assured that the general, not to say universal, principle is: no peace with Bonaparte; or, if a peace is made with him, let it be such as to put his malice and skill in such a state of infirmity that we are as easy as if we replaced the Bourbons on the throne." But they considered themselves bound to leave, in appearance, freedom of choice to the French, except to make impossible for them any choice which would not be that of the Bourbons. It would therefore suffice for Castlereagh to oppose the other combinations for this one to end up prevailing, as the only one capable of reconciling all interests: Austria not wanting to hear of Bernadotte, nor Alexander of a Napoléon.

Such were the ulterior motives with which Castlereagh prepared to assume the part of arbiter between Metternich, who wished to treat with Napoléon, by weakening him, and Alexander, who wished to dethrone him. "The rage to go to Paris made him deaf to all remonstrances," wrote Gentz on 8 May. By personal taste, by fear of adventures, above all by concern to contain the ambitions of Russia, Castlereagh was going to find himself closer to Austria, whatever secret desire he kept to overthrow Napoléon and whatever his conviction that England would know no lasting peace with Napoléon, in agreement, in this, with the opinion of his country, "where the fury against Napoléon has become a veritable delirium." To enter into the views of Metternich, and by the very negotiation, conducted in agreement with him, to lead him to the downfall of the Bonapartes and the restoration of the Bourbons, such was his secret plan from then on. Alexander, he thought, would eventually go there, seeing it as the only way to involve his allies in revenge. But then he would not dictate peace alone, and the new government of France, a government of principles and no longer of expedients, would be neither the obligee nor the client of any of the allies. The great design of Russian supremacy would thus be thwarted.

Castlereagh arrived on 18 January at Freiburg, a character who appears on the stage when the drama comes to an end; he will therefore remain in the front ranks; he will contribute powerfully, both from his character as the representative of England and from his very person, to prepare the denouement. Robert Stewart, Viscount Castlereagh, Marquess of Londonderry, was in his 45th year, and from his 21st he lived in politics as MP, Under Secretary of State, Minister,

Colonies, War, Foreign Affairs in 1811, and since then a leading Minister. A friend of Wellington, he formed with him the formidable duumvirate which led English policy to its ends in this great catastrophe of the supremacy of France. Castlereagh prided himself on the principles to which he held with an unshakable constancy, which in affairs was confused with stubbornness; but his "principles" were in no way abstract or speculative, they all boiled down to one, the higher interest of England; they all proceeded from this high *raison d'État*. Castlereagh spoke with authority and expressed himself inelegantly, the authority bordering on stiffness and the lack of elegance bordering on confusion. In the commerce of life, the gentleman dominated the politician, courteous, of noble manners, of an intimacy difficult to penetrate, sure when one was admitted there. He loathed the Revolution in itself, and because it was French and turned to the greatness of France. To annihilate the Revolution, to bring France back to its former limits, that was all his policy; he was the man behind the Treaty of Utrecht and the treaty of 1763: the barrier and point of extension of France, neither on the continent nor elsewhere; on this model he conceived the peace of 1814 and worked on it. But persistent as his hostility was so long as France remained a threatening rival of England, this hostility was to cease the day when England had won these guarantees. Castlereagh wanted neither the total ruin and obliteration of France, nor the triumph and preponderance of Russia. These views estranged him from Alexander. Alexander always worried him without ever seducing him; everything in this elusive Slav led him into distrust; this comet upset his system. Metternich, without inspiring him with more confidence, reassured him by his method: he was tacking in the same waters. From their first meeting, they had the impression that they would easily manage to get along.

  Alexander set out for Langres, where he arrived on the 22nd, resolved to press on the offensive and impose a *fait accompli* on his opponents. He found General Schwarzenberg resistant to the impetus he wanted to give to the war, that is to say to the direct march on Paris. Metternich showed himself even more resistant to it when he rejoined the Tsar on the 25th, accompanying Franz II and followed by Castlereagh. As Münster said to the Prince-Regent of England:

The main reason for all these disagreements, is that Russia does not decide how far she wishes to extend her limits in Poland.[12] Austria suspects that she is fomenting trouble in Gallicia, that she is aiming to restore the kingdom of Poland in favor of the Emperor Alexander, and that is why she would like to give Alsace to the Austria.[13] The promise which is said to have been made to Prussia by Russia to grant her all electoral Saxony, with the exception of a small increase for Weimar, operates in the same direction. Finally, there is plenty of room for quarrel between the two great powers of the continent, which, in the event of a reverse, could produce very disastrous consequences.

It is probable that Metternich touched on this with Castlereagh; that he informed him, at the same time, of Alexander's designs on the French monarchy and on Bernadotte. Castlereagh always remained indifferent on the fate of the King of Saxony, and it mattered little to him to see the Prussians at Dresden, but he had no desire for the Russians to push themselves into the heart of Europe; he wished even less to restore in France, for the honor and profit of Russia, a kind of Poland before 1792: finally he held to the "old limits" which would allow a lasting peace, at least with England. He easily won over Metternich, who considered Alsace to be the most perfidious of those present. For fear of seeing the Russians at Cracow and the Prussians at Dresden, this Austrian concluded to keep Strasbourg for the French. Castlereagh had a long talk with Alexander. The Tsar denied any agreement between him and Bernadotte on the subject of France. Castlereagh convinced himself that Alexander was deceiving him; that, at the very least, he was playing on words, and that his views for the Prince Royal of Sweden were to be taken very seriously. This duplicity threw him decidedly on the side of Metternich.

## II. Protocol of Langres

The allies being assembled at Langres, the deliberation opened on the conduct of the war. On 26 January, Schwarzenberg handed the Franz II a long memo in which the advantages and disadvantages of a march on Paris were discussed. He avoided concluding; however, his considerations turned to prudence infinitely more than to audacity. He wrote that very day to his wife, "We should make peace here, that's my opinion. Our Emperor, Stadion, Metternich, even Castlereagh are of this opinion. But the Emperor Alexander! This is the moment for decisive resolutions; may Heaven protect us in this crisis!"

Franz II asked Metternich for a report on Schwarzenberg's memo. Metternich gave it to him the next day, the 27th. He recalled the stipulations of Tœplitz, the object then given to the war: "the re-establishment of the balance of the powers of Europe and a distribution of their respective forces capable of ensuring this balance; ... the repression of French power within limits compatible with a system of balance in Europe."[14] To achieve this object, the powers deemed it necessary... "the re-entry of France within the limits of the Rhine, the Alps and the Pyrenees, the Rhine and the Alps offering lines to be determined." Here, finally, was Frankfurt's great secret leaking out. It was because the allies no longer had to pretend. They could say what they always wanted, and impose it. Napoléon, continued Metternich, "sent a plenipotentiary, Caulaincourt, to Châtillon to negotiate peace. Will he accept negotiation on these bases? We will know soon, if we want to enter into conferences." There remained the question of the internal government of France. Metternich was of the opinion not to raise it, "to reserve the initiative for it to France itself, not to provoke it and not to prevent it." The English believed that this neutrality would lead to the restoration of the Bourbons. Metternich harbored other thoughts. It was, he continued, "to derive from the existence of Napoléon, tolerated by the nation, all possible advantage, and the same, as regards the general point of view, that it would be just and reasonable to want to achieve by the reintegration of the Bourbons carried out by the nation." On Bernadotte he was formal:

> I do not admit the possibility of the establishment of another dynasty and will not stop to demonstrate that the powers could never manage to give a great people a sovereign taken from a relatively weak party.... It will not be Bernadotte who will replace him (he had already written on 16 January). It is not necessary to know France to admit the most remote supposition.

He concluded by proposing a conference between the allies on the following six points: 1) Are the allies ready to deal with France on the bases agreed among them "and with a fixing of limits on the side of the Alps and the Rhine, on which the four cabinets would have to agree without loss of time?" 2) Are they ready to stipulate in the name of Europe and to exclude France from the reconstitution of Europe fixed by them and which one will state summarily to the French?

3) Are they, if the negotiation drags on, prepared to make their proposals known, by way of a manifesto, to the French people? 4) Should the question of dynasty be put first or second? 5) Are the powers determined to declare themselves only against the person of Napoléon, or also against his succession and in favor of a Bourbon? 6) Are the cabinets, if they have changed their minds on the reconstitution of the great powers as they were in 1805, prepared to determine their new views and fix them?[15] Finally he tackled the question, still uncertain, of the compensations reserved for Austria and Prussia. Believing himself sure of Hardenberg, having won Castlereagh to his views, he wanted to get rid of the nightmare of Russian claims to Poland.[16] Franz II, in a reasoned resolution, approved the conclusions of his minister. Memo and imperial resolution were communicated to the allies.

Around Alexander opinion was divided. The generals leaned towards Schwarzenberg, towards caution. Nesselrode persisted in advising moderation: spare France, while driving it back to its old limits, not humiliate it too much, make peace, give itself the glory of restoring balance in Europe. Pozzo di Borgo, having returned from London, where he had seen the Prince Regent disposed to the House of Bourbon, worked in their favor. The French *émigré* Rochechouart, a friend of the Duc de Richelieu and consequently in a very good position in the Russian general staff, came to the rescue. La Harpe,[17] who had gone to Paris to speak with the opposition, dreamed of a plebiscite, of a constitution; he advised his former pupil to take advantage of the discontent of the French against Napoléon and pleaded for Bernadotte.[18]

On the article of the Bourbons, all the dialectics of Pozzo could not shake Alexander. "Let the French speak out," he repeated; "then many difficulties will be smoothed out."[19] And he fully expected that they would decide for Bernadotte. He had authorized the insinuations to Saint-Aignan, under the assurance given by Metternich that Napoléon would not listen to them and that it would only be a ruse of war. Now that the ruse had succeeded and that the manifesto of 1 December had publicly thrown all the responsibility for the war on Napoléon, Austria still claimed to be negotiating! Alexander lost his temper, announced that he was going to leave, put himself at the head of his army.

On the evening of the 27th, Hardenberg tried to mediate. We read in his diary:

Saw the King and Emperor of Russia. Discussion on the plan of operations and misunderstandings. Intrigue of Stein to make the army go straight to Paris, which the Emperor Alexander wants. The Austrian party is against it; others don't know what they want.

These words were for the King of Prussia. This king did on that day what he had been doing ever since the famous visit to the tomb of the Great Frederick, in Potsdam, in November 1805 when he yielded to the prestige of Alexander and threw himself into his arms. "The King of Prussia has promised to stay with him until the last extremity."[20] It was in the same evening, after dinner, that it is appropriate to place an interview told by Metternich and of which all the details cannot be admitted without reservation.[21] Metternich having an interest, at the time when he wrote his memoirs, in showing himself to be more far-sighted, and above all more favorable to the Bourbons than he was then.[22] Alexander said:

> France is hostile to the Bourbons. To want to bring them back to a throne which they were unable to keep would be to expose France and Europe to new revolutions whose consequences are incalculable. Choosing a new sovereign is a big undertaking for the foreigner.

Returning then to the plan which he had elucidated in 1804, which he then very keenly desired to apply and which he tried to resume, after Waterloo, in 1815, he proposed to press vigorously on Paris, to seize it, to address a declaration to the French telling them that they were free to choose their sovereign, to convene the primary assemblies, which would have to deliberate on two questions only: the form of the government, the choice of the sovereign; but with the implication that neither the government would be the republic, nor the sovereign Napoléon. "An essential point will be to lead the assembly well. I have at hand the man I need. La Harp."

Metternich supported his plan of negotiation; then he went to take orders from Franz II and returned the next day, 28 January, to Alexander. "I went as far as the threat of a breakup and took the piece away," he wrote. Alexander understood that anything was better than the retreat of the coalition Austrians. With the Austrians, he could go to Paris, and victory would carry the rest. He consented to a conference where the bases of the instructions to be given to the envoys who would meet with Caulaincourt at Châtillon would be established.[23]

However, before sending his minister there, Alexander wanted to clarify his views, to state his reservations, and to this end he had Pozzo write, it is believed, "observations" on Metternich's memo.[24] "No one can decide, while the war is still going on, whether the purpose of the alliance has been achieved. The probability of reaching the goal depends on the victory." Moving to the successive negotiations of Prague, Toeplitz, Frankfurt, the Russian note defined exactly their spirit: they were overtures which did not commit anything, a means for starting preliminary negotiations, reserving the right to raise the requirements according to the events of the war: what, in reality, had happened.

> At the time when a large part of Europe was still occupied by the French armies, and when the hopes of success were uncertain, the allies had to circumscribe their pretensions to the nature of their situation; but these terms are not a renunciation of all the other advantages to which Providence and the immense sacrifices which the powers have already made allow them to aspire. The bases which were spoken of in an unofficial way in Frankfurt are not those to which we would like to adhere strictly today; the ideas of Freiburg differ from those of Basel, and the latter may not conform to those of Langres.
>
> If it is therefore permissible – as it is true – to extend one's claims in such a serious way..., no previous transaction between the allies obliges them in any way towards their enemies...

There was no need, continued the note, to discuss with France the arrangements relating to Europe; one had only to determine and notify them of "future limits" The note concluded to negotiate by fighting:

> This view does not imply or hurt the question of dynasty, but if Providence were to convert the events and the popularity of Napoléon into instruments of destruction against his political existence, neither justice nor the interests of Europe would would have to suffer from such a result.

Alexander had consented to conferences at Chatillon, a dilatory means, but with the ulterior motive of breaking their effects. So in Prague and Frankfurt. Münster wrote: "Metternich has made every possible effort, since the sojourn in Freiburg, to stop the military operations. The Emperor Alexander always escaped him by going forward."[25] He left, in fact, on the 29th, leaving the diplomats to parley. However, he was careful to order his ministers to adjourn the first conference at Châtillon to 3 February, "probably" wrote Münster, one can say certainly, "with the intention of dealing a blow to the enemy and overthrowing the freak."

The conference between the allies took place on 29 January. There were present Metternich and Stadion for Austria, Nesselrode and Rasoumovsky for Russia, Castlereagh for England, Hardenberg for Prussia. Pozzo di Borgo kept the protocol.[26]

It was agreed that Caulaincourt would be informed of the arrival of the envoys at Châtillon, for 3 February, to open "preliminary conferences for general peace"; that in these conferences the four would stipulate in the name of Europe. Castlereagh, was very keen to correct the kind of tacit admission given by Aberdeen to the "natural limits," in November, in Frankfurt; he decreed that the limits of 1792 would be proposed to France as the basis of peace. It was added, at Metternich's request: "except to enter into details of arrangement of a reciprocal convenience on some portions of territory beyond the limits, on both sides." It was a loophole for him, a specious way of linking the Châtillon negotiations with the insinuations and declaration of Frankfurt, the Rhine, the Alps and the expanse of territory that France had never known under its kings.

The Russians would have liked to forbid any communication to the French on the future arrangements of Europe. The proposal seemed hurtful in these terms; it was set aside, and they limited themselves to stipulating: "That they will be made aware of the general arrangements without however making it a subject of negotiation"; finally, "that in the event of a breakdown in the negotiations, the proposed conditions would be brought to the attention of the French nation." Before the conference was adjourned, Castlereagh declared that his Government hoped that none of the allied sovereigns would oppose the restoration of the Bourbons, should it be the work of the French nation, and he reserved the right to break off the negotiations the day when Napoléon's situation no longer ensured the execution of the engagements which he would have made. The plenipotentiaries had to carry a common instruction. Metternich was commissioned to write it.[27]

The ardor of Alexander, and the audacity of Blücher, cut short the hesitations of the politicians: in 1792-95, the diplomats stopped the armies; in 1814, the armies took after the diplomats who were often frightened, always cabalant and murmuring. However, the ferment remained, and Napoléon could still hope, by defeating them in detail, to separate them in the negotiations. He defeated Blücher on 31 January at Brienne; Blücher defeated him on 1 February at La Rothière.[28] On the 3rd, the plenipotentiaries of the allies left for the congress, and took away these written instructions under the impression of the success of Blücher to divide the negotiation into two parts: 1) the return of France to the *anciennes limites*; 2) the summary communication to France, which was to exercise no influence there, of the views of the allies on the reconstruction of Europe, namely: Germany composed of sovereign and confederate states; Confederate Switzerland; Italy partitioned into independent states; Spain to the Bourbons; independent and increased Holland. To these written instructions, Alexander added the verbal injunction to his representative "not to precipitate anything, but to allow the events of the war time to develop their results."

### III. First Talks

The plenipotentiaries were for Russia, Count Rasoumovsky; for Austria, Count Stadion; for England Castlereagh, Aberdeen, and Stewart; for Prussia, Humboldt, plus a whole staff of chancellery, scribes and officials. The small town, deserted by the peasants, no longer had a market: "We are stocking up as if it were a question of going to India," Stadion wrote to his wife.

On the evening of the 4th, meeting at Stadion's place, the allies found themselves in the presence of the question which they had in turn asked themselves in Prague and Frankfurt: "And if he agrees to everything," said Rasoumovsky, "shall we sign?"[29] Castlereagh and Stadion protested against the misguided curious and the inconvenient questions. It was decided to postpone notification of terms of peace.[30]

Caulaincourt was waiting for them. He spent the day of the 4th in a state of extreme agitation and depression. The news of the war, a retreat on Paris in prospect, Alexander's resolution to push to the limit, lastly and very probably some notions collected on the designs of the allies, all contributed to disturb his spirits. Was he beginning to suspect how shifting and slippery these Frankfurt bases were, of which his imagination had made a kind of rampart, and how they would collapse as soon as one tried to fix oneself there? However, he still clung to it. "Certainly, we must not give up any of our natural limits," he wrote to Maret on 4 February. Above all, he feared Napoléon's stubbornness in the game of war, postponing everything in the hope of revenge if he was defeated, withdrawing all concessions and raising demands if he were victorious. He addressed Berthier, as the Emperor's most devoted servant:

> So bring the truth to His Majesty, show him how serious the circumstances are, all that the slightest delay can cause to be risked without being able to assure any advantage. Tell me the truth, my prince. Do you still have an army? Can we discuss the conditions for fifteen days or must we accept them immediately? If no one has the courage to tell me where things really stand, I remain in the vagueness of news from M. de Bassano's gazettes and I cannot know what I should do.

He was asking for full powers, the power to seize on the fly this opportunity which he believed he had glimpsed in Prague and which, he thought, if it reappeared, would still escape. He wrote to the Emperor,

> All the plenipotentiaries, notably the English, have expressed to me their desire to conclude peace promptly; but it was easy for me to see in the midst of these protestations that people would be very exacting. I cannot urge Your Majesty too strongly to send me the general powers which I have requested.[31]

The conference was opened on 5 February only to be suspended after twenty minutes, Rasoumovsky declaring that he did not yet have the signed copy of his instructions. Humboldt also lacked his, but he thought it more expedient not to say anything about it. After the session, Castlereagh made this declaration to his allies: even if Napoléon subscribed to all the demands of the coalition, the English envoys could not sign the peace before the organization of Europe was decided among the allies, and that they had not fixed among them "their respective state of possession"; "What are the arrangements made between Austria, Russia and Prussia? What will be the lot of Holland? What indemnity will be assigned to the King of Sicily, if he has to renounce Naples?" He said, "He is considering the possibility of

France agreeing to all the conditions, and in that case he would find himself embarrassed." Stadion said, that very day,

> Our work here takes on the whole turn of a bad comedy which can only interest by its flatness; unless our whole conference is broken up by the force of events, we will be in the unfortunate situation of having been, from beginning to end, completely wrong towards a power which until now had been wrong towards everyone.

Napoléon had received at Troyes, on the night of the 4th, the courier from Caulaincourt. At the same time as he demanded powers, Caulaincourt signaled the immense development of the enemy's forces and means. Napoléon then sought to calm his spirits and exhorted himself to constancy by leafing through a volume of Montesquieu. He pointed to Maret this passage from *Grandeur et décadence*, which applied to the trying times of Louis XIV:

> I know of nothing so magnanimous as the resolution taken by a monarch who has reigned in our day, rather to bury himself under the ruins of the throne than to accept propositions a king cannot hear; his soul was too proud to stoop lower than his misfortunes had placed him; and he knew well that courage can strengthen a crown and that infamy never does.[32]

"And I," cried Maret, who had been a journalist for emphatic ages and remembered it in meetings, "I know something more magnanimous, it is to throw away your glory to fill the abyss into which France would fall with you!" Napoléon cried, "Well! gentlemen, make peace! Let Caulaincourt do it, let him sign everything necessary to obtain it; I can bear the shame, but don't expect me to dictate my own humiliation." He wrote to Caulaincourt: "The conditions are, it seems, decided in advance between the allies. As soon as they have communicated them to you, you are free to accept them or to refer them to me within twenty-four hours."[33] Maret added this comment: "The Emperor's intention is that you consider yourself invested with all the powers and all the authority necessary in these important circumstances, to take the most suitable course in order to stop the progress of the enemy and to save the capital." These credentials were dispatched with a second letter from Napoléon, dated the 5th, at one o'clock in the morning.[34]

He accentuated his restrictions there, because, during this campaign, he only signed anything with the ulterior motive of "giving the war time to develop its results." So he added:

> We must end things quickly and, from the first conferences, we should be able to stop things; for finally, in a few days, there will be a general affair which will decide everything. As the allies have already stopped the bases, you must have already accepted them, if they are acceptable, and, if not, we will run the chances of a battle, and even the loss of Paris and all that will follow.

The mail gone, Maret realized that these reservations strangely limited the "full powers." The hazards of the great battle doubtless terrified him. Napoléon always believed himself on the eve of Castiglione, Rivoli, Marengo, Austerlitz, and Friedland! He insisted near him, Napoléon listened to him, discussing "a great part of the night," through the military orders he was dictating for Berthier. He finally gave in. A second courier was dispatched to Chàtillon, with this letter from Maret for Caulaincourt:

> At the moment of leaving this city (Troyes), His Majesty instructs me to let you know in my own terms that His Majesty gives you *carte blanche* to lead the negotiations to a happy end, to save the capital or to avoid a battle and the last hopes of the nation.

And, to remove any ambiguity, this note to La Besnardière, which accompanied Caulaincourt: "Here, in a few words, is the meaning of my letter to the Duc de Vicence. The Emperor gives him *carte blanche*."[35]

Caulaincourt had asked for full powers; he received *carte blanche*, and found himself neither more sure of himself nor more reassured about his master's thoughts. What he would have liked was the firm acceptance of definite conditions, and that is what Napoléon did not give. He did not think, however, that he should delay. Napoléon ordered people to move quickly. Caulaincourt demanded a meeting for the following day.

It took place on the morning of the 7th.[36] The powers were found to be in order and the allies declared their terms of peace. Caulaincourt fell from a height. He said to the allies:

> You see me in a very painful position. When I came here, I anticipated that I would be asked to make great sacrifices. What we are asking for today is so far removed from the bases proposed to M. de Saint-Aignan, and which had been much more positively stated in a later declaration, that we should in no way have expected it.[37]

Then, recovering little by little, he objected, not on the bases, he seemed resigned from then on, but on the other terms of peace. He said, "Old France consisted of its provinces and colonies; will England restore all those she has conquered?" They replied, "The old limits!" Caulaincourt continued:

> Since we are asking France for cessions, we must at least know the use that will be made of them, in favor of whom we dispose of these countries, because it could not be indifferent to France to have as a neighbor a large power or a little prince. Being part of the system of Europe, it has the right to know how Europe would be composed. Moreover, if the principle is laid down that France will restore all that it has gained since the Revolution, it would not be fair not to apply the same principle to other powers.[38]

They were, quite simply, dividing Poland, Venetia, and Illyria. Caulaincourt, moreover, only seemed to observe it for the sake of principle; "very slightly." They answered again: "The old limits!" By this refrain one recognized that this time England was present, and that the negotiation was taking on seriousness. So Caulaincourt: "Finally, if I accepted your proposal, would you sign immediately and would the bloodshed be stopped at this moment?" This was the indiscreet question, and which, since Prague, the allies always dreaded and eluded. They could not, this time, repeat their antiphon "the old limits!" and they remained in embarrassment. Stadion pulled them out: "The answer, he said, is in our full powers." Whereupon Caulaincourt, who in turn feared being taken at his word, asked for time to reflect. The rest of the conference was postponed until the evening. "He is a man devastated by the misfortune of the circumstance, desiring only the end of the war, whatever it was, only asking to grant everything that one would propose, provided that one puts him in the case to present a signed treaty to his master," Stadion wrote.[39] "A treaty, whatever it is, provided that it is Napoléon who signs it."

Now, that was precisely what Alexander didn't want. Rasoumowsky received a letter from Nesselrode: "Events continue to be so favorable that we do not think we can be eager enough to inform Your Excellency of them."[40] Namur, Givet, and Philippeville had fallen; Bülow in Brussels. "These satisfactory notions will convince you, Monsieur le Comte, that every day new reasons are added on the necessity of not hastening the progress of the Châtillon negotiations." The allies dined at four o'clock at Rasoumowsky's. During the meal, Stewart learned of the occupation of Troyes by the allies, the arrival of the Cossacks at Melun, marching on Fontainebleau. Humbolt, Castlereagh, and Rasoumovsky concluded from this that Napoléon was down, that the war would soon end "and with his entire downfall"; that one could not deal with a man who, "at the very moment of signing, could neither fulfill nor guarantee the conditions thereof." Rasoumovsky said, "Don't make peace with him he's on the verge of being overthrown!" Humboldt agreed. They agreed that in the evening they would confine themselves to taking Courtliness's observations *ad referendum.*

At eight o'clock they met again. Caulaincourt read a protocol text which he had had La Besnardière write; he recalled there "the bases proposed by the allied powers at Frankfurt, and founded on what the allies called the natural limits of France." Whereupon the allies to interrupt, rectify, attenuate or crudely dispute the assertion. Count Rasoumovsky pretended not to know that these bases had been proposed at Frankfort. His instructions didn't mention it. "M. de Stadion seemed doubtful. Lord Aberdeen seemed to want to evade the question." Caulaincourt persisted in asking it, and the sitting was closed, after having taken the note *ad referendum.*

Then the allies assembled at Stewart's. Aberdeen showed himself greatly moved by this disavowal of insinuations which he had involuntarily witnessed. He understood the comedy and found that his lordship played in it a character unworthy of his rank. Stadion wrote to Metternich, 8 February 1814,

> If you leave us here a little longer, we will all mourn at poor Lord Aberdeen's funeral. His diplomatic innocence will kill him by dint of horror and scandal at everything he sees happening here and the part he must take in it. He melts into groans, and whatever expressions of unhappiness we see on Caulaincourt's

face are nothing compared to the deep annihilation that is painted in the features of his English colleague. Humboldt enjoys it like corpses between Leipzig and Frankfurt.

Rasoumovsky had his secret orders; he proposed to adjourn the conferences and ask for instructions. Stadion wrote to Metternich:

> Do we still want peace with the sovereign of France, whoever he may be, or do we want the person of Napoléon? Do we believe that Napoléon can sustain himself on the throne, or should we regard his fall as almost certain? Do we think that a peace made with France and signed by Napoléon would also be peace with the sovereign who would succeed him? Staying here is a kind of hell. We dine every day with people who must hate us with good reason. Rasoumovsky received a letter from Pozzo which drove him to extremes. We have all the trouble to keep it decent *vis-à-vis* the French plenipotentiaries. It is all the more unreasonable at conferences.[41]

However Caulaincourt wrote to Napoléon on 8 February 1814:

> Your Majesty has given me *carte blanche*, it is to give me necessity as a rule; but necessity emerges from events, it is in the situation of things, and as long as I am unaware of this situation, when I know nothing of what is going on, when Your Majesty gives me no news, I find myself reduced to walking in darkness and without a guide. What I know for certain is that I am dealing here with men who are nothing less than sincere, that to rush to make concessions to them is to encourage them to ask for new ones, without knowing where they will stop and without obtaining any result.

This was what Napoléon had discerned from the first conversation with Dubna, and had known since Dresden. Caulaincourt had come a long way: the reality that imposed itself on him at Châtillon, he had refused to see in Prague, in Paris: it was because then he only listened to Metternich. He understood now what peace meant in 60 hours and what Metternich's secret word was. He saw the four in front of him, and without knowing the agreements of Reichenbach, Toeplitz, of Langres, he saw their strength. He concluded: "The Austrians show us an apparent interest and deceive us. Not an ally, not a friend, not even an indifferent one. I await Your Majesty's orders."

The Austrians are deceiving us! However, he still found help only on their side; try as he may, Metternich still held him. He wrote to him on the 9th: "I regret more every day that it is not with you that I have to deal. Do the allies want to make time to get to Paris?" What then would be the fate of the Empress, reduced to fleeing before her father's army! He begged him to come to Châtillon with Nesselrode and Castlereagh, to hold a three-hour conference with him.

> I propose to ask the plenipotentiaries of the allied courts if France, by consenting, as they have requested, to return to her old limits, will immediately obtain an armistice. If by such a sacrifice an armistice can be obtained, I will be ready to do so, I will still be ready, on this assumption, to immediately restore part of the places that this sacrifice will have to cause us to lose.

On the same day, Rasoumovsky received this letter from Nesselrode: "The Emperor cannot yet send you his orders today. The conferences will therefore have to be suspended until he is able to address them to you." The secretary of the Austrian legation, Floret, took a letter from Maret to Caulaincourt. "I felt," reports this secretary, "that what he could say to me would be as unpleasant to hear as it would be difficult to answer." Caulaincourt emptied his entire bag .... "You consigned me here. You are stopping my mails. You ask me to make great sacrifices. I ask if after all these sacrifices we will finally finish. You answer with subtleties. Don't miss the moment. You want to go to Paris. You don't know what you are preparing for"; and Rayneval, one of the secretaries of the French legation, added: "You are going to rekindle the Revolution." But however much the Austrians complained, Lord Aberdeen rolled his forehead in the ashes, the Russians did not yield, supported by the other allies.

A short conference was held on 9 February 1814. Rasoumowski declared "that His Majesty the Emperor having deemed it expedient to consult with the allied sovereigns on the subject of the talks in Châtillon, His Majesty had given orders to his plenipotentiary to declare that he desired them to be suspended." It was done. That same day Castlereagh left for Troyes, where the allies had just established their headquarters and where Metternich called him to his aid.[42]

## IV. Napoléon at Nogent-sur-Seine

A few leagues away, at Nogent-sur-Seine, on the night of 7-8 February, Napoléon was struggling in abominable anguish, passing through one of those crises of uncertainty which, for a man of his temperament, were the worst of all ailments.[43] His army retreated before the Prussians; Schwartzenberg urged him; he wanted to separate them, they threatened to stifle him. Joseph, from Paris, cried out in misery, as before from Madrid, without energy, in the midst of intrigues; Belgium was lost, finally Murat betrayed! The letters follow one another, "loaded with misfortunes." At headquarters, it was a gloomy stupor: Napoléon sometimes dismayed, languishing, sometimes as if awakened with a start, dictating letter after letter, heaping up details as if to delude himself about the coolness he lacked, the power that he no longer practiced. They talked to each other as in sickrooms, during desperate nights; they murmured the name of Caulaincourt: he was the doctor of the last illusions.

A messenger arrived bringing the mail from Châtillon. Caulaincourt possessed powers: he did not dare to use them, faced with this implacable ultimatum: the old limits! Napoléon read the letter, then crumpling it in his hands, returned to his room. Maret and Berthier found him there "with his elbow resting on the table, forehead compressed in hand, the other hanging down and abandoned, still holding the letter."

They dared to call him to himself and talk about peace. Then he lost his temper, recalling all his youth and that famous day in Brumaire when he had hurled the formidable apostrophe at the Directory. He imagined he heard the echo of those words which had overthrown a government. He exclaimed:

> What! You want me to sign such a treaty, that I trample my oath underfoot! Unheard-of reverses have wrung from me the promise to renounce my conquests; but that I abandon those of the Republic! That I violate the deposit which was given to me with such confidence! That I leave France smaller than I ever found it! What will I be for the French when I have signed their humiliation? What shall I have to reply to the Republicans of the Senate when they come to ask me again for their Rhine barrier? You are afraid of the continuation of the war, and I am afraid of more certain dangers, which you do not see.

What he discovered with this intuition of the force of things which had so often enlightened him, was the necessary consequence of peace within the old limits: the return of the old monarchy, the eternal problem of Year III: that is to say for him forfeiture, for his faithful exile, for the others treason, for his son captivity.

After a discussion, or rather a monologue, interrupted here and there by exhortations from the Duc de Bassano and the Prince de Neufchâtel, he stopped in his agitated walk: "Answer what you will! I will never sign." In the end, however, he seemed to consent. France would withdraw by stages, give way first on Belgium, then on the left bank of the Rhine. Maret went out with Berthier to write to Caulaincourt. Napoléon tried to sleep. Ten times he called, dismissed, and called back his *valet de chambre*; sometimes asking him for light, sometimes making him take it away. In these alternations of drowsiness and insomnia, the catastrophe unfolded before his eyes in haunting visions. He perceived all the horror of the future. Towards morning he wrote Joseph this letter of agony.[44]

Nogent-sur-Seine, 8 February 1814
4 am

Paris will never be occupied in my lifetime...

If Talleyrand has anything to do with this opinion of leaving the Empress in Paris in case the enemy approaches, it is betrayal; I repeat to you: beware of this man; I have practiced him for sixteen years, I have even had favor with him, but he is surely the greatest enemy of our house, now that fortune has abandoned it for some time.

If a lost battle were to arrive and news of my death, you would be informed of it before my house: send the Empress and the King of Rome to Rambouillet, order the Senate, the Council of State, all the troops to unite on the Loire... Never let the Empress and the King of Rome fall into the hands of the enemy. Anything left that way would be destroyed... What would you say of the Empress? That she has abandoned her son's throne and ours!

I would rather have my son slaughtered than see him ever brought up in Vienna like an Austrian prince.

> I have never seen *Andromaque* represented that I did not feel sorry for the fate of Astyanax surviving at his house, and that I did not consider it a happiness for him not to survive his father...
>
> Besides, it is possible that the enemy, approaching Paris, I would defeat them!

At daybreak, around seven o'clock, a courier arrived from Marmont. Blücher's four corps marched past, at long intervals, on the two roads that go to Paris, one by Epernay and Chateau-Thierry, the other by Champaubert and Montmirail. Napoléon jumped out of bed, threw himself on the maps, compass in hand, staking out the paths with pins. He discerned an action to take, he pulled himself together. Maret surprised him at work; he brought the telegram to be signed for Caulaincourt. Cried the Emperor:

> Oh! here you are! Now it's a whole other thing. I am currently beating Blücher with my eye! I'll beat him tomorrow, I'll beat him the day after tomorrow; the face of things will change. Let's not rush anything. There will always be time to make a peace like the one we are being offered!

Thus on the same day that Alexander, for fear that Napoléon would accept the allies' conditions, gave the order to suspend talks, Napoléon suspended the sending of instructions to Caulaincourt.

## V. The Bases of Troyes

Hardenberg wrote in his diary, "Alexander wants to drag out the negotiation, to arrive, in the meantime, in Paris, and to make peace there."[45] To so many causes of disagreement were added the pretensions of the Prussians: the conquest delivered to their covetousness beautiful vacant lands, and they thought of settling there.[46] It was no longer just Saxony, but "all the countries on the left bank of the Rhine," which Humboldt said "would offer a sufficient mass to complete the lot that would be necessary for Prussia." Whereupon Stadion, who never ceased to squint in the same way towards Milan, Venice, the Legations, even Piedmont, to cry foul, and Aberdeen to observe that, for 20 years "Prussia had had an unstable policy, that she had been the first to bind herself with France, that one could not answer that she did not do so again, and that then her power reunited with France would again put Europe in danger." All the more reason, according to Castlereagh, to insist on the prior settlement of "the arrangements of Europe." Must Austria and Prussia be rebuilt exactly as they were in 1805, or by equivalents, and which ones? Will they add enlargements and where to take them? What will Russia demand? Stadion, who found the demand for the Rhine by Prussia "scandalous" claimed for Austria the restitution of the Low Countries and moreover "ample compensation" for Gallicia, if Russia annexed this province. He thought of Swabia, of pieces to be taken in Lusatia, Silesia, in case Prussia should take Saxony. Castlereagh cried out. So Stadion: "First of all, Russia should be forced to decide on her projects in western Poland, because all our calculations depend on it, and those of Prussia could only then be put into balance." Castlereagh seemed to abound in this direction. "One cannot admit a kingdom or a separate duchy of Poland, neither in fact nor in name, neither in avowed form nor in concealed form." It was Russian supremacy and the Eastern Question opened by Russia, and this Englishman did not consent to it at any price; with such signs as to contain Alexander, in his invasive march, he thought expedient to arrest it, on the road to Paris; he would not allow him to give the French a king from his hand. Metternich opposed it with as much energy. And there followed this remarkable consequence: Castlereagh willing to treat, if necessary, with Napoléon, and Metternich inclined, if necessary, to the restoration of the Bourbons, to prevent Russia from dominating Europe. These complicated combinations, this impatience to "fix prizes," these underground struggles for influence, recall the impediments of the beginnings of the Great War, at the time when people were talking about barter for Bavaria and the Low Countries and the partition of Poland

It all came down to this preliminary question posed by Stadion to Metternich: "Do we still want peace with the sovereign of France, whoever he is, where do we want the person of Napoléon?"

The parties were agitated in Paris; the letters of the secret agents were beginning to speak of the Bourbons. "I fear for our poor empress," Metternich told Hudelist.

> The Duke of Angoulême has passed over dry land. This is a second-line affair for us.... The Duke of Angoulême lands at Saint-Jean de Luz, the Duke of Berry in Brittany, Monsieur (the Count of Artois) goes to Switzerland. What effect will this appearance have? The event will tell. Here there is only one cry: peace, and not from Napoléon, because with him peace is impossible. But what will we put in its place? Some say: the Bourbons. It was the former and the emigrants who already shared the places at court. Most say regency. The people say nothing but Peace, and end it at all costs The knot will only be cut in Paris.[47]

The regency still remained the thought behind the head, a thought *à la* Kaunitz, conceived in these days by Talleyrand; but it was a quarter century too late, and Metternich, who brooded over it, did not risk proposing it. He confided to Hudelist:

> The public voice is in France: Down with Napoléon! These frivolous people have not yet considered what could be put in Napoléon's place. A regency becomes in this horrible crisis something that can hardly be thought of anymore.[48]

The Prussians had only one idea: to overthrow Napoléon in Paris; after which, anyone, the Comte d'Artois, for example, who was there and whom, said Blücher, the French would gladly take. Hardenberg asked Münster: "wouldn't it be possible to bring in a Bourbon."[49]

Royalist emissaries endeavored to approach the headquarters, above all to circumvent Alexander. He turned them away, as much from an inveterate prejudice against the Bourbons as from a presumption of his own glory.[50] Bernadotte remained his favorite combination. In the absence of this former Minister of the Directory, and if he could not avoid the Bourbons, at least one cadet, of this house, the Duc de Berry, an Orléans more willingly, who would further distance himself from this legitimacy, as they were beginning to say, by appropriating a word from Louis XVIII in 1804, which had hurt Alexander too much for him to ever forget it. To Louis XVIII, he reproached his height, the infatuation of his blood, his precedence, his claim to be enthroned in the first rank of kings, the closest to the right hand of God! Finally, what he could not confess, the capitulation to which Napoléon had twice forced Russia, the banishment of this prince, the expulsion of a guest. An Orléans offended him the less there were two scaffolds between this Orléans and the royal house: that of Louis XVI and that of *Égalité*. He speculated about it as in France, the Orleanists of 1802: "We need a king who has a crown because I have this place deriving its rights from ours."[51]

La Harpe, the Tsar's great prompter in his subtle speculations on France, provided him with fine pretexts for liberty, respect for the law, and the sovereignty of the French people. Alexander intended that this people be consulted, in the Polish manner of course, under Russian guns, and the ingenious La Harpe would insinuate the response to the "representatives of the French people" hand-picked by his cronies. For if the Tsar drew his doctrines from Switzerland, he borrowed his constitutional practices from Poland. Münster wrote,[52]

> The Emperor relating a conversation of February 11, spoke to me for a long time of his projects. He assured me that he was far from any idea of revenge, but that he believed he had to do the impossible to overthrow Napoléon; that it was for this end that he wanted to push on Paris and, however, to drag out the negotiations, in order to be able to take advantage of them, in the unexpected case of a reverse. I do not think I am mistaken in supposing that the Emperor had the idea of wishing to favor the projects of the Prince of Sweden.

He summed up the state of affairs thus:

> The French want to end the negotiation with a peace at all costs; perhaps Metternich desires it just as keenly. The political religion of the English ministers is reluctant to drag out a negotiation with the secret design of not giving it a follow-up; they believe that it would be dishonorable, after having consented to negotiate, not to sign the peace if Napoléon wished to grant everything.

This is where the allies stood at Troyes, where their headquarters had been established on 10 February. Alexander received there, on the 11th, a courier from London which somewhat changed the picture of things. It was a long report from Lieven on a talk he had had with the Prince Regent. This prince, finely constitutional, explained himself only as a "particular." He admired, he said, with England, with all of Europe, in the Emperor of Russia the liberator of Europe, the leader of "this immortal coalition"; he admired "the sublime will" to give peace to the universe, and it would be, "to deceive the wish of Providence not to establish this peace on unshakable bases." Which led him to this declaration: "A peace, however advantageous it might be, made with Napoléon would never ensure more or less a truce for mankind." He was inclined to warn the French of this, to invite them to "separate their interests from those of their tyrant," to promise them to "conclude with such master as they would like to give themselves, except the one on good faith to which neither they nor the allies cannot count." However, by allowing them freedom of choice, as befit "a respectable nation," the Regent was of the opinion to "remind them of the existence of a legitimate dynasty." He said: "I can only take a keen interest in the Bourbons and I am persuaded that the Emperor's political interest and his intimate conviction also dispose him in their favour, but in any case this interest must be subordinated to the wish of the nation." Finally, and this was the main thing, Lieven "acquired the certainty" that Liverpool, head of the Ministry, basically shared the Regent's view "and that he feared this extraordinary propensity of the Austrian cabinet for peace at a time when the most brilliant chances seemed to open the road to Paris to the allied armies."[53]

These communications fortified Alexander; they disarmed Castlereagh and Metternich in the most immediate affair: peace without Napoléon. As to the second point, the future government of France, Alexander remained in disagreement with Metternich, who desired the regency *in petto*, and Castlereagh, who declared himself personally for the Bourbons; Alexander relied on events. The Prince Regent tended to the restoration of the Bourbons, without proposing it; it was enough for Alexander to avoid a disagreement, not to exclude them. Besides, he felt comfortable with them. They had made their pledge on the essential article, the limits. Metternich wrote to Hudelist on 9 February: "The question of the Bourbons, which is growing every day, is still very problematic. The Bourbons have very recently consented to the peace we are asking for: thus little by little we are getting what we wanted."

In the meantime, Metternich received Caulaincourt's letter, asking if France, by consenting to return to the former limits, would immediately obtain an armistice. Metternich was inclined to it, and he seized the allies on the question.[54] But the scene suddenly changed. Napoléon had entered the campaign, and on the 10th at Champaubert, on the 11th at Montmirail, on the 12th at Château-Thierry he defeated the Russians and the Prussians. With this return of genius and this return of fortune, the danger that France would rise up, this national resistance which everything had been done to paralyze seemed to be announced: the peasants fired on the Cossacks, killed the stragglers, finally and from above all the sign which astonished and alarmed at the same time the allies: one did not find spies![55]

All was in question. It was important at all costs to postpone their quarrels, to tighten the bonds and to rush *en masse* on Napoléon; his very victories weakened him, because his army could no longer be recruited. It was under these impressions that the parleys which had been called the conferences of Troyes were carried on. The ministers of the four met twice during the day of the 12th, once on the 13th, not to mention visits and private meetings. "Austrian dissatisfaction with Alexander," Hardenberg noted in his journal: "Outraged Austria threatens to separate. I do everything in the world to reconcile. Written to the Emperor of Russia. Night spent in worry."

Metternich asked the questions; there were seven. What will they say to the Duke of Vicenza? Will they decide for Louis XVIII or leave the initiative to the French? How to be sure of the dispositions of the French on a change of dynasty? What will be the last term assigned to them to decide? If Paris decides for the Bourbons and if Napoléon remains in arms, what will the allies do? In the meantime, what course to take with regard to Louis XVIII, the Comte d'Artois and their emissaries at headquarters? How to govern Paris when one will be master of it?[56]

The answers, qualified as votes, were given in writing and inserted in the protocol. Castlereagh declared: "The allies entered France to win the peace which they thought they could not make on the Rhine"; if Napoléon accepts a peace which seems suitable, treat with him, unless a national movement, "makes doubtful his competence to contract," but, the peace obtained, there would be no need to continue the war "to dethrone the individual placed at the head of the government of France." Under no circumstances agree to an armistice.

Austria and Prussia came to the same conclusions: by the return of France to the old limits, "the object of the war is entirely achieved." If Napoléon agrees, sign with him. Paris cannot suffice to ascertain the general opinion of the country. If the national wish is for the Bourbons, Louis XVIII must be preferred. "Do not support the claims of one of the princes of the house of Bourbon to the detriment of the principle of legitimacy"; but, in any case, with respect to everyone, to maintain a passive role.

The Russian vote differed significantly from the other three. Do not pronounce for Louis XVIII; leave the initiative to the French; "the provisions of the capital will guide the steps of the powers in this respect"; if Paris does not decide against Napoléon, to treat with him; a governor of Paris will be appointed; "the Emperor wants it to be a Russian Governor."

Between the vote of Austria and that of Russia, there was a very significant opposition on a very delicate point of public law: in the eyes of Alexander, brought up by La Harpe, at the school of the philosophers, and according to the precedents of the Revolution, Paris represented France, and the assembly which would be supposed to represent Paris would stipulate for the whole of France; Metternich, on the contrary, felt agitated by legal scruples: an enemy invasion did not seem to him "conducive to making the people express their independent will." He perhaps remembered the votes in Belgium in 1793 and the plebiscites in Italy in 1796. He did not allow, and it was a corollary of his concept of the regency, that bodies formed by Napoléon should become sovereign by the very fall of their author and competent to declare fallen a prince whom they would not have had the right to elect. Finally, "he considered it no less impossible to attribute to the votes of an assembly of individuals called and chosen by foreign powers the value of the expression of the national will." Thus, in their formal forms, the proposals of the allies contradicted each other. In the remarks, the opposition grew strangely accentuated. Hardenberg wrote to the King:

> Austria's exasperation and jealousy of this sort of dictatorship of Russia, as it is called, is extreme. The Austrians talk of nothing less than making separate arrangements with France rather than allowing themselves to be dragged off to Paris following the Emperor of Russia, without knowing what he will do there. They want to induce Your Majesty to join forces with them. They say they are sure Bavaria and Württemberg would side with them. What a pity if this was realized![57]

Hardenberg stepped in. Metternich had a long conference with Alexander on the morning of the 14th. He indoctrinated him and he suggested the idea of a preliminary treaty to present to Caulaincourt.

Alexander rallied to it. The day of the 14th was employed in the preparation of this project.[58]

The allied powers imposed on France the limits of 1792 and they guaranteed them:

> They do not intend and will not allow any power to extend views of conquest, following new successes of the allied armies, beyond the limits mentioned above.... The person of the sovereign and the national institutions being regarded by them as so many objects which must remain placed outside any foreign influence, they make the formal commitment not to interfere directly or indirectly in the internal relations of France. However desirable a spontaneous movement on the part of the French in favor of the former royal family expelled following the Revolution might appear to them, they are none the less determined to follow the line of conduct observed hitherto by them with the princes of the house of Bourbon. In the event that a spontaneous movement of the nation decides in favor of one of the younger princes of the house of Bourbon, the powers will only bring him help and assistance insofar as the head of this house formally renounces his rights.

The allies undertook to treat with Napoléon on the bases proposed at Châtillon unless negotiation failed at Châtillon; before the entry of the allies into Paris, the "wish of the capital," at the time of this entry, in favor of the old dynasty, did not deprive Napoléon of the means of dealing with sufficient guarantees.

This wording, of extreme dexterity, suspended and veiled the difficulties; it made it possible to press on to the goal, without compromising anyone's resolutions for the next day. Only the cadets of Bourbon, in fact the Orléans, remained excluded from the national choice; but the vote, more or less prepared and dictated, remained with the French, which left the illusions and calculations of Alexander on Bernadotte and the handling of assemblies by the "virtuous" La Harpe sufficient license. It was also possible that Napoléon would abdicate, that there would be no revolution and that the public authorities would come out in favor of a regency: this was the part of the hopes for Austria, failing which Metternich, out of Bernadotte's antipathy and jealousy of Russia, would fall back on the Bourbons, the preferred solution of the English and which events made more and more probable.

This project, adopted by Castlereagh, Hardenberg, and Metternich, was submitted on 15 February to Alexander, who adhered to it. The news of Napoléon's fourth victory, on the 14th, had something to do with it.[59] England, moreover, had its deposit. On 15 February, that is to say at the same time as the draft treaty to be imposed on France, Castlereagh and Nesselrode exchanged identical notes in which it was said that peace with France could be concluded before the arrangements for European peace were achieved among the allies, they already agreed: 1) that the countries located between the Meuse and the former border of France, on the one hand, between the Meuse and the Rhine from Maastricht as far as Cologne, would be ceded to the Prince of Orange to be reunited forever with Holland; that the other countries of the left bank would be united with Holland or distributed, in agreement with England, for the better protection of Germany; 2) an indemnity to the King of Sicily; 3) the cession to England of all the vessels and all the war material captured in the ports.[60] Metternich also received his spices, and it was a splendid piece: Italy. He wrote to Hudelist on the 14th: "We have just received the news that the King of Naples has ratified his treaty of alliance with us, and that his army is in full march on Piedmont."

Castlereagh set out on 16 February from Troyes for Châtillon, with the project of a treaty, or rather of capitulation. It was worse that forfeiture was opprobrium and a certain fall for a sovereign whose power was made up of glory and prestige:

> France brought back to the frontiers of 1792 the Emperor's renunciation of all constitutional influence, direct or indirect, beyond these limits; the renunciation of the titles of King of Italy, King of Rome, Protector of the Confederation of the Rhine, Mediator of the Swiss Confederation; Germany made up of independent, confederate states; Italy made up of independent states; Holland, increased, to the House of Orange; independent Switzerland; Spain to the Bourbons; the visitation by England of the French colonies, except Tabago. The Emperor of the French recognizes, moreover, the right of the allied powers to determine, according to existing treaties, the limits and relations both of the countries ceded by France and of their States between them, without France being able to do so in any way to intervene. Immediate evacuation of the ceded countries and surrender of all the fortresses, notably Mainz, Hamburg, Antwerp, Mantua, Venice, Peschiera, the places on the Oder and the Elbe.

And it would still only be a preliminary peace. France would remain excluded from the discussion of the general peace. After having stripped it of its absolute power, they reserved, without even hearing it, to attack it in its relative power and to organize Europe against it, or it would be struck, in a way, by legal prohibition and stripped of his political rights! When Napoléon had appeared on the point of negotiating, the allies had broken off the negotiation, hoping to annihilate him; they offered to reconnect, hoping to drive him to abdication or suicide.

## VI. Alliance of Chaumont

On the 10th, after Champaubert, Napoléon said to Marmont:

> On what does the destiny of empires depend! If tomorrow we have a success over Sacken similar to that which we had today over Olsoufieff, the enemy will recross the Rhine more quickly than he crossed it; and I am still on the Vistula.

He was "drunk with joy." He believed himself to be the master of affairs again. People around him were alarmed at this reversal of things. He realized this: "And then," he went on, "I will make peace on the natural borders of the Rhine!" On the 11th he defeated Sacken at Montmirail, and on the 12th again at Château-Thierry. "The day was decisive. The army of Silesia no longer exists. I put her in complete rout. Russia's best army no longer exists." He commanded "proclamations so that everywhere people rise up and stop them. It is time for the French people to rise up to fall on them." He believed that "the enemy must be stricken with singular terror."[61] On the 14th, Blücher returned to the charge; Napoléon defeated him again at Vauxchamps. However Maret warned Caulaincourt:

> It is considered probable that these events will dissipate the foolish illusions of the Emperor of Russia. There can be no reasonable peace except on the basis laid by the allies themselves in Frankfurt. Any other peace would only be a truce.[62]

Here then was Caulaincourt without powers, and it was up to him to delay things when the allies, on the contrary, said they were ready to negotiate. He lamented, complaining that he was being abandoned.

He wrote to Maret on the 14th:

> All of Europe is against us. They will have no qualms about any way if we don't end quickly. There should be no illusions. They don't want to negotiate with us. They want to dictate conditions to us and deprive us of even the means of complaining.

Act on the Emperor; the emperor decides. "Let posterity not believe that ... when all that was needed to save everything was a word from the Emperor, no one was found to lead him to say this word or to say it in his name."

In the conference of the 17th, Stadion read the draft treaty preliminarily drawn up by his colleagues and himself, as a result of the resolutions taken at Troyes. When Caulaincourt heard the article relating to the fortresses, he found it difficult to contain himself; he requested adjournment to a later sitting. Returning home, the allies realized that this article was too hard, offensive, useless finally, said Aberdeen. An Austrian wrote, "To suppose that Napoléon could subscribe to a condition so humiliating for himself and for the nation, he would have to be at the last extremity. The reverses of Blücher's army must have proved the contrary to us."[63]

Maret wrote to Caulaincourt on 16 February: "If fate is against the Emperor, everything is useless. Everything depends on the outcome of the three days that will happen."[64] The 17th: "Luck has changed, we are no longer in a hurry. Preliminaries on the bases of Frankfurt would put an end to the difficulties immediately."[65] And the 8th? Napoléon to Caulaincourt:

> I gave you *carte blanche* to save Paris and avoid a battle which was the nation's last hope. The battle has taken place. Providence has blessed our weapons. Yesterday I surrounded Prince Schwarzenberg's army, which I hope to destroy before it crosses our borders.
>
> My intention is that you should not sign anything without my order, because only I know my position.
>
> I am ready to cease hostilities and let the enemies go home quietly, if they sign the preliminaries based on the Frankfurt proposals.

The same day he defeated the Austrians at Montereau, and Schwarzenberg demanded a suspension of arms. It was then that he received the draft treaty communicated by the allies, on the 17th. He wrote to Caulaincourt who urged him to resign and showed him the danger of Bourbon restoration:

> I consider you as ... knowing nothing of my affairs and influenced by impostors. As soon as I will be in Troyes, I will send you the counter-proposal that you will have to give. I want to make my ultimatum myself. I would a hundred times prefer the loss of Paris to the dishonor and annihilation of France. I am so moved by the infamous proposal you send me, that I think I am dishonored, just to have put myself in the situation that it was proposed to you. You always speak of the Bourbons; I would rather see the Bourbons in France on reasonable terms than the infamous proposals you send me.

And he claimed the "natural limits" in compensation for the partitions of Poland, the secularizations of Germany, the conquests of England in Asia. In short, he ordered his negotiator to enter into the affairs of Europe from which the allies claimed to exclude him.

The motives which dictated the Emperor's reply were the same as those which had inspired 22 years previously, in analogous circumstances, the acts of the Provisional Executive Council. When the enemy was repulsed at Valmy, this Council demanded a retreat beyond the frontiers of old France; when the enemy had crossed these frontiers, the Council demanded that they withdraw beyond the Rhine; when they were beyond the Rhine, the Council ordered that they be pursued there, to ensure the effects of victory and to consolidate the new frontier of the Republic, whence a war of prestige within the France, of supremacy abroad, which became the law of all Republican governments. Napoléon and his empire had emerged from it, and he could maintain himself in power only by defending the avenues by which he had gone there. The Republic and the Empire which had sprung from it remained linked to the frontier of the Rhine: in conquering it, the Convention had consecrated the Republic; in claiming it, Napoléon was only supporting the work and rebuilding the foundations, without which everything would crumble.

Raising his voice everywhere, he asked Savary, who had thought it witty, to enhance the master, to say that he was fighting one against three:

> You must have lost your mind. I say everywhere that I have 300,000 men. The enemy believes it. With strokes of the pen you destroy all the good that results from victory. The enemy pillages, massacres, rapes, burns; it is necessary to publish the letters which tell it, very crudely, and not in tables of genre. We must excite the people by publishing these excesses.

To Augereau, who grew numb and complained of running out of equipment:

> Augereau! I destroyed 80,000 enemies with battalions composed of conscripts without pouches. If you are still the Augereau of Castiglione, keep the command; if your sixty years weigh on you, leave it. The homeland is in danger, it can only be saved by audacity. You have to take back your boots and your resolution of '93.[66]

On the 21st he sent a long letter to Franz II. The conditions presented at Châtillon would make France a slave to England.

> It is the realization of the dream of Burke, who wanted to make France disappear from the map of Europe. That England wants to destroy Antwerp! But you, Sire, what is your interest in the annihilation of the navy of France, in putting the Belgians under the yoke of a Protestant prince whose son will ascend the throne of England?[67] I will never give up Antwerp and Belgium. (He concluded by proposing to) sign the peace, without delay, on the Frankfurt terms.

The fact is that the allies no longer felt safe. At all costs, Schwarzenberg intended to deny Napoléon the chances of a new battle. He resolved to withdraw, if need be, to Langres. The royals left Troyes on 23 February. To cover the retreat, Schwarzenberg began, at the outposts, a dilatory armistice negotiation, which was not to succeed. Napoléon wanted to insert in the convention, in the form of a preamble, the recognition of the bases of Frankfurt; but the allies refused.[68] On the same day, 25 February, at Bar-sur-Aube, Alexander had his allies adopt a protocol, the text of which he had written in pencil with his own hand: "The great army will refuse battle and will continue to withdraw to Chaumont. Blücher, fortified by Bülow,

Winzingerode, and Woronzof, will continue to march on Paris." This combination brought together the Austrians, partisans of the defensive, and the Prussians, partisans of the offensive; it offered the advantage of threatening Paris and obliging Napoléon to divide his forces.

Napoléon had entered Troyes on the 24th. He set out again on the 27th. Leaving it to Macdonald to contain Schwarzenberg's army, he resolved to attack Blücher from behind. It was important to him to mask his movements; this is why he renewed armistice negotiations and asked Caulaincourt to prevaricate at Châtillon. "Try to make the negotiation work." He sent him documents, arguments, adding: "It is of the utmost importance that the enemy does not doubt that I am between Bar-sur-Aube and Vandeuvre."[69]

From Chaumont, where they had withdrawn, the allies decided to put Napoléon on notice and to prescribe an end to him. They drew up, on the 26th, an instruction for the plenipotentiaries. It said that the draft treaty which they demanded acceptance or rejection was based, in substance, on an offer made by the French negotiator in a letter to Metternich, dated the 9th of this month, namely "that France was ready to accept as the basis of a general peace the old limits and to immediately cede to the allies several fortresses as pledges of her intention to sign peace on the conditions announced."[70] The envoys could accept a discussion, but, on the detail and the forms, nothing "which differed essentially from the spirit of the arrangement already agreed upon"; otherwise, immediate rupture, and they would leave it to the fate of arms.

By sending this piece to Stadion, Metternich, always trying to insinuate himself into a place apart, and to create a way back, sent him to tell Caulaincourt: "If we were alone at war, peace would be made, assuming that the Emperor Napoléon would have sincerely wanted it." But "the questions are all squarely placed now." And as he foresaw a claim, difficult to evade, on the bases of Frankfurt, he suggested an answer, the one, probably, that he had prepared from Frankfurt: "The Emperor Napoléon wanted to have the bases of Frankfurt admitted by signing an armistice. These bases are the same as those from Châtillon, except that the latter are detailed and the others were not." He added, hoping to hang up the case again: "Let the Duke of Vicenza present a counter-project, and we will no doubt meet halfway." The powers would not bend on the article of the old limits, but France could perhaps obtain something in addition![71]

These instructions arrived at Châtillon on the 27th of February.

The plenipotentiaries were greatly discouraged. Over dinner at Aberdeen's, Stewart kept saying, "Congress will get you nowhere." In the evening, they met to decide on the terms of the declaration to be delivered to Caulaincourt, one of them, and to observe that the instruction contained an inaccurate quotation. Caulaincourt had neither offered nor accepted the allies' project. The letter to Metternich of 9 February posed only one question: "If France, by consenting, as they (the allies) have requested, to return to its former limits, will immediately obtain an armistice"; in this case, Caulaincourt would be ready to give places. An hour-long discussion ensued "in an indecent manner" over the quote from Caulaincourt's letter.[72]

> Aberdeen declared that, as a man of honor, he would never sign a lie. Humboldt maliciously maintained that the statement should be given as prescribed by the court order, saying that if the courts wanted one to sign a lie, that was their business, and he did not see why they should refuse it.[73]

Cathcart, like a good soldier, demanded instructions. Rasoumovsky left it to the majority. Finally, Stadion found an expedient, which consisted in analyzing the declaration instead of quoting it. It was done. The conference passed, on the 28th, in proceedings. It was stipulated that if on the 10th of March, at midnight, no answer had arrived from the Emperor, "in agreement in substance with the basis established by the allies," the negotiation would be regarded as terminated, and the allied plenipotentiaries would withdraw.[74]

Napoléon had resumed his march. He was going to succeed. Blücher seemed lost, provided Soissons held out for 24 hours: "He ran the risk of being cornered in the Aisne. He was desperate. What would he have done if he had found the place closed and defended by a commander determined to sacrifice everything?"[75] The commander, a General Moreau, a tired soldier, placed there as an invalid, was no longer in his head or heart to support such tragic circumstances. He had the weakness to allow entry into the place and receive a Russian officer, Loewenstern. This leader of partisans, as insidious as he was daring, frightened him in such a way that Moreau capitulated on 4 March with military honors. Russians immediately occupied the gates. Blücher managed to escape; he joined Winzingerode and Bülow; instead of a routed army, the Prussians were able to oppose Napoléon more than 100,000 men.

The allies had retired to Chaumont, where they waited in perplexity. Fierce battles were fought around Laon; Blücher was not retreating, but he was no longer advancing. With fear, political divisions reappeared between the allies. The Russians and the English suspected Metternich to negotiate secretly with the French; and the fact is that he was tempting it. He sent, under the pretext of carrying letters to Stadion, a diplomat of his entourage, Esterhazy, to Châtillon, and instructed him to admonish Caulaincourt.[76] He wrote on 8 March to this diplomat, "the good duke," as Stadion described him, "and who sincerely wanted peace." He revealed to him that day what he had concealed from him in Prague and Frankfurt and what should have been discovered sooner or later, when it came to drawing up the articles, namely the commitment made not to deal without England and England's willingness to impose the old limits:

> Let the Emperor convince himself that he will have done nothing if he does not achieve general peace. England is going smoothly. The ministry is strong enough to want peace. If it is not made at this moment, no other occasion will present itself on which it can be permitted to hope even for a negotiation. It will be the triumph of the supporters of the war of extinction against the Emperor of the French. The world will be turned upside down and France will fall prey to events.

It was then that, to put an end to machinations which they dreaded and which only too clearly explained the softness of Schwarzenberg, Castlereagh returned to his favorite combination, the plan prescribed by the Prince Regent and Liverpool: a general alliance which would summarize and seal all the particular treaties of 1813, and would tie the bundle so tightly that no part could detach itself from it. On this point he found himself in agreement with Alexander, and as he held the keys to the subsidy box, Metternich had to pass by whatever he wanted. The talks, although pursued under the influence of necessity, did not fail to be thorny.[77] It was because, to guarantee the outcome of the war, it had to be defined, and that was to tackle the chapter of compensations. The English would have liked to have the greater part of the left bank of the Rhine attributed to Holland; the Prussians protested. If they were not left, on this bank, "a territory capable of being defended and of maintaining an army of 100,000 men, the king would not consent to take his indemnities on the left bank of the Rhine."[78] Finally, on 9 March, the work was on its feet. This treaty, "my treaty," said Castlereagh to Hamilton, 10 March 1814 was antedated and carried forward, in the instrument, to 1 March.

It was the famous Treaty of Chaumont,[79] "the great treaty of alliance," said Münster, "perhaps the most extensive that has been concluded," wrote Metternich to Merveldt. It governed Europe until 1848 and founded this coalition of four which, so often broken up, was reconstituted each time France showed some inclination to go beyond the limits which the allies then claimed to impose on it. It constituted, in a way, the executive power of Europe, of which the treaties of Paris of 30 May 1814 and of Vienna of 9 June 1815 formed the charter. The object declared by the preamble was "to draw closer (among the powers) the bonds which unite them for the vigorous pursuit of a war undertaken with the salutary aim of putting an end to the misfortunes of Europe; to ensure the peace of Europe by the re-establishment of a just balance," and to "maintain against all attack the order of things which will have been the happy result of their efforts." In the event of refusal of their terms of peace by France, the allies would devote "all the means of their respective States to the vigorous pursuit of the present war"; each one would deploy at least 150,000 men, that is to say an army of 600,000 men; England to pay for 1814 a sum of £5 million. They undertook "not to negotiate separately with the common enemy, and to sign neither peace, nor truce, nor convention except by mutual agreement." They promised to "not lay down arms until the object of war, mutually agreed and understood, has been achieved." They will enter "without delay, into defensive commitments for the protection of their respective States in Europe against any attack that France would like to bring to the order of things resulting from this pacification." If France attacked one of them, the others would intervene diplomatically, first, then each by a corps of 60,000 men. The command and pay of the auxiliary army were regulated. The treaty was for 20 years, and renewable. The monarchies of Spain, Portugal, Sweden and the Prince of Orange (future King of the Netherlands) would be invited to access it. The treaty finally posed the bases of peace already so many times drawn: Germany composed of sovereign princes, confederates; independent Switzerland under the guarantee of the powers; Italy into independent states; Spain to the Bourbons; Holland, augmented, to the Prince of Orange.

The treaty was signed, but to have engaged with this

solemnity, the allies had not abjured their disagreements and their rivalries: in the background, for general peace, the question of Poland and the question of Russian supremacy; in the foreground, the question of peace with Napoléon or the decline of the Empire.

## VII. Ultimatum of the Allies

Caulaincourt meditated, in the bitterness of his heart and the disaster of his thought, on a catastrophe which henceforth seemed to him inevitable. He revealed to Napoléon what he learned of the intrigues of the Bourbons and the complacency of Austria in letting the Comte d'Artois approach. "Austria, since she is no longer ashamed of such conduct, is ready to disown you." He reported the last words of Metternich's emissary, Esterhazy. He concluded, "Peace is most urgent for Your Majesty, one cannot know where things will go. Should they momentarily retreat beyond the Rhine, and take new chances, the game is tied in such a way that the greatest reverses would not change the claims that have been made." He added, on the suggestion of Metternich: "Austria and Prussia, defeated by Your Majesty, gave him more than one example of resignation: this virtue has benefited these cabinets, for they speak today as victors. Imitate them, Sire, while your capital is not yet overrun." This advice was "Austria's last act of kinship."[80]

On 10 March there was, as agreed, a conference at Châtillon.[81] Caulaincourt read a long memo probably drawn up by Besnardière, according to instructions from the Emperor. These were indisputable observations on the effects of the partitions of Poland, the increases obtained in 1793 and 1795 by Russia, Prussia and Austria, the Russian acquisitions of the Treaty of Yassy, that of Tilsit and Finland, and the secularizations in Germany.

The allies, said this memo, spoke of equilibrium: would it be a stable one which would consist in bringing France back to the limits of before 1792, while the others would retain or recover their limits extended since 1792, Austria and Prussia restored to the state of 1805, England keeping the Indian Empire, Ceylon, and the Cape?

> When everything has changed around France, how could she retain the same relative power by being placed back in the same state as before? Replaced in this same state, it would not even have the degree of absolute power which it

then had, for its overseas possessions were incontestably one of the elements of this power.

Historical arguments, political arguments, excellent in themselves, and which would have carried if the balance, in the language of the allies, had meant something other than the displacement, to their advan-tage, of the old balance of power. This is how they understood it in 1709, in 1792, in 1793, in 1799. The Executive Council, the Committee of Public Safety, and the Directory, Bonaparte, in 1797, had also invoked, to justify their pretensions to the left bank of the Rhine, the partition of Poland; but France then occupied this left bank, and part of the right bank, and Holland, and Italy as far as Venice and the Legations: it held the balance, it could speak of balance! In turn, the allies let Caulaincourt read his "long and tedious dissertation." He produced, in support, "the note sent to M. de Saint-Aignan, with the letter from M. de Metternich which establishes," he said, the authenti-city of this document. Alleging the "Frankfurt bases," claiming to establish its authenticity, was inevitably to stir up a storm. "A lively discussion arose. It was represented that this was not the answer to be expected, that they had to decide, that they had set a deadline.[82] One of the English demanded a counter-proposal; Caulaincourt replied on all the articles. "The conference became increasingly stormy. The plenipotentiaries of Russia and England seem strongly decided to break off. Aberdeen was the most moderate of the whole assembly, and indeed the only one." Stadion asked: "Is this a denial of our peace terms?" Caulaincourt didn't let him even finish his sentence. It's not a refusal; France refuses nothing; these are observations which he pres-ents for the consideration of the plenipotentiaries. It was discussed academically for some time, when the allies pretending to rise, Cau-laincourt took from his papers a writing which he read, in the form of a verbal declaration: Napoléon was ready to renounce all titles expres-sing relations of sovereignty, supremacy, protection, mediation bey-ond the limits of France; to recognize the Bourbon restoration in Spain; the independence of Italy, Switzerland, Germany; Holland to the Prince of Orange; transfers of colonies in return for compensation. These were, implicitly, the "natural limits" that he claimed, and he used the very expressions of the Frankfurt declaration, in abdicating "the preponderance beyond the limits of his empire."

The allies asked to refer and the conference was adjourned *sine die*. Stadion wrote to Metternich:

> There's plenty to break up if you like, and there's plenty to stay on forever, all up to you. Your tapestry figures from Châtillon have held the doors open to whatever the powers of Chaumont will want to decide. I believe that for straw men, we have done beyond what we should have expected.

At Chaumont, where they had this news on the 11th, they began by arguing about it, then fell back, finally, into misunderstandings.[83] Several letters from Maret to Caulaincourt had been intercepted;[84] in the interval of time when the outposts had seized them and when Stadion had received them, resealed them, and delivered them to Caulaincourt, the black cabinet of Austria, worthy of its old reputation, had partly deciphered them. Metternich considered them peaceful. He communicated to the Tsar what was necessary to make him believe that on 9 February, when this emperor had broken, "peace would have been made on the most beautiful conditions." He thought, "We bitterly repented of not having signed peace at that time, when Napoléon implored it as a pardon, on our most extreme terms."[85]

The allies refused to take Caulaincourt's historical considerations and deductions seriously. They invited him once again to produce a counter-project, which was not the negation of the allies' project: in short, the old limits, with some amendments perhaps on the other articles.[86] They thus agreed to leave the protocol open, hoping: Alexander that the war would close it brutally, Metternich that a few insinuations could be slipped into it, if events turned out badly. He commanded Stadion,

> Speak secretly to Caulaincourt, and make him understand, if you deem it useful, that the ships of Antwerp, if the rest is granted, cannot make a condition *sine qua non* in England. Caulaincourt is so animated by the best spirit that I beg you to put yourself in direct contact with him.

He arranged a secret mode of correspondence with Stadion, through his wife.[87] The next day: "Let Caulaincourt know that I find the dissertation detestable, the articles insufficient and that if he does not know how to do the best job, we will not achieve peace, despite the desire we have for it, with him." He would send a final ultimatum. "If Caulaincourt fattens it up a bit, we may lure him here to end up jointly with you in twice twenty-four hours... We must be at peace with France in a few days, or be able to serve as powerful weapons to act on the public opinion that the breakdown of negotiations by France will provide us with."[88] "A more beautiful manifesto has never been written," he said a few days earlier.[89]

So well did Metternich hide his game, his colleagues suspected it: "We are all suspects to the envoys.... You have no idea how much those in our headquarters make us suffer. I can't stand it any longer, and the Emperor is sick of it. They are all crazy."[90] Singular remarks by Schwarzenberg were peddled. This generalissimo was on the defensive. Was it wise to engage in battle with this army? he asked. And he wrote to his wife: "If this army is beaten too, what a triumph for Napoléon and what role will the sovereigns play if they cross the Rhine at the head of the beaten army?"[91]

On 12 March there was held at Chaumont a most stormy conference at Hardenberg's. Did Franz II forbid the Generalissimo to fight? asked Alexander of Metternich; had he already given him the order to recross the Rhine? Friedrich-Wilhelm III pronounced the word treason; they wanted to push Blücher to extremes: Austria certainly agreed with France! Metternich, on leaving, wrote to Schwarzenberg on 13 March 1814: "Please speak very loudly to the Emperor Alexander; don't be confused by anything. It's about beating the enemy, not fighting. Let the boasters do the talking." It was important to await the result of the duel between Blücher and Napoléon, and, in the meantime, to preserve for Austria the famous "flanking position" which would make them arbiter of affairs.

The conference of 13 March in Châtillon was only a formal notice to Caulaincourt to file a new counter-project.[92] The allies demanded it within 24 hours; Caulaincourt asked for 48. Moreover, he stiffened, assuring that if precise declarations were wanted, he could not provide any more precise than Saint-Aignan's note. This note thus returned incessantly. Until then the allies had avoided discussion. This time, and especially after the memo of 10 March, they judged it essential to break the ambiguity which had lasted since 9 November, and they dissipated the phantom. Stadion reported,

> As for the bases of M. de Saint-Aignan, we positively refused to admit them, and we declared that, if he wanted to persist in them or base the counter-project on them, that could only be regarded as a refusal. The English ministers especially took great care in rejecting the Frankfurt documents as being officially unknown to them, and quite foreign to the

negotiations at Châtillon.

These feigned proposals had never been, as they liked to believe in France, a stopping point in the war, and in trading an era, in a way, where the course of things could have changed. They were an episode which suspended nothing, stopped nothing, and flowed away like the rest, according to the fortune of arms. However, arms turned against Napoléon. He had had to give up trying to tumble Blücher at Laon. He retired, 9-13 March, and Schwarzenberg resumed the offensive. The English, having forced Soult to fall back, had entered Bordeaux, where, on 12 March, the mayor proclaimed the Bourbons and raised the white flag. At the same time an emissary from the Comte d'Artois presented himself at the headquarters of the allies.

## VIII. Royalists

Royalists infiltrated all frontiers, prowled around the staffs, seeking audiences, playing the envoys of importance, great promises, solicitors more eager again. All the old cronies of the agencies got back into the campaign, beating the bushes, the great political poaching being reopened. In the front line stood the Baron de Vitrolles. This former officer of Condé's army[93] had slipped into Talleyrand's, and Dalberg's, who only asked to be informed of the views of the allies, and those of the "princes" about whom they were very worried, acting for them to be the artisans, beneficiaries and dignitaries of the future monarchy, or the dupes of the next revolution, which was neither in their tastes nor in their habits. Vitrolles offered to go as a scout, and Dalberg handed him a nice letter in ink for Stadion, and another for Nesselrode, with a sign of recognition. "The person I send to you is with all confidence; listen to him and thank me. It's time to be clearer. You walk on crutches, use your legs and want what you can." We know that for a long time he corresponded with the Russians.

Vitrolles and the lesser-known agents of whom he is, thanks to his political fortune, his narrative verve, his art of staging, having become like the type and the leader having neither more politics, nor more daring, nor more interpersonal skills than so many of their predecessors, couriers, clerks and brokers, knights-errant or diplomatic condottières of the monarchy, since 1790. They had, on that day, at least, the air of the "commercial traveler" who, instead of obsessing the people he visited with his offers, presented them the intermediary they needed for a business that urged them.

Vitrolles landed, he said, on 10 March, at Châtillon, at Stadion, under the name of Saint-Vincent. Stadion thought he spoke well and reported things worth hearing; he sent it to Metternich. Vitrolles went to Troyes, where Metternich arrived on the 16th with the sovereigns and the ministers. Vitrolles brought news from Paris, information on public opinion, people who were stirring, people with whom one had to count, those on whom one could count. Nesselrode reported, "M. de Vitrolles made me aware of the state of minds in Paris, of the facility we would have to master them, by giving more vigor to our military operations, and of the welcome we would find there.[94] Received for a moment on the evening of the 16th, he had his audience the next day, first from Metternich, then from Nesselrode. Metternich asked,

> Finally, what would we want in France? – France asks for a rest that has been stolen from it for twenty-five years. In short, there will be no peace with Bonaparte, and there will be no France without the Bourbons. – But, resumed Metternich, we are crossing this France, we have been living in the middle of it for more than two months, and nothing similar has revealed itself to us, neither the need for rest, nor the memories of former times, not even a general expression of displeasure against the Emperor. We did see a few *émigrés* come up to us and ask us very quietly in our ears if we intended to bring the king back.

The interview passed off fairly coldly, a little sour on Metternich's side, pressing on the other. The Austrian noted,

> That France decides is, moreover, its business and not ours. It is yours, replied Vitrolles, for you want peace, and otherwise you will not have it. So decide, and France, which is unaware of your intentions, which Bonaparte still terrifies, will then decide.

Metternich reserved his regency. Alexander reserved his arbitration, his notables, and his candidate. He had refused to receive the Comte des Cars and the Duc de Polignac, who had presented themselves on behalf of the Comte d'Artois. He consented to hear Vitrolles, and said to him with a cold and constrained air:

> The proof of attachment you give to your former masters is certainly commendable, but the obstacles which now separate the princes of the House of Bourbon from the throne of France seem to me insurmountable. They would return embittered by misfortune; they would not be masters of moderating those who suffered for them and through them. The spirit of the army, of this army so powerful in France, is opposed to them. The influence of the new generations would be contrary to them; the Protestants would not see their return without fear and without opposition; the spirit of the times is not for them. Besides, do you know the princes of the royal family?

Vitrolles had known only the three Condés under whom he had served. The Emperor resumed, "Well! if you knew them, you would be persuaded that the burden of such a crown would be too heavy for them... Some time ago, we thought of Bernadotte... several reasons came to keep us away from it. We talked about Eugène Beauharnais... After that, maybe a republic?" Vitrolles pleaded, preached, exhorted. He saw Castlereagh, "noble, quiet, cold, polite," a very distinguished Englishman. He saw Hardenberg, who jumped on his neck, crying like a deaf man; it was his infirmity:

> You are a good man! Why didn't you come sooner? – Finally we discussed with him about the possible things, about the means and the people. – "Where is the Count of Artois, where will he find men?" Vitrolles insinuated: "The Abbé de Pradt and so many others. Help us only to create for ourselves an existence and a power, and you will see more of them rushing in from all sides than we would like. "But," said a minister, "you will see that their prejudices will prevent them from bringing closer to them men placed high in public opinion, and who can carry them away: M. de Talleyrand, Fouché? "And why not M. de Talleyrand?" retorted Vitrolles, a little embarrassed; you must consider him fully committed to this cause, at least in his heart.

They laughed: "Ah! in his heart is a very good joke!" – Finally, would his prince know how to attach himself to Fouché? "Fouche," replied Vitrolles, in a low voice, "that's a bit much; but finally, if it was necessary."

"You are going to return to Paris," said Metternich, "you will see your friends, so that they may give us their assistance; then you will come back to consult us, according to the circumstances, the subsequent execution of your plans." – Vitrolles declared that he must first take orders from the princes, from the Comte d'Artois, who was in France. They answered him:

> It is a waste of time; we do not need him to serve him. We are sure of his approval. It is a great cooperation in Paris that you have promised us; this is what must be obtained as soon as possible; it is there that it is necessary to act, time presses; on the other side, we will always arrive.

Vitrolles struggled so well that he "snatched" rather than obtained safe-conducts to find the Comte d'Artois. He left on the 20th or 21st of March, and ran after his prince as far as Nancy, where he stayed until the 25th or 26th, which meant that he did not arrive before Paris until the 31st and had no part to the decisive crisis.

He was not alone in Troyes. There was another emissary there at the same time as himself, and this one directly accredited by the Comte d'Artois. He was a Swiss from Bienne, Wildermeth, who had a sister attached to Princess Charlotte of Prussia, daughter of the King.

> He was responsible for asking the allies for the recognition of Monsieur as lieutenant general of the kingdom of France in the name of Louis XVIII, in return for which Monsieur offered: 1) to make peace on the conditions on which it was desired to obtain it from Napoléon; 2) not to operate in the current French constitution of other loadings than those which one would judge necessary, and which would tend to give a peace more assured to France and to Europe; 3) to make the most suitable declarations with respect to the national domains, to the various bodies of the State and to all persons in place; 4) as far as Marie-Louise was concerned, Monsieur offered the Prince de Metternich to sign whatever he asked of him. There was no mention of religion or public debt.[95]

Metternich received it on 20 March and concluded, as with Vitrolles, that it was up to France to declare itself.

The Bourbons had lawyers who were better accredited in the general staff, even in the chancellery of the allies: Rochechouart, close to Alexander, and above all Pozzo di Borgo, the most listened to, because he was a politician and gave the only reasons that carried, the *raison d'État*. As he said and repeated often,

Legitimacy was not the only one and certainly not the first motive which decided the sovereigns of Europe in favor of the restoration of the Bourbons. The most effective reason, the most practical, and, without a doubt, the most permanent came from the good which would result from it for Europe by the tranquility of France. A government which signed the peace and which, wishing to keep it, would guarantee it.[96]

As for Bernadotte, each progress of events, by rendering the Bourbons more necessary, diminished his chances and his credit. It must be said that he did it himself by the tangle of his intrigues and the contradiction of his remarks. Secured by Norway by his treaty of 14 January with Denmark,[97] he offered himself to all as the savior of all, to the Republicans, to the Constitutionalists, to the Bourbons, to Napoléon himself;[98] lavishing promises and handshakes with the magnificence and cordiality of a candidate. "He is doing everything possible to embroil Prussia with us," wrote a Russian. "Our Emperor has been warned of all this, and we are not sending this boy back with his 20 or 25,000 Swedes to Sweden!"[99]

## IX. Breakup of the Congress

On 15 March the congress held a session where Caulaincourt exhibited a counter-proposal: Napoléon ceded to Eugène the crown of Italy, diminished by Venice; he demanded the restoration of the King of Saxony; he claimed his voice in the congress which would regulate the future organization of Europe. "We should be driven back to Vienna," wrote Metternich, "that we could not make a worse peace."[100] Napoléon was condemned less by his pretensions than by the event. Intercepted letters betrayed the desperation of French affairs: "The young guard is melting like snow. We must give your orders for redoubts to be started in Montmartre."[101] On 14 March, on the advice of Napoléon's failure at Laon and the capture of France by the Russians, the allies had ordered, at Châtillon, "to break off if the project of France was not like we wanted it." On the 16th, headquarters returned to Troyes. They conferred there on the 17th on declarations of rupture. Metternich wrote to Stadion at midnight: "Napoléon has a great interest in dragging out the Châtillon negotiations, he is profiting from the simple fact of their existence, therefore they must be broken off and put in the position of negotiating only in the form of capitulation." The severance order went out the same day; the envoys were to notify it on the 18th and leave immediately. That day, Caulaincourt wrote to the Emperor: "My presentiments have been confirmed only too well. The negotiations are broken off. It is to return, more or less, to our old limits that we are required to consent to." The rupture was notified on 19 March. Everything, in reality, was collapsing in Paris.

Joseph wrote, "Everyone wants peace with natural boundaries. No one today would want the old boundaries."[102] But, at the same time, he showed the State in ruins: he conferred with the Minister of the Interior, the Minister of Police, the Archchancellor: Toulouse and Bordeaux were detestable: "A Bourbon would be welcomed if he presented himself. The current state cannot last. The administration everywhere falls into dissolution." A note from d'Hauterive to Caulaincourt, 25 February, said a lot about the state of minds in Paris:

> This morning the cannon sounded. I am not afraid to say it: when we know the reason, the first feeling will be that of regret to see that it is only a victory. The first of all needs is a beginning of agreement, preliminaries and an armistice.

On 12 March he wrote again: "The Emperor is warned." For a fortnight, the truth has been coming to him from all sides: none of his ministers were hiding with him anymore. King Joseph wrote to him four days before: "Sire, you are alone, your family, all your ministers, your army want the peace you refuse."[103] Ministers were summoned yesterday. The language of all of them had been firm, negative, and unanimous. An eminent personage, who was however never known for the boldness of these speeches, said "we could not ask now for 20,000 men, that France could rather demand an account of the two million men she has lost." Moreover, the wording of the opinion of the ministers was extremely simple: "Sire, peace or death, such is the opinion of all your ministers," and they signed.

It was to letters of this kind that Napoléon replied when he wrote to Savary on the 14th: "I do not want any intrigue in the State. I would have had the king arrested, my ministers. I do not want a tribune of the people; let it not be forgotten that I am the grand tribune!"[104]

More and more irritated, worried also by Joseph's insubordination, the intrigues of his friends, their cajoling of the National Guard, all this game of a Gaston d'Orléans doubled by a Lafayette, he wrote to him on 16 March, reiterating his orders from Nogent, of 8 February: "You must not allow, in any case, the Empress and the King of Rome to fall into the hands of the enemy." If resistance was impossible,

> send in the direction of the Loire, the regent, my son, the great dignitaries, the ministers, the treasury. Do not leave my son, and remember that I would rather throw him in the Seine, than in the hands of the enemies of France. The fate of Astyanax prisoner of the Greeks has always seemed to me the most unfortunate in history.

On 17 March in Reims, he touched the bottom of the abyss. He very probably received advice from the faithful Méneval, which was confirmed shortly after by a letter from the Empress.[105] "I read," reported Pasquier, who had received them on deposit from Savary,

> the last letters written to this minister by the Emperor, on leaving Rheims. They were largely based on suspicions he had entertained with regard to the Empress Marie-Louise, or rather her brother Joseph, whom he accused of having made the most odious attempts on her. I have since learned from M. de Saint-Aignan, who, owing to his very intimate liaison with the Duchess of Montebello, must have been very well informed on this subject, that the suspicion was only too well founded, and that the empress, at that time, had been much annoyed and had much to complain about the attentions of her brother-in-law.[106]

On the 20th and 21st, Napoléon attempted to arrest Schwarzenberg; after fierce battles at Arcis-sur-Aube, he was forced to give it up. He then resolved to make a point at Saint-Dizier and take the allies from the rear. A daring combination which would have been formidable if the allies had not known the secret. It was revealed to them on 22 March by an intercepted letter from the Emperor to Maria-Louisa.

On the 28th at Saint-Dizier, Caulaincourt brought him Wessenberg who had been captured by a cavalry picket. He had a long interview with this Austrian diplomat.[107] He said to him in substance,

I am ready for great sacrifices: I abandon Spain, I renounce Germany, Italy, Switzerland; I will recognize the Prince of Orange in Holland, although I would have preferred a republic. I return to Holland all that she possessed on the left bank of the Meuse and the Rhine. I insist on Antwerp. I am ready to give up all the colonies if I can, at this price, obtain the mouths of the Scheldt. England cannot persist in demanding them if Austria does not support her. Austria has nothing more to desire, for she will obtain everything she has always wanted in Poland, in Italy, in Germany. Can Metternich forget that my marriage to an Austrian princess is his work? Your Emperor doesn't seem to love his daughter; if he loved her, he couldn't be insensitive to her pains. I made a big mistake when I married her. If I had married a Russian princess, I wouldn't be where I am. I would never have believed that the Empress could become a stranger to her father. I repeat that I made a big political mistake by marrying an Archduchess of Austria, but I cannot deny that the Empress is an incomparable woman. You do not know her merit; I couldn't have made a better choice. I guarantee you that she will get along better in government than the famous Anne of Austria. I count my life for nothing, I play it every day, but the Empress will be loved by the French. You will prefer this regency and that of the Senate to the government of the Bourbons. She has, during my absence, gained much in public opinion, and I am a man to put power in her hands.

During this monologue, he insinuated this proposition:

The courts should give full powers to Austria, and peace would be made in two hours. England is the most reasonable of allies, and Castlereagh seems to me an estimable man. Your accident will be good fortune for me, he concludes, if it gives me the opportunity to enlighten your court about my feelings and bring us closer to each other.

It was the abdication offered to Austria as the price of the regency guaranteed by Austria. But the allies had taken their part. Alexander prevailed. The forfeiture was resolved. Hardenberg wrote in his diary on the 20th: "The generals would have to commit extraordinary faults for us not to be masters of Paris in ten or twelve days." The moment seemed to have come to launch this manifesto, of which Metternich said that a finer one would never have been written. Dated from Vitry, 25 March, it was printed in Dijon and published on 28 March.[108] The famous sentence to Saint-Aignan on the "natural limits," already concealed, under the whitewash, in the Frankfurt manifesto, was drowned here in diplomatic rigmarole. This is the last word in the long process of treachery that continued from Prague:

> France, restored to the dimensions which centuries of glory and prosperity, under the domination of her kings, had assured her, was to share with Europe the benefits of liberty, national independence, and peace. The powers had offered to discuss, in a spirit of conciliation, wishes on objects of possession of mutual convenience which would go beyond the limits of France before the wars of the Revolution. France can only blame her government for the ills she suffers. Peace will be that of Europe; any other is inadmissible.

This was a judgment on Napoléon: the downfall of the Emperor after the destruction of the Empire. "Therefore the peace of Europe is assured, and nothing can disturb it in the future."

On the 29th the allies arrived before Paris. On the 30th, after a battle fought for honor, they seized the heights which overlook the capital. The victorious Germans contemplating, from the foot of the windmills of Montmartre, the great city stretched below them, the city of august towers, sacred cupolas, cast bronze columns with cannons, Notre-Dame, the Pantheon, the Invalides, and in the mist, the Arc de Triomphe, the giant in freestone, still informed. A German wrote, "Nine and a half centuries had passed since our Emperor Otto II had planted his eagles on these hills and terrified the great city with the Hallelujahs! of his fighters."[109] Gneisenau wrote: "What patriots have dreamed of and what egoists have mocked is accomplished." And Stein, "The man is down!" On 31 March, Paris surrendered.

1 *Journal de Hardenberg*, 10 December 1813.
2 To Hudelist, 3 January 1814. See the letter to the Princess de Lieven, 18 October 1819. Daudet, *Revue hebdomadaire* (29 juillet 1899).
3 See on this state of mind the letters of Woronzof to his son, who was at war in Holland, December 1813-January 1814. Letters from Gentz to the hospidars, I, p. 72-77, April 1814, retrospective. (Fournier, Chatillon.)
4 Czartoryski to Novossiltsof, *Société d'histoire de Russie*, IX, p. 435.
5 "Immediately after the receipt of the replies (from the allies, i.e. from England), negotiations may open." Metternich to Caulaincourt, 10 December 1813.
6 Fournier, *Châtillon*, p. 49, note.
7 Arriving on 18 January 1814.
8 Oncken, II, p. 723; Fournier, p. 51-52. Letter in German.
9 Castlereagh, *Letters and dispatches*, IX; Wellington, *Supplementary dispatches*, VIII; Instructions to Castlereagh, 24 December 1813; Castlereagh to Hamilton, 10 March 1814; Martens, XI, p. 199-200, 218; Arneth, *Wessenberg*, I, p. 175 et suiv.
10 Edward Cooke to Castlereagh, 5 January 1814.
11 Memo relating to the Saint-Aignan. Castlereagh, note. I, p. 139.
12 30 January 1814. Fournier, in French.
13 Memo to Nesselrode, 23 janvier 1814. This project deprived France of a part of Lorraine and Alsace, and seemed to leave it the left bank of the Scheldt. (Martens, VII, p. 153.)
14 Preamble to the separate and secret articles of the treaty of 9 September 1813.
15 Text in *Publications de la Société d'histoire de Russie*, XXXI. The brief is dated 14-26 January. Metternich's minute, in his own hand, bears the date of the 27th. (Fournier.)
16 Memo to Friedrich-Wilhelm III, 27 January 1814. (Fournier.)
17 Preceptor of Alexander, in relations of friendship with the French liberals.
18 *Mémoires de Moriolles*, p. 138, 144.
19 Note of Rochechouart, 27 janvier 1814. Conversation with Alexander, same day. *Mémoires de Rochechouart*.
20 Münster to Prince Regent, 30 January 1814. (Fournier.)
21 *Autobiographie*: on the alliances, sojourn in Langres: *Mémoires*, I, p. 183; Fournier, p. 70, note; Report of Castlereagh, 29 January 1814.
22 Bailleu, "Die Memoiren Metternich's," *Historische Zeitschrift* (1880).
23 Metternich to the Emperor, 28 January; to Schwarzenberg, 30 January. (Fournier.)
24 Russia, XXXI: Deliberations between the allied cabinets at Langres.
25 Reports of Münster, 30 January, 2 February 1814. (Fournier.)
26 Protocol of the conference in Langres, 29 January 1814. (Russie, XXXI.) Metternich to Hudelist, 30 January, 1 February 1814. (Fournier, Oncken, II, p. 763-64.
27 Bar-sur- Aube, 2 February 1814. (Fournier.)
28 Henry Houssaye, 1814; Thiers, XVII, books LI and LII.
29 Notes and protocol, in Angeberg, p. 104 et suiv; reports of Stadion, journal of Stadion, in Fournier; *Letters of Castlereagh;* notes of Stewart; Caulaincourt to the Emperor, 5 février 1814.
30 On their installation, see *Mémoires* of Mme Chastenay, II, p. 278; Ségur, VI, p.

289.
31 Caulaincourt to Berthier, 3 février; to Napoléon, 4 février 1814.
32 Ernouf, *Maret*, ch. LXVI.
33 Napoléon to Caulaincourt, 4 février 1814, first letter.
34 Maret to Caulaincourt, Troyes, 5 février; Napoléon to Caulaincourt, second letter, 5 février, 1AM.
35 Maret to Caulaincourt, Troyes, 5 février 1814; to Besnardière, 5 février 1814. [The footnote in Sorel says 1813, but I have corrected this error. - FW]
36 Caulaincourt to Napoléon, 8 février 1814; Report of Stadion; *Journal de Floret*. (Fournier.)
37 Memory confusion. The declaration, much less positive than Saint-Aignan's note, did not specify the limits.
38 Compare the text of the protocol the same arguments formatted by La Besnardière. (Angeberg.)
39 Metternich, 8 February 1814.
40 6-7 February. Russie, XXXI, p. 271; *Journal de Floret*; Fournier.
41 The diplomats, including Caulaincourt, received each other to dinner.
42 Metternich to Stadion, 9 February 1814.
43 Ségur, VI, p. 302 et suiv. Notes of Maret. Ernouf, p. 622-23.
44 Ducasse, *les Rois frères*.
45 9 February 1814. (Fournier, p. 362.)
46 Letter to Stadion, 9 February 1814; *Journal de Floret*; Fournier, pièces.
47 Letters of 1 and 3 February 1814. (Fournier.)
48 To Hudelist, 9 February 1814. (Fournier.)
49 Blücher to his wife, 18 February 1814; Blücher, *Briefen*; letter of Münster, 2 February 1814. (Fournier.)
50 *Mémoires de Rochechouart*: letter of 27 janvier 1814; *Souvenirs du comte de Semallé*, Paris, ch. V: Comte d'Artois in Vesoul.
51 Conversation of Antraigues with Champagny, 21 avril 1802. (Pingaud, p. 209.)
52 Letter of Münster, 12 February 1814. (Fournier.)
53 Castlereagh, I, p. 267. Cf. Arneth, *Wessenberg*, I, p. 177.
54 From 9 February 1814, arrived on the 11th at Troyes.
55 Treitschke, I, p. 542-43.
56 Fournier, annexes, III. Crisis in Troyes. Letter of Münster, 14 February 1814; Russie, XXXI: conferences at Troyes.
57 At Troyes, 14 February 1814. (Fournier.)
58 Metternich to Alexander, 14 February 1814. (Fournier.) Text in French, in Bailleu. Notice on the *mémoires* of Metternich, *Historische Zeitschrift*.
59 Hardenberg, *Journal*, 14 February 1814.
60 Martens, XI, p. 200.
61 To Joseph, Savary, and Marmont, 12 février 1814. *Mémoires de Marmont*, VI.
62 Maret to Caulaincourt, 12 février 1814. (Bignon, XIII, ch. VI.)
63 Cf. Stadion to Metternich, 18 February 1814. (Fournier.)
64 Bignon, XIII, p. 343.
65 Napoléon to Joseph, 18 février 1814.
66 To Savary, 19, 21 février; to Augereau, 21 février.
67 By a planned marriage to Princess Charlotte.
68 Russie, XXXI, p. 364. Instruction of Napoléon to Flahaut, 24 février 1814;

*Journal* of Hardenberg, 24-25 February 1814.
69  Berthier, for Flahaut, 28 février; to Caulaincourt, 26-27 février 1814.
70  Instruction, 26 February 1814. (Fournier.)
71  Metternich to Stadion, 26 February 1814. (Fournier.)
72  *Journal de Floret*, 27 février 1814; Russie, XXXI.
73  [One must assume this quote is from the same source as note 72. - FW]
74  Angeberg, p. 114 et suiv.
75  Loewenstern, *Mémoires*, II, p. 309-32, 430. "If the place had held for twenty-four hours, the army of Silesia would have been crushed and would have lost at least all its artillery." (Langeron, p. 410.)
76  3 March 1814. (Fournier.) Stadion to Metternich, 9 March. – On the mission of Esterhazy, see Bignon, XIII, p. 379 et suiv.
77  Around the 7th, said Hardenberg, in his journal. He noted a conference with Castlereagh on the 3rd, until one o'clock.
78  Letter of Munster to the Prince Regent, 10 March 1814.
79  Renewals of the Treaty of Chaumont: Vienna, 25 March 1815; Paris, 20 November 1815; Aix-la-Chapelle, 15 November 1818.
80  Caulaincourt to Napoléon, 3-5 mars 1814.
81  Angeberg; Ranke, IV, p. 428-29; Notes of Stewart; Castlereagh, I, p. 556; Stadion to Metternich, 10 March; Caulaincourt to Napoléon, 11 March 1814.
82  Caulaincourt to Napoléon, 11 mars 1814.
83  *Journal de Hardenberg*, 11 March 1814. (Fournier.)
84  36 hours. Caulaincourt complained about it to the conference on the 10th. (Fournier, p. 339.)
85  See these documents in Fournier, appendices, p. 340-42. Metternich to Stadion, 11 and 12 March; to Hudelist, 2 March 1814. (Fournier.)
86  Instruction for Châtillon, 11 March 1814. (Fournier.)
87  To Stadion, 11 March, 2AM.
88  To Stadion, 12 March 3AM.
89  To Stadion, 26 February 1814.
90  To Stadion, undated, but probably 13 March.
91  Schwarzenberg to his wife, 12 March 1814. (Fournier.)
92  Angeberg. Report of Stadion, 13 March 1814. Notes of Stewart, Castlereagh, I, p. 560.
93  *Mémoires de Vitrolles*; *Mémoires de Talleyrand*, II, p. 147; Pasquier, II, p. 151, 175.
94  Nesselrode, *Autobiographie*.
95  *Souvenirs du comte de Semallé*; *Journal de Hardenberg*, 19-20 March 1814.
96  Report to Nesselrode, 2 mars 1816. *Correspondance of Pozzo di Borgo*. "It was given, said the *Aperçu de la politique russe*, to the energy of a superior man to exert a great influence on the state of things and to fix the ideas of the Emperor Alexander." Memo presented to Alexander before the entry of the allies into Paris. (*Russie*, XXXI.)
97  Denmark ceded Norway in exchange for Swedish Pomerania and Rügen.
98  D'Hauterive wrote on 26 March to Caulaincourt. He saw King Joseph twice. "The king (Joseph) is in confidential communication with the prince of Sweden and the emperor wants the king to maintain this communication. The Prince of Sweden wants the preservation of the Emperor, and would have liked peace with

the natural limits of France. The fact, as to the first point, is indisputable: this prince expressed his opinion in a completely public manner, and then in the most intimate secrecy, he made known dispositions from which it would be possible to draw great advantage. " But it would require skill, courage, responsibility and troops.

99 Pingaud, ch. XVI, XVII; letter of Woronzof, Londres, 15 December 1813; Langeron, p. 455.
100 To Hudelist, 16 March 1814.
101 Napoléon to Joseph, 11 mars 1814.
102 21, 22 février 1814, *Mémoires*, X.
103 Paraphrase of letter, Joseph to Napoléon, 11 mars 1813. (*Mémoires*, XI, p. 193.)
104 To Savary, 14 mars. Lecestre.
105 To Cambacérès, 16 mars: "I received your three letters. No one has slandered anyone near me; for all that I know of this affair I know from a letter from Méneval, which was followed six hours later by a letter from the Empress. I'm sure you weren't told these crazy plans." (Lecestre.) On this extraordinary and significant episode, see Pasquier, II, p. 229, 236-37.
106 "Eugène has honor, the king has none." Conversation with Roederer, 12 novembre 1813. (III, p. 581.)
107 Arneth, *Wessenberg*, I, p. 188-93. Résumé of the conversation of Napoléon.
108 Angerberg, p. 143. (Fournier, p. 237, notes.)
109 Treitschke, I, p. 553.

# Chapter V: The Peace of 1814

## 1814

### I. Talleyrand

    The allies, living in the tradition of the old monarchy, renewed by the Revolution, expected everything from Paris, as in the time of Henri IV, of the Fronde, as of 10 August, 9 Thermidor, 19 Brumaire, constituting the whole of France. *Roma locuta est!* But Paris was silent, inert. Among the people, where the old national spirit and the revolutionary spirit subsisted, confusedly mixed, there were no leaders, no rallying words, except the old national maxim, the permanent maxim of public safety: no foreigners! But what could the disarmed people do, restrained by the police and under the influence of terror, who, having changed hands from Robespierre to Fouché and having organized themselves, still governed from afar, like the horrific images of the gods? at the bottom of the temples, and up close, tangible, by spies and henchmen. What remained of the Republicans felt, and the masses instinctively felt like them, that nothing that followed the invasion would turn to the advantage of their cause. The rest, civil servants, moneyed men, bourgeois subjected to the Empire, rallied nobles, and returned *émigrés*, thought only of their own business. Some were looking for the possible, others were resigned to it, hardly anyone had yet discerned it. As in the camp of the allies, they were advancing blind. In this indecisive state, the first impulse was to cause the mass to oscillate. But one need dominated the others: peace. The allies demanded a government which made it; Paris accepted it as soon as it offered itself. Talleyrand's hour was coming.¹

He did not see it coming without anguish, not that he lacked courage at the hour of action; but this man of such subtle sagacity and rare firmness in encounters suffered from not yet discerning what it would be in his interest to want. He smelled the wind, and all political Paris was waiting for him to announce the change. He was still all for the regency: "What to do?" he replied to Mme de Coigny, who vaguely insinuated her princes. "What to do? Don't we have his son?" – Nothing else? "It can only be a question of regency," he said, lowering his eyes and the serious tone he affected when he did not want to be annoyed. He speculated sometimes on the death of the Emperor killed in one of the harsh hand-to-hand combats of the campaign, sometimes on peace. He followed the ups and downs of the Châtillon talks. "I have," he confessed, "with Caulaincourt an agreed number and sign by which he will inform me, for example, whether or not the Emperor accepts proposals for peace." Napoléon not dying, peace not taking shape, he began to listen when people "whispered" around him the name of the Bourbons. Mme de Coigny recalled, "One day he got up, went to the door of his cabinet of pictures, and after making sure that it was closed, he came back to me, raising his arms and saying to me: "Mme de Coigny, I want the king, but." The ex-*Jeune captive* interrupted him, embraced his neck; he moderated her and resumed:

> Yes, I do, but have to know how I am with that family. I would still get on quite well with the Count d'Artois, because there is something between him and me which would explain much of my conduct to him. But his brother doesn't know me at all; I do not want, I admit it to you, instead of a thank you, to expose myself to a pardon or to have to justify myself. I have no way to get through.

The next day they resumed the subject. Mme de Coigny's great friend, Boisgelin, who worked for the Bourbons, was about to leave to join them. Talleyrand would have said,

> Well! I'm all for this business, and from this moment you can look at me. Let us work to deliver the country from this madman. We must speak loudly of his faults, of his lack of faith in all the commitments he had made to reign over the French. We should not be afraid to utter the words nation, people's rights again.

These were not precisely the watchwords of "legitimacy." Talleyrand would therefore have revealed in part the plan he was hatching in his head, infinitely more practical than that of Sieyès in Brumaire Year VIII: a senator will denounce Napoléon; Napoléon failed in his oaths, the contract is cancelled; Napoléon is outlawed; the Senate declares France a constitutional monarchy, with three or four laws clearly indicating the liberties of the people; Louis XVIII will be called by a plebiscite. Foreigners will be invited to recross the Rhine, "to begin there the preliminaries of peace." France would have a constitution, the Brumairians their guarantee, Talleyrand his *habeas corpus*. He learned on 24 February that, for the first time, the name of the Bourbons was mentioned in a Prussian proclamation. He allowed Vitrolles to "whisper" his name to the headquarters of the allies.[2] After the occupation of Bordeaux by the English on 12 March, and the proclamation of Louis XVIII by the mayor of this city, he wrote to Mme de Dino:

> If peace is not made, Bordeaux becomes something very important in affairs: if peace is made, Bordeaux loses its importance. We would lose her likewise if the Emperor were killed, for we would then have the King of Rome, and the regency of his mother. The Emperor's brothers would indeed be an obstacle to this arrangement, by the influence they would claim to exercise; but this obstacle would be easy to remove: they would be forced to leave France, where neither of them has a party...

And again, on 20 March: "If the emperor were killed, his death would ensure the rights of his son. The regency would satisfy everyone because a council would be appointed which would please all opinions."

Eight days later his decision was taken. He saw "social decomposition" increasing every day. "No one obeys, and no one commands."[3] In his uncertainty about the plans of the allies, he speculated about them, and he speculated wisely.

> It became more urgent every hour to prepare a government that could quickly replace the one that was collapsing. A single day of hesitation could give rise to ideas of partition and enslavement which silently threatened this unhappy country. There were no intrigues to link, all would have been insufficient; what was needed was to find just what France

wanted and what Europe should want. France, in the midst of the horrors of invasion, wanted to be free and respected; it was to want the House of Bourbon in the order prescribed by legitimacy. Europe, still uneasy in the midst of France, wanted it to disarm, to return to the old limits, that peace no longer need to be constantly watched; it asked for guarantees: it was also to want the House of Bourbon.[4]

His reason, his political sense led Talleyrand there, but it seems that he did not decide until the last hour, and it was the force of circumstances that decided him.

The need to impose and defend the conquest of the "natural limits" commanded all foreign policy since 1792; the need to return to the "old limits" governed internal policy in 1814. The question of limits had remained so intimately linked, since the beginning of the Great War, to the question of the internal government of France, the governments resulting from the Revolution had so much identified with the conquest and conservation of natural limits, that to destroy these limits was to destroy these governments, and to bring about by the very reflux of things, with the return to the old limits, the restoration of the Bourbons. The Bourbons alone could consent to the peace of Europe with dignity, because they attached to this peace their own principle, old frontier, old monarchy, peace and legitimacy; it was the whole continuation of their policy in emigration.[5]

Similarly, on the plot so often torn and taken up again in Talleyrand's career, this concept of peace alone maintained a kind of consequence in his conduct, at least a permanent mental restriction to so many denials that he had given himself to stand in place. He returned there after strange ramblings, but he found himself at home. He saw the cycle closing at the point where it had opened. The peace which was imposed by the allies in 1814 was that which in 1792 he advised the nascent Republic. He had discerned the aberrations of conquest, he had shown the external conditions of a free government in France. Far from repugnant to the old limits, he was one of the few men in France who consented to them by knowledge and advice. It would be the bond between the Bourbons and the allies, and it would be up to him to form the knot. However antipathetic he felt to Louis XVIII, so suspicious to the allies, he knew that neither the king would take it into account if he brought him the Crown, nor the allies if he procured them peace at their convenience. The defile opened before him; he entered it with a measured but sure step, like a great lord who holds court, and the equal, in this solemn passage of his destiny, of the most famous kingmakers and negotiators of treaties.

France needed peace and Talleyrand needed this peace to become a minister. France needed a guarantee of its liberties, and nothing less than a constitution was needed to give Talleyrand the letters of remission, the security of his person, of his titles and of his property; his private interest was at this moment confounded with the public interest. It is these sorts of encounters which can turn a man of great skill and good manners into a statesman.

His resolution was arrested when, on 28 March, the Regency Council met, which, despite repeated orders from Napoléon, separated the Empress and the King of Rome from the government and ordered Maria-Louisa to leave for Rambouillet. On 31 March the capitulation was signed, Joseph left in his turn, and following him what remained of the Government. Talleyrand should have gone out with the regency council, of which he was officially a member. He managed to remain by force, and by a trick of comedy worthy of his illustrious patron, the Cardinal de Retz, he was arrested at the barrier, in the name of the people of Paris, by the National Guards of Auguste-Laurent Rémusat, who combined this command with the prefecture of the palace.[6]

Paris preserved from an assault, the announced peace, Napoléon lost, everything changed, everyone thought they were saved, and from extreme consternation Paris passed to unalloyed blooming. Business people congratulated each other. The liberals erupted in effusions. Allies stopped looking like enemies. Alexander, preceded by the most prestigious of advertisements, appeared as the savior of national independence, restorer of French liberty. March 31$^{st}$ was a Sunday. "The weather was superb," says Nesselrode. "The boulevards were covered with people in their Sunday best. We seemed to be gathered there for a party and not for the entry of an enemy army." Paris gave the counterpart of Napoléon's entry into Milan, nine years before. As in Italy, the little people stayed at home, fierce, feeling invaded, overwhelmed, under the boot and the spur, like the native land and the cobblestones of the city under the shoes of the horses. The fashionable world crowded; an elegant, sumptuous procession, Splendid skies, bright sunshine, upholstery of light toilets, fluttering feathers and ribbon bows. At the barriers, allied generals, the Prince of Württemberg, formed the line.

Finally he arrived, accompanied by the King of Prussia, the Prince of Schwarzenberg, Marshal Barclay de Tolly, Marshal Blücher, preceded by a detachment of Cossacks, all superb men; columns of infantry, with excellent music; artillery and the finest cavalry imaginable followed the Emperor. This superb procession crossed the Porte Saint-Martin and headed for the Champs-Elysées. The handkerchiefs began to flutter at the windows. Everywhere cries of: *Long live the Emperor Alexander! Long live our liberator!* And a few cries of *Vivent les Bourbons!*... The Emperor Alexander was superb. He wore the little uniform of the knight-guards and rode a gray horse. The retinue was formed of more than a thousand general officers, princes, etc.[7]

All of old Europe, freshly decked out, disgorged itself on Paris, and this frivolous Paris, with the same eye that it had contemplated the Federations and the processions of the Supreme Being, was amused by the spectacle of these uniforms that for twenty years only the backs had been seen, and the barbarous names spelled out in Napoléon's bulletins of victory were repeated, with fattening and softening.

The King of Prussia seemed touching and noble, in his past misfortunes, almost a companion in misfortune, escaped, like Paris, from the jail of the tyrant; Schwarzenberg, long ambassador, and known to everyone by his ball and his fire during the wedding feasts, seemed a friend returning among his own; Alexander, handsome, young, smiling, radiant, in the serenity of the day, amidst these cries of enthusiasm, this shimmering of colors, this quivering of crumpled stuffs and softened women, produced the effect of a young god; to see him sensitive, the moist eyes under the radiant forehead, these deluded incorrigibles concluded that he paraded triumphant, no doubt, in his conquest, but subjugated by them, by the enchantment of their Parisian spring, the charm of their city, the surges of their hearts, the spectacle of their enthusiasm, and believing conquered, they considered themselves delivered.[8]

Nesselrode, preceding his master, had arrived in the morning at Talleyrand's. He found him at his *toilette*. He said,

> Talleyrand rushed in, half wearing his hair, to meet me, threw himself into my arms, and covered me with powder; he summoned the men with whom he was in full conspiracy. They were the Duke of Dalberg, the Abbe de Pradt, Baron Louis. I told them that the Emperor still had only one fixed idea, that of not leaving Napoléon on the throne of France; that he would only make a decision after having gathered the enlightened opinions of the enlightened men with whom he was going to come into contact.

Alexander reviewed the troops on the Champs-Élysées, then he installed himself at Talleyrand's, at the Hôtel Saint-Florentin, where, since the morning, everyone who mattered in Paris had been flocking there to appear or only sought their ease there. There he found a whole court of soldiers and dignitaries, eager to collect from his lips the password and the safe-conduct to the new regime. Was he still thinking of Bernadotte? He saw him out of place, in a way, and as if lost in Paris. He didn't insist on it anymore. He understood that to appoint a marshal would be to unite all the others; they would only be held in check by putting them back in the ranks, and aligned. It was the secret of the Empire; Alexander was able to penetrate the reason. "Why a soldier when we reject the first of all?" asked Talleyrand. Then he pleaded his thesis:

> Neither you, Sire, nor the allied powers, nor I, in whom you believe to have some influence, none of us can give a king to France. Any king, imposed, would be the result of intrigue or force; either would be powerless. To establish something lasting and to be accepted without complaint, it is necessary to act according to a principle. With one principle, we are strong; the opposition will disappear in a short time; and there is only one principle: Louis XVIII is a principle, he is the legitimate king.

The Tsar possessed political flair, he was aware of the necessary and the possible; flexible to necessity, skillful in taking advantage of circumstances and calculating the rocket of a phrase as one calculates that of a piece of firework. The "principle" that Talleyrand invoked for France was that which Alexander claimed in Russia and which he claimed to make prevail throughout Europe, except in France, where he would have preferred some vague symbol or simulacrum of popular sovereignty. Seeing them all converted, and judging that, to come to this, they risked more and came from further afield than he did, he allowed himself to be inclined, not without some reluctance out of self-esteem and political uneasiness. However, he avoided pronouncing the name of the Bourbons, still flattering himself that the French would pronounce another.

He held a sort of council attended by the King of Prussia, Talleyrand, Schwarzenberg, Dalberg, Nesselrode, Pozzo, Prince Lichtenstein, then the Abbé de Pradt and Baron Louis, who declared France royalist: it was not waiting to show that the example of Paris and the guarantee of the allies. Paris had set the example; the allies gave the guarantee. It was the declaration of the Tsar, dated 31 March, drawn up by Dalberg and Nesselrode, signed by the Tsar and published at three o'clock in the afternoon.

> If the conditions of peace were to contain stronger guarantees when it was a question of chaining the ambition of Bonaparte, they must be more favorable when, by a return to a wise government, France itself will offer the best insurance. The sovereigns therefore proclaim that they will no longer treat with Napoléon Bonaparte, nor with any member of his family; that they respect the integrity of old France, such as it existed under its legitimate kings they can even do more... because it is necessary, for the happiness of Europe, that France is great and strong. They will recognize and guarantee the constitution that the French nation will give itself. They invite, therefore, the Senate to designate a provisional government on the spot ... and to prepare the constitution which will suit the French people.

There had to be an appearance of consulting the people, at least by figure and metaphor. Said the Tsar to Talleyrand, "How can I know that France desires the House of Bourbon?" "By a deliberation, Sire, which I undertake to cause to be taken to the senate, and the effect of which your Majesty will immediately see." – "Are you sure?" – "I answer for it, Sire."

Talleyrand knew, for having practiced it many times, this august body, pivot of the constitutions of the Empire and which it was enough to strike according to the rites to draw oracles from it, like hollow statues of the ancient gods. No one was more expert at moving the plank at the *senatus consulta*. He knew, and from personal experience, that notwithstanding the noble endowments and qualifications, the princes, the dukes, the counts, the senators, this body had no other dignity, the other soul and, at bottom, of other power than those of the rump parliament from which it came and which, on the night of 19 to 20 Brumaire Year VIII, had undone the Constitution of Year III, confiscated the Republic and legitimized Bonaparte's *coup d'etat*. Talleyrand expected from the Senate the counterpart, without more effort and by the same means, the servitude of interests. He promised places of safety, the guarantee of titles and endowments; he got what he wanted. The conservative senate, born from the ruin of the Republic, ruined an Empire; by an implacable logic, it came to ruin itself and, by the absurd, by dint of wanting to live, it was on the way to suicide.

On 2 April, Talleyrand presented to the Tsar the "memorable deliberation" which he had had all the senators present sign individually: 64 out of 140; the others, as in Brumaire, had not come, or had not received a summons.[9] This deliberation created a provisional government, composed of Talleyrand, Jaucourt, Dalberg, Beurnonville, the Abbé de Montesquiou, and would prepare a constitution. Talleyrand and Jaucourt had been noted for years among the "friends" of Austria. Dalberg was a friend of Russia, Beurnonville a jack of all trades, who had studied *coups d'etat* in Paris in 1792 and 1793, then in Holland; the Abbé de Montesquiou represented, in this council, the plots of the royalist and Catholic emigration. These gentlemen proclaimed the guarantees which the future constitution would give to France: they were the permanence of the Senate, or rather that of the present members of this assembly, during the famous decree of the Convention on the two-thirds, in 1795; the guarantee of ranks to soldiers, of national property to purchasers, of rents to rentiers, liberty of conscience, and finally the promise not to seek out any Frenchman "for the opinions and votes he may have expressed." The members of the government were the first interested in these guarantees. With this program, they could count on the majority of senators and deputies, on the adhesion of the general staffs and the commanders of the army corps. The same day, 2 April, the senate, after long recitals, an act of accusation against the Emperor, a pitiful confession of the servility of a body which had approved everything since the year VIII, pronounced the forfeiture of Napoléon and of his family: the French people and the army were released from any oath of loyalty.[10]

Alexander was stupefied when he learned the number of senators who demanded the return of the Bourbons, and found among them the names of several who had voted for the death of Louis XVI. In reality, on 2 April 1814, they were asking Talleyrand and the allies what they had asked for in January 1793 to Robespierre and the Jacobins: they demanded their lives. His perspective in power had long been the substance of their politics and the whole spirit of their recantations.

In the evening there was a grand dinner at the Hôtel Saint-Florentin, a dinner of emperors and kings, of allied generals and united generals. Everyone went to the Opéra: the *Clemency of Trajan* had been announced. This title "thwarted Alexander's modesty"; on the other hand, it was remembered that the play was only a panegyric of Napoléon, and the poster had to be changed. They took the Vestal, which did not offend Talleyrand's modesty. The sacred fire had changed altars, not hands, and it was still burning; but for whom?

The Provisional Government, and more than anyone, Talleyrand, who led it, had openly compromised for the Bourbons.[11] Now, Alexander still hesitated: the civilians declared themselves, but whatever the constitutional prejudices of the pupil of La Harpe, the essential sanction was lacking in his eyes, and he waited for the army to decide; he judged in the Russian way, where the barracks bring about revolutions. Finally, what he had observed of the royalists for two days justified his prejudices, awakened his unpleasant memories of the *émigrés* in the time of Mittau: haughty, infatuated, deluded. However, as long as Alexander had not formally recognized Louis XVIII, one could fear everything from the agents and advisers who abounded around him.

The forfeiture itself was only a decree of the Senate, but without an executory force, was worth no more than the former *senatus-consultes* without the sword of the Emperor. Napoléon, with his shred of an army, remained embarrassing, disquieting, almost threatening still. He could attempt a desperate blow, throw himself in the rear of the allies, while an insurrection would break out in Paris, where the patriots, beginning to understand, were agitated. "If a daring and devoted leader to the emperor would have liked to seize the command," said the man best placed to know what was going on in Paris at the time, the prefect of police Pasquier,[12]

> all the soldiers and almost all the second-ranking officers would have taken the road to Fontainebleau with him, at all risk and peril.... I knew the anxieties and fears which the Emperor inspired in the general staff of the allied army. When generals, in such a position, with such a superiority of forces, have such

> obvious fear of the one they are going to fight, how can one not foresee the possibility of a great reverse!

The fact is that on the night of 2-3 April they thought of evacuating Paris, expecting an attack from Napoléon and not wanting to give battle in the city for fear of being caught in the crossfire, the Emperor and the insurgent population.[13] It would have been for the members of the government and their cronies their heads at stake, and they were very concerned about it. As long as Napoléon had a troop of soldiers, he would remain formidable; as long as he even lived, and as long as an army held out for him, Alexander would oppose the wish of this army to the decrees of the Senate for the Bourbons.

The idea naturally arose to take the army away from the Emperor and, if necessary, to get rid of his person. Marmont commanded the bulk of the troops and the best; we had reason to believe it accessible in the rue Saint-Florentin. Roux-Laborie and the former Abbé Louis unearthed a M. de Montessuy who had served under Marmont in Egypt. He was sent to him on the night of 2 to 3 April, in the name of the Government, to persuade him and hire him. The Emperor had also been taken care of. Napoléon remained an obstacle on the avenues of the king, as in the days of his consulship, when he refused the role of Monk. They returned to the expedients of the time. When these designs were fermenting in the mind, henchmen never fail to carry them out. A famous swordsman, the Comte de Maubreuil, or Marquis d'Orsvault,* who had fought in the war of partisans in Vendée, had gone from there to the venery of Jérôme, squire and captain of the hunts of the King of Westphalia, then had waged war in Spain, worked in military supplies and had signalized himself, during the capitulation of Paris, by the fervor of his royalism; riding through the streets, his cross of honor (removed during his adventures) at the tail of his horse. This profession of faith led him into the secret corridors and closets of the Hôtel Saint-Florentin, where he soon appeared to be in confidence with Roux-Laborie, who passed for the official of unmentionable jobs. "We will anticipate the chance that we must, in fact, dread," Dalberg said on 2 April to Pasquier. He said that a number of determined individuals, led by a vigorous "bugger," would put on the costumes of *chasseurs de la garde*, approach Napoléon and deliver France from him. Maubreuil maneuvered in such a way as to make people believe that he was that "bugger there," that Laborie had

---

\* Jacques Marie Armand de Guerry de Beauregard (1788-1868).

provided him with the necessary means to carry out the *coup* from 2 to 3 April; that Talleyrand had approved; in short, he compromised the whole Provisional Government in the ambush. If he did not carry out with his false *chasseurs*, on the road to Fontainebleau, the *coup* that Cadoudal had planned to accomplish with his *chouans*, also disguised as soldiers, on the road to Malmaison, in 1804, it is because on the 3rd, in the morning, there was "good news" from Marmont which caused the *coup de main* to be postponed.[14]

    Alexander thought only of disarming Napoléon, and, knowing his character, he did not despair of bringing him, in the words of an officer in the service of Russia, to "end with inexcusable weakness a military life so stormy and so brilliant." The defection of Marmont would reduce him to capitulate without a fight, and the abdication, betraying "his lack of firmness in reverses" would lose him before his faithful, who disbanded. The Tsar approved of the steps taken near Marmont. He took care, in person, of the abdication. It seems in this last resumption of the duel which had lasted for two years, to have drawn from the zeal, the boiling heart and the agitated brain of Caulaincourt the same party as at the time of the talks of Petersburg, the conferences of Pleiswitz, those of Prague, of Châtillon, and he employed to persuade Napoléon to abdicate the same means that had been employed to reduce him to peace. He received Caulaincourt at Bondy. He received him again at the rue Saint-Florentin;[15] he listened to his warm pleas, he let him unfold once more the antiphon of illusions, the conditions of Châtillon accepted, on 25 March, by Napoléon, as before, the bases of Frankfurt; he replied that peace with Napoléon would only be a truce, that the Emperor's friends had only one more service to render him, and that was to persuade him to resign himself, that it was the only way to obtain for him a less severe fate. Did he speak of a "throne" for Napoléon II, what Caulaincourt would have interpreted by the regency and by the throne of France? to report the abdication and then they would see "for the regency"? In any case, Caulaincourt left for Fontainebleau as convinced of the necessity of abdication as he had been in Prague of the necessity of gaining access to Austrian mediation, then to the bases of Frankfurt, then to the ultimatum of Châtillon, and resolved to use his influence with the Emperor to induce him to do so, the only means of saving Napoléon's person from captivity, and perhaps of preserving the crown for his son.[16]

## II. The Abdication

It was on Napoléon's order that Caulaincourt went to see Alexander.[17] Napoléon fell back on Fontainebleau on 31 March. Caulaincourt found him there on the night of 2-3 April. He informed him of the votes of the Senate and the latest decisions of the allies: they demanded abdication, the Senate had voted forfeiture. Napoléon was indignant. He counted the senators for less than nothing; they busied themselves in translating the *ukases* of Alexander into decrees, with the same obedience as they had formerly done in *senatus-consults* the decrees of Caesar![18] He listened to Caulaincourt; it was only to indignantly reject his advice. He still flattered himself that he terrified the allies. He hoped to disconcert them by a stroke of audacity and to defeat them by a stroke of fortune. He spent the day of the 3rd in combining his measures and inspecting his troops. He gathered the officers and non-commissioned officers, made them form a circle, and said to them:

> I had the Emperor Alexander offered a peace bought by great sacrifices: France with its old limits. He refused. He authorizes emigrants to wear the white cockade, and soon he will want to substitute it for our national cockade. I will attack him in Paris. I count on you.

The officers listened in silence. The Emperor resumed: "Am I right?" Then, a thunder of cries: "Long live the Emperor! In Paris!" One witness said, "We were silent, because we thought it was useless to answer."[19] "Communicate these sentiments to your soldiers!" said Napoléon. The soldiers responded with cheers.

But most generals reserved themselves, anxious, weary to the point of nausea from war and adventures, obsessed to the point of defection, with peace, and with the enjoyment of wealth acquired through so many chances and a last chance could annihilate; no longer merely rebellious, as on the eve of Austerlitz or Eylau, irritated as in Moscow, demoralized as at Beresina or Leipzig, but, in the surprise of finding themselves still alive after so many catastrophes, exasperated at the thought of facing a new one, probably the last and the definitive one; decided at last, as they refused to put an end to the game of death, to put an end to him. Add the tensions, the words whispered in the ear by the officials of the Provisional Government, the perfidious advice which veiled the defection of patriotic pretexts and the personal concerns of *raison d'État*. "Only abdication can get us out of here," Ney said.

At the end of the day, some, and among them, the most glorious and the best endowed, Ney, Lefebvre, Moncey, talked about this abdication which would consume everything, and of the war which would call everything into question. The abdication imposed itself on their imaginations, like the position to be taken, the redoubt to be taken, Pratzen or Borodino. A dog kick! and they would sleep peacefully. They got excited. "One declares that he will know how to wrest the emperor from his downfall ... Another even says much more." These illustrious upstarts, threatened in their conquest, find themselves soldiers, and soldiers, as in the days when it was a question for them of climbing to the first ranks of the State, passing on the belly of the "lawyers" of the Councils and the Directory. From the Tuileries to the Kremlin they had mounted an assault on so many palaces! They had, to carry off their duchies, swept away so many princes! To keep these things, it remained to give Napoléon one last sweep: at bottom he was no more than a man on the ground, and a very small man! Ney, the most excited of all, and by his own passions and by the anger of his colleagues, abruptly passed from words to action, and dragged them into the Emperor's study. He said to him, "Sire! it's time to end it! Your situation is that of a desperate patient! You must make your will and abdicate for the King of Rome." The Emperor, master of himself, disputes and discusses: he could still regain victory. "It's impossible," cried the marshal; the army would not follow you; you have lost its confidence." Napoléon replied, "The army will still obey enough to punish you for your revolt." Ney exclaimed, "Hey! if you had the power, would I still be here right now?" "Lunging like a charger," he spoke loudly, the gesture menacing. The Emperor, astonished, worried perhaps in spite of himself, gazed at him with that gaze which Ney could not bear, which suddenly threw upon himself that tumultuous, heroic soul which had remained ingenuous in its sudden reversals. He became confused, stopped: "Don't be afraid, we're not coming here to make a scene of Petersburg for you!" The storm began to calm down; the generals allowed themselves to be dismissed; but they promised each other, if this first blow failed, to come back to the rescue, and Napoléon, feeling abandoned, inclined towards this abdication which he still flattered himself, an hour before, to avoid.

Meanwhile Macdonald was moving towards Fontainebleau with the remnants of his troops. On 4 April, in the morning, Gerard and several other generals came to see him, in the name of their soldiers. Gerard represented:

> that everyone had had enough of it, that our misfortunes were great enough not to aggravate them by mad resistance and expose Paris to the fate of Moscow, if, as rumor had it, we wanted to try to drive the enemy out of it; that he and his people were in no way disposed to contribute to new disasters.

Macdonald replied that he thought like them, and that he would make it plain to the Emperor. They cried, "In that case you are our leader, we will obey!" They all set off again and arrived at Fontainebleau in the morning. Macdonald went to the palace with Oudinot, several generals and their staffs. These officers feared that Napoléon would do a disservice to their leaders. Macdonald reassured them. He said to them, "The times are changed, he would dare the less because the army is for us." The fact is that Napoléon was closer to the times of Paul I than to those of the Duc d'Enghien, Pichegru, Moreau, and Pius VII. The court of honor and the apartments were then filled with officers of all ranks, all heated, noisy and violent. Ney, Berthier, Caulaincourt, Moncey, Maret, Lefebvre awaited the Emperor in his dining room. About eleven o'clock he arrived, sat down to table, breakfasted hastily, and led them into the adjoining drawing-room. They stood in a circle, silent. Napoléon, who had restrained himself the day before, was in great agitation. "He came and went, with great strides, his eyes fixed on the ground." Finally, stopping in front of Caulaincourt, he uttered the word they had all been waiting for: "I will abdicate!" Then Moncey shouted, "Ah! Sire, you save France! Make no mistake," he added; "that is my feeling, sire; but give orders, and wherever you want, I am none the less ready to follow you!"

The others were silent. Fain had prepared an act of abdication. Caulaincourt declared it insufficient: the allies would reject it. He indicated other terms; Napoléon discussed them. Then Ney, getting carried away, "with burning eyes, exclaimed that time was pressing, that they had to hurry, that there was no longer a moment to lose." The Emperor approached a console and made some corrections; Caulaincourt glanced at it: "It wouldn't end anything," he said. Then Napoléon went into his study and soon came out with a third draft. He said, "This time I won't change anything about it." The Duke of Vicenza read it.

As he was finishing, Macdonald entered, "head held high and determined, for such was his usual countenance." The Emperor came to him:

> Hello, Duke of Taranto, how are you? – Very sadly, so many unfortunate events! Succumb without glory! Not having made an effort to save Paris we are all overwhelmed by it! Humiliated! – It's a great misfortune, it's true, and what are your troops saying? – That you call us to march on the capital they share our pain, and I come to declare to you, in their name, that they do not want to expose it to the fate of Moscow.

He relayed their fatigue, their misery, their decay; he showed the improbability of success, the horror of a defeat, and he added:

> For the rest, our part is taken, and whichever one we take, we are very determined to put an end to it; as for me, I declare to you that my sword will never be drawn against Frenchmen nor tinged with French blood, whatever side one takes, enough of this unfortunate war without kindling civil war! "No, no," said the Emperor, "we have no intention of marching on Paris.

This response was made with calm and gentleness, he repeated: "It is true, the capture of Paris is a great misfortune." Macdonald represented the state of opinion, the need not to waste time. Then the Emperor: "I wanted the glory and the happiness of France. I have not succeeded, I abdicate and retire. All the dignitaries present, challenged successively by the Emperor, declared themselves for the King of Rome with the Regency of the Empress.

Napoléon appointed negotiators: "I will have their instructions prepared." Then, suddenly, abruptly changing attitude and language, he threw himself on a sofa, and, slapping his thigh with his hand, he continued with a relaxed air: "Bah! gentlemen, let's leave that, and march tomorrow, we'll beat them!" Macdonald objected: "No, we have had enough, and take care that every hour that passes turns against the success of the mission which the commissioners have to fulfill." Napoléon did not insist and said to the plenipotentiaries: "Get ready to leave at four o'clock."

In Paris Talleyrand awaited with equal anxiety for news of

Marmont's defection and Napoléon's abdication. An emissary from Fontainebleau arrived at full speed: the act was signed. Macdonald and Ney followed, with Caulaincourt. Talleyrand convened the Provisional Government urgently, and Napoléon's envoys find this council united. But the two marshals, or rather Caulaincourt, who was trying to conduct the negotiation, intended to treat only with Alexander, and they went to his apartment. Did Alexander find himself flattered by the new arbitration offered to him, did he feel annoyed by the undertakings of Talleyrand who was forcing his hand, disgusted with so many outrageous defections, fed up with indiscretion and arrogance? royalists who made their king, instead of the obliging the allies, the savior of the coalition in embarrassment? Was there a sudden reversal in this mobile soul? Was he moved at the sight of such a fall, the colossus at his feet, asking for mercy for his person, and protection for his child? Or did he give himself the spectacle of a drama in which he excelled, author, actor, and audience at the same time of his imperial theater? Did he feel a need to confess his feelings, to defend his policy? Explaining himself in front of the gallery, displaying his greatness of soul and, all at once, seducing his victims and flattering his dupes, having the decision he had made months ago, that he burned to execute, but which seemed to him, at the moment of pronouncing the irreparable word, to lack poetry? Still, he harangued them: "He was no longer the enemy of the unfortunate Napoléon; he had been his friend, his faithful ally against England." Napoléon had forced him into war, and the climate had decided that. He teased them: "You were only passive instruments, gentlemen; I esteem you all the more for it." He praised their loyalty to the master, "while so many others come to throw themselves into our arms and bring about his overthrow, that of the French empire." He wanted neither to humiliate France, nor even to diminish it!

 He stopped. So, Ney interrupting Caulaincourt, "Let me speak, you will have your turn!" He expressed himself, as a soldier, very interested, but very little political, and the others after him poured out compliments on "the magnanimity of Alexander," "the generosity of the allies," then they came to the point: the King of Rome and the Regency. The Regency had been the bait. The monster trapped, Alexander evaded. "It's too late; public opinion has made too rapid progress. Why didn't you get along with the Conservative Senate?" At these words, they exclaimed: "By what right does he act? He lied to his title! He held its existence from the constitutions of the empire;

they are reversed; he is nothing!" As for public opinion, the Tsar was deceived: everyone trembled before the resentment and revenge of the *émigrés*.

> All the institutions, all existences will be threatened: the purchasers of national property will be sought; a frightful civil war will arise from it, the army will not allow the glory with which it has covered itself, the liberties, the national independence, to be trampled underfoot. Sire! be our mediator!

Alexander listened to them, obviously impressed. This role was the one he had destined for himself and which Talleyrand, with his superior near-digitation, was in the process of evading. Did he foresee a passage to his favorite combination?

> I don't care about the Bourbons, I don't know them. I have no objection to your seeing the Senate. It will be impossible, I fear, to obtain the regency; Austria is against it; I would gladly consent to this, but I must act in concert with my allies.[20]

This statement, perfectly inaccurate, having opened the way, he insinuated: "As the Bourbons are not suitable, take a foreign prince, or choose from among your marshals as Sweden has done of Bernadotte; there is no shortage of illustrious men in France." He promised to tell his allies about it, and he dismissed them.

They met in the antechambers with the members of the Provisional Government that Alexander had summoned. To their profound surprise, Alexander pleaded the cause of the Regency, and holding to each the language which suited his designs: "The very lively interest that Austria cannot help taking in the imperial dynasty offers an assured guarantee." Talleyrand, Dalberg developed their arguments, and the most convincing of all against the Regency: the inevitable return of Napoléon; and how to oppose it? What would they do with him! They probably did not think of keeping him in prison. On the other hand, the royalists had revived everywhere. Bordeaux had spoken. The Senate recognized the rights of the Bourbons. It meant civil war! There were *raisons d'État*, and in conclusion, legitimacy. The Provisional Government refused to hear a half-word, to divine Alexander's thoughts. This prince then called in the marshals and Caulaincourt; then he saw again, after them, Talleyrand and his colleagues. Pozzo, who was watching at the gates, sent him a note on the inconveniences of the Regency. Talleyrand launched the argument he had kept in reserve: the Emperor Alexander could not forget that the members of the Government and all those who had been trained by their example had been determined only by its word, which would no longer be treated with Napoléon or with any member of his family. Terrible vengeance would befall them. They would have no other salvation than to give themselves to the Tsar, to follow him, to ask him for asylum in Russia!

Alexander, more impressed than he wanted to appear, and more embarrassed too, closed the meeting: "I will have decided tomorrow at nine o'clock!" These crossovers had lasted until two o'clock in the morning.

During the night, Marmont effected his defection, and this act decided the event: no revolt of the soldiers was henceforth to be feared. Alexander received the Marshals and Caulaincourt on the morning of the 5th, in the company of the King of Prussia. Well-to-do, open, cheerful at heart, and reassured by the news, he declared that the question of the Regency had been resolved by his allies and by him negatively. He returned to the extension that would be granted to France, beyond the old limits, and in such a way as to suggest that it would be obtained on the left bank of the Rhin. Then he passed to the lot that the allies reserved for Napoléon. "I have," said Alexander,

> executed his continental system, and yet this treaty was the misfortune of my country, and while I was ruining my subjects he was enriching himself by issuing licenses. But he is unhappy today, I become his friend again and everything is forgotten. He will have the island of Elba for sovereignty, or something else; he will keep this title under which he is generally recognized; his family will have pensions. Tell him if he doesn't want this sovereignty and he finds no asylum anywhere, he comes to my States. He will be received there as a sovereign; he can count on Alexander's word.

The marshals returned to Fontainebleau, where they arrived around midnight. Napoléon was dozing, they woke him:

Did you succeed? – Partly, Sire, answered Ney, but not for the regency. Revolutions never retreat; this has taken its course; it was too late. The Senate will recognize the Bourbons tomorrow. – Where can I live with my family? – Where Your Majesty wishes, for example on the Isle of Elba, with six millions in revenue. – Six million! that's a lot; what will I do with it? I don't need a *louis* a day. I become a soldier again. I wanted the happiness of France, I was wrong.[21]

Chateaubriand's pamphlet appeared that day, an extremely violent invective against Napoléon, an exalted apology for the recalled former dynasty: a political counterpart to the *Genie du Christianisme*, inspired by the divination of general anxiety. Talleyrand had given politicians the word: legitimacy; Chateaubriand presented an image to the imaginative: the King. Talleyrand brought everyone the deal everyone needed. Chateaubriand provided Louis XVIII with "a certificate of life.... I taught France what the old royal family was. It was as if I had counted the children of the emperor of China." He did more. If we think of the state of mind, not only of the people who ignored them entirely, but of the bourgeoisie who had forgotten them, of the youth who knew nothing about them, of the officers, even the nobles of birth, who hated them instinctively, to see them buzzing around the allies, prancing about in their staffs, following, alongside, escorting; if we weigh these words of a man of the birth of Fezensac, and he was legion: "They did not come like Henri IV to reconquer their kingdom; they marched behind foreign bayonets; they triumphed over our reverses; they were saddened by our successes"; the irritation of the officers was at its height. A young officer who was told the King was coming back replied with surprise: "I thought the king had perished in the Revolution!"[22] If from these soldiers, brought closer to the people by the very ranks where they commanded, we move on to people of the world and onlookers and ponder this story of a Russian officer, quite impertinent moreover:

> Finding myself in a box, for barely in Paris the allies rushed to the Opéra and the All-Paris of the Opéra gave them a gallery there, finding me in a box with ladies, they asked me after we had sang verses in honor of the Bourbons: – Tell us, I beg you, what are these Bourbons whose virtues we are so much praising for. We never heard of them. – And I was compelled, smiling, to tell them the story of their king.[23]

If we gather these testimonies, we will understand how effective was this voice which, in magnificent phrases, justified the necessity, ennobled the capitulation and attached to France these ghosts of a glorious past.

On 6 April the Senate voted and, on the 9th, the legislative body in turn accepted the constitutional articles: Article 2 stipulated: "The French people freely call to the throne Louis of France, brother of the last king"; "this constitution will be subject to acceptance of the French people"; and Article 29: Louis-Stanislas-Xavier, proclaimed King of the French, as soon as he had sworn and signed an act stating "I accept the constitution, I swear to observe it and cause it to be observed." The rest of the articles, which guaranteed what were commonly called "the principles of 89," strongly resembled what was to become the Constitutional Charter of 1830.

All that remained was to accommodate the Emperor. The English found the island of Elba too close to France, too worrying for Italy. Castlereagh suggested the idea that Napoléon should seek asylum from the English. Napoléon had said a word about it to Caulaincourt. Metternich, who arrived on 10 April, supported the objections to Elba, but to all these criticisms Alexander gave the same answer: "I gave my word." The abdication in form was handed over to the allies on 11 April, and on the same day Napoléon signed a treaty with them which recognized the sovereignty of the island of Elba, with the title of Emperor and two million annuities on the ledger; Parma, Piacenza, and Guastalla to Maria-Louisa; pensions to Mme Mère, brothers and sisters.[24] On the night of the 12th to the 13th, Napoléon tried to poison himself. Not having succeeded, he resigned himself, reduced to the character of a spectator in the catastrophe of his own history.[25]

The entries followed one another in Paris, always, officially, in celebration. On the 11th it was the Duc de Berry; on the 12th, the Count of Artois, whom the Senate, impatient to create titles and to give themselves patents of survival, invested power, under the title of lieutenant general of the kingdom; on the 15th the Emperor of Austria This, even at this time, caused a scandal.

The sovereigns, with their escort of Prussians, Russians, and Austrians, went to meet him. The Comte d'Artois, inaugurating his lieutenancy general, came to fetch him at the head of national guards on horseback, and the whole procession went to the Place Louis XV, where a solemn parade of allied troops took place. It was a lot of people and pomp to notify the universe that the Emperor Franz II was going to take up residence in a capital from which he had driven his son-in-law, his daughter, and his grandson.

Metternich, under the auspices of this sacred Majesty, employed the subtlety of his art to separate the mother from the child. The wife, neither widowed nor divorced, but now vacant, of Napoléon, was sent on the road to Italy, to Aix in Savoy, where she found Neipperg, qualified as a knight of honor, destined to watch over her and, if necessary, to distract her.[26] As for the child, they packed him up for Austria with his cradle with golden eagles, his imperial toys, his nurse, and they sent him to Schoenbrunn to get away from the air of France, until he withered away in the air of Vienna. Finally, for Napoléon, General Baron Koller was sent to him, with the mission of rendering him the kind of service rendered to political prisoners by the police inspectors who accompany them to the frontiers.

These services were not useless, because on the night of the 18th, the "vigorous bugger," the Duke of Dalberg, and the Marquis d'Orsvault, left Paris with a band of scoundrels on horseback, provided with safe-conducts and requisition orders signed, for the allies, by the Russian Sacken, and for the Provisional Government, by General Dupont, Minister of War, representing Pichegru, his former general, who died before his time; by Bourrienne, Minister of Posts, and by M. Angles, Director-General of the Police. The avowed object was to recover the treasures, crown diamonds and other works of art that the princes of the imperial family could take away. The real object was to get rid of Napoléon, by attacking him *en route*. Napoléon escaped the ambush; it is that Maubreuil, more avaricious than bloodthirsty, and, by temperament, more swindler than assassin, used it like those champions of divine right who under the Directory and the Consulate armed themselves for the crusade and stopped on the highways robbing stagecoaches. It is doubtless said to himself that when the tyrant is dead, the tyrant's head no longer has any price; to this compromising trophy he preferred the diamonds of his former sovereign, the Queen of Westphalia; he removed them most gallantly in the world, after the manner of the companions of Jehu. As for the plan of assassination, he reserved it for the future, like a good note of blackmail on the Provisional Government, which he did not fail to use afterwards, and very scandalously.

Napoléon left on 20 April, accompanied by Russian, English, Prussian, and Austrian commissioners. The Austrian saw him weep at the thought of the abandonment into which the Empress was abandoning him, of the solitude into which the King of Rome was thrown, without his exiled father, without his mother interned in a palace in Italy. He said to her, "I am not ashamed to show you my grief, for you know how much I have exposed myself in affairs." The Midi was a prey to an attack of that recurrent fever which had formerly caused the massacres of Avignon. It was now the massacre of Nîmes, the atrocious white terror, which was distinguished from the other only by the quality of the massacred: in 1792 the royalists and the priests; in 1814 the Liberals and the Protestants.[27] It was the enraged pack; the horrible and infamous death, the flaying, the gallows, the slaughterhouse! Napoléon concealed himself; he was not destined for this kind of torture. He was not recognized, the foreigners imposed on these furious people, and the populace allowed the justice of Europe to pass.

### III. Treaty of Paris

Thus was accomplished, by the help of all, this restoration which most of those who made it did not want, and which each of them needed. It was, from top to bottom, Brumaire returned. Everything was against it, and everything worked. A fortnight before, no one thought of it, and everyone rallied around it. The Revolution ended with one of those ground swells which had made all *journées*. This one took place like the others, by a stroke of prestige from Paris to France, a committee of a few men, with no other mandate than that which they arrogated to themselves, engineering the affair. An anonymous crowd acclaimed the revolution, the army brought order to it, and the assembly brought legality to it. The habit was so inveterate that no one, either among the royalists, or among the allies, or among the former Constitutionalists, contested for a moment this prerogative of Paris. As for the country, what had it not allowed to be destroyed since 1792? And the royalty of Louis XVI, "restorer of liberties," and the Republic of the Girondins, humanitarian and emancipator of peoples, and that of Danton, citizen and national, and that of Citizen Robespierre, theocratic, inquisitorial, and international like religions, and that of the Directory, debauched, bankrupt and conquering! If the people did not rise up against the invader, it was because the allies had maneuvered so well and their cronies from France had served them so well, as dupes, but not as victims, that France believed it had nothing to be feared for the two causes to which it had sacrificed so much since the Republic: the Rights of Man and natural limits.

The obstacles to anyone who had planned to undertake this restoration of concerted design would have seemed insurmountable. The worst came from the King himself who, in his manifestos, had imperturbably maintained his "right," his flag, that is to say condemned national sovereignty; who had guaranteed nothing from the Revolution and who never ceased to identify his re-establishment with the return to the old limits, that is to say the opposite of what France wanted, and precisely against what it had for 22 years been constantly armed. It knew only that of these princes, and that was enough to make them impossible.

But France wanted, above all, peace, and rushes there blindly. As in all of its crises, it ran to the most urgent thing: to get rid of Napoléon. They contented themselves with a vague guarantee, entirely verbal, of fundamental rights; the very limits faded into the background. As it appears that no one could either make peace or receive it but the Bourbons, so France accepted them, made of the necessity that it undergo the illusion of hope, and even resigned itself to the white [Bourbon] flag.

This peace demanded by France, was something Louis XVIII also wanted. He declared it from the beginning of the great conquests: "The king hopes that the balance of Europe will become the guiding principle of the sovereigns." His only desire would be to achieve this without seeking for himself any advantage other than his recovery. He will therefore not suffer the peace of the allies, he will sign with them his royal peace, as King of France; if the allies wanted it, in 1814, in Paris, just as he wanted it, in 1795, in Verona, the meeting neither humiliated nor diminished him. It was as natural for him to consent to it as it was against nature for Napoléon to accept it.

Despite the tangle of plots that occupied the backstage, the backstage, and the stage, all these actors and all these extras, however agitated they showed themselves, and puffed up with their character, were neither the author who composed the play and arranged the outcome, nor even the stagehand who operates the change of scenery. "The more one will prove that no general will, no great force, internal or external, called for and brought about the Restoration," said a great historian, then in a condition to take history in the act, "the more one will will shed light on the specific and intimate force of this superior necessity which determined the event.[28]

Alexander in triumph, lieutenant-general of this Providence

which, through him, destined and accomplished everything. And here was '89 at the feet of this autocrat, like the *philosophes* of old, fathers of '89, at the feet of the great Catherine, "on all fours!" as she said to Grimm in her German haughtiness, irreverently. He wallowed in the incense of men of letters, exalted coquettes and mystical coquettes, captivated lovers, and spellbound enchantresses, ideologues, politicians, intellectuals of all origins, of all sexes and of all doctrines, the human aviary who cackles, struts around, and gets caught in the mirror.

> It is a rightful king and a free government that your victorious arms have given.... It is an event like no other in history and which is due to you alone. I saw you, Sire, as great in adversity as you are now, at the pinnacle of human prosperity.[29]

This is how Corinne expresses herself, an irreconcilable denigrater of Napoléon who had refused him with so much noise the glory of his praises. After the Constituent Assembly, here comes the old Court: "What about the Emperor? We must kiss his footprints. He will be the savior of Europe, and in particular of France, which could have so little right to claim his benevolence."[30] And this consecration of his prestige: Chateaubriand was dazzled by it and seemed not to see the artifice:

> There was something calm and sad about Alexander: he strolled through Paris, on horseback or on foot, casually and without affectation. He looked astonished at his triumph; his gaze, almost tender, wandered over a population he seemed to consider superior to him: one would have said that he was a barbarian in our midst, like a Roman who felt ashamed in Athens.[31]

A first work was necessary if the allies wanted to justify their promises and the provisional government its *coup d'état*: to give France material peace, to save it from the excesses and humiliations of foreign occupation, to restore its dignity and free possession of itself. This was the object of the armistice agreement of 23 April: it suspended all military operations; the allies must evacuate the French territory as France evacuated the places which it still occupied beyond its old frontiers.[32] This act being necessary, only its advantages must be considered, and they were great: the end of the sufferings of war and of the state of conquest; the restitution to France, with arms and baggage, of the French garrisons abroad, in reality an excellent army which France recovered, and of which a few months later recognized the full value. Without the abandonment of these places, Antwerp, Danzig, Hamburg, Magdeburg, Mainz, Luxembourg, the allies would never have consented to evacuate France, and without the immediate evacuation of France, there was no possible government.

Louis XVIII, very kingly in all his attitude towards the allies, awaited the news. The convention concluded, that is to say, in law, the kingdom being free, he came to take possession of it. He crossed the Channel on 24 April. He brought to the restoration of the monarchy ideas very different from those of the men who had just made themselves its instruments. He held his "right" from God through the mystery of his birth, and this right, with which he had been invested with his very life, did not depend on any person in the world, not even on his own person, to modify it or harm it. His royalty was one and indivisible, like the Republic conceived in his image. Louis XVIII kept its integral and intangible dogma. His reign began with the declaration, made to the Convention, 31 Prairial Year III, on the death of his nephew Louis XVII. From that day, he considered himself King of France and for the duration of his existence. Events had prevented him from exercising his right; circumstances now permitted him to exercise it. That is all he consented to know of these two capitulations, that of Paris and that of Fontainebleau: facts, and nothing more, which could not alter the principle. Peace remained a political matter to be negotiated according to form; as for the act of the Senate, which recalled Louis to the throne, qualified him as King of the French and adorned him with a constitution, subject to popular ratification and condition of oath, he considered it as a paper without value. It was up to him alone to define, as absolute legislator, the character and forms of his Government: he received the oath, but did not take it. He did not have to submit to or discuss any constitution whatsoever: he would make a declaration of his views and, if it suited him, he would grant his subjects a charter which, without infringing on his rights, would regulate their exercise.

As had been the tradition and in a way the law of the French monarchy for centuries, as all the rulers, legislators, civil servants and soldiers of 1814 had completely compromised themselves in the party of monarchical restoration, and as there was no monarchy without the "king" they had to go where the King wanted; they passed through it, and Talleyrand the first. After having imprisoned Alexander in legitimacy and principle, he found himself imprisoned there himself, with all the Senate. Louis stopped at Compiègne, from 29 April to 2 May. He received Alexander and Talleyrand there. With Talleyrand everything accommodated itself and the most "honest" in the world. Talleyrand was well acquainted with this mixture of dogmas, reasons of State, and political precedents which were not written in any book, which were always evoked without ever quoting the text, and which were described as "public law." He thought of them as things of religion and, without believing in them any more, he reasoned about them like a subtle theologian. He learned from his master Retz that under this "fundamental law," the rights of the King and those of the people only agreed in silence. Louis XVIII needed Talleyrand, Talleyrand needed Louis XVIII. These two men, the most political and shrewd of their century, had perhaps, to understand each other, only to exchange these two words: Sire! my cousin! Talleyrand avoided speaking of the Senate and its constitutional articles; Louis deigned not to speak of Vincennes or of the bishopric of Autun, and, thanks to the majesty of the King, to the perfect bearing of the prince, the audience ended to their common satisfaction. The prince paid homage to his King; the King accepted the homage of his Minister for Foreign Affairs.

Alexander had the taste and even the coquetry of gratitude. He flattered himself that he received the testimony of it. Louis was not of the character to experience this feeling, and if he did, extraordinarily, he prided himself on not showing it. Alexander treated Louis as pretending to be ruined. Louis treated Alexander as an upstart. The descendant of Saint Louis established as a dogma the precedence of the Crown of France over all the crowns of the universe. He considered the proud successor of that Napoléon of the North, who was called Peter the Great, and whom Louis XIV hardly distinguished from the Khan of Tartary, to be a trifle. He spoke of men as a skeptic and acted believing in legitimacy. Alexander discoursed like a mystic and behaved like a realist. It was in his propriety that the Restoration should remain obsequious and subordinate towards him. Louis intended that the Restoration, although condemned to temporary effacement, should show itself worthy and independent. He also felt that by returning to his throne, he would put Europe back in balance. According to him, legitimacy was a right, victory an effect of force: this right should take precedence over this force. Alexander considered (with all of Europe) that the legitimate consequence of victory was the sharing of the spoils of the vanquished and that the most precious attribute of monarchy was to legitimately conquer kingdoms, legitimately dethroning kings. To consent to the Restoration was equivalent, in his eyes, to granting Louis XVIII a vacant throne, like Saxony to the King of Prussia, Holland to the Prince of Nassau.

Louis received Alexander, leader of kings and the savior of Europe, as if there were no Agamemnon except at the Comédie-Française. "He affected a dignity quite out of place towards a sovereign to whom he owed his return to the throne," wrote Nesselrode, and this sentence reveals the abyss which separated them. The meeting was icy. Strict etiquette took a discourteous turn. There were ways of going to meet them, of going through the doors, of driving back, of finally sitting down at the table, where the King occupied an armchair and had a chair offered to the Tsar, which at the same time offended, in Alexander and the lofty idea he had of his power, of the services rendered, of the effort made over himself to overcome his repugnance, and his magnanimity, very sincere but very touchy, his elegant sensitivity, the cordiality of morals with which he was used to and that he had enjoyed so much at the Prussian Court. However, in the spectacle of this impotent King without an army, without treasure, camped in a castle of which not a piece of furniture belonged to him and could not have been paid for by him, carrying in his person this ironic and paradoxical presumption of grandeur, one cannot overlook a superior *je ne sais quoi* by which Alexander felt affected in the prestige of his victory. The King and he never understood each other. The Russians remarked on "the painful impression which this interview made on the mind of the Emperor and the sad presentiments which he experienced from it." He came back ulcerated. This king remained for him the most infatuated of *émigrés*. How far this Compiègne was from the raft of Tilsit, from the theater of Erfurt, from the embraces, the reviews, the endless chats where he shared the world and competed in gallantries, where he played a role no doubt learned and wanted, but what a role and in what a theater, before such a gallery! Where a compliment from Napoléon seemed the flattery of a god and was worth a note on immortality, where however (and it was an exquisite tickle) victorious and deified as he was, the Bonaparte before the Romanof remained the upstart. What a fall into the pettiness of the ceremonial of Versailles! Was it calumniating Alexander to suppose that on this return from Compiègne he regretted Napoléon, and reproached him-self, at the very least, for having yielded too easily on Bernadotte's article?

On 2 May, Louis XVIII enacted the so-called Saint-Ouen Declaration which maintained the rights of the King, but contained the fundamental provisions of representative government and political liberty: the two chambers, the tax-free vote, civil liberty, religious liberty, equality before the law. The solemn entry into Paris took place on 3 May. It looked like a procession: the houses draped in white, the streets strewn with flowers, the crowd of believers in ecstasy. For the royalists, for the people of the Catholics, old French royalty revived for a moment with its mystical halo and its sacerdotal character. The King, returning from such distant exiles, emerging from lost horizons, seemed in his feeble old age like a symbol of the perpetual miracle of royalty which cannot die. He was the merciful and tutelary Majesty. He imposed a respect mixed with filial tenderness and his followers surrounded him with tears in their eyes. For the others, those who had crossed the Republic and tasted if not freedom of thought, at least the pagan skepticism of the Revolution and the Empire, it was a pomp as empty as that of the Supreme Being of Robespierre or of Napoléon's coronation. A spectacle after so many other spectacles of which, the relaxed draperies and the dispersed processions, nothing remains. The monarchy? A label on a poster glued to the wall that the rain takes off, that the passer-by tears off; the King? an obese old man who can't ride a horse, who can barely stand. The Marshal-Dukes, Macdonald, Ney, Moncey, Berthier, swords raised, cried: *Long live the king!* and commanded to repeat the cry; after them the generals, the sonorous voice, then with less authority the colonels, the squadron leaders; order fades away with the ranks, the cry lost in the regiments without an echo, and here and there, at the rear of the columns, a dull murmur: *Long live the Emperor!*[33] It was a regiment of the Old Guard on foot which formed the hedge from the Pont-Neuf to Notre-Dame. Chateaubriand said, "I don't believe that human figures ever expressed something so threatening and so terrible. When they presented arms, it was with a movement of fury, and the noise of these arms made one tremble."

The King appointed his first council of ministers on May 5. Apart from the immense work of personal interests and the pretensions to be satisfied by places and ranks, two arduous tasks imposed themselves on this government, which carried them out in front. One was to develop the Charter. The King gave a commission. Alexander, in spite of Compiègne's warning, dared to intervene. All the Constitutionalists of France, all the publicists in need of a constitution, formed around him a sort of legislative court or academy of liberalism. Alexander was all the more attached to it as he had, before leaving for glory, dismissed Speransky more harshly. To this was added a highly political calculation which was realized: in the absence of the deference of the King, to constitute in the chambers, in the liberal public, a party which would make it possible to balance, even to dominate, the bad will of the monarch; and he succeeded.[34] The English, on the contrary, affected to take no interest in the work; they paid their court to the king, who had a strong taste for it. All the tastes of Louis XVIII were on their side; not only the hospitality received, the encouragements of the Prince Regent, the first, the only ones, when all of Europe showed itself hostile;[35] but still the good tone of the English, who didn't bother to take the King of France to law school. The fact is that the English professed the haughtiest indifference to this article, and this was the very spirit of their Magna Carta, entirely insular, the least rational, the least intellectual and universal of constitutions, the exclusive and privileged heritage of England, rebellious to any acclimatization on the Continent.

However, they agreed with the Tsar on one point: to hurry the accomplishment of the work, for they were in a hurry to get away. Alexander only wanted to leave Paris with a constitution promulgated and peace concluded. Peace was brewing, concurrently with the Charter.

The bases of peace with France were laid; all that remained, it seemed, was to write the articles. But the allies did not agree on the accommodations of the general peace, that is to say, on the convenience of Russia, the reconstitution of Austria, and that of Prussia in the proportions of 1805. They used the expedient of Toeplitz, Frankfurt, Langres, and Chaumont. They adjourned to a congress to be held at Vienna the settlement of these great affairs, and they confined themselves to stipulating the provisions to which France should subscribe in advance, and as if with eyes closed to Europe. As for the particular arrangements that would follow, they flattered themselves that they would complete them among themselves, as a foursome, before the congress. They could not, however, treat the France of the Bourbons, the France brought back, and by their hands, and according to their wish, into the European order, the France which they had declared that they wanted to restore and maintain in its former dignity, in the degree of consideration due to the nation, France "great, strong and happy," as they claimed to treat Napoléon reduced to capitulation, and to exclude him from the congress. They had announced it formally.[36]

But they arranged their measures in such a way that the King's ambassador should appear at the congress only for pomp and ostentation, that he would not have to attend but only carry his pen and the seal of his arms, and nothing to do but put his signature at the bottom of the deliberate protocol, at four, before his arrival. Alexander, moreover, had taken his precautions on the subject which he had most at heart, the kingdom of Poland, and he could believe that Talleyrand was won over to it. Talleyrand had then too much need of Alexander to refuse a misunderstanding. He played, it seems, as skillfully on the word "Poland" as Metternich once did on the word "Rhine" and he avoided defining the character and dimensions of this future kingdom. It did not appear that Alexander talked to Louis XVIII about it, and without the King's consent, Talleyrand's advice was not binding. We will see it soon.

It was a question of elaborating the articles which directly affected France, that is to say the conditions of the particular peace between them and the allies, stipulating in their name and in the name of Europe. They had promised France "an expanse of territory that France had never known under her kings." They had consented to discuss "on objects of possession of mutual convenience which would exceed the limits of France before the Revolution."[37] All that remained was to translate these promises reiterated verbally by Alexander into border realities. Talleyrand took note of it in the King's name. He renewed Caulaincourt's arguments at Châtillon: the same as La Besnardière and Rayneval, who then wrote the notes, had resumed their places in Foreign Affairs, excellent publicists, educated in history. They discussed the partitions of Poland and the secularizations of Germany; but Talleyrand had to recognize that the discussion would remain academic. The allies appointed him to half a million more subjects than in 1790, and only accepted discussion on the territories in which to take them.[38]

Commissioners were appointed on both sides. The one from the King, the Comte d'Osmond received, on 10 May, instructions "to procure for France the points necessary to complete her system of defense."[39] The allies had spoken of 500,000 souls beyond the state of possession of 1792; the King wished to obtain a million of them, and to the north, along Belgium, between the ocean and the Rhine, a line from Nieuport to the confluence of the Spierbach, by Dixmude, Ypres, Courtray, Tournay, Ath, Mons, Namur, Dinant, Givet, Neufchâteau, Arlon, Luxembourg, Saarlouis, Kaiserslautern. The foreign commissioners "constantly rejected the idea that an increase in population had been promised to us by the allies." Everything remained a matter of conciliation, an arrangement "of mutual convenience." Osmond pointed out "the king's reluctance to receive part of Savoy." But nothing helped.

The allies, who were busy re-establishing the treaty of barriers and organizing a large guard post on the northern frontier, did not intend to leave France any lead on those countries on the left bank of the Rhine so desired, so loved, so missed by the French and where they retained so many ties. As the French insisted, they quibbled; then they dictated: Avignon and the Comtat, Montbeliard, Mulhouse were calculated in the total figure; one granted part of Savoy with Chambéry and Annecy; to the north, on the side of Belgium, Philippeville and Marienbourg; on the side of Germany, Sarrelouis and Landau: in all, 450,000 souls. It was not admitted that the colonial domain was part of the body of ancient France, which enabled England to carve out its indemnities and conveniences in the two Indies: the Isle of France, Tabago, Saint Lucia, Malta, the Seychelles; Santo Domingo returned to Spain, for the part ceded in 1795. But, Sweden renounced Guadeloupe and Portugal to Guyana, which treaties with the allies attributed to them and which returned to France. This was, for Louis XVIII, the painful part of the treaty, and in spite of his taste for under-standing with England, in spite of the services which the English Government had rendered to the restoration of the monarchy, he felt it for a long time, without, however, obtaining either concession or complaisance. On this article and on that of the Low Countries, which were the articles of her own interests, England never compromised.[40]

The article on good graces and consideration appeared elsewhere, negatively, indeed, but in a very notable way. The works of art stolen since 1795 were left to France; these were the trophies that the vanquished peoples were most anxious to recover; they were also those of which France was most proud, and kept them.

The Prussians produced at the conference of 17 May a bill for 169,785,859 *francs*. It caused a scandal even among the allies.[41] They had spoken too loudly of a "great, strong, happy" France, "because the great and strong French power is one of the fundamental bases of the social edifice," of a France "sharing with Europe the benefits of liberty, national independence and peace."[42] This Prussian claim detonated and distorted the treaty; it made it impossible for the monarchy to reconstitute the military state of the French. It uncovered an ugly character of avarice which diminished the fine effect of Russian magnanimity, of Austrian high propriety, of British correction. The two emperors, having no memorial to produce on their own account, abstained from supporting the Prussian claim. Louis XVIII protested: he would rather let himself be imprisoned in his palace, like Pius VII, than consent to this degrading sacrifice. He appealed to the Tsar, and the Prussians were in favor of their bills; they put the paper back in the portfolio, value on the future, and reserved it for any due date.

Peace was concluded by identical acts, signed on 30 May, between France on the one hand, and on the other hand Austria and Russia, Great Britain, Prussia, Sweden, Portugal; Spain acceded to it on 20 July, which brought to eight the number of powers said to have signed the Peace of Paris. Subject to the above arrangements, France waived all rights to countries located outside the new frontier. It was stipulated that "within the period of two months, all the powers which have been engaged, on both sides, in the present war will send plenipotentiaries to Vienna, to regulate, in a general congress, the arrangements which must supplement the provisions of this Treaty."[43] Nothing in the articles limited the rights of the King of France to negotiate, in this congress, on the same footing as the other powers. It was the ostensible portion of homage rendered to the dignity of his Crown. The restrictions figured in the secret articles: it followed (which was of considerable consequence) that these restrictions remained strictly limiting, that apart from these secret engagements, the King found himself master of his action, and that nothing in the congress, not even the articles on which he committed himself in advance, could not be definitively concluded without his participation. The secret articles began with a rather equivocal statement:

> The disposition to make of the territories which His Most Christian Majesty renounces by article III of the patent treaty, and the relations from which must result a system of real and lasting equilibrium in Europe, will be settled in Congress on the bases decided upon by the allied powers among themselves and according to the rules contained in the following articles...

They were: Lombardy and Venetia to Austria; the re-establishment of the King of Sardinia, diminished by part of Savoy, but increased by Genoa; the organization of Switzerland; the union of Belgium and

Holland into a kingdom of the Netherlands; the countries on the left bank of the Rhine reserved "for the aggrandizement of Holland and compensations for Prussia and other German states." Nothing from Poland, nothing from the rest of Italy, and in particular from Naples, nothing about the future organization of Germany. The allies could not oblige France to subscribe to their arrangements on these matters, since they had not yet succeeded in agreeing themselves on the way of settling them. They measured the inconvenience. The rivalry of France with Austria in Italy, and the game of French diplomacy in Germany against the unity of the Empire were classic, to the point of passing for maxims of the old monarchy. Louis XVIII would not fail to return to it; grandson of a Polish woman, son of a Saxon woman, allied to the House of Savoy, he would claim, without any doubt, to support these two crowns; reduced to his old frontier, he would resume the old policy of his house, the protection of small States, the patronage of princes in Italy and Germany. Talleyrand excelled at these, and had practiced them on a large scale, and in particular in 1803. At all costs the allies wanted to avoid them; they knew only one sure way: "stop the bases"; but that is precisely what they were most incapable of. They therefore had to adjourn and leave this dangerous lizard within the walls of their building. They vaguely protected themselves in a secret protocol which postponed until the stay in Vienna any arrangement on the countries ceded by France and on those which remained at the disposal of the allies. It regulated the provisional occupation and already prejudged the final attribution of certain vacant lands:[44] the Duchy of Berg, the lands between the Rhine, the Meuse and the Moselle, to Prussia; the left bank of the Meuse to the Dutch; the countries on the right bank of the Moselle, Würzburg, and Aschaffenburg to the Bavarians. It was, in principle, the division of the left bank of the Rhine between Holland for the smallest part, Bavaria for a larger part, and the main lot to Prussia, that is to say roughly what had been done.[45]

    Their work completed, the allies could retire, which they did on 2 June. On the 4th, Paris evacuated, France restored to itself, Louis XVIII, sole king in his capital, held the royal session of his Parlement; then he granted the charter which organized representative monarchy and promulgated the treaty which, after 22 years of war, gave France a peace which everyone had desired, but which no one already dared to believe would last. France was too restricted, the monarchy too precarious, the Revolution still too ardent in souls, Europe too divided and Napoléon too near.

Meanwhile, the imperial edifice was lying on the ground and the debris was being swept away. The re-established King of Piedmont at Turin, the Bourbons of Spain at Madrid, the Austrians in Venice and Milan, the Pope in Rome, the scattered Bonapartes, of all that brilliant tribe which had conquered the old world, only the two Gascons, that in Naples and that in Stockholm, and the first hardly held to Europe, if one dares to say, that by the cord intended to strangle it. Bernadotte had arrived in Paris a little late, as anxious not to compromise his Swedish heritage as to save himself as a snack for France, if by chance or inadvertence the throne should become vacant again. He resumed the role he had played in Brumaire Year VIII, and, remarkably, with as much profit.[46] In 1799 he formed the reserve of Republicans; there he won the baton of marshal and the principality of Ponte-Corvo. He remained in 1814 the favorite expedient of the liberals, and gained there, with Norway, the favors of the Holy Alliance. One saw it in processions; the public hardly noticed that he had changed sides, passing from the rank of the marshals of France who escorted the allies to the rank of the princes in a row who paraded in front of the marshals. His fate was enough to satisfy this very wise ambitious man. Alone of all his "promotion" he continued to reign and made a line of kings. The Swedes celebrated his return. Sergeant Belle-Jambe was born a king. Stripping away the draft and the rebellious, he displayed on the throne the superior qualities of a statesman. It wasn't just the symbolic marshal's baton he had carried in his pouch, it was a crown, and it went to his head. Also, dynasties begin with someone: "The first who was king was a happy soldier."

There must be a first rung in the mysterious ladder of legitimacy if the top does not necessarily touch heaven, the foot, as holy scripture says, "always rests on the earth."

1  Talleyrand, 1814, extracts from letters to the Duchess of Dino, *Revue d'histoire diplomatique*, II; Lamy, *Aimée de Coigny et ses Mémoires*.
2  "His mission had been conceived with Talleyrand, who had put himself at the head of a party working for the fall of Napoléon." (Nesselrode, *Autobiographie*.)
3  To Dino, 17, 20, 27 mars 1814.
4  *Mémoires*, II, p. 156 et suiv.
5  *Essais d'Histoire et de critique*: "Talleyrand au congrès de Vienne."
6  Pasquier, II, p. 231.
7  Loewenstern; Langeron; Henry Houssaye. Enthusiasm of the women, Mme de Chastenay, II, p. 306-307, 312-15; Letters of Mme de Staël, *Revue de Paris* (1 janvier 1897).
8  Michelet wrote, "Anyone who knows France and its rapid training knows that, in these moments, the avalanche rushes, every obstacle disappears, every care; no care to spare the nuances, to soften the transition." (*Histoire de France*, XII, the entry of Henri IV into Paris, into the Paris of the League.)
9  Duvergier de Hauranne, *Histoire du gouvernement parlementaire*, II, ch. I, "Fin de l'empire."
10 This decree was published on 3 April and approved by the Legislative Body, 3-4 April 1814.
11 Pasquier, *Mémoire,* II, ch. XIV, XV; Houssaye, 1814: liv. VIII, ch. II-IV: the provisional government, the defection of Marmont, the abdication; Viel-Castel, *Histoire de là Restauration*; Vitrolles, II.
12 *Mémoires*, II, p. 284, 313, 327.
13 Langeron, p. 481; Loewenstern, II, p. 412.
14 Pasquier, II, p. 286, 375-76. Cf. 195, 198. Vitrolles, II, p. 68- 94. Welschinger, *l'Affaire Maubreuil*; Houssaye, 1814, p. 595 et suiv.
15 On these interviews: Pasquier, II, p. 296-97; Thiers, XV II, p. 631, 635,683. Thiers seems to me to have completely misunderstood Alexander's feelings. See Henry Houssaye, p. 550, 588; Fain, *Manuscrit de 1814*.
16 His Majesty's opinion "on the Duke of Vicenza has not been contradicted under any circumstances; the courage with which he combated, in all times, the exaggerated ideas of Bonaparte and all the atrocity of his system, the essential service which he has recently rendered, and in particular to the king and his country, by preventing civil war by all that he has done to bring about the abdication, have further added to the esteem owed to him." (Nesselrode to Pozzo, 22 June 1814.) Polovstoff.
17 To Caulaincourt, 30 mars. – Thiers, XVII, p. 621-29.
18 Houssaye, liv. VIII, ch. II: Napoléon at Fontainebleau; Theirs, XVII, liv. LIII: first abdication; Ségur, VII, liv. X, ch. V-VII; Macdonald, *Mémoires*; Pasquier, II, ch. XIV.
19 Speech to the Old Guard. 3 avril 1814. *Corr.* after notes of General Pelet.
20 We have seen above that it was precisely the opposite.
21 Russie, XXXI. *Aperçu*.
22 *Souvenirs militaires*. "Campagne de Saxe," ch. VII. Compare Castellane, Ségur.
23 Loewenstern, II, p. 401.
24 Du Clercq, II, p. 402. England ratified on 27 April 1814.
25 Masson, *Marie-Louise*, ch. XII.
26 Conversation of Napoléon with Roederer, 13 novembre 1813. "Marie-Louise

was innocence itself, she always wanted to be with me. And then her father brought that rascal Neipperg with her." (Conversation of 26 septembre 1817. Gourgaud, II, p. 330.)

27 D'Espinchal, II, ch. XXVIII-XXIX.
28 Guizot, *Mémoires*, I, p. 30.
29 Mme de Staël to Alexander, 25 avril 1814.
30 Le duc de Richelieu to Rochechouart, 16 mars 1814.
31 *Mémoires d'outre-tombe* [n.p.].
32 De Clercq, II, p. 410; Talleyrand, *Mémoires*, II, p. 172 et suiv.
33 Castellane, I, p. 255.
34 See letters of Pozzo, I; esp. those of 15 juillet, 13 décembre 1816.
35 Pasquier, I, p. 400, 402; Duvergier de Hauranne, I, p. 154, 155.
36 Declaration of 1 December 1813, manifesto of 25 March 1814; declaration of 31 March on the entry into Paris.
37 Declaration of 1 December 1813; manifesto of 25 March.
38 Thiers, XVIII, liv. LIV; Bignon, XIV; Viel-Castel, *Histoire de la Restauration*, I.
39 Report of Osmond, 20 mai; Osmond to Talleyrand, 16 mai 1814.
40 The allies had some merit there, carding their European public, this measure, very political, was generally blamed. A friend of the Countess of Albany wrote to her from Naples on 25 July 1814: "It is truly to consecrate injustice and brigandage. Far from producing a good effect, such moderation is only done to revive the insolence momentarily dejected, and in the country where we laugh at everything, we are already laughing no doubt at this moderation so out of reason and so contrary to the French spirit." (Pélissier, *Le portefeuille de la comtesse d'Albany*.)
41 Oncken, II, liv. IX, ch. III.
42 1 décembre 1812, 25 mars 1814.
43 Article XXXII, Treaty of Paris, 30 May 1814.
44 31 May 1814. Martens, III, p. 168.
45 Except this difference: Mainz to Hesse and Trier to Prussia.
46 Around 12 April; lured recently. Léonce Pingaud.

Page left intentionally blank.

# Section Two: Treaties of 1815

## Chapter I: The Congress of Vienna

### 1814 - 1815

#### I. Restoration

Louis XVIII knew Europe, but he did not know France. If he had the highest concept and the clearest idea of his royal dignity, if he possessed the office and the liturgy marvelously well, he was unaware of the first elements of his profession as King: to come out of oneself, to tear oneself away from one's milieu, to the people, and in default of the popular heart and instinct, which are the very virtues of the prince, to acquire an intelligence, an entirely national *raison d'État*. He could neither look nor listen. If he passed through the streets, it was in a carriage at full gallop, running towards the suburbs to seek fresh air, shaking his numbed limbs, endeavoring, by the work of the horses and the carriage, to supplement the movement that he could not take on his own. He showed himself, but did not see. His Government was worn out in Court intrigues and police maneuvers: titles, endowments, employments, ranks, nothing but rivalries, inquisitions, the eagerness of people; everything there remained petty, emigrant. Little by little, however, the atmosphere of France, without his suspecting it and even lending himself to it, was penetrating him; but this treatment needed time and new trials. This prince, destined to return from a second exile, began with the most deplorable of routines.[1]

At the end of three months, everyone was in opposition to the new regime, even the princes, who found it too liberal. Those who rallied and those who returned complained alike, those who joined because they did not receive enough, those who returned because they did not monopolize everything; the rallies, claiming the Charter to keep their places, the ghosts, of their pretended privileges, to usurp them. The bourgeois feared for national property, income, equality. The soldiers, enslaved to intruding officers, execrated and despised, carried like a chain an odious discipline as soon as the superiority of merit no longer justified it, or else, reduced to half pay, idle, interned and under high police surveillance, they saw themselves treated as prisoners of war in their own country: all recalled Napoléon. The people felt in a way tolerated from on high, after having believed that they reigned and having heard themselves proclaimed so many times sovereign, creator of all sovereignty. Seeing the former nobles raise their heads, the priests raise their voices, they began to dread the return of the *ancien régime* and to miss the Empire. Add the excesses of the fanatical royalists, the White Terror. The crime of this Government was attributed to its own *raison d'être*: peace, a return to the old limits. It had been called upon and invoked to deliver France from foreigners; the war over, the foreigners gone, it was reproached for having returned to France following them, "in their vans," and for having capitulated into their hands.[2]

    Napoléon, by counter-stroke, regained all the ground lost by the Bourbons: they fell through where they had come up; he threatened to bounce back where he had fallen: war, glory, resistance to foreigners, and those three things that the French had so long used to confuse in the same passion, which was for them all the revolution, all liberty, the whole Republic: civil liberty, equality, and natural limits. Political liberty, which would, as a gift of joyful advent, reconcile the people to the new regime, distinguished them on the contrary, turning as at the time when it had tired everyone, under the Directory, to the despotism of a vindictive and insatiable minority, only used to stir up hatred, to unleash the counter-revolution, as detestable to the French as terror itself.

    Thus, in France, where everything was once conspired by the success of the monarchy, catering killed this monarchy under it. In Europe, where everything conspired to erase this monarchy, its weakness and its guardianship, it got up, on the contrary, and put, at the same time as it, France in the front row, in dignity as in influence. Louis XVIII and his Minister of Foreign Affairs carried out a political masterpiece outside, and of a quality that is all the more rare, even, as the force entered for nothing. Everything proceeded from the knowledge of men, the intelligence of affairs, the higher art to make virtue of necessities. Everything was arranged to relegate France to the Congress vestibule; Louis XVIII brought it back to the council room, to a place of honor, his former square; and if he saw it falling, shortly after, it was by the backlash of his own fall inside the country.

It is necessary, to well appreciate this work, of a frame so strong and so subtle at the same time, with tight knots, with so elegant embroidery, to put itself in mind the conditions where the government of catering was going to operate. The superior view of this government was to draw from these very conditions, from its principle, on the one hand, and, on the other hand, the commitments that the allies had imposed on it, a political system of an imperturbable logic and whose allies could not contest the foundation. The skill consisted to establish this system, to take advantage of the divisions of the allies, which had precisely led them to demand in advance from France a kind of capitulation, and to impose on it when its representatives would arrive in Vienna the facts accomplished, a note that part of the arrangements of Europe being in advance granted by it, would, for the other part, have where its consent remained free, in theory, only to subscribe to the agreements of the allies between *carte blanche* they gave in Paris and the forced signature that they would give to Vienna, to remain as strangled.[3]

## II. Conflict Among the Allies

On 30 May 1814, by dictating peace in Paris, the allies achieved the object that all coalitions had pursued since 1792 and that in 1804-1805 England and Russia had clearly defined to bring France back to its former limits, to "chain" it there, to oppose barriers to it in the event that it should again seek to overflow into Belgium or onto the left bank of the Rhine, and finally to keep the monarchy there under guardianship and quarantine, weakened by its own charter, re-established to give peace and unpopular by that very peace. This was the thought of Austria from 1791, it was the thought of England from 1792: they remembered Louis XIV. It was in 1814, after the Republic and Napoléon, the common thought of England, Austria, Prussia, and Russia. "From then on," said Alexander in 1815, speaking of the constitutional monarchy, "this nation, at peace with itself, will cease to be aggressive towards Europe."

The four, the allies of Chaumont, reserved for themselves to found, among themselves, the bases on which European peace would rest. They did not intend to admit any other State, and especially France, to these deliberations. By a protocol of 31 May, Metternich, Castlereagh, Hardenberg, and Nesselrode had decided to adjourn "until the stay in Vienna any discussion on the final arrangements for the countries ceded by France, as well as for those which, in Germany, remained available to the allies." This last stipulation applied especially to Saxony, whose king, remaining faithful to the French alliance, was considered on this account as struck down and held prisoner in Berlin. This forfeiture resulted in the vacancy of the Duchy of Warsaw, of which the King of Saxony was sovereign. The allies flattered themselves, by these precautions, of binding France entirely, of concealing their differences from them, and of forestalling the attempts which they might make, thanks to these differences, to insinuate France into great affairs, to establish itself in Congress, and regain consideration and credit in Europe. However, these differences were deep and the talks that followed during the summer, far from appeasing them, on the contrary only made them worse.

Alexander, who reserved the senior management of the congress, had its opening adjourned to 1 September, then to 2 October.[4] In the meantime he visited the Prince Regent of England, experienced "little satisfaction" there, according to Nesselrode, conferred with the King of Prussia, and took care of arranging affairs according to his designs.

The allies, in their manifestos, had invoked great principles: imprescriptible rights, the re-establishment of legitimate governments, the preservation of public law, the independence of peoples. They had opposed these principles to the irregularities, the violence, "the ignominious yoke" of the French Republic and Empire. But this empire now destroyed, the principles had finished their work. The four had no intention of encumbering the satisfaction of their respective gains with vain words. These conveniences they had declared in the treaties which had formed the coalition in 1813. It was now a question of reconciling these engagements with each other, and the allies counted on providing for it by means of the "right of conquest," the most imprescriptible of all, in their eyes.

Alexander found the ministers neither embarrassing nor embarrassed on principles in general: they professed only one, the interest of England.[5] But he saw them very busy finishing their war with the United States. This war, the last repercussion of the immense struggle begun in 1793 for the supremacy of the seas, had dealt to this supremacy the only sensible blows that England had experienced. It was a question, and the fall of Napoléon provided the means, of pushing the Americans to the limit and striking them with terror. This is what the army was working towards, which broke through the hearth of the United States and burned all the public monuments in Washington, symbols of American independence. This enterprise diverted the English from the European continent. Alexander could discern the most complete indifference to the fate of the King of Saxony, his person and his legitimacy; few provisions, on the contrary, for the development of a kingdom of Poland linked to Russia, which would be too powerful in the East. Finally, tendencies which corresponded to those which Louis XVIII had manifested in Paris, the taste for a rapprochement, if not an understanding, with France. He took umbrage at it and ordered it. The duration of the Government of Louis XVIII seemed less than assured; a return of the Revolution, a resumption of arms were possible. England, Russia, Prussia, and Austria, considering that the object of the alliance "cannot be considered as attained until the arrangements concerning the different countries (of Europe) have been finally settled at the congress," judged it necessary to confirm their alliance of Chaumont, and to keep on foot, each, an army of 75,000 men.[6] It was to tighten the alliance against France. On this article unanimity existed among the four, but this article did not suppress the disagreements which, between these four allies, labored to break the alliance.

These disagreements arose above all from the dispositions of Kalisch, Reichenbach, and Toeplitz relative to the reconstitution of Prussia and Austria. Alexander, far from renouncing his designs on Poland, returned to it on the contrary; the magnanimous ambition still tormented him to regenerate this nation and to accomplish there the fine liberal task which he had been unable to accomplish in Paris.

He would not have to reckon with the pretensions of any "legitimist"; there were none in ancient Poland, where the Crown was elective, and Alexander would himself be the "constituent" of this kingdom. But he had to reckon on the one hand with his subjects to whom this plan remained "so antipathetic,"[7] on the other hand and above all with his allies. He had found a combination which seemed to him to reconcile everything: the King of Saxony was Duke of Warsaw; he had lost all his states: the German part, Saxony, would be attributed to Prussia; the Polish part, the duchy, to Russia. Austria, for what it would not reprove in Gallicia, would be indemnified in Italy. Prussia would be concentrated in Germany, would establish itself in the heart of the old Empire; from a power two-thirds Slavic, and drifting towards the east, that the partitions of Poland had made it, it would become a power more than two-thirds German, and of all the States of Germany, that which would count the largest with more German subjects.

The Prussians did not contradict it, especially those who intended for Prussia a great role, the preponderant role in Germany and saw the constitution, in its hands, of a confederation of the North, then later, perhaps, of an empire more firmly cemented than the old one, which would satisfy the wishes of the patriots and fulfill the ambitions of Prussia. Saxony suited them perfectly and they had indicated it a long time ago.[8] But they also reserved for themselves, for the same future, and as a title in the eyes of national Germany, the defense of the eastern marches against the Slavs. Warned by the events of 1805 and 1812 of the short space which separates the friendship of a Tsar for a King of Prussia from the invasion of the Prussian States by the Russian armies, they demanded Warsaw, the line of the Vistula, and their ambitions, which were not small, tended to renew through the Duchy of Posen, between old Prussia and Silesia, the communication promised by Alexander to Kalisch. Saxony would find itself ready to compensate for the territories of Westphalia and the left bank of the Rhine, lost in 1795 and 1807, and to fulfill, in addition, the article of districts and indemnities. As for the other countries on the left bank of the Rhine, which they had occupied since the invasion, Mainz, among others, they would not mind keeping them, but it was the last quarter of Germany where it suited them to expand. In the first place, these territories, separated from the bulk of the monarchy, would be difficult to defend; they would not offer to Prussia, for means of communication, only easements of passage over the territories of sovereigns, brothers no doubt, but easily enemies. The experiments of 1794 and 1806 had shown the danger of these scattered and diverse possessions. Finally, these territories remained too close to France, exposed to its first blows. The day when France would come out of its enforced lethargy, it would be through this that it would take and push forward an offensive, that it would seek its compensations. The Prussians greatly feared this vanguard post detached from the coalition. They advocated an ingenious combination which was, since some showed scruples about the total expropriation and confiscation of the King of Saxony, to transport him on the Rhine with his crown, his gallery and his *Grüne Gewölbe*, his porcelains and his fairy tale trinkets.[9] This prince, a Catholic, related to the King of France, would undoubtedly fall into the French clientele, but it would only be more difficult for the French to despoil him.

Alexander saw his design for Poland opposed by his own ministers and by the ministers of the King of Prussia, his friend, his ally, and the main beneficiary of the coalition. These hidden oppositions had already produced many complications since the beginnings of the alliance; they had almost prevented Kalisch, they had slowed down the march of the invasion. Alexander never found but one remedy: an interview, exalted admonitions and exhortations, the call for brotherhood in arms, hugs, tears, direct agreement with Friedrich-Wilhelm III and the disavowal of their respective ministers, his own, which cost him little, and those of the King of Prussia, whom he took pleasure in disconcerting. But it would have been compromising this agreement to seek prematurely to form the spoils and to fix the limits. Alexander and Friedrich-Wilhelm III therefore simply renewed the promises of Kalisch: "It is to your loyalty, to your imperturbable firmness, that the success is largely due," wrote Alexander; and Friedrich-Wilhelm III:

> The feelings that I have dedicated to you will only end with my life. It is to Your Majesty that Europe owes the example of this noble courage and this fine perseverance which has just broken its chains. It is a real need to be with Your Majesty and to talk to him about all the matters which interest us reciprocally.[10]

Alexander enjoined his ministers to support Prussia's claims in the congress to the greater part of Saxony, and Hardenberg continued, while claiming that same Saxony, to claim the line of the Vistula, thus thwarting Alexander's claims to the Duchy of Warsaw.[11] In this respect he found favorable dispositions in Vienna and London; he did not despair, thanks to the mobility of Alexander, to his passionate desire to keep the upper hand over the alliance, finally thanks to the hidden assistance of Nesselrode and his colleagues, to win Saxony and recover the Duchy of Warsaw.

Austria nourished the same fears as England, closer, more direct still for the East. Metternich had resigned himself to handing over Saxony to Prussia only in the confidence that Prussia would oppose the acquisition of the Duchy of Warsaw by the Russians. Moreover, Prussia established in Saxony, on the frontier of Bohemia, having become the preponderant power in Germany, would become a threat, a cause of forfeiture that Austria could not tolerate. At least, if they were to suffer the inconvenience of the Russians in Warsaw, they would renounce the parts of this duchy ceded by them in 1809 only in exchange for territories in Italy.[12] Metternich would take up Thugut's plans; he was preparing to reopen with the Russians the markets of Campo-Formio and Lunéville, that is to say the division of the Papal Legations. "Your Majesty will not take them for himself?" Pius VII's envoy to Vienna, Consalvi, asked Franz II. He had great difficulty in obtaining from this devout prince this ambiguous answer that "he would not have taken them for himself"; and according to another version: "But if others want to dispose of it, I cannot wage war against it."[13] The statement was equivocal and full of ulterior motives, those of Austria itself, which wanted the border to be rectified towards the Po, which would affect the legation of Ferrara. The remains of this legation, those of Bologna and Ravenna, could serve to settle some thorny affair: Louis XVIII wished to compensate Maria-Louisa of Spain for the lost royalty of Etruria, which Franz intended for an archduke. Franz, on the other hand, was looking for an estate for his daughter Maria-Louisa, and the allies had guaranteed it to him. But only Parma remained available. Whence this expedient, to indemnify with the Legations that of the two Maria-Louisas who would not go to Parma. This ex-pontifical domain, in its quality of Church land, seemed suitable for any secularization, and the Prussians were thinking of transporting the dynasty of Saxony there, as the Lorrains had formerly been transported to Tuscany.[14] Finally, Austria had promised Murat a good frontier and 400,000 souls, which could only be found at the expense of the Holy See. But although the Pope, who suspected the arrangement, was greatly frightened by it, this article was, in reality, much more formidable to Murat himself than to Pius VII.[15]

Murat, by the fall of Napoléon, ceased to be useful, and he began to become dangerous. At his first imprudence, that is to say, at his first attempt to take his alliance with Austria and the promise of indemnity in the Papal States literally and seriously, he would become a criminal. Then they would suddenly discover his machinations with the Unitarian sect, his plans to unite "under one man all the peoples, from Calabria to the Alps," and who knew, to reach out to Napoléon on the island of Elba, to reconcile with his brother-in-law and help him to become Emperor again, if Napoléon recognized him as king of Italy? Then, too, it would be seen that the treaty of 1 January was not expressly ratified by any of the allies, and only committed Austria alone. The Russians hadn't signed anything. When the Duke of Orléans went to London in June to talk to Alexander about the restoration of Ferdinand IV: "My dear Duke of Orléans, as for me, I am quite ready, replied the Tsar; but it is from here that it depends." The Prince-Regent did not hide his feelings: "I don't know how they were making all these arrangements with Murat. It is detestable." The ministers did not accede to the treaty. Liverpool had only one desire, to get rid of Murat, "without being reproached for missing any commitment."[16] Now they had only one quasi-engagement, with Austria. They would leave everything to Metternich, and Metternich will let Murat lose himself, helping him there if necessary. On 29 July, Saint-Marsan, who had served in Sardinia and represented Victor-Emmanuel in Vienna, reported that he had told the Emperor of the fears that Murat's revolutionary intrigues were causing his king: "You are right, but I hope that he will make himself the instrument of his ruin," replied Franz II.

Ferdinand IV, the Bourbon of Sicily, had dispatched to Paris, then to Vienna, a plenipotentiary, Commander Ruffo, responsible for asserting his rights to a "restoration" in Naples. This diplomat wrote, "We believe, from our conferences with Prince Metternich, that Austria has completely abandoned the idea of supporting Murat." Metternich admitted it. He told Saint-Marsan, "I would give the whole world to receive the news that King Ferdinand is restored to his throne. Unfortunately we cannot, at the moment, use our weapons there."[17] The first shots had to come from Murat. When the time came, Italy induced into revolution by Murat, Austria would intervene there to restore order. It would then make itself the arbiter. It would have the passages of the Alps allocated under the pretext of setting up a barrier against the French. It would secure Piedmont for itself, with the marriage of an archduke with the eldest daughter of Victor-Emmanuel, who had no son; it would have the female succession established at the expense of the Carignans; an archduke in Tuscany, an Austrian prince in Modena, the Austrian Maria-Louisa in Parma, the Austrian Maria-Carolina in the Two Sicilies and the Austrians massed in Venice, Verona, Mantua, Milan, the Legations, would pass there, at the end. Austria protecting the restored princes, incapable of imposing itself on their subjects without the support of its arms, would form of all these clients a confederation, like the Confederation of the Rhine, of which Franz II would be the protector, and which would put the whole of Italy at its discretion.[18] But Russia would consent to it only in return for the Polish provinces, Prussia only in return for Saxony; the two affairs therefore linked everywhere, and everything else depended on them.

Three parties were thus formed between these four allies. The summer of 1814 passed in vain parleys. Meanwhile, the German peoples to whom Koutousov, in March 1813, had promised independence, a constitution "modeled on the ancient spirit of the German peoples," which would enable "a regenerated Germany... rejuvenated, vigorous, united, to reappear with advantages among the nations of Europe," agitated, murmured, and demanded the fulfillment of these promises, the re-establishment of the Germanic Empire and were irritated at the thought that so much bloodshed, so many sacrifices would have had no other effect than the extension of Prussia, the destruction of an old German state and the distribution of peoples among new masters.

### III. Instructions of Louis XVIII

Such were the secrets of the allies, which they were so anxious to conceal from France. But they perspired little by little, through the confidences of the interested parties, the future victims or dupes of these great transactions which the four were plotting so painfully. Saint-Marsan, still loyal to Talleyrand, revealed to his minister of the day before Austria's plans for Italy and all the shrewd comedy to destroy Murat after having betrayed him.[19] Metternich himself, in a moment of ill humor against Prussia, fearing to see the old coquetry and the old agreements of 1740 and 1795 revive between Paris and Berlin, not very desirous of establishing the Prussians in Dresden, preferring, if only to make them irreconcilable with the French, to install them on the left bank of the Rhine, and occupy the compromising position that Alexander and Friedrich-Wilhelm III had for a moment intended for Austria, in Alsace, denounced to Talleyrand the designs of Prussia on Saxony, the plan to transport the King of Saxony first to Münster, further on afterwards, to Bonn, to Cologne, and to get rid of the onerous and precarious guard of the left bank. Add the grievances of the petty Courts of Germany and Italy, some of which felt threatened by Austria, others by Prussia. Talleyrand had "practiced" and exploited this personnel of wandering diplomats, always intriguing. Greedy and enriched, filled with ecclesiastical and seigniorial lands, confederates and protected, these German sovereigns had more or less conspired, like him, the fall of Napoléon and the restoration of the "legitimate" princes, which enabled them to "legitimately" preserve the property acquired from the usurper and to evade services promised in exchange. Like Talleyrand, it was not to lose their benefices that they had betrayed the Emperor, and, naturally, they approached him; jealous above all, of what was called "their independence."

The allies did their best, the logic of things prevailed over their combinations of chancery. By restoring the old dynasty, by driving France back to its old limits, by excluding France from the great partitions of vacant territories, they made it, at the same time, return to its old policy, and restored to it the clientele of the small states. The adjournments imposed on the congress sufficed to show that the four were not in agreement on the articles which they had reserved for themselves to settle among themselves. From the silence observed with regard to France, it was evident that they persisted in wanting to exclude it from these great affairs. Castlereagh wrote it to Wellington, ambassador in Paris, and Wellington informed Talleyrand of it: there had been engagements entered into "at a time when England was far from being able to count the French government among her friends."[20] On the other hand, the Duc de Berry, who had gone to London, where he informed Louis XVIII that Castlereagh was about to leave for Vienna, that he would arrive there before the opening of the congress, and that the object of his visit would be to concert, without the intervention of France, the preliminary measures which would regulate the progress of the congress. Invited to stop in Paris, Castlereagh came there on 26 August, was received there by the King, and reassured him: the anticipated meeting of the allies in Vienna was, he said, only intended to agree on a few particular points of their previous conventions, and "not to decide, without France's knowledge, the general or particular questions on which she was naturally called upon to give her official consent." Talleyrand took note of it, and he concluded from it, with good reason, that England found itself hampered by its engagements, that it would therefore be possible to break the beam; that if France claimed its right to the congress, it would find support in England, and that in the congress the dissidences of the allies, if they did not succeed in agreeing by then, would open the breach to them through which they could return to Europe, and perhaps, in time, dissolve the coalition formed, renewed and united against France.

This was the great object of the policy of Louis XVIII, and it was for this purpose that the subtle, ingenious, and profound plan of diplomacy which he adopted, in agreement with Talleyrand, was conceived. Above all, the King had to seek to draw France out of the isolation to which the allies had relegated it, to which they claimed to keep it. Fear and jealousy of French power had been the object and bond of the coalition. To provide any pretext for suspicion, to allow the slightest territorial ambition to be glimpsed, to worry the English on the side of Belgium, the Prussians and the Germans on the side of the left bank of the Rhine, was to immediately bring the allies closer together, and to furnish a weapon to those who, like the Prussians, were animated against France by implacable rancor. France therefore had only one means of dividing them: it was to reassure them. They had imposed disinterestedness on them: that was their only strength. They had organized a skillful system of precautions against ambition and duplicity: they had foreseen neither the case in which France would give up being ambitious, nor that in which, making itself a virtue of necessity, would show itself sincere. They had forbidden the policy of expedients and intrigues: they dictated, in a way, the policy of principles. Louis XVIII and Talleyrand understood this, and their art consisted in extracting from the obligations they suffered their resources and their instrument of action. It was in the name of the public law of Europe that the coalition had fought France and forced it to sign the Peace of Paris; it was by virtue of this public law that France was going to intervene in the congress, demanding from everyone the application to everyone of the rules that had been imposed on them; proving respect for the commitments entered into by the very energy that it would bring to make the principle prevail everywhere. Talleyrand said,

> It was necessary to make it understood that France only wanted what she had; that it was frankly that she had repudiated the heritage of conquest; that it was strong enough within its old limits; that she had no thought of extending them; that finally she placed her glory today in her moderation; but that if she wanted her voice to be counted in Europe, it was to defend the rights of others against any kind of invasion.

This self-sacrificing role could "not be devoid of grandeur"; it was not lacking in skill: "It is through the utility she could be in supporting the weak," that France would seek to place itself "in a worthy and honorable position."[21]

It was a return to politics which excellent minds considered the true tradition of French diplomacy. France had done itself the honor and advantage of it in prosperous times; but made the mistake of abandoning it out of incompetence under Louis XV, out of fury of propaganda or magnificence under the Republic and under the Empire. To renounce for oneself great conquests because they could not be accomplished without great divisions; to prevent the strong from becoming too powerful; to defend the small states against the covetousness of the big ones; to maintain a balance of power between all which, while guaranteeing peace, would ensure for France, alongside a divided Italy, a fragmented Germany, an influence all the more effective as it would be more moderating, this policy which claimed the great name of Henri IV, had been that of Richelieu and Mazarin. Vergennes had resumed it with discretion, but with dignity, under Louis XVI. He had been Talleyrand's first adviser to the nascent Republic, in 1792; it had been the first intention of Louis XVIII when he had thought of returning to the throne in 1795. Starting out, the King from a principle, the minister from a calculation, they came to the same conclusions, both guided and enlightened by the experience of facts, the feeling of the force of things and instinct of the permanent interests of France in Europe. Thus were composed under the direct inspiration of Louis XVIII, on the indications and notes of Talleyrand, the Instructions of September 1814. The first clerk of foreign affairs, La Besnardière, was the editor. These instructions were until the Treaty of Paris of 1856, a brilliant consecration and last manifesto of this policy, the code and the rule of French diplomacy: "France is in the happy situation of not having to desire that justice and utility be divided and (of not having) to seek its particular utility outside of justice, which is the utility of all." Justice asked that "a sovereign whose states are under conquest does not cease to be sovereign, unless he has ceded his right." Public law had two fundamental principles: that conquest, by itself, does not confer sovereignty unless the legitimate sovereign cedes the conquered territory; that no title of sovereignty exists for States except insofar as they have recognized it. It followed that the King of Saxony must send a plenipotentiary to the congress and claim his right; that Murat, recognized neither by the

English, nor by France, nor by Russia, could not send an envoy as the King of Naples. Justice and public law required that States cannot be confederated among themselves in spite of themselves; it followed that the States of Germany, whose independence had been recognized by the Treaty of Paris, must take part in the deliberations of the Congress and, in particular, on the confederation which they were called upon to form among themselves. "To these reasons for justice is added a reason of utility for France: what is in the interest of the small States is also in its interest." They would want, in Italy and in Germany, to recover, to preserve their independence: it must help them there. Austria was no longer formidable in Germany, but its ambitions were directed towards Italy, and in Germany Prussia tended to take its place.

In Italy, it was Austria that must be prevented from dominating by opposing to its influence contrary influences; in Germany, it was Prussia. The physical constitution of his monarchy made ambition a sort of necessity. No scruple stopped them. Its emissaries agitated Germany, painted France as ready to invade him again, and asked that it be delivered to Prussia to preserve it.

Whence these consequences: to restore the King of Saxony, to restore the Bourbon King in Naples, to restore the Legations to the Holy See, to ensure, in the mountains, the male succession, the traditional succession, at the House of Carignan; to make consequently impossible with Austria to seize this monarchy by the marriage of an archduke with the eldest daughter of the King; to restore Austria and Prussia to their former state of possession, by compensating Austria for the loss of the Low Countries by the former territory of Venice. It would have been fair to extend this work of reparation to Poland, no doubt, and to restore, at the same time, the balance of forces as it was in 1792, because France was brought back to its frontier of that time. But they would come up against the impossible. Neither Prussia, nor Austria, nor Russia would consent to bring back to this succession of Poland what they had usurped in 1772, 1793, and 1795. No Russian would lend himself to the restitution of Lithuania:

> Russia does not want the restoration of Poland in order to lose what she has acquired from it; she wants it in order to acquire what she does not possess... If nevertheless, against all probability, the Emperor of Russia would agree to give up what he possesses of Poland (and it is probable that he could not not

without exposing himself to personal dangers on the side of the Russians) ... the king ... without expecting a happy result ... would put no opposition to it.

But if Russia kept Lithuania, as simply a matter of annexing to the Russian Empire the Duchy of Warsaw, more or less increased on the side of Gallicia, at the expense of Austria, the question of principle disappeared. It was no longer anything but a question of interest, and it was not in Europe's interest to push such a tremendously increased Russia to the Oder. Under these conditions, the wisest thing was to restore things to the state they were in before 1807.

Switzerland would form an independent and neutral confederation. "The Ottoman Porte is a European power whose preservation is important for the maintenance of European balance. It is therefore useful that its existence is guaranteed." And at the same time France would maintain its ancient prerogatives in the East, its old commerce, its capitulations, the protection of Catholics, of European residents, of the Franks, as they used to say. It would resume, thanks to this very system, its former influence everywhere.

> Recent times have left impressions that need to be erased. France is such a powerful State that other peoples can only be reassured by the idea of its moderation, an idea which they will accept all the more easily because she has given them a greater sense of her justice.

Everything fit in this system. "Nearly all the objects to be regulated by Congress depend on one and the same principle, and to abandon it for one point would be to abandon it for all." Hence the extreme importance attributed to preliminary questions, to the organization of the congress, to declarations of principles; the minute prescriptions made to the French envoys so that no one was admitted to the congress who did not have the right to sit there, so that no one was excluded from it who would have the right to be admitted; so that the congress really met, constituted, and determined, above all, which States should have plenipotentiaries there and what objects should be settled.

The position thus taken by France was unassailable. France opposed to the allies a right which they had solemnly proclaimed. Certainly, the sovereigns and diplomats of Russia, Prussia, and

Austria had only one design: to imitate Napoléon after having killed him, to treat the French Empire in disherence as they had treated Poland in anarchy, and they considered that to owe it to no one but themselves. But the fourth ally, the English, could not follow them that far. It was obliged to publicly justify its conduct. Doubtless the representative of England, Castlereagh, was personally as indifferent as his colleagues to principles and public law; but not everyone in Parliament was. By the mere fact that there was in London a tribune, the press, where the transactions of congress would be discussed, its acts would find public sanction. It was by this that Talleyrand would hold the English, and it was what made the impact of the notes of principles that he wrote, less to edify his colleagues than to move public opinion, thanks to happy indiscretions which delivered his notes in the gazettes.

Certainly, to anyone who considered Talleyrand's past and the winding paths he had traveled from the bishopric of Autun to the Congress of Vienna, passing through Danton's cabinet, the chancellery of the Directory, Napoléon's Court, Berlin, Tilsit, Erfurt, the role was scabrous. Talleyrand had to impose not only the principles of his new master, but his own person, strangely coupled. It required, on his part, a force of effrontery which perhaps did not exceed his means, and on the part of his colleagues a prodigious complaisance. But the role and the character imposed themselves. Gathering around the green carpet, the former partners of so many illustrious parties were compelled to all look new again. None of them was there on their own; they all represented something else, and it was precisely the principle by virtue of which Louis XVIII, restored by them, reigned in France, and which Talleyrand, Louis XVIII's ambassador, invoked at the Congress. Talleyrand spoke in the name of an irreproachable king on this article. Besides, who would have dared to reproach him for his palinodies? If he had served the usurpations of the Republic and the Empire, the others had, in turn, participated in them; they had sealed the pact, Prussia at Basel, Berlin, Rastadt; Austria in Campo-Formio, in Lunéville, in 1810 at the time of the marriage; Russia in Tilsit and Erfurt. Only one could have looked down on him, it was the English, but they were instructed to keep quiet. All therefore agreed to throw the veil. In the secret articles for which there is no reason, they could still make light of public law; in their protocols, in their declarations, they could not. And it was thus that these old augurs, skeptics, and libertines, were obliged to look at each other without laughing, and, while grumbling, to follow the office celebrated by their master in skepticism and licentiousness, the "lame devil" as they said, become pontiff of their own church by the effect of their coalitions and the grace of their victories.

However, there were weak points in France's position. It was not necessary that on the most insignificant article, it departed from disinterestedness. From then on everything collapsed, and suddenly its declarations, taxed with hypocrisy, lowered this beautiful negotiator in principle to the most vulgar game of intrigue. Never has a policy demanded more dress. Now it was in the interest of those whom this policy thwarted, to divert it, to disconcert, in short, to induce the French agents into temptation, into a bargain, and to compromise them. Metternich was not to be missed. Moreover, what was serious, the policy adopted by Louis XVIII implied a complete antagonism with Russia and Prussia, whose interests were united, whose sovereigns were united by the most tender, and firmest friendship. Louis XVIII considered them, with good reason, as inseparable, and not wishing to sacrifice, in the person of the King of Saxony, his principle to Prussia, nor to serve, in any degree, the plans of this Crown, he was led to thwart Russia. He agreed to it effortlessly. The progress of Russian power worried him, and I don't know what excessiveness there was in that nation offended his classical mind; the contrasts in the character of Alexander, generous and cunning, but politic even in magnanimity, passed in the eyes of this pure Voltairian for masks of comedy.

During Alexander's stay in Paris, there had been talk of an engagement between the Duc de Berry and the Grand Duchess Anna Paulovna. Difficulties of conversion and chapels, moreover very serious, because they concerned the very tradition of the two sovereign families and touched on the very foundation of the two monarchies, were raised on both sides. The game seen at the time of a similar project of Napoléon with the Grand Duchess Catherine began again, but with this difference that, this time, the Russians showed themselves eager, without however wanting to yield on the essential article, the [religious] conversion, and that Louis XVIII, on the contrary, entrenched himself in absolute principles, and pleas of inadmissibility which concealed his lack of zeal. Pozzo wrote, "This is an opportunity that should not be missed. France is no longer that of Bonaparte, nor that of Louis XVIII at Hartwell: it is the French monarchy."[22] It was precisely what Louis XVIII allowed too much to be seen, what Alexander felt with too much displeasure, and what added to so many other feelings of vexation experienced since the interview at Compiègne: the *cordon bleu* sent to the Prince-Regent of England and not offered to Alexander, the Russian embassy requested by Alexander for Caulaincourt and refused by the King, Caulaincourt excluded from the peerage. "His Majesty was keenly wounded, and charges Your Excellency to bear witness to this without reservation," wrote Nesselrode to Pozzo.[23]

Finally, Louis XVIII sincerely wanted peace, to re-establish his monarchy, restore the strength of the nation, reconcile the French with their former kings; his policy accorded with his personal tastes, which leaned towards England. The interests at this time were analogous. As for the future, the King did not worry about it, knowing that the day when France would be reconstituted, when Russia would need them and when France would find their advantages there, the rapprochement would happen by itself. Until then, and in particular in Vienna, Louis XVIII, by lending himself to the proprieties of Alexander, by placing himself among his clientele, would diminish himself in the present and would lose for the future the chance of becoming an ally that one sought and rewarded. By appearing to solicit from Alexander some vague promise of aggrandizement, by reducing himself to the policy of "tips," he exposed himself to suspicion, he justified the denunciations of his enemies, he isolated himself, England being unshakeable on this article, hostile Austria and intractable Prussia. It would place itself at the discretion of Russia alone, which, therefore, holding it, would take care, to satisfy it, to quarrel with its other allies. Louis XVIII was incapable of penetrating the genius of the Russian people; but his extreme shrewdness made him divine the very skillful combinations which Alexander so elegantly concealed from superficial observers under the guise of enthusiasm, sensibility, and liberalism. Alexander had no thought of breaking the coalition which was his work and the instrument of his lofty ambition, hegemony over Europe. He had no thought of enlarging France, and the purpose of the coalition was precisely to contain it. But having brought it to the point which suited him, he desired to remove it from Austria and England, while remaining united with these two Courts. He wanted France to have no other ally but him and to become for him an always available helper. It never occurred to him to sacrifice Prussia; but he found it in his interest to keep on his right and on his left, equally devoted, equally subordinate, the King of Prussia and the King of

France, auxiliaries of his policy. It would therefore not be to break the quadruple alliance that he could attract Louis XVIII, it would be to fortify himself in this quadruple alliance, by the addition of France, and to remain there incontestably the first, the master. But, to this very combination, he preferred the four-way arrangement of all affairs, and that was what seemed to be in Vienna from the first meeting.

## IV. Prejudicial Questions

It had been agreed between the four that in the first days of September they would meet in preliminary conferences. Before the sovereigns, before the other plenipotentiaries arrived at Vienna, where Metternich represented Austria, Nesselrode for Russia, Humboldt and Hardenberg for Prussia, Castlereagh and his brother, Charles Stewart, for England, they did precisely what Talleyrand had foreseen that they would make a program for the work of the congress. This program, drawn up by Humboldt, was communicated on 16 September to the four allies, and on the 18th they decided to settle the affairs of Poland, Italy, and Germany among themselves. But, the next day, they had to realize that the agreement between them was far from being made. They began with the thorniest of all these affairs, the division of the Duchy of Warsaw. Hardenberg claimed for his master a share of this duchy. Nesselrode replied that his master wanted everything. Metternich pointed out that the duchy had not been conquered by the Russian armies alone, that the Austrians had contributed to the conquest, that they did not dispute Russia's right to indemnify itself, although Alexander had declared that he would not make a conquest, but that he could not agree to abandon the provinces which had formed part of Austria: Cracow and Zamoisk were too close to Vienna for Austria to let the Russians settle there; the restoration of the name of Poland would, in itself, be a peril, and would constitute an infraction of the treaties.[24] Nesselrode replied that Cracow and Zamoisk were absolutely necessary for the defense of Russia. Hardenberg added that Thorn was no less committed to the defense of Prussia, that Prussia, in any case, could not consent to the restoration of Poland. Castlereagh said, on the contrary, that this restoration would be very well seen in the English parliament; but it was understood that it would be a total, independent Poland, not a Poland restricted and subordinated to Russia.

Under these conditions, it was more necessary than ever to

close the door to the French and, unable to deliberate on the substance, they discussed the forms. This was the subject of a conference held on the 22d at Metternich's. The text of the Treaty of Paris was taken up again. The first secret article was re-read: "The dispositions to be made of the territories will be settled in Congress on the bases decided upon by the powers allied among themselves." It was recognized that the terms agreed upon and agreed upon between them clearly expressed that it was not a question of conferences where France would sit; that, moreover, it was fitting that France should not attend the first discussion, for, if it attended,

> it will take sides for or against every issue, whether related to its own interests or not; it will favor or oppose such and such a prince according to particular views, and the petty princes of Germany will thereby be invited to start all over again all that trickery of intrigues and cabals which, in large part, has caused the misfortune of recent years. This is why it is of the utmost importance not to enter into conference with the French plenipotentiaries until this object has been settled.

But if one excluded France, then one had to exclude at the same time Spain, Portugal, and Sweden, which were also signatories to the Treaty of Paris. The protocol of the 18th was thus confirmed. Metternich, Hardenberg, Humboldt, and Nesselrode signed the deliberation; Castlereagh dared not adhere to it wholeheartedly, and his reservation prepared the way for the French: "I nevertheless consider that the arrangements thus put forward will be open to free and liberal discussion with the other two powers as friendly and not hostile parties." The other two were Spain and France, which Castlereagh dared not officially rule out. For the arrangements themselves, he was very anxious that unanimity be established, but, he said, "I cannot consent to be absolutely bound by a majority."

The four met again on the 23rd, to settle the terms of the communication which they would make to the French and the Spanish; for of Portugal and Sweden there was no longer any question. As a result, a protocol was signed in which it was said that the questions would be divided into two series: 1) those relating to "the great interests of Europe, including the relations of the powers among themselves, the fixing of limits and the disposition to make countries temporarily occupied and administered by the allied powers," that is to say, the affairs of Poland, Germany and Italy: the four allied courts would deliberate among themselves, and when they were in agreement, they would communicate their work to the representatives of France and Spain, and "invite them to make known their opinions and wishes"; 2) the preparation of the federative pact of Germany: the Courts of Austria, Prussia, Bavaria, Württemberg, and Hanover would be in charge of it. To this protocol was added a draft declaration stating that the signatory powers of the Treaty of Paris would direct the work of the congress, but would not decide any question without the concurrence of the powers which appeared to have the right to intervene therein.[25]

Such was the state of things when, on 23 September, Talleyrand arrived, accompanied by Dalberg, La Tour du Pin, Alexis de Noailles, for the official conferences, La Besnardière for the drafting of the reports, notes, and protocols, the Duchess of Dino for the charm of her life, the spirit of her letters, the enchantment and seduction of her receptions, the supreme art of making others speak and of throwing about, without seeming to touch them, disturbing or attractive insinuations: an auxiliary which was not useless with two partners as refined in female diplomacy as Alexander and Metternich.

All the States or pseudo-States which, since 1789, had been despoiled or despoilers, mediatized, secularized, or demanded the restitution of their property, or sought the confirmation of their titles. All old Imperial Germany, and even the Order of Malta, had sent representatives or agents. There were 216 heads of mission. The sovereigns arrived in their turn. The Emperor of Russia and the King of Prussia made their entry on 25 September. The Court of Vienna united all the former spectators of the theater of Erfurt and guests of the castle of Dresden, except the King of Saxony, who was in captivity in Berlin; Maria-Louisa, who was on retreat at Schoenbrunn, and Napoléon, who was interned on the island of Elba. The parties began and did not stop. They have remained legendary. The chronicle says that the cost amounted to 40 million. On 27 September 1814, Nesselrode wrote to Pozzo di Borgo, Alexander's ambassador to Paris:

> If Austria does not yield with good grace, I do not know where we will go. The support of England and France would only be of negative use to them. We have the Russian army and 500,000 men; there will therefore be nothing to employ against us but friendly representations if they fail, there will only be any more to do than to yield.

If they were celebrating, they were far from being at peace. A German diplomat, Gagern, reported that when he arrived on the 15th, he had already heard of the war on the 21st. "We only agreed against the French; this situation soon turned to their advantage," he added.

But at first they felt terribly isolated. Talleyrand expected it, and he needed all his self-assurance, all his dexterity to avoid stumbling in the first encounters, in those sorts of reconnaissances on which the success of his entire plan of conduct depended. Gagern said,

> He was hated. How many times, at parties given to welcome the Congress, have I seen him alone, neglected until the moment when I came to him, helping him out of embarrassment or out of bad humor. The English exchanged with me in this role. Even his hôtel was seldom visited. But that didn't last long, and that changed completely. His intelligence, his consistency, the principles he upheld, his friendliness when he was good enough to show it, triumphed over all obstacles.

He found the big ones haughty, but withdrawn he found the little ones suspicious. The former repeated that in Paris they had been too easy on money and borders. "I saw them," said Talleyrand, "very *blasé* about the pleasures that generosity gives." He knew he had nothing to expect from them. He turned to the others. Above all, he had to reassure them of France's intentions. The disinterestedness which he would declare everywhere was bound to find incredulous people. One would believe in it only on behavior; nevertheless, it was necessary to dispose people's minds, and Talleyrand did his best to do so. He recognized that the sensitive point was the silence that the four kept towards everyone, the claim of the four to do everything among themselves. There was a link between Talleyrand and everything that was not the four. He took advantage of it. He wrote,

> I didn't complain. I confined myself to making known all the discontent I felt to the ministers of the secondary courts who had common interests with me. Finding also in the old policy of their countries old memories of confidence in France, they soon looked on me as their support.

The fact is that among the signatories of the treaty of 30 May who arrogated to themselves the leadership of the Congress, Talleyrand was the only one who could and wanted to speak for them. Having an interest in believing him, they believed him. He said to Gagern,

> The will to peace is the only opportunity for strength for France. She must give good examples after so many bad ones. You have to be a good European, moderate. France asks for nothing, absolutely nothing, except what is expressed in the prologue to peace: a fair distribution of forces among the powers.

This is how, having guessed the game of the allies, he warned them precisely in this "merry-go-round" that they had tried to forbid him. Besides, he was informed. The Spanish plenipotentiary, Labrador, excluded like him from important affairs, was not the object of the same mistrust; Saint-Marsan penetrated everywhere: both informed Talleyrand of the plot formed against him. Finally, to Castlereagh's embarrassment, Talleyrand had no difficulty in discerning that this ambassador had entered into commitments which weighed heavily on him and for which he would be afraid, if necessary, to render an account to Parliament. Also, without wasting a day, on 28 September, detaching from his instructions one of the most studied pages, the best disposed to be distributed or published, he made a note of it in which he demonstrated that nothing would be fairer than to re-establish a independent Poland, but that nothing would be more dangerous than the establishment of a Russian Poland. On the same day, Alexander, dissatisfied with the Prussian ministers and their pretensions to the line of the Vistula, had a conference with Friedrich-Wilhelm III. Following this interview, Hardenberg, Nesselrode, Humboldt, and Stein signed a protocol stating that Saxony would be allotted entirely to the King of Prussia, on condition that it would retain in the States of this prince the name of Kingdom of Saxony.[26] It was the first chapter and the first condition of the attribution of the Duchy of Warsaw to Russia under the name of kingdom of Poland. The protocol, moreover, was to remain strictly secret until the day when the Tsar saw fit evacuate Saxony and hand over its administration to the King of Prussia.

However, the opening of the congress having been publicly announced for 2 October, it was not possible to postpone it any longer without giving explanations, and without the signatories of the treaty of 30 May having met to deliberate. Metternich summoned the six: Austria, Spain, France, Great Britain, Prussia, Russia, to his home on 30 September. This preparatory meeting was to decide the progress of the congress and, in particular, the role of France.

Talleyrand had to take a position there, and how he behaved would depend on his erasure or his influence. He played his character masterfully. Metternich communicated to him the protocol of 22 September. Talleyrand read it calmly; he noted there the term *allied powers* which came up several times. He said,

> Allies and against whom? It's not against Napoléon: he's on the island of Elba. It is certainly not against the King of France, he is the guarantor of the duration of this peace. Gentlemen, let's speak frankly: if there are still allied powers, I am too many here.

They replied that they did not want the term. Seeing that this first skirmish had impressed them somewhat, Talleyrand grew bolder and pushed a forehand:

> And yet, if I wasn't here, you would essentially miss me. I may be the only one who doesn't ask for anything. Great consideration, that is all I want for France. It is powerful enough by its resources, by its extent, by the number and the spirit of its inhabitants. I want nothing, I repeat it to you; and I bring you immensely. The presence of a minister of Louis XVIII consecrates here the principle on which the whole social order rests. The first need of Europe is to banish forever the opinion that one can acquire rights by conquest alone, and to revive the sacred principle of legitimacy from which flow order and stability...

Then, passing to the projected declaration, he asked when the conferences of the general congress would open, in which, according to the Treaty of Paris, the representatives of all the powers engaged in the war were to participate. If the signatory powers of this treaty were to assume the role of directors, they needed at least a mandate from the others, and this mandate could only be given by the congress. "There were measures which ministers without responsibility could easily adopt, but he and Lord Castlereagh were in a different case." Castlereagh confessed that "those thoughts came to mind." A general conversation ensued.

It was necessary that they talk about Murat. Talleyrand had prepared his attacks and Metternich was to experience all of their sharpness. It was an opportunity for revenge against this rival, whom he had known in Paris as such a slender courtier, so "scamp" at Court and State, and whom he found again in Vienna in this personage of "prime" minister of the coalition, so haughty, so remote from the day when he inquired about the health of the King of Rome and displayed his gallantries with Caroline Murat.[27] Talleyrand was well acquainted with his intrigues with this beautiful princess, mad about her crown, and whom Metternich abused with so much perfidy after having so insolently displayed her favors. He knew the machine set up to dump Murat. You have to remember these little adventures, these undersides, to taste all the salt of the scene that happened that day.

Someone pronounced the name of the King of Naples, and he heard dire Murat. Labrador expressed himself bluntly about this prince, and Talleyrand, now feeling at ease, dared to throw out this sentence: "Which king of Naples are we talking about? We do not know the man in question." The insolence on the part of Napoléon's former minister, creator of the kingdom and brother-in-law of the king, was unheard of. The man! he had plotted with him, in 1808, against Napoléon;[28] they had figured together in a number of processions, if only at the coronation of the Emperor. The silence that greeted this question proved that it was appropriate. Metternich, who had quite recently again made a pact with Murat, was forced to remain silent, for he dared not reveal his treaty. Neither the Russian nor the English had consented to recognize Murat. A single Prussian, Humboldt, who, moreover, was disinterested in the affair, pointed out that the powers had recognized him and guaranteed him his states. "Those who guaranteed it to him couldn't," said Talleyrand. Thereupon, they adjourned to prepare another draft declaration. In his diary, Frederic de Gentz, congress secretary, reported,

> The intervention of Talleyrand and Labrador furiously disturbed our plans. They protested against the form we have adopted. They scolded us for two hours. It's a scene I will never forget. Prince de Metternich does not see as I do what is embarrassing and even dreadful in our situation.[29]

Talleyrand had henceforth his admission to all the conferences, he had his role in Vienna, and from that day his isolation ceased. On October 1st, taking advantage of his opportunity, he wrote a note which he sent to his colleagues in Austria, Spain, England, Prussia, Russia. He maintained that the eight signatory powers of the Treaty of Paris were alone qualified to prepare the congress; that this congress should meet, were it only to verify credentials; then they could divide into committees. He went the same day to Alexander and found him very irritated at the intervention of the previous day. He might have been embarrassed in the presence of this prince, for whom he had, at Erfurt, and since, betrayed his then master, Napoléon; with whom he had once worked on the restoration of his new master, Louis XVIII; but this collaboration in such diverse affairs, so many common secrets that they now had a common interest to erase, on the contrary put him at ease. Alexander and Talleyrand spoke to each other as if they had only known each other the day before, in Paris, during the restoration of the monarchy in France, a prelude to the restoration of public law in Europe, which led to this singular dialogue:

> Let's talk about our business, said the Emperor. We have to finish them here. – It depends on Your Majesty. They will end quickly and happily if Your Majesty brings to them the same nobility and the same greatness of soul as in those of France. – But everyone has to find their convenience. – And everyone has their rights. – I will keep what I occupy. – Your Majesty will only want to keep what is rightfully yours. – I agree with the great powers. – I don't know if Your Majesty counts France among these powers. – Yes surely; but if you don't want everyone to find their convenience, what do you expect? – I put the law first, and the proprieties later. – The proprieties of Europe are the law. – This language, Sire, is not yours; it is foreign to you, and your heart disavows it. – No, I repeat, the proprieties of Europe are the law.

Then Talleyrand banged his head against the paneling, lamenting: "Europe, Europe, unhappy Europe!" And Alexander, waving his arms, exclaimed: "Rather war, than give up what I occupy!" Then he abruptly corrected himself: "It's time for the show," and he left. He was really angry; but Talleyrand had faced more formidable assaults, and he was not unduly troubled by them. He wrote to Louis XVIII: "Our position is difficult. It can become more so every day. Your Majesty's ministers might encounter such obstacles that they would have to give up all other hope than that of saving honor. But they are not yours."

On 3 October there was a meeting at Metternich's, and this minister asked Talleyrand to withdraw his note. Talleyrand refused. Metternich again insinuated that everything should be settled at four. Talleyrand replied:

> If you take the question from this side, I'm quite your man; I'm ready, I don't ask for more. – How do you understand it? – In a very simple way. I will not take part in your conferences, I will only be a member of the congress here, and I will wait for it to open.

The allies' plan could only succeed through secrecy. Talleyrand threatened to reveal it with scandal, and if we let him do so, he would transform himself from agent of defeated France into advocate of a Europe played or exploited by those who had undertaken to give it order and peace. Decidedly, however dangerous it was to admit him to the conferences, it was better to have him inside than outside. Anything suited the allies better than declaring their intentions. Talleyrand was therefore retained; but at each step he raised his voice. He drew up a new note, according to his instructions, stating that there would be a congress and that this congress would really be open; he discussed it with Castlereagh and found that this Englishman agreed with him in form and, in part, in substance.[30]

But before resigning himself to releasing the Chaumont alliance, to confide in France, much more, to ask her assistance, Castlereagh and Metternich exhausted all the means of convincing their allies and of compromising with them. Castlereagh composed, on 4 October, a memo in which he was clearly inspired by the note that Talleyrand had given him on 28 September. He concluded with the *status quo ante* in Poland. Could they suppose, he said, that Austria and Prussia entered into the alliance, treated at Kalisch and Reichenbach "for the sole aggrandizement of Russia, and that by destroying their own frontiers and thus leaving their capitals exposed and defenseless?" To make Poland a free nation, an independent state, would be a just work; but one could not, by giving it to Russia, make it "a formidable military instrument"; therefore, "as long as His Imperial Majesty holds to this unfortunate project, it is impossible that any plan of arrangement for the reconstitution of Europe can be proposed or that this present congress can be assembled..."

However, with great effort of innuendos, misunderstandings, and chancery equivocations, Gentz had drafted a declaration suspending the opening of the congress until "the questions had reached a sufficient degree of maturity so that the result answered to the stipulations of the Treaty of Paris and to the fair expectation of contemporaries." The congress would thus be adjourned until 1 November. The six were summoned on 8 October to Metternich to deliberate. Talleyrand, invited to go there a little before the time of the conference, found Metternich eager to make him speak, to lead him above all to some compromising imprudence, to ask something, to at least accept the conversation on some subject of special interest to his master. There never was but one, and it was illusory, the Naples affair. It was known that the King had some passion for dethroning Murat to restore his cousin Ferdinand. But it was to misunderstand the character of Louis XVIII, his policy and his patience, to believe him capable of sacrificing his principle at a point where, precisely, this principle was to triumph by itself. Forced to renounce the Legations, Metternich would abandon Murat and seek to get rid of him. Now, the reinstatement of the Pope in the Legations was a question related to that of the reinstatement of the King of Saxony, and the direct application of the principle of legitimacy as understood by Louis XVIII. By defending the rights of the King of Saxony, he was defending those of the Pope, and the Pope restored to his States, Murat would be no more than an embarrassment and a danger to Austria, as was already the case. Prince Metternich no longer dreamed of stripping the Holy See of Legations; no one encouraged him to do so. From then on Murat was sacrificed, and all of Metternich's game was to lure this unfortunate king into some trap into which he would let himself fall blindly. Talleyrand was informed of these arrangements by Saint-Marsan and by the other Italians. He would therefore be careful not to accept as a service rendered to his King an act to which Metternich would be constrained by his own interest.

Metternich noticed this from the first insinuations he made of it that day to Talleyrand. The latter showed himself disposed to come to an understanding with Austria on important matters; but, he said, they were moving away from him, they were surrounding themselves with mystery!

> As for me, I don't do it, and I don't need it. That's the advantage of those who only negotiate with principles. Here are paper and pens. Do you want to write that France asks for nothing, and would not even accept anything? I am ready to sign. – But you have the Naples affair, which is properly yours. – No more mine than anyone else's. It's just a matter of principles for me.

And, becoming animated, he declared what he meant by these "matters of principles": the Bourbon King in Naples, the King of Saxony in Dresden, no Prussians in Saxony, no Prussians in Luxemburg, nor in Mainz; no Russians in Warsaw. These "principles" accorded with the "interests" of Austria. Talleyrand knew this well, and he was not surprised to hear Metternich answer him:

> We are much closer than you think. I promise you that Prussia will have neither Luxembourg nor Mainz. We do not want Russia to grow beyond measure any more than you do, and as for Saxony, we will do what we can to preserve at least a part of it.

Whereupon they moved on to the conference. Talleyrand accepted Gentz's project and the preparatory conferences to be held before the opening of the congress, because he was sure of being admitted to them, and because they gave up settling everything in advance among the four. But he asked that to the sentence stating that the opening of the congress would take place on 1 November should be added these words: "It will be done in accordance with the principles of public law." This proposal raised a storm. The Prussians especially flew into vehement indignation. Hardenberg, very deaf, stood up, banging on the table, threatening, uttering broken words: "No, sir! public law? it's useless...it goes without saying. – If that goes without saying," replied Talleyrand, "it will go even better by saying it." Humboldt also cried, "What is public law doing here?" "It made you," replied Talleyrand, who remembered how, at Tilsit, Prussia had almost disappeared from the map of Europe. Castlereagh took him aside and asked him if, once satisfied on this article, he would show himself easier. Talleyrand asked him, in his turn, how by showing himself easy he could have hope from England in the Naples affair. Castlereagh promised to support it with all his influence: "I will speak to Metternich about it; I have the right to have an opinion on this matter. – Will you give me your word? – I give it to you." After two hours of debate, they ended up adopting the sentence, which was placed a few lines higher: "So that the result meets the principles of public law, the stipulations of the Treaty of Paris, etc."

Talleyrand had come a long way. He had recognized the weak point of the allies; nevertheless he was not blinded to the difficulty he had in making himself believed, he, Talleyrand, speaking of law, of disinterestedness; on the impossibility of making the most just principles prevail if some force did not support them. This is why he wrote to the King on 13 October: "Those who know that we are contrary to their pretensions think that we have only reasons to oppose them." Alexander said a few days ago: "Talleyrand seems to be the minister of Louis XIV." Humboldt, seeking to seduce at the same time as to intimidate Schulenburg, Minister of Saxony, said to him:

> there is nothing behind to support them. Woe to those who would believe it! The way to get rid of all these talks and put an end to all these irresolutions would be for Your Majesty, in a declaration which you would address to your peoples, after having made known the principles which you have ordered us to follow and your firm resolution to never to deviate from it, only to let it be seen that the just cause would not remain without support.

In the meantime, Talleyrand undertook the representatives of the small states, and said to Gagern:

> Unreason stirs, everything was done with extreme disregard. We are not prepared on any question. We forget that we are no longer in Chaumont. We want nothing, absolutely nothing, not a village; but we want what is right. And if we refuse, I will go as far as retirement, protest. Personally, I don't want Belgium... Do you know where my Belgium is? She's in the freedom of the rivers, that's all I want.

## V. The Question of Saxony and Poland

The declaration, adopted on the 8th, was brought to the attention of the plenipotentiaries on the 13th. And, in the midst of banquets, parties, opera, and comedy galas, the work of notes, counter-notes, memoranda, confidences, and cabals began again. Nothing was possible as long as the question of Poland and that of Saxony were not resolved, and it was through underground approaches, mines, and counter-mines that they fought around this labyrinth. This work only resulted in opening wider the breach in the coalition. Castlereagh and Metternich campaigned together over Poland; but Metternich, not daring to put himself forward, pressed Castlereagh. On the other hand, the Prussians, sure of Russia in the affair of Saxony, as the Tsar had undertaken, on 28 September, to hand over this kingdom to them, now sought to get rid of the counterpart, the attribution to Russia of the Duchy of Warsaw, especially the country of Posen. They attempted a secret opening on the side of the Austrians and the English. They recognized the danger of establishing the Russians in Poland, so they insinuate that if they were given Saxony, they would be disposed to unite with Austria to contain Russia.[31] Castlereagh and Metternich were too shrewd to fall into the trap. Suspecting some secret agreement between Prussia and Russia, Castlereagh replied to Hardenberg on 11 October that he would be prepared to cede Saxony to Prussia on condition that Prussia should not receive it in compensation for acquisitions which the Russians would do in Poland. At the same time, Castlereagh requested an audience with the Tsar.

Alexander took the lead and went to Castlereagh. The conversation was followed by a letter and a long memo which Castlereagh addressed to Alexander on 12 October, developing his memo of the 4th. He added:

> The plenipotentiaries of Great Britain, France, and Spain, and probably those of the other States of Europe, large and small, have the same view of this project. In what unfortunate situation will Europe be if Your Imperial Majesty does not want to give up your project and is determined to take possession of the Duchy of Warsaw against general opinion!

The French plenipotentiaries wrote: "It places the question as we conceive it. It demonstrates that the situation in Europe demands either the re-establishment of the old Poland or that this source of troubles and pretensions be forever removed from discussions in Europe." Castlereagh had confided to the French his notes and his interview with the Tsar. Metternich gave them a try. Said a confidant of Metternich to Dalberg: "You seem to us like dogs that bark very skillfully, but do not bite. We don't want to bite alone." He added that if he was more sure of the firmness of France, he would be more energetic; Russia would yield and Prussia would have to comply. Bavaria, so interested in the defense of the rights of the secondary states, and consequently in the re-establishment of Saxony, was also tested. Metternich asked Marshal de Wrede if Bavaria would be disposed to join forces with France and Austria.

Talleyrand wrote letter after letter to Paris, demanding new instructions, especially a military demonstration. Bavaria was arming;

the petty German sovereigns, worried about the intentions of the Prussians to dominate the future confederation, Württemberg and Hanover in particular, declared that they would consent to nothing in Germany until the question of Saxony was resolved. On this question, Castlereagh was still stubborn, out of the resentment of a coalition against a German king loyal to Napoléon, out of complacency also towards his Prussian colleagues with whom he had been waging war since 1813. He hoped that by drawing up and publishing large notes of principles on Poland, he would apologize, in the eyes of his Parliament, for this concession. Talleyrand, knowing his embarrassment, pressed him with arguments, showed him to what extent the two questions were linked. Castlereagh persisted in believing that by satisfying the Prussians, he would detach them from Russia, and thus settle the Polish affair without the aid of France. Talleyrand said in his letter to the King, of 31 October,"In his way of estimating our forces, we can judge that it is France that he fears the most." – "You have," he said, "twenty-six million men; we estimate them at forty million." Once, it escaped him to say: "Ah if you had not had any view left on the left bank of the Rhine!"

Alexander grew impatient. His ambassador in Paris, Pozzo, summoned to Vienna, brought the impression that France was not in a position to act; the army was unsure, barely reorganized, insufficient. So, all of Talleyrand's words and writings were nothing but merry-go-rounds and bluster! Alexander engaged the King of Prussia to execute the secret convention of 28 September, and to occupy Saxony. Then he sounded out Talleyrand, who, on this matter, showed himself intractable. So he summoned him to his house, hoping to subdue him, confuse him or seduce him; however, he preferred the first method, which was more flattering for his self-esteem and more convenient for his policy. The interview took place on October 22. It began with an apostrophe *à la* Napoléon.

> In Paris, you were of the opinion of a kingdom of Poland. How come you changed? – My opinion, Sire, is still the same. In Paris, it was a question of the re-establishment of all Poland. I wanted then, as I would now, its independence. But now it is something quite different. The question is subordinated to a fixing of limits which puts Austria and Prussia in safety. – They shouldn't be worried. Besides, I have 200,000 men in the Duchy of Warsaw; chase me away! I gave Saxony to Prussia, Austria consents. – I do not know whether

Austria consents to this. I would hardly believe it, as it is against their interest. But can the consent of Austria make Prussia owner of what belongs to the King of Saxony? – If the King of Saxony does not abdicate, he will be taken to Russia, he will die there. Another king has already died there.

Then after this significant allusion to the partitions of Poland and to the end of Stanislas Poniatowski, he resumed: "I thought that France owed me something. You always talk about principles. Your public law is nothing to me; I don't know what it is. What do you think I think of all your scrolls and treatises?" Now was the time to move on to seduction and if he had any means of temptation in reserve, to produce it. But he did not, he never had the intention of gaining France by land cessions, he only thought of taking it, gratuitously, on his own bait, and because it was nourished by principles, of satisfying it on this article outside of Germany. He said, "The King of Prussia will be King of Prussia and Saxony, as I will be Emperor of Russia and King of Poland. The complacency that France will have for me on these two points will be the measure of that which I will have for her on everything that may interest her." This phrase applied only to the Naples affair. Talleyrand was not the man to give up a very skillfully chosen position for an illusory concession.

He emerged more convinced than ever of the impossibility of separating Prussia from Russia, or rather of detaching the King of Prussia from Alexander. Metternich and Castlereagh experienced this at this very time. In imitation of his colleague from England, Metternich addressed a note to Hardenberg on 22 October: he declared in it that he consented to the provisional occupation of Saxony by Prussia, on condition that Prussia would join forces with Austria and England to oppose Russian projects in Poland. Metternich and Castlereagh had been able, unless they were the dupes, to negotiate with Hardenberg some underhand transaction against Russia; the King of Prussia must not have known of it; any desire for dissimulation towards the friend of his youth, twice savior of his monarchy, to whom, on the battlefields, he had sworn, before God, faith and eternal alliance, was repugnant to his soul, like a felony. Hardenberg was obliged to submit Metternich's note to him. Without knowing that this note was a response to an insinuation from his own ministers, Friedrich-Wilhelm III, indignant, took it to the Tsar, who was was about to leave for an excursion to Hungary. He summoned Metternich and had with him, wrote Talleyrand, "a conversation in which it is taken for granted that he treated this minister with a haughtiness and a violence of language which might have seemed extraordinary, even with regard to his servants." To crown his disgrace, Metternich, dismissed in this way by the all-powerful Tsar, for having tried to save Saxony, saw himself accused by the Germans of surrendering this kingdom out of complacency towards Russia. He had a moment of confusion and spoke of withdrawing. As for Castlereagh, the Tsar sent him a letter on October 30th, accompanied by a memorandum drawn up by Czartoryski; there he discussed, point by point, the English memo.

At the end of October everyone was alarmed, demanding the opening of the congress. Would so many efforts end in a solemn disappointment, in the bankruptcy of victorious Europe, and would the war be resumed for the division of Napoléon's spoils? to prevaricate, to expedients of procedure. On 30 October the eight signatory powers of the Treaty of Paris met at Metternich's: Portugal and Sweden had taken back the places to which they were entitled, and it was, with Spain, a reserve corps ready to support Talleyrand. Metternich warned that serious questions were still pending, but that nothing stood in the way of the verification of the credentials of the plenipotentiaries of the States which had deputed to the Congress. A commission drawn by lot, and formed of the representatives of England, Prussia, and Russia, was charged with the verification of credentials. A discussion ensued on the distribution of work between committees, which would be led by a delegation of eight; these, as intervening powers, would serve as intermediaries between the powers interested in each affair. It was not possible, in fact, to call the congress into a plenary assembly and transform it into a diplomatic parliament. But to propose to distribute the work was to raise the preliminary question of the admission of the envoys of the King of Saxony and those of Murat. The process continued to drag from protocol to protocol. However, for less contentious matters, committees were gradually formed. There was one for German affairs, in which figured Austria, Prussia, Bavaria, Hanover, and Württemberg; he had already been working since 14 October. Another was formed on the 14th of November, for the affairs of Switzerland, in which figured Austria, Prussia, England, and Russia.

Meanwhile, Talleyrand received from Paris the declarations and instructions he had requested from the King. It was first a note, published in the *Moniteur* on 22 October: France was not jealous of anyone, it only aspired to the re-establishment of a fair balance. It was not looking for anything

> beyond its limits; it does not listen to any insinuation tending to establish systems of simple convenience; and, resuming the role which once assured it the esteem and recognition of the people it wants to become once again the support of the weak and the defender of the oppressed.

Then a letter from the King, dated 27 October, which approved Talleyrand's declarations. Other letters informed Talleyrand that the King had conferred with Wellington, the English ambassador in Paris, that they had come to complete agreement; that Wellington had written of it to London, that Castlereagh was about to receive the order to defend Saxony. Consequently, by additional instructions, dated 25 October, Louis XVIII authorized his ambassador to act in concert with Austria and Bavaria, to open up to them, if necessary, to Castlereagh, and to declare that these Courts "could count, on the part of the king, on the most active military co-operation, to oppose the designs of Russia and Prussia, both on Poland and on Saxony."

Feeling supported, Talleyrand took the offensive and launched a reasoned memo on Saxony, dated 2 November and intended to stir public opinion in Germany and England: in Germany, by the scandal of a dethroned king, by the danger of example, by the peril of the increase of Prussia; in England, by this argument which the history of the century had confirmed:

> One alleged pretext in favor of the union of Saxony with Prussia is that it is desired to make the latter a barrier against Russia. But the sovereigns of the two countries are united by bonds which mean that as long as they both live, one will have nothing to fear from the other; this precaution could therefore only look to a very distant future, but what would those who so warmly support the project of reunion say if, witnesses of this future, they saw Prussia relying on Russia to obtain an extension in Germany? that they would have facilitated, and in turn support Russia in undertakings against the Ottoman Empire? Not only is the thing possible, it is also probable, because it is in the natural order.

The fact is that it happened and Europe was shocked by it. The intimacy of sovereigns passed from fathers to children, continued between Nicolas, brother of Alexander, son-in-law of Friedrich-Wilhelm III, Friedrich-Wilhelm IV, and Wilhelm I, son of this king, brothers-in-law of Nicolas, Alexander II their nephew. It led Prussia to realize, even to exceed, its dreams of 1814: Prussia increased by a third, brought into the Empire of Germany; France dismembered from Alsace and Lorraine, 1866-1871. The alliance did not come to an end until, in 1878, Russia having won its share in the East, Prussia thought fit to break the pact and, having received in excess, having nothing more to receive, to oblige Russia to return.

## IV. Treaty of 3 January 1815

Everyone was talking about war, and Talleyrand, far from stifling the rumor, spread it. They were no longer trying to create a vacuum around it. Alexander then struck the blow which, he believed, would put an end to the maneuvers of his adversaries. On November 8th, Repnin, who commanded the Russian occupation corps in Saxony, bade farewell to the Saxons and announced to them that they were going to pass under the supreme administration of Prussia, "in consequence of an arrangement agreed between Russia and Prussia, and to which Austria and England adhered." On 10 November the Prussian generals took possession. The news was still ignored in Vienna, when on Saturday, 12 November, Alexander sent for Talleyrand again. The fact was accomplished, but it was a question of the congress ratifying it, and it was not indifferent to the Tsar that France should give its consent. It was, with a more softened tone, with more consideration, the repetition of the preceding interview. Alexander endeavored to reduce the question of Saxony to a family affair (Louis XVIII's mother was Saxon) and to insinuate that the Bourbons, as a family, had a more direct interest elsewhere. He had previously only hinted at it; this time he found himself:

> I hope that these cases will lead to a rapprochement between France and Russia. What are the king's intentions in this regard? – The King will never forget the services your Majesty has rendered him... – Listen, let's make a deal: be kind to me in the question of Saxony, I will be kind to you in that of Naples. I have no commitment on this side. – Your Majesty knows very well that such a bargain is not feasible. There is no parity between the two questions. It is impossible that Your Majesty does not want, in relation to Naples, what we ourselves want. –

> Well then, persuade the Prussians to give me back my word! – Your Majesty has all power over the mind of the king; moreover, he can satisfy him. – And how? – By leaving them something more in Poland! – Singular expedient that you propose to me; you want me to take it upon myself to give it to them.

Talleyrand's impression was that the Tsar was basically weakening, and that if a way was found to satisfy the Prussians, without forcing him to sacrifice too many of his pretensions, he would compromise in the face of the fear of a general war. Coming out of the audience, Talleyrand learned of the taking possession of Saxony by the Prussians and the strange way in which Metternich and Castlereagh had been played by Hardenberg. This minister, taking their conditional propositions for an unconditional consent, had transformed into a definitive authorization to occupy Saxony the offer to give this authorization if Prussia should unite against Russia, and he had proclaimed this consent in official form. Talleyrand found them, Castlereagh especially, very irritated: the part of dupe being not one which an English minister had the good grace to play before Parliament. But he made no secret of the fact that only in cases of absolute military necessity would the English resign themselves to breaking the pact of Chaumont. Alexander, on his side, turned to attentions and dispatched Czartoryski to Talleyrand; but the emissary, like the Tsar, limited himself to vague words and, on this chapter, Talleyrand could never write anything more precise than these words, on 20 November: "The Emperor Alexander testifies the intention to approach us." Louis XVIII, moreover, would not have wanted to go any further.[32] He wrote to Talleyrand on 26 November:

> For the first time, I see ideas of justice floating around. The Emperor of Russia has taken a retrograde step, and in politics, as in everything else, the first was never the last. This prince would be mistaken, however, if he thought I was committing myself to a (political) alliance with him. As you know, my system is a general alliance, no particular ones; these are a source of war, the other is a guarantor of peace.

It was with a view to peace and to force it, so to speak, that Louis XVIII armed and authorized Talleyrand to form a league with Austria, Bavaria and, if need be, the English.

The declaration of Repnin and the Prussian generals in Saxony, confirming all fears, unleashed general anger in Vienna. It was, cried the Germans, a usurpation more odious than all those of Napoléon. Castlereagh and Metternich were assailed with questions they could not answer, and with reproaches which they were powerless to justify. To crown the agitation, a proclamation was received from Warsaw from the Grand Duke Constantine to the Poles, inviting them to unite under the old flag of Poland, to defend their threatened rights. One heard everywhere only recriminations. Schwarzenberg said very loudly that if he had suspected these designs of the Russians, he would not have retired before them, he would not have signed the armistice of 30 January 1813. These discords, this impotence of Europe, would affect the exile on the island of Elba, and what a dramatic change would occur in the world if Napoléon suddenly reappeared on the scene. Between the English and the Austrians, the forces were calculated: Austria and Germany could field 350,000 men; Russia and Prussia had about as many. To tip the scales, a supplement was needed. Talleyrand repeated that the king had 130,000 men on foot, and one was forced to admit that this addition would be decisive. Alexander complained about the Bourbons, and dropped phrases like these: "If they force me, the monster will be released on them."

But, the bad humor poured out, each, in his heart of hearts, recognizing that war would be a disastrous bankruptcy, a political and social peril for each monarchy, and each continued to threaten the others only out of countenance, to force them to yield before a combination of forces that, on paper, would make the struggle too unequal, and justify accommodation. The Prussian soldiers alone arrogantly, and perhaps with sincerity, expended courage, but their diplomats, wiser, while showing themselves intractable on their pretensions, began to discuss the means of execution. Willingly or unwillingly, they had to come to terms with it. Notes were exchanged during the second part of December, one, among others, on the 19th, from Talleyrand to Metternich, intended for the public: there he recalled, in very fine form, his declarations of disinterestedness; he announced this important concession that, the King of Saxony being restored to the integrity of his rights, the King of France would be the first to engage him to use these very rights to abandon to Prussia such portions of his territories as seemed necessary for the restoration of Prussia, by means of equivalents, to its territorial state prior to 1806.

The Prussians argued tenaciously: they had been promised, they said, not only restoration, but districting; one could, moreover, transport the King of Saxony, and they indicated a part of the vacant territories on the left bank of the Rhine, with Bonn as its capital, the Moselle as its limit. They would take for themselves the contact, the outpost, the vanguard, the point on the French frontier, not that they wanted to, but because they thought that the allies and, especially the English, would not yield on this article.[33] Alexander, seeing that he would not succeed in having the entire Duchy of Warsaw granted to him, and that he would have to renounce demanding from Austria the cession of Gallicia, constantly opposed by the Russians themselves in his Polish design, began to get discouraged. A combination whom the best of his advisers blamed, who was unpopular in his empire, of which the Poles showed themselves by no means enthusiastic, was it worth the peril of restarting the war, of breaking the alliance of Chaumont?

He admitted that the King of Saxony should be restored, that this prince should cede a part of his States to Prussia, that Prussia should recover, in Poland, the country of Posen and should only renounce, subject to compensation to be taken both in Saxony and in Germany, on its part of the dismemberment of 1795, that is to say in Warsaw. Austria and England showed themselves disposed to enter into an arrangement on this principle, and they began to discuss the number of inhabitants, the extent of territory, the lines of frontiers. As the Prussians disputed the assessments, Castlereagh imagined setting up a statistical commission. Only the four were to be part of it. He thought it useful, however, to inform Talleyrand of this. The latter took care not to object to it; he consented as if he were consulted and as if, by obvious right, a Frenchman had to sit on the commission. Then he added that it would be better first to agree, to three, England, France, Austria, that the rights of the King of Saxony should be recognized. Castlereagh retired very perplexed: he had not dared to tell Talleyrand that the French were excluded from the commission. He referred to the four. The Prussians would not hear of Talleyrand. Neither Metternich nor Castlereagh had the courage to admit that they had entered into confidence with the French ambassador, and Charles Stewart was charged with the unpleasant mission of announcing to Talleyrand his exclusion. It was, after three months, to risk repeating the scene of 30 September.

Talleyrand did not believe that the admission of the French plenipotentiary could be in doubt. "We oppose it," Stewart told him. – Who opposes it? – He is not my brother (Castlereagh). – And who?"

He replied hesitantly: "But they are..." And he ended up stammering out the word allies. At this word, Talleyrand lost patience; it showed the conduct that Europe expected of an English ambassador; he said that Castlereagh had deviated from it since the beginning of the negotiations; that this conduct would not go unnoticed; that it would be tried in England, and that Castlereagh would suffer the consequences; he complained about the complacency of the two Englishmen for Prussia, and ended by declaring "that if they still wanted to be Chaumont's men and still form part of the coalition, France should withdraw from the congress"; that he would not remain a day in Vienna if a plenipotentiary of the King were not called to the commission. Stewart reported this ultimatum to the four, and, despite the Prussians, the Frenchman was invited.

It was 23 December. That evening, Talleyrand and Metternich agreed on the order and the nature of the work. Talleyrand proposed that the valuations should be made according to the population, and that the population should not be valued "under the simple relation of the quota, but also under that of the species or of the quality." He said, "Because a Polish peasant without capital, without land, without industry should not be put on the same line as an inhabitant of the left bank of the Rhine or of the most fertile or richest regions of Germany. Metternich agreed, put down on paper, in the form of instructions, these proposals of high political anthropology, and the commission met on 24 December. Dalberg represented France.

It sat on 24, 25, and 28 December. But somehow it only had to unravel the matter. The distribution of men and lands was being prepared on the side, and this again the allies tried to settle by four, in great secrecy, in conferences which were held on 29 and 30 December. On the 29th, Hardenberg proposed to transport the King of Saxony to the left bank of the Rhine, where he would no longer have Bonn, but part of the old archbishopric of Trier and Luxembourg. He claimed all of Saxony for his king. On the 30th, Rasoumowsky developed, in the name of the Tsar, an overall project: Prussia would recover Posen and take the whole of Saxony; the King of Saxony would be transported to the Rhine, he would have Trier, Bonn, and Luxembourg; Alexander would take the rest of the Duchy of Warsaw, as a State united with Russia, to which he would reserve the right to give an independent constitution and, on the side of Russia, such extension of limits as he thought fit. They adjourned 2 January 1815.

On 1 January, Castlereagh received news which singularly

changed the face of things. Peace was made between England and the United States; England henceforth had all means at its disposal, and the Prince Regent found himself in complete agreement with the King of France on German affairs. With more freedom, Castlereagh showed more energy. Let us add that the jealousy and fear of France also found their account there. The idea of carrying the King of Saxony across the Rhine worried the English. Liverpool wrote, "The King of Saxony, on this hypothesis, would probably be the creature of France, and therefore disposed to support the views of the French government on the Low Countries, rather than to resist them." The pretensions of the Prussians therefore appeared inadmissible to the English, and the Prussians themselves impertinent. As for the Russians, Castlereagh's opinion was made up. He opened up to Talleyrand on 2 January, "The Russians want to impose the law on us; England is not made to receive it from anyone." Talleyrand went from there to push the insinuation of a three-way agreement. Castlereagh became animated to the point of offering to write down his thoughts on this agreement. He brought them the next day, 3 January. They were submitted to Metternich, and in the evening a secret treaty was signed between France, Austria, and England.

The three powers engaged to act in concert, "with the most perfect disinterestedness," to carry out the Treaty of Paris; if they could not succeed by peaceful means, they would set up, to defend whichever of them was attacked, each a corps of 150,000 men. Bavaria, Holland, Hanover, and Sardinia would be called upon to accede to this agreement.

It was the triumph of Talleyrand who wrote to the King:

> The coalition is dissolved. France is no longer isolated in Europe. Your Majesty marches in concert with two of the greatest powers, three States of the second order, and soon all the States which follow other principles and other maxims than revolutionary principles and maxims. She will truly be the head and soul of this union, formed to defend the principles she was the first to proclaim.

It was a policy. Several of those who most strongly criticized it at the time of the Restoration, or later most strongly reproached Louis XVIII and Talleyrand for it, did not fail to praise its conception, as conforming to the traditional policy of France, to do honor to the Government of July and to deplore, as a defection to the interests of France, the abandonment of it under the Second Empire.[34] This was the rationale.

The treaty produced its effects immediately. The concerted language of Austria, England, and France demonstrated their agreement, and they did not need to threaten to convince. The Prussians still resisted; they absolutely wanted Leipzig, insisting on establishing themselves in the heart of old Germany. They argued about the figures and the limits; but by 5 January Castlereagh was able to write that all danger of war had disappeared. He was called back to London when Parliament returned, and he was anxious to bring about general peace, at least in these essential articles. Alexander, from the moment that he had entered into composition and that it was no longer a question of simple quarrels over limits, was in a hurry to get it over with.[35]

Apart from the details of execution, the following principles were fixed during February: the King of Saxony, restored to his hereditary throne, renounced the Duchy of Warsaw, and ceded part of his kingdom to Prussia; Austria takes over the districts of eastern Gallicia ceded to the Duchy of Warsaw in 1809; it renounces Western Gallicia, which it had possessed from 1795 to 1809. Prussia renounces to take back the parts of Poland which had, in 1807, served to constitute the Duchy of Warsaw, except the territories which, under the name of Grand Duchy of Posen, will serve to re-establish communications between old Prussia and Silesia. It completes its reconstruction with Swedish Pomerania, part of Saxony, territories on the right bank of the Rhine, remnants of the kingdom of Westphalia, and, under the name of Rhine Province, Cologne, Bonn and Trier, on the left bank of the Rhine.[36] Prussia and Austria recognize a new kingdom of Poland, of which the Tsar will be king and which will enjoy a distinct administration. Krakow will form a neutral free city. These arrangements were the subject of separate treaties between Austria and Russia; Russia and Prussia; Prussia, Austria and Russia; Saxony and Prussia.[37]

These arrangements were far from satisfying the Prussians. Instead of making Prussia, as they wanted, the most coherent and German of the powers of Germany, giving it Leipzig and Dresden, it was left in the air, cut off in two disparate pieces, separated by rival states, suspicious, probably hostile, in case of war, Hanover for example; finally, it was exposed in point on the side of France, the first to receive the blows, without having time to hasten, and threatened above all with suffering conquest on the day when the map could be reorganized for the benefit of France. Instead of Lutheran Saxony and, although strongly anti-Prussian, assimilated over time, thanks to the community of morals and interests, the Prussians were given Catholic Rhinelanders, more imaginative, more mobile, who had dabbled in French administration, who held to the Civil Code, in which France had left great and vivid memories. These Rhinelanders were all the more inclined towards France as the new government, preserving the Civil Code, guaranteeing the purchasers of national property, favored the Catholic Church and practiced the policy of peace. It thus offered them the advantages which, since the Consulate, had won them over to France, and it freed them from the charges which detached them from it at the end of the Empire.

It was a side of things that was not considered in France. They only wanted to see a hostile and aggressive Prussia, placed there, in the vanguard of the coalition, by the English, to watch over Germany and the Low Countries. Talleyrand has been much reproached for not having supported the proposal which would have taken the King of Saxony to the Rhine. But besides the abandonment of the principle which was all the strength and all the policy of Louis XVIII, besides the inconvenience of concentrating Prussia in Germany, we forget that by establishing the King of Saxony on the Rhine, France would have had to give up, forever, to any claim on these territories. It would have found itself with this prince, its client, in the position in which it had found itself with Bavaria. It could not at the same time practice, in Germany, the policy of protecting the secondary States, and retain, on the Rhine, the ulterior motive of despoiling these same props. Finally, the King of Saxony, a Catholic, would have met with as many facilities in the assimilation of the Rhinelanders as Prussia met with obstacles. France threatened Prussia infinitely more in these countries than Prussia threatened France there. Talleyrand noted,

> Nothing, when pressed on this article, would be more simple, more natural than to take back from Prussia those of the provinces which had been ceded to her, whereas if they had been given to the King of Saxony in compensation for his former States, it would be difficult and far too hard to strip him of it.

## VII. Fall of Murat

"The Naples case will now be pursued with heat," wrote Pozzo.[38] It was unraveled by the force of circumstances, by the very character of the prince [Murat] who had received this kingdom from the hands of Napoléon and who claimed to survive the Empire whose convenience had been its sole *raison d'être* in Europe. Talleyrand wrote on 28 December 1814, "Your Majesty has seen by the documents I sent him that I do not lose sight of the Naples affair. I don't forget the *Delenda Carthago* either, but that's not where you can start." Talleyrand had rightly foreseen that, the French expelled from Italy, the work of restoration being accomplished everywhere, Austria would have an interest in suppressing a center of revolution as Naples would be under Murat, and in substituting this ally, always doubtful, for a Bourbon, who would always be docile and only ask to be protected. But, in this false betrayal, Metternich felt some embarrassment in front of Talleyrand. He would have exposed himself too much to his colleague's irony by confessing his secret. Failing to have been able to sell Murat to the ambassador of Louis XVIII, he tried to earn the merit of abandoning his second-hand ally from this king. It was the object of a negotiation, rather obscure, in Paris, for the King, between Louis-Philippe Bombelles, envoy of Metternich; Pierre-Jean-Louis Blacas, confidant of Louis XVIII, and Wellington, who pursued Napoléon's last lieutenant in Murat and wished to win for England, with the Bourbons of Naples, a naval station in the Mediterranean. Wellington arrived at Vienna on 3 February, to replace Castlereagh, who left on the 14th. He declared that France would, if need be, be in a position to compel Murat to leave Naples, and to restore Ferdinand there; that England would support France in this affair, on condition that France would second them on the question of the slave trade. Whereupon Talleyrand went on to publish that France, supported by Spain, would undertake the operation alone, if Austria had any reluctance to interfere. Austria, by the treaty of January 1814, had undertaken to defend Murat. Murat demanded the execution of this promise and demanded passage for the troops he intended to march to meet those of Louis XVIII.[39] Metternich also wanted to withdraw from this engagement and drive the French away from Italy. He formally declared to Talleyrand that Austria would consider the entry of the French into Italy as a case of war;[40] but, the next day, he declared to Campo-

Chiaro, Murat's envoy, that this guarantee should be sufficient for him; that Murat's armaments had, consequently, no *raison d'être*; that they were agitating Italy uselessly, and that any movement of the Neapolitan army beyond the frontiers of the kingdom would be considered as a rupture of the alliance and an attack on Austria. This master in cunning reckoned that, France not disarming, Murat would march all the same and, by this whim, would untie Austria and bring it to restore Ferdinand itself. Circumstances served this purpose even better than Metternich could have foreseen.[41]

The Austrian alliance weighed heavily on Murat. Convinced that he would draw from it no shred of the States of the Pope, and that, in Italy reconstituted in Vienna, his reign would be nonsense, the same motives which had led him to betray Napoléon led him to break his pact with Austria. He dreamed to raise Italy against the Austrians, to make himself the national sovereign there, the liberator; then, being informed that Napoléon was thinking of leaving the island of Elba, fearing that the Emperor, to punish and drive him out of Naples, he wanted, in advance, to secure himself, make himself indispensable, and he hastened the event. His correspondence with Napoléon was intercepted and taken to Paris, in copies. Blacas communicated these documents to Wellington, who, on 4 March, made them known in Vienna. Metternich felt at ease, and Murat was decidedly doomed. The next day he was lost.

1. From the dissolution of the *Chambre Introuvable* to the fall of the Decazes ministry to the death of the Duc de Berry, September 1816 to February 1820.
2. On this reaction and the formation of the legend, since 1814, see *Mémoires d'une inconnue*, p. 229, 249, 250. Cf. Thiébault, p. 214, 218, 228, 232; D'Espinchal, Fezensac, Castellane
3. Lavisse and Rimbaud, *Histoire générale*, X. Congress of Vienna, ch. I. See my "Talleyrand au congres de Vienne," *Essais d'histoire et de critique*. I have given in the above-mentioned chapter of the *Histoire générale*, p. 61, a summary bibliography of the history of the Congress. I am content to mention here the main collections of printed documents: Angeberg, *Le congrès de Vienne et les traités de 1815*. - Talleyrand, *Mémoires*, II, III. - Pallain, *Correspondance du prince de Talleyrand et du roi Louis XVIII*. - Castlereagh, Wellington, Pozzo di Borgo, letters. - Gagern, *Mein Antheil an der Politik*. - Gentz, *Tagebücher et Dépêches aux hospodars*. - Martens, *Traités de la Russie*, III, VII, and XI. - Polovtsoff, *Correspondance des ambassadeurs, France et Russie, 1814-1816*. Bianchi, *Storia documentata della diplomazia europea in Italia*. - Rinieri, *Correspondenza dei cardinali Consalvi e Pacca*.
4. Talleyrand to Noailles, in Petersburg, 22 juillet 1814.
5. Green, *Histoire du peuple anglais*, II, p. 418.
6. Convention of London, 29 June 1814; Martens, XI; Angeberg.
7. Nesselrode, *Autobiographie*.
8. See the memoirs of Stein, of Hardenberg. Oncken, II, ch. VI.
9. Hardenberg, memo of 29 April 1814; he was thinking of constituting a life duchy of Münster-Paderborn for the King of Saxony. (Oncken, II, p. 842.)
10. Alexander to Friedrich-Wilhelm III, 2 August; Friedrich-Wilhelm III to Alexander, 19 August 1814. (Bailleu.)
11. Convention of August 1814. (Martens, VII.)
12. *Lettres de Gentz aux hospodars*, 21 June 1814, 14 January 1815, I, p. 80, 141.
13. Report of Consalvi, 17 September 1814; report of Saint-Marsan, 17 October 1814; Rinieri; Bianchi.
14. Alexander thought about it.; Rinieri, p. 67, 99; 101, 104.
15. Treaty of 11 January 1814.
16. Orléans to Ferdinand IV, 10 juillet 1814; Weil, *Revue d'histoire moderne* (1904).
17. 12 September. Report of Saint-Marsan, 20 octobre 1814. (Bianchi.)
18. On these plans for an Italian, conservative, anti-Jacobin, anti-unitary league, see Metternich's conversations with Consalvi; in particular Consalvi's report of 17 September 1814. (Rinieri.)
19. Rinieri, *Journal de Saint-Marsan*.
20. Castlereagh to Wellington, 14 August 1814; Talleyrand, *Mémoires*, II, p. 276, 277; Pozzo to Nesselrode, 28 August 1814.
21. "Replaced within its ancient limits, it no longer dreamed of extending them, like the sea which only crosses its shores when it has been raised by the storm." (Talleyrand to Metternich, 19 December 1814.) "The king," wrote Pozzo on 28 August, "has neither the intention of enlarging his territory, nor that of putting forward proposals opposed to the principles of balance that it is proposed to establish, but he feels that his own dignity and his duties towards the nation prescribe to him to participate with perfect equality in the arrangements and stipulations destined to fix the interests and the justice of all."

22 The affair dragged on and was definitely broken off on 2 January 1815. See Pozzo's correspondence with Nesselrode in Polovtsoff, p. 10, 18, 29, 30, 38 et seq., 53 et seq., 64, 70, 85, 86, 93, 128, 135; and the *Correspondance de Talleyrand avec Louis XVIII*.
23 Nesselrode to Pozzo 22 June, and *id.*, 6 July 1814. (Polovtsoff.)
24 Compare Alexander's insistence on obtaining this declaration from Napoléon" "The Kingdom of Poland will never be restored." Convention of 4 January 1810, not ratified by Napoléon.
25 "The three continental courts seem animated by an equal jealousy against any idea of admitting France to take any serious part in the decision of the questions, consequences of the peace." (Report of Castlereagh, 24 September 1814.)
26 Martens, VII, p. 157.
27 At Saint-Cloud in 1810, "when he wore a bracelet of hair from C.... M., so beautiful then." (Henri Beyle to Balzac, 30 octobre 1840.) – "The beautiful and benevolent gaze of Mosca. The look with which M. de Metternich would deceive God." (Balzac, *Études sur M. Beyle*, 1840.) Balzac knew Metternich by hearsay from the Duchesse d'Abrantes, who had known him too well, doubly deceived then by Caroline, who had begged her husband, Junot, and her consoler, Metternich. *Fragments inédits*, from the office of Spoelberch de Lovenjoul. – Turquan, *La duchesse d'Abrantès*.
28 Like all words, this one was sharpened in advance, and Talleyrand had recently tried the effect. – 27 September: "Dinner at Talleyrand; the Princess of Isembourg asks him for news of the Duc de Bassano; he replies that he has never heard of him." (*Journal de Saint-Marsan*. Rinieri.) And this precedent that Talleyrand must have forgotten was so far away! In 1803, regarding a protest by Louis XVIII against negotiations with the first consul: "The first consul did not know that there was a count in Warsaw than by this publication." (Circular of Talleyrand, 23 août 1803; Boulay de la Meurthe, *Corr. du duc d'Enghien*.)
29 Cf. Nesselrode to Pozzo, 27 September 1814. (Polotsoff.)
30 "As the return of the King caused the disappearance in France of all the ideas which had produced and which had propagated the Revolution, it is to be hoped that in Europe one will cease to transform force into right, and that one will take for rule, not propriety, but equity." (Circular to French agents, 3 October 1814.)
31 Hardenberg to Metternich, 9 October, sent to Castlereagh on the 10th.
32 Nowhere has there been found any proof or presumption whatever that Russia and Prussia offered or even gave hope to France, at Vienna, for an increase in territory on the left bank of the river, as asserted by Thiers, XVIII, p. 639: "Alexander and Friedrich-Wilhelm ... would have offered him everything and, as on the Rhine there were only English or Austrian interests (?) they would have conceded to us on this side what we would have wanted ... The conflict being pushed to the point of war, it is indisputable that at least part of the left bank of the Rhine would have been returned to us..." "If there is," writes Lytton Bulwer, *Essay on Talleyrand*, "an extravagant idea it is this that Prussia or even Russia would have consented to reinstall France on the Rhine." It was, on the contrary, the article on which the allies had never varied and which had formed the basis of all their agreements since Langres; it was a fundamental article of the Treaty of Chaumont." This retrospective discussion point was elucidated by Albert Pingaud, "Le congrès de Vienne et la politique de Talleyrand," *Revue historique*

LXX (mai 1899).

33 Metternich to Hardenberg, 10 December 1814; Hardenburg to Alexander, 16 December; to Metternich, 2 and 16 December. See Oncken, II, ch. IX, IV, V: the reconstitution of Prussia; Albert Pingaud, p. 44, 45.

34 Compare the reviews of Thiers, XVIII, p. 433, 436, 638, 640 written in 1860, with the famous speech of 3 May 1866: "I must show you how the law has been outrageously violated. There are two powers whose union is already complete, because it is invariable and no one can destroy it: it is the union of Prussia and Russia. In the presence of such a state of things, what is France's essential power? This is Austria." It shows the Prussians "wanting to use German ideas" to rebuild the empire; he condemns the idea that France could receive "a salary" to support this policy. These are Talleyrand's own reasons. Cf. *Mémoire sur la Saxe*. Bismarck, who judged it as a man of action, judged it more fairly than Thiers, "I was already afraid, at Versailles, that France's participation in the London conferences would be used to graft, with the audacity that Talleyrand had shown in Vienna, the Franco-German question on the discussions provided for in the program." (*Mémoires*, II, p. 273, 274.)

35 "M. de Talleyrand has encountered many obstacles, but the consummate prudence with which he has supported the cause entrusted to his talents has brought about a result which, under the given circumstances, must, in my opinion, be regarded as very happy." (Pozzo to Jaucourt, 7 February 1815. Polovstof.)

36 Treaty of Kiel, 14 February 1814: Denmark cedes Norway to Sweden and receives Swedish Pomerania and Rügen; Treaty of 4 June 1815: Russia takes Swedish Pomerania and Rügen, cedes Lauenburg to Denmark, and pays it 2,600,000 crowns.

37 3, 18, 22 May 1815. Final act of Congress, 9 June 1815, articles 1 to 26.

38 To Jaucourt 14 February 1815. On the adventures of this affair, Bianchi, and reports them from Consalvi, in Rinieri.

39 Note of 25 January 1815 delivered to Vienna on 23 February. (Bianchi.)

40 Note of 25 February 1815.

41 Notes of 26 February. "Murat's loss is resolved." Report by Consalvi, 25 February 1814. (Rinieri.)

# Chapter II: Final Act in Vienna

## 1815

### I. Return of Napoléon

Napoléon was consumed on the island of Elba.[1] The adventure which had tempted him at Fontainebleau and which he regretted not having risked, obsessed him again.[2] Add the mirage of the return from Egypt. The gambler within him, as soon as he came back to himself, the despondency gone, began to believe in his star again and burned to start the game over again, part in despair, all for all, but he had won it so many times! Circumstances compelled him to break his ban, as they formerly urged him to declare war. In Vienna, the Congress in full crisis, they seemed ready to come to blows; in Italy Murat was agitated, returned to his Emperor, proposed an insurrection in the peninsula; from France, finally, came letters and emissaries depicting the general discontent, the rapid decay of the Restoration, the change of heart in favor of the Empire, the forgetting of the last setbacks and the invasion, the memory, on the contrary, of lost greatness, and the illusion of the Consulate reborn by comparison with the new regime, just as popularity was formerly born of comparison with the Directory. A pretext was needed. Napoléon found it in the refusal to pay his pension, in the threats to deport him, to lock him up, even to assassinate him, the plots of Bruslard, following the plot of Maubreuil.[3]

He went. He landed in France on 2 March. The populace of Provence, who wanted to kill him ten months before, acclaimed him: Down with the nobles! Down with the priests! This was the rallying cry; the old soldiers returned to their ranks, and the people who performed the miracle hastened to admire the popular miracle.[4] He had a nation, he had an army and he marched on Paris in the midst of villages adorned with the tricolor flag. The Government tried to resist. The royal guard, the musketeers waved their plumes, put on their beautiful new uniforms, sharpened their sabers, pointed their spurs. Marshals parodied the gestures of the distribution of the eagles: one hand on the heart, the other brandishing the sword, they uttered all the oaths of the political liturgy. But if some of the chiefs marched, the troops refused. What does not disband, gives itself. Leipzig returned. Ney, who had promised to bring Napoléon back in a cage,[5] advanced towards him with his hand raised, to apprehend him seeing the tricolor flag, the furry caps of the grenadiers, the little hat, the gray frock coat, and threw himself, weeping, into the arms of the Emperor:[6] a soldier at heart, who found himself a people, a child of the Revolution and whirl about himself in the vertigo of his life that arose in his brain. He died of it, six months later, his senses turned. Before them everything dispersed, dissolved, fled. The King gave up and set off at a gallop in his carriage, surrounded by this famous "house," which in eleven months had kindled more hatred in the French army, launched under the skies of France more irritating challenges than the *émigrés* to the stranger for 23 years.

Napoléon said, "They let me come, as they let them go!" He was not mistaken. It was not the return from Egypt, it was neither the same France, nor the same Europe, nor the same Bonaparte. Then the horizons opened up unlimited and luminous: the horizon was now obscured by clouds. The Revolution was not beginning again, it was continuing. In 1799, it continued against the Directory. In 1815 it continued against the Bourbons. Napoléon had absorbed it for fifteen years: he was no longer anything more than its temporary nominee.

Louis-Mathieu Molé exclaimed to him, greeting him at the Tuileries, on the evening of 20 March,

> Sire, only your Majesty can perform such prodigies. – I only had to show myself to succeed; they made so many mistakes, so indisposed the nation and the army, that all the troops sent against me lined up for me, and if I had wanted to, I would have arrived in Paris followed by 70,000 armed peasants. Do not believe in an alleged conspiracy. What idea have you formed of the king's character? – Sire, there is reason to believe

him to be good, just, and lacking neither shrewdness nor courage. – Yes, it is Louis XVI with less frankness and more wit. But, how did he allow so many mistakes to be made? Nothing surprised me more on my return to France than this hatred of priests and the nobility, which I find as universal and as violent as at the beginning of the Revolution. They questioned everything that was decided. I find all the parties, all the renewed hatreds, they have given back to liberal ideas, to the ideas of the beginning of the Revolution, all the strength they had lost. Also, I announced on disembarking that I was going to give a constitution more liberal than the charter of the Bourbons, and on which, above all, the nation would be consulted...

But if the people seemed to give themselves up, if the mass of the French seemed to submit, the royalists did not surrender. It was necessary to start again the work of high police of the Consulate, to hunt down the *chouans*, the henchmen of the party, to contain the Vendée, and, at the same time, to practice the Jacobins, the former revolutionaries, finally to supervise the faction of which they always spoke of, which was nowhere and which brooded everywhere, a faction without a leader, but where the lieutenants were legion and which pushed its affiliations to the leaders of all the other parties, the faction of Orléans.[7] There was only one man suited to this work; he imposed himself: Fouché.[8] Napoléon took him back, as he had placed Talleyrand in the Council of Regency in 1814, flattering himself to compromise him, to restrain him, to oblige him to act in broad daylight, outside his underground passages. He composed his ministry, with a view to the future constitution, with everything that still belonged to the Republic and everything that had offended the Restoration: Caulaincourt in foreign affairs, Fouché in the police, Decrès in the navy, Mollien in the treasury, Cambacérès to justice.

Then he turned towards Europe, trying to resume the game of divisions and to take advantage of those which were represented to him as so bitter and so ardent at Vienna. However, he had few illusions. On arriving in Paris, his first orders were to arm to excess. He said to Davout,

> I will speak to you with an open heart, tell you everything. I left and I must let believe that I act in concert with my father-in-law, the emperor of Austria. It is announced from all sides that the Empress is on her way with the King of Rome, that she will arrive at any moment. The truth is that it is not so, that I am alone in before Europe. This is my situation.

He nevertheless tried all possible steps to initiate a negotiation to least to gain time. Caulaincourt tried to restore affairs to the point where it had broken off at Châtillon. Napoléon could imagine for a moment that he was holding an important card. Both Reinhard and Jaucourt, in hastily leaving the Hôtel des Affaires Etrangères, had forgotten the treaty of 3 January there. Napoléon, as soon as he learned of it, had foreign agents who demanded their passports detained in Paris. Caulaincourt took advantage of this to communicate the treaty to Boutiaguine, *chargé d'affaires* of Russia, and to deliver to Vincent, the Austrian ambassador, a letter from Napoléon to Maria-Louisa.

It was a question of embroiling Alexander with Metternich and Talleyrand, and, on the other hand, perhaps, of chilling Franz II. Caulaincourt saw Vincent with Mme de Souza and Boutiaguine with Mlle Cauchelet. Vincent took the letter, Boutiaguine read the treaty, but Vincent said nothing. Boutiaguine was no more reassuring: "However great may be the just dissatisfaction of my master against the King of France on learning of the existence of this treaty, I dare not flatter myself that it results the slightest change in dispositions." Napoléon then wrote a letter to the sovereigns, demanding, promising peace, announcing "the holy struggle for the happiness of the peoples."[9] He didn't believe in it enough to hope to make people believe in it. On 5 April the Council of State took a deliberation which was a veritable manifesto: "What does Napoléon want? What the French people want: independence for France, internal peace, peace with all peoples, the execution of the Treaty of Paris of 30 May 1814. Nothing has changed!" This is what Napoléon had come to: he demanded, he guaranteed the treaty of 30 May, that is to say the work of the Restoration. Whether the policy of Louis XVIII and Talleyrand needed a counter-proof, it would find Napoléon obliged to use the same language and declare the same disinterestedness.

## II. Outlaw Napoléon

During the night of 6-7 March, Metternich was informed that Napoléon had left the island of Elba. There was general consternation, immediately followed by fury.[10] Alexander, who formerly, in his irritation against Talleyrand and Louis XVIII, spoke of unleashing "the monster," spoke now only of exterminating him. He exclaimed that "the affair concerned him personally, that he had to reproach himself for an imprudence, to clear himself of a wrong (having left Napoléon on the island of Elba), and that he would put to this resurgent war through his fault his last man and his last crown." The Prussians, sensing the occasion of a more complete revenge than that of 1814, and of conquests, which had then escaped them, stirred up the irritation of their ally. One could see what a chimera would have pursued those of the French who would have tried to separate Prussia from Russia, and to give themselves to Alexander with the ulterior motive that Russia would procure for France a piece of Germany or Belgium. The mere threat of renewed ambition on the part of France, the mere thought that the Treaty of Paris might be called into question, brought the allies closer together, and the pact of Chaumont was formed, firmer than ever. On 13 March, the eight signatory powers of the Treaty of Paris declared that Bonaparte had broken "the only legal title to which his existence was attached," placing him "outside civil and social relations," and delivered him up "to public vindictiveness." He was the outlaw of the Convention, the outlaw of Brumaire, translated into monarchical language. They promised, at the same time, their support to the King of France and to the French nation against the usurper. Talleyrand signed this pact which made Louis XVIII the ally of Europe against Napoléon.

It was soon learned that, having landed in France, Napoléon was acclaimed there; that his march towards Paris recalled, at least, by the popular spectacle, his triumphal return from Egypt in 1799; that the troops were defecting from the King, that France refused the Bourbons, and that Louis XVIII was forced to flee. France thus tore up the Treaty of Paris. The allies had no doubt that by giving themselves up to Napoléon, the French wanted, with him, through him, to reconquer the frontier of the Republic, the natural limits, always sacred in their imaginations, and the only condition in their eyes of glorious and enduring peace. "There is no doubt that to retake

Belgium and move back to the Rhine, all the soldiers and even the recruits will run," wrote the acting foreign minister, Jaucourt. The allies were not mis-taken. Their main guarantee of peace was Louis XVIII, the monarchy, the Charter. The restored monarchy manifesting its impotence to love the nation, to govern it; the French declaring their repugnance for this monarchy, the allies found themselves in the conditions which had preceded the fall of Napoléon; but they returned to it with the disap-pointment of a failed operation, the regret of having shown them-selves too moderate towards the French, the desire to seek more real guarantees against the bellicose mood and the revolutionary spirit of this nation.

On 25 March the allies solemnly renewed the alliance of Chaumont to "maintain" the Treaty of Paris, with this threatening clause: "with the aim of completing the provisions of this treaty." In vain Napoléon, trying to adopt the policy which Louis XVIII was reproached for not having followed, wanted to reconnect with Russia, to detach it from England and Austria. The revelation of the treaty of 3 January had no effect. But the treaty was already no more than a dead letter. Alexander, who did not like Metternich, showed some resentment against this minister. This did not prevent them from agreeing in all things. Alexander did not conceive of it, or at least did not show any irritation against the English.[11] He even caused Castle-reagh to write a letter full of the spirit of 1813. As for Talleyrand and the Bourbons, if he affected to be indignant at this treaty which they had signed with Austria and England, and that he forgave Austria and England so easily, it was because it suited him to have an ostensible grievance against Talleyrand and a reason for not engaging in a new restoration of the eldest branch.

Napoléon's return to Paris, and Louis XVIII's flight to Ghent had suddenly overthrown Talleyrand's skillful and subtle scaffolding. All this scaffolding rested on the restoration, the principle of legiti-macy, by virtue of which this restoration had been accomplished, the proclamation of this principle by the allies, the identity of this princi-ple with the interests of France, the necessity in which the allies to support the restored monarchy, the guarantees of peace which, by its own interest, by the reiterated declarations of disinterestedness, this monarchy gave them. The return of Napoléon threw Europe back into politics *de facto et de force*. The "principles," to use a very apt word from Talleyrand, had been recognized by the allies only insofar as they in no way ran counter to their conventions; they were no more than an abstract formula, without political value. It came back to the maxim of Alexander, which was that of all ancient diplomacy: "The proprieties of Europe are the law." The allies made this harshly felt by the envoy of Louis XVIII. The role Talleyrand had composed for himself and the character he had played were artificial. His strength had been the strength of things; his art had consisted in understanding it and making use of it. When this support failed him, the mask fell. There remained only a man of extraordinary poise, of consummate dexterity, but contradicted by the facts, baffled in his calculations, unbearable, hated. He was no longer "the minister of Louis XIV." He was no more than the minister of James II. He struggled vainly in this impasse. He exhausted the ambiguities. He tried to have the allies declare that the object of the war would be the restoration of the Bourbons. He endeavored to induce the allies to respect the limits granted to France by the Treaty of Paris, and, to obtain this guarantee, he insinuated himself into the coalition, associating Louis XVIII with it, and adhered to the renewal of the Treaty of Chaumont.[12] He hoped thus to make it very difficult for the allies to despoil a prince who made common cause with them. But he was a dethroned prince, a fugitive, without an army, without popularity. He was the "suitor" of 1795, returned to his exile, and everyone reserved, according to their interests, to treat him as a client or an outcast. Talleyrand got off with giving the repugnant spectacle, although correct from the dynastic point of view, from the point of view of legitimacy and according to ancient European public law, of a French ambassador signing, in the name of the King of France, declarations and combined acts against France and the French armies.

The allies had been, in 1814, very divided and for a very long time, on the government to be established in France. Except for the English, they had undergone the Restoration much more than they had made it. In 1815, these discussions began again.

English diplomats, Castlereagh detained in London, Clancarty who replaced him in Vienna, Wellington who was preparing to return from Congress to the army, remained convinced that restoration of Louis XVIII would be, in 1815, as in 1814, the only serious guarantee of the Treaty of Paris. They felt that any other combination would require a war footing, "ruinous armaments for all of Europe."[13] But, as in 1814, they were obliged to be officially silent. As in 1813 and 1814, Parliament opposed a war whose interference in the internal affairs of France would have been the object. It wanted the expulsion of "Bonaparte" and the taking of more effective guarantees: money, land, fortresses. The Ministry even feared that the accession of Talleyrand to the treaty of 25 March, confirming the alliance of Chaumont, would raise storms. Napoléon, because he came from the Revolution, kept some supporters among the irregular Whigs. On 3 April a pacific motion of Whitbread, in favor of peace, was rejected, in the House of Commons, by 220 votes against 27; the Commons approved the arms announced by the Prince Regent.[14] It seemed very clear that England did not want to incur expenses for the Bourbons. On the 8th Castlereagh wrote to Clancarty:

> You will appreciate how important it is from the parliamentary point of view that it cannot be said that Louis XVIII, being our ally against Bonaparte, has become a member of the coalition for his own restoration. His Majesty cannot wish us to feel more than we feel how important the restoration is. We will make every effort to ensure that the war produces this result; but we cannot make it a *sine qua non*.

Officially, England reserved itself. Castlereagh declared it when sending the ratification of the treaty of 25 March. "It is not to be construed as obliging His Britannic Majesty to prosecute the war for the purpose of imposing any particular government upon France."[15]

In Austria, some resumed thinking, *in petto*, of the combination abandoned in 1814, a regency with Napoléon II.[16] Gentz wrote,

> When one thinks how high Austria could rise by frankly embracing the interests of Napoléon's son, one is doubtless astonished – posterity will be even more so – that such a resolution is not even counted today among the probable chances, barely among the possible chances. But we are too committed to the opposite system, too accustomed to sacrificing our own interests for fear of compromising ourselves with our allies! The Emperor would never lend himself to it... Consequently, Austria will join England in working heart and soul for the restoration of the Bourbons.

Although Austria remained discreetly supportive, Prussia showed itself violently, noisily, hostile not only to Bonaparte, but to everything that could furnish a pretext for accommodating him. German politicians demanded 1814 guarantees, and at least a strong contribution, against a new uprising by France. The fact justified, according to them, their complaint. Throughout Germany, the volunteers, just dismissed, ran to arms again. Add to this the end of great dreams, Germany one and powerful, and this new fall into the swamp of the old empire, which had again become the market of diplomacy. The indignation of disappointed hopes turned into fury against the common enemy, the hereditary enemy. It was no longer against the person of Napoléon that Germany persisted, it was against France itself. It was with France that the German patriots wanted to put an end to it. Stein wrote to his wife,

> The upheaval of France is a consequence of the deep corruption of the nation, which, driven by vengeance and brigandage, prefers the government of a tyrant to the legitimate government of a pious and intelligent king; who receives everywhere this tyrant with enthusiasm and who prepares with joy for the war of conquest and pillage.

Was Germany condemned forever by these turbulent and frivolous adventurers to know neither tranquility nor lasting happiness in the work of the home, nor the sweet and lofty speculations of the mind![17] Gagern, representative of Nassau and the House of Orange, refused to ratify the treaty of March 25 and where the treaty of May 30 was as guaranteed: "The forces of turbulent France are deploying to take provinces from us. Ours will deploy for the same intentions. Our borders are bad, they must be rectified."

They returned suddenly to 1792, at the time of the Antwerp conference. This was its language, and they saw its combinations revived. The Prussians, Hardenberg, Humboldt and all their cortege, thought only of extorting the millions which they were wronged in 1814, of gnawing at the frontiers, and they did not intend to commit themselves to anything towards any French government, especially the one that, for its so-called "principle," one had so recklessly managed in Paris and which had just shown the value of its rights! However, they concealed these plans of revenge under the insidious declaration that the French would be free to give themselves the government they wanted, provided that this government assured Europe of the means to peace, but such guarantees they wanted in land and cash.

Alexander was fed up with the Bourbons. The prejudices of 1814 turned to aversion, it was even said to horror.[18] Legitimacy, with its fundamental laws written nowhere, its untraceable Salic law, its holy chrism and its Holy Spirit, always made this emperor impatient. The mere word *legitimacy* offended him like an impertinence, a lack of regard for his Crown. His self-esteem was more than ever, on this article, in harmony with his interests. The language he held moreover was in conformity with that which he held in 1804 when he meditated his great enterprise of reconstituting Europe under Russian supremacy. He had, in 1814, brought it to its ends, and it was a question of consummating it. He wrote,

> It is necessary that in France the constitution be monarchical. The cabinets will agree on the individual and the family who might be called upon to reign in France. If it's the Bourbons, which of them... the conduct that will be required of him, the conditions to which he will have to subscribe.[19]

The King, thus restored, would owe everything to Alexander and, before him, would no longer pretend like Louis XVIII to treat Catherine's heir from the full height of the dynasty of Hugues Capet. The King of France would be a little less than a King of Prussia. It would only date from 1815, with a stroke of majority, and all the monarchical prestige would pass from protege to protector, from Paris to Petersburg, where the new Charlemagne would reign. The Tsar needed a monarchy less proud of its origins, which was at his discretion, and a monarch both more popular in France and more dependent on Russia. He returned to the plebiscite, the people, of course, voting by delegates, sorted and indoctrinated. As for the candidate, King Bernadotte, worn out from the first try, no longer counted. The favor passed to Orléans, Louis-Philippe and the tricolor, a medium term, it was said, between Louis XVIII and Napoléon II.

### III. Fouché

This party came to him in the most captious form, by embassies of the man (whom Talleyrand disconcerted, baffled, worn out), then passed, in Paris as in Vienna, in Vienna as in Ghent, to the hôtel furnished by Louis XVIII and Napoléon's Tuileries, for the only one to know France and to hold it, a necessary instrument of the inevitable and imminent revolution, Fouché. This man was absent in March of 1814. He had failed in this crisis and the intrigues had been tied up without him. Talleyrand had been the craftsman and the great beneficiary of the Restoration, and this is where Talleyrand had led France, the Bourbons and Europe: the Bourbons into exile, France into the Empire, and Europe into war! Everything therefore has to be started over again, and here was the hour that Fouché had been waiting for for fifteen years to work in the great, to show what he was capable of, what statesman, what diplomat Robespierre and Napoléon had misunderstood in him. Let us add the main idea: his places and his possessions, his tomorrow, his person, his pride, which he no more separated from the history of France than Napoléon separated his person from the Revolution and Louis XVIII his from legitimacy. This former pedant of the Oratory thought highly of himself in the world; he had made his career and his security a public right which, in his eyes, was equal to that of peoples and that of kings. Which party would win? He knew nothing about it, but whoever he was, Napoléon II, Louis-Philippe, or even Louis XVIII, he was determined to make himself the necessary minister.

One saw him in those weeks of April 1815 maneuvering everywhere with his superior astuteness, multiplying the emissaries, the nets, the hooks, dispatching travelers everywhere, open eared, insidiously worded, to praise the brand of his house and place his goods, seeking to discern the demand, to specify offers.[20] Napoléon took him as minister against the Bourbons; at Ghent, the purest and most enraged recommend him as the King's minister against Napoléon.[21] In Vienna, Alexander expected from him the name that would come out of the plebiscite ballot boxes. With all, against all, this astonishing craftsman of intrigues remained the rough draft that he was in the soul and which prevented him from realizing in himself the statesman of which he had forged the image. However, we discover a background in the troubled cabals of Paris and also in Fouché's plots a favorite deceit. If he leaned towards the King of Rome, he found the Bonapartes, Joseph, Lucien, and behind the scene, moving all of the puppets, Metternich. On the way to Louis XVIII, the regicide and the scaffolds. With Louis-Philippe everything agreed, including 21 January, which sealed the alliance, confused adversaries, and bound the interests.[22]

This name of Orléans floated on all lips in the circumspect and wise world of politicians who intended to push the grass. It was the seed of 1830 which germinated. We see ideas and men insinuating themselves, those who have sown and those who will reap, the day which will bring together in a common federation Fructidor and Brumaire, 10 August and 20 March, around Talleyrand, officiating as in 1790, the elders, the Senate, the peers of 1814, the peers of the Hundred Days, and all the marshals, except the exiled Duc de Raguse, Ney shot, except Fouché finally, but by the sole effect of premature death. A line painted the actors, in this episode, and gave the spirit of the play.

  A very active agent in the restoration of the monarchy in 1814, Pasquier was not without fears after the return from the island of Elba. He put up with an exile on his lands; but he dreaded Vincennes. He had known how to retain, among his former colleagues in the imperial service, trustworthy and devoted friends. He went to visit them. Caulaincourt already saw France invaded a second time and only saw salvation in the Bourbons. La Valette made remarks reminiscent of those that Champagny made to d'Antraigues in 1802. He related that he had conspired against Louis XVIII, but that it was not for the benefit of Napoléon: "We would have given ourselves a sovereign who would hold the crown of France and abroad. But as sovereign where would you have taken it? – Who knows, perhaps the Duc d'Orléans, if he had wanted to be intelligent and reasonable. This one would have had to be sincerely constitutional; I don't think he would have scared Europe." Pasquier doubtless considered this statement sensible and worth remembering; but he also considered it very premature. He continued his tour and went to Fouché's. The dialogue which took place between them is a marvel of tact. Rarely has the political game been conducted with such a skillful and sure hand, the ball pushed from a lighter stroke to finer effects; nothing seems to hit, everything carries and everything ricochets towards the goal.

  Fouché, after dismissing a few intruders, took Pasquier into the garden and, when they were in the middle of the lawns, which have no ears, Fouché took the lead and began confidences: He said, speaking of the sovereign who gave him the mandate to prevent royalist plots, "This man is corrected for nothing and returns as despotic, as eager for conquests, finally as mad as ever." It was a theme that lends; Fouché extended there. Said Pasquier to let him breathe for a moment,

These are, serious matters I cannot allow myself to discuss them. – Let's go! replied Fouché, who caught his breath, leave this reserve: I am giving you the example; to conclude, I declare to you that in spite of the assurance that he has given of it, all of Europe is going to fall on his army; it is impossible for him to resist it; his affairs will be done within four months. – When that happens, I will resign myself to it; but, in good faith, Monsieur le Duc, I do not see what use the confidence you have made me can serve. – I am going to tell you. I ask nothing better than the Bourbons to return; only things must be arranged a little less stupidly than they were last year by Talleyrand; not everyone should be at their mercy. We need well-made conditions, good and solid guarantees. – Wonderfully, I don't object to any of this; I could manage it as well as you, but what can I do? – Nothing, for the moment, a lot perhaps in some time. When the decisive moment arrives, I will need capable and reliable men to back me up, men who inspire confidence in everyone, even the royal family. You are that man, I'm counting on you.

Pasquier thought that was going very quickly and very far; he knew Fouché familiar with all betrayals and with all trickery. Napoléon was standing, all-powerful in appearance, and Fouché, officially, his Minister of Police. "You do me a lot of honor by telling you the truth, I'm not tempted to run such great risks," said Pasquier. He talked about traveling. Fouché perfectly measured the degree of confidence he was worthy of inspiring:

> You affect to turn a deaf ear, he resumed; I'm sure you understood me correctly. So then you're going to go. You are intimate with Mme de Vaudemont: leave her your address and I will ask her to write to you when the time comes. – Since you open this way for me, I will use it in a month, not for such a serious matter, but to ask your permission to pass through Paris on the way to Mont-Dore. – Perfectly! whatever you want; this is our established means of correspondence.

Then, as if changing his mind: "Why would you allow yourself to be exiled? Ask to return to the Council of State; he will be only too happy to grant it to you." Pasquier declined the overture. Fouché cried,

> Oh! I see what it is: scruples of fidelity which you now pride yourself on for the House of Bourbon, as if, in order to do something really useful to those one wants to serve, one should not, above all, have a hand in the dough? What, pray tell, would you have been good at last April, if you hadn't been prefect of police?[23]

These confidences were exchanged in the last days of April 1815.

Fouché found it amusing, stretching under Talleyrand's feet the ropes where he would stumble on descending the steps, to enlist the most renowned, the most influential of his cronies, the most skillful in soliciting fortune in all games of politics and chance, Montrond. He thought it very clever to mingle his intrigue with the secret steps with which Napoléon charged the same personage with Maria-Louisa, Alexander, and the ministers at the Congress. Despite all his know-how, Montrond obtained nothing from the allies, less than nothing even. When he tried to speak of the Emperor, he was turned down: "We don't even want the regency," said Metternich; and Nesselrode: "No peace with Bonaparte!" So there remained the "intermediate shades"; and here the mission produced its effects. Montrond very likely undertook to test Talleyrand, Fouché preferring to have him as a partner than as an adversary.[24] Talleyrand himself probably reasoned the same way as Fouché. If the next day Orléans was called, then Talleyrand needed Fouché; if tomorrow Louis XVIII was called, then Fouché would need Talleyrand; hence the number of nocturnal meetings, masked visitors with raised collars, the rustling of steel in the shadows, parades, and dirty tricks. The fact is that they both became ministers of Louis XVIII, as they had been of Bonaparte after Brumaire, of Napoléon after 1804, and as they would have been of Louis-Philippe, if the July revolution, anticipating the time of fifteen years, would have anticipated their desires. Basically, all these detours and all these mines are things that are rather indifferent to history, and one need not trouble one's mind to untangle their inextricable skein;[25] no other secret can be discovered there than the personal interest of a few men, struggling, wading, or swimming in the great overflowing river; none of these men did the current nor the storm change; they were looking for the edge or the pass and we must retain of their adventures only what explains and depicts the general pace, which carried everything, them and the rest.

In this respect, Fouché's steps in Belgium, in Brussels with

Wellington, in Ghent with Louis XVIII's agents, were infinitely more significant than Montrond's fiddling in Vienna. He first occupied himself with providing for his own safety, and confided to Wellington "his anxieties as to the stability of the affairs of France and the dangers he was running from Napoléon, adding that he hoped to find an asylum in England, in case he should be forced to take refuge there." Then he offered his services and took care, by a signal blow, to show them off. No one knew better than him the underside of royalist plots, that of Georges in particular, and it would be calumniating to suppose him ignorant of the recent "missions" of Maubreuil and Bruslard. He knew how far he could push his points with princes and ministers who had been involved in these affairs, and allies who figured more than one confidant, if not an accomplice, of the death of Paul I. He awaited the opportunity; it introduced itself.[26]

Vitrolles had been arrested at Toulouse. Mme de Vitrolles was in Brussels; she trembled for her husband. The Comte d'Artois gave him this note: "I will be eternally grateful to whoever saves time and restores liberty to M. de Vitrolles." Mme de Vitrolles, armed with this talisman, left for Paris; she knew one of Fouché's cronies, Gaillard; she showed him the writing. Gaillard took it, carried it to Fouché, returned to find Mme de Vitrolles, took it to the Duc d'Otrante; this noble consoled her: "Your husband is saved; I wrung the promise of it from the Emperor. You must leave for Ghent; I have had a carriage prepared for you and will have a trusted man accompany you." The trusted man was received by Louis XVIII and told him

> that Fouché was ready to get rid of Bonaparte if he obtained the promise to remain Minister of Police and if M. de Talleyrand were placed at the head of the administration. Louis XVIII had too much shrewdness and he was too jaded, since the Consulate, on insinuations of this kind, to compromise himself in such a shady business. He spoke only of Vitrolles, and contented himself with encouraging the emissary, adding, in this connection, that he would always be ready to recognize the services that Fouché would be in a position to render to him and to France.[27]

Was the confidant able to insist? Pozzo wrote three days after this first interview: "Mme de Vitrolles is leaving today. The king has charged her to assure Fouché that the services he can render will be approved and rewarded; we will see what he will do."[28] But it is probable that his heart failed him. He reserved himself, negotiating and haggling.[29] Pozzo wrote on 23 May:

> If he wanted and, even more, if he could, destroy Bonaparte, there is no doubt that he would do it without hesitation, because then he would find himself the most powerful man in France. But he is far from possessing the power or the courage necessary to risk such an enterprise. My language, when circumstances have led me to express myself on this subject, has always been very encouraging for Fouché, saying to those who could repeat it to him, what he himself feels, that the man who, at the head of any party, would succeed in delivering Europe from Bonaparte, would have no conditions to ask for, because he could prescribe them all.

We can suppose that Fouché judged more finely. To rid Europe of Napoléon, he would be playing a fool's game, for once the monster had been exterminated, Europe, reassured, they would think only of separating from the liberator, who had become a nuisance. On the contrary, leaving the allies to defeat Napoléon, he gained everything by waiting for them at the gates of Paris, the silver platter in one hand and the keys in the other. The allies would need him; he would make his price with them more advantageously and with less danger to his person. The death of Robespierre had not made him a member of the Committee of Public Safety; Brumaire had made him minister, senator, and duke.

In Vienna the allies elaborated draft declarations, in response to Napoléon's manifesto, and this work reveals their deep differences. Lord Clancarty would have liked a sentence inserted "on the benefits of a paternal government under the legitimate king," instead of leaving the future of France vague.[30] Alexander did not consent to this. He invited Clancarty to come to his palace, and asked him the reason for the amendment he proposed. Clancarty replied:

> It's not enough to overthrow Bonaparte; the door must not be opened to the Jacobins. – First of all, said Alexander, we must overthrow Napoléon. There are three parties: the army, the Jacobins, the royalists. The army is attached to Bonaparte, but several of the leaders are also Jacobins. Among the Jacobins there are men of great talent, of indefatigable activity, of considerable influence, Fouché, for example. You have to win

them. They arrived, enriched, they have an interest in stopping the revolution. The royalist party is chiefly composed of peasants and married men, from whom no effort can be expected to restore the king. We need, he continued, a government that suits everyone. – France, resumed Clancarty, was happy under the paternal government of her legitimate king. He has for him the wishes of the whole nation. – Yes, said Alexander, from that part of the nation which has never been anything but passive; who, for twenty-six years, has endured all revolutions, who can only moan about them and does not prevent any. But will the other part, which seems to be the entire nation, because it alone shows itself, acts and dominates, submit? Will you impose on her the government she has just abandoned? Will you impose it on her in spite of herself? Will you wage a war of extermination for this? – I feel, replied Clancarty, that duty ends where impossibility begins. But until the impossibility arrives, I hold that the duty of the powers is to support the legitimate king. – Our first duties, resumed the Emperor, are to Europe and to ourselves. What is the probability that the king's government would be more stable than it has been? Last year, the regency could have been established; but the Archduchess Maria-Louisa, to whom I have spoken, does not wish, at any price whatsoever, to return to France. Her son must have an establishment in Austria, and she desires nothing more for him. I am completely against the elevation of any of the French marshals or generals to the throne of France, like Soult, Prince Eugène and others of that caliber. They can only disturb the peace in Europe. If the French want the king back, that's fine; if they want the Duke of Orléans as king of the revolution, there is nothing to object. I see no one fit to reconcile everything except the Duc d'Orléans. He is French, he is Bourbon, he is the husband of a Bourbon; he has sons; he served, when young, the constitutional cause; he wore his tricolor cockade which, as I have often said in Paris, we should never have taken off. It would unite all parties.

Neither the Tsar convinced the English nor did the English shake the Tsar's prejudice. The consequence was the declaration of 12 May, that the consent of the French nation to the return of Bonaparte to the throne would amount to a declaration of war; Europe would never make peace with Bonaparte, but the allies would "respect the liberty of France wherever it was not incompatible with their own safety and with the general tranquility of Europe."

Murat followed the fate of his master. On 28 March, the allies decided to act against him. Murat had left Naples on 17 March, flattering himself that he was supported by Napoléon and supported by the English who, until the last hour, had lured him with equivocal words. He occupied Ancona, pushed on to Bologna. On the 29th, he crossed the line of demarcation established between his armies and those of Austria. On the 30th, at Rimini, he called Italy to arms and to independence. The nation was exhorted to unity, under a national, powerful, feared, valiant king. On 2 April, he entered Bologna, on the 4th in Modena. But the nation did not rise. On the 9th and 10th he was beaten; on the 13th he retreated, on the 21st he negotiated. As he had abandoned the cause of France for the Crown of Naples, he was ready, to preserve this Crown, to abandon the cause of Italy. England declared war on him on 5 April. He asked Austria for peace and his kingdom. The obsession with the throne drove him crazy. Everything was refused to him, negotiation and armistice. On 29 April, Austria signed a treaty of alliance with Ferdinand IV. On 2 and 3 May, at Tolentino, Murat lost, at the same time, in two hours, the battle and the throne. He fled to Naples, ahead of his routed army. Then, on the night of 19 to 20 May, he embarked; on the 25 to arrive in Cannes. However, Naples capitulated, the Austrians entered there on the 28th; Ferdinand again became King of the Two Sicilies. Murat was Napoléon's only ally in the war; he was its first victim.[31]

## IV. Treaty of 9 June 1815

The restoration of the Bourbons in the Two Sicilies was thenceforth an accomplished fact, and at Vienna the eight recognized it. The solution of this affair facilitated the settlement of other questions relating to Italy. It was decided that Parma would be assigned to Maria-Louisa of Austria, Napoléon's wife, on a lifelong basis. On her death, Parma would pass to Maria-Louisa of Spain, former Queen of Etruria, and her children; in the meantime, this princess would have Lucca, who, after her, would return to Tuscany. Tuscany passed in heredity to Archduke Ferdinand of Austria, and Modena to Archduke Francesco d'Este. The Pope recovered the Legations of Ravenna, Bologna, Ferrara, La Marche, and finally Benevento, and Ponte-Corvo. The King of Sardinia received Genoa, and the succession was assured, in spite of the claims of Austria and according to the wishes of France, to the branch of Savoy-Carignan. Finally Austria which, by its alliances, dominated the peninsula, took for itself Lombardy, all the territory of the ancient Republic of Venice, Trieste, Dalmatia and Illyria.

German affairs had occupied many conferences.[32] All who, in Germany, thought and aspired to constitute a great fatherland, all who had armed themselves, in 1813, for the emancipation of this very fatherland, all who had then recognized the power of the nation when it was united, and desired, for this nation, a greatness and a role in conformity with its real strength, aspired to the reconstitution of the Empire under a federal and national form. Stein had made himself, with Alexander, the convinced advocate of this party. It was, he wrote to the Tsar on 5 November 1814,

> in conformity with the principles of justice and liberality of the allied powers, that Germany enjoy political and civil liberty, that the sovereignty of princes be limited, that abuses of authority cease, that an ancient and illustrious nobility by its feats of arms, its influence in the councils, its preeminence in the Church, is not delivered to the caprices of despots guided by a Jacobin and envious bureaucracy; that the rights of all be fixed and guaranteed, and that Germany cease to be a vast receptacle of oppressors and oppressed.

Among the princes of Germany, no one had any interest in seeing these wishes fulfilled. All the princes wanted to be sovereign masters at home, to dispose of their subjects according to their conveniences and to be in no way hindered, either internally or externally, in the exercise of their sovereignty. The idea of forming a powerful empire offended and frightened all the German princes, except one: they saw in it a lessening of their sovereignty. The only one who could expect an aggrandizement from it was the King of Prussia. But as long as he didn't become emperor, he didn't want an empire. Now Austria, which neither dared nor could aspire to the empire for itself, did not want it for Prussia. The German Empire fell at the same time as the idea of endowing the German nation with national public law.

The neighboring powers, Russia and France above all, could only fear a united, concentrated German nation, constituted as an imperial state. It was in their interest to neutralize, in some way, that Germany which the years 1813 and 1814 had shown so formidable. It could not be more effective than by itself, by the particularism of the German States, by that of the populations, by the opposition of North and South, by the jealousy of the great among themselves and of all the small against the great, the conflict between subjects and governments, the league of governments to keep their subjects submissive and divided, in short the impediment of everything by all, and the opposition of all particular forces to the force of the together. This object was attained by the Germanic confederation, a tutelary work for the peace of Europe, for the tranquility of Germany's neighbors, but a profound disappointment for German patriots.

The 34 sovereign princes and four free cities of Germany, all equal in rights, formed a confederation "for the maintenance and external and internal security of Germany, of the independence and inviolability of the Confederate States." A federative Diet, composed of diplomats, representing each of the States, and presided over by Austria, was charged with the affairs of this confederation. In the event of war declared against the Confederacy, none of the Confederates was to enter into negotiations with the enemy. The Confederate States were not to contract any engagement contrary to the security of the Confederation but, subject to this reservation, they could contract alliances. In case of conflict between them, they had to submit to the mediation of the Diet. If this mediation did not succeed, arbitration would be held and the sentence would be without appeal. This was, in broad outline, the plan of perpetual peace set forth by the Abbé de Saint-Pierre.

We have seen the reconstitution of Prussia. The remains of the former Rhine Palatinate, a part of the country between the Rhine and Moselle, were assigned to Bavaria; Mainz was assigned to Hesse-Darmstadt and became a federal stronghold; the same was true of the town of Luxembourg, assigned, with the Grand Duchy, to the King of the Netherlands, by a personal union. Electoral Hesse, with Cassel as its capital, was re-established, and its sovereign qualified as elector, the last vestige of the Holy Roman Empire. Hanover was erected into a kingdom, in the hands of the King of England. The Kingdom of the Netherlands, composed of Belgium and Holland, was given to the Prince of Orange-Nassau;[33] with the Grand Duchy of Luxembourg, on a personal basis. Switzerland, in which Valais, Geneva, and Neuchatel were included, formed a confederation of 19 free, independent and neutral cantons.[34]

The congress made a declaration relative to the freedom of the rivers; a regulation on precedence between diplomatic agents, and a declaration relative to the abolition of the slave trade.

All of these transactions were the subject of special treaties between the powers interested in each of them, and they were all, in their main provisions, united in a body of the treaty signed at Vienna, 9 June 1815 by the eight signatory powers of the Treaty of Paris and took the title of the *Final Act known as the Congress of Vienna*.[35]

Alexander and his advisers would have liked to include in this treaty provisions relating to the Ottoman Empire. By a note of the month of January 1815 the Russian government called the attention from the powers to the excesses committed by the Turks against the Christians, notably in Serbia; on the need for Christian states to protect Christians in Turkey; on the quality of natural protector of Greek Christians which belonged to the Tsar of Russia, just as the quality of protector of Eastern Catholics belonged to the King of France: by virtue of the "August Code..., palladium of political order," the cause of "the Negroes has been brought to the court of sovereigns; it is by invoking the same principles that the heads of the European family have the right to demand from the Porte the cessation of so many atrocities." The Greek Capo d'Istria, in great favor with Alexander, supported the cause of his compatriots and co-religionists; as sincere, ardent advocate of the Greeks, the Corfiots, the Serbs, Alexander proposed to declare as a right of Europe the permanent intervention of Russia in favor of the Christians of the East. This would have been to recognize the Russian protectorate in favor of the Greeks, transforming the obscure clauses of the Treaty of Kainardji into clear and general stipulations, to give Russia the legal mandate to pursue its own policy, its own interests in the East and to make Russian supremacy in Turkey an article of European public law. It was explained that Tsar Alexander sought this; it is understandable that the English did not lend themselves to it. On the other hand, Talleyrand was instructed to place the Ottoman Empire under the guarantee of Europe. Metternich considered "this guarantee as an essential point for the interests of Austria." To put this affair under deliberation would have been to note the deep dissidence of the powers; it was avoided. It was therefore only an attempt, which was dissipated in conversations and did not even give rise to a protocol.

1  For the whole and particularly for the war: Henri Houssaye, *Les Cent jours. Waterloo*.
2  At the moment of departure, he said again to the Austrian Koller: "I am going to address the troops Soldats! I'm not leaving anymore. My abdication is void. I will gather a nucleus of 30,000 men, I will increase it, and I will have a formidable army." (Report of Schouvalof, 21 avril 1814.)
3  On these cases, see Houssaye: liv. II, ch. I, and especially p. 174-75. "Bruslard, one of the men most ardently involved in the conspiracies of the *Chouannerie*, was appointed commander of Corsica. I saw M. de Bruslard almost at the moment of his departure. He had just taken leave of the royal family, and M. le Duc de Berry had said to him: 'Won't you find a way to get him to give him the boost?'" (Barante, *Souvenirs*, I, p. 120; cf. Fournier, *Napoléon*, III, p. 224.) One of the objects of the refusal of the pension was to oblige Napoléon to dismiss his guard, which would have delivered him defenseless to the police or the assassins. "We show a fairly firm intention to keep Bonaparte away from the island of Elba. I suggested the Azores." (Pallain, *Lettre de Talleyrand au roi*, 13 octobre 1814, and related notes, p. 42.)
4  "France recognizes him, the sacred cuckoo flies from steeple to steeple and all of France shouts: Long live the Emperor! He had taken back his dear France and picked up his troops, saying only two words to them: Here I am! greatest miracle that God has done! Before him, had a man ever gained sway just by showing his hat?" (Balzac, *Le Napoléon du peuple*.)
5  Don Quixote's cage! Liv. IV, ch. XLVI.
6  Henri Welschinger, *Le maréchal Ney*. – See the study, "Le procès de Ney," *Nouveaux essais d'histoire et de critique*.
7  Report of Pozzo, Bruxelles, 17 April 1815. (Polovtsoff.)
8  Madelin, *Fouché*, ch. XXIV.
9  14 avril 1815. Circular of Caulaincourt, 30 mars 1815.
10  *Mémoires de Metternich*, I, p. 205; *Journal de Saint-Marsan*, 7 mars; Report of Consalvi, 8 March 1815. (Rinieri.)
11  "I flatter myself that this cannot make any bad impression on the Emperor of Russia, after all he has seen for a long time. The affair, on the whole, came from the dissidences actually arranged." (Castlereagh to Wellington, London, 29 March 1815.) Alexander took this as a pretext to oppose moderation, constancy, equity in the principles of his policy, to "the ascendant exercised over the advice of sovereigns by weakness, levity and ambition." He contented himself with this scratch. (Nesselrode to Pozzo, 3 May 1815. Polovtsoff.) Wellington's explanation and agreement: Pozzo to Nesselrode, Brussels, 23 May 1815, *id*.
12  Note of 27 March 1815. (Angeberg.)
13  Wellington to Metternich, 20 May 1815.
14  Same motion, also rejected, on 28 April 1815.
15  Declaration of 25 April 1814.
16  Gentz to hospodars, 19 July 1815; Pozzo to Alexander, 7 October 1815.
17  18 March 1815. – Pertz, Treitschke, Oncken.
18  Gentz, letter of 19 July 1815.
19  Memo of the Russian Cabinet, 1815; *Correspondance de Pozzo di Borgo*, I, p. 128, 134, 169; Clancarty to Castlereagh, 11-15 April 1815.
20  Pasquier, *Mémoires*, III, VIII, IX; Houssaye, liv. III, ch. V; Welschinger, *le Roi*

*de Rome*, ch. VIII; Madelin, *Fouché*, ch. XXV.
21 Chateaubriand, *Mémoires*, III. Barante, II, p. 134.
22 Barante, II, p. 130, 149, 199. On the views of Fouché, Pozzo to Nesselrode, 3 May 1815. (Polovtsoff.)
23 Compare Bonaparte's word to Bourmont in 1800.
24 "7April. Dined at Talleyrand. Montrond comes and goes." *Journal de Saint-Marsan* ; Reports of Consalvi, 12 and 30 April 1815. (Rinieri.)
25 On another emissary of Fouché, and Orléanist, Saint-Léon, see Pasquier, III, p. 190; Pallain, p. 380; Welschinger, p. 150.
26 Report of Pozzo, Bruxelles, 17 April 1815; Conversation with Wellington. (Polovtsoff.)
27 Pozzo to Nesselrode, Bruxelles, 3 May 1815. (Polovtsoff.)
28 Pozzo to Nesselrode, 6 May 1815.
29 Throughout this period there was a remarkable levy of spies and a strange deal of treason. Numerous reports of agents in Wellington's correspondence, supplement. See Pozzo to Nesselrode, 4 June 1815. (Polovtsoff.)
30 Clancarty Reports, 11, 15 April 1815; Talleyrand to Louis XVIII, 23 April 1815. Talleyrand got Clancarty's account, partly, at second hand, from Stewart; he arranged it to the King's taste, and in his own interest.
31 Houssaye, Dufourcq, Helfert, De Sassenay: *Les derniers mois de Murat*.
32 Oncken, II, liv. IX, ch. VI: the final act of the congress and the foundation of the Germanic Confederation. – Treitschke, I, liv. II, V: the Germanic confederation. – Hausser, IV, liv. VI, ch. XI, the German Confederation. – Ranke, IV, p. 446. – Gervinus, I, III. – Martens, III, p. 232; VII, p. 154.
33 These combinations, Hanover and Holland, are the end of the grand design of the Guelph kingdom.
34 Declaration of neutrality 27 May; 20 November 1815.
35 Anckeberg, Partial Treaties and Final Act.

Page left intentionally blank.

# Chapter III: Waterloo

## 1815

### I. The Last Battle

The Congress had placed Napoléon outside the law of nations. In the House of Commons, a Whig, Graham, dedicated him to the execration of the human race and to the vengeance of England.

> The French government is war, its armies live to fight and fight to live. Their constitution has war as its essence, and the object of this war is the conquest of Europe. It was not an army, it was a military government which was on the march, similar to those Roman legions of the worst time in Rome, the Italica, the Rapace, troops without law, without checks, without responsibility before God or before man. He took possession of most of Europe and formed his plan to conquer the Crown of England. England defeated her designs with a stroke of her trident, she overthrew her empire.[1]

The Prussians claimed the line of the Vosges, the Dutch, French Flanders; all the Germans, the revenge and purification of modern Babylon, by the cosmopolitan plunder of the Croats, Hungarians, Cossacks, and Prussians. It was necessary to humiliate France, to drag it into ashes, to confound it in shame and to reduce it, for half a century, to have no power to harm!

So it was, again, for existence and independence that the French army was going to fight, and it seemed, to see the Prussians advancing through the Low Countries, flanked by Wellington's English, the Austrians, and the Russians arriving from the east to the rescue, that the invasion of 1792 and the flood of 1799, the great national perils must begin again. However, it was not by war, this time, that France was preserved, nor by the skill of its diplomacy: it was made so only from the arguments of the victors over the division of spoils, the will of the most powerful to re-establish a lasting peace and to enjoy it, the impossibility of obtaining this peace from any government other than that of the Bourbons, and the impossibility of obtaining from these princes a peace which, by lowering their crown, would have restored their hateful return to the French people. France was lost by the greatest soldier who had commanded its armies, and saved by the impotent king whom they had allowed to flee. Louis XVIII was to exercise between Europe and France that arbitration which the last counselors of the Crown intended for Louis XVI and to gain the restoration of his throne by the same services to the State from which the politicians of 1791 thought that Louis XVI would draw the regeneration of his monarchy. But before that, France experienced one of its most tragic adventures and endured one of the cruelest invasions it had ever suffered.

When he entered Belgium on 15 June 1815, Napoléon counted on striking a sudden and decisive blow, breaking the coalition before the enemy armies had joined, separating the English from the Prussians, defeating them one after the other, disconcert the Russians, stop the Austrians, force victory and rush peace. He had prepared his plan of war with superior art. He thought he had won the victory twice on 16 June at Ligny; the morning of the 18th, at Waterloo. He lost the opportunity on the 16th; on the 18th he was still saying, "Wellington has rolled the dice, and they are for us." The chances of success disappeared one by one, victory slipped away in pieces and the battle turned into a rout. It was to be a new beginning; it was the catastrophe of the Grand Army, of the Emperor and of the Empire.

A Wellington spy compared the army reformed by Napoléon to that of 1792; a historian shows it "more fiery, more exalted, more eager to fight than any other republican or imperial army. Never had Napoléon had in his hands such a formidable or fragile instrument of war." It was distorted in his very hand and broke, without either he, who believed himself sure of his combinations and saw them destroying themselves one after the other, nor his soldiers, who gave themselves the same heroic dash as at the days of great triumphs, could understand why the day did not end like Austerlitz or Jena.

Physicists, to explain the phenomena of light, sound, and heat, suppose the existence of an imponderable fluid in which we live as if bathed and whose vibrations shake our nerves. We must admit something analogous in the world of souls, in the world of emotion, human passion and action: a sort of atmosphere which changes incessantly and imperceptibly, which has its heavy depressions and its flights of invigorating breezes, its calms and its storms; it seems, in crises, to denature itself and denature us to the point that our impressions and our actions surprise and disconcert us; we no longer recognize ourselves. In short, as the people say, there is the spirit of the times, which influences all things. But the tide had turned. It blew like a hurricane against the French, it blinded them, sometimes with dust, sometimes with rain, always with the smoke of their own weapons. On the contrary, it bore the enemy and made daylight before its steps.

Napoléon's lieutenants awaited his orders and fulfilled them badly. Those of Wellington warned of the instructions he neglected to give them. While Napoléon was preparing to surprise and cut him off, he was at the ball in Brussels, where he paraded in solemn boldness and a demigod of the salon. His orders were pitiful. If they had been executed, he himself opened the way to the French. Fortunately for him, his lieutenants saw the danger and took it upon themselves to counter it; mediocre, however, Napoléon had a different seed than those; but the cause of the defeat was precisely that which caused Wellington's lieutenants to show themselves above their task, above themselves, and that those of Napoléon, even as their masters, failed in the work and failed in the council.

Wellington left the ball and found his army ready. On the battlefield, he took his revenge: "There is no other order than to hold out until the last man!" he said in the midst of the furious assaults of the French. "Twice I saved the day by my stubbornness; but I hope never to have to fight such a battle," he said. He held on, convinced that the Prussians would arrive and decide the victory. Holding on in this way, arming oneself with this confidence, were new things in the history of coalitions. From 1792 to 1799 no one expected an ally, because they knew themselves incapable of joining. Things went on like this again, on more than one occasion, in the campaign of France, in 1814. Wellington, however, was right to hold on: his desperate persistence had its reward, and the rabid ardor of Blücher proved him right.

The latter surprised and disconcerted Napoléon still more by his impetuosity than Wellington had done by his resistance. Beaten and wounded at Ligny, clinging to the field of battle, and forced in spite of himself to let go, he had pulled himself together in retreat. Grouchy was looking for him wherever, according to custom and precedent, he should have found him, that is to say, very far away. Blücher appeared where he was least expected, and his scarred, exhausted, starving Prussians reappeared, frantic and ferocious, to attack the French army. Napoléon was caught between two fires. Suddenly, the cry "guard back!" resounded like the knell of the Grand Army. The English masses stabbed fugitives with this ferocious cry: *No quarter! no quarter!* Napoléon still hoped to organize the retreat. He established three battalions of the guard in as many squares. In a heroic retreat, the guard marched literally flooded with enemies.

But why kill them? Some were coming, some would always come, and after those of today, those of tomorrow; they would come from everywhere, even from those confines of Illyria where Napoléon had carried his outposts, even from that Russia where he had tried to penetrate and which had thrown him to shreds. Napoléon's conquests over Europe resembled those made by the peoples of the coasts on the shores of the ocean. He had, to protect his empire, tried to enchain the sea, he had extended ever further his dykes and his booms. The force of the waters had swept away everything and the sea was coming in more fatal, more irresistible, because it was coming from further away and the obstacle had held it back longer. What made the power of the Prussians at Waterloo was that they were the vanguard of an innumerable army of peoples, of a colossal invasion which pushed them, to tell the truth, more than it supported them. They came, in a formidable flow of Europe, like the first waves of the roaring, furious tide, which collide with the rocks of the shore, envelop them, break there, crash down and spread out in foam, relieved immediately and brought back to the assault by the massive, crushing weight of the ocean which falls from the other hemisphere and rises in deluge behind them. The guard squares were a wreck, the Avenger's raft spitting its last grapeshot, saluting death rather than threatening the enemy, and sinking, overrun by the waters.

Every war is fought with a view to peace, every battle fought with a view to tomorrow. There was no longer, in 1815, either peace possible for the Emperor, or tomorrow for victory. Napoléon had drawn up his plans as Carnot had drawn up his in 1794, as he himself had drawn up so many other admirable ones in 1800, 1805, 1807, 1809. Everything, once again, was going to depend on a only battle he could, he had to win: but what would he do with it? When he thought of starting over Marengo, Austerlitz, Jena, he forgot that after the Battle of Marengo and to complete it Hohenlinden had been needed; that to preserve the conquests of Marengo and Hohenlinden it had been necessary to make Austerlitz; that to draw the consequences of this Austerlitz, that is to say, to paralyze Prussia after Austria, it had been necessary to have Jena; that to draw conclusions from Jena, that is to say, to paralyze Russia after Prussia, Friedland had been needed; and that after this victory it had been necessary to start over with Austria, that everything had nearly been called into question at Essling, and that it had taken Wagram to bring things back to the point they were in the day after Friedland.

Now, since October 1812, Napoléon had been beating a retreat, and the worst thing was that Europe was concentrating around him. He no longer acted like the wedge that sinks into the wood and splits it; he himself was caught between two enormous jaws which were closing on him. The fortune which abandoned Napoléon, and with him the Grand Army, and with them France, was the revolution which had formerly driven them into Europe and which was now turning against the French. Neither the generals nor the soldiers recognized it; and how would they have recognized it "in this horde of slaves, traitors, conspiratorial kings?" For they were still at the heroic age, at the time when they were young and when they had committed themselves for life. The revolution, for them, was 14 July, the French embracing each other with tears of joy; it was the federation, the country in danger, royalty broken because the King made a pact with the foreigner; public safety, France delivered, France enlarged to the Rhine; peoples who were proclaimed brothers, called to liberty; republics which they gave themselves as sisters, founded on the frontiers of republican France, extended to the limits of Caesar's Gaul; it was the triumphal way of Milan, Rome, Naples, Vienna, Berlin, even of Moscow. As through this sublime adventure, they judged themselves to have always remained the same, having passed without knowing it from the war of defense to the war of conquest, from the Jacobin Republic to the Consular Republic, then to the Caesarian Republic, from which Napoléon was made the Emperor, and did not imagine that the other peoples had changed, that a revolution had taken place around France and by their own work, reverse and counterpart of that which they had glorified, but just as powerful in war, just as fearsome and conquering. This strange harvest of peoples which they had sown surprised them. No doubt they had met here and there, in the past, strange resistances in Vendée, in France, in Calabria, in Abruzzi, in Italy; then all of Spain, which was only a vast Calabria. But they had an explanation ready: fanaticism, superstition, monks, brigands, *chouannerie*! And they had preserved the illusion that they carried at the same time, in their pouches, the marshal's baton for every soldier of France, the Civil Code and liberty for every child of Europe conquered by the French.

They were still at the time when, in Italy, the partisans of the Directory of Paris were called patriots, and the partisans of Italy to the Italians were called anarchists. What were these barbarous peoples getting into? What did these so-called nations want? Was the "great nation" no longer sufficient for the liberty of peoples? Was there no longer room in the Emperor's Pantheon for all the icons and all the gods, as in his church of the Invalides for all the trophies? What delirium swept away these wretched and enslaved Russians and made them burn their hovels, their towns, their harvests in the footsteps of the liberator? What were these absurd and denatured Germans getting into? Ferocious Germans who marched on the attack, Prussians who no longer fled, no longer spared themselves, as in the days of Brunswick and the "virtuous" Moellendorf; the very Austrians who went ahead! The allies entering Paris, Pitt and Cobourg resurrected in flesh and blood; the returned *émigrés*, the Bourbons re-established on the throne, the white flag, the processions, and on the frontier, tightened to the lines of the old maps, Wellington arriving from Portugal, passing over the body of France; the English in Belgium, who did not re-embark on first summons as in Brune's time; allies who did not disperse as in the time of Jourdan, Pichegru, Hoche. It was the world turned upside down for these souls who remained enthusiastic and naive, despite the plumes and crowns of princes, dukes and counts, some of whom some had adorned themselves. The last *voltigeurs*, in this respect, knew as much and understood as little as the first of the marshals. "I fear only one thing, that is that the sky will fall on my head," said the Gaul to the great Alexander. The sky had fallen.

## II. Second Abdication

On the morning of 21 June, Napoléon was at the Elysée, his body shattered, his soul dejected. He threw himself into a bath and had Davout called: 1 "What do they say in Paris, what do you think it will become?" He had a long lunch with Queen Hortense, then went to the Council. Each offered the recipe for its heroic times: Carnot, a dictatorship, the country in danger, a mass uprising of federals, withdrawing behind the Loire; Lucien, a *coup d'État*: necessary, he says, that in 24 hours the authority of the Emperor or that of the assembly will have ceased to exist: another 19 Brumaire! But time passed and opportunity passed. The Chamber of Deputies met at noon, a second edition of the Legislative of 10 August. The outburst was general against the fallen Emperor. "This man is without an army," wrote a Constitutionalist, son of a prefect, and himself, once, prefect of the empire;[2] "He has had his army exterminated in a terrible way, and he is coming back just like from Russia and Leipzig. The deputies and we are cowardly enough not to stop at any part. What does he want?" said the novelist and hero of the novel who had believed himself the statesman of the Hundred Days, Benjamin Constant, "No sooner had the news of his disasters reached the frontier than the idea of abandoning him crossed all minds. The first word was that the Emperor should abdicate." Fouché sowed fear with perfidious little notes, alarming words propagated by his cronies. Napoléon was preparing a decree of dissolution, an expulsion, another Saint-Cloud.

And, like Carnot, like Lucien, Lafayette threw himself back on his youth. He returned to debiting his repertoire role: he believed little in the furious crusade of the peoples of Europe. There was misunderstanding between France and the peoples of Europe; that France evoked 1789, and the peoples would acclaim it, the invasion would of course stop by itself! He believed in the magnanimity of Alexander, who did not want the Bourbons, who only wished the happiness of France. A single man stood in the way: let him go, and France was saved! The hour was propitious to avenge Brumaire and to establish liberty!

As Napoléon did not act, his adversaries took the lead. The Chamber declared itself permanently, declared that a decree of dissolution would amount to a crime of treason: in fact, it was the vacancy of power, and the Chamber seized it. Lucien ran to the Elysée and demanded the decree; but the ministers remained gloomy, Napoléon inert. He adjourned, he only came out of his apathy to utter vague words, words of forfeiture, words *à la* Louis XVI: "We have to see what will become of it!" He awaited the stroke of genius, of fortune. Thus fifteen years earlier, at Saint-Cloud, when he came out of the orangery half-suffocated and the Five Hundred shouted: *Outlaw!* But nothing happened. He was no longer 30 years old, he no longer came from the East, prestigious savior, before the discredited Directory. It is he, it is his empire that the chamber denounces, that Paris condemns. The wave that carried him receded, and he did not even struggle: he sank and abandoned himself.

Ministers conferred with deputies. It was decided to appoint a commission of plenipotentiaries to negotiate with the allies. Power was being detached, piece by piece, from the Emperor. The mainspring of a *coup d'État*, force, was lacking, especially moral force, and opinion. Paris was calm, as if indifferent. The National Guard remained impassive. All that rises for Napoléon were bands of federals, troops of the populace who surrounded the Elysée, vociferated, sang, demanded revolution, and a few soldiers always ready to rush on anyone, anywhere, in desperate charges. It was no longer even for Napoléon the heroic temptation of Fontainebleau, a last maneuver, a last combat, the bloody sacrifice to destiny. To march on the Assembly at the head of these hordes would be worse than the abdication of one's life, of one's glory, of one's honor, a riot, a 20 June, an August 10th returned! Perhaps he was tempted for a moment to see the turn the deliberations of the Chamber were taking. But was Paris incubating a revolution? Could Napoléon make himself its leader and climb all the slopes descended from the steps of Saint-Roch in a few hours? Often at Saint Helena he discussed the plan which, on that day of the 11th, that night of the 11th to the 12th, when the mob howled under his windows, agitated his mind.

This plan was quite frankly a government of public safety of which he would have been the dictator, as he had made himself, in 1804, Emperor of the Republic. A ministry which would have brought together several members of the old committee, Cambacérès, Carnot, Merlin, and the means of '93, and of '94, because like Robespierre, he discovered no others: terror. It was the complete return of the Revolution on itself. After Waterloo as after Neerwinden, same danger and same remedy:

> If after Waterloo, I had stayed there (in Paris), if I had had a hundred heads cut off, Fouché's first, with the rabble I could have held Paris. On my return from Waterloo, I was of the opinion that Fouché's neck should be cut off. I had already composed the military commission, it was that of the Duc d'Enghien, all people who risked. (His Majesty makes a sign with his tie). I was well served by it; they were of my opinion, and I regret not having done so. But who thinks that Louis XVI perished for not having had the Duc d'Orléans' neck cut off? I should have gone to the rooms while arriving. I would have moved them and carried them away, my eloquence would have filled them with enthusiasm. I would have had the heads of Lanjuinais, Lafayette, or a dozen others cut off. – First of all, I made a mistake by leaving Lanjuinais as president: Carnot had to be put there. He is a man who knows revolutions and has a lot of courage... Carnot alone assured me that it was a rout like those of the Revolution and that the army would rally under Paris, where they had cannons. Everyone else thought all was lost.

It would have been necessary to arrive at the Chamber as Cromwell, and Napoléon was not Cromwell.[3]

> At that time could one stir up the people, have the guillotine erected? And then, you have to say the word, I didn't have the courage. In 1793, we chose terror, because it was the only way out. Besides, I wouldn't have succeeded: I had too many enemies; I would have put myself in horrible peril. Much blood and little success; whereas, when I saw that the chambers were coming against me, I said to them, 'You believe, gentlemen, that I am an obstacle to peace. Well! get on with it.' I preferred to abdicate in favor of my son and let them fend for themselves and show them that it wasn't my person alone they were after, but France.[4]

"Rule by the axe!" what's the point? what if he failed? to have been the Bonaparte of Lodi, of Milan, the legislator consul and pacifier of civil wars, the man of Austerlitz, to perish in the boots of Henriot; to begin again on 2 June 1793, to direct the cannons of Vendémiaire against the Assembly! having been elected by the French nation, consecrated by the Pope at Notre-Dame, having married an archduchess of Austria, to fall, like Robespierre, at the town hall, his jaw shattered, hideous, disfigured under the chin, jeered at by the scoundrels, dragged to the road, and perhaps even worse, the Conciergerie, the scaffold in the Place du Trône, the wall of Vincennes, or, as a last resort, Pichegru's cravat! He was horrified. "We want it," he said to Davout, who represented to him the abomination and the uselessness of the adventure, "it won't cost me more than the rest." And he signed the abdication, 22 June 1815, for the second time. Then he left for Malmaison, where Josephine had died, Malmaison still enchanted with greenery and flowers, to breathe one last time the air of its spring, before leaving for exile from which he felt he would never return.

### III. Wellington

A provisional government was appointed, escaping Lafayette, as power always eluded him. Fouché was its head and president. Everything came to him, as in 1814 to Talleyrand. He triumphed, he was to triumph to the end, to hyperbole, regicide in the king's council! He resumed the work, the weft of which had been laid down in 1809 in the time of Walcheren and had remained on the job since 1810. He issued proclamations in the style of the Convention. He raised and federated National Guards. He reopened clubs. He invoked the public safety and proclaimed that he was its instrument. It excited all that still fermented of the old Jacobin and revolutionary spirit in France. After releasing this other "monster" he persuaded the royalists that he was the only man capable of muzzling it. He persuaded patriots and republicans that he was the only man capable of saving them from vengeance and proscriptions. He negotiated with the English, alone of the allies who sincerely wanted the restoration of the Bourbons, and he persuaded them that he was the only man capable of accomplishing this restoration. He persuaded liberals that he alone was capable of guaranteeing the independence of the nation before the allies, and public liberties before the Bourbons. He persuaded the Bonapartists that he was the only one capable of securing the throne for Napoléon II, and the monarchists that he was the only one capable of removing the Prince Imperial from this same throne.

Things just went faster than he wanted. Napoléon had been defeated too soon; his empire was crumbling too quickly and too easily. It was in France's interest that the Bourbons should return to Paris before the foreigners and that the allies should find before them, re-established by the force of circumstances and supported by national opinion, a Government which they would be bound to spare. It was not in Fouché's interest, because then he would become useless and lose all market value. He therefore endeavored to confuse everything, to delay everything, to the point of compromising everything. He showed even more astuteness in this counter-mine than he had brought into his plots of the Hundred Days. He had imposed himself on Napoléon by conspiring to bring down his empire, he made himself necessary to the Bourbons by thwarting the restoration of their monarchy. Never had such a complicated, subtle and audacious game been seen, except perhaps at the time of the great libertinism of the Fronde, and it was not for better ends.

The deputies, both Lafayette and his friends and the survivors of the Empire, all those who, after rallying in April 1814, had broken away in March 1815 and who knew full well that, this time, the famous article, the article of oblivion, the article of votes would be repealed, all those, finally, and there were many, for whom the first restoration remained a disappointment and for whom a second restoration would be ruin, exile, death perhaps, were struggling furiously. They no longer wanted Napoléon, they no longer wanted Louis XVIII. The cautious murmured the name of Napoléon II, hoping to reach Austria; more skillful was the name of Orléans, counting on Russia, and doubtless imagining that it would interest the English, because the English had had William III. They were wary of Fouché, even while submitting to him. They guarded themselves against the intrigues and the designs which they supposed of him to confiscate the government in the manner of Talleyrand last year. So there was no Hôtel Saint-Florentin, no secret meetings. Everything would happen officially, by delegations and commissioners, with reports and speeches.

The first point was to ascertain the disposition of the allies. The novelists, the pledged confidants or the voluntary confidants, the friends of La Harpe, the emissaries of the clan of liberals and idealists who surrounded Alexander, went away buzzing, insinuating that the Tsar more than ever was the master of affairs, hated the Bourbons as much as the French hated them themselves, as disappointed in them as the Constitutionalists of 1814 adding that France remained free to give itself a leader, that the allies would not interfere, and all that transpired in English and German gazettes gave the same impression. It was important to obtain direct assurance of this. A commission of five plenipotentiaries, Sébastiani, Pontécoulant, Laforest, Lafayette, and Voyer d'Argenson, with Benjamin Constant as secretary, was instructed to go to the headquarters of the coalition. Their instructions carried the devolution of the Empire to Napoléon II, the integrity of the territory with, at least, the limits of 1814, the security and inviolability of Napoléon's person.[5]

These words: at least the limits of 1814, revealed the immense ingenuity of their illusions, and this ineradicable belief that Napoléon defeated, Europe reconciled and peaceful, would return to France, once again become the the borders of the Republic, the limits of the Rhine! The official, concerted language of the allies was to maintain in the minds, stubborn for fifteen years of the same prejudice, an ambiguity which once again nearly became disastrous for France.

The commissioners demanded an ostensible declaration; the allies could only respond to them on the terms agreed between them, that is to say that they would not meddle in the internal affairs of France: the English because of their parliament, the Prussians because they reserved to trim further and to ransom more thoroughly France with any Government which would not be the Bourbons, the Russians because they observed their instructions of plebiscite.[6]

The commissioners met the coalition diplomats behind the army, in Haguenau, on 26 June.[7] Sebastiani said, "We only want independence and liberty for our country. No question is prejudged, no commitment is made." They said they were ready to negotiate. The allies refused, the English having no powers. They intended moreover that Napoléon should be handed over to their custody. They would impose, they said, on France neither the Bourbons nor any other particular government; but they were "resolved to demand the strictest precautions and guarantees that Napoléon should not reappear on the world stage." The commissioners wanted Napoléon II or Orléans, Napoléon II seemed to them in the exclusions of the allies, and Orléans, at bottom, the object of secret preferences. As for the precautions demanded against Napoléon, these negotiators were not frightened by them; they did not even suspect that this respect for the independence of the French, on the part of the victors, could hide some insinuation, if not some trap. They took away the answer they had come to fetch, and they needed no more: France was mistress of her destinies, the deputies had full license to decide.

However, if the allies made dupes, they did not deceive themselves, and this parade diplomacy did not suit their main business, which was to conclude peace. Allowing the Prussians and other Germans to grumble, very much occupied besides in pressing, plundering, frightfully vexing, even hanging and shooting to satiety,[8] the English and the Russians, rather embittered and very jealous, moreover, of each other, but equally interested in organizing a stable government in France, which could be for each of them, if need be, an ally against the other, endeavored to show, the Russians to their Tsar, the English to their Ministry, things as they were. Pozzo di Borgo and Wellington played a truly superior role in this encounter, Pozzo with his Corsican suppleness and friendliness; Wellington, haughty, stiff, phlegmatic; Pozzo endeavoring to please the French even more than to serve them, Wellington putting his British pride to serve them without pleasing them. Pozzo had to struggle against the prejudices of the Tsar, his wounded self-esteem, his constitutional whims: knowing better the public law of old France, he showed him the plebiscite which was vain, useless, even dangerous. Monarchy was nothing, he said, if it was not a principle, and this principle was nothing if it was put to the vote, especially to the votes of regicides. "The Bourbons are an institution, not a family. Europe needs them to be at peace, France cannot dispense with them to be free."

Wellington shared these views.[9] In London public opinion demanded stronger guarantees with other rulers; serious, however, with the Bourbons themselves: "a few frontier fortresses, including Lille." Wellington showed himself to be the rare politician[10] and army leader who, being victorious, takes his declarations before the battle literally and prides himself on remaining faithful to them. He had promised Vienna the Treaty of Paris of 30 May; he had declared himself, in all his conversations, the partisan of the Bourbons, as the only guarantors of this peace, the only lasting peace according to him; he had made this proclamation, crossing the border: "I am entering this country not as an enemy, except the enemy of the human race, with whom I do not want to have either peace or truce, but to help the French to shake off the iron yoke under which they are oppressed." And as he had said, he was fulfilling it.

Blücher claimed to hunt Napoléon, take him, "have him shot at the place where the Duc d'Enghien had fallen." Wellington wrote to Blücher: "We have, you and I, played too distinguished a role in recent events to stoop to the role of executioner." He represented to Castlereagh, who came to join him and whom he promptly convinced with Liverpool, who judged from afar, according to the rumors and passions of London, that restoration alone was possible, that being possible it ought to operate; that the interest of the allies was to render it honorable and beneficial to France, to render it popular at the present time and powerful in the future. He did better. He urged Louis XVIII to return in all haste, to occupy the place, to warn the allies in Paris. The allies finding him restored to his throne, all conspiracies would cease; fact would prevail over cabals; forced to treat with him, the allies would spare him, and he, before them his throne, freed from the equivocation of 1814, he could speak to them as a sovereign by right, who discusses the interests of his people. He urged Talleyrand to follow the King. He spoke with Fouché, whom he considered the necessary instrument, and over whom he exercised a prodigious ascendancy, that of a limited, stubborn, but straight mind, on a dazed draft of his own verve, and who, as he wasn't hunting short-sighted, his nose level with the ground, losing track in the fog. "The important point is that the king be restored first unconditionally, then without the force of the allied armies appearing to restore him to his throne," he wrote to Talleyrand.[11]

Time was pressing, the allied army was arriving under Paris; Fouché on the one hand, Talleyrand on the other, negotiated with Louis XVIII the charter of the French and their private capitulations; the King was in no hurry, haggled, refined his words, and, in the misunderstanding, the opportunity threatened to vanish. Wellington made up his mind to tear the veil.[12] On 29 June, new commissioners (the first were, at that very time, in Haguenau) presented themselves at Wellington's headquarters in Louvres: they were Andréossy, Flaugergues, Boissy d'Anglas, de Valence and La Besnardière; a former Bonaparte ambassador to London, a former member of the Year III committee, a general in Dumouriez's army. They demanded a suspension of arms. Wellington refused it. They talked about the future state of France, trying to sort out whether the allies would be inclined to recognize the Regency, or what could replace it, of which they did not speak. Wellington eluded the answer, except on one point: the allies, he said, declared that they did not want to make peace either with Napoléon or with any member of his family. It was there that these political ends awaited him. They confusedly insinuated vague combinations, a foreign prince, and finally they stammered the name of the Duke of Orléans.[13] Wellington saw where they wanted to come from. His answer left no ambiguity:

> According to me, Europe has no hope of preserving peace if any other person than the king is called to the throne of France; anyone so called should be considered a usurper; he would seek to distract the country's attention from the illegitimacy of his title by war and foreign conquests; the powers of Europe should, in that case, be on their guard against such an evil, and all I can assure you is, that unless I have orders to the contrary from my government, I will use all the influence I have with the allied sovereigns to induce them to insist on guarantees for the preservation of the peace, besides the treaty itself, if the arrangement of which you have just spoken is adopted.

It was clear: the Bourbons, or dismemberment, the war contribution, the dismantling of the fortresses, occupation. The deputies left as they had come, and, despite the perfect clarity of this language, without understanding things any better than their colleagues in Haguenau.

## IV. Second Restoration

On 3 July, Paris capitulated. The capitulation, signed for England by Colonel Herney, for Prussia by the General Müffling, and ratified by Davout, carried, Article XII:[14]

> Particular persons and properties will be respected; the inhabitants and in general all the individuals who are in the capital will continue to enjoy their rights and liberties, without being able to be disturbed or sought in any way, relative to the functions they occupy or would have occupied, to their conduct and their political opinions.

This article, counterpart of the declaration of Brunswick in 1792, deserves to be quoted at the end of a book in which we have recorded so many broken oaths, retracted promises, broken treaties, so many recantations, denials, and denials of justice to peoples and individuals; which began with the partitions of Poland, and ended with the cynical retort of the most precise text ever written by negotiators. Ney, Labédoyère, peers of France, were in Paris; a good number of regicides sat in the chambers, in the magistracies, in the Institute: this stipulation placed them under the safeguard of the law of nations, it made their safety a synallagmatic condition, inseparable from the capitulation of

Paris. The honor of the allies was engaged there, like that of Davout, who had signed for France. Davout defended his, the allies made good use of theirs and gave free rein to the vindictiveness of the factions, which led Ney and Labédoyère to the wall, and the regicides into exile.

The commissioners had returned from Haguenau and Wellington's headquarters. The deputies, considering themselves informed, deliberated to vote for a constitution and to send a deputation to the camp of the allies to propose "a completely different sovereign than a prince of the house of Bourbon." It was, in the meeting, to propose the dismemberment of France. But the delegates could not cross the frontier, and that was fortunate. The Restoration was done without their knowledge. Louis XVIII had set out. He stopped on 5 July at Arnouville. It was there that he received Fouché, indoctrinated by Wellington at Neuilly, where he had been to see him in secret.[15] Fouché was playing the same game, he made the same calculation as Talleyrand in 1814, and the transaction was the same between the King and him. The King took Fouché, turning his head away. Fouché gave himself up, rather lent himself, received his pledge and forgot the rest. He had his place of safety, the ministry of the police, that was, ultimately, in his eyes, what France needed, and all the spirit of its royalist conversion in 1815, as of its republican virtue in 1793.[16] Fouché did not impose just himself; it was enforced by the whole Court. Talleyrand said to Pasquier,

> What do you want? Everyone has come together to impose this law on us. The Duke of Wellington, who has his head turned, has himself come to conjure the king. That's not all; the Faubourg Saint-Germain swears only by M. Fouché, all that has reached the princes in letters and emissaries for the past fortnight has spoken only of him and of the great services he rendered to the royal cause. Finally the bailiff of Crussol arrived yesterday and indoctrinated Monsieur so well that, this morning, he came to find the king, preached from the housetops that the salvation of the king and of royalty lay solely in the person of Fouché. I had believed until then that these movements of opinion were reserved for the ignorance of the people, and I was astonished to see the salons of the Faubourg Saint-Germain easier to carry away than the cabarets of the Faubourg Saint-Antoine.

The two accomplices of the time of Barras, the two associates of Brumaire, the accomplices of the time of Marengo, of Madrid, of Wagram, one prince, the other a duke of the Empire, left the cabinet of the brother of Louis XVI, one tall, powdered, insolent, club-footed and limping [Talleyrand], leaning on the arm of the other, spindly, pale and grimacing.[17] "I would love to hear what those lambs are saying," whispered Pozzo as he met them.

On 6 July, Blücher and the Prussians entered Paris, the English remaining encamped in the Bois de Boulogne.[18] They expelled from the Luxembourg the peers of Napoléon, who were still deliberating under the presidency of Cambacérès. Decazes, Prefect of Police, took the keys to the Chamber of Deputies. The *Moniteur* announced on the 8th that the Chamber was dissolved. Fouché officially passed from the Provisional Government, made against the Bourbons, to the Ministry of the Bourbons, made against the Provisional Government. The deputies who presented themselves to sit found closed gates and bayonets, a Royal Fructidor returned home, as in Brumaire, happy not to be taken to Guyana, as under the Directory, and to feel their heads more solid on their shoulders than after 2 June 1793. Louis XVIII made his entry on the 9th, more simply, more militarily than in 1814, but in the midst of a more general eagerness, which here and there took the form of enthusiasm.[19] He said: "I had foreseen the evils with which Paris was threatened, I wish to prevent and repair them." It was his wish, it was his *raison d'être* before the French and all the strength he possessed with regard to foreigners.

Faced with the *fait accompli*, everyone bowed. Wellington, Castlereagh, and Pozzo satisfied, Alexander resigned, and concerned only with creating for Russia, for the French monarchy, a clientele, for the French public a clientele.

## V. Exile of Napoléon

The difficulties were immense, one might say atrocious. There were very painful ones; the invasion with its train of unfulfilled vengeance the year before; there was none more urgent and more embarrassing than the presence of Napoléon. This man who had filled the world for 19 years, now reduced to impotence, no longer knew what to do with himself and the victors did not know what to do with him. He was decidedly too big for all the molds of the old world.

As he could not be sent either to Russia, or to Germany, or to

Italy, where his wife was held in a sort of semi-captivity, or to Austria, where his son was interned in order to hand him over to Court and state pedants; as everyone feared to see him leave for America, from where one returns with too much ease, England, the only government which possessed distant islands and was able to prohibit the approach and to block them, in some way, saw with humor and inevitably threatened with the custody of the prisoner. The English Ministers would have preferred to leave this discourteous task to others and get rid of the Emperor by other means. Let him die! Why not do justice to himself! Liverpool reasoned by dilemma: "One of two things, either Napoléon must resume his primitive character as a French subject, or he is nothing at all, and he led his expeditions like an outlaw, of an outcast who is outside of society, outside of the laws, *hostis generis humani*."[20]

In the first case, it was up to the justice of the King of France: "We would like that the king of France would have Bonaparte shot or hanged; that would be the best way to end the deal," said Liverpool to Castlereagh. And he said to Lieven, Alexander's ambassador: "The lawyers of this country were generally of opinion that H.M. Most Christian would have had every right, and without much scrutiny, to have him tried and convicted."[21] We add: "and execute without stopping": in a procedure like the arrest and the death of the Duke of Enghien. For the operation, in the absence of the court martial of Vincennes, one had provost courts, "this is the best, said Napoléon, to contain the common people and the rabble. To hang, to exile, to drive out, that is what the Bourbons must do; in 1814, they had only acted with rose water, so they were overthrown."[22] But Louis XVIII did not see it that way, and he was right to judge. The court of peers, which sufficed for Ney, was not sufficient for Napoléon.

There remained the other end of the dilemma: kill him. He was an outlaw, even in Europe and its representatives in Vienna. All that was needed was a man of goodwill: Maubreuil was available, Bruslart at his command, and there was no lack of Chouans, companions of Jehu, eager to get their hands dirty and create titles of recognition by the civilized world. But this expedient, which would have had the advantage of reconciling the precedents of the *ancien régime* and the Revolution, the banishment of the Empire, and the outlawry of the Terror, suited neither Alexander, who had solemnly guaranteed Napoléon's life, nor to Wellington, who had assumed his protection. "If the King of France does not feel strong enough to treat him as a rebel,"

Liverpool wrote then, "we are ready to take care of his person."

Napoléon gave himself up, either because he understood that he had no other destiny and preferred to hasten the arrest, or because he kept England, the English, their character, their constitution of the illusions which had been those of almost all the men of his age; or that he imagined that, having taken refuge in England, he would be free there to go, to come, to write, to act, to speak to Europe and to make a party, a sort of Charles-Quint ready to come out of the cloister or of Charles XII among the Turks, or that he remembered Corsica, Theodore the false king, and Paoli the great citizen, both taken in by British hospitality.[23] When very young, he had composed, as one composes a little poem, a letter from Theodore in prison to Walpole: "Unjust men! I wanted to contribute to the happiness of a nation. I succeeded for a while, and you admired me. Fate has changed. I am in a dungeon, and you despise me." And Voltaire's friend, the English *philosophe*, Walpole, answered: "You are suffering and you are unhappy. These are indeed two titles for having a right to the pity of an Englishman. Come out of your prison, and receive £2,000 pension for your subsistence." He sketched these lines, around 1788, probably at Auxonne, lieutenant of artillery. From the island of Aix, where he had been transported, deposed emperor and captive, he wrote, on 14 July, to the Prince-Regent of England:

> Faced with the factions which divide my country and the enmity of the powers of Europe, I have finished my political career, and I come, like Themistocles, to sit at the hearth of the British people. I put myself under the protection of its laws, which I claim from Your Royal Highness, as the most powerful, the most constant and the most generous of my enemies.

This step led him to Saint Helena, where England set itself the task of history, for lack of having been able to suppress his person, to suppress his name and to annihilate his memory. He was embarked on the *Northumberland*. Cockburn, who commanded this ship, was known to be a "rough-mannered" Englishman. After he had landed his prisoner, Bertrand, Napoléon's companion in exile, wrote to him, and in the letter mentioned the title of Emperor: in this island, "no person invested with this dignity, as you tell me, traveled with me on the *Northumberland*." It was the instruction. Hudson Lowe applied it until after death. He did not allow Napoléon's name to appear on the Emperor's coffin, and Napoléon's tomb was sealed on an anonymous grave: *Here lies! no name!*

1. 23 May 1815, translation of Villemain. *Cours de littérature*, VIII. Compare the philipics of 1800-1803, VI, p. 35, 101, 166-169, 206-08, 297.
2. Barante, 21 June 1815.
3. *Journal de Gourgaud*: "There is no comparison to be made between Cromwell and me; I was elected three times by the people."
4. Conversations of 31 août, 23 septembre 1817; *Journal de Gourgaud*, II, p. 283, 231. Compare Montholon, same dates; II, p. 179-80, 201-02, and 12 July 1817, II, p. 150: "It is true that although it was necessary to reign by the axe, that was repugnant to me."
5. This article was not superfluous. We read in a letter from Pozzo to Nesselrode of 27 June, if Dessoles had wanted to agree to kidnap Bonaparte, he could have; but he "refused an act which he considered contrary, according to him, to his personal delicacy."
6. Nesselrode to Pozzo, 17 June 1815.
7. Instructions, 25 June 1815. – Asngberg. – Pasquier, III, p. 315. – Pontécoulant, *Souvenirs*.
8. On this excess, see my study: *Le traité du 20 novembre 1815*, p. 68 et suiv; Pozzo to Nesselrode, 9 July 1815. (Polovtsoff.)
9. Pozzo di Borgo to Nesselrode, 13, 23 May; 4, 17 June 1815. (Polovtsoff.)
10. Memorandum from Liverpool to Castlereagh, 30 June 1815.
11. Wellington to Talleyrand, 24 June 1815. Cf. Letters of Pozzo to Ne»Nesselrode, 23 May, 26 June 1815.
12. Wellington to Bathurst, 2 July; Pozzo to Nesselrode, 1 July 1815.
13. In 1817, people thought, in the same world, of the Prince of Orange. In 1791 we thought of Brunswick, in 1799, of Prince Henry of Prussia. See Barante, letter, July 4, 1815, II, p. 165, 315-17. The commissioners of Haguenau would have spoken of a Prince of Saxony. (Pasquier, III, p. 316.)
14. Angeberg, p. 14, 63.
15. Pozzo to Nesselrode, 4, 8 July 1815.
16. "I am of Fouché's opinion," wrote Proudhon, "and I think that the shortest thing then was to return to the Bourbons. Fouché does not betray. He was then, as always, the representative of that immense party of patriots, or moderate revolutionaries, who never loved the Emperor more than the Terror, who asked nothing better than to be reconciled with the Bourbons if the Bourbons offered them guarantees, that is to say the preservation of their fortunes and their jobs and the new rights created by the Revolution." (*Commentaires sur les mémoires de Fouché*.)
17. "Vice leaning on crime," Chateaubriand, *Mémoires*; Broglie, *Souvenirs*, I, p. 310.
18. Pozzo to Nesselrode, 2 July 1815. (Polovtsoff.)
19. Barante, I, p. 164; Castellane, I, p. 295.
20. To Eldon, in Lord Roseberry, *Napoléon*. (Trans. Filon.)
21. Lieven to Nesselrode, 28 July 1815. (Martens, XI, p. 239.)
22. Gourgaud, 27 décembre 1816.
23. Masson, *Napoléon inconnu*; manuscript of Napoléon, VII: Théodore to Walpole.

Page left intentionally blank.

# Chapter IV: Treaty of 20 November

## 1815

### I. *Objets d'Art*

Louis XVIII had returned to his Tuileries; but he lived there as a sequestered king of Europe, as Louis XVI was sequestered from his people after the days of October 1789. XVI had to wait after Varennes for the constitution given to him by the National Assembly. Government conditions were appalling. North of the Loire, the invasion with all its excesses; south of the Loire, White Terror with all its fury. Between the two, the quivering, starving French army, a wandering revolution, always ready to bite, to run to arms, fermented of revolt, wherever it was sown, which could not be deported, which had to be dispersed, like the Huguenots under Henri IV and the Vendéens at the time of the Consulate. The allies monopolized the country, masters of the finances, disposing of resources; they hindered all policing, prevented all administration. They had organized in Paris, under the name of Conference, a kind of provisional government which, if it respected, in theory, the power of the King, paralyzed its exercise. This Conference was composed, for England, of Castlereagh and Wellington; for Russia, Rasoumowsky and Capo d'Istria; for Austria, Metternich and Wessenberg; for Prussia, Hardenberg and Humboldt. They spoke neither of shortening nor of lightening the occupation. Public monuments were threatened. Louis XVIII, during the festivities of 1814, had been able to become dazed with the joy of reigning and had truly believed, by so many cheers and illuminations, that the catastrophe of the French armies was turning into a blessing for the dynasty and for France. A dreadful ambiguity disguised this entire first Restoration. In July 1815, Louis XVIII saw himself as both necessary and powerless. He felt French, he suffered, and he became King. He found words that remained, and he added to them a kind of poignant majesty by the spectacle of his infirmities. Blücher wanted to blow up the Pont d'Iéna. Louis wrote that he would be carried there in his armchair. These were all the resources of prestige and influence of the French monarchy.

In 1814, it was a decision, on the part of the allies, to displace the dignity of the French, the self-esteem of the Parisians. The Germans were chomping at the bit: they were forced to hold themselves to the port of arms, and when they went out into the streets, to hold their hands to their bodies, closed and clasped. In 1815, they were given license. In 1814 the allies left to the museums the works of art conquered by the Republic and by the Empire. The diplomats cared nothing about it, the Prussians protested little, for lack of masterpieces to lay claim to; the Dutch were left to moan and the Italians to cry. In the way of granting to "French vanity" this alms of trophies, when France was stripped of so many conquests, there entered somewhat of that proud contempt which made an illustrious German historian say, marking with the seal of nonsense the first hero of the French national legend, the Gaul Vercingetorix: "Everything is said about the Celtic nation, when we say that its greatest man was only a knight!"[1] They disdainfully left the knights their outfits, the people their rattles. In 1815, it was out of counsel, and to strike the French at the most sensitive point, to humiliate them before themselves, to castigate them before the universe, that the allies decided to return to the Italians, the Flemings, the Dutch, the Rhinelanders, and the Spanish what they had had to yield or let take. The English Ministers betrayed some inclination to enrich the museums of London by retaliation, seizing, by right of windfall, these masterpieces which they described themselves as "looted" by the French.[2] They reasoned about it as they did in Paris between 1794 and 1797. Said one of the first collectors of paintings, statues, and trinkets, "Too long have these masterpieces been sullied by the aspect of servitude!" In London, they would decorate these three deities of British Valhalla: Religion, Commerce and Liberty! Castlereagh, who opined purely politically, felt that the King could hardly "maintain himself in France if, after presenting himself to the nation, as a means of placating the allies, they disavowed him to such an extent." Wellington considered the measure not "prudent." But Liverpool, very insular, very Anglican, persisted: "We must give the French a lesson in high political morality." The Conference diplomats adjourned. Unable to prevent anything, Louis XVIII found it more worthy to allow himself to be stripped by force than to compromise and ratify, even in part, the operation. While waiting for it to be officially decided, Italian, Dutch, and German commissioners spread through the galleries, marking the rooms, and the removal began.

## II. Projects of Dismemberment

The museums contained only the rooms of honor, the crown jewels of the building; it was the very edifice that the majority of the allies claimed to undermine, dismantle, and strip. While officers and soldiers in the occupied departments ransomed and wrapped up, in Paris ministers and publicists reasoned and deliberated on the surest means of cutting off and enervating the vanquished, of enriching and fortifying the victors.[3] The Prussians demanded, bitterly and greedily, their double revenge, that of their losses in 1807, and that of their disappointments in 1814. One wonders what revenge could well satisfy the Bavarians, Württembergers, Badois, Hessians of Darmstadt and other Confederates of the Rhine, showered by Napoléon with German crowns, abbeys, and seigniories. They nevertheless showed themselves to be the most rapacious, the most insatiable, and they remained, in this, in their character, having never acted except in this way, in all diplomatic ways, and having become the allies of France against the Holy Roman Empire only by the effects of this same greed which threw them then on the spoils of France.[4]

Their agents besieged the Conference and the embassies with notes, speeches, pamphlets, and innumerable gazette articles. Hatred, revenge, covetousness, were confused there in the most cynical way with motives of interest, reasons of strategy and legal deductions according to the maxims of the "law of nations." Because it was not enough for them to enrich themselves and to retaliate, they claimed to rob only to ensure public peace, guarantee civilization and do the work of historical truth, transcendent justice, Christian morality above all, by inspiring, with skillful penances combined, to the sinner hardened the horror of his sin. Stein said,

> The people rightly demand from sovereigns that they be accounted for the blood they have shed, the property they have sacrificed to repel the insolent and greedy Frenchman. Everyone now agrees that the first Treaty of Paris left France with a military power that is a constant threat to European security.

He designated the Archduke Charles "as the character best suited to overcome the Alsatians-Lorrainers." Gagern said to Humboldt, "The monarchs of Prussia and Austria could not return with honor and security to their own capitals leaving the borders of France intact." Münster, the Minister of Hanover, held for "natural limits" according to his German notion: "The Pyrenees, the Alps and the sea present limits to the ambition of France; why should the Jura, the Vosges and the Ardennes not return to Germany the guarantees enjoyed by Spain and Italy?" They needed French Flanders to ensure peace in Dutch Flanders; they needed Dunkirk, otherwise the capture of Antwerp meant nothing. They needed Franche-Comté, where, said Gneisenau, there remained so many memories, so many monuments of the golden age (*Goldenen Zeit*) of Charles V, and of the attachment of the peoples to the House of Habsburg: *Deo et Caesari semper fidelis!* They had to dismantle this fortress because it was offensive in the hands of the French, annex this other because it would immediately become defensive in the hands of the Dutch or the Germans, conquer this territory because it seemed useful for the defense of Germany, and this other because they had once been part of it.

No interest, according to them, in sparing the French a pure deception, on the contrary. What the French would never forgive was the loss of the left bank of the Rhine, the loss of supremacy, in defeat they would not be grateful to the allies for taking a little less instead of a little more, so politics therefore required taking a lot, everything necessary, everything superfluous, everything possible. Stein declared "The neighbors, the allies, will always be threatened by the offensive constitution of the old frontier, by the systematic ambition of the French government, by the ardent vanity of the people, who will not cease demanding the conquest of Belgium and left bank of the Rhine." Gagern wrote, "To possess the Rhine, to have Alsace, is for them only a source of pride, a temptation to have the entire limit of the Rhine."[5] Schoepflin alleged: "Alsace, that guardian power of the Upper Rhine, which once opened France to the Germans, now opens Germany to the French." Finally, Hardenberg,

> France must return to her defense formed by art or by nature, and return to her neighbors the defense she has taken from them, that is to say, Alsace and the fortresses of the Low Countries, the Meuse, the Moselle and the Saar. For the good of Europe, for the good of France, let's not miss the opportunity. The hand of divine Providence has obviously brought about this occasion.

Alexander showed himself both what he was and what he wanted to appear, both political and magnanimous. Until then, politics had prevailed in his character. This greatness of soul, of which he felt capable, of which he had made an ideal since his youth, he had rather put on the stage and had given himself the spectacle of it in 1814 rather than he had experienced it in effective and operated in action. In 1815, he saw high, he saw clearly, he saw far, and he acted with as much simplicity and uprightness as energy and skill. He showed all the more merit there in that part of the role, perhaps the most cherished by the artist, the reconstitution of France as a free country and the creation of a new dynasty, under the Russian aegis, escaped in 1815 as in 1814. He knew how to overcome his prejudices. Louis XVIII no doubt bothered him. He felt powerless to trick this prince as subtle as himself and to dazzle with his prestige this Voltairian armored against all phantasmagoria. But Louis XVIII would live for a short time, and his eventual successors only asked, by taste, by heir-presumptive reaction, to give themselves to Russia. Alexander could accomplish this remarkable prodigy of dexterity, becoming the ostensible idol of the royalists while remaining the hidden god of the liberals. He displayed as much art in asserting his actions as in making his designs prevail. He knew how to marvelously play on the imagination and sensitivity of the French, affecting before them, with the disinterestedness of all conquest and the detachment of all pride, a profound contempt for the gross greed of the Germans; offering his moved grace in contrast with British haughtiness presenting itself as the sole savior of the old frontier, honor and dignity of the monarchy, condition for the consolidation of the Crown, necessity for the recovery of the country; gaining by his familiar majesty the alliance of the Court and that of the enlightened public, the mystical legitimists and the philosophical intellectuals; finally assuring France, thus bound by feelings to Russia, the resources capable of making it, when the time came, a profitable ally. But first, precautionary measures: a temporary occupation, and a contribution, because it was necessary to make allowance for the avarice and the indigence of the Germans. Capo d'Istria, in a memo drawn up under the inspiration of the Tsar, very highly developed the very intelligent motives for these measures, and, in the name of his master, invited the allies to deliberate on them, 28 July 1815.

It was above all against the English that Alexander wanted to secure an ally in France, and it was in the East, against the Turkish Empire, with a view to establishing Russian supremacy over the Orthodox peoples that he sought the effects of this alliance. It was against Russia, for the preservation of the Ottoman Empire, that Wellington and Castlereagh thought that France might one day be necessary to them. For opposite reasons, they concluded, like Alexander, to strengthen the restored Government, to render it popular, to assure it guarantees of duration and the means of recovery. They brought to it no good grace, no search for skill, but they put into it a tenacity as active as the Russians, and from this competition came the event. Their task was singularly more arduous than that of the Tsar. Alexander had only to command his ministers. The English ambassadors first had to convert their Government. They had started, they continued.

The letters which were then exchanged between Paris and London, between Castlereagh and Liverpool, are remarkable bits of politics. Out of taste, out of consideration of the chambers, of the press, of public opinion, of the City, out of British and Protestant pride, Liverpool stubbornly took something, if only for a work of evangelization and a measure of penance from the place of France. He decided and argued from afar, according to doctrine, precedents, prejudices, his own passions, those of the public. The ambassadors in Paris judged on the spot, and directly they did not put an idealized England in opposition to a denatured France. They saw France alive, and spoke of a France that England had an interest in seeing live and which could only live by its own life; ministers and ambassadors moved, moreover, solely by the superior interest of their country. The eternal dispute between those who imagine the world according to their politics and those who arrange their politics according to the realities of the world.[6] Castlereagh wrote to Liverpool on 17August,

To take away from France a few portions of territory and a line of fortresses is to exasperate it without weakening it, to depopularize the king or to force him to throw himself into the arms of his people, to deprive peace of any chance of lasting and to inaugurate for a long time in Europe the system of standing armies. Certain satisfactions must, however, be given to the German powers. This will be achieved by restricting France to the 1790 border, by allocating the enclaves to neighboring countries. France will keep Avignon, and Germany will get Landau. A peace concluded on this principle will not be popular either in Germany or in England. But our object is not to collect trophies. It is to bring the world back to peaceful habits. I do not think that this goal can be reconciled with the idea of materially altering the situation of France. Nor am I quite convinced – provided that by putting a straitjacket on her for a few years we can bring her back to these habits – that France, with her present dimensions, cannot become a useful member rather than a dangerous one to the European system. (Add Russia, which had taken a position, and very clearly) Russia, because of its remoteness, inclines rather to protect France; the principles of the Emperor Alexander naturally push it in this direction. He would also be inclined to remain allied with France, and he would not like to see her reduced too low.

Metternich leaned towards the Russian side; but, said Castlereagh, "he fears to give Russia too preponderant a role, and to favor, by seconding the views of Alexander, too close an alliance between Russia and France." Gagern reported, "Castlereagh's main arguments, spoken by ear, revolved around the need to maintain the alliance, to contain Russia, which had a penchant for linking up with France, and to enter into a rivalry with her for generosity and moderation."

Thus Alexander spared the Bourbons because he wanted to spare France; the English spared France because they wanted to secure the alliance of the Bourbons; the Austrians saw themselves brought to the same temperaments so that neither France would give itself to Russia nor the Bourbons to England. The fear of the Revolution, of Jacobinism, was added to this in Metternich and, consequently, the need to consolidate the Restoration. A league was formed between the three which broke, for a moment, the famous alliance of four. The Germans, by their indiscretion, their intrigues, their brutally, displayed voracity, did the rest. "The Prussians cannot be supported: their conduct tends to unite the French and divide the allies," wrote

Castlereagh.

The Prussians constituted themselves the *ex officio* advocates of Germany in this affair. All the Germans ran towards them, harassing them with representations, complaints, exhortations, indignant harangues, threatening notes. They circumvented and solicited, in London, the Hanoverians, the Prince Regent and his ministers. They cried misery, they cried persecution. They saw themselves rejected everywhere. Alexander exhaled in a conversation with Stein the disgust he felt at this:

> I have a very high regard for the Prussian army, but it sullies and profanes the great and beautiful cause of the allies by the vengeance, the ill-treatment, the violence of its soldiers. The Prince of Wurtemberg is too indulgent towards his troops; he exaggerates his pretensions to the diminution of France, claims to deprive her of Alsace and Lorraine. This is contrary to the promises given in Vienna at the beginning of the war. Alsatians are reluctant to become Germans.

A Prussian gentleman discussing politics before Alexander exclaimed: "We have bayonets." Whereupon the Tsar, angrily: "And I too have bayonets!" And he left the apartment.[7] They did so much that Liverpool, without going to the merits and for the future, ended up writing Castlereagh on 18 August: "I entirely share your opinion and that of the Duke of Wellington about the extravagance of Prussian proposals in the present circumstances."

These discussions filled the month of August. Proposals presented by the various powers, in their notes and memoirs, can be summed up as follows:

RUSSIA: Temporary occupation and war contribution to be fixed by mutual agreement.

ENGLAND: Temporary occupation, war contribution, return to the 1790 border, Savoy and Landau, as maximum territorial cessions.

AUSTRIA: Occupation by 150,000 men, contribution of war, return to the border of 1790, cession or dismantling of the fortresses of the first line, Flanders and Alsace.

PRUSSIA: Occupation by 240,000 men, war contribution of 1.2 billion, cession of the strongholds of Flanders, Alsace, Lorraine and Savoy.

LOW COUNTRIES AND GERMAN STATES: Occupation, contribution, cession of Flanders, Alsace, Lorraine, Savoy. The dismemberment, the most extensive that had been thought of, involved the loss of 4,762,000 inhabitants and included Franche-Comté, Alsace, Lorraine, Burgundy, French Flanders. The border left out Dunkirk, Lille, Metz, Strasbourg, Besançon, Chambéry, and part of Dauphiné.

It was Paris open, "a masterpiece of destruction," said in a report to the Tsar from Pozzo di Borgo. As soon as the opposition of the Russians and the English was known, there was a clamor in all the inns and *tables d'hôte* where the Germans met. Stein said: "The Russians want Germany to remain vulnerable." Gneisenau wrote on 18 August to his friend and fellow fighter the poet Arndt:

> We are in danger of concluding a new Treaty of Utrecht, and the danger comes from the same side as before. England does not want anything bad to happen to France: not the cession of territory! That Russia uses such language is explained by her selfish policy, by her design to leave Austria and Prussia threatened within their frontiers, and always to arrange for an ally in France. But, for England, one can only conclude from such perversity an effort to maintain the war on the Continent and Germany in her dependence. Austria, or rather Metternich, is tottering, doubtful, she is considering alliances with France. Bavaria and Württemberg join us. If everyone were safer and more capable of following a higher policy, we could well, in common, with the small States, make the law, and the others would have to be silent.

But this community, precisely, was what was most lacking, and it was lacking by the very motive of the German claims and by the particular character of the small states: greed, which brought them together to plunder and pitted them against each other for the division of the spoils. Flanders? They held to it only for the principles: historical right, and the lesson of morality; it was, moreover, up to the English to build the "barrier" and to fortify their client in the Low Countries. The big problem remained Lorraine, Alsace, Franche-Comté. Now, who would keep them?[8] Prussia, which was overwhelmed, and the small States found Prussia already too powerful. Austria neither condescended nor wanted, and we have seen how much, in 1792 and 1813, it dreaded this dangerous present. However, if Prussia took Alsace, Austria would claim compensation; it would also claim one in the event that Bavaria was awarded the "German Marches" as guard: Bavaria must not become a Prussia of the south. Besides, who could count on Bavaria? Would Austria be safer because the Bavarians would garrison Strasbourg and Metz? The examples of the War of Succession were not forgotten; those of the war of 1805 and that of 1809 would have sufficed to revive them. If they did not entrust Strasbourg and Metz to the Bavarians, confer them to the Badois, to the Württembergers? Then the Bavarians protested in their turn. If the Marches were divided among the small States, the guard seemed insufficient; if it were attributed to one alone, it would become too strong. There was talk of giving Alsace to Prussia, and Lorraine to an archduke; but the small States immediately protested against the usurpation of the great, that is: no Lorraine to Austria, and Alsace to Prussia; but where to compensate the Austrians for this increase in Prussia? It was, in all its swamp, the historical mess of Germany's quarry, after the hunts of the Holy Roman Empire. Letting the pack howl, the older ones retreated to the hall of honor, where their meal was served.

    Wellington had taken the initiative on the explanations, with Pozzo, on 1 August.[9] Pozzo wrote, "He seemed convinced to me that unless the two Russian and English cabinets agree, we will never reach a conclusion." He knew the hesitations of Metternich and the repugnance of this minister against any clear and definitive party; he was alarmed at the temerity of the Prussians. They agreed in principle to a temporary occupation by an army of which "Wellington would willingly take command." According to Pozzo, "This project, gives to Lord Wellington the guard of the interests of Europe towards France; but he is, in fact, the only man who can undertake it with more probability of success and less inconvenience." Metternich was the first to let go of the Germans, and his defection, highly political, highly calculated, led to the bankruptcy of Prussia, which found itself alone with its starving clientele. If Metternich had retained some regret over his compromised popularity in Germany, he would have consoled himself with the rather pitiful spectacle of the retirement to which Hardenberg and Humboldt were condemned and, behind them, the whole "clique" of small diplomats from the princely, the whole hated clan of Jacobins, revolutionaries, patriots, supporters of a great national and united Germany, Stein, Gneisenau, Arndt, Austria's worst enemies henceforth and those whom peace was precisely going to give Metternich the means to reduce to inaction and silence.

Things thus arranged and judging that it was proper to finish, Castlereagh sent, on 2 September, to his colleagues, a memorandum which was the real ultimatum of England to France, even to the allies. Russia joined on 7 September.[10] Austria allowed itself to be led back to it. With Prussia, Alexander had recourse to great means, those of Kalisch, of Langres, of Vienna: he had an interview with Friedrich-Wilhelm III. Hardenberg struggled, jotted down desperate notes, then capitulated. On 12 September, agreement was restored among the four: they had adopted the English project. There remained the question of works of art. Restitution and removal were decided. Alexander was not interested in it. The English found in it a means of giving, by vexing the French, satisfaction to British rancor and puritanism. Public opinion in France was grateful to the Emperor of Russia for his abstention; as for the English, who put their arrogance on concealing their concessions on the essential articles, we only knew of them their demands on this article, and they were not forgiven for it. Gagern wrote, "The murmurs are high, and especially directed against the Duke of Wellington. Lord Castlereagh assured me yesterday with a laugh: We are worse and more horrified than the Prussians!"

On 20 September, the four handed Talleyrand their ultimatum; it carried: 1) Cession of a territory equal to two thirds of what had been added to old France by the treaty of 30 May 1814, which involved the loss of Savoy and the places of Condé, Philippeville, Marienbourg, Givet, Sarrelouis, Charlemont, Landau, Fort-Joux, Fort de l'Ecluse; 2) The dismantling of Huningue; 3) The payment of 600 million as a war indemnity and 200 million for the construction of fortresses in the countries bordering on France, notably the barrier of the Low Countries; 4) The occupation for seven years of a line of territory and strongholds along the northern and eastern borders.

Savoy had not formed part of ancient France; but the other places required by the allies had belonged to it: Condé and Charlemont, by the Treaty of 1679, the Lock in 1602, Marienbourg and Philippeville in 1659, Landau in 1680 and 1714; Sarrelouis had been fortified by Vauban in 1680.

### III. Duke of Richelieu

Until this day, the French Government knew nothing of the fate reserved for it by the allies. All the diplomacy of Talleyrand had worn itself out fighting over the article on works of art. He had suffered haughty refusals and submitted to the imperious injunctions of the Conference. The King, Paris, the whole of France, waited with an anxiety that rose to anguish. The King maintained only official relations with the sovereigns.[11] The whole train of galas, dinners, and spectacles of 1814 was restricted to courtesies and ceremonial gestures. The allies shut themselves up among themselves, creating a vacuum around the Tuileries and Foreign Affairs. Talleyrand, since Napoléon's return, had lost all prestige and credit. Louis XVIII, who did not love him and, despite all the spirit of his letters from Vienna, liked him little, never forgave him for having imposed in 1814, in Paris, in Ghent; crumpled, at bottom, of the quasi-tutelage of a character who, despite all his apparent deference, raised the pretensions of a feudatory of Hugues Capet by the pride of a feudatory of Napoléon; too old nobility, too recent nobility, both equally disagreeable to the King. Finally, he held a particular grudge against him for having introduced Fouché into the Council. Talleyrand annoyed the King, but Fouché revolted him, and more so as both seemed less useful, especially Fouché. Louis had not yet swallowed the bitterness of this forced choice. It was for this end and political patient a diversion to his forced inaction, a revenge against his relatives, the coterie of Artois, Angoulême and Berry, to use between his soft and fat hands, to reduce to the state of revolutionary puppet, this once so redoubtable man, imposed as necessary and becoming so quickly cumbersome.

The Faubourg Saint-Germain's craze for Fouché passed with fear. Thus Tallien and his associates after 9 Thermidor. Once in the Council and in the normal government, Fouché was no longer there.[12] The salons which had evoked him as a savior remembered that this savior had been a regicide and a Terrorist, and demanded his exclusion. Louis XVIII appointed him, on 14 September, envoy in Dresden, where he was soon to pass from the personage of resident to that of proscribed.

It was a warning for Talleyrand, although having neither voted in January 1793, nor ordered executions, nor made a profession of purveyor to the guillotine, he had only to fear, in terms of exile, than the idleness of the peerage. Reduced to inertia, for the allies heard no complaints and revealed no design, he affected casualness and dissipation. They spoke only of his autumn love with the Duchesse de Dino, and of the melancholy into which he was plunged by the departure for Vienna of this enchantress. Talleyrand, without a doubt, was affected by it, being taken by the senses, the mind, the heart perhaps, as much as he was susceptible, and, at his age, these grips are tyrannical; but it did not displease him to be said so: it was a gallant attitude of a great lord, while disgrace would carry off one of those affronts from which one does not easily recover. However, it was coming, and he felt it coming, and from the very side whence the favor had come in 1814: Russia.

The King was antipathetic to the Tsar, and the Minister was odious and suspicious to him. Talleyrand had, in Paris, in 1814, given all hope to Alexander, who believed him to be at his discretion. In Vienna, he showed himself the constant adversary of the designs of the Tsar. The Frenchmen of Alexander's entourage attributed to Talleyrand alone all the machination of the January treaty. They asserted that Louis XVIII knew nothing of it. Alexander, suspicious of the King, refused to negotiate with the Minister. He even had his agents, Nesselrode and Pozzo, working against him.[13] Louis XVIII had no taste for receiving a foreign minister from Alexander; necessity compelled him to it. His temper against Talleyrand found in it a pretext for satisfying himself; he knew how to bring him, and in rather dry form, to resign. On 20 September, informed that the allies said they were in a position, he appointed Talleyrand, Dalberg and Baron Louis "to confer relative to the definitive arrangement which must be made with the powers assembled in Paris."[14]

Talleyrand, for his part, never failed to break through the game, and seeing himself threatened, he planned his outing, thinking of a future comeback. He used it with the King as well as formerly with the Emperor. As he had been able to blame Napoleon for the unpopularity of conquests, he tried to blame Louis XVIII and the successor that this king would give him for the unpopularity of concessions. He found in the demands of the allies the most honorable of motives for resignation, and he contrived once more to do himself honor to necessity. On the same day they adopted it, September 20, the allies communicated their ultimatum to Talleyrand. We find in Foreign Affairs this note:[15]

> Here are the proposals from the allies. The king is to hear them this evening at nine o'clock. Two copies are needed. M. de Talleyrand begs you to have them done by the bureaus. I'll come and pick them up before nine o'clock. Make your thoughts. I cannot sign such agreements. There is neither France nor king with that.

Talleyrand thought the same and said so out loud. He had La Besnardière compose a response to the note from the allies: it was dated 21 September, a publicist's memo, an academic dissertation on the right of conquest.[16] The allies recognized the style and the spirit of the notes of Caulaincourt at the congress of Châtillon, of the notes of Talleyrand on Saxony at the congress of Vienna, and returned the document to the same archives. It spoke rhetorically of "the spirit of conquest inspired by usurpation." A German, Gagern, observed, ironically:

> When M. le Prince de Talleyrand or my honorable friend M. le Chevalier de la Besnardière tell me that they detest the spirit of conquest, I believe them. I gladly pay them this personal tribute. I witnessed this noble sentiment in calamitous times. But if they speak in the name of France, we cannot help seeing, in this horror of the forbidden fruit, the application of a fable by Gellert and La Fontaine.

However Talleyrand admitted the discussion, he admitted cessions "on what was not the territory of old France," that is to say Savoy, and perhaps Landau.

But the allies seemed at the end of their concessions. The English had had too much trouble leading their own government there; the Prussians had complied with it with too much humor to risk starting the debate over again. Alexander alone, who from the beginning had spoken against any territorial cession, would perhaps consent to some amendment; would he decide his allies there? To tempt him, he had at least to find in it a serious political interest or some fine motive for disinterestedness. He discovered no interest in showing himself magnanimous through the Talleyrand channel, and, for Louis XVIII to obtain a new token of friendship from Russia, he was to bring him some pledge of the sincerity and duration of his gratitude.

Louis XVIII saw Alexander on 22 September, and he got almost nothing from him: words, "opinions not very different from the terms of the transaction."[17] Louis XVIII did not know or did not want to find what he would have had to tell Alexander to earn it. Alexander no doubt judged that it would have been too condescending to insinuate it himself. It was then that Pozzo intervened. This very slender Corsican had been able to please Louis XVIII, who even thought of attaching him as Minister of the Interior.[18] He desired the covenant; he knew perfectly well what value Alexander would place on his intervention. He said so, and managed to get Louis XVIII to admit it. He doubtless gave him to understand that Alexander had, in Paris and Vienna, experienced disappointments too painful to face new ones; he blamed Talleyrand for the error of the treaty of 3 January; he spoke of this treaty as if the King had neither approved nor even known of it; but he insinuated that Alexander, to intervene with his allies, needed a pledge of the King's intentions, and it was thus that the expedient of a letter from the King to the Tsar was devised. This letter was destined to remain in the Russian archives, as a bill of exchange in royal form, an authentic testimony of the solicitations of the King of France and of the obligations contracted by him towards Russia. Pozzo prepared the minute, Louis XVIII probably wrote the passages relating to his person. He was not lazy to write; he wrote in elegant form, and when it was a question of his honor and the integrity of old France, in grand style:

> It is in the bitterness of my heart that I appeal to Your Majesty. I felt the need to renounce this surplus territory which had been devolved to France by the Treaty of Paris. But could I have presumed that instead of these conditions, already quite onerous, I would be offered others which combine ruin with dishonor? No, Sire, I still cannot persuade myself that your opinion is irrevocable. The confidence that your great and generous soul inspires in me still resists the sad reality.
>
> But if it were otherwise; if I had the misfortune to deceive myself; if France no longer had to hope for the revocation of the decree which is intended to degrade her; If Your Majesty remained inflexible, and did not want to use with your august allies the ascendancy given to you by your virtues, friendship and a common glory, then, I no longer hesitate to confess it to you, Sire, I would refuse to be the instrument of the loss of my people and I would descend from the throne rather than condescend to tarnish its ancient splendor by an unexampled

abasement.

> Your Majesty will no doubt resonate in the sincerity of this confession, which is based on an unshakeable resolution, the full extent of my pain, as well as the courtesy of the feelings with which I am...

These expressions seem rather disproportionate if one thinks only of the extent of the territories which had to be saved. What did the King mean when he speaks of the conditions "which unite ruin with dishonor?" For ruin, it was the excess of the contribution (800 million) and the duration of the military occupation by 150,000 men, during seven years, at the expense of France. For dishonor, it was the cession of Condé, Givet, Charlemont, Philippeville, Marienbourg, Sarrelouis, Landau, the forts of Joux and Écluse, the dismantling of Huningue. Shacks, you will say; was it appropriate to view the abandonment of it as shameful, when a year before one had not been dishonored to renounce the kingdom of Italy, the entire left bank of the Rhine and Holland? But the territories abandoned in 1814 were conquests of the Revolution; vitiated conquests in the eyes of Louis XVIII. By renouncing it, this king restored, but did not yield. The territories claimed by the ultimatum of 20 September had belonged to old France, and came from Louis XIV; to give up a particle of it was, for Louis XVIII, to alienate a sacred heritage and to capitulate on his principle almost as seriously as if he had accepted the plebiscite. This explains the solemnity of the expressions of the letter.

Louis signed it on 23 September. He did more. He decided to dismiss Talleyrand and to appoint to the presidency of the Council, with the portfolio of foreign affairs, a man whose entry into the ministry would be for Alexander the living guarantee of the King's sincerity. This statesman, who passed for a "good Russian," was, at the same time, the best Frenchman in the world, the most enlightened of royalists and the most apt not only to put France back on its feet in Europe, but to put the monarchy on foot in France, to make of Louis XVIII, in Europe, something other than the lieutenant general of the coalition, a true King of France, and, in France; something other than the king of emigration, the king of all the French. Absent from France since 1790, the Duc de Richelieu had not emigrated: he had taken service in Russia, in good standing and form, and by temperament, by public education, by heart he was also the least "emigrated." He knew affairs, and he had proved himself as an administrator in his government of Odessa. Finally, he had taken no part in the wars of the coalition. He did not return to France as a winner. A man of old France, capable of understanding and loving the new, Richelieu possessed, to the highest degree, qualities which Talleyrand lacked and which nothing, in the crisis of affairs, could supply: dignity, purity of life, nobility of character, sincerity which commands confidence and attracts sympathy: from head to toe, a perfect gentleman in the service of the State.[19]

However, he hesitated, knowing the disagreements of the royal family and being wary of the pitfalls of the ultras. It was the Tsar who decided it, and the words he addressed to him on 24 September shed light on the whole story.

> Intriguers of the worst kind, he told him (Talleyrand), nearly embroiled us, the king and me, by unjustifiable steps, harmful to the true interests of France (understand the treaty of 3 January). I cannot trust them; You alone offer me enough to forget this act of ingratitude; I release you from all your engagements towards me, on the condition that you will serve your king as you have served me. Be the link of the sincere alliance between the two countries, I demand it in the name of the salvation of France.

Richelieu placed himself at the disposal of Louis XVIII. Talleyrand, however, without response from the allies, asked the King to intervene personally with them. Louis XVIII answered him, with the most cruel, but the most constitutional irony: "It is up to the cabinet to get out of the difficulty." Talleyrand understood and resigned. Then he presented it to the public as an act of patriotism. "Why don't you want to be Minister for Europe with us?" asked Castlereagh. "Because I only want to be the Minister for France, and you can see that by the way I responded to your note," he reportedly replied. The King accepted the resignation "with the air of a very relieved man."[20] "My retirement was also a relief for the Emperor of Russia. He needed a dupe, and I couldn't be."[21] Fifteen years later, he wrote from London, where, representing Louis-Philippe d'Orléans, he had just had Belgium declared neutral: "The humiliating conditions proposed in 1815 then decided my retirement."[22]

On 26 September, the Ministry was constituted. Two days later, 100 million was deducted from the war contribution and the dismemberment of the frontier reduced, besides Savoy, to the places of Philippeville, Marienbourg, Sarrelouis, Landau. France saved Condé, Givet, Charlemont, Joux, Fort de l'Écluse. This was the Duke of Richelieu's joyful advent gift. Alexander declared that he would go no further, and the representatives of Louis XVIII struggled in vain, but obtained nothing more. As Richelieu insisted to the Tsar, this prince showed him a map on which was drawn the maximum line of the claims of the allies:[23] "Here is France such as my allies wanted to make it; only my signature is missing, and I promise you it will always be missing." He could not end with more nobility, grace, and skill a negotiation into which he had introduced a policy so firm, so skillful, with so much real grandeur.

Richelieu wrote to him on 17 October: "May your Majesty please say that France exists, and support this will, and I dare to hope that we will save ourselves." Alexander had remade Prussia; Richelieu called him the savior of France: let him complete the reconstruction of Poland, and his dream would be accomplished. Less than a century after the death of Peter, who was the first to make known to Europe that the Tsar of Muscovy was one of the great princes, Alexander had led the victorious Russian armies to Paris, he posed as the protector of the heir of Louis XIV and the heir of Frederick, and he raised Russia to continental supremacy.

## IV. The Signature

The detailed arrangements, notably those of occupation and contributions, filled the month of October and part of the month of November. In the meantime, Murat, after having wandered like an outlaw in Provence, attempted one last adventure. Carried away by the vertigo of the Crown like others by the vertigo of the abyss, he landed on the shores of his ancient kingdom with the insane design of unleashing a revolution there. He was arrested and shot at Pizzo on 13 October 1815.[24] Pozzo di Borgo wrote on November 7, "You know the end of Murat. Ney will be judged within the week." Arrested on 5 August in violation of the capitulation of Paris and by the unpardonable denial of speech and of the foreigners who had signed this capitulation, and of the Government which had profited from it, Ney appeared before the Court of Peers, transformed into a provost court, where sat so many of his companions arms of the Republic and his classmates in the Imperial nobility. He was condemned to death on 5

December and executed on the 7th. Murat was 44, Ney 48.

The peace treaty was signed on 20 November.[25] The districts of Belgium and Germany, indicated above, as well as the parts of Savoy added in 1814 to the former French territory, were separated from it. Huningue was dismantled. France paid a war indemnity of 700 million and underwent an occupation of 150,000 men at French expense, on the northern and eastern frontiers. The duration of this occupation was set at a maximum of five years; however, the sovereigns reserved the right to shorten the term, by mutual agreement, after three years, if the state of France allowed it. This occupation presented the double character of a taking of pledge for the payment of the indemnity and of a guarantee against the danger of a new revolution. Against this peril, the four renewed on the very day of the treaty, 20 November, their alliance of Chaumont.

This treaty confirmed the executive power of the alliance. This alliance had constituted a charter for Europe, the final act of 9 June 1815, which determined the state of possession of each power. The allies tried to go further, to give this Europe, provided with a law and a police force, principles and a system of government.

Principles had been stipulated in the mystical contract signed, on 26 September, by Alexander, Friedrich-Wilhelm III and Franz II, said to be the Treaty of the Holy Alliance. The three sovereigns, before separating, wished to address a solemn thanksgiving to heaven, to call the universe to witness of the beauty of their oaths, and, considering themselves invested with a political apostolate, erect its symbol. They declared themselves brothers, delegated by Providence to the government of branches of the same family: Austria, Prussia, Russia, and, considering themselves as compatriots in the same Christian city, they would lend themselves on all occasions, and in all location, assistance, aid and relief. England joined. These principles, one could say this manifest political religion, they organized its rites and decreed its canon law. They sought in the means they had employed to restore peace a means of maintaining it. They decided to make congresses a European institution intended to prevent and settle disputes between states and nations, "To ensure and facilitate the execution of the present treaty – 20 November – and to consolidate the close relations which today unite the four sovereigns for the happiness of the world, the high contracting parties have agreed to renew at determined times meetings devoted to the great common interests and to the examination of the measures which, in each of these epochs, will be judged most salutary for the peace and prosperity of the peoples and for the maintenance of peace in Europe."[26]

This peace was placed under the regime of congresses, and to regulate this regime, the four set themselves up as a directory. France was excluded. It had ceased to be outside conquest only to pass under guardianship. It remained subject to foreign occupation, for the police, and to the Conference, for politics. The ambassadors of the four continued to sit in Paris, in this form, supervising everything, interfering in all the operations of the French Government, because there was no essential measure of government which was not connected with the execution of the Treaty of Paris: maintenance of peace, payment of the war contribution, maintenance of the army of occupation. That way, they touched on the administration in the occupied departments and, through finance, to the whole Government.

Louis XVIII and Richelieu therefore had only one political object: to liberate French territory, to liberate French finances, to restore to the nation its independence, to the Crown its liberty of action, and to France its dignity among the nations. However, it was not enough for them to pay, they had to reassure the allies on the duration of the government of the Restoration, and obtain from them, in reality, the right to exist. They succeeded in a Government which was, during three years, 1817-1820, one of the most beneficent that France had known and which, for the foundation of the free government, can be compared to the four years of the Consulate of Bonaparte, for the establishment of civil liberty. They achieved this, thanks to the generous and political support which had saved the integrity of old France in 1815, that of Tsar Alexander and that of Wellington, who commanded the army of occupation and chaired the Conference. Alexander expressed the wish that France should be restored to itself, and Wellington certified that it could be so without danger to the peace of Europe. Thus were negotiated and signed, in 1817, a convention which alleviated the occupation of 30,000 men; in 1818, at the Congress of Aix-la-Chapelle, another convention which accepted for the remainder of the war indemnity a loan guaranteed by bankers from Holland and England.[27] On 4 November, in this congress which once again brought together the three sovereigns, army chiefs, and chiefs of peoples of 1813, Alexander, Friedrich-Wilhelm III, and Franz II, with the principal diplomats of the coalition and the treaties of 1815, Castlereagh, Wellington, Metternich, Nesselrode, Capo d'Istria, Hardenberg, the representatives of the four invited the Duc de Richelieu to come and sit on their councils and henceforth to take part in their deliberations. On 15 November, the high government of Europe by the five great powers was really declared to the world and governed by the principles laid down in Paris three years earlier.[28] On 30 November 1818, the last foreign soldiers left French territory. The Great War, the Twenty-Three Years' War, was definitely over.

Considering only the surface of things, the colors of the map, the letter of the treaties and the arrangement of the charters, it seems that France had simply returned to its starting point. It had undertaken the war in 1792 to defend its national independence, the integrity of its territory, the reforms which it had accomplished in the laws (civil liberty) and the guarantees which it had given itself of it rights by its political institutions. War had been declared by Louis XVI, the constitutional king of the French; peace was signed by Louis XVIII, the King of France, governing according to the charter which guaranteed civil and political liberties to the French brought back to their territory of 1790. The body of the nation was not affected. The essential results of the Revolution remained. France retained the Civil Code with its social effects. It possessed representative government with its political consequences. The cycle was closed.

1. Mommsen, *Histoire romaine*.
2. "Either we return them to the countries where they were taken, or we share them among the allies." Liverpool to Castlereagh, 15 July 1815.
3. Pieces in Angeberg-Schaumann: *Geschichte des zweiten pariser Friedens*; Gagern, *Mein Antheil an der Politik*; Pertz, Stein; Gervinus, Varnhagen von Esse; Treitschke; Oncken; Martens; Arndt, *Hardenberg's Leben*; Gentz, *Briefe an Pilat*; Correspondence of Wellington, Castlereagh, Pozzo di Borgo. One will find a summary and numerous extracts from these pieces in the study entitled. *Le Traité de Paris du 20 novembre 1815*, ch. II, projects of dismemberment.
4. Compare the negotiations of Gertruydenberg, of The Hague, in May 1700, in particular the Prussian memorandum on Franche-Comté, the necessity of humiliating France, of exhausting it, of freeing the course of the Rhine. Masson *Journal de Torcy*; De Courcy, *La coalition de 1701*; Émile Bourgeois, *Neufchâtel et la polilitique prussienne en Franche-Comté*.
5. Compare German claims in the 17th and 18th centuries, and in the first conflict of 1790. Also compare Bismarck's circulars, 13 and 16 September 1870. Same motives, same reasoning, almost the same terms.
6. Liverpool to Castlereagh, 15, 29 July; 11, 18, 23 August; 29 September. Castlereagh to Liverpool, 24, 29 July; 3, 17 August. Wellington to Liverpool, 11 August 1815.
7. Private intelligence from Paris, 7 August 1815. Corr. de Wellington. Supplement.
8. Compare the conflicts to the time of the first coalition.
9. Note of Pozzo, 2 August 1815.
10. Schaumann, exhibit no. XII; Treaty of 20 November, p. 119 et suiv.
11. Pasquier; Vitrolles.
12. Pasquier; Madelin, ch. XXVIII.
13. Pasquier; Pozzo: letters of August and September 1815.
14. The order signed "Louis" is in the hand of Talleyrand.
15. Note to La Besnardière, without signature; the archivist who classified the papers attributed it to Dalberg.
16. Angeberg.
17. Louis XVIII to Alexandre, 23 septembre 1815. (*Corr. de Pozzo*, I, p. 209.)
18. Report of Pozzo to Alexander.
19. Rochechouart; Barante; *Correspondance de Richelieu*: Société d'histoire de Russie.
20. *Mémoires*, II, p. 141, 298. Valençay, 1816.
21. To Sebastiani, 21 janvier 1831.
22. Instruction to Pozzo, 20 September 1815. Secret protocol of 2 October 1815.
23. Angeberg.
24. Marquis de Sassenais, *Les derniers mois de Murat*. – Dufourcq, Desvernois, Helfert.
25. Protocols and exhibits in Angeberg.
26. Art. VI of the Treaty of 20 November 1815, which renewed the Treaty of Chaumont of 1 March 1814.
27. 2 and 8 October 1815, Protocols and Acts, Angeberg; Creux, *la Libération du territoire*.
28. Declaration of the protocol of 15 November 1815, signed by Richelieu and by the ministers of the four. (Angeberg.)

# Chapter V: Europe and the French Revolution

## I. War

The cycle is closed, the cycle of this book; but a book does not stop the development of history at its last page any more than a picture encloses the immensity of the sky within its frame. It is only ever a slice in the endless tapestry that is constantly unfolding. Everything continues, evolves and bears its effects. Everything is detached from the past, everything is linked to the future, and the era that the historian thinks he is grasping is never more than an in-between. However, at the moment of seeing the end of this period and the beginning of a new one, it is permissible to stop at the bend, to consider, as a whole, the region traversed, to seek the direct and continuous lines, to clear in the uninterrupted transformation of life, what remains of the permanent, what appears to be particular, in a word, the characteristics by which this period cut out by the historian from general history nevertheless enters it and forms a moment of it.

However, in this history of a quarter of a century which put all of Europe at odds, the permanent thing is the struggle for limits. It is in this way that the history of Europe and of the French Revolution is linked to the previous struggles of Europe and France and contributes to explaining the sequence of struggles to come. France wanted to conquer the limits of Caesar; it was a tradition of royal chancelleries; it was the teaching of scholars, a suggestion of poets, an ambition of chiefs, kings, general ministers, assemblies or committees, an article of interest for economists, a *raison d'État* for politicians, a national utopia for the people, and all history has marched there, since Charlemagne, first by instinctive impulse, and later by concerted design.

With the same tenacity as France pursued this design of growth, the other states of Europe pursued their plans of compression; they brought as much obstinacy to pushing France back into its "old limits" as France put momentum into leaving them, to give itself its "natural limits." The pretexts of the war changed, like the weapons of the combatants but it was the same war which continued, and which did not end any more in Vienna in 1815, than it had ended in Utrecht, Nijmegen, the Pyrenees, Osnabrück, and Münster. From time immemorial, it was in Holland that France had conquered and lost Belgium and Flanders; at all times when it wanted to expand towards the north, it was England it found in the way, in arms, at the passages, and, once peace was made, blocking the exits and fortifying the barriers. From time immemorial, the Rhine valley had been the battlefield of the two empires that emerged from the empire of Charlemagne; France had always conquered and lost the Rhine in Italy and Germany. This is the mark of origin and the sign of the species in all coalitions, from Bouvines to Fleurus, from Crécy to Waterloo, from Pavia to Lodi, whether the pretext be reform or revolution, the succession of Naples or the succession of Spain, whom the protagonists called Louis XIV or William III, Wellington or Napoléon. Under this relation, which is a continuous relation, the Revolution is no more separated from the *ancien regime* than the Empire from the Republic. The stops that one tries to introduce into this march are only artifices of bookish composition; they have no more bearing on the events of the story than the snips at the displeasing, embarrassing, or saddening pages in the book in which the story is told.

Why didn't Louis XIV stop after the Peace of Nijmegen, the Republic after Campo-Formio, Napoléon after Austerlitz? Childish questions, verbal phantasmagoria, which suppose a France isolated in the world, mistress of a docile and disinterested Europe, a France controlling the course of things and the passions of men, led to port by a wind that will not change, carried by a tide that will never ebb. Of so many ambitious and skillful politicians, two only knew how to mix moderation with force, and saw themselves stopped in full success, Henri IV by the dagger of Ravaillac, Richelieu by disease; but the death of Henri IV, instead of dissolving the coalition, the reform, and the weakness of the regency, instead of appeasing Europe, excited it with the revenge; but, Richelieu dead, the enemies rushed on the kingdom, with no other view than to tear it to its bowels and dismember it at its extremities.

Consider the motives these enemies gave themselves, always the same. When France was barely emerging from the feudal silt, as early as François I, they spoke of reducing it to its ancient limits, and their publicists of the sixteenth century expressed themselves no differently than those of the seventeenth. To read the protocols, notes and memoirs of 1709 and 1710, one seems to read those of the Treaty of Paris in 1815, and Bismarck, in 1870, to justify the reunion of Alsace and Metz, did not invoke other pretexts then those of Gagern, Hardenberg, and Humboldt in 1815. Except for Russia, which then did not figure in the coalitions, the same English, Austrian, Prussian, German, and Dutch allies uttered, a century earlier, the same threats of extermination and demanded the same punishments and the same dismemberments against the legitimate kings of ancient France. The Spanish had meditated the same destructions against the Catholic Henri III and the Huguenot Henri IV. William III spoke like Graham or Stein, acted like Blücher and Wellington. They were no more relentless, at the Antwerp conference, against revolutionary and Republican France than they had been against the France of Louis XIV, and we were to see most of them relentless against the France of Louis XVIII. It is therefore not the excess of victory alone, however real it may be and however disproportionate it may seem, from 1805 onwards, which explains the persistence of coalitions under such diverse regimes and under such different political conditions.

To observe only in itself and apart from the others each of the coalitions which succeeded one another from 1792 to 1815, one confuses the pretexts of pageantry with the real causes, and, in this great trial of France, one forgets the bottom of the dispute to judge only on the procedure and on the incidents. We have to put things back in line. In 1812, what the coalition aimed at was the Grand Empire, France raised to 130 departments, overflowing beyond the mouths of the Elbe, embracing Holland and Rome, dominating Germany by the Confederation of the Rhine, pushing its captures as far as the Vistula through the Duchy of Warsaw, mistress of Italy through the kingdom of Italy under Napoléon and the kingdom of Naples under Murat, disposing of Switzerland, occupying Spain. During the previous coalition in 1809, neither the Hanseatic cities and northern Germany, nor Holland, nor Rome were annexed to the Grand Empire: it was therefore because Napoléon placed his brothers in The Hague, in Madrid, in Dusseldorf, his brother-in-law in Naples, because he was protector of the Confederation of the Rhine, and Poland, through the Duchy of Warsaw, march of the Empire. Agreed: but during the previous coalition, in 1806, there was no Duchy of Warsaw, nor Bonaparte in Spain and Dusseldorf; it is therefore the Confederation of the Rhine, Louis in Holland and Joseph in Naples. During the previous coalition, in 1805, the Confederation of the Rhine did not exist, the Bourbons still reigned in Naples and they even figured among the allies; Austrians ruled Venice, Istria, Dalmatia; it was therefore the Kingdom of Italy, Milan, the Legations, Genoa, and Piedmont annexed. During the previous coalition, in 1798, we see neither the kingdom of Italy nor Piedmont in departments: these are therefore the republics, Batavian, Helvetic, Cisalpine, Ligurian. In 1795, these republics did not exist, and if the war was doggedly pursued by England and Austria, it was therefore for these Low Countries and the left bank of the Rhine, the "natural limits." In 1793, when the grand coalition was formed, that which united all of Europe, not only did France not invade, but it was invaded; it was not even a question of pushing it back into its old limits, it was a question of cutting into it there: Flanders, Picardy as far as the Somme, Lorraine, Alsace, the Comté, Dauphiné perhaps. It was therefore revolutionary propaganda and regicide, the scandal given to monarchical Europe, the exit of the conquerors of 1792, the danger for all thrones. Granted, but when in February 1792, the first alliance was formed between Austria and Prussia, the matrix of all future coalitions, Louis XVI was on the throne and propaganda was only a subject of harangues. It was therefore old France being blamed, and it was necessary to come to this to discover the foundation, or, as we say of ships, the lifeblood of all coalitions.

  In 1791, Louis XVI was in danger and the monarchical principle was threatened by the very constitution which the French had imposed on him; now, when they spoke of rescuing him, that is to say of protecting themselves in his person, what speeches were made by those who sought to tie the alliance of kings against these turbulent Frenchmen? The same ones that, some eighty years earlier, the allies of the time at the conferences of Gertruydenberg had insisted on trimming France, taking Alsace and Lorraine away. Louis XIV reigned then: if he threatened anything, it was certainly not the "monarchical principle." The future allies, in 1791, thought so little of defending this "principle" that they were happy to see the French monarchy weakened by its new constitution, eating away at itself in its interior, while waiting for it to give the opportunity to start it from the outside. Kaunitz wrote,

> The experience of more than a century, which made all of Europe often feel the preponderance that the physical situation and the infinite resources of France procured for this kingdom in the general balance under the government of an absolute monarch, had especially convinced Austria that nothing was more compatible with the security of her own States than a relaxation and a complication of the internal springs of this formidable monarchy, which would in the future divert her energy from foreign enterprises.[1]

Instead of Austria, read Europe, England included, of course, and, at the very heart of the league, you will know the spirit of all the coalitions, the link which bound them together, since that fomented in 1790, the Diet of Ratisbonne, judging the occasion good to demand the denunciation of the Treaty of Westphalia and the restitution of Alsace and Lorraine to the Empire, because France had abolished, at home, seigneurial rights,[2] until that of 1815 when the same Germans claimed the same Alsace and the same Lorraine under the pretext of protecting the peaceful, modest and disinterested Germanys against "the ardent vanity of the people who will not cease to claim the conquest of Belgium and the left bank of the Rhine."[3] Hardenberg said, "For the good of Europe, for the good of France, let us not miss the favorable moment. Divine Providence obviously brought about this occasion."[4] All the policy of the English, all the magnanimity of Alexander, went to weld the broken mesh to the point where, in 1792, the first allies would have liked to forge it the constitutional monarchy, the limits of 1790 and the barrier of the Low Countries.

The coalition of 1805, in which were drawn all the plans which were accomplished in 1815, marks about the middle of this history of twenty-three years, from 1792 to 1815. To seize then the businesses, with the passage and in the fullness of their growth, one discerns direction and flow. Lunéville and Amiens destroyed each other by the same movements which brought them Europe, because it did not want to, France, because it could not hold on to it. To impose them, it was necessary to occupy Italy, Switzerland, Germany, and Holland, and to preserve them it was necessary to dominate these countries, without which the allies settled there and, from there, carry out their parallels and their approaches on the place conquered in

1801 and in 1802. It is thus necessary to follow this war of mines between the allies who always wanted to drive back France beyond the limits which they had recognized, in 1795, 1797, 1801; and France, constantly led to push its bridgeheads, advances, detached forts beyond these same limits, if it wished to defend them against the contrary tide whose tide incessantly came to beat them. Everything always depended, from beginning to end, from 1792 to 1815, on an accident, on the genius of a man, on the tenacity of an army, on a day of battle, and the last battle, uncertain like all precedents, tossed between the success which would renew everything and the catastrophe where everything would sink, as Fleurus, Castiglione, Zurich, Marengo, Austerlitz, Jena, Friedland, Wagram, Moskova, and Leipzig were tossed about, ended in the collapse of the Empire and the disaster of France.

We have considered the ups and downs of this struggle, we know its origins and circumstances; considered the measures taken by victorious Europe to prevent its return. We've seen what they are, let's see what they're worth.

## II. Treaties of 1815

The war, despite its enormous proportions, was a war of limits; treaties, however extensive their stipulations, were also treaties of limits.

Of all the congresses, the Congress of Vienna was the most considerable in terms of the importance and the number of affairs settled by it. The Final Act of 9 June 1815 was the largest treaty ever signed. It dealt only with state formation, borders, and legacies. It was the first attempt that had been made to give Europe a charter, at least territorial, to determine the state of possession of each, and to base it on the solemn recognition which was made of it, on the guarantee which was therein given by the signature of the eight principal European powers, on the impossibility of breaking this pact without placing oneself outside public law, on the possibility, on the contrary, of modifying it with the consent of those who had sanctioned it; in short, to found general peace on a collective contract. It was a new fact. A Europe where the rights of each result from the duties of all was something so foreign to the statesmen of the *ancien régime* that it took a quarter of a century's war to impose the notion of it on them and demonstrate the need. Yet they only came there out of weariness of fighting, out of exhaustion of men, money, blood, and expedients. France tried to make this great settlement of affairs proceed from a higher principle, legitimacy, considered as the principle of the transmission of power in monarchies, an essential form of sovereignty. Emperors and kings put this principle as a kind of epigraph to the first chapter of their official public law; they displayed it in the galleries and manifested it in their proclamations to the people; but when applied, they only complied with it according to the measure of their interests and conveniences. The final transaction proceeded much less from common submission to a higher principle than from the contradiction of respective pretensions. It was, in fact, a combination of balance.

Treaties are the expression of the relations which exist, at the time when they are concluded, between the material forces and the moral forces of the States which conclude them. Depending on whether these forces are evaluated with more or less accuracy and breadth of mind, whether the men who measure them go back further to their origins, see further into the consequences, take less account of accidental facts and more, taking into account the permanent conditions of the politics of states and nations, treaties are more or less durable. The rights they stipulate never survive the conditions under which these rights were established.

However incomplete its conception may seem, however empirical, arbitrary and even abusive that certain applications have been, the work of Vienna has none the less procured for Europe the longest and most fruitful period of peace and civilization which it had hitherto enjoyed. However, this edifice crumbled, and the places where it broke are precisely those to which the diplomats had applied their most subtle art; but these were only diplomatic expedients. They had calculated with sufficient approximation the number of inhabitants in the territories to be distributed; they had even, according to the formula of the statistical commission, assessed the economic, military, agricultural, industrial value of the inhabitants, their productive power, their capacity to to serve; but of the state of their souls, of their consciences, of their traditions, of their aspirations, of what made each of them a man, and of these grouped men, nations, nothing. That is to say, the material forces had been evaluated, the moral forces had been neglected or misunderstood; it is through this that the work perished.

The diplomats of Vienna carved out territories and made lots of peoples, as the co-partitioners of Poland had done. They were not concerned with the relationship between the territories and the peoples who inhabited them, nor with the disposition of these peoples to confine themselves within the borders assigned to them or to cross these borders. They organized Europe into States, and organized it as if there were no nations in Europe. Now, States only exist, and live, through the nations they represent. These facts could have been misunderstood before, just as the laws according to which the phenomena of nature operate regulate these phenomena long before the scientists expose and determine their conditions. But, after 1814, this ignorance became a capital error. The French Revolution had given rise everywhere to the idea that peoples alone have the right to self-determination, that men who are conscious of belonging to the same nation have the right to constitute themselves as a nation. The diplomats of Vienna considered these principles subversive of the monarchical order; they wanted to annihilate them forever; they believed that to suppress the effects of the French Revolution, it sufficed to declare it null and void and to move barriers over the surface of Europe. It was too late. The treaties of Vienna were broken successively by all the parts where they had disregarded or violated this principle of life of the new Europe: nationality.

In the Low Countries, first, where the Catholic Belgians, very attached to their Church and their traditions of local liberties, were subordinated to the Government of the Protestant Dutch, opposed in morals and interests; they had arbitrarily brought together what had never been linked except by constraint and what had been separated for more than two centuries.

In Poland, where a generous, valiant nation, perhaps incapable of governing itself, but also incapable of forgetting that thirty years earlier it had been independent, remained dismembered, subject to foreign masters, associated with peoples different from it by religion, origins, interests thus sacrificed, in scandalous contempt of the public law of the old regime, and in painful contempt of the public law of the new regime.

In Italy, where a nation gathered, in fact, under French domination and united in armies by the French saw itself reduced to being no more than an expression of geography.

In Germany, where the peoples, armed for independence of their fatherland, were condemned to dream of the greatness of this fatherland only in the history of the past, and saw themselves obliged by Europe to seek their destiny only in the convenience of their neighbors.

These were so many centers of revolution which were forming in Europe and which were to, with their successive explosions, first shake and then overthrow the work.

Finally, victorious Europe had not taken enough account of the French nation. They had calculated that by depriving France of its conquests, it would be made to forget its glory. They claimed to restrain and humiliate it: they offended it. Considering only the system of equilibrium, it was not an exact calculation of forces to drive France back to its pre-1792 limits. Austria and Prussia recaptured and even increased the possessions they had acquired since that time. It was a fact that the French had, since 1792, identified the idea of the republic and of national independence, with that of the limits of Gaul, the "natural limits." Europe had never consented to this; but was it wise to consider, here again, as null and void a concept so national and so passionate? Would it not have been prudent to facilitate the acceptance of the new order of things for the French, by arranging their interests and their ideas? They would thus, little by little, have recognized its advantages: homogeneous and concentrated France, between divided nations, weak and dispersed States, Holland, Germany, Italy. On the contrary, France was thrown back on its Revolution, it was brought back to identify, as in 1795, liberty and natural limits; to supplement its claims, within, against the charter granted, by claims outside, against the "odious" treaties of 1815, and to make, of the destruction of these treaties, a question of French patriotism. Against the well-understood interest of France, the French nation was made the natural ally of all the peoples who revolted against these treaties, and the French governments which sought popularity in glory were necessarily led to associate, in Europe, to the governments which their ambition impelled to tear up the pact of Vienna and to exploit, for the profit of their dynastic greatness, the national passions of the people.

It was thus that in 1830 the revolution took place as much for the charter as for the limit of the Rhine; that Belgium, animated by the example of France, rose up and was separated from Holland; that Poland rose in revolt, and that the cry of "Long live Poland!" was in the streets of Paris, in 1830-1832, in 1848, a cry of French revolution; that in 1859-1860 the Emperor Napoléon III joined forces with Piedmont and united Italy; that in 1866 he allowed the Prussians. He said in May 1866, "I hate like the majority of the French people, these treaties of 1815, which we would like to make today the sole basis of our foreign policy."⁵

Thus undermined from their origin and in their foundations, shaken in 1830, overturned, in part, in 1848, then raised with great reinforcement of props and scaffolding, the Treaties of Vienna were destroyed in 1860, 1866, and 1870, by the creation of an independent and neutral Belgium, by that of an Italian monarchy, by that of a German empire. Nothing remains of what was essentially the work of Vienna, either in fact or in principle, and, except as regards Belgium, this ruin has not been more damaging to any nation than to the French nation, which has so often cursed these treaties and which has contributed so much to their destruction.

## III. The Revolution

The war of 1792-1815, was an immense war of limits, the treaties which ended it were treaties of limits, and, therefore, the struggles of France and Europe during the Revolution, continued the history of France and Europe under the *ancien régime*. But whosoever stops at this aspect of things would only see the figure, and of the men who supported these struggles, he would know nothing, except the map of the countries where they carried their arms. There is something else, and this other thing is essential, the spirit which moves the human masses, the soul which animates the matter of history. The shape of the earth does not change; the concept that men have of the earth and of human existence, their reasons for living and dying are modified: to the same attachment to the city of their birth, to the same covetousness of the city of others, to the same jealousy from their own independence to the same ambition of subjugating that of others, the times bring various reasons, feed this perpetual fire with varied nourishment and fan it with new breaths.

The English of the Black Prince were the same as that of Cromwell and that of Wellington: the Catholic piety of the soldiers of Henry IV, invading France with their clergy at their head, singing psalms and going to confession on the eve of Agincourt; the fanaticism of Henry VI's lieutenants, who burned Joan of Arc as a heretic and a witch, sprang from the same funds as the pietism of the Puritans of William III, who claimed to confuse Baal and Nebuchadnezzar in the person of the very Christian king, and chastise Babylon in the halls of Versailles. All the soul and all the spirit of the wars of the

Revolution, such as led them by the French, appeared in the Crusades, from the first, very popular and spontaneous, which went away in tumultuous procession to deliver the holy places, until to those which mixed sacred enterprise and political combination, led Saint Louis to Egypt, put him to death in Tunis and degenerated into the conquest of a Christian empire in Byzantium, into the carving up of fiefs in the Holy Land, benumbed the knights in the delights of the harems of the East and left no other trace of their passage than the names of extinct dynasties or castles in ruins. You will find similar in the conquest of Naples at the time of the Renaissance and in those of the Revolution.

And yet the Englishman of the Hundred Years' War, the Puritan, the colonizer of the 17th century, the manufacturer, exporter and hoarder of the 19th; the French of Saint Bernard and that of Vergniaud, the soldier of Charles VIII and that of Championnet, General Louvois and that of the Committee of Public Safety, the musketeer of Louis XIV and the grenadier of Napoléon, if they speak the same language, express themselves in idioms of such different ages and translate ideas so different into such disparate images, that, following the same roads to march towards the same goal, if they met, they would not know how to recognize and understand each other.

What was new in 1792 was the Declaration of the Rights of Man, which gave natural proselytism to the French conquest the special character of the century, the form appropriate to the genius and passions of contemporaries: the abstract and universal idea. By assimilating it to their genius, the French transformed it into their blood and their flesh, and if the maxims remained abstract and universal, the idea became real and particular: in this way, it entered into facts, but propaganda, therefore, became confused with the conquest. Nothing helped, neither the ardor of convictions and the humanitarian and civilizing enthusiasm of some, nor the harsh theocratic and converting genius of others, nor the apostolate, nor the inquisition. Nature as always, swept away the theory. The French routed the Revolution along the great Roman road of French history: they made it a living work, and the nationalized Revolution made the French people the great nation. French democracy thus resumed and accomplished, for a time, the classic design of kings: the military, political, legal, and the intellectual supremacy of the continent; it surpassed Louis XIV, began Charlemagne anew and realized the age-old dream: the Roman Empire of the modern world, Roman peace by and for the French.

This hyperbolic enterprise succeeded because the French

realized in themselves the Revolution, that of a cosmopolitan entity they made a French reality, confused the Rights of Man with the rights of the Frenchman and their supremacy over the old world with the emancipation of the peoples of Europe. The enterprise crumbled by the very effect of its success: following the example of the French, the conquered peoples each made human rights their own rights and did not want to know of any other emancipation than that which they operated themselves by freeing themselves from foreigners.

The power of the Revolution in the world therefore came from the particular character of applications by each of the peoples where it spread. It had been everywhere as in France, exclusively national, which had been its driving force in the hands of the French and its power of assimilation in the souls of other peoples. It had become for each his thing and the main thing, the one that takes precedence over all the others and from which all the others proceed: national independence, which is for the peoples what the first aspiration of the air is for the child which is born into the world, the first manifestation and, until the end, the necessary condition of life.

The struggle of peoples to conquer each the government of themselves, or democracy, to conquer their independence with regard to other peoples, or nationality, fills the 19th century: it has made Europe, deeply national, where we live. The two facts are correlative. They emerge together from the French Revolution; they express, in two forms, the same principle, that of national sovereignty. France, which was the first to proclaim it, understood it with justice and magnanimity: "I love, therefore I am!" This, in the true spirit of the French Revolution, is the fundamental axiom of nationality. In this sense the principle of nationality becomes a principle of justice. It is an honor that France is entitled to claim, to have founded its public law on this principle, which gives the only sanction of conquest, namely that the peoples alone have the right to self-determination and that no change in their national destiny is legitimate to unless it is ratified by their direct, universal, and free suffrage. It proclaimed this principle and applied it at the first meeting operated by the Convention in 1792, that of Savoy, and more than half a century later it invoked and consecrated it at the last reunion it had operated in Europe, that of this same Savoy, by Napoléon III, in 1860. They would have been entitled to claim, they will always remain entitled to hope from the justice of men, the application of the same principle, their own, to populations which the war, in 1870, violently separated from its body.

Certainly, in the course of its struggle with Europe, it had too often made little use of this principle; victorious over the ancient monarchies, it compromised and made a pact with them, according to their customs and conveniences. They entered into their public rights and it sacrificed its own. Victorious in their turn, these monarchies had not modified their custom, and it is thus that conquest governed Europe from 1793 to 1815. The nations which fought with the most energy for their independence, this independence won, claimed to turn it to supremacy. Following their traditions, they used "modern science" like the French Revolution of pure reason: diplomacy, archaeology, philology, ethnography, palaeography, anthropology, origin and evolution words, the measure, the countenance and the deformities of skulls have served as a pretext to classify, divide, and enslave men. Historical "missions" have been imagined which are nothing other than a very crude application to politics of the hypothesis of final causes. The struggle for independence of each has degenerated into a struggle of all against all for land and power. Barely delivered from Napoléon, the Germans dreamed of Barbarossa and Otho, masters of Italy, Lotharingia, Burgundy, and Flanders. After the *Risorgimento* in Italy, arose, and without transition, the *primato*. What is called "imperialism" is born, of a necessary generation, wherever popular pride ferments with the feeling of sovereignty. It is the child of democracy in England, as it is in the United States, as it was in ancient Rome.

Thus, the ideas, the passions, the forces which the French Revolution threw into the world survived it, subsisted and were transformed according to the genius and the traditions of the people. Such a formidable overflow of men and thoughts has given irresistible impulses to the world, unleashed currents, dug new beds of great waters in the ground. For 23 years the sovereigns of ancient Europe struggled against this deluge and tried to drive it back. They failed. The most ambitious and intelligent among them then tried to harness its power. Thus were formed the new national dominations, Italy and Germany.

The princes who have accomplished, for their own profit, these great changes have conceived the European revolution and the nationalities, as Napoléon had conceived the French Revolution and the sovereignty of the people. They built their monarchies with the materials and on the dismantled bastions of the Grand Empire. All their designs spring from the meditations of Saint Helena, as from a

*Discourse on Method*, from which were deduced, for years, all the theories of *philosophes* and all the hypotheses of scholars.

Napoléon thus remains in the consequences of this history what he was in the crises, the executor and the organizer of the French Revolution in Europe. He laid the stakes, opened the avenues, erected the foundations, leveled the ground; the nationalities prevailed in Italy, in Germany, and later in the Christian countries of the East, according to directions which he had arranged for them. Napoléon, who had fallen, appeared immense;[6] the conqueror and the despot disappeared, one discovered the prodigious laborer of the land of Europe, the work of the statesman and its endless repercussions in history. "The halo that journalists, historians and poets have spread around Napoléon disappears before the implacable reality of this book," said Goethe, in 1827, after reading a collection of memoirs; "but the hero is not diminished, on the contrary; he grows as he becomes more true."[7]

I would like this work to leave the same impression not only of the great man who occupies so much space in it, but also and above all of the French nation which fills it and which is its soul. Napoléon engendered from it an incomparable epic, but without it he would have been only a magnificent and sterile force, like lightning in the mountains and a hurricane on the seas. I would like, after having resumed one last time and knotted in their last knot the guiding threads of this story, to gather in a single image the scattered views that I have sown there and to print this image, which is all the light and all the life of this book, as enduring and significant in the memory of the reader as it is in my thought. It is the image of the Frenchman, our father, a poor devil, glorious and generous in soul and person, bruised in his body, crippled, scattering the shreds of his broken limbs on the roads; voluntarily to defend the fatherland, "to drive the foreigners out of the kingdom," to found for the French, the French Republic, to bring to peoples hungry for justice the new gospel; then a soldier, by vocation or career, armed for the splendor of this Republic, the splendor of the empire born of it, the beneficent supremacy of France; exposing themselves, exhausting themselves, sacrificing themselves in blood and breath to pursue the ancestral chimera, the human idol of spirit and flesh, the enchanting liberty, the peace that heals the wounds of the wounded, quenches the thirst of the feverish, comforts the infirm, blooms around them the children and the flowers, matures the crops and the generations, consecrates by its benefaction the anonymous heroes who have conquered it. None of them would have dared to say: "I am France!" but of all we say: "Without them France would not have been what it was." It is to them that I turn when closing this book, companion of my youth, friend of my mature age, where I put thirty years of my life, and tried to translate into words my love for my country, my admiration for its genius, my worship for its history, my tenderness for its illusions, my pity for its misfortunes, my pride in its triumphs and my unshakable faith in its destinies.

Paris, 1874. – Honfleur, 1904.

1. Kaunitz to Cobenzl, 12 November 1791.
2. See vol. II, Sec. I, ch. III.
3. Stein, 18 August 1815.
4. Hardenberg, 4 August 1815.
5. Speech in Auxerre, May 1866.
6. "The solitude in which Bonaparte left the world." (Chateaubriand, *Mémoires*, November 1828.)
7. Conversation with Eckermann.

# Index

*Note*: volume IX is the General Index for all previous volumes.

There are no entries for Bonaparte / Naopléon, because he is on almost every page. I follow Sorel in this regard.

18-19 Brumaire, 187, 221, 257, 259, 265, 279, 291, 347, 354, 356, 358, 373, 383

abdication, 165, 232, 251, 268, 269ff, 270, 271, 273, 277, 292(n11, 16), 264(n2), 373ff, 374, 376
Aberdeen, Lord, 164, 169, 171, 172, 173, 174, 175, 183, 184, 186, 190, 191, 194, 195, 203, 204, 212, 213, 218, 220, 223, 233, 237, 241
Abo, 9
Abranowics, Count, 3
Abrantès, Duchess of, 341(n27)
Abruzzi, 372
Adriatic, 59, 141, 159
Agamemnon, 154, 284
Agincourt, 420
Aix, island of, 385
Aix-la-Chapelle, Treaty of, 259(n79), 408
Aisne, 237
Albany, Countess of, 293(n40)
Alexander, Tsar, 4, 5, 6, 7, 9, 10, 11, 17, 21, 22, 26, 38, 39, 42, 43, 44, 45, 46, 47, 48, 50, 51, 52, 55, 57, 62, 65, 80, 81, 88, 89, 90, 91, 94, 96, 98, 99, 100, 102, 103, 104, 105, 106, 110, 111, 115, 121, 122, 128, 129, 132, 140, 151, 153, 154, 157, 158, 161, 162, 163, 164, 165, 166, 167, 169, 170, 172, 174, 175, 179, 183, 201, 202, 205, 206, 207, 209, 210, 211, 212, 213, 218, 223, 224, 225, 226, 227, 228, 229, 230, 231, 235, 238, 242, 243, 245, 247, 251, 255(n96), 261, 262, 263, 265, 266, 267, 268, 269, 273, 274, 275, 277, 280, 281, 282, 283, 284, 285, 286, 287, 292(n15), 297, 298, 299, 300, 301, 303, 304, 311, 312, 313, 315, 317, 320, 324, 325, 326, 327, 330, 331, 332, 333, 334, 336, 341(n24, 32), 346, 347, 348, 349, 351, 352, 353, 356, 358, 359, 361, 363, 364(n11), 372, 373, 377, 383, 384, 393, 394, 395, 396, 399, 401, 402, 403, 404, 406, 407, 408, 415
Alps, 8, 27, 59, 65(n12), 117, 156, 166, 171, 173, 184, 185, 191, 204, 208, 212, 302, 303, 392
Alsace, 141, 187, 207, 253(n13), 304, 330, 392, 396, 397, 398, 413, 414, 415
Amiens, Treaty of, 15, 30, 141, 177, 179, 182, 415
*ancien régime*, 85, 296, 384, 412, 416, 420
Ancillon, Jean-Pierre, 14, 16
Andréossy, Antoine-François, 380
Angles, 278
Angoulème, Duke of, 225, 400
Anna Paulovna, Grand Duchess, 311
Austria, Anne of, 176, 251
Anstett, 10, 38, 47, 49, 123, 130, 135, 139, 147(n115), 169
Antraigues (Emmanuel Henri de Launay), Comte d', 151, 177, 354
Antwerp, 141, 170, 175, 231, 235, 242, 251, 282, 351, 392, 413
Arcis-sur-Aube, Battle of, 250
Ardennes, 201, 392
Argenson, René-Louis de Voyer d', 378
Arndt, publicist, 6, 397, 399
Arnouville, 382
Artois, Comte d', 225, 228, 240, 244, 245, 246, 247, 258, 277, 357, 400
Aschaffenburg, 290
Asia, 234
*assignats*, 69
Asturias, Prince of, 180
Augereau, Charles, 14, 15, 21, 23, 42,

44, 235
Austerlitz, 31, 59, 63, 81, 102, 152, 182, 216, 269, 369, 371, 375, 412, 416
Austria, 1, 3, 5, 6, 8, 9, 10, 13, 14, 15, 19, 21-30, 32-43, 50, 51, 53, 55, 56, 60, 61, 62, 63, 69-80, 82, 83, 84, 87-113, 115-142, 145(n54), 148(n128), 149(n135, 136, 155), 151-67, 170, 171, 172, 175, 176, 177, 181, 188-97(n5), 202, 205, 207, 209, 210, 212, 213, 214, 219, 220, 222, 224, 227, 228, 229, 230, 233, 234, 236, 240, 242, 243, 245, 250, 251, 265, 268, 274, 277, 278, 286, 289, 291, 297, 299-304, 308, 309, 310, 312, 313, 315, 317, 319, 321, 322, 323, 325-33, 335, 336, 338, 339, 341(n32), 342(n34), 346, 348, 350, 359-63, 368, 371, 372, 375, 377, 384, 389, 392, 395, 396-99, 407, 413, 414, 415, 419
Autun, Bishop of. *See* Talleyrand.
Auxonne, 385
Avignon, 61, 279, 288, 395
Azores, 364(n3)
Avout, Louis-Nicolas d'. *See* Davout.

Baal, 420
Babylon, 367, 420
Baltic, 141
Bar-sur-Aube, 235-36
Barbarossa, 423
Barclay de Tolly, Michael, 100, 262
Barras, Paul-François, 383
Basel, 9, 65(n25), 185, 201, 203, 211, 310
Bassano, Duc de. *See* Maret.
Batavia, 84, 414
Bautzen, Battle of, 99, 101, 105
Bavaria, 7, 70, 93, 94, 99, 126, 157, 158, 161, 163, 164, 189, 224, 229, 290, 315, 325, 328, 329, 331, 335, 337, 362, 391, 397, 398
Bayonne, 124, 176, 180, 199(n49)
Béarn, 178, 187
Beauharnais, family, 22

Beauharnais, Eugène de, 83, 99, 100, 101, 180, 191, 246, 248, 256(n106), 359
Beauregard, Jacques Marie de Guerry, 267n
Belgium, 58, 60, 61, 62, 117, 141, 142, 156, 170, 174, 176, 204, 221, 222, 229, 235, 287, 288, 289, 297, 306, 324, 347, 348, 356, 362, 368, 372, 392, 405, 407, 412, 415, 419, 420
Benevento, 176, 360
Bentinck, William, 78, 84, 85, 86, 115, 150(n158), 191, 192, 194
Beresina, river, 2, 3, 28, 269
Berg, Grand Duchy of, 52, 112, 182, 290
Berlin, 12, 14, 15, 17, 22, 23, 24, 29, 30, 37, 39, 42, 44, 46, 57, 67(n92), 100, 148(n128), 151, 152, 162, 298, 304, 310, 315, 371
Berry, Duke of, 225, 277, 305, 311, 340(n1), 363(n3)
Berthier, Pierre, 12, 21, 82, 100, 106, 107, 115, 133, 153, 182, 214, 216, 221, 222, 271, 285
Bertrand, Henri-Gratien, 104, 385
Besançon, 397
Besnardière, J.-B. de Coucy, Comte de La, 33, 196, 216, 218, 240, 254(n38), 287, 307, 315, 380, 402
Bessières, Jean-Baptiste, 127
Beurnonville, Marquis de, 265
Bignon, Louis-Pierre, 3
Binder, 41
Bismarck, 342(n34), 409(n5), 413
Blacas, Pierre-Jean-Louis, 338, 339
Black Prince, 420
Blockade, Continental, 7, 42, 74, 141
Blücher, Gebhard von, 55, 153, 155, 162, 170, 175, 201, 213, 223, 225, 232, 235, 237, 238, 243, 244, 262, 369, 370, 379, 383, 390, 413
Bohemia, 56, 73, 74, 89, 90, 98, 107, 121, 128, 139, 152, 302
Boisgelin, Bruno, 258
Boissy d'Anglas, 380

428

Bologna, 302, 360
Bombelles, Louis-Philippe, 338
Bonaparte, Caroline, 189, 195, 319, 341(n27)
Bonaparte, Joseph, 9, 32, 63, 64, 78, 119, 145(n45), 178, 179, 180, 187, 188, 196, 221, 222, 249, 250, 255(n98), 261, 353, 376, 414
Bonaparte, Louis, 82, 176, 179, 187
Bonaparte, Lucien, 353, 373
Bondy, 268
Bonn, 333, 336
Bouches-de-l'Elbe, 52
Bordeaux, 244, 249, 259, 274
Borodino, Battle of, 270
Boulogne, 383
Bourbon, House of, 9, 63, 78, 84, 94, 112, 119, 122, 123, 142, 146(n67), 158, 165, 171, 177, 178, 179, 185, 187, 195, 196, 204, 205, 208, 209, 210, 212, 213, 224, 225, 227, 228, 230, 231, 234, 239, 241, 244, 245, 246, 247, 248, 249, 251, 258, 259, 260, 262, 264, 265, 266, 267, 274, 276, 280, 286, 291, 296, 303, 308, 323, 330, 332, 338, 344, 345, 348, 349, 350, 351, 352, 353, 354, 355, 356, 359, 360, 368, 372, 373, 376, 377, 378, 379, 381, 382, 383, 384, 387(n16), 395, 414
Bourbon, Louis (Condé), 178
Bourrienne, 278
Boussay. *See* Menou.
Boutiaguine, agent, 10, 346
Bouvines, Battle of, 412
Boyen, Colonel, 10, 21, 42
Brabant, 98, 117, 187
Braganza, House of, 32, 119
Bremen, 145(n49)
Breslau, 42, 43, 46, 48, 49, 51, 57, 100, 106
Brandeis, 121, 124, 134
Brandenburg, Count of, 45
Brittany, 225
Broglie, Victor de, 28
Brünn, 7-8

Brunswick, 19, 108, 156, 178, 372, 381, 387(n13)
Brunswick-Lüneburg, House of, 156
Bruslard, Louis-Guérin de, 343, 357, 364(n3)
Brussels, 218, 356, 357, 369
Bubna, General, 29, 32, 33, 35, 36, 38, 60, 92-98, 100, 101, 105, 114, 124, 134, 138, 139
Bülow, Friedrich, 218, 235, 237
Burgundy, 423
Burke, Edmund, 235
Byzantium, 421

Cadiz, 59
Cadore, Duke of. See Champagny.
Cadoudal, Georges, 268
Caesar, 5, 31, 269, 371, 392, 411
Calabria, 59, 302, 372
Cambacérès, Jean-Jacques, 33, 114, 196, 345, 374, 383
Cambon, 52
Campo-Chiaro, 338-39
Campo-Formio, Treaty of, 302, 310, 412
Cannes, 360
Canning, 122
Capo d'Istria, Jean-Antoine, 363, 389, 394, 409
*carbonari*, 84, 193
Cariati, Prince, 83, 125, 144(n30)
Carignan, House of, 303, 308, 360
Carnot, 152
Carrousel, 64
Cars, Comte des, 246
Cassel, 161, 362
Castiglione, 160
Castlereagh, Lord, 79, 80, 122, 128, 148(n128), 173, 174, 194, 203, 204, 205, 206, 207, 209, 212, 213, 214, 218, 220, 224, 227, 228, 231, 238, 239, 246, 251, 277, 298, 305, 310, 313, 314, 317, 318, 321, 323, 324, 325, 326, 327, 328, 329, 331, 332, 333, 334, 335, 336, 338, 348, 349, 350, 364(n11), 379, 383, 384, 389,

390, 394, 395, 396, 399, 405, 409, 410(n2)
Cathcart, Lord, 80, 87, 128, 153, 169, 175, 237
Catherine II, 4, 78, 281, 352
Catherine, Grand Duchess, 311
Catholics, 61, 285, 309
Cauchelet, Mlle, 346
Caulaincourt, Armand, 33, 87, 95, 97, 98, 99, 100, 102, 103, 104, 105, 106, 107, 115, 125, 126, 127, 129, 129, 130, 131, 132, 133, 134, 135, 136, 137, 138, 139, 140, 146(n69), 148(n134), 149(n135, 136), 167, 168, 172, 177, 181, 182, 183, 184, 185, 186, 188, 196, 202, 203, 208, 211, 212, 213, 215, 216, 217, 218, 219, 220, 221, 222, 223, 227, 229, 232, 233, 234, 236, 237, 238, 240, 241, 242, 243, 248, 249, 250, 254(n41), 255(n98), 258, 268, 269, 271, 273, 274, 275, 277, 287, 312, 345, 346, 354, 402
Ceylon, 240
Chambéry, 288, 397
Champagne, 19
Champagny, Jean-Baptiste, 33, 354
Championnet, 193, 421
Champaubert, 223, 227, 232
Champs-Elysées, 262, 263
Channel, English, 282
Charlemagne, 352, 412, 421
Charles, Archduke, 392
Charles V, Emperor, 385, 392
Charles XII, 385
Charles XIII, 421
Charlotte, Princess, 247, 254
Chastenay, Mme de, 176, 178
Chateau-Thierry, 223, 227, 232
Chateaubriand, 178, 200(n82), 276, 281, 285, 387(n17), 426(n6)
Châtillon, Congress of, 54, 201ff, 402
Chaumont, 232, 235, 238, 239, 242, 243, 255(n79), 286, 298, 299, 321, 324, 331, 333, 334, 341(n32), 347, 348, 349, 350, 407, 410(n26)

*chouans*, 268, 345, 364(n3), 372, 384
Cisalpine, 192, 414
Civil Code, 337, 372, 409
civilization, 178, 391, 417
Clausewitz, Karl von, 17, 18
Cockburn, Capt., 385
Coigny, Mme de, 176, 181, 258
Cologne, 8, 162, 231, 304, 336
Comédie Française, 114-15, 284
Committee of Public Safety, 23, 71, 141, 241, 358, 421
Commons, House of, 350, 367
Compiègne, 283, 284, 285, 312
Concordat, 61
Condé, county, 399, 404, 406
Condé, Prince of. *See* Bourbon, Louis.
Congress of Vienna, 136(n90), 248, 410
Consalvi, Cardinal, 302, 340(n18)
Constant, Benjamin, 9, 123, 178, 373, 378
Constantine, Emperor, 20, 419
Constantine, Grand Duke, 331, 332
Constantinople, 78
Constituent Assembly, 281
Constitutional Charter of 1830, 277
Constitutionalists, 81, 248, 279, 285, 377
Consulate (1799-1804), 278, 337, 343, 345, 357, 389, 408
Continental System, 72, 74, 96, 141, 275
Convention, 6, 54, 282, 347, 376, 422
Convention of 4 January, 340(n24)
Convention of 28 September, 326
Convention of 30 June,
Convention of August 1814, 340(n11)
Convention of London, 340(n6)
Cooke, Edward, 205
Copenhagen, 147(n107)
Corfu, 34
Corsica, 364(n3), 385
Cossacks, 17, 104, 218, 228, 262, 367
*coup d'état*, 265, 281, 373, 374
Courlande, Dorothée de, 176, 259, 315, 401
Cracow, 31, 56, 207

430

Crécy, Battle of, 412
Croats, 367
Cromwell, Oliver, 9, 375, 387(n3), 420
crusade, 5, 50, 52, 278, 373, 421
Czartoryski, Adam, 5, 6, 7, 46, 328, 331

Dalberg, Baron of, 176, 181, 244, 263, 264, 265, 267, 274, 278, 315, 325, 334, 401, 410(n15)
Dalberg, Duchess of, 176
Dalmatia, 91, 101, 361, 414
Danton, Georges, 279, 310
Danube, 121
Danzig, 46, 98, 109, 110, 136, 138, 141, 282
Darmstadt, 391
Daru, Pierre Antoine, 183
Dauphiné, 397, 414
Davout, Louis-Nicolas, 44, 82, 114, 345, 373, 376, 381, 382
Decazes, Élie, 340(n1), 383
Decrès, Denis, 345
Denmark, 40, 65(n17, 81, 121, 138, 248, 255(n97), 342(n36)
Desaix de Veygoux, Louis-Charles-Antoine, 42
Dessoles, Jean-Joseph, 387(n5)
Diebitsch, Hans Karl von, 16-18
Dijon, 252
Dino, Duchess of. *See* Courlande.
Directory, 82, 84, 141, 188, 221, 225, 241, 270, 278, 279, 296, 310, 343, 344, 372, 374, 383, 408
Dohna, Count, 18
Dorogobuje, 1
Doulcet. *See* Pontécoulant, Comte de.
Dresden, 3, 12, 13, 29, 87, 88, 89, 93, 111, 113, 115, 124, 126, 131, 132, 133, 137, 138, 140, 152, 153, 163, 168, 173, 188, 207, 219, 304, 315, 323, 336, 400
Dumouriez, Charles-François, 87, 197(n2), 380
Dun Castle, 154
Dupont de l'Étang, Pierre-Antoine, 278
Durant, 82, 85, 188, 193

Duroc, Géraud-Christophe, 101, 127
Düsseldorf, 414

Eastern Question, 224
Eckermann, 426
Egypt, 3, 267, 343, 344, 347, 421
Elba, island of, 276-77
Elbe, river, 46, 59, 80, 130, 145(n36)
Elbing, 22
Elysée, palace, 373, 374
*émigrés*, 81, 84, 151, 245, 257, 266, 274, 284, 344, 372
Ems-Oriental, 108, 145(n49)
Ems-Supérieur, 108, 145(n49)
Enghien, Duke of, 271, 375, 379, 384
Epernay, 223
Erfurt, 87, 103, 148(n133), 161, 284, 310, 315, 320
Essen, general, 11
Essling, Battle of, 371
Este, (Archduke) Francesco d', 360
Esterhazy, Nicolas, 238, 240, 255(n76)
Etruria, King of, 83(n130), 95, 178
Etruria, Queen of, 302, 360
Eylau, Battle of, 269

fanaticism, 372, 420
Ferdinand IV, 303, 360
Fernando, Don, 64, 84, 180
Ferrara, 302, 360
Fezensac, 276
Finland, 240
Five Hundred, Council of the, 374
Flanders, 141, 197(n2), 367, 392, 396, 397, 412, 414, 423
Flaugergues, Pierre-François, 380
Fleurus, Battle of, 59, 412, 416
Floret, 26, 29, 220
Fontainebleau, 61, 185, 195, 218, 266, 268, 269, 271, 273, 275, 282, 343, 374
Fort de l'Ecluse, 399, 406
Fort-Joux, 399, 406
Fouché, Joseph, 81, 176, 180, 181, 188, 189, 192, 246, 257, 345, 352, 353, 354, 355, 356, 357, 358, 364(n22),

373, 375, 376, 377, 380, 382, 383, 387(n16), 400
Franche-Comté, 187, 382, 397, 410(n4)
Frankfurt, 54, 97, 162, 169, 170, 175, 181, 182, 184, 186, 188, 189, 191, 194, 203, 208, 211, 212, 213, 218, 219, 232, 233, 235, 236, 238, 241, 243, 252, 268, 286
Franz II, Emperor, 7, 27, 29, 32, 33, 35, 37, 38, 39, 60, 66(n50), 76, 90, 91, 96, 97, 98, 100, 102, 105, 107, 111, 112, 124, 127, 128, 129, 139, 144(n18), 160, 164, 165, 166, 167, 169, 193, 195, 200(n82), 206, 207, 209, 210, 235, 243, 277, 302, 303, 304, 346, 407, 408
French Revolution, 20, 53, 67(n66), 78, 162, 411, 418, 419, 422, 423, 424
Friedland, Battle of, 59, 141, 152, 216, 371, 416
Friedrich Augustus, 55, 88, 89,
Friedrich-Wilhelm III, King, 10, 12, 22, 39, 42, 43, 44, 45, 46, 47, 48, 51, 57, 59, 100, 121, 123, 243, 301, 304, 317, 327, 407, 408
Friedrich-Wilhelm IV, King, 330
Friends of England, 81, 177
Fronde, 176, 257, 377
Fructidor, 14, 82, 354, 383

Gaillard, Maurice, 357
Gallicia, 25, 35, 117, 162, 202, 207, 224, 300, 309, 333, 336
Gallo, minister, 83
Gagern, Hans Christoph Ernst von, 316, 317, 324, 351, 392, 395, 399, 402, 413
*Garde nationale. See* National Guard.
Gaul, 371, 372, 390, 419
Geneva, 362
Genoa, 141, 289, 360, 414
Gentz, Friedrich von, 26, 75, 132, 135
George, Prince-Regent, 206, 226, 303, 312, 385
George III, King, 27
Georges. *See* Cadoudal.

Gerard, Maurice, 271
Gertruydenberg [Geertruidenberg], 410(n4), 414
Ghent, 348, 352, 353, 357, 400
Girondins, 279
Gitschin, 105, 107, 111, 115, 146(n72)
Givet, 218, 287, 399, 404, 406
Glogau, 98
Gneisenau, August, 51, 170, 252, 392, 397, 399
Goethe, 20, 424
Goltz, Count, 23
Goritz, 138
Gourgaud, Gaspard, 107
Gouvion Saint-Cyr, 152
Graham,
Gravier, Charles de. *See* Vergennes.
*Grande Armée. See* Grand Army.
Grand Army, 1, 4, 14, 15, 19, 28, 82, 86, 87, 88, 203, 368, 370, 371
Grand Empire, 25, 54, 58, 59, 95, 97, 140, 141, 151, 154, 179, 185, 413, 423
Grawert, 11
Grosbois, 115
Grossbeeren, Battle of, 153, 154, 157
Grouchy, Emmanuel, 370
Guadeloupe, 81, 288
Guelph, 80, 81, 174, 365(n33)
Gumbinen, 82
Guyana, 288, 383

Hague, The, 150(n159), 413
Hake, 44
Hamburg, 59, 100, 102, 104, 106, 109, 114, 136, 138, 140, 145(n49), 175, 231, 282
Hamilton, agent, 239
Hamilton, Lady Emma. *See* Lyon, Amy.
Hanau, 162
Hanover, 27, 40, 45, 47, 79, 80, 82, 107, 108, 156, 159, 315, 326, 328, 335, 336, 362, 365(n33), 392, 39
Hanseatic cities, 66(n48), 74, 75, 95, 109, 141, 159, 413
Hardenberg, Karl August Fürst von, 7,

432

10, 12, 13, 14, 15, 16, 20, 21, 22, 23, 27, 28, 29, 35, 40, 42, 43, 44, 45, 46, 47, 48, 49, 70, 77, 79, 80, 90, 94, 109, 120, 129, 139, 140, 157, 163, 169, 170, 173, 175, 195, 202, 209, 212, 223, 225, 228, 229, 231, 243, 246, 251, 298, 301, 313, 314, 317, 323, 324, 325, 327, 331, 334, 351, 389, 392, 398, 399, 409, 413, 415
Harpe (La), 209, 210, 226, 229, 230, 266, 377
Hartwell, 311
Hatzfeld, Prince of, 21, 22, 23, 46
Hauterive, Alexandre-Maurice d', 33, 186, 249, 255(n98)
Henckel von Donnersmarck, Wilhelm Ludwig, 17, 20
Henri IV, King of Navarre, then France, 178, 257, 276, 292(n8), 307, 389, 412, 413
Henriot, 375
Herney, Colonel, 381
Hesse-Darmstadt, 197(n19), 362
Hildesheim, 107
Hohenlinden, Battle of, 9, 59, 122, 371
Hohenzollern, 80, 163
Holland, 53, 58, 60, 63, 72, 74, 78, 80, 84, 91, 92, 93, 95, 112, 117, 128, 137, 141, 142, 156, 159, 168, 170, 171, 174, 175, 176, 179, 182, 185, 187, 204, 213, 214, 231, 238, 239, 241, 251, 253(n3), 265, 284, 290, 335, 362, 365(n33), 404, 408, 412, 413, 414, 415, 419
Holy Alliance, 291
Holy Alliance, Treaty of the, 407
Holy Roman Empire, 157, 362, 391, 398
Holy See, 61, 302, 308, 322
Honfleur, 425
Hortense, Queen, 373
Hudelist, Josef von, 156, 173, 175, 224, 225, 227, 231
Huguenots, 389
Hugues Capet, 352, 400
Humboldt, Wilhelm von, 35, 40, 70, 77, 96, 120, 123, 124, 135, 137, 139, 169, 213, 214, 218, 219, 223, 237, 313, 314, 317, 319, 323, 324, 351, 389, 392, 398, 413
Hundred Days, 354, 373, 377
Hundred Years' War, 421
Hungary, 327
Huningue, 141, 399, 404, 407

Illyria, 28, 32, 34, 41, 73, 74, 91, 92, 93, 94, 95, 97, 109, 116, 117, 136, 138, 139, 142, 145(n36), 147(n94), 176, 188, 195, 217, 361, 370
India, 79, 213, 240
indemnities, 20, 63, 129, 142, 157, 238, 288, 300
Inn, district, 93
Inn, river, 101
inquisition, 295, 421
Israel, 142
Istria, 101, 138, 140, 363, 389, 394, 409, 414
Italy, 27, 28, 35, 47, 51, 53, 58, 60, 63, 76, 78, 83, 84, 85, 86, 91, 92, 93, 94, 95, 96, 100, 112, 177, 126, 128, 137, 141, 142, 145(n54), 148(n128), 154, 156, 159, 160, 161, 171, 176, 181, 182, 188, 189, 190, 191, 192, 193, 195, 213, 229, 231, 239, 241, 248, 251, 261, 277, 278, 279, 290, 300, 302, 303, 304, 307, 308, 313, 315, 338, 339, 343, 360, 372, 384, 392, 404, 412, 413, 414, 415, 418, 419, 423, 424

Jackson, envoy, 149(n139)
Jacobi, agent, 79
Jacobins, 9, 52, 69, 97, 266, 340(n18), 345, 358, 361, 371, 376, 395, 399
James II, 349
Jaucourt, 265
Jehu, companions of, 278
Jemappes, Battle of, 44
Jena, Battle of, 31, 59, 71, 87, 369, 371, 416
Joan of Arc, 420

433

Jomini, Antoine-Henri, 151
Jourdan, Jean-Baptiste, 147(n103), 372
*journées*, 279
Julius Caesar. *See* Caesar.
Jung-Bunzlau, 121
Junot, Jean-Andoche, 341(n27)
Jura, 392

Kainardji, Treaty of, 363
Kalisch, 41, 49, 52, 54, 56, 79, 93, 107, 108, 110, 141, 155, 199, 300, 301, 321, 299
Katzbach, Battle of, 153-54
Kaunitz, Austrian Chancellor, 202, 225, 415
Kellermann, François-Étienne-Christophe, 87
Kherson, Ukraine. *See* Cherson.
Kiel, Treaty of, 342(n36)
Kleist, Friedrich, 22, 103, 104
Klodova, 46
Knesebeck, Karl Friedrich, 14, 149(n155)
Kœnigsberg, 17, 48, 57
Koller, Baron, 278, 364(n2)
Kremlin, 270
Krusemarck, Friedrich Wilhelm von, 21, 43, 48
Koutousof, 4, 38, 49, 52-55, 69, 164
Kutno, 3

Labédoyère, François-Huchet, 381-82
Laforest (Antoine René Charles Mathurin, Comte de), 180, 377
Laforêt. *See* Laforest.
Lainé, Joachim-Joseph, 186
Landau, 288, 295, 396, 399, 402, 404, 406
*Landwehr*, 42, 67(n66), 152
Langeron, Louis-Alexandre Andrault, Comte de, 100, 146(70), 149(138), 197(n2), 255(n75)
Langres, 175, 203, 206, 211, 219, 235,
Langres, Protocol of, 207ff, 286, 341(n42), 399
Laon, 238

Lauter, river, 8
Laval, Mme de, 181
Lavalette, 181
*lazzaroni*, 193
Lebzeltern, envoy, 39, 50, 51, 55, 56, 70
Lefebvre, François-Joseph, 270-71
Legations, 223, 241, 302, 303, 308, 322, 360, 377, 414
Leipzig, Battle, 121, 153, 158, 160, 161, 219, 269, 336, 344, 373, 416
Leoben, 129
Léopold, 202
*lèse-majesté*, 52
*levée en masse*, 31, 52, 67(n66), 140
Lichtenstein, Johann of, 264
Liegnitz, 103
Lieven, envoy, 10, 21, 42, 80, 226, 227, 384
Ligny, Battle of, 368, 370
Lippe, 52, 145(n49)
Lisbon, 63
Lithuania, 308, 309
Liverpool, Lord, 228, 238, 303, 335, 379, 384, 385, 391, 394, 396, 410(n2)
Lodi, 59, 375, 412
Loewenstern, 237
Loire, river, 222, 250, 373, 389
Lombardy, 112, 289, 361
London, 15, 39, 51, 77, 78, 79, 80, 84, 85, 115, 122, 148(128), 150(n158), 156, 175, 197(n2), 205, 209, 226, 301, 303, 305, 310, 329, 336, 342(n34), 349, 364(n11), 379, 380, 390, 394, 396, 405
London, Bank of, 78
Lorraine, 98, 117, 253(n13), 330, 392, 396, 397, 398, 414, 415
Lotharingia, 423
Louis XIV, 59, 60, 141, 150(n159), 166, 176, 215, 283, 297, 324, 349, 404, 406, 412, 413, 414, 421
Louis XV, 59, 277, 307
Louis XVI, 44, 165, 226, 279, 345, 368, 375, 389, 383, 409, 414
Louis XVIII, 9, 192, 225, 228, 229,

247, 259, 260, 263, 266, 276, 280, 282, 283, 284, 285, 286, 287, 288, 289, 290, 295, 297, 299, 302, 304, 305, 306, 307, 310, 311, 312, 313, 318, 320, 322, 329, 330, 331, 335, 337, 338, 341(n28), 346, 347, 348, 349, 350, 352, 353, 354, 356, 357, 368, 377, 380, 382, 383, 384, 389, 390, 391, 393, 400, 401, 402, 403, 404, 405, 406, 408, 409, 413
Louis-Philippe, 9, 338, 352, 353, 405
Louis Stanislas Xavier. *See* Provence.
Louvois, 421
Low Countries, 78, 141, 198(n44), 224, 288, 308, 335, 337, 368, 393, 397, 399, 414, 415, 418
Lowe, Hudson, 385
Lübeck, 109, 136, 138, 140
Lunéville, Treaty of, 15, 30, 54, 91, 103, 114, 129, 138, 141, 173, 177, 202, 203, 302, 310, 415
Lusatia, 224
Lutzen, Battle of, 87, 89
Luxembourg, 282, 287, 323, 334, 362,
Luxembourg Palace, 383

Maastricht, 231
Machiavelli and Machiavellianism, 32, 36, 192
Mack. *See* Leiberich, Karl Freiherr.
Madrid, 64, 125, 221, 291, 383, 413
Magdeburg, 282
Magna Carta, 286
Maine, Duke of, 197(n24)
Maintenon, Mme de, 197(n24)
Mainz, 127, 133, 162, 170, 201, 231, 282, 293(n45), 300, 323, 362
Malet, Claude-François, 31
Mallet-du-Pan, 1-2
Malmaison, 168, 376
Malta, 63, 288
Malta, Order of, 315
Mantua, 51, 231, 303
Marbois. *See* Barbé-Marbois.
Marche, La, 360
Marcolini Palace, 115

Marengo, Battle of, 59, 216, 371, 383, 416
Maret (Hugues-Bernard), Duc de Bassano, 2, 3, 13, 14, 15, 26, 33, 34, 37, 38, 62, 63, 101, 102, 111, 115, 118, 119, 125, 127, 129, 134, 137, 138, 139, 146(n35), 147(n93), 148(n123, 134), 149(n135), 173, 181, 182, 183, 214, 215, 216, 220, 221, 222, 223, 232, 233, 242, 271, 341(n28)
Maria-Carolina, 84, 195, 303
Maria Feodorovna. *See* Mother Inmperial.
Maria-Louisa, Archduchess, 359
Maria-Louisa, Empress, 57, 61, 75, 127, 165, 196, 250, 261, 277, 302, 303, 315, 346, 356, 359, 360
Maria-Louisa of Spain, 302, 360
Marie-Antoinette, 85, 165
Marienbourg, 288
Marmont, Auguste, 101, 223, 232, 267, 268, 273, 275, 292(n11)
Marracq, castle of, 199(n49)
Massenbach, Christian Karl, 18, 19
Mathurin. *See* Laforest.
Mazarin, Cardinal, 141, 176, 307
Mecklenburg, 52
Mediterranean, 78, 141, 160, 338
Melun, 218
Memel, 18
Méneval, Claude-François, 250
Mercy-Argenteau, François, 41
Merveldt, Maximillian (Count), 158, 160, 164, 169, 239
Metternich, Clement, 10, 12, 24-29, 32-42, 55, 56, 59, 60, 62, 69-77, 83, 86, 87, 89, 90, 91, 92, 95, 96, 98, 99, 102, 103, 105, 107-13, 115-20, 123, 124, 125, 126, 127, 128, 129, 130, 131, 132, 133, 134, 135, 136, 137, 139, 140, 141, 144(n30), 146(n69), 147(n94, 95), 148(n128, 134), 149(n136), 154, 156, 157, 161, 162, 163, 164, 165, 166, 167, 168, 169, 170, 171, 172, 173, 174, 175, 17776,

435

177, 181, 182, 183, 184, 185, 186, 188-92, 194, 195, 201-12, 218, 219, 220-31, 236-40, 245, 242, 243, 245-48, 251, 253(n5), 278, 287, 298, 301, 303, 304, 311, 313-25, 327, 328, 331-35, 338, 339, 340(n18, 21), 341(n27), 346, 347, 348, 353, 356, 363, 389, 395, 397, 398, 399, 409
Meuse, river, 8, 174, 231, 251, 290, 393
Midi, 175, 279
Mier, Count, 86, 124, 189, 190, 191, 192, 193
Milan, 63, 97, 99, 142, 223, 261, 291, 303, 371, 375, 414
Mincio, 27, 91, 93
Mittau, 11, 12, 266
Moellendorf, Richard, 65(n25), 372
Molé, Louis, 181, 196, 344
Mollien, Nicolas-François, 182, 345
Moncey, Bon-Adrien Jeannot de, 270, 271, 285
Monk, 9, 123, 267
Monsieur. *See* Provence, Count of.
Montbeliard, 288
Montebello, Duchess of, 250
Mont-Dore, 355
Montereau, Battle of, 234
Montessuy, 267
Montesquieu, 155, 178, 215
Montesquiou, Abbé de, 265
Montesquiou, General, 2, 65(n3),
Montmartre, 34, 142, 248, 252
Montmirail, 223, 227, 232
Montrond,
Moreau, Jean-Victor, 9, 81, 122, 123, 151, 152, 153, 157, 197(n2), 237, 271
Mortefontaine, 179
Moscow, 3, 5, 24, 59, 71, 124, 132, 154, 168, 179, 269, 271, 272, 371
Moselle, river, 8, 174, 290, 333, 362, 393
Moskva, 141
Müffling, General, 381
Mulhouse, 288
Müller, Johann von, 6, 106

Munich, 41
Münster, Ernst Friedrich, 77, 79, 129, 157, 206, 212, 225, 226, 239, 304, 392, 412
Münster-Paderborn, Duchy of, 340(n9)
Murat, Joachim, 22, 32, 78, 81, 82, 83, 84, 85, 86, 115, 124, 140, 153, 161, 185, 188, 189, 190, 191, 192, 193, 194, 195, 199(n78), 200(n82), 221, 302, 303, 304, 307, 318, 319, 322, 328, 338, 339, 342(n41), 343, 360, 406, 413

Namur, 218, 287
Nancy, 247
Naples, 32, 58, 82, 83, 85, 86, 112, 119, 124, 141, 142, 150(n158), 161, 188-95, 197(n15), 214, 231, 290, 291, 293(n40), 303, 308, 319, 322, 323, 327, 330, 338, 339, 360, 371, 412, 413, 421
Napoléon II. *See* Rome, King of.
Napoléon III, 420, 422
Narbonne, Louis, 4, 12, 15, 21, 22, 23, 61, 67(n91), 71, 72, 73, 74, 75, 76, 87, 88, 91, 92, 93, 95, 98, 119, 120, 125, 126, 127, 129, 131, 134, 139, 148(n134), 149(n135, 136)
Nassau, Prince of, 284, 351, 362
National Guard, 35, 250, 261, 277, 374, 376
natural limits, concept, 8, 27, 54, 55, 58, 82, 103, 171, 172, 173, 174, 183, 184, 196, 204, 212, 214,, 218, 234, 241, 252, 256(n98), 260, 280, 296, 347, 392, 412, 414, 419
Natzmer, Major, 22, 42
Nebuchadnezzar, 420
Neerwinden, Battle of, 374
Neipperg, Colonel, 191, 192, 193, 194, 195, 199(n50), 278, 293(n26)
Nesselrode, Karl Robert, 5, 7, 8, 47, 52, 56, 71, 93, 94, 96, 97, 99, 102, 103, 105, 109, 111, 112, 120, 169, 170, 172, 174, 182, 186, 195, 109, 212, 218, 220, 231,, 244, 245, 261, 262,

436

264, 284, 298, 301, 312, 313, 314, 315, 317, 356, 401, 409
Netherlands, 80, 112, 239, 290, 362
Neufchâtel, Prince de, 222
Neuilly, 382
Ney, Marshal, 2, 42, 44, 153, 270, 271, 273, 276, 285, 344, 354, 381, 382, 384, 406, 407
Niemen, river, 2, 17, 30, 71, 73
Nieuport, 288
Nijmegen, Peace of, 412
Nîmes, 279
Noailles, Alexis de, 9, 315
Nogent-sur-Seine, 221
Northern Germany, 50, 120, 413
North Sea, 59, 141, 159
Norway, 81, 122, 248, 255(n97), 291, 342(n96)
Notre-Dame de Paris, 252, 285
Novossiltsof, 81

Oder, river, 21, 22, 37, 40, 46, 98, 110, 231
Oglio, 91
Oldenburg, 66(n48)
Opéra, 266
Orange, Prince of, 178, 231, 239, 241, 251, 362, 387(n13)
Oratory, 353
Orléans, Duc d', 354, 359, 375
Orléans, Gaston d', 250
Orsvault, Marquis d', 267
Orthodox Church, 394
Osmond, Comte d', 287, 288
Osnabrück, 412
Ost-Friesland, 107
Otranto, Duke of, 176, 192, 357
Otto II, Emperor, 252
Otto, French ambassador, 28, 29-30, 33, 37, 39, 61
Otto, Russian agent, 10
Ottoman Empire, 102, 309, 329, 363, 394
Oudinot, Nicolas, 152, 153, 271

Palermo, 194, 195

Palatinate, 362
Paoli, 385
Paris, Treaty of, 279ff, 314, 321-23, 335, 347, 349, 379, 392, 403, 413
Parlement of Paris, 290
Parliament, of England, 84, 165, 265, 310, 313, 317, 326, 328, 331, 336, 349, 378
Parma, 112
partition, 6, 15, 52, 73, 162, 213, 224, 234, 240, 241, 259, 287, 300, 305, 327, 381, 418
Pasquier, prefect of police, 181, 182, 250, 266, 267, 354, 355, 382
patriotism, 5, 46, 405, 419
Paul I, Tsar, 31, 271, 357
Paulucci, Filippo, 11, 17, 21
Pavia, 412
Péluse. *See* Monge.
Persia, 181
Peschiera, 231
Petersburg, 176, 268, 270, 352
Phélypeaux. *See* Maurepas, J.-F.
Philippeville, 218, 288, 399, 404, 406
*Philosophes*, 281, 424
Phull, Karl Ludwig von, 107
Piacenza, 66(n48), 277
Piacenza, Bishop of, 185
Pichegru, Jean-Charles, 9, 151, 271, 278, 372, 376
Piedmont, 66(n48), 112, 181, 223, 231, 291, 303, 414, 419
Pilnitz, 202
Pitt, William (the Younger), 80, 204, 372
Pius VII, 61, 185, 271, 289, 302
Pizzo, 406
Place du Trône, 376
Pleiswitz, Armistice of, 87, 106, 268
Po, river, 93
Poland, 5, 6, 10, 13, 19, 24, 35, 38, 52, 53, 56, 58, 70, 73, 74, 96, 99, 100, 117, 155, 162, 164, 179, 195, 202, 207, 209, 217, 224, 226, 234, 240, 241, 251, 287, 290, 299, 300, 301, 308, 310, 313, 315, 317, 321, 324,

437

325, 326, 327, 329, 331, 332, 333, 336, 341(n41), 381, 406, 414, 418, 419
Polignac, Duc de, 246
Pomerania, 151, 255(97), 336, 342(n36)
Poniatowski, Stanislas, 56, 162, 327
Pont-Neuf, 285
Pontécoulant (Louis-Gustave Doulcet), Comte de, 377
Porte, Turkish, 27, 262, 309, 363
Portugal, 32, 63, 78, 239, 288, 289, 314, 328, 372
Poscherun, 18
Posen, 10, 45, 162, 300, 325, 333, 334, 336
Potsdam, 13, 20, 42, 210
Pozzo di Borgo, 151, 157, 169, 175, 209, 211, 212, 219, 247, 264, 274, 311, 312, 315, 326, 338, 340(n21), 342(n35), 357, 364(n11), 379, 383, 387(n5), 397, 398, 401, 403, 406
Pradt (Dominique Dufour), abbé de, 246, 263, 264
Prague, 40, 54, 62, 93, 101, 107, 119, 120, 123, 124, 128, 129, 130, 135, 136, 137, 139, 141, 142, 146(n69), 148(n123, 128), 156, 158, 164, 177, 181, 182, 183, 203, 211, 212, 213, 214, 217, 219, 238, 252, 268
Pratzen, 270
Pressburg, 138, 141
Prince-Regent. *See* George, Prince-Regent.
propaganda, 307, 414, 421
Protestant, 141, 178, 235, 246, 279, 394, 418
Proudhon, 387(n16)
Provence, 60, 343, 406
Provisional Government, 264, 265, 266, 268, 270, 273, 274, 278, 281, 292(n11), 376, 382, 389
Pyrenees, 8, 27, 65(n12), 117, 120, 166, 171, 173, 184, 204, 208, 392, 412

Radetzky, Johann Josef, 128, 170
Ragusa, Duke of, 104, 354

*raison d'État*, 61, 102, 142, 206, 247, 270, 295, 411
Rambouillet, 222, 261
Rapp, Jean de, 115
Rasoumowsky, ambassador, 218, 334, 389
Rastadt, 133, 310
Ratisbon, Diet of, 415
Ravaillac, 412
Ravenna, 302, 360
Raynouard, François-Marie, 186
Regency, putative, 27, 33, 57, 61, 75, 82, 122, 127, 165, 166, 176, 180, 188, 196, 225, 227, 229, 230, 245, 251, 258, 259, 261, 268, 272, 273, 274, 275, 276, 345, 350, 356, 359, 380, 412
Regnaud. *See* Saint-Jean-d'Angely.
Reichenbach, 107, 108, 110, 112, 113, 115, 123, 128, 141, 144(n21), 149(n136, 146), 155, 156, 219, 299, 321
Reims, 250
Reinhard, Karl-Friedrich, 161, 346
Regnault, 59
Rémusat, Auguste-Laurent, 261
Rémusat, Mme de, 114, 261
Renaissance, 421
Restoration, 85, 178, 187, 195, 205, 208, 212, 224, 227, 234, 248, 260, 279, 280, 282, 283, 284, 288, 295, 320, 335, 343, 345, 346, 348, 349, 350, 353, 354, 368, 376, 377, 381, 382, 390, 395, 408
Retz, Cardinal de, 261, 283
Revolution of 1789. *See* French Revolution.
Rhine, river, 7, 8, 15, 24, 27, 30, 41, 52, 53, 54, 58, 59, 65(n12), 71, 73, 74, 76, 78, 87, 88, 91, 92, 93, 94, 95, 98, 102, 109, 112, 117, 128, 136, 140, 141, 142, 154, 156, 157, 160, 162, 163, 164, 166, 167, 170, 171, 173, 174, 175, 176, 179, 183, 184, 185, 201, 204, 208, 212, 221, 223, 228, 231, 232, 234, 238, 240, 241, 243,

251, 259, 287, 290, 297, 300, 301, 304, 306, 326, 333, 334, 335, 336, 337, 341(n32), 348, 362, 371, 378, 390, 391, 392, 404, 410(n4), 412, 413, 414, 415, 419
Rhine, Confederation of, 15, 24, 52, 53, 58, 73, 74, 78, 87, 88, 92, 93, 94, 95, 98, 109, 128, 136, 140, 141, 142, 154, 156, 157, 163, 231, 304, 413
Richelieu, Cardinal, 307, 412
Richelieu, Duc d', 209, 400, 404, 405, 406, 408, 409
Riel, Pierre. *See* Beurnonville.
Riga, 11
Rights of Man, 280, 421, 422
Rimini, 360
Riqueti, Honoré Gabriel. *See* Mirabeau.
*Risorgimento*, 423
Rivoli, Battle of, 216
Robespierre, Maximilien, 257, 266, 279, 285, 353, 358, 374, 375
Roche, officer, 4
Rochechouart, 151, 157, 158, 209, 247
Roederer, Pierre-Louis, 179, 256(n106)
Romana, La, 11, 65(n17)
Rome, 112, 185, 191, 193, 199(n778), 291, 367, 371, 413, 423
Rome, King of, 32, 33, 61, 97, 127, 196, 222, 231, 250, 259, 261, 270, 272, 273, 297, 319, 346, 353, 378
Roumiantsof, 7
Roux-Laborie, Antoine-Anasthase, 176, 267
royalty, 9, 44, 78, 83, 178, 279, 282, 285, 302, 371, 382
Ruffo, Commander, 303
Rügen, 255(n97), 342(n36)
Ryswick, Treaty of, 133

Saar, 393
Sacken, Fabien, 232, 278
Saint-Aignan, Baron de, 167-74, 181, 182, 183, 184, 186, 195, 198(n36), 204, 209, 217, 241, 243, 252, 253(n11), 254(n37)
Saint-Antoine, faubourg, 382

Saint-Bernard, 421
Saint-Cloud, 179, 180, 341(n27), 373, 374
Saint-Dizier, 250
Saint-Florentin, Hôtel, 263, 267, 268
Saint-Germain, faubourg, 382, 400
Saint Helena, island, 374, 385, 423
Saint-Jean de Luz, 225
Saint-Léon, 365(n25)
Saint-Lucia, island, 288
Saint-Marsan, Philippe-Asinari, 12, 13, 15, 21, 22, 23, 42, 46, 148(n128), 303, 304, 317, 322
Saint-Ouen Declaration, 285
Saint-Pierre, Abbé de, 362
Saint-Roch, 374
Saint-Simon, 150(n159)
Saint-Vincent, 25
Salic law, 352
Salzburg, 101
*sans-culottes*, 14
Santo Domingo, 288
Sardinia, 148(n128), 289, 303, 335, 360
Savary, Anne Jean Marie René, 114, 182, 182, 195, 234, 249, 250
Savona, 195
Savoy, 150(n159), 278, 288, 289, 290, 360, 396, 397, 399, 402, 406, 407, 422
Saxony, 11, 41, 45, 47, 52, 55, 62, 67(n70, 73, 76, 77, 85, 87, 88, 89, 96, 117, 121, 138, 144(n18), 152, 162, 164, 202, 207, 223, 224, 248, 284, 298, 299, 300, 301, 302, 304, 307, 308, 311, 315, 317, 322, 323, 324, 325, 326, 327, 328, 329, 330, 331, 332, 333, 334, 335, 336, 337, 340(n9), 387(n13), 403
Schack, Captain de, 12
Scharnhorst, Gerhard, 43
Scheldt, 8, 54, 65(n12), 80, 82, 112, 156, 170, 251, 253(n13)
Schinina, 190
Schoenbrünn Palace, 278, 315
Schroeder, Paul W., *xiii*
Schoepflin, Jean-Daniel, 392

Schouvalof, 103, 104, 105, 146(n69)
Schulenburg, Friedrich Wilhelm, 324
Schwarzenberg, Karl Philipp, Prince, 10, 25, 38, 62, 63, 64, 72, 74, 90, 106, 107, 111, 116, 118, 119, 128, 132, 151, 169, 170, 172, 175, 201, 203, 206, 207, 209, 233, 235, 236, 238, 243, 244, 250, 262, 264, 332
Sébastiani, Horace François, 42, 377, 378
secularization, of principalities, 141, 234, 240, 287, 302
Seine, river, 250
*senatus-consultum*, 33, 34, 59, 61, 125, 269
Senfft, 89
Serbia, 363
Serra, minister, 12,
Seven Years' War, 55
Seychelles, 288
Seydlitz, Major, 17, 18
Sicily, 32, 78, 83, 84, 85, 192, 214, 231, 303
Sieyès, abbé, 31, 141, 259
Silesia, 37, 42, 44, 46, 47, 62, 67(n86), 70, 73, 100, 107, 121, 138, 139, 152, 158, 224, 232, 255(n75), 300, 336
Slavs, 300
Smolensk, 1, 5, 27
Soissons, 237
Sorel, Albert, 200(n88), 254(n35)
Soult, Jean-de-Dieu, 107, 244, 359
Souvaroff, 4
Souza, Mme de, 346
Spain, 2, 3, 26, 32, 34, 58, 63, 64, 65(n17), 72, 74, 78, 84, 92, 93, 96, 112, 115, 119, 124, 125, 133, 150(n159), 160, 171, 180, 185, 187, 188, 195, 213, 231, 239, 241, 251, 267, 288, 289, 291, 302, 314, 315, 317, 319, 325, 328, 338, 360, 372, 412, 413, 414
Speransky, Michael, 103, 286
Stackelberg, Gustav Ernst von, 39, 69, 77
Stadion, Johann Philipp, 36, 71, 73, 87, 90, 91, 93, 94, 100, 107, 109, 121, 122, 132, 145(n54), 164, 169, 207, 212, 213, 215, 217, 218, 219, 223, 224, 233, 236, 237, 238, 241, 242, 243, 244, 245, 248
Staël, Mme de, 9, 81, 122, 123, 178
Stahrenberg, 96
Stein, Freidrich, 6, 7, 15, 17, 18, 42, 43, 46, 48, 49, 52, 55, 67(n66), 88, 151, 163, 164, 169, 210, 252, 317, 351, 361, 391, 392, 396, 397, 399, 413
Stewart, Charles, 80, 87, 149(n139), 169, 313, 333
Stockholm, 81, 291
Strasbourg, 170, 207, 397, 398
Strogonof, 9
Stuttgart, 41
Swabia, 224
Sweden, 40, 49, 71, 82, 100, 102, 110, 121, 122, 151, 155, 156, 178, 207, 226, 239, 248, 255(n98), 274, 288, 289, 314, 328, 342(n36)
Sweden, Prince Royal of, 207
Switzerland, 141, 175, 213, 225, 226, 231, 239, 241, 251, 289, 309, 328, 362, 413, 415

Tabago, 231, 288
Talleyrand, Charles Maurice de, 31, 33, 81, 103, 166, 167, 169, 171, 176, 177, 180, 181, 182, 188, 196, 201, 222, 225, 244, 246, 257, 258, 259-66, 268, 272, 274, 275, 276, 282, 283, 287, 290, 304, 305, 306, 307, 310, 313, 315, 317, 318, 319, 320, 321, 322, 323, 324, 325, 326, 327, 328, 329, 330, 331, 332, 333, 334, 335, 337, 338, 340(n21), 341(n28, 32), 342(n34, 35), 345, 346, 347, 348, 349, 350, 352, 353, 354, 355, 356, 357, 363, 365(n24, 30), 376, 377, 380, 382, 383, 399, 400, 401, 402, 403, 404, 405, 410(n14)
Tallien, Jean-Lambert, 400
Taranto, Duke of, 160, 272
Tauroggen, 12, 17, 19, 22, 39

Terror, The, 189, 384, 387(n16), 400
Terror, White, 296, 389
Thugut, Johann von, 302
Tilsit, 12, 16, 17, 18, 27, 43, 141, 154, 155, 240, 284, 310, 323
Toeplitz, Treaty of, 147(n114), 151ff, 154, 155, 156, 157, 160, 164, 197(n5), 208, 211, 219, 286, 299
Tolentino, 360
Toll, Charles-Ferdinand, 94
Toulouse, 249, 357
Tour du Pin, La, 315
Trachenberg Castle, 121, 125, 128
Tracy. *See* Destutt.
Trautmansdorf, Count of, 105
Trier, 293, 334, 336
Trieste, 138, 139, 361
Troyes, 215, 216, 218, 220, 223, 226, 228, 231, 233, 234, 235, 236, 245, 247, 248
Tuileries, 167, 180, 270, 344, 352, 389, 400
Tunis, 421
Turin, 99, 148(n128), 291
Turkey, 34, 363
Turks, 363, 385
Tuscany, 66(n48), 97, 98, 112, 188, 302, 303, 360
Tyrol, 51, 91, 93, 99, 138

utopia, 412
Utrecht, Treaty of, 185, 206, 397

Valais, 362
Valençay, 180, 185, 195
Valence (Alexandre de Timburne), Comte de, 380
Valletta, 182
Valette, La, 196, 354
Valhalla, 390
Valmy, Battle of, 20, 44, 59, 234
Vandamme, 152, 153, 154
Vandeuvre, 236
Varennes, 202, 389
Vauban, 399
Vaudémont, Mme de, 176, 181, 355

Vauxchamps, 232
Vendée,146(n67), 267, 345, 372, 389
Venice, 63, 97, 98, 138, 140, 223, 231, 241, 248, 291, 303, 308, 361, 414
Vercingetorix, 390
Vergniaud, 421
Verona, 280, 303
Versailles, 284, 342(n34), 420
Vicenza, Duke of, 139, 168, 172, 182, 228, 236, 272, 292(n16)
Victor-Emmanuel, 303
Vienna, 39, 10, 14, 21, 24, 27, 30, 39, 41, 42, 44, 51, 57, 75, 82, 87, 89, 93, 94, 105, 120, 141, 148(n128), 156, 163, 190, 202, 222, 239, 248, 278, 286, 289, 290, 295, 297, 298, 301, 302, 303, 305, 310, 312, 313, 315, 319, 326, 330, 332, 334, 338, 339, 341(n32), 342(n34), 343, 345, 349, 352, 353, 357, 358, 360, 363, 371, 379, 384, 396, 399, 400, 401, 402, 403, 412, 416, 417, 418, 419, 420
Vienna, 148(n28), 310, 402
Vienna, Congress of, 202, 295ff, 310, 363, 402, 416
Villach, 138,
Vilnius, 3, 4, 11, 26, 28, 29
Vincennes, 283, 376, 354, 376, 394
Vincent, ambassador, 346
Vistula, river, 21, 30, 44, 56, 59, 60, 62, 98, 100, 232, 300, 301, 317, 413
Vitrolles, Eugène, 181, 244, 245, 246, 247, 259
Vitrolles, Mme de, 357
Vitry, 252.
Vittoria, Battle of, 120, 125, 147(n92)
Voltaire, 385
Vosges, 367, 392

Wagram, Battle of, 59, 88, 141, 152, 371, 383, 416
Walcheren Affair, 376
Walpole, Horace, 385
Warsaw, 3, 5, 10, 23, 28, 29, 32, 34, 37, 38, 39, 43, 45, 47, 48, 52, 56, 60, 62, 73, 74, 78, 90, 92, 93, 94, 95, 98,

104, 109, 113, 117, 136, 138, 141,
142, 154, 256, 160, 162, 298, 299,
300, 301, 302, 309, 313, 317, 323,
325, 326, 332, 333, 334, 336,
341(n28), 413, 414
Waterloo, 161, 162, 210, 367ff, 368,
370, 374, 375, 412
Wellington, Duke of, 120, 147(n91),
206, 305, 329, 338, 339, 349, 357,
364(n11), 365(n29), 368, 369, 370,
372, 376, 379, 380, 382, 383, 384,
389, 391, 394, 396, 398, 399, 408,
409, 412, 413, 420
Wessenberg, Johann, 39, 78, 79, 250,
389
Weser, river, 80, 145(n49)
Westphalia, 7, 52, 58, 62, 73, 98, 107,
112, 133, 162, 176, 182, 267, 278,
300, 336, 415
Whigs, 350
Wildermeth, 247
Wilhelm, Prince, 20
Wilhelm I, King, 330
William III, 377, 412, 413, 420
Wilson, 153
Winzingerode, Ferdinand, 236
Wittgenstein, Ludwig Adolf Peter von
Sayn-, 17, 18
Wolkonski, 94
Woronzof, Simon, 5, 236, 253(n2)
Wrede, Marshal de, 325
Wurschen, 94, 121
Württemberg, 114, 197(n19), 229, 261,
315, 326, 328, 391, 397, 398
Würzburg, 148(n123), 290

Yassy, Treaty of, 240
York, Friedrich von, 11, 12, 13, 16, 17,
18, 19, 20, 21, 22, 35, 37, 42, 43, 46,
59
Ypres, 287

Zamoisk, 313
Zeycs, Armistice of, 35, 38, 39
Zichy, Count, 37, 39
Zurich, Diet of, 201

Made in the USA
Middletown, DE
14 August 2023

36669752R00272